THE ENCYCLOPAEDIA OF EVERYTHING ELSE

THE ENCYCLOPAEDIA OF EVERYTHING ELSE

William Hartston

First published in hardback in Great Britain in 2022 by Atlantic Books,
an imprint of Atlantic Books Ltd.

10 9 8 7 6 5 4 3 2 1

A CIP catalogue record for this book is available from the British Library.
Hardback ISBN: 978-1-83895-723-0
E-book ISBN: 978-1-83895-724-7

Designed and typeset by carrdesignstudio.com
Printed and bound by CPI Group (UK) Ltd, Croydon, CR0 4YY

Atlantic Books
An imprint of Atlantic Books Ltd
Ormond House
26–27 Boswell Street
London
WC1N 3JZ

www.atlantic-books.co.uk

PREFACE

Most encyclopaedias are dull. They are so full of dreary, worthy and important facts that everything else is squeezed out.

Not this one.

This is *The Encyclopaedia of Everything Else.*

Enjoy it.

Please note: The cross-references – indicated by at the end of entries – are not *everything* else, just the items I think add most to what has been said.

AA

Apart from being a useful way to get rid of surplus vowels in Scrabble, aa is a type of volcanic lava flow.

There are also rivers called Aa in France and Germany. These may be considered alphabetically the first places on Earth, but the village of Å in the Moskenes municipality in Norway also has strong claims to that title. It took its name, which was originally spelled Aa, from an Old Norse word meaning 'small river', but the spelling was changed to Å in 1917 in accordance with Norwegian language reform. There are also several other places named Å in both Norway and Sweden.

AARDVARK

Aardvark means 'earth pig' in Afrikaans. In African culture, the aardvark is thought very brave for its skill and willingness to hunt termites.

Charms made from parts of the aardvark are said to give the wearer the ability to pass through walls in the night.

Aardvarks have only 20 teeth, but their ears may be 25 centimetres (10 inches) long.

At the beginning of 2006 there were only four known aardvarks in the UK but, thanks mainly to the breeding techniques at Colchester Zoo, the number has since grown, with nine baby aardvarks born there since 2007.

ABORIGINE

In 1957, researchers at Darwin University in Australia conducted interviews and experiments to examine the efficiency of the Aborigine habit of standing on one leg to rest. No definite conclusions were reached other than that further research was needed.

In the Pitta Pitta Aboriginal tongue, *kanga* means 'alcohol' and *kangamarru* is 'drunk'. The word for 'kangaroo' is *kulipila*, *matyumpa* or *warrhaputha*.

⚲ *DIDGERIDOO, KOALA, QUEENSLAND*

ABORTION

In 1920, the USSR became the first country to legalise abortion. Malta, El Salvador, Nicaragua and the Dominican Republic are the only countries in the world where abortion is illegal under any circumstances – even when the mother's life is at risk.

1

In North America, beavers' testicles were once thought to be useful for procuring an abortion. In 1984, however, China had about 18 million births and nearly 9 million abortions without harming any beavers.

⚲ GERBIL, HIPPOCRATES

ACCIDENTS

Research in the USA has shown that the average American is more likely to die from an asteroid hitting Earth than as a result of a flood, but is more likely to die in an aircraft accident than from an asteroid impact.

In the years from 2008 to 2015, the chance of an American being killed by an animal (most likely are bees, wasps, hornets and dogs) was calculated to have been one in 1.6 million, and of being killed in a terrorist attack was about one in 30 million.

In the UK, December is the worst month for both road accident deaths and fatal falls, but drowning is most common in July.

⚲ CANADA, CRASH, DEATH, HORSE, ROAD
FATALITY

ACCORDION

The modern accordion was patented by Anthony Faas of Philadelphia on 13 January 1854. However, an earlier patent for an instrument called an accordion was issued to Cyrill Demian in Vienna in 1829. Both inventions shared the principle of a bellows and keys, but Faas's creation looked much more like a modern accordion. In the introduction to his patent, Faas said that he had 'invented certain new and useful Improvements in Accordions'.

ACNE

A survey in 2017 reported that 68 per cent of teenagers believe that most of their peers who suffer from acne will alter their photos on social media to hide it, while 67 per cent of teenagers who have had acne say it had a negative effect on their self-esteem.

ACNESTIS

In quadrupeds, the acnestis is the point or area on the animal's back between the shoulder blades and the loins which it cannot reach to scratch. In humans, the word has been used for the part of the back between the shoulder blades, whether it can be scratched or not.

ACTRESS

On 8 December 1660, Margaret Hughes appeared as Desdemona in Shakespeare's *Othello* at the Vere Street Theatre in London. This is said to be the first time a professional actress appeared on the British stage.

Margaret Hughes was the mistress of Prince Rupert, Duke of Cumberland, and may also have briefly been a lover of King Charles II. In 1662 Charles II issued a royal warrant decreeing that all female roles should be played only by female actresses. Until then men had taken female roles and 'actress' meant 'a woman performing an action'.

All four Best Supporting Actress Oscars from 1978 to 1981 were won by people with the initials M.S.

Maggie Smith won hers for *California Suite* (1978), playing an actress nominated for an Oscar.

ADAMS, Douglas (1952–2001)

Hitchhiker's Guide to the Galaxy author Douglas Adams died at the age of 49 on 11 May 2001; Spencer Perceval, the only

2

British Prime Minister to have been assassinated, died at the age of 49 on 11 May 1812. William Pitt the Elder died on 11 May 1778, but not at the age of 49.

ADDAMS, Charles (1912–88)

The cartoonist Charles Addams, creator of *The Addams Family*, liked to use headed notepaper identifying itself as being from 'The Gotham Rest Home for Mental Defectives' when he replied to letters from fans. When he married his third and final wife, both bride and groom dressed in black for the ceremony, which took place in a dog cemetery. They subsequently lived together in a New York estate which they called 'The Swamp'. When Addams died, he was cremated and his ashes buried in a region of The Swamp that had been used as a pet cemetery.

ADDRESS

In 1463, Paris became the first city to use house numbers. London did so exactly 300 years later in 1763.

The Duke of Wellington's London home at Aspley House had the address Number One, London, because it was the first house encountered from the countryside after passing the tollgates at the top of Knightsbridge.

HITLER

ADMIRALTY ISLANDS

Elisha Fawcett was a one-legged Manchester clergyman who, in the words of a contemporary, 'devoted his life to teaching the natives of the Admiralty Islands the Commandments of God and the Laws of Cricket'. When he died, his parishioners in the islands were too poor to afford a tombstone, so planted his wooden leg at the head of his grave. Miraculously, it took root and provided a bountiful harvest of wood from which they are said to have made cricket bats for generations.

ADOLESCENCE

A long-term study at Northwestern University medical school in Chicago showed that memories of middle-aged men concerning their adolescent years are highly unreliable. By comparing answers given at the age of 14 about family relationships, home environment, dating and sexuality, religion, parental discipline and general activities with their memories of the same events 34 years later, results published in 2000 showed that the likelihood of accurately remembering events from adolescence was no greater than chance.

'Adolescence: a stage between childhood and adultery.' Ambrose Bierce, The Devil's Dictionary, 1906

HAMSTER

ADRENALINE

The use of gerbils to detect undercover agents and terrorists by smelling out their adrenaline has a history dating back to the 1970s when MI5 looked at the possibility of using trained gerbils for that purpose.

They had been impressed by trials at Tel Aviv airport where gerbils were being used at security check areas to sniff a suspect's hands as fans wafted the aroma in the gerbil's direction.

The gerbils were trained to press a lever if they detected increased adrenaline, thus identifying passengers under stress.

Unfortunately, the plans had to be abandoned when it was found that the gerbils could not distinguish between terrorists and people who were afraid of flying.

The adrenaline-sniffing skill of the gerbils began with their use by the Royal Canadian Mounted Police in the 1970s to sniff out drugs in Canadian prisons.

Their ability to do so was undoubted, but a number of suspicious deaths among the gerbils suggested they were being murdered by drug-dealing prisoners and the project was abandoned.

There was also the problem of getting rid of the smell of the gerbils' urine.

More recently, however, gerbils have been performing excellent work in detecting landmines in Africa.

ADULTERY

In ancient Greek, the meaning of the verb *rhaphanizo* was 'to thrust a radish up the fundament'.

This was a punishment for adulterers, but before we condemn it as severe, it should be compared with the penalty in ancient India, which consisted of having the nose cut off, and the still more severe punishment in Britain at the time of King Canute, when an adulteress was liable to lose both her nose and ears.

♀ *ADOLESCENCE, BRANDING, DRAMA*

ADVERTISEMENT

In September 2010, a Chinese female lawyer issued a lawsuit against a cinema and a film distribution company for showing 20 minutes of advertisements before the main feature. She said the company and the cinema should have told her how long the adverts would last and accused them of wasting her time and violating her freedom of choice. Chen Xiaomei demanded a refund of the money she'd spent on the ticket, an equal amount in compensation, a nominal amount for emotional damages, and a written apology.

In 1996, Daihatsu became the first car manufacturer to advertise a new model by placing stickers on condom machines in pubs and wine bars. 'The stickers are a further element of Daihatsu's campaign to poke fun at the pretentious nature of the car market,' said a spokesman for the advertising agency marketing the new Daihatsu Hijet.

♀ *RECRUITMENT, UNITED STATES*

AESCHYLUS (525–456 BC)

The Greek tragedian Aeschylus is said to have been killed when a tortoise fell on his head. According to legend, the tortoise was dropped by an eagle which mistook Aeschylus's bald head for a rock which it could use to crack the shell of the tortoise. What happened to the tortoise is not known.

Pliny the Elder, who first recounted the tale of Aeschylus's death, said it was a lammergeyer (also known as a bearded vulture) not an eagle.

'It is in the character of very few men to honour without envy a friend who has prospered.' Aeschylus

AFGHANISTAN

Afghanistan comes first if you arrange the nations of the world in alphabetical order. From 1918 until 1991, Afghanistan was the only country on Earth whose name began with A but did not also end in A. After the Soviet Union collapsed, it was joined in that respect by Azerbaijan.

A traditional sport in northern Afghanistan is Buzkashi, played by horsemen who try to dump a headless calf in the enemy goal. Players are allowed to whip or kick the man holding the calf, but off-the-calf fouls are penalised.

There are two UNESCO World Heritage Sites in Afghanistan: the Minaret of Jam, and the Buddhas of Bamiyan.

Afghanistan is four and a half hours ahead of Greenwich Mean Time.

📍 *CARROT, TALIBAN*

● AGATHOCLES (361–289 BC)

Machiavelli described Agathocles as an example 'of those who become princes through their crimes'. Known as the 'Tyrant of Syracuse', Agathocles was the son of a potter who achieved considerable military success largely through nefarious means and conquered most of Sicily, of which he considered himself the King. He is said to have died through using a toothpick poisoned by his enemies.

Agathocles is also the name of a heavy metal band from the city of Mol in Belgium.

● AGNOSTIC

The word 'agnostic' was coined by Thomas Huxley one evening at a party at Mr James Knowles's house on Clapham Common, specifically to describe Charles Darwin's attitude towards religious belief.

● AGRICULTURE

A world record was set at the Alton and North East Hampshire Agricultural Show in the UK in 2009 for running the longest distance while on fire. Amateur stuntman Keith Malcolm ran 79 metres (259 feet) while on fire, beating the previous record by 9.75 metres (32 feet). He wore several layers of fire-resistant clothing and had a man with a fire extinguisher in close attendance.

The record was subsequently beaten several times and now stands at 205.23 metres (almost 700 feet), set by stuntman Antony Britton in 2017. He also set a record for 'fastest 100-metres [328-foot] sprint (full-body burn, without oxygen)', completing the run in just 24.58 seconds.

● AIDS

In 2001, King Mswati III of Swaziland invoked an ancient chastity rite known as umchwasho in an attempt to curb the AIDS epidemic in his country. This involved banning all young maidens under the age of 50 from having sex for five years. Two months later he violated his own decree by taking a 17-year-old girl as his thirteenth wife and was made to pay a fine of one cow.

King Mswati rules in conjunction with his mother, who is known as the Great She-Elephant. He currently has 15 wives and 23 children. His father and predecessor, King Sobhuza II, had 125 wives in his 82-year reign.

According to tradition, the King may only marry after his 'wife' becomes pregnant. Until then she is known only as a 'bride'.

📍 *NIGERIA*

● AIR HOSTESSES

Miss Ellen Church of Iowa became the world's first air stewardess on 15 May 1930 after writing to United Airlines with the suggestion that suitably qualified young ladies might be useful on flights. The airline not only employed Ms Church but asked her to draw up qualifications for further recruits. Her resulting specifications were modelled on her own best points: applicants had to be registered nurses aged no more than 25; they must not weigh more than 52 kilograms (115 pounds) or be more than 1.6 metres (5 feet 4 inches) tall.

The first British air hostess was Miss Daphne Kearley, who served on her first flight on 16 May 1936. Typing and cocktail-mixing were among the skills specified, though her own account of the job suggested that calming down anxious passengers and politely turning down marriage proposals were the main parts of the role. By 1943, the major qualifications demanded by the British Overseas Airways Corporation (BOAC) were 'poise' and an 'educated voice'.

'Stewardesses' is the longest common word that is typed entirely by the left hand of a trained typist on a QWERTY keyboard. However, it is two letters shorter than the uncommon 'after-cataracts' (an eye condition that may follow an operation for cataracts) and 'tesseradecades' (groups of 14).

● ALASKA

The Alaskan coastline is 10,686 kilometres (6,640 miles) long, which is longer than the combined coastlines of all the other US states. If Alaska were a country, it would be the sixteenth largest in the world.

Alaska is the only US state whose name can be typed on a single row of letters on a standard keyboard.

Alaska was transferred from Russia to the United States on 18 October 1867 for $7.2 million, which is why 18 October is Alaska Day. Since then, Alaska has remained about 500 miles from the rest of the USA but is still only 55 miles from mainland Russia.

Under Alaskan law, wanton waste of a moose carries a maximum penalty of one year in jail and a $10,000 fine. Taking the antlers without salvaging all the edible meat constitutes 'wanton waste'. The town of Talkeetna, Alaska, used to hold a Moose Dropping Festival,

dropping pieces of moose poo by crane onto a target. This festival was last held in 2009, after which it was judged to have become too popular for the town's good.

Waking a sleeping bear for the purpose of taking a photograph is prohibited in Alaska.

The Nenana Ice Classic is an Alaskan sweepstake that has been running since 1917. It started when bored railway engineers erected a wooden tripod on the frozen Tanana River and placed bets on the exact moment in spring when it would fall through the ice. A paper in *Science* journal in 2001 was devoted to demonstrating that the records of the Nenana Ice Classic are a valid measure of global warming.

Until 1995 it was illegal to keep an elephant in Alaska. In that year, however, they changed the law regarding exotic pets specifically to allow an ex-circus elephant to stay there.

The state sport of Alaska is dog mushing, which is racing on sleds pulled by dogs.

Of the 20 highest mountains in the USA, 17 are in Alaska.

♀ BACULUM, DRAGONFLY, MOOSE, TREADMILL

● ALBANIA

One official motto of Albania is: 'The faith of the Albanians is Albanism'. The Albanians call Albania 'Shqiperia', which means 'land of the eagle'.

In 1967 Albania became the world's first officially atheist state. In 1976 the official name of Albania was changed to People's Socialist Republic of Albania. In 1992, after the fall of communism, the name changed again to simply Republic of Albania. During the communist era, private cars were illegal in Albania.

Probably the most famous Albanian was Mother Teresa of Calcutta, born

Agnes Gonxha Bojaxhiu. Her middle name means 'little flower' in Albanian.

In 1995, a traffic light tax of 2,000 lek (about £14) was imposed in Albania, but drivers in the northern city of Shkodra refused to pay it on the grounds that their city had no traffic lights.

The oldest known name of the main island of Britain was Albion. Around the 11th century, writings in Latin referred to it as Albania. Albania is the name of at least three towns in Colombia.

The Albanian currency, the lek, was named after Alexander the Great, whose name was often shortened to Leka in Albanian.

From the 14th to the 20th century, Albania did not have a king. Charles I was king from 1272 to 1285 and was succeeded by his son Charles II from 1285 to 1294. The next king was Zog I from 1928 to 1939.

HOXHA, WISDOM, ZOG I

● ALBATROSS

According to a recent study, a large proportion of female albatrosses in Hawaii are lesbian. A pair of lesbian albatrosses in the world's only inland breeding colony in New Zealand were reported in 2010 to be bringing up a chick together. The identity of the chick's father is unknown.

● ALBERT I, King of Belgium (1875–1934)

King Albert I was killed in a climbing accident in Belgium. His last reported words were addressed to his valet, whom he instructed to wait in the car: 'If I feel in good form, I shall take the difficult way up. If I do not, I shall take the easy one. I shall join you in an hour.' When he did not return, a search began and eventually found his body. Rumours of foul play circulated, including a suggestion that he was murdered elsewhere and his body brought to the mountain. In 2016, however, a DNA analysis of blood samples found on March-les-Dames above the place where the body was found confirmed that he had died in an accident there.

In 1914, when presented with an ultimatum by Germany demanding safe passage for the German army to France, King Albert replied: 'Belgium is a country not a road'; Germany then declared war on Belgium, and the king assumed personal command of the Belgian army while his wife, Queen Elisabeth, worked as a nurse at the front.

● ALCHEMY

In the 4th century BC, Plato and Aristotle developed alchemy from the idea that everything was made of earth, air, fire and water. Each of those was said to combine two primary qualities: hot or cold, and wet or dry. Earth is cold and dry, air is hot and wet, fire is hot and dry, water is cold and wet. When fire loses its heat, it becomes earth – in the form of ash; when water is heated, it becomes air – in the form of steam. It followed that anything could be turned into anything else by reducing it to its basic components, then remixing them with a little heating, chilling, wetting or drying.

Sadly, it didn't work in practice, so the early alchemists decided that something must be missing. That something was the legendary Philosopher's Stone, which supposedly had the power to turn all things to gold and to bestow eternal life by transforming a person from earthly impurity into heavenly perfection. It was, in short, the answer to everything.

'I have seen and handled more than once the Stone of the Philosophers,' said the 17th-century Belgian alchemist J.B. van Helmont. 'In colour it was like powder of saffron but heavy and shining even as powdered glass.'

John Damian was court alchemist to James IV of Scotland. In 1507, he built himself a pair of wings and tried to fly from the ramparts of Stirling Castle but fell to the ground and broke a leg. He blamed the feathers he had used, which came from barnyard fowl unaccustomed to flying. Despite this failure, James IV still paid £15.16s.0d for Damian's alchemist's gown of damask and £4 for his velvet socks.

Edward Kelley claimed to have discovered the Philosopher's Stone among the ruins of Glastonbury Abbey around 1583. He was sent to the pillory at Lancaster and had his ears cropped after a conviction for forgery.

John Dee employed Kelley and never noticed the latter's mutilated ears (which were hidden beneath a skull cap). Dee sent Queen Elizabeth a piece of gold that he said he had made from metal cut from a warming pan, and gave his son quoits which he claimed were made from transmuted gold. In 2011, John Dee was himself transmuted into an opera, *Dr Dee*, directed by Rufus Norris with music by Damon Albarn.

The French alchemist Nicolas Flamel, whose search for the Philosopher's Stone inspired parts of J.K. Rowling's Harry Potter stories, lived from 1330 to 1418. The house he built in 1407 is now considered the oldest building in Paris and houses a restaurant, the Auberge Nicolas Flamel, which in 2021 sold a three-course lunch for 38 euros.

● ALCOHOL

The word 'alcohol' was first used in English in the early 17th century as a name for ore of antimony, a fine metallic powder used as eye make-up. By extension, the word then came to be applied to any fine powder produced by grinding or distillation, and finally it took on the meaning of the distilled liquid itself rather than its powdery residue.

Samuel Johnson's *Dictionary* defined alcohol as: 'an Arabic term used by chymists for a highly rectified dephlegmated spirit of wine, or for any thing reduced into an impalpable powder'.

Alcoholic drinks are very old. There is evidence of beer-drinking in Mesopotamia around 8000 BC, while the sediment in a pottery jar excavated in northern Iran indicates that man was drinking a retsina-like wine in 5000 BC. Workers on the Egyptian pyramids around 4,500 years ago had three drink-breaks each day, when five types of beer and four varieties of wine were available.

In the early 18th century, Empress Catherine I of Russia banned women from getting drunk. This may explain the large number of female transvestites at Moscow balls, where wine ran freely. Catherine's husband and predecessor, Peter the Great, had the lover of one of his mistresses executed and his head preserved in alcohol and kept by his bedside.

The effects of alcohol on goldfish and humans have been found to be remarkably similar. For both species, experiments have shown that anything learned in a state of mild inebriation is liable to be forgotten when sobriety is restored, but a subsequent return to the inebriated state may be accompanied by a return of the forgotten memories. So if you have forgotten something that you learned when you were drunk, your best chance of recalling it may well be to get drunk again. If you drank so much that you blacked out, however, all memories of what you said, did or learned while intoxicated are liable to vanish for ever, whether you are human or goldfish. Mildly inebriated goldfish, however, have been shown to learn simple tasks more quickly than sober goldfish.

As to the effects of alcohol on lechery, a porter explains all to Macduff in Shakespeare's *Macbeth*: 'It provokes the desire, but it takes away the performance.' Studies have confirmed that alcohol increases subjective estimates of sexual arousal but diminishes physiological symptoms.

According to a poll in 2008, the average British man will drink 11,616 pints of beer in his lifetime as well as 1,089 pints of cider, 5,082 glasses of wine, 4,356 single measures of spirits. This will cost him £24,357.30.

⚲ *ALE, BEER, HANGOVER, WHISKY*

ALDRIN, Edwin Eugene ('Buzz') (b. 1930)

Appropriately enough for the second man to walk on the Moon, Buzz Aldrin's mother's maiden name was Moon. His own name, remarkably enough, really was 'Buzz', but not until 1988. Prior to that it had been a nickname which began with his little sister's attempt to pronounce the word 'brother', which came out as 'Buzzer'. In 1988, he legally changed his first name to 'Buzz'. In 1963, Edwin Aldrin, as he then was, received a doctorate from MIT for his thesis on orbital mechanics.

⚲ *MOON*

ALE

In July 2010, the Aberdeen brewery BrewDog created 12 bottles of a super-strength ale, which they placed inside the dead bodies of seven stoats, four squirrels and one hare and sold for £500 a bottle.

At 55 per cent alcohol by volume (ABV), the brewers claimed it was the world's strongest beer. A week later, however, the Dutch brewer Jan Nijboer produced a beer that was 60 per cent alcohol. Since 2013, the world's strongest beer has been Brewmeister's Snake Venom at 67.5 per cent.

⚲ *BEER, URINATION*

ALEXANDRA, Queen (1844–1925)

Wife of Edward VII, Queen Alexandra admitted she had no interest in intellectual pursuits and was notoriously unpunctual. According to one contemporary historian, she 'had no brain'. When she was left with a limp after an illness in 1867, ladies at court copied the limp to be fashionable.

ALFRED THE GREAT (849–899)

During the reign of Alfred the Great in England, laws were introduced to make people convicted of crimes give compensation to their victims. A 2.5-centimetre (1-inch) wound required a payment of one shilling; a broken tooth was worth six shillings; and an ear cost 20 shillings. The scale for toes specified 20 shillings for a big toe, 15 shillings for the second toe, nine shillings for a middle toe, five shillings for the little toe and only four shillings for the fourth toe.

Alfred is the only English or British king to be known as 'the Great'.

⚲ *WESSEX*

ALGERIA

Algeria is the largest country by area in Africa. Before 2011, when South Sudan became independent, Sudan was the largest.

The only people born in Algeria to have won Nobel Prizes were Albert Camus (Literature, 1957) and Claude Cohen-Tannoudji (Physics, 1997). Camus played as goalkeeper in the football team for the University of Algiers, which may therefore be the world's only university to have had a Nobel Prize-winning goalkeeper in its team.

In 2007, a court in Algeria had to rule on the ownership of a donkey that had eaten the money brought by a purchaser for its sale.

St Augustine of Hippo (354–430) was the most famous Algerian of all. The city of Hippo is now Annaba.

ALLIGATOR

Alligators have five toes on their front feet and four toes on the back feet.

In the US state of Florida, intentionally feeding a wild alligator is a misdemeanour of the second degree, but killing or injuring an alligator is a third-degree felony. Except in extreme situations, an alligator must be at least 1.2 metres (4 feet) long before it is considered by law to be a nuisance.

In Louisiana, theft of an alligator, whether dead or alive, is a crime punishable by imprisonment for not more than 10 years with or without hard labour and/or a fine of not more than $3,000 if the value of the crime is more than $500, or two years' imprisonment and/or a $2,000 fine if the value is between $300 and $500.

♀ CROCODILE

ALPACA

The alpaca is a sort of soft-haired llama and is found mainly in Peru. Alpacas can breed with llamas; a cross between a male llama and female alpaca is called a 'huarizo'. The offspring of a male alpaca and female llama is a 'misti'.

In Andean mythology, alpacas were associated with the Earth Mother goddess Pachmama. They were said to have been given to mankind as a gift at Mount Ausangate in Peru and to be left on Earth for only as long as they were properly looked after.

Alpaca wool comes in 22 natural colours, the most of any wool-producing animal.

A baby alpaca is called a cria.

ALPHABET

The technical name for the dot above a letter 'i' is a 'tittle'. Curiously, the *Oxford English Dictionary* gives 'The dot over the letter i' as one of the meanings of 'tittle' but does not say that it can also mean the dot over the letter j. It does, however, include a citation from 1676 saying that the dot over a j is formed the same way as that over the i.

'The person said the Duke [of Marlborough] puts no tittles upon the i's. "O", says the Prince [Eugene of Savoy], "it saves his Grace's ink".' Mary Delany, Autobiography and Correspondence, 1783

♀ CROATIA, FIJI, GEORGIA, PI, POLAND, THAILAND, TWENTY-TWO

AMAZING

'Amazing' was voted top of the list of overused words nominated for banishment in 2012 in the annual poll conducted by Lake Superior State University. It was closely followed by 'baby bump'. The 2021 list, published at the end of 2020, gave the top place for proposed banishment to COVID-19, followed by the phrases 'social distancing' and 'we're all in this together'.

AMAZON

There are no bridges across the Amazon anywhere along its 6,437-kilometre (4,000-mile) length. There is some dispute over the width of the mouth of the Amazon owing to the position of the large island of Marajó, where the Amazon meets the ocean, but according to one measure, the width is greater than the entire length of the River Thames in England.

The Amazon is responsible for about 17 per cent of all the fresh water discharged into the world's oceans each day and about 50 per cent of the water discharged into the Atlantic.

With a net worth approaching $200 billion, Jeff Bezos, founder of Amazon.com was ranked the richest person in the world in 2021, ahead of Elon Musk. Among his other accomplishments, Bezos played an alien in the movie *Star Trek Beyond*.

COMPUTATION, MARSTON, OIL

AMERICA

We have long thought that America was named after the explorer Amerigo Vespucci, but another candidate has recently emerged. Richard Amerike, a Bristol merchant, knew about North America long before Columbus and Vespucci 'discovered' it. Bristolians had for many years been buying salted cod from Icelandic fishermen which had been caught in Newfoundland.

Not wishing to spread the word about their new fishing grounds, they kept this knowledge secret, but Amerike was a major sponsor of John Cabot's voyages to North America around 1497–99, and documents found in recent years suggest that Cabot gave a map to Columbus which may have had Amerike's name on it. Another piece of circumstantial evidence is Amerike's family banner: a flag in red, white and blue, depicting stripes and stars.

The German cartographer Martin Waldseemüller was the first known person to call the New World 'America', having inscribed the name on his engravings for a world map in 1507. Later in life, Waldseemüller changed his opinion, believing that 'Columbia' might have been a better name, but by then the name of America had established itself too well to be altered.

The country Colombia was given its name in 1819 by Simón Bolívar. In 1825 Bolivia was named after Bolívar, who was Venezuelan.

According to some official estimates, the number of soldiers killed in conflict in the American Revolution was 4,435, which is fewer than the number now killed on America's roads every 40 days.

According to a nationwide survey in 2022, one in three people across America have detectable levels of a toxic herbicide linked to cancers, birth defects and hormonal imbalances.

CHIPS, COLUMBUS, CRIME, FOOD, POPULATION, RUBBISH, TELEVISION

AMMONIA

For a curious reason, the gas ammonia (NH_3) takes its name from the Egyptian god Ammon.

Ammonium chloride, also known as sal ammoniac, was discovered by accident in classical times as a by-product of burning camel dung in the temple of

11

Jupiter Ammon at Siwa oasis in Egypt, not far from the Libyan border.

The marine fossils known as ammonites are also named after Ammon, because their spiral structure was reminiscent of the ram's horns that Ammon was said to have had.

AMNESIA

In October 2011, the *Journal of Emergency Medicine* reported the case of a woman who went to the emergency room of Georgetown University Hospital complaining of lack of memory of the previous 24 hours, about an hour after she had had orgasmic sex with her husband.

Doctors diagnosed a rare condition known as transient global amnesia (TGA), caused by the scrambling of the memory circuits of the brain, often brought on by physical or emotional triggers.

ℙ *ALCOHOL*

AMPUTATION

During the American Civil War, 75 per cent of all battlefield surgery involved amputations. A total of more than 50,000 such amputations were performed.

A man with no arms and no legs swam the English Channel in September 2010, thanks to his motor-propelled, flipper-shaped artificial legs. Philippe Croizon, 42, lost all his limbs in an accident in 1994 when he was hit by a 20,000-volt charge from a power line while removing a television aerial. The Channel crossing took him 13 and a half hours. He said he had done it to inspire all those 'who think life is nothing but suffering'.

ℙ *NAPOLEON BONAPARTE, PORTER*

AMUSEMENT

A thief in the German town of Hamelin was reported in 2010 to have robbed an amusement arcade by threatening the attendant with a cup of coffee. 'He wasn't going to pour coffee over her,' a police spokesman explained, 'he was going to hit her with the cup.'

ANAESTHETICS

On 30 March 1842, Dr Crawford Long became the first to use ether as an anaesthetic, when removing a cyst from the neck of a student named John Venable. In the USA, 30 March is celebrated as Doctors' Day in commemoration of this.

Before 1842, the only medicament available to dull the pain of an operation was whisky or some other alcohol. Surgeons were also known to partake of the whisky during operations to help dull their own sensitivity to the screams of the patient.

Nitrous oxide, or 'laughing gas', was used purely for entertainment before its use as an anaesthetic. Charlie Chaplin made a 16-minute comedy short called *Laughing Gas* in 1914.

In 2002, researchers at the University of Louisville reported that people with ginger hair require 20 per cent more anaesthetic before surgery than people with hair of another colour.

In 1981, 17 doctors in South Africa used enough anaesthetic to kill 70 men when performing dentistry on an elephant.

ℙ *ELEPHANT, LONGFELLOW*

ANAGRAMS

Notable people whose names are anagrams of a single word include: actress Meg Ryan (Germany), singer Britney Spears (Presbyterians), former

US vice-president and Nobel Prize winner Al Gore (gaoler), singer Roger Daltrey (retrogradely), musician Eric Clapton (narcoleptic), actor Tom Cruise (costumier) and conservationist Steve Irwin (interviews).

Britain's first chess grandmaster Tony Miles was an anagram of 'solemnity', and Britain's world chess title challenger Nigel Short is an anagram of 'holstering'.

♀ *COVID-19, LEWINSKY, SHAKESPEARE*

● ANATOMY

In 1997, after eight years of discussions, the International Federation of Associations of Anatomists (IFAA) finally reached agreement on the correct term for the area between a woman's breasts.

The expression they settled on was 'intermammary sulcus'. The creator of the term was the 77-year-old Brazilian Liberato DiDio, who was secretary-general of the IFAA's committee on anatomical terminology. The committee also agreed that the area at the bottom of the breast where it meets the chest was to be known as the 'inframammary sulcus'.

Another part of the body renamed by the same committee was the part formerly known as the Adam's apple, which is now the 'laryngeal prominence'.

♀ *FOOTBALL, SLOTH*

● ANCHOVY

The first screenplay Quentin Tarantino ever wrote – at the age of 14 – was called 'Captain Peachfuzz and the Anchovy Bandit'. It has never been filmed.

Anchovy-flavoured popcorn was one of the bedtime treats offered to cats at the Sutton Place Hotel in Vancouver in 1998 when it started its 'Pampered Pets' service.

● ANDERSEN, Hans Christian (1805–75)

The great Danish writer of over 150 fairy tales, Hans Christian Andersen, was born two months after his parents married. He never married, but carried a letter from his first love, Riborg Voigt, in a pouch around his neck until he died. He also expressed attraction for other men but apparently never acted on this.

Andersen parted his hair on the right and had a big nose. He never ate pork, and when staying in hotels carried a coil of rope with him in case he needed to escape from a fire. He was also afraid of dogs and suffered from taphophobia – a fear of being buried alive. As a precaution against this, he left a note by his bedside at night saying: 'I only appear to be dead'.

♀ *MERMAID*

● ANDORRA

Andorra is the world's only co-principality, with two princes jointly sharing authority over it. The two princes are the President of France and the Bishop of Urgell, a Roman Catholic diocese straddling both Andorra and Spain.

Andorra has no unemployment, no airports, no US ambassador, only one prison, and one of the world's highest life expectancies at 83 years (80.8 for men, 85.4 for women).

The flag of Andorra is the world's only national flag with two cows on it.

♀ *BRUNEI, FLAGS, INCOME TAX*

● ANIMAL NOISES

In Germany, horses go 'prrrh'; in ancient Greece, dogs went 'au au'; Danish pigs go 'knor'; Japanese cats 'nyaa' in Japanese; cows 'baeh' in Urdu; geese tööt in Finnish; snakes 'hvese' in Norwegian.

By contrast, Italian humans sneeze 'ecci ecci'.

 UKRAINE

ANORAK

The word 'anorak' first appeared in English in 1924. It comes from the Canadian Inuit *annuraaq*, meaning 'a piece of clothing'.

In 1996, Swedish artist Ann-Kristin Antman produced an anorak made from salmon skins toughened and made waterproof by soaking in human urine. 'It is a method used in the Stone Age in Sweden,' she explained. 'The smell disappears when you rinse the skins in water.'

The first recorded use of 'anorak' in its more recent sense of (as the *OED* puts it) 'a boring, studious, or socially inept young person' was in 1984.

ANOREXIA

Although we often see anorexia as a modern problem, the word first appeared in English in 1605. The complaint of anorexia nervosa was given its name in 1873 by the physician Sir William Withey Gull, who proposed 'apepsia hysterica' as an alternative.

 BARBIE

ANTARCTICA

The ancient Greeks gave Antarctica its name, calling it 'Anti-Arktikos', which literally means 'opposite the bear'. The Great Bear (Ursa Major) is above the North Pole, so the South became Anti-Arktikos and the North was identified as Arktikos.

On 17 January 1773, Captain James Cook became the first European to sail south of the Antarctic Circle, and on 17 January 1912, Robert Falcon Scott reached the South Pole.

Present-day Antarctica contains between 1,000 and 4,000 people (depending on the season) from 27 nations (the signatories to the Antarctic Treaty). The number of penguins is less clear. Some estimates put it as high as 100 million, but the State of Atlantic Penguins (SOAP) survey in 2020 listed 5.77 million breeding pairs in 698 locations. Antarctica also has one active volcano, Mount Erebus.

There is about eight times as much ice in Antarctica as in the Arctic. If all the ice in Antarctica melted, the global sea level would rise by about 60 metres (200 feet).

The first person to be born in Antarctica was the Argentine Emilio Marcos Palma on 7 January 1978. The first person to be buried in Antarctica was the Norwegian zoologist Nicolai Hanson on 14 October 1899.

 HILLARY, OCEAN, PENGUIN

ANTELOPE

The mating behaviour of antelopes is called lekking. In 2008, it was reported that high-quality male African topi antelopes are so much in demand that they have to fight off female admirers. This is against the normal male mammalian behaviour of mating with as many females as possible. Given the choice, a male topi antelope will choose a new partner over one he has mated with before.

 BERLIN, CHAMOIS

ANTIQUES

A giant egg laid in the 17th century was put on sale for £5,000 at the Chelsea Antiques Fair in 2009. The egg, which is more than 90 centimetres (3 feet) in circumference, is probably the biggest in the world at present. It was laid by the Great Elephant Bird of Madagascar which became extinct about 1,000 years ago.

APATHY

At an election in the North Dakota city of Pillsbury in 2008, nobody turned out to vote. The mayor and two aldermen were standing for re-election unopposed, but even they could not be bothered to get to a polling station. The county auditor ruled that those in office could stay there and appoint people, including themselves, to the jobs until the next election. The mayor commented that council members are paid $48 a year, but most of that goes on doughnuts eaten at the meetings and gas to get there.

APHRODISIAC

As long ago as the 16th century, the English were using the word 'venereal' (from Venus, the Roman goddess of love) for anything connected with sexual desire. By the 17th century, however, the word had become so strongly linked with venereal disease that another word was needed for its positive aspects. Swap Venus for her Greek equivalent, Aphrodite, and the word 'aphrodisiac' was born.

Pliny the Elder, in his *Natural History*, wrote that the philosopher Democritus considered radishes to be an aphrodisiac. Radishes have also been praised for their aphrodisiac qualities in Japan and other oriental countries.

The 12th-century rabbi and physician Maimonides is also said to have recommended a radish ointment as an early form of Viagra. His recipe was to mix radish oil with mustard oil and carrot oil, then add live ants.

The Indian elephant god Ganesh is also often depicted holding a radish, which some say is connected to its supposed aphrodisiac qualities.

CARROT, CELERY, CHOCOLATE

APPLE

87.24 million tonnes of apples were produced in the world in 2019. By far the largest producer is China, with almost half of the total.

Apples are the second most valuable fruit crop in the USA behind grapes but ahead of oranges.

The apple that is said to have struck Isaac Newton and inspired the theory of gravity is a large green-skinned variety called Flower of Kent. There are over 7,000 varieties of apple in the world.

Steve Jobs, co-founder of the Apple Computer Company in 1976, said that the name of the company was inspired by his visit to an apple farm when he was on a fruitarian diet. He described the name 'Apple' as 'fun, spirited and not intimidating'.

GRAVITY, HEDGEHOG, POMEGRANATE, TURING

APRIL

The name of this month comes from the Latin 'Aprilis', though nobody is sure why the Romans gave it that name. Some say it is connected to the verb '*aperire*', to open, referring to the opening of flowers. Others say it refers to the goddess Aphrodite.

In Old English the month was also called 'Eastermonad'.

The term 'April gentleman' in English used to refer to a newly married man (by implication, a fool).

In Finland April is known as 'Huhtikuu' or 'Burnwood' month.

APRIL FOOLS

A judge in Melbourne told two robbers they were a 'pair of fools' before sending them to prison for a robbery committed on 1 April 2007. Benjamin Jorgensen, 38, and Donna Hayes, 36, were jailed for seven and eight years respectively for robbing a restaurant of a bag which they believed contained the day's takings. Later they discovered that the bag was in fact filled with bread rolls. Jorgensen also fired his gun accidentally during the heist, shooting Hayes in the buttocks.

1 April is also the date each year of the International Edible Book Festival. The date was chosen to celebrate the birthday of French gastronome and writer Jean-Anthelme Brillat-Savarin, who wrote *Physiologie du Goût* (*The Physiology of Taste*) (1825).

Since 2004, 1 April has also been celebrated as Fossil Fools Day, with demonstrations against the use of fossil fuels as sources of energy.

In Ancient Rome, 1 April was the date of the festival of Veneralia, praising the goddess Venus.

Since the early 16th century, French children have celebrated '*poisson d'Avril*' (April fish) on 1 April by sticking pictures of fish on people's backs.

On 1 April 1698, many were fooled into going to the Tower of London to 'see the lions washed'.

On 1 April 1889, the first successful dishwasher went on sale in Chicago. Its inventor Josephine Cochran said it washed faster than her servants.

♀ *DANCING, ELASTIC*

AQUARIUM

A woman at an aquarium in the Ukraine dropped her mobile phone, which was eaten by the crocodile she was trying to photograph. Staff called her number and the crocodile started to ring. 'This should have been a very dramatic shot, but things didn't work out,' the woman said.

♀ *HEADS, WEDDING*

ARACHNOLOGY

The singers David Bowie and Neil Young, the film director and actor Orson Welles, the actress Angelina Jolie, the actor Harrison Ford and the satirist Stephen Colbert have all had species of spider named after them.

So have Nelson Mandela and Frank Zappa.

Orson Welles towers above the others, however, as he had a whole genus of spiders named after him, though Frank Zappa also had a jellyfish and a fish genus named in his honour.

♀ *SPIDER*

ARCHERY

In 1545, the scholar Roger Ascham published a treatise on archery which he called *Toxophilus*. He coined the name from two Greek words meaning 'lover of the bow', and the science of archery became known as toxophily or toxophilism.

Archery itself, however, is far older. The earliest known use of bows and arrows in warfare was in 2340 BC, when Sargon of Akkad in Babylonia defeated the Sumerians with an infantry of archers.

In the 1900 Olympic archery event, live pigeons were used as targets.

The first woman to kill an elephant with a bow and arrow is believed to be the American Teressa Groenewald-Hagerman, who achieved the feat in Zimbabwe in May 2009. She says she worked out for four hours a day for eight months in order to develop the strength to draw the bow needed for the task. She says she did it to win a bet with a male colleague. Previously, the last person to have killed an elephant with a bow and arrow is thought to have been a man called Howard Hill, 60 years earlier.

Great archers:

- Lottie Dod won the Wimbledon ladies' singles championship in 1887 when she was 15, won the British Ladies Amateur Golf Championship in 1904, and took silver in the Olympic archery in 1908.
- Sybil Fenton Newall known as 'Queenie Newall' was the woman who beat Lottie Dod to win Olympic gold in 1908. She was aged 53 at the time and is still the oldest female winner of an individual Olympic gold.
- Geena Davis, the Oscar-winning actress, reached the semi-finals of the US women's archery championship in 1999 and eventually finished 24th.

♀ *BHUTAN, FOOTBALL, GOLF, OLYMPIC GAMES*

● ARGENTINA

In 1995, the first International Housewives Congress was held in the Argentine capital Buenos Aires, and in 1966 the Free Tramps Federation staged the first World Tramps Congress in the coastal resort of Mar del Plata. Among the proposals suggested at that event was the official introduction of an International Day of Idleness on 2 May as a response to Labour Day on 1 May.

The Argentine lake duck, *Oxyura vittata*, has the largest penis of any bird. In 2001, researchers from the University of Alaska discovered that its penis, when fully extended, measures about 42.5 centimetres (17 inches), which is about the same as the entire length of the duck. When not in use, the corkscrew-shaped penis retracts into the duck's abdomen.

In a paper in the journal *Nature*, Kevin McCracken explained that previously the duck's penis length had been thought to be only about 20 centimetres (8 inches), however measurements had only been taken from dissected birds: 'but in April we were in Argentina collecting birds for another genetic study, and we found this bird running around in its natural form, with its penis hanging out, which was something we'd never seen before.' He said that the trait deserved further study.

Quite apart from its length, the existence of a penis is unusual in a bird. Most male birds do not have one as they copulate by touching genital openings for a brief time.

♀ *CARNIVORE, FALKLAND ISLANDS*

● ARISTARCHUS of Samos (c.310– 230 BC)

The astronomer Aristarchus of Samos was the first person to argue that the Earth orbits the Sun rather than the other way around. A crater on the Moon and a telescope at the National Observatory of Athens are named after Aristarchus.

● ARISTOTLE (384–322 BC)

When Alexander the Great was a child, Aristotle was hired to be his tutor. Aristotle believed that the Universe had no beginning and will have no end, and that women are inferior to men.

'There was never a great genius without a tincture of madness.' Aristotle

♀ *GIRL, GRAVITY, PREGNANCY, SEX*

ARIZONA

A woman was arrested in Phoenix, Arizona, in 2010 for attempting to exchange a two-year-old child for a gun. Police said that she thought the friend to whom she offered the swap would make a better job of bringing up the child than she would. She was charged with the unlawful sale of a child and solicitation to possess a weapon by a prohibited person.

♀ CARROT, RUBBER BANDS, TRAFFIC

ARMADILLO

It is frequently stated that the nine-banded armadillo is the only animal other than the human that can suffer from leprosy. That is not quite true, as mice and rhesus monkeys have also been infected with the leprosy virus, but the armadillo is certainly the most useful experimental animal for leprosy research. Up to 5 per cent of wild armadillos are thought to suffer from leprosy.

Without its shell or carapace, an armadillo is said to resemble a rabbit.

ARMENIA

The Armenian company Grand Candy was awarded a certificate by Guinness World Records in September 2010 for making the world's biggest bar of chocolate. It weighed 4,410 kilograms (9,720 pounds) and measured 5.6 metres (18.4 feet) by 2.75 metres (9 feet). The previous record had been set by a 3,580-kilogram (7,892-pound) bar made in Italy in 2007.

ARMOUR

Under a statute of 1313, enacted during the reign of Edward II, it is illegal for a British Member of Parliament to enter the House of Commons wearing full armour. It decrees, in Anglo-Norman dialect, 'that in all Parliaments, Treatises and other Assemblies which should be made in the realm of England for ever that every Man shall come without all Force and Armour'. It has never been formally repealed.

ART

The Chilean artist Marco Evaristti displayed an exhibit at a museum in Denmark in 2000 that featured 10 blenders containing live goldfish. Guests were invited to turn on the blenders. This led to the museum director being charged with animal cruelty, though he was later acquitted.

In 2004, Evaristti's Ice Cube Project set itself the objective of painting the exposed tip of a small iceberg in Greenland red. This was achieved with the help of two icebreakers and a 20-man crew. Three fire hoses and 3,000 litres (660 gallons) of paint were used to paint the iceberg blood-red. The artist commented: 'We all have a need to decorate Mother Nature because it belongs to all us.'

In 2007, Evaristti hosted a dinner party at which he served agnolotti pasta that was topped with a meatball cooked in the artist's own fat, removed earlier in the year in a liposuction operation. Later the same year, he draped the peak of Mont Blanc with red fabric. He was arrested and detained for attempting to paint the peak red.

♀ MATISSE, PAINTING, STRESS

ARTICHOKE

The first 'Californian Artichoke Queen', crowned in 1948 in Castroville, California, was Marilyn Monroe. Castroville calls itself the Artichoke Capital of the World.

In 1959, the Castroville Artichoke Advisory Board was formed and the town has held an annual Artichoke Festival ever since, with the food available including fried, grilled, sauteed, pickled, marinated and fresh artichokes, as well as artichoke cream soup and artichoke cupcakes.

In 2018, the countries eating most artichokes were Italy (394,000 tonnes), Egypt (319,000 tonnes) and Spain (196,000 tonnes), with these three accounting for more than half the global consumption. The countries eating most artichokes per capita were Italy, Peru and Spain.

ARTIFICIAL LEG

When a plastic right leg, dressed in a stocking and a black shoe, was found in a street in Newport, Isle of Wight, in 1996, a police inspector who was trying to trace its owner commented, 'I would have thought that the person concerned has noticed it is missing.'

AMPUTATION, FLAMINGO

ASCENSION ISLAND

In January 2005, the Royal Mail admitted that the British dependency of Ascension Island in the South Atlantic had not received any post since the previous October because they had been sending it to Asunción, the capital of Paraguay, by mistake.

Ascension Island was discovered by the Portuguese navigator João da Nova on 21 May 1501, which was Ascension Day. Hence the name.

ASCOT

In 1711, Queen Anne decided that a patch of land in an area of England called East Cote was ideal for 'horses to gallop at full stretch', and that was the start of Ascot Racecourse. It was then more than century before the British parliament passed an Act of Enclosure in 1813 ensuring that Ascot Heath, though Crown property, would be kept and used in perpetuity as a public racecourse.

The regulations for Royal Ascot week range from mildly eccentric to very strict. For example:

- Divorcees were banned from the Royal Enclosure until 1955; convicted criminals and undischarged bankrupts are still banned. In the 1920s, women in the Royal Enclosure were forbidden to smoke.
- According to Ascot's Royal Enclosure dress code, 'Her Majesty's Representative wishes to point out that only formal day dress with a hat or substantial fascinator will be acceptable.'
- Gentlemen must wear morning dress, including a waistcoat, with a top hat. 'A gentleman may remove his top hat within a restaurant, a private box, a private club or that facility's terrace, balcony or garden.'
- It is traditional that when the reigning monarch finishes lunch in the Royal Box, everyone else must stop eating.
- The late Princess Diana is the only woman to have been allowed in the Royal Enclosure bare-legged.

ASH

The name of the ash tree comes from the Old English word aesc, meaning spear. Winged seeds of an ash are called samara. They are also known as keys, wingnuts and helicopters.

Ash was the name, in Old English, for the letter æ, formed by joining an 'a' and 'e' together.

The first man to have his ashes taken into space was Star Trek creator Gene

Roddenberry in 1992. Those ashes were brought back to earth but 7 grams of them were scattered in space in 1997.

'Ashes will always blow back into the face of the thrower.' Nigerian proverb

♀ *TREES*

ASH WEDNESDAY

The name of Ash Wednesday comes from the practice of placing ashes from palm branches on the heads of Christian worshippers and blessing them with the words 'remember that you are dust, and to dust you shall return'. Ash Wednesday is 46 days before Easter, being the 40 fasting days of Lent plus six Sundays, which are seen as feast days.

Until 1715, Ash Wednesday was marked in the British royal household by an officer known as the King's Cock Crower imitating a cockerel, in remembrance of St Peter being called back to repentance by a cock crow. An 18th-century account explains how this grand tradition came to be abandoned:

'On the first Ash Wednesday after the accession [in 1714] of the House of Hanover, as the Prince of Wales, afterwards George II, was sitting down to supper, this officer suddenly entered the apartment, before the chaplain said grace, and crowed "past ten o'clock". The astonished Prince, not understanding English, and mistaking the tremulation of the crow for mockery, concluded that this ceremony was intended as an insult, and instantly rose to resent it; when, with some difficulty, he was made to understand the nature of the custom, and that it was intended as a compliment, and according to court etiquette. From that period the custom was discontinued.'

♀ *LENT*

ASHES, The

The idea behind the Ashes cricket trophy dates back to England's first home cricket defeat by Australia in 1882, which led to a mock obituary in *The Sporting Times*: 'In affectionate remembrance of English cricket, which died at the Oval on 29th August, 1882.' A note at the end said: 'The body will be cremated and the ashes taken to Australia.' However, there were no physical ashes until the following year when two Australian sisters, remembering the *Sporting Times* obituary, burned the bails after an English cricket victory in Australia to give the English some real ashes to return to the motherland. The ashes now found inside the urn at Lord's Cricket Ground in London are from those bails burned in 1883.

ASPARAGUS

People have been eating asparagus since ancient times, with both the Greeks and Romans providing records detailing instructions for growing it and for medicinal uses. The Greeks in particular recommended using asparagus to cure everything from toothache to heart disease.

Roman emperors employed people with the specific job of collecting wild asparagus, and Roman aristocrats took asparagus with them when they conquered new lands.

In the early 17th century, King Louis XIV of France ordered special greenhouses to grow asparagus.

Peru is the world's largest exporter of asparagus; the largest importer, by a very long way, is the United States.

The word 'asparagus' comes from the Greek *asparagos*, meaning a shoot or sprout. The word has been known in English since the 16th century, when it was also known as 'sperage' or 'sparage'. In the 17th and 18th centuries it was commonly also known as 'sparrow-grass'.

In his diary for 20 April 1667, Samuel Pepys wrote: 'Brought home with me from Fenchurch-Street a hundred of sparrowgrass.'

♀ *CUPCAKE, CURRY, HERON-ALLEN, SHOPPING TROLLEYS*

● ASSHOLE

In 2010, the American Civil Liberties Union sued the police on behalf of a woman who had been issued a disorderly conduct citation when she yelled 'asshole' at a motorcyclist who swerved close to her.

As a result, Philadelphia State Police agreed in January 2011 to stop issuing citations to people who call motorcyclists assholes, or for similar uses of bad language.

♀ *BLACK HOLE*

● ASTROLOGY

The Babylonians invented the Zodiac signs around 700 BC, but the Greeks, in the 4th century BC, were the first to cast personal horoscopes. The Iranian calendar is based on Zodiac signs.

According to a 1998 survey by Touchline Insurance in the UK, people born under the sign of Sagittarius make fewer insurance claims than those born under any other Zodiac sign. Cancer, Aquarius and Aries make the highest number of claims, while people born under Capricorn were revealed as the clumsiest, with the most claims for accidental damage.

According to a more recent survey, Australians born under the sign of Gemini are most likely to be involved in road accidents. Research in 2011 suggested that Aquarians belong to the sign most likely to drive a Peugeot 106.

In the 1980s, Nancy Reagan used to consult an astrologer to predict assassination attempts on her husband, President Ronald Reagan.

♀ *ECONOMICS, SYPHILIS*

● ASTRONAUTS

Orbiting astronauts on the International Space Station can see 16 sunsets and 16 sunrises in 24 hours.

The furthest anyone has flown from Earth is 400,171 kilometres (248,655 miles). This record was set by the Apollo 13 crew on 14 April 1970.

According to NASA, the items most missed by astronauts on space missions are pizza, ice cream and fizzy drinks.

♀ *GRAVITY, PEANUT*

● ASTRONOMY

On 4 March 1675, John Flamsteed was appointed England's first Astronomer Royal. Astronomer is an anagram of 'moon-starer'.

Our Sun is only one of about 400 billion stars in the Milky Way galaxy, and the Hubble Telescope has revealed that the Milky Way is only one of at least 100 billion galaxies in the Universe. The Sun orbits the Milky Way galaxy about once every 200 million years.

One light year, which is the distance light travels in a year, is equal to about 5,880 billion miles. Andromeda, the nearest major galaxy to the Milky Way, is almost 3 million light years away.

Weight-loss tip: stand on the Moon and your weight will be reduced by about five-sixths. A full Moon, incidentally, is nine times as bright as a half Moon. Every year, the Moon moves about 3.8 centimetres (1.5 inches) further away from Earth.

If you want to remember the order of the planets around the Sun, one recommended mnemonic used to be the sentence 'MEn Very Easily MAke Jugs Serve Useful Nocturnal Purposes' (Mercury, Venus, Earth, Mars, Jupiter, Saturn, Uranus, Neptune, Pluto), but that was before 2006 when Pluto was downgraded to the status of 'dwarf planet' alongside Ceres and Eris. *National Geographic* held a planetary mnemonic contest to devise a new way to remember the eight planets and three dwarf planets and their order in distance from the Sun. The winner was a girl called Maryn Smith, whose award-winner was 'My Very Exciting Magic Carpet Just Sailed Under Nine Palace Elephants'.

♀ *ECLIPSE, MARS, NEPTUNE, PLUTO, SUN*

● ATHLETICS

The word 'athlete' was first recorded in English in the early 15th century, but it took another 300 years before various sports came to be referred to as 'athletics'.

The Welsh athlete Griffith Morgan ran 19 kilometres (12 miles) in 53 minutes in 1732. He won a prize of 100 sover-eigns, but fell and died when slapped on the back in congratulations.

On 24 April 1909, Harry Hillman and Lawson Robertson set a record that has still not been broken: they ran the 100-yard three-legged race in 11.0 seconds. Both men were Olympic medallists, Hillman winning three gold medals at St Louis 1904 in the 400 metres and both the 400-metre and 200-metre hurdles, while Robertson took bronze in the standing high jump in 1904, silver in the same event in 1906,

and another bronze in the long jump in the same year.

In 2013, Mark Howlett (England) and Rab Lee (Scotland) set a record by running 109.8 kilometres (68.23 miles) three-legged in a 24-hour trail race. This was not only the furthest ever three-legged run in 24 hours, but the furthest ever three-legged run with no time limit. Howlett and Lee employed a technique known as 'The Maverick', which they had invented, where one of the pair leans slightly in front of the other to help them go faster.

It is illegal to run a three-legged race for money in British Columbia. Killing a sasquatch (also known as Bigfoot) is also illegal there.

♀ *FINGER LENGTH, OLYMPIC GAMES, SEX TEST, SPRINTING*

● ATLANTIC

The word 'Atlantic' originally referred to the mythical Mount Atlas in Syria, on which the heavens were said to rest. It was subsequently applied to the sea near the west coast of Africa, and finally to the whole ocean.

In 1957, the US air force completed a survey of the Atlantic Ocean but refused to divulge its width on the grounds that the information might be of military use to the Russians.

In 1995, two Englishmen – Jason Lewis and Steve Smith – became the first to cross the Atlantic from east to west on a pedalo.

The Atlantic Ocean contains 23 per cent of the world's seawater. The Pacific contains 48 per cent. There are roughly 20.8 trillion trillion tablespoons of water in the Atlantic.

♀ *LINDBERG OCEAN, PANAMA, PUERTO RICO*

ATOMIC ENERGY

The word 'atom' comes from a Greek word *atomon*, meaning 'that which cannot be divided'. We have known this was wrong since 1932 when John Cockcroft and E.T.S. Walton split the atom for the first time. Soon after, science made another big mistake in estimating the power of atomic energy. This came in 1933, when Ernest Rutherford said, 'Energy produced by the breaking down of the atom is a very poor kind of thing. Anyone who expects a source of power from the transformation of these atoms is talking moonshine.'

The first atom bomb, which was exploded in New Mexico in 1945, released 1,000,000,000,000,000,000,000 ergs of energy. Einstein commented, 'The release of atom power has changed everything except our way of thinking.' He went on to say, 'If only I had known, I should have become a watchmaker.'

ATTRACTIVENESS

Why are men attracted by the colour red? A paper published in the online science journal *PLoS ONE* in 2012 reported research showing that one common explanation was probably wrong.

Earlier research had established that women associated with red objects or red surroundings are seen as more desirable, and the hypothesis was that women use the colour red to announce impending ovulation and sexual receptiveness. It was thought this might be associated with genital colour, making men more attracted in consequence.

The new research at the University of Kent, however, set about determining whether men really do prefer women with red genitals, and their conclusion is summarised in the title of their paper: 'Red Is Not a Proxy Signal for Female Genitalia in Humans' by Sarah E. Johns, Lucy A. Hargrave and Nicholas E. Newton-Fisher.

The experiment involved showing heterosexual male subjects 16 pictures of female genitalia, which had been obtained by modifying the colours in four different pictures so that each original was presented in four versions: pale pink, light pink, dark pink, red.

The men were asked to rate the sexual attractiveness of each picture on a scale from 0 to 100.

Summarising the results, the researchers state: 'We found a relative preference for pinker genital images, with redder genitalia rated significantly less sexually attractive.'

They further point out that this effect was independent of the prior sexual experience of the men doing the rating or variations in the shape of the female genitals.

BEAUTY, HIPS, VOICE

AUCTION

The highest recorded price paid for bottled ghosts at auction is NZ$1,983 (US$1,410). A woman from Christchurch said that she had captured the spirits of an old man and a young girl in vials after an exorcism session at her house. She offered them for sale in an online auction in 2010.

AUGUST

August was named in 8 BC after the Roman Emperor Augustus because it was the month in which many significant events in his rise to power occurred.

In the USA, the first Saturday in August is National Mustard Day.

The Anglo-Saxons called August by the name Weod-monath (weed month) because it is the month when weeds and other plants grow most rapidly.

In Sweden, the third Thursday in August is known as Surströmming-spremiär – the first day for selling surströmming, which is fermented Baltic herring.

Henry VI, Part 1 and *The Tempest* are the only Shakespeare plays that mention the month of August.

'In August, choler and melancholy much increase from whence proceeds long-lasting fevers and agues not easily cured.'
Richard Saunders, 1679

AUGUSTUS (63 BC–AD 14)

Augustus was the first Roman Emperor. The name he was given at birth was Gaius Octavius, but he changed it to Gaius Julius Caesar Octavianus when he was adopted by his great-uncle Julius Caesar. Seventeen years later, in 8 BC, the Senate voted to give him the name Augustus, meaning 'Revered One'. He was 1.7 metres (5 feet 7 inches) tall but is said to have worn thick-soled shoes to make him look taller. According to the historian Suetonius, his teeth were small, few in number and decayed. He softened the hairs on his legs by singeing them with red-hot walnut shells and he carried a seal-skin amulet, which he believed protected him from his greatest fear: lightning.

AUSTEN, Jane (1775–1817)

Jane Austen brewed her own beer, flavoured with spruce buds or needles and molasses to give added sweetness. She was the earliest known writer to use the expression 'dinner party', in *Mansfield Park*, Chapter 41: 'To have had him join their family dinner-party, and see all their deficiencies, would have been dreadful!' Other words Austen introduced include 'sponge-cake' and 'doorbell'.

According to her niece, Jane Austen always wore a cap.

♀ BASEBALL, CHRISTMAS, MARRIAGE, SLIME

AUSTRALIA

Australia Day, on 26 January, marks the anniversary of the arrival of the British First Fleet at Port Jackson, New South Wales, in 1788, and the raising of the British flag at that site by Governor Arthur Phillip. The first celebrations of 26 January were in 1808 but it was not called Australia Day until 1935.

More than 25 per cent of all people living in Australia today were born in another country.

The world's largest cattle station is Anna Creek in South Australia. It is bigger than Belgium.

Australia has more kangaroos than people and more wild camels than any other country. They even export camels to Saudi Arabia. China is the only country with more sheep than Australia.

Mount Disappointment in Australia was given its name in 1824 by explorers Hamilton Hume and William Hovell, who were disappointed with the view from the top.

An emu and a kangaroo are on the Australian coat of arms as they rarely walk backwards.

Sydney is Australia's biggest city, Mount Kosciuszko its highest summit. Both are named after men who never visited Australia. Mount Kosciuszko is named after a Polish patriot who fought alongside Washington in the American

Civil War, and the largest city is named after Lord Sydney.

The first man to fly an aeroplane in a public display in Australia was the escapologist Harry Houdini.

The first Australian animals in space were spiders that perished on the US Shuttle Columbia in 2003.

The Indian cobra is the 15th most deadly snake on Earth; the top 14 are all found in Australia.

♀ *DINGO, KANGAROO, KOALA, WOMBAT*

AUSTRIA

The world's biggest liver dumpling was cooked in the Austrian village of Zams on 16 September 1996. It weighed 1.8 tonnes.

In 1998, Austria held the first international tennis tournament for over-85s.

Austria has more accountants per head of population than any other country.

AVOCADO

The name of the avocado comes to us from the Aztecs, who called the fruit *ahuacatl*, which was the word for 'testicle' in the Nahuatl language.

The avocado was so named because of its shape. The Spanish conquerors of the Aztecs adopted the word, changing it to *aguacate* and later to avocado, which was also the Spanish word for a lawyer. Lawyers, however, were not named after testicles, the same word in their case

coming from the Latin verb *advocare* meaning 'to call to one's aid'.

The liqueur advocaat, made from eggs, sugar and brandy, is so called because it was seen as a lawyers' tipple.

AZERBAIJAN

The first time Pope John Paul II stayed in a hotel was during his visit to Azerbaijan in 2002. Avoiding expectations that they would choose a five-star international hotel, the papal delegation settled instead for the Hotel Irshad, whose name meant 'spiritual guide'. Rooms included views over the Caspian Sea, jacuzzi-style bathtubs and around 30 satellite TV channels.

The national animal of Azerbaijan is the Karabakh horse, which is praised for its speed, intelligence and endurance. Horsemeat was once widely eaten in Azerbaijan, but has now fallen out of favour.

'Cheap meat never makes a good soup.'
Azerbaijan proverb

♀ *AFGHANISTAN*

AZTEC

The *Oxford English Dictionary* lists eight words that may have come into English from the Aztec: avocado, axolotl, jalap (a purgative drug), ocelot, shack, tacamahac (an aromatic resin), teguexin (a South American lizard) and tule (a species of bulrush).

BABBAGE, Charles (1791–1871)

As a student at Trinity College, Cambridge, the mathematician and computer pioneer Charles Babbage was a member of the Ghost Club, investigating supernatural phenomena, and the Extractors Club, dedicated to ensuring that its members were freed from the madhouse, should any be committed to one.

He had a strong dislike of 'the Mob', which led him to write 'Observations of Street Nuisances' in 1864, including a tally of 165 such nuisances over a period of 80 days. He particularly disliked organ-grinders, of whom he wrote: 'It is difficult to estimate the misery inflicted upon thousands of persons, and the absolute pecuniary penalty imposed upon multitudes of intellectual workers by the loss of their time, destroyed by organ-grinders and other similar nuisances.' In the 1860s, he also took up a campaign against hoop-rolling in the streets, which he held responsible for many accidents. Half of Babbage's brain is kept at the Hunterian Museum in the Royal College of Surgeons in London; the other half is on display in the Science Museum, London.

Babbage once wrote to Alfred Lord Tennyson to point out his dissatisfaction at the poet's lines 'Every moment dies a man, every moment one is born.' As he pointed out, to reflect accurately population growth, the correct version should, at the time of writing, have said: 'every moment one and one-sixteenth is born'.

The moon crater Babbage is named after him.

⚲ *BYRON Ada, COMPUTERS*

BABIES

Experiments at the Munich Institute of Medical Psychology in 2001 showed that men were more successful than women at correctly identifying from the smell whether T-shirts had been worn by newborn babies or older children.

⚲ *NAMES, PREGNANCY, SEX, TWINS*

BABOONS

The gelada baboon of Ethiopia is the only monkey that lives entirely on grass.

According to research published in February 2013 ('Evidence for tactical concealment in a wild primate' in *Nature Communications*), 91 per cent of copulations between gelada baboons are between the dominant male in a group and females in the same group. The other 9 per cent are between females and other males. In 20 per cent of those extra-pair copulations, however, the dominant male finds out about it and becomes very aggressive towards both the male and female involved.

To avoid this danger of reprisal, cheating pairs were found to significantly suppress their copulation vocalisations, keeping down the volume while having sex, though females tend to be noisy when having sex with the dominant male.

Researchers also found that infidelity to the dominant male was far more common when the dominant male was more than 20 metres (66 feet) away.

In 2019, a paper in the journal *Animal Behaviour* reported that female baboons in Senegal grunt more frequently when infants are present.

⚲ *BERLIN, MERMAID*

● BACCARAT

The Gaming Control Board of Nevada fined Caesars Palace Casino $250,000 for allowing a high-stakes baccarat player to dance on a card table while the game was in progress. The Board complained that the casino had failed to take action to protect the game and the customer, who had climbed onto the table three times, and even placed a bet while standing on the table.

In the first James Bond book, *Casino Royale*, published in 1953, the plot centres on a game of baccarat between Bond and the SMERSH agent known as Le Chiffre. The full version of the book even included an introduction to the game. In the 1967 film of *Casino Royale*, the game was still baccarat, but in the 2006 film it was changed to poker, with Bond, Le Chiffre and others staking all on a game of Texas Hold'em.

● BACH, Johann Sebastian (1685–1750)

The only grandson of J.S. Bach to make his living as a composer was Wilhelm Friedrich Ernst Bach, who was born nine years after the death of J.S. Bach and died on Christmas Day 1845 at the age of 86. Despite being on record as saying that 'heredity tends to run out of ideas', he composed a number of well-received works, including a concerto for six hands on one piano, which is written to be performed by one large male and two petite female pianists. The man sits between the two women, stretches his arms around their waists, and plays at the opposite extremes of the keyboard while the ladies play their parts in the middle register.

J.S. Bach died on 28 July 1750; Antonio Vivaldi died on 28 July 1741. Other less musical 28 July deaths include Thomas Cromwell, executed on that day in 1540, and Maximilien Robespierre, guillotined on 28 July 1794.

● BACHELORS

The only bachelor ever to be President of the United States was James Buchanan, who was elected in 1857. While he was in office, his niece, Harriet Lane, served as First Lady.

By contrast, men who were still unmarried at the age of 30 in ancient Sparta forfeited the right to vote.

⚲ *ITALY, MARRIAGE, OSTRICH*

● BACON

Making bacon by preserving and salting pork bellies began with the Chinese around 1500 BC. The earliest account of bacon and eggs for breakfast dates back to 1560.

The earliest known use of the phrase 'streaky bacon' was in Dickens's *Oliver Twist* in 1838, though Shakespeare had mentioned bacon in both *Henry IV, Part 1* and *The Merry Wives Of Windsor*.

The earliest reference to a 'bacon sandwich' listed in the *Oxford English Dictionary* was by George Orwell in 1931, while the first mention of a 'bacon sarnie' was in the *Daily Express* on 21 August 1986.

Almost a third of all pork consumption in the UK is accounted for by bacon. According to the Office for National Statistics, the average household in the UK spent about 80p a week on bacon and ham in 2019, which works out at a total of around £1.24 billion every year.

The US gift company Archie McPhee has a range of bacon products including bacon soap, bacon bandages, bacon-flavoured toothpicks, bacon air freshener and bacon dental floss.

⚲ *BAUDELAIRE, BREAKFAST, SMELL*

BACON, Francis (1561–1626)

Francis Bacon became the first QC when Queen Elizabeth I made him her legal advisor as Queen's Counsel in 1597. He later became Lord High Chancellor of England, but after being fined £40,000 for 23 charges of corruption including accepting bribes, he devoted his life to science and knowledge.

His scientific experiments, however, did not always go well and he died from a severe cold in 1626, which he is said to have contracted while attempting to stuff a chicken with snow in an early attempt to invent frozen food. It was almost another 300 years before Clarence Birdseye succeeded in inventing frozen food in 1923.

⚲ *BREAKFAST, URINATION*

BACULUM

The baculum, or penis bone, is present in all carnivorous and insectivorous mammals except the human being and the hyena.

In Latin, the word originally meant a rod or stick. In Alaska, the baculum of a walrus, seal, sea lion or polar bear is known as an oosik.

The longest baculum is that of the walrus. In 2007, a 1.4-metre (4.5-foot) long fossilised penis bone from an extinct species of walrus, believed to be the largest in existence, sold for $8,000.

In 2015, Professor Ziony Zevit of the American Jewish University in Los Angeles came up with the interesting theory that when God created Eve, she was made not from one of Adam's ribs but from his penis bone. If she had been made of a rib, he argued, then women would have one more rib than men. She must have been made from a bone that men originally possessed but then lost, and he saw the baculum as the most likely answer.

⚲ *BAGUETTE*

BADGER

The honey badger – which is not a badger but its own species, probably more closely related to the polecat – has the reputation of being the most fearless and vicious of all mammals.

When attacking a male of another species, the honey badger is said to go for the genitals. The first published record of this behaviour was an account in 1947 of a honey badger reportedly castrating an adult buffalo.

Other animals alleged to have been castrated by honey badgers include wildebeest, waterbuck, zebras and humans.

The honey badger is very difficult to kill owing to its remarkably tough skin, which can deflect spears and arrows. This also helps it when it tears bees' nests apart in search of honey and grubs, when it seems immune to the stings of the annoyed residents.

The male honey badger makes a low grunting noise when mating.

BAGHDAD

Baghdad was founded on 30 July 762. It was probably the largest city in the world until about AD 930.

⚲ *PYRAMID*

BAGUETTE

The baguette became popular in France around 1920 and is said to owe its existence to a French law that banned bakers from working before 4am. That gave them insufficient time to make freshly baked loaves for their customers' breakfasts, so they started making long, thin loaves that baked more quickly.

Under French law, the dough for a baguette may not contain any fat or oil. Under European law, however, such additions are not prohibited, which is why Fosters Bakery in Barnsley, Yorkshire, began selling baguettes to French railways in 2008. The buffets on SNCF trains wanted baguettes that did not go stale as quickly as usual, and the Barnsley bakers achieved that objective by adding fats, which their French competitors could not do.

On 5 November 2009, overheating in the Large Hadron Collider at CERN in Switzerland, which necessitated a shut-down of the system, was blamed on a bird dropping a piece of baguette into a part of the Collider's outdoor machinery.

The word baguette literally means 'little rod', and is derived from the Latin *baculum*, a stick or staff, which is also the name for a mammal's penis bone.

BAHAMAS

When Christopher Columbus discovered the New World in 1492, the first land he saw was probably one of the 700 islands of the Bahamas. He called it San Salvador, but it is unclear whether this is the same island that was named San Salvador in 1926; since the 1680s it had been known as Watlings Island.

Woodes Rogers, who was appointed the first Royal Governor of the Bahamas in 1718, had been a pirate and slave trader. He is remembered as the captain of the ship that rescued Alexander Selkirk – the original inspiration for Daniel Defoe's Robinson Crusoe – from the island of Juan Fernández.

Perry Christie, who was Prime Minister of the Bahamas from 2002 to 2007 and from 2012 to 2017, won a bronze medal in the triple jump at the Central American and Caribbean Games in 1962.

Bahamas has won 16 Olympic medals (8 gold, 2 silver, 6 bronze) which is more than any other country with a population less than 1 million, and more per head of population than any other country, just ahead of Finland, Hungary and Sweden.

⚲ *BRANDING, EDWARD VIII, INCOME TAX*

BAHRAIN

Bahrain is the third smallest independent nation in Asia and the smallest in the Middle East. Despite this, it has the world's largest underwater theme park, called Dive Bahrain, spread across 100,000 square metres (just over 1 million square feet) and includes a 70-metre (230-foot) fully submerged Boeing 747 jumbo jet.

There were officially 36 Jews living in Bahrain in 2007. Current estimates vary between 30 and 50.

♀ CONSENT, INCOME TAX, KUWAIT

● BAIL

In 2004, a special court in Ahmedabad, India, turned down a prisoner's request to be allowed bail so that he could go home and have sex with his wife. The man, who had been charged under an anti-terrorism law, said that he had been in jail more than 30 months and he and his wife were suffering mental trauma because they had not had sex for a long time. The court turned down his request, saying that if it granted bail in this case, many other prisoners would ask for the same thing.

♀ RICHARD III

● BAIRD, John Logie (1888–1946)

When John Logie Baird made his first successful transmission of a television picture on 2 October 1925 (of a ventriloquist's dummy known as 'Stooky Bill', incidentally), he went to the offices of the *Daily Express* to tell them of his invention. The news editor, however, is reported to have been less than impressed. According to one of his staff, he said, 'For God's sake, go down to reception and get rid of a lunatic who's down there. He says he has a machine for seeing by wireless! Watch him – he may have a razor on him.'

Before he invented television, Baird briefly ran a jam factory in Trinidad and Tobago.

● BALFOUR, Arthur (1848–1930)

Arthur Balfour, who was British Prime Minister from 1902 to 1905, was the nephew of Robert Arthur Talbot Gascoyne-Cecil, 3rd Marquess of Salisbury, who preceded him as PM. Their relationship is probably the origin of the phrase 'Bob's your uncle'.

When Major Clopton Wingfield invented a game he called 'Sphairistike' in 1872, it is said that Balfour was the person who suggested to him that 'lawn tennis' would be a better name.

Balfour was the first British Prime Minister to own a motorcar.

♀ DAYLIGHT SAVING

● BALI

The Balinese traditionally forbade sex for the sick or malformed. This may be connected with another traditional Balinese belief, that hurried love-making will result in deformed babies.

The names given to children in Bali indicates their birth order: The first born are called Wayan, Putu, Gede, or for a girl, Ni Luh. Which of those is chosen indicates the caste or social status of the child. Second-born children are named Made, Kadek or Nengah. The third born is given the name Nyoman or Komang, and fourth-born children are always named Ketut.

Wayan is a Balinese name meaning 'eldest'; Made and Nengah mean 'middle'; Kadek means 'little brother' or 'little sister'.

● BALLET

In February 2008, in western Romania, ballet classes were instituted for police officers. A spokesman explained: 'The aim is to develop an ability to regulate traffic and achieve elegance in their movements, which will not only be agreeable to the eyes but could also help drivers waiting at a red light get rid of their stress or sadness.'

Two thousand ballet-goers had to be evacuated from London's Royal Opera

House one evening in 2001 when a fire alarm was triggered by an exploding baked potato.

♀ DONKEY, TURKMENISTAN, YEARS

⬤ BALLIOL COLLEGE

Balliol College, Oxford, was founded in 1263 by John de Balliol, who was the father of King John I of Scotland. According to the Prime Minister, Herbert Asquith, Balliol men display 'the tranquil consciousness of an effortless superiority'.

Balliol has produced four UK prime ministers (Herbert Asquith, Harold Macmillan, Edward Heath and Boris Johnson), which is a long way behind the 13 produced by Christ Church but ahead of all other Oxford colleges.

♀ CHOCOLATE

⬤ BALLOON

The first living creatures to take to the skies in a hot-air balloon were a sheep, a cockerel and a duck, launched by the Montgolfier brothers in September 1783. All survived the flight, but the cockerel broke a wing, thought to be the result of its being kicked by the sheep.

The first recorded manned flight was made two months later by Jean-François Pilâtre de Rozier and the Marquis d'Arlandes. The balloon caught fire but both were unharmed. Another pioneer balloonist who narrowly avoided disaster was Jacques Charles, who also made a flight in 1783, from Paris. When he drifted low over fields, his balloon was attacked by farmers who thought he must be the Devil. He placated them with champagne.

On 4 June 1784, in Lyon, France, the opera singer Madame Elisabeth Thible became the first woman to fly in a Montgolfier hot-air balloon. King Gustave III of Sweden was among those who came to watch, and the balloon was named *Gustave* in his honour. Madame Thible was accompanied by Monsieur Fleurant, who acted as pilot of the balloon. As soon as the balloon took off, they sang two operatic duets together.

In 1808, two men called de Grandpré and le Pique had a duel from balloons after a dispute over a woman. Le Pique's balloon was shot and he crashed to his death.

In 1999, Brian Jones of the UK and Bertrand Piccard of Switzerland became the first people to fly round the world non-stop in a balloon. It took them 19 days, 12 hours and 47 minutes. On completing the flight, Jones said: 'The first thing I'll do is phone my wife, and then, like the good Englishman I am, I'll have a cup of tea.'

The first person to cross the English Channel in a wicker basket carried by a cluster of helium-filled balloons was Jonathan Trappe, who did so on 28 May 2010. The flight used 55 balloons, took four hours and landed – by cutting loose some of the balloons – in a cabbage field in France.

The toy balloon owes its invention to Michael Faraday, who used balloons to store gases produced in his chemical experiments in 1824.

♀ CHANNEL, LITHUANIA, SPORT, WASHINGTON

⬤ BALLPOINT

The first patent for a ballpoint pen was awarded to John Loud, an English leather tanner, on 30 October 1888. The instrument was intended only for the purpose of marking leather and the patent was never exploited to create a more universal writing device.

Research conducted for National

Office Week in the UK in 2008 revealed that the average Bic ballpoint pen can draw a line 3 kilometres (1.9 miles) long.

BALZAC, Honoré de (1799–1850)

The author Balzac was suckled by a wet-nurse and did not meet his rich mother until he was four years old. After returning to his family home, he was kept away from his parents then sent to a grammar school where he spent a great deal of time in a punishment cell. At the age of 15, he attempted suicide by jumping off a bridge on the Loire River.

Always in debt through bad business ventures, he seemed destined to fail at everything until he developed a passion for writing, intricately describing French society after the revolution.

According to one account, a typical meal for the writer during the periods between his compulsive writing episodes might have comprised 100 oysters, 12 lamb cutlets, two roast partridges, a duckling, various fruits and vast quantities of coffee.

BANANA

Botanically, the banana is not a fruit but a berry. It is the largest known plant without a solid trunk. If we do classify them as a fruit, however, then bananas, by weight, are the world's second highest fruit crop, just behind oranges but ahead of grapes. India and Brazil produce more bananas than any other countries.

Bananas were first sold in Britain on 10 April 1633. Three hundred and forty-seven years and one day later, Dr Canaan Banana became President of Zimbabwe.

In February 1946, a girl in Bridlington, Yorkshire, died after eating four bananas from the first crop to reach Britain's shops after the war.

European Commission Regulation (EC) No 2257/94 of 16 September 1994 consists of 1,831 words, including specifications for the length (not less than 14 centimetres/5.5 inches) and shape ('free from abnormal curvature') of bananas. It does not apply to plantains.

Bananas contain more vitamin B6 than any other fresh fruit. This vitamin is commonly associated with creating a good mood and may justify the Latin name for the banana, which is *Musa sapientum*, meaning 'fruit of the wise men'.

When stealing bananas, elephants in Burma have been known to silence bells hung round their neck by clogging them with mud so they won't be caught.

The first banana-eating championship in Estonia in 1997 was won by Mait Lepik, who ate 10 bananas in three minutes. His secret was to save time by eating the skins as well. The world record for the most bananas peeled and eaten in one minute is eight, set by Patrick Bertoletti (USA) on 14 January 2012. His compatriot and rival Matt Stonie, however, ate 23 already peeled bananas in two minutes in 2013.

Because of their potassium content, bananas are slightly radioactive.

More than 40,000 bananas were ordered for the players at Wimbledon in 2019.

COLOMBIA, FRUITFLY, HOXHA, ST LUCIA

BANGLADESH

Bangladesh is the most crowded country on Earth, with 1,265 people per square kilometre (3,277 per square mile).

In February 1986, the Bangladesh government offered a bounty of about £7 for every 1,000 dead rodent bodies in a campaign to eliminate rodents that were destroying food crops worth £350 million a year.

During the 2010 World Cup, Bangladesh power authorities asked shops and shopping malls in the capital Dhaka to shut in the evening so that fans could watch the football on television without overloading the power supply. This followed attacks on several power distribution centres after a loss of transmission from South Africa.

⚲ EXAMINATIONS, HAIL, MUGGING

BANKING

In a rare interview given by a living goddess in Nepal in April 2010, Chanira Bajracharya said that she hoped for a career in banking when her term as a goddess was over. The interview took place after the Nepalese government ruled that goddesses must be properly educated and she had become the first goddess to take the school leaving certificate examination. The 'Kurami' or 'living goddess' renounces her status as adulthood approaches. Chanira, who retired as a goddess at the age of 15, had held the post since she was six. She then became a business student.

BAR CODES

The first three digits of a 13-digit bar code (the standard type on products sold in Europe) identify the country of origin. For example, codes beginning 000 to 139 are from the USA or Canada; 300 to 379 indicate France or Monaco; 400 to 440 Germany; 500 to 509 the UK.

This national identifier, however, gives the country of origin of the bar code itself, which may not be the country of origin of the product it is attached to. Irrespective of the nation of origin, newspapers and magazines always have a code beginning 977 and books are 978.

On 26 June 1974, in Troy, Ohio, a packet of Wrigley's chewing gum was the first item to be scanned by a bar-code reader.

BARBADOS

Barbados was the only foreign country George Washington ever visited. He spent six weeks there when he was 19.

Under the Barbados Slave Code of 1661, a slave was guaranteed one new set of clothes every year. The official title of this Slave Code was 'An Act for Better Ordering and Governing of Negroes'. A slave's master could face a fine of $15 if he intentionally burnt the slave to death for no particular reason other than 'Bloody Mindedness'.

Several amendments to the Code were made in the later 17th century, including a clause in 1688 ruling that: 'No person of the Hebrew Nation residing in any Sea-Port Town of this Island, shall keep or employ any Negro or other Slave … for any Use or Service whatsoever.'

⚲ GRAPEFRUIT, NELSON

BARBER

Historically, barbers were also dentists and surgeons, practising tooth extraction, bloodletting and leeching, which did far more harm than good.

In England, barbers were chartered as a guild, the Company of Barbers, in 1462 by Edward IV.

The barbers and surgeons guilds were merged into one by a statute of Henry VIII in 1540. In 1745, George II passed several acts to separate surgeons from barbers.

In ancient Rome, barbers dressed cuts with spiders' webs soaked in vinegar.

In 2011, Nabi Salehi of Putney, London, set a record by giving 526 haircuts in 24 hours. The record for most people cutting hair at the same time is 552, set at a cosmetologists' convention in the US in 2010.

The correct term for a fear of having your hair cut is tonsurephobia.

♀ MEDICINE, STRIKE, URINATION

● BARBIE

The Barbie doll made her first appearance on 9 March 1959, which is therefore her official birthday. Her designer Ruth Handler named her after her daughter Barbara, and Barbie's full name is in fact Barbara Millicent Roberts.

A standard Barbie doll is 29 centimetres (11.5 inches) tall, and is said to be one-sixth lifesize, which corresponds to a height of 1.75 metres (5 feet 9 inches). Barbie's scaled-up vital statistics have been estimated at 36 inches (chest), 18 inches (waist) and 33 inches (hips). With a supposed weight of 50 kilograms (110 pounds), Barbie would have a body mass index (BMI) of 16.24, which fits the criteria for anorexia. According to research in Helsinki, she would lack the level of body fat required for a woman to menstruate.

In 2012, when the West imposed sanctions against Iranian oil exports, the Iranians retaliated by banning the sale of Barbie dolls to protect the country from decadent Western cultural influences.

Worldwide, around three Barbie dolls are sold every second.

Bettina Dorfmann of Germany owns a record number of Barbies, estimated in 2019 to be over 18,000 dolls.

A Barbie with a genuine diamond necklace was sold at auction in New York in 2010 for $302,500.

Barbie split up with her boyfriend Ken in 2004 after dating him for 43 years.

♀ CHICKEN

● BARCELONA

There were no beaches in Barcelona until 1992. It was decided to create seven beaches for the city when it staged the Olympic Games that year.

Statistical information for Barcelona:
- 1.4 million trees including 90,924 palm trees (2017)
- 1.62 million people living in Barcelona (2018)
- 3,180 kilometres (1,976 miles) of single carriageway roads (2018)
- 2.5 million square metres (27 million square feet) of cemeteries (2019), containing 336,000 graves
- 30 million: average number of tourists every year who visited Barcelona in 2010–19 (2020). Each tourist spent on average 2.7 nights in the city.

♀ COLUMBUS, MADONNA

● BARKING

In 2009, 30 dogs in Finsbury Park, north London, set a record for the loudest collective bark. Their final attempt of three reached 115 decibels. That record was beaten later the same year by 76 dogs in Colorado whose bark measured 124 decibels.

● BARLEY

Seven per cent of the Irish barley crop goes to the production of Guinness.

♀ PREGNANCY TEST, WHISKY

● BARNACLE

Barnacles are hermaphrodites, which means they have both male and female sex organs and can reproduce without the help of a friend. However, barnacles prefer mating with other barnacles rather than inseminating themselves, which poses a problem as they spend their entire lives anchored to the same spot. Barnacles have therefore evolved very long penises, about eight times as long as their body, the longest penis–body ratio in the animal world.

In 2008, Christopher Neufeld and Richard Palmer, of the University of Alberta, published research showing that barnacles can change the width and length of their penises to adapt to sea conditions. Their experiments involved transplanting barnacles from rough sea to calmer waters and vice versa to see if their penises changed shape. A major difficulty of the research, as Neufeld put it, was that 'It's hard to get barnacles to extend their penises on demand in the lab.' To get round this problem, they artificially inflated the barnacles' genitalia with seawater using a custom-made penis pump built out of tubes and hypodermic syringes. The results showed that barnacles living in rough waters have shorter, stouter penises that are better suited to withstand strong waves.

BARRIE, Sir James Matthew (1860–1937)

J.M. Barrie, the author of *Peter Pan*, was impotent, ambidextrous, refused to pay income tax for many years and is claimed by some to have invented the name 'Wendy'. He is said to have coined the name from the utterings of a little girl called Margaret Henley who always called Barrie 'my friendy', which came out as 'my fwendy' or sometimes 'my fwendy-wendy'. Margaret Henley died when only six years old, but Barrie perpetuated her memory in the name of Wendy Darling. Actually there were earlier records of Britons called Wendy. There were two in the 1881 census, and there is a record of a boy named Wendy in the late 18th century, but it

was certainly Barrie's *Peter Pan* that popularised the name.

Barrie was godfather to the naturalist Sir Peter Scott, who was the son of his friend, the Antarctic explorer Robert Falcon Scott.

⚲ PETER PAN, ROSES

BASEBALL

The earliest recorded use of the word 'baseball' in an English novel is in Jane Austen's *Northanger Abbey* written in 1798–99, though the word had appeared in print some 50 years earlier.

A 1791 bylaw in Pittsfield, Massachusetts, banned the playing of baseball within 80 yards of the town meeting house.

In 1996 in Los Angeles, a couple found guilty of lewd conduct after engaging in a sexual act during a baseball game at Dodger Stadium were ordered to buy 50 tickets each for games that season and donate them to charity.

According to the paper 'Life Expectancy of Major League Baseball Umpires', published in the journal *The Physician and Sportsmedicine* in May 2000, baseball umpires have exactly the same life expectancy as anyone else.

In 2013, an appellate court in Kansas City ruled that 'The risk of being hit in the face by a hot dog is not a well-known incidental risk of attending a baseball game. Consequently, a plaintiff may not be said to have consented to, and voluntarily assumed, the risk by attending the game.' The ruling overturned the verdict of a lower court in a case brought by a man who had suffered a detached retina and facial injuries when hit by a foil-wrapped hot dog thrown by the local team's mascot. The court in 2011 had ruled that anyone purchasing a ticket for a baseball game assumes the risk of a hot-dog related injury.

♀ *COSTA RICA, DOLPHIN*

BASKETBALL

On 15 January 1892, the Massachusetts physician and sports coach Dr James Naismith published the rules of his newly invented game of basketball. His motivation is variously given as a desire to have a game less injury-prone than football, or to give his young sportsmen something to do when it was too cold and wet to play outside.

Some suggested that it be called 'Naismith's Game' but Naismith proposed basketball. In 1891, his original game was played with peach baskets and a soccer ball. At first, the basket had its bottom still in place, so someone had to climb up and remove the ball after anyone scored.

His original rules insisted that the ball be thrown from where it was caught, so no dribbling.

Basketball is the national sport of Lithuania. It has been included at every Olympic Games since 1936 and was a demonstration sport in 1904.

Players in the US National Basketball Association (NBA) are said, on average, to be the world's best paid sportsmen. The average height of players in the NBA in 2021–22 was 198.6cm (6ft 6.2in).

Pope John Paul II (2000) and Pope Francis (2015) were both made honorary members of the Harlem Globetrotters basketball team.

♀ *LITHUANIA, VASECTOMY, VOLLEYBALL*

BASS

The sea bass always reaches maturity as a male, then after one or two spawnings, it changes sex and becomes female.

BASTARD

In 2012, the Alabama Alcoholic Beverage Control Board banned the sale of Dirty Bastard beer, though Fat Bastard wine and Raging Bitch beer had been approved for sale for some years.

Officially, the ban was because of 'profanity on the label' and was motivated by a desire to 'keep dirty pictures and dirty words away from children'.

The state has drawn up a list of words that they think ought to be banned from labels, including the word 'bastard', but the approval for Fat Bastard wine dates back to before the list was compiled.

The first article of the constitution of the Old Bastards Vintage Motorcycle Club in Bastard Township, Ontario, reads as follows: 'The official Club name shall be "Old Bastards Vintage Motorcycle Club". It may also be referred to as "OB"s or "OBVMC" but hereafter in this document is referred to as "the Club". The headquarters of this Club will never be changed from Delta, Ontario, Bastard Township. This article shall not be subject to amendment.'

Quentin Tarantino's 2009 Oscar-winning film *Inglourious Basterds* takes its misspelt title from a 1978 Italian war film, *The Inglorious Bastards*, directed by Enzo Castellari. Castellari himself appeared in cameo roles in both films, as a German mortar squad commander in his original film and as a German general in Tarantino's film.

♀ *TEQUILA*

BAT

In 1943 the US army developed a novel incendiary bomb involving bats with napalm strapped to their wings. This bat bomb project was abandoned in 1944, after the USA decided that the atom bomb might be a better idea.

The earliest known use of the term 'batshit crazy' cited in the *Oxford English Dictionary* is from 1993, but it tells us that 'batshit' has been used as a synonym for 'insane' since 1971. 'Apeshit', however, has been used in the same sense since 1955.

In 2010, after monitoring the calls of 30 species of bat, researchers in Australia announced their finding that bats speak with regional accents.

♀ *BAUDELAIRE, DICKENS, FRUIT BAT, MOTH*

BATMAN

Since 2013, the University of Victoria in British Colombia has offered a course in 'The Science of Batman'. According to the university, it covers: 'The extreme range of adaptability of the human body explored through the life of the Caped Crusader; examines human potential using Batman as a metaphor for the ultimate in human conditioning; evaluates the concepts of adaptation to exercise and injury from the perspective of science and exercise training; examines the multiple sciences behind exercise adaptation, musculoskeletal injury and concussion, and limitations of the human body and mind.'

In a phone-in poll in 1988, readers of Batman comics voted by 5,343 to 5,271 to have Robin the Boy Wonder killed by the Joker.

Batman first appeared in *Detective Comics* on 30 March 1939.

♀ *DOLPHIN*

BAUDELAIRE, Charles Pierre (1821–67)

The favourite foods of the French poet and critic Baudelaire were onion soup and bacon omelette. He kept a pet bat in a cage on his desk. At the age of 21, he came into a good inheritance which he squandered on laudanum and prostitutes. He died at the age of 46, probably as a result of syphilis.

♀ *CHURCHILL*

BEANS

On average, there are approximately 465 beans in a standard 415-gram (14-ounce) can. Every hour, 32.7 tons of baked beans are eaten in Britain. In the year 2019–20, the average Briton ate 4.2 kilograms (9.25 pounds) of baked beans, four times as much as the average American. According to a survey in 2020 by Heinz, 44 per cent of Irish people eat baked beans at least once a week and one in 10 eat them cold.

In Nicaragua, newlyweds are given a bowl of beans for good luck.

In ancient Greece, minor officials were elected by putting one white bean with many black beans inside a pot. All the candidates then picked a bean and whoever picked the white bean got the job. In the 19th century, the Russian army used the same system to give a conscript his freedom.

BEAR

There are eight species of bear: American black, polar, giant panda, Asiatic black, sloth, spectacled, sun and brown.

A male bear is a boar; a female is a sow.

Bears can eat up to 15 per cent of their body weight in one day and are partial to salmon.

Black bears can run at up to 56 km/h (35 mph).

The skin of a polar bear is black, which helps them to absorb more heat from the Sun.

♀ *LIVER, PULSES, PYTHAGORAS*

BEARD

The average human beard, if left untended, will grow 14 centimetres (5.5 inches) a year. The longest ever beard was that of the Norwegian Hans Langseth – it stretched 5.33 metres (17 feet 6 inches) when measured on his death in Kensett, Iowa, in 1927. The beard was presented to the Smithsonian Institution in Washington in 1967.

Positive aspects of beards were revealed in 2020 in the journal *Integrative Organismal Biology*, in a paper with the title 'Impact Protection Potential of Mammalian Hair: Testing the Pugilism Hypothesis for the Evolution of Human Facial Hair'. The researchers measured the impact force and absorbed energy of blows delivered to an epoxy composite (representing bone) covered by 'furred', 'plucked' or 'sheared' sheep skin. Their findings that 'fully furred samples were capable of absorbing more energy than plucked and sheared samples' supported the hypothesis 'that human beards protect vulnerable regions of the facial skeleton from damaging strikes'.

In 2016, model and body positivity campaigner Harnaam Kaur, 24, from Slough, Berkshire, was named by Guinness World Records as the youngest woman in the world to have a full beard. Her facial hair was 15 centimetres (6 inches) long. She said it was 'humbling' to be included.

The medical word for 'growth of beard by a woman' is 'pogoniasis'. Fear of beards is called pogonophobia, while the study of beards is pogonology. 'Barbatulous' is an obsolete word for 'having only a small beard'.

♀ *HAIR, MOUSTACHE, WHISKERS*

BEATLES

Announcing a new MA course entitled 'The Beatles, Popular Music and Society' in 2009, Liverpool Hope University said this qualification would be the first of its kind in the world. The course consists of four 12-week lecture modules and a dissertation.

♀ *CHRISTMAS EVE, LENNON*

BEAUTY

The scientific unit of beauty is the millihelen, defined as the amount of beauty required to launch one ship. The argument is that if Helen of Troy had a face that launched 1,000 ships, a millihelen must be enough for one. The idea came from Christopher Marlowe's 1592 play *Doctor Faustus*, in which he wrote of Helen: 'Was this the face that launch'd a thousand ships, And burnt the topless towers of Ilium.' The word 'millihelen', however, had to wait until the 1950s when it is was coined by the science fiction author Isaac Asimov, though some give the credit to Cambridge mathematician W.A.H. Rushton.

According to research at the Polytechnic University of Hong Kong, the best measurement of a woman's attractiveness is given by taking her volume in cubic metres and dividing it by the square of her height. Sadly, the researchers did not give any conversion formula between this measurement and the result in millihelens. Their calculation, however, is very similar to the formula for body mass index but with weight in the BMI formula replaced by volume.

King Philip the Fair of France had such high standards of beauty that he made skin diseases a punishable offence. In 1313, he decreed that all lepers should be burned at the stake, though it is not clear whether this included skin diseases milder than leprosy.

The first international beauty contest was held in Folkestone on 14 August 1908.

In 2006, when Miss Israel winner Yael Nezri was called up for national service in the Israeli army, she was exempted from carrying a rifle because it was liable to bruise her beauty queen legs.

⚲ CAMEL, CRUSTACEAN, MANSFIELD

◉ BEAVER

The testicles of a beaver are internal. Despite the difficulties posed by that arrangement, minced beavers' testicles were sometimes added to tobacco in the olden days in North America to sweeten the flavour. According to the 1945 book *Cooking Wild Game* by Frank Ashbrook and Edna Sater, the tail and liver of the beaver are special delicacies. 'The tail is fatty tissue, rich and palatable when cooked, and was greatly relished by early trappers and explorers.'

It has been calculated that a beaver that was 21 metres (68 feet) long with a 15 metre (51 foot) tail could have built the Kariba dam.

Beavers are strict vegetarians.

According to the *Oxford English Dictionary*, the word 'beaver' has been used to mean a beard or a bearded man since 1910, while it has also meant a woman's pubic area since 1927.

⚲ ABORTION, FLEAS, PLATYPUS

◉ BEDROOM

A study in Italy in 2006 reported that couples who have a TV set in their bedroom have sex half as often as those who don't. 'If there's no television in the bedroom, the frequency [of sexual intercourse] doubles,' said Serenella Salomoni, whose team of psychologists questioned 523 Italian couples to see what effect television had on their sex lives.

On average, Italians who live without TV in the bedroom have sex eight times a month. This drops to an average of four times a month for those with a TV, the study found. For the over-50s the effect is even more marked, with the average of seven couplings a month falling to just 1.5.

No evidence was offered to suggest whether the televisions caused a decline in sexual activity, or whether the decline in sexual activity was the reason for bringing a TV into the bedroom in the first place.

According to a survey by the Duvet and Pillow Warehouse in the UK in 2012, 14 per cent of people eat in bed, with the figure rising to 48 per cent for 18–24 year-olds; 41 per cent of people play with technology in bed; 36 per cent watch TV in bed; and 32 per cent talk on the phone while under the covers.

A survey in 2021 reported that eating in bed was the greatest source of annoyance between married couples, and nearly 44 per cent of respondents said they'd rather sleep in the spare room than put up with their partner repeatedly chomping food in bed.

⚲ DUVET, SNORING, ST CLARE

◉ BEDS

Research in 2001 showed that couples who slept in beds less than two years old were far more likely to share intimate secrets with each other at bedtime than those whose beds were eight years old or more. It has been estimated that one in 10 living Europeans were conceived in an Ikea bed.

In 1985, the Hurricane Bed was patented in the USA. It consists of a bed in a drawer which can be closed into a cabinet to protect you from hurricanes.

Pull-down beds called 'Murphy beds', made to be folded into the wall, were patented by William Lawrence Murphy of San Francisco around 1900. In 1982, a drunken man died from suffocation in Los Angeles after passing out in a Murphy bed.

Several beds were found in the tomb of Tutankhamun, including one that folded up for travelling. The most impressive of these was made of ebony and gold with a base of woven string to lie on. Ancient Egyptians did not use pillows on their beds but had a carved headboard shaped to allow their neck and head to rest on it to sleep.

The first waterbeds were goatskins filled with water, used in Persia nearly 4,000 years ago. The first modern waterbeds were used at St Bartholomew's Hospital in London as a way to treat and prevent bed sores.

LOUIS XIV, PHOBIAS

● BEE

Until the late 17th/early 18th century, queen bees were thought to be kings.

Research published in 2008 reported that Asian and European honeybees can understand each other through waggling dance movements, though they need to learn each other's dialects. On first waggling at each other to communicate the location of pollen sources, they tended to misunderstand distances, but quickly learned to recalibrate their measurement systems and understand each other's instructions.

The flapping of the wings of 1,000 bees generates seven watts of heat. This means that the continuous wing-flaps of 6.6 trillion bees could provide the entire energy consumption of the UK.

Bees cannot see the colour red – it looks the same as black to them.

LABRADOR, SKUNK, SNIFFING

● BEE KEEPING

The first eyewitness report of a flight by the Wright brothers appeared in a magazine called *Gleanings in Bee Culture* in January 1905. Despite their achievement in flying heavier-than-air machines, the Wright brothers attracted little publicity in their early years, but one man who did notice them, and even took part in their first flight, was Amos Root, publisher of *Gleanings in Bee Culture*. After travelling to witness an early flight, Root wrote: '… these brothers have probably not even a faint glimpse of what their discovery is going to bring to the children of men.

'No one living can give a guess of what is coming along this line, much better than any one living could conjecture the final outcome of Columbus' experiment when he pushed off through the trackless waters. Possibly we may be able to fly over the North Pole…'

After seeing and writing about the Wright brothers, Amos Root went back to his main business, making beehives and designing bee-keeping equipment. His factory was one of the first to have mandatory breaks for workers, during which hymns were played on a piano. Some years after Root died in 1923, the factory changed from making beehives to making candles. Root's Candles has remained in the family and is now run by his great-great-grandson.

In 2019, there were about 90.11 million beehives worldwide, increasing from around 89.56 million the previous year. There are more beehives in India than any other country, an estimated

12.25 million. Second place is taken by China with 9 million.

♀ HILLARY, ST BERNARD

● BEER

The first brewers of beer were probably the Sumerians around 10,000 BC. Ninkasi, the Sumerian goddess of alcohol and beer, was reputedly 'born of fresh sparkling water'.

Louis Pasteur developed pasteurisation for beer more than 20 years before he did it for milk.

The total amount of beer drunk in the world in 2019 was around 189.05 billion litres. People in the Czech Republic drink more beer than anywhere else, an average amount of 191.8 litres per head per annum. The figure for the UK is only 72.9 litres per head. The only drinks that are more widely consumed than beer worldwide are water and tea.

In 1814 London suffered the Great Beer Flood when about 388,000 gallons of beer flooded the streets around Tottenham Court Road after vats in a brewery ruptured. At least eight people drowned but a judge and jury ruled the beer flood was an Act of God.

In medieval Britain more beer was drunk than water as the alcohol made it safer. The weekly ration allocated to each child in Norwich children's hospital in 1632 included two gallons of beer.

Deprivation from beer is also an old British punishment. Among the regulations applying to Officers of the Bedchamber at the court of Henry VIII was this: 'Such pages as cause the maids of the King's household to become mothers shall go without beer for a month.'

One of the miracles that led to the canonisation of the 16th-century abbess St Brigid of Ireland was her feat of transforming her bath water into beer for visiting clerics.

A few dozen bottles of Allsopp's Arctic Ale made for an Arctic expedition of 1875 were found in a garage in Shropshire, England, and one of them was allegedly sold in an eBay auction in 2007 for $503,300, though it is very unclear that this bid was honoured. A bottle of the same beer was sold at auction in 2016 for £3,300 ($5,131).

The lead ship of the Arctic expedition, HMS *Resolute*, became stuck in ice and was abandoned but was later found by an American whaler. It was bought by the US Congress and presented to Queen Victoria as a gift in 1856. In 1880, the Resolute Desk, made from the ship's timbers, was given by the Queen to US President Rutherford B. Hayes, who put it in the White House, where it has remained ever since.

♀ BODY ODOUR, GUT BARGING, OCTOPUS, SPA

● BEER MATS

The first modern beer mat, made of wood pulp, was created by Robert South of Dresden in 1892, though cardboard beer mats had been known since 1880. There are now around 5.5 billion beer mats made every year, 75 per cent of them by the Katz Group, based in Weisenbach, Germany.

The hobby of collecting beer mats is called tegestology.

There is a type of flea that lives and breeds only in beer mats in Germany.

Octopuses in Monterey Bay in California have shown no particular fondness for beer mats but have been observed making their homes in discarded beer cans.

The world's largest beer mat was 15 metres (49.21 feet) in diameter and was made in 2002 by Carlsberg in Denmark.

On one day in July 2010, Dean Gould of Felixstowe, Suffolk, set three beer-mat-flipping world records: he flipped and caught 35 beer mats with two fingers while blindfolded; he set a new 'speed flipping' record with 1,000 successful flips (comprising 20 flips of piles of 50 mats) in 41.06 seconds; and he set a new 'snatch' record by catching 108 mats after dropping them from his elbow. His current records include 36 beer mats successfully flipped with two fingers blindfolded, and 114 beer mats in a single pile on a table flipped and caught in one go.

BEETHOVEN, Ludwig van (1770–1827)

Beethoven was 1.65 metres (5 feet 5 inches) tall. When drinking coffee, he insisted that every cup was prepared from exactly 60 coffee beans. His last words are said to have been: 'Pity, pity, too late,' when he was delivered a crate of wine from his publisher.

Beethoven died at the age of 56 and his autopsy gave his cause of death as cirrhosis of the liver, with pancreatitis and peritonitis as contributing factors. In 2013, however, a toxicology analysis found poisonous concentrations of lead in his hair and bones at the time of his death. This may have been caused by the lead crystal in his wine glasses, but in 2020 another theory was advanced: that the low-quality wines he liked to drink from Hungary and Germany may have been treated with a form of lead monoxide to soften their taste.

In October 1996, the conductor Daniel Barenboim, wearing a hardhat and overcoat, set 19 construction cranes dancing to the 'Ode to Joy' from Beethoven's Ninth Symphony to celebrate the completion of a stage in the building of a Daimler-Benz project. Around 2,000 guests watched this 'dance of the cranes' on Potsdamer Platz, the cranes slowly swinging back and forth in perfect time to the music as Barenboim, on an elevated platform, conducted their drivers with red and blue signalling flags. To add another coincidental musical touch, the building project had been designed by Italian architect Renzo Piano.

ALCHEMY, COMPACT DISC, MUSIC

BEETLE

In January 2008, Quentin Wheeler, an entomologist at Arizona State University, announced to a Roy Orbison tribute concert that a new species of beetle would be named *Orectochilus orbisonorum* in honour of the late singer and his widow, Barbara.

Other people to have had beetle species named after them include David Attenborough, Che Guevara, Adolf Hitler, Robert Redford, Arnold Schwarzenegger, Liv Tyler and Kate Winslet. Darth Vader has also had a beetle, *Agathidium vaderi*, named after him.

BRAZIL, FIJI, HITLER, LAOS

BEIJING

According to the official Chinese news agency, Beijing has more public lavatories than any other city in the world. In February 2008, the figure stood at 5,174 public toilets, but after an intensive effort to improve facilities, the number was reported to be over 6,000 in 2016, out of 68,000 in the whole of China. A paper in the *Journal of Architectural Education* in 2000 reported that: 'Communist Urbanism, defined as the spatial order of communal living, reserves a place of honor for the public toilet.'

In 2012, the Municipal Commission of City Administration and Environment Authorities in Beijing set a new standard for public toilets called the 'two fly rule', specifying that no toilet in a public place should contain more than two flies.

⚲ *CHINA, SPITTING*

BELCH

The longest recorded belch in history is 1 minute 13.057 seconds achieved by Michele Forgione (Italy) at the 13th annual Hard Rock Beer Festival 'Ruttosound' competition, in Reggiolo, Italy, on 16 June 2009.

'If an Asthmatical Person comes to belch, it is a good Sign.' Richard Bradley, Family Dictionary, *1727*

⚲ *KOALA, METHANE, ORANGUTAN*

BELGIUM

There are approximately 3,000 castles in Belgium, which gives the country a good claim to having more castles per square mile than anywhere else.

Over 1.6 kilograms (3.5 pounds) of chocolate is sold every minute at Brussels airport, which is more than any other place in the world.

In some parts of Belgium, cabbage is eaten on Shrove Tuesday in the belief that this will save other cabbages from being eaten by caterpillars and flies.

There was no Christmas Day in Flanders in 1582; in that year the change was made from the Julian to Gregorian calendar and the last 10 days of the year, from 22 to 31 December, were omitted.

The Belgian hare is not a hare but a rabbit.

⚲ *BRUSSELS SPROUTS, CARROT, SPA*

BELL, Alexander Graham (1847–1922)

At his baptism, Alexander Graham Bell was simply given the name 'Alexander Bell'. Since this was also the name of his father and grandfather, he always wanted a middle name, and on his 11th birthday was given permission by his parents to adopt the middle name 'Graham'.

Alexander Graham Bell's patent for the telephone modestly titles the invention as 'Improvement in Telegraphy'. When he tried to sell this patent to Western Union in 1876, he was turned down with the words: 'This electrical toy has far too many shortcomings to ever be considered a practical means of communication.'

Bell's claim to have invented the first working telephone is dubious for several reasons: first, he only beat Elisha Gray by a couple of hours in registering a preliminary telephone patent in February 1876, and later research suggests that Gray's device would have worked while Bell's would not. Secondly, documents found in 2003 seem to confirm that the German Philipp Reis had invented a working telephone in 1863. Thirdly, the US House of Representatives passed a motion in 2002 crediting the Italian Antonio Meucci with the invention of the telephone as long ago as 1849.

Around 600 lawsuits were brought against Bell's patent in the US, but his 1876 patent number 174,465 for the telephone is said to be the most valuable of all time.

Bell recommended answering the phone with the word 'Ahoy'. It was Thomas Edison who suggested 'Hello'.

When President James Garfield was shot in 1881, Bell quickly devised an electromagnetic device to locate the bullet in Garfield's body, but it was not enough to save the President's life.

In 1919, Bell collaborated on a hydrofoil design that set a world water speed record which stood until 1963.

In 1929, seven years after Bell died, the scientific community named the standard unit for the intensity of soundwaves, the 'bel', after him. A decibel, one-tenth of a bel, became the most commonly used metric for the magnitude of noise.

♀ *NOVA SCOTIA, TELEPHONE*

BENFORD'S LAW

First stated by Dr Frank Benford in 1938, this is the law that tells us, surprisingly, that numbers are far more likely to begin with a '1' than any other digit. Benford first confirmed this by looking at tables of statistics from a variety of sources – lengths of rivers, heights of mountains, street numbers in addresses, baseball averages, areas of countries – then reasoned out the process by which so many began with the digit '1'.

Effectively, such numbers arise from a counting process. Counting up to nine uses each digit once (we exclude zero as a possible starting digit). From 10 to 19, everything begins with 1, which puts 1 in a big lead. All the others have caught up by the time we get to 99, but from 100 to 199 the '1' numbers storm ahead again. The same thing happens from 1,000 to 1,999. With all the other digits always playing catch-up, whatever range a group of numbers inhabits, those beginning with 1 are likely to be ahead.

In fact, both theory and practice suggest that the percentage of randomly selected statistics beginning with each digit are as shown in the following table:

1	2	3	4	5	6	7	8	9
30.1	17.6	12.5	9.7	7.9	6.7	5.8	5.1	4.6

BENNETT, Alan (b. 1934)

Alan Bennett is the only person to have turned down a CBE, a knighthood and an honorary doctorate from Oxford University. He refused the last of these in protest at Oxford accepting funding for a Chair named in honour of Rupert Murdoch.

In 2010, a contestant on the TV quiz *Mastermind* chose 'The Plays of Alan Bennett' as his specialist subject. A BBC Radio 4 arts programme then challenged Alan Bennett to answer the same questions, and he did less well than quiz contestant Robin Seavill.

♀ *EDUCATION*

BENTHAM, Jeremy (1748–1832)

Philosopher and social reformer Jeremy Bentham is said to have fed his favourite cat on macaroni. The name he gave to the cat was Langbourne, which later became Sir John Langbourne, and later still the Reverend Sir John Langbourne, D.D. (Doctor of Divinity). When the cat died, Bentham buried it in his garden.

He donated his own body to science, inviting his friends to watch its dissection. He also instructed that his skeleton be later reconstructed as an 'Auto-Icon' – a mixture of mummy and waxwork of himself. His precise instruction, as laid out in his will, requested that the skeleton 'be given to my good friend Dr Southwood Smith ... to be put together in such a manner as that the whole figure may be seated in a chair usually occupied by me when living, in the attitude in which I am sitting when engaged in thought'. He also asked that the skeleton, when prepared according to those wishes, be dressed in one of his black suits and placed on a chair holding his favourite walking stick, which he called 'Dapple'. He also suggested that, if his friends would like to meet for the purpose of paying respect to him, he would like his executor to arrange for his body to be wheeled in to join them. His wishes were followed, though the model was made with a wax head rather than Bentham's own skull, which had deteriorated too badly during the preservation process. In 1850, the body was moved to University College, London, where it can still be seen in a glass case in the Student Centre.

BEQUEST

The German poet Heinrich Heine left his estate to his wife, Mathilde, when he died in 1856, on the condition that she remarry, so that 'there will be at least one man to regret my death'. Mathilde remarried, inherited the estate, and lived comfortably until she died in 1883. Whether her second husband regretted Heinrich's death is not known.

BRITISH MUSEUM, TWELFTH NIGHT

BERGMAN

The 1978 film *Autumn Sonata* was the last film made by the great Swedish actress Ingrid Bergman (1915–82). It was directed by the great Swedish film-maker Ingmar Bergman (1918–2007; no relation) and was shot in Norway after accusations of tax evasion had forced the director out of his native country.

Ingmar Bergman's fifth and last wife was Ingrid von Rosen. They had a daughter, Maria von Rosen in 1959, but their marriage, which made Ingmar's wife another Ingrid Bergman, did not take place until 1972.

Ingrid Bergman (the actress) died on her 67th birthday on 29 August 1982.

SHAKESPEARE

BERLIN

It is frequently claimed (over 6,000 times on the Internet) that the first bomb dropped on Berlin during the Second World War killed the only elephant in Berlin Zoo. Anyone repeating that claim, however, has clearly not read *Von der Menagerie zum Tierparadies: 125 Jahre Zoo Berlin* by Heinz-Georg Kloss, which gives a detailed account of the fatalities at Berlin Zoo caused by wartime bombing.

The zoo was hit by bombs 12 times between 1941 and 1945, with the worst raids on the nights of 22–23 November 1943 and 29–30 January 1944. During the two nights in January, Kloss says that one-third of all the animals were killed, including one rhino, two giraffes, 17 antelopes, 11 bovines, 25 deer, 15 monkeys, one chimpanzee, one orangutan and seven elephants. At the beginning of the war, the zoo held 3,715 animals. By the end, only 91 animals survived, including two lions, two hyenas, one Asian elephant bull, one hippo bull, 10 sacred baboons, one chimpanzee, one oriental stork and one shoebill.

BEETHOVEN, ENVIRONMENT, SEX WORK

BERLUSCONI, Silvio (b. 1936)

A 'Pizza Berlusconi', made in Finland and topped with smoked reindeer, won first prize at the 2008 New York Pizza Show. Named for the Italian Prime Minister, it was created by the Kotipizza chain in Finland following derogatory remarks about Finnish cuisine made by Silvio Berlusconi in 2005 during discussions about the location of a meeting of the European Food Safety Authority.

When Berlusconi was accused in 2009 of having sex with an underage prostitute, several references were made to a bed, with curtains around it, which Berlusconi referred to as 'Putin's bed', claiming it was a gift from the Russian leader. This has never been confirmed or definitively denied by Mr Putin's office.

According to the 2011 Forbes List of richest people in the world, Mr Berlusconi was in 118th place. By 2021, he had gone down to 327th.

'Silvio Berlusconi' is an anagram of 'invisible colours'.

♀ *BUNGA BUNGA*

● BERWICK-UPON-TWEED

Contrary to popular belief, Berwick-upon-Tweed was not at war with Russia for most of the 20th century. This myth was based on the Treaty of Perpetual Peace between England and Scotland, signed by Henry VII of England and James IV of Scotland in 1502, which solved the contentious issue of the status of Berwick by declaring that the town was in neither England nor Scotland.

For many years thereafter, Berwick was always mentioned separately in any laws relating to England as the town was deemed to be 'of' the Kingdom of England but not 'in' it.

The Berwick–Russian war myth was based on the idea that when the Crimean War was declared in 1853, Berwick was specifically mentioned, but was omitted from the Treaty of Paris ending the war in1856. Actually, this is all nonsense, as Berwick was not mentioned in the declaration of war, and even if it had been, there would have been no problem as the Wales and Berwick Act of 1746 had already stated that any mention of England was to be taken to include Berwick.

Despite this, in 1966 the Mayor of Berwick did sign an official peace treaty with a Russian official.

● BESTIALITY

A man who appeared in court in Zimbabwe in October 2011 charged with bestiality admitted the offence but said that the donkey with whom he was caught having sex was in fact a prostitute whom he had paid $20 for her services at a nightclub and who had mysteriously turned into a donkey overnight.

In his defence in court, Sunday Moyo was reported to have said: 'Your worship, I only came to know that I was being intimate with a donkey when I got arrested.' He was remanded in custody and ordered to undergo psychiatric tests.

● BETHLEHEM

Palestinian police had to storm the Basilica of the Nativity in Bethlehem at Christmas 2011 to break up a fight between rival groups of Orthodox and Armenian clerics. The dispute, leading to a pitched battle fought with brooms by about 100 priests and monks, was over the boundaries of their respective jurisdictions at the church while it was being cleaned in preparation for Orthodox Christmas celebrations.

● BHUTAN

Responding to criticism of its economy in 1987, the King of Bhutan said that Gross National Happiness is more important than Gross National Product. The term Gross National Happiness was coined in 1972 by the 4th King of Bhutan, King Jigme Singye Wangchuk.

In a survey in Bhutan in 2010, 8.3 per cent of respondents were found to be deeply happy, 32.6 per cent were extensively happy, 47.8 per cent were narrowly happy, and only 10.4 per cent were unhappy. Nevertheless, in 2017, when the UN released its own happiness survey, Bhutan was only in 97th place.

On the day of the World Cup final in 2002, Bhutan played football against Montserrat. They were ranked the world's two worst national teams. Bhutan won 4–0.

The national sport in Bhutan is archery.

In 1999, the government in Bhutan lifted its ban on TV and the Internet.

The official language of Bhutan is Dzongkha. The currency is the ngultrum, which is divided into 100 chetrum. 'Ngultrum' means 'silver coin'; 'chetrum' means 'half coin'.

Bhutan has no formal relations with the US, Russia, China, the UK or France. Tourists are only allowed to visit Bhutan in official groups. Single tourists are not allowed in.

Bhutan is known to its own inhabitants as Druk Yul, 'Land of the Thunder Dragon'. The wearing of traditional robes is mandatory in Bhutan, with a sash indicating a person's status.

In Bhutanese Buddhism, there are 81 types of violence. For that reason, it is considered unlucky if a member of the family dies at the age of 81. If that should happen, the family is advised to hang the body upside down in the house until the 82nd birthday would have arrived, and then burn it.

Gangkhar Puensum in Bhutan is the highest unclimbed mountain in the world. In 1994, for religious reasons, Bhutan passed a law prohibiting mountaineers from climbing a mountain higher than 6,000 metres (20,000 feet), which may explain why no one has climbed Gangkhar Puensum since then as it is more than 7,500 metres (25,000 feet). Attempts have been made to climb it from its Chinese side, but the Bhutanese asked the Chinese to respect their laws and the Chinese agreed to ban such attempts too.

Over 600 species of orchid grow in Bhutan.

BIBLE

The 46th word of Psalm 46 in the King James Bible is 'shake', and the 46th word from the end of the same Psalm is 'spear' (if you ignore the final 'selah', which is generally taken just as an instruction to pause or reflect). William Shakespeare was 46 when the Bible was being translated; the above 'coincidence' in Psalm 46 was presumably a well-hidden birthday gift from the translators.

The animal most frequently mentioned in the Old Testament is the sheep (191 references), followed by the lamb (182), ox (149), ram (164), bullock (148), horse (147), ass (140), lion (133), goat (122) and camel (53).

The longest name in the Bible is that of Isaiah's son Mahershalalhashbaz, who is mentioned twice in the first chapter of Isaiah.

The words 'girl' and 'girls' each occur only once in the entire Authorised Version. 'Eternity' and 'grandmother' also occur only once each in the King James Bible, in Isaiah 57:15 and 2 Timothy 1:5 respectively.

ETHIOPIA, POMEGRANATE, SHEEP

BICYCLE

The bicycle developed from the velocipede, a sort of hobby horse patented in England in 1818 by Denis Johnson of London.

Count Leo Tolstoy, author of *War and Peace*, was given a bicycle by the Moscow Society of Velocipede Lovers for his 67th birthday in 1895. He promptly learnt to ride it '… in a hall large enough to drill a division of soldiers' – and he knocked down the only other person in the room.

In June 2001, Javier Zapata of Colombia cycled up 1,200 stairs at the Parque Central Tower in Venezuela.

POVERTY, TRANSPORT, WRIGHT

BIDEN, Joseph Robinette (b. 1942)

In 2016, Joe Biden said: 'I don't drink. I don't smoke. But I eat a lot of ice cream.' During his successful presidential campaign in 2020, he was calculated to have spent $10,000 on ice cream as gifts to campaign donors.

In 2008 he said his favourite movie was *Chariots of Fire*.

BUSH George Walker, GLOBAL WARMING

BIKINI

The French designer Louis Réard generally takes the credit for designing the bikini in June 1946, though another Parisian, Jacques Heim, had produced a two-piece swimsuit several months earlier. Heim had called his the 'Atome'; Réard named his after Bikini Atoll where atomic bomb tests took place. His reasons are ascribed either to the bikini's appearance of having been blown apart, or the explosive reaction he expected it to create. Réard described it as 'Four triangles of nothing.'

When it was displayed at a Paris fashion show, the bikini was modelled by Micheline Bernardini, a stripper at the Casino de Paris. Sweden, Spain, Portugal and Italy promptly banned it.

The bikini came into fashion after Brigitte Bardot wore one in the film *And God Created Woman* in 1956. Four years later, Brian Hyland's song 'Itsy Bitsy Teenie Weenie Yellow Polka Dot Bikini' led to a bikini-buying spree.

In 2001, the Nuclear Claims Tribunal awarded the Bikini islanders $563,315,500 in damages for destruction and suffering caused by US nuclear testing.

The world record for the number of women photographed wearing bikinis in the same place at the same time stands at 3,090 participants for an event in China in 2011.

BILLIARDS

In the 15th and 16th centuries, billiards was definitely a game for royalty. The earliest known verified account of a billiard table was found in a 1470 inventory of the possessions of King Louis XI of France. His table comprised a bed of stone, a cloth covering and a hole in the middle of the playing area, into which balls could be driven.

Mary, Queen of Scots, was also a keen player and complained when she was not allowed use of her billiard table when she was imprisoned. After her execution, her body was wrapped in the blue Strachan tartan cloth torn from her billiard table.

Most scandalous of all, when British Prime Minister Lord Palmerston died two days short of his 81st birthday, it was strongly rumoured that his body was found on a billiard table where he had suffered a heart attack while seducing a maid at Brocket Hall in Hertfordshire.

The only mention of billiards in Shakespeare is in *Antony and Cleopatra* (Act II, Scene V) when Cleopatra says to her maid: 'Let's to billiards, come Charmian.'

Billiards was the first game or sport to hold an official world championship. It was won by a Frenchman called Gamier in 1873. The second game to have a world championship was chess in 1886.

On 7 December 1873, 'The quaintest billiard match ever played' is said to have taken place between Mr Jefferson of America and William Dufton of England. Dufton, as usual, played with his cue, but Jefferson played the balls with his nose and won by a margin of 47 points.

⚲ *MOZART, WHITE HOUSE*

⬤ BIRMINGHAM

A survey in 1999 revealed that holiday-making Britons who make love on a foreign beach are more likely to be from Birmingham than any other part of the country. Explaining this finding, a researcher commented, 'There aren't many beaches in Birmingham, so it's a bit of a novelty.'

There are 22 more miles of canal in Birmingham than in Venice.

You are more likely to have an injury at work in Birmingham than in any other British city.

According to Bill Bryson's 1990 book *Mother Tongue*, the expression '*être de Birmingham*' in French slang means to be bored to death. French sources, however, are not so sure. At least one agrees with Bryson, but specifies that it is Parisian slang, while another dates the expression back to the 18th century, saying that it was used in praise, reflecting the sharpness of razors from Birmingham.

⚲ *UNIVERSITIES*

⬤ BIRTH

Around 140 million babies are born into the world every year, which works out at an average of just over 4.4 babies born every second. There were 3,605,201 births registered in the USA in 2020, which means that on average one American was born every 24 seconds.

⚲ *MARRIAGE, POPULATION, PREGNANCY*

⬤ BIRTHDAY

'Happy Birthday to You' was composed as 'Good morning to you' by Mildred and Patty Hill and published by Clayton F. Summy in 1893. The Summy company registered a copyright on the song in 1935, and in 1988 Warner Chappell Music bought the company for US $25 million, of which $5 million was the estimated value of 'Happy Birthday'. Warner claimed that unauthorised public performances were illegal without the payment of royalties, which in 2010 were quoted at £700.

In 2013, Good Morning to You Productions sued Warner, alleging false claim to the copyright, and in 2015 a federal judge declared the copyright claim invalid. Warner Chappell agreed to pay back $14 million in licensing fees, and in 2016 the court declared that 'Happy Birthday to You' was now in the public domain.

⚲ *SONGS*

⬤ BISCUITS

The word 'biscuit' comes from the French for 'twice cooked'.

In September 2001, a biscuit taken from the *Titanic* before her ill-fated maiden voyage fetched £3,525 at auction in London. Sotheby's catalogue described the biscuit as 'in almost perfect condition with signs of moulding'.

The World Biscuit Throwing Championship is held annually at the Glendale Show near Wooler, Northumberland. Contestants have to throw a McVitie's Rich Tea biscuit as far as they can. All biscuits are closely inspected before they are tossed to ensure they conform to the strict regulations, which specify that they must be perfectly circular and un-nibbled. The winner receives the Biscuit Medal, a Rich Tea thickly dunked in varnish.

In 1991, a VAT tribunal in the UK was called upon to specify the precise difference between a biscuit and a cake. According to their regulations, 'a cake is zero-rated even if it is covered in chocolate, whereas a biscuit is standard-rated if wholly or partly covered in chocolate'. Specifically, the question was whether the jam filling of a Jaffa Cake transformed it from a biscuit to a cake. Lawyers for Jaffa convinced the tribunal of the cake-ness of their product, thus saving Jaffa 17.5 per cent tax.

In 2008, a survey by Holiday Inn reported that around 80 per cent of business professionals believe the outcome of a meeting can be positively influenced by the choice and quality of biscuit on offer.

The reason biscuit tins are not square is to enable them to be stacked inside each other to save space when being transported.

⚲ FOOD, TURKEY (country)

BLACK HOLE

The term 'black hole' for a massive collapsed star from whose gravitational field not even light can escape, was coined in 1967 by the American physicist John Wheeler.

The term was strongly opposed for several years by the French, because it translates into their language as 'trou noir', which was a slang term for what the Americans call an 'asshole'.

The first black hole was discovered in 1969, two years after Wheeler named it.

⚲ TOILET PAPER

BLACKBERRIES

The blackberry is botanically not a berry but an aggregate fruit composed of many small drupelets.

Batology is the scientific study of brambles, especially blackberries. This should not be confused with battology, which is a needless and tiresome repetition in speaking or writing.

In south-west England there was a superstition that the first blackberry picked each year would banish warts. There was also a more general superstition in the UK that blackberries should not be picked after Michaelmas (29 September) as the devil has then claimed them, having left his mark by urinating on the leaves.

The BlackBerry smartphone was given its name because its small buttons reminded its creators of the fruit – and it was a fun name.

Troilus and Cressida is the only Shakespeare play containing the word 'blackberry', but Falstaff in *Henry IV, Part 1* twice says 'blackberries'.

BLACKBIRD

Authorities in the town of Beebe, Arkansas, celebrated the start of 2012 with an announcement that only about 100 blackbirds had died as a result of New Year celebrations compared with thousands last year.

Large numbers of blackbirds roost in the community and they are apparently driven to panic by the fireworks, when they fly into homes, cars, telephone poles or each other.

⚲ GOLF

BLACKCURRANT

Thirteen billion blackcurrants are cultivated every year in Britain – enough to give everyone on Earth almost two

British blackcurrants. However, 95 per cent of the British blackcurrant crop is used for making Ribena.

The Latin for blackcurrant is *Ribes nigrum* – hence the name Ribena.

In 1911, New York State banned the growing of blackcurrants as a public nuisance. The ban was lifted only in 2003.

BLACKPOOL

If Blackpool Tower in the north of England were 4 metres (13 feet) higher, it would be exactly half the height of the Eiffel Tower.

DAVIDSON, DIVORCE, HEALTH, ROLLER-COASTER

BLAKE, William (1757–1827)

The visionary English poet, painter and print-maker William Blake held only one exhibition of his paintings in his lifetime and it was not a success.

He displayed the paintings in a room above his brother's drapery shop in Golden Square in London's Soho, opening in the summer of 1809 when he announced that customers could take their purchases away at the end of September. Unfortunately, none of the paintings were sold and they stayed on the walls for a year.

The only review of the exhibition was in *The Examiner* by Robert Hunt, brother of the poet Leigh Hunt. He wrote that Blake could not draw and his paintings were 'the ebullitions of a distempered brain'. He also described Blake as 'an unfortunate lunatic' suffering from 'egregious vanity'. William Wordsworth was slightly more complimentary, saying: 'There was no doubt that this poor man was mad, but there is something in the madness of this man which interests me more than

the sanity of Lord Byron and Walter Scott.'

Blake's painting *The Great Red Dragon and the Woman Clothed with the Sun*, which inspired the killer Francis Dolarhyde in Thomas Harris's novel *Red Dragon* (the first of the Hannibal Lecter books), can be seen at the Brooklyn Museum of Art.

BLANKET

The first weaving looms in Bristol were established by Thomas Blanket (or Blanquette) in the late 1330s. In 1339, he was given formal permission by a Bristol magistrate to set up a loom on which to make a 'well raised surface fabric' for use as a bed covering.

The common belief that he gave his name to bedclothes, however, is probably wrong, since the word 'blanket' dates back to around 1300, so it is more likely that Thomas Blanket's family took their name from the industry. In any case, the 14th-century Thomas Blanket ought not to be confused with the 21st-century 'Thomas Blanket', which is a blanket displaying a Thomas the Tank Engine motif.

GHOSTS, MUMMIFICATION, YEARS

BLINDNESS

In 1985, an unusual case of erratic driving in Chesapeake, Virginia, involved a policeman who was almost run off the road by a weaving car. He pursued the vehicle and stopped it, suspecting a drunken driver. This was confirmed, but may not have been the sole cause of the incident as the driver was also blind. He was aged 24 and had lost his sight when he was 12.

CENSUS, EVEREST, MOUNTAINEERING

BLOOD

The average adult human has 5–6 litres (1.2–1.5 gallons) of blood in their body. There are 60,000 miles of blood vessels in the human body. An individual blood cell takes about 60 seconds to make a complete circuit of the body.

Since the heart pumps all of your blood around your body about once a minute, this adds up to a weight of about ten tonnes of blood a day being pumped. A human heart pumps enough blood in a lifetime to fill 100 swimming pools.

Octopus blood is blue in colour.

The first successful blood transfusions took place between dogs in the 1660s.

Dr Bernard Fantus began a blood storage and transfusion service at Cook County Hospital, Chicago, in 1936 and his daughter Ruth suggested calling it a 'blood bank'. On 15 March 1937, this became the world's first official blood bank. Britain's first was in Ipswich later in 1937.

⚲ *FLEAS, LUCK, OCTOPUS, UNDEAD*

BLUE

The third Monday in January is known as 'Blue Monday', supposedly the most depressing day of the year. The idea of 'Blue Monday' originated with an advertising campaign in 2005 and was based on a very unconvincing formula to calculate happiness.

The colour blue has been associated with depression since the 15th century, but the earliest known reference to blues music was in 1912.

The psychologist Charles Spence has shown that food tastes saltier if served in blue dishes.

Studies have shown that weightlifters can lift heavier weights in gyms with blue walls.

Many ancient languages did not have a word for the colour blue. The Himba people of Namibia still have no word for blue in their language.

The only national flag without red, white or blue is that of Jamaica. Until 2017, the Mauritanian flag also had no red, white or blue, but after a national referendum held in that year, two red stripes were added at the top and bottom.

Around 8 per cent of the world's population have blue eyes, though a study in 1914 reported that in the UK the figure is 48 per cent.

The Russian Blue species of cat was brought to England from Archangelsk, Russia, in 1875 by sailors and was first called the Archangel Cat. Its name of 'Russian Blue' is curious as Russian has two words for blue: голубой (*goluboy*), meaning light blue, and синий (*siniy*), meaning dark blue.

The first of these, голубой, is also slang for a male homosexual, because gays in Moscow used to hang out by a metro station that was coloured light blue.

'The blueness of a wound cleanseth away evil.' Proverbs 20, King James Bible

⚲ *BOWERBIRD, ISLAM, MOSQUITO, NAVEL*

BLUEBOTTLE

Henry IV, Part 2 is the only Shakespeare play that uses the word 'bluebottle', in Act V, Scene IV when Doll Tearsheet calls First Beadle a 'blue-bottle rogue'.

⚲ *BUCKLAND*

BLYTON, Enid Mary (1897–1968)

Having written over 700 books and 10,000 short stories, with total sales of over 600 million books, Enid Blyton is possibly the most prolific author of all time. She comes fourth in the list of most-translated authors, behind Agatha Christie, Jules Verne and William Shakespeare.

Born Enid Mary Blyton, she wrote under the name Mary Pollock between 1940 and 1943 when she was married to Hugh Pollock. Her second husband was Kenneth Darrell Waters, which is why her full name is sometimes given as Enid Mary Blyton Pollock Darrell Waters.

One of her daughters said that Blyton had no time for her own children; the other described her as a mother who picked her up from school, took her on wonderful walks and read her the adventures of the Famous Five direct from the typewriter.

Enid Blyton created Noddy in 1949 and Noddy books stayed unchanged until 1989 when the golliwogs were changed to goblins to avoid charges of racism. Scandinavian countries protested, taking the change as an insult to trolls. In America, Big Ears had his name changed to Whitebeard to avoid offending the aurally advantaged.

Noddy is known as Oui Oui in France, Doddi in Iceland, Purzelknirps in Germany and Hilitos in Spain.

BOAR

The upper tusks of a wild boar are called 'honours', the lower tusks are 'rippers'. When the boar opens and closes its mouth, the tusks rub against each other, which keeps them sharp.

Both Adonis, in Greek myth, and Gwydre, son of King Arthur, are said to have been killed by wild boars.

According to the 15th century *Book of St Albans*, the collective noun for a group of 12 or more wild boar or other swine is a 'sounder'.

♀ *BEAR, COSMETICS*

BOATS

The basic difference between a boat and a ship is that boats are designed for rivers and inland waterways, ships for seas and oceans. More technically, there is a difference in their centre of gravity, which makes a boat lean in when turning, while a ship leans outwards.

There is only one mention of a boat in the Old Testament of the King James Bible (2 Samuel 19:18), but 37 references to ships.

♀ *BOUNTY, BRAHMS, NAVIES*

BOB

For most people known as Bob, the name is a diminutive of Robert, but Bob as a given first name has experienced great changes in popularity. In 1959, the number of boy babies in the USA given the name 'Bob' was 2,826, but in 2020 the figure was only 12. In that year, Bob was only the 6,558th most popular name for a boy baby, being given to one in 152,619 boys.

There are more people named Bob living in California than in any other US State.

♀ *BALFOUR, COLORADO*

BODY

About 96 per cent of our body is made of four elements: oxygen (about 65 per cent), carbon (18.5 per cent), hydrogen (9.5 per cent) and nitrogen (3.3 per cent). The greatest contributor to the remainder is calcium at 1.5 per cent.

Parts of the body that you may not have realised have names include the following:

- Canthus: the corner of the eye where the upper and lower eyelids meet.
- Columella: the partition between the nostrils.
- Dewlap: the fold of loose skin hanging

under the chin (originally of cattle, but extended to humans and other animals).

- Glabella: the smooth part of the forehead above the eyebrows.
- Nasion: the point where your nose meets your forehead.
- Niddick: the nape of the neck.
- Philtrum: the groove down the middle of your upper lip.
- Popliteal: the hollow at the back of the knee.
- Rhinarium: the tip of a nose, especially a mammal's cold, wet nose.

The only two parts of a woman's body that are anagrams of each other are the elbow/bowel. Men also have the spine/penis.

BODY ART

A tattoo of a helicopter shooting a peanut vendor led to a murder conviction in Los Angeles in 2011. Anthony Garcia, 25, was first suspected of the gangland killing, which took place in 2004, when he was stopped for driving on a suspended licence and a detective noticed his tattoo.

Investigations revealed that Garcia's gang nickname was 'Chopper', which prosecutors said explained the helicopter, and that 'peanut' is a derogatory term for a rival gang member.

'This is completely one-of-a-kind,' a Los Angeles Deputy District Attorney said.

The mother of the victim's daughter told Garcia that he should blame only himself: 'You were stupid enough to get the tattoo that convicted you,' she said.

BODY ODOUR

Mosquitoes prefer the body odour of beer-drinkers to that of people who have drunk only water. Malaria-carrying mosquitoes track their victims by smell, and research published in 2010 showed that they are more likely to follow the smell of beer-drinkers than water-drinkers.

⚲ SMELL

BODYGUARD

The first meeting of the World Bodyguards Association (WBA) was held in Budapest in September 1995, attracting 130 delegates from 40 countries. The WBA now 'counts more than 25,000 professionals', whom it no longer calls 'bodyguards', saying instead that it provides 'modern and sophisticated services, provided by skilled and properly educated Executive Protection Officers'.

The oldest and largest such association is the International Bodyguard Association, which was founded in Paris in 1957.

⚲ GADDAFI

BOGART, Humphrey (1899–1957)

The actor Humphrey Bogart was born on Christmas Day 1899. Before making his name as an actor, he added to his meagre income by hustling as a chess player in New York parks.

⚲ BURIAL

BOLEYN, Anne (c.1501–36)

Henry VIII's second wife, Anne Boleyn, was long rumoured to have had six fingers on her right hand and was also sometimes described as having three breasts, but both claims seem to have been part of a campaign to discredit her, as such imperfections were often seen as signs of witchcraft.

According to the exiled Catholic priest Nicholas Sander (or Sanders): 'She had a projecting tooth under the upper lip, and on her right hand six fingers,' but her alleged sixth finger may have been no more than a fingernail deformity; when Anne's body was exhumed from the Tower of London in the 19th century, no evidence was found of a sixth finger.

As for the third breast, Sander also wrote: 'There was a large wen under her chin, and therefore to hide its ugliness she wore a high dress covering her throat.' Others have described the alleged extra breast as a cyst on the neck. Sander never met Anne Boleyn so this may all be fiction.

After Anne Boleyn was executed in 1536, her heart was apparently stolen. It may have been discovered just over 300 years later, during renovations in 1837 at St Mary's Church in Erwarton, Suffolk, where a heart-shaped casket was found in the chancel wall. Anne and her family certainly had strong connections with the church, and the casket was reburied beneath the organ with a small plaque to mark the spot, claiming that the casket had contained Anne Boleyn's heart.

BOLIVIA

Bolivia has a 5,000-man navy but no coastline. This is the largest navy of any landlocked country. The only other country in South America that is totally inland is Paraguay.

It is often claimed that Bolivia once had three presidents in one day. That is not quite correct but it came very close in August 1825: from 6 to 11 August, the acting president was Jose Mariano Serrano, who was succeeded by Antonio José de Sucre, who held the post for only one day before being followed by Simón Bolivar on 12 August.

AMERICA, NAVIES

BOMB

The word 'bomb' comes from the Greek *bombos*, which means a humming noise or a boom.

BAT, BERLIN, BIKINI, WELLS

BOOKS

Since 2007, every published book has been assigned a unique 13-digit ISBN (International Standard Book Number). The final digit of any ISBN is included as a way for computers to make an instant check for incorrectly entered numbers: if you add together all the digits in odd-numbered places then add to that total three times all the digits in even-numbered places, the resulting figure will always, if no mistake has been made, be divisible by 10.

For example, the ISBN of the first edition of my book *Sloths!: A Celebration of the World's Most Maligned Mammal* is 9781786494221. The above process gives us $(9 + 8 + 7 + 6 + 9 + 2 +1) + 3(7 + 1 + 8 + 4 + 4 + 2)$, which equals $42 + 78 = 120$ which is 10 x 12. The final digit of the ISBN is calculated to make this happen. Before 2007 any ISBN had only ten digits, with a completely different rule to check for mistypings.

The average UK household spends £1.50 on books every week. The average British male aged 15 to 24 spends only 3.1 minutes a day reading books.

The Japanese spend more on books than any other nation. Norway comes second.

The top three best-selling books of all time are: 1. The Bible, 2. *Quotations From Chairman Mao Tse-Tung*, 3. *Lord Of The Rings*.

The three countries with most Nobel Prize for Literature winners are: 1. France, 2. USA, 3. Britain.

There were 188,000 different books published in Britain in 2018, which works out at one new book every 2 minutes 48 seconds. In 2020, around 202 million books were sold in the UK.

BLYTON, HEALTH, LITERACY, INTERNET

BORDEN, Lizzie Drew (1860–1927)

Lizzie Borden had an axe,
Gave her mother forty whacks.
When she saw what she had done,
She gave her father forty-one.

This verse, however, gives a misleading account of the facts. In fact, on 19 June 1893, Lizzie Borden, the alleged axe murderess, was acquitted of killing her parents in Fall River, Massachusetts.

Her great-great-great-great-great grandfather, Thomas Cornell, however, was executed in Rhode Island in 1673 for killing his mother. He was almost certainly innocent, as the main evidence against him was the testimony of a man who said that the late Mrs Cornell had come to him in a dream and accused her son of having killed her.

BORGIA

The power of the House of Borgia in Italy and the Vatican began when the pious Alfonso Borgia was elected Pope Calixtus III in 1455. Corruption and nepotism started in 1456 when the Pope made his nephew Rodrigo a cardinal. Despite being a gambler and womaniser, Rodrigo became Pope Alexander VI in 1492.

Unusually for a Pope, Rodrigo had a wife, four legitimate children and several more children from various lovers. He is said to have had an incestuous relationship with his daughter Lucrezia. Rodrigo died in 1503, allegedly from a poisoned apple, though medical evidence suggests malaria. Lucrezia's brother Giovanni was

murdered by her other brother Cesare Borgia, and Cesare then became the first person to resign as a cardinal.

Lucrezia was first married at the age of 13 and later declared to be a virgin, despite being pregnant.

Pope Innocent X was the great-great-great grandson of Pope Alexander VI. He died in 1655, exactly 200 years after a Borgia first became Pope.

The actress Brooke Shields is a direct descendant of Lucrezia Borgia.

BOSCH, Hieronymus (c.1450–1516)

In 2003, the journal *Mycological Research* published a paper entitled 'Amanita muscaria: chemistry, biology, toxicology, and ethnomycology', which drew attention to Hieronymus Bosch's triptych *The Garden of Earthly Delights*, which included a depiction of the hallucinogenic mushroom *Amanita muscaria*, supporting suggestions that the mushroom may have been at least partly responsible for the fantastic visions portrayed in many Bosch paintings.

Another detail from the same painting also led to a piece of music first recorded in 2013 based on some musical notes that appear on the buttocks of a man being crushed by a harp and some sort of mandolin. The notes, written in a curious medieval notation, were transcribed and translated into modern notation by Oklahoma music student Amelia Hamrick and played on a piano. She called the piece '600 Year Old Butt Song From Hell', which was later amended to '500 Year Old Butt Song From Hell' when her arithmetic was corrected. A choral arrangement was later made, with the words: 'Butt song from hell, This is the butt song from hell, We sing from our asses while burning in purgatory, The butt song from hell, The butt song from hell, Butts.'

BOSNIA

Bosnia-Herzegovina has never won a medal of any sort in either the Winter or Summer Olympics. Apart from microstates and Albania, it is the only European sovereign country that has never won an Olympic medal.

BOSTON

In 2011 in Boston, Massachusetts, the emergency services unveiled an ambulance modified for the obese. It included a stretcher that can hold 385 kilograms (850 pounds) and a hydraulic lift with 453-kilogram (1,000-pound) capacity. This was designed both to ensure the safety of the sick and to reduce injuries among crews lifting even larger patients. It cost about $12,000 to retrofit the vehicle.

TOOTHPICK

BOSWELL, James (1740–95)

Best known as Samuel Johnson's biographer, James Boswell was a remarkable person in his own right. After suffering from depression and possibly bipolar disorder in his youth in Scotland, he decided to become a monk but was taken back to Scotland by his father, who was an esteemed judge.

He travelled to the Netherlands to continue his law studies at Utrecht University, met Voltaire and Rousseau, became attached to the latter's mistress and brought her back to England. It is not known whether this had any connection with his suffering from gonorrhoea, of which between 12 and 17 episodes are recorded. He also had an ingrowing toenail.

Boswell was introduced to Samuel Johnson by the actor and bookseller Thomas Davies. In his *Life of Samuel Johnson,* Boswell quotes Thomas Davies' description of Johnson's laughter: 'He laughs like a rhinoceros.'

Boswell's family surname was spelled with only one final L when he was born, but he added another later. In 1782, when his father died, he succeeded to the title of 9th Earl of Auchinleck.

CELIBACY

BOTSWANA

According to a report in 2007 by the International Union for Conservation of Nature, there are more African elephants in Botswana than any other country. The number of elephants in Botswana was given as 133,829, with Tanzania in second place on 108,816.

Despite increased poaching, the figure for Botswana has remained roughly the same since then, though in 2019 a five-year hunting ban on elephants in Zimbabwe was lifted. In the same year, it was estimated that some 216,000 African elephants migrate freely between Angola, Botswana, Namibia, Zambia and Zimbabwe, making it difficult to assess how many live in each country.

In 1930, close to 10 million wild elephants are thought to have roamed the African continent, but conflicts and poaching reduced this number to around 415,000 by 2016.

CLICK, ZEBRA

BOTTOM

All three of the medallists at a chilli-eating contest in the Philippines in 1996 had to be treated in hospital afterwards for a condition known in Mexico as Gringo's Bottom, characterised by painful burns to the bottom area. They were also treated for dangerously high blood pressure and severe bowel pain. The winner, Mexican Bert Gonzalez, had eaten a world-record 300 chunks of the lada pepper from the Philippines, one of the hottest varieties in the world.

'Chilli eating should be an Olympic sport,' he said, while lying face down on his hospital bed.

'It's very strenuous and taxing to the body and I shall have to spend some time recovering.'

The words 'bottom' or 'bottoms' occur only once in the King James Bible, in Jonah 2:6, but 'bottomless' occurs seven times in the Book of Revelation, always followed by the word 'pit'.

♀ *BUTTOCKS, CARUSO, RENOIR, TOILET PAPER*

BOUNTY

HMS *Bounty* was originally built at Blaydes shipyard in Hull as a coal-carrying vessel. The ship was on a trip to collect breadfruit from Tahiti when the infamous mutiny took place. The mutineers cast Captain Bligh adrift with 18 loyal crew members who successfully steered their boat on a 47-day journey to Timor. Bligh later rose to the rank of vice-admiral and became governor of New South Wales.

Fletcher Christian, who led the mutiny on the *Bounty* in 1789, named his first son Thursday October Christian, apparently because he was born on a Thursday in October 1790.

Only when Pitcairn was rediscovered years later was it realised that a miscalculation had been made because of the International Date Line and he should have been Friday October Christian. Thursday October Christian's fourth son, born in 1820, also began

life on a Thursday in October so he was given the same name. Thursday October Christian II went on to become chief magistrate on Pitcairn.

The wreck of the *Bounty* was found in 1957. Luis Marden, the American diver who found it, wore cufflinks made from the ship's nails. Bounty Day is celebrated on 23 January on Pitcairn, marking the day in 1790 when the *Bounty* mutineers set fire to the ship to avoid detection.

BOURDALOUE

A bourdaloue was an elegant porcelain chamber-pot designed for women. Shaped rather like a gravy boat, it was designed to accompany ladies on journeys or at events where they might find it difficult to rush off to use a lavatory. The bourdaloue was held between the lady's legs beneath her petticoats, then removed and taken away by her servants when she had urinated into it. It was very popular throughout the 18th century.

The origin of the name is uncertain, but some say it was named after the preacher Louis Bourdaloue, whose sermons were said to be so good and so long sometimes that ladies in the congregation did not want to tear themselves away to go to the lavatory.

Bourdaloue pear tart has nothing to do with urination but was named after a bakery in a Paris street named after Louis Bourdaloue.

♀ *LAVATORIES*

BOWERBIRD

The bowerbird of Australia and New Guinea has an elaborate and extraordinary mating ritual. The males build complex and highly decorated bowers on the forest floor from twigs, leaves and moss, which have also been described as 'love-nests' or 'bachelor pads' with the sole purpose of enticing female birds. The decorations include colourful feathers, pebbles, berries, snail shells and kangaroo bones. When a female shows interest in the bower, the male struts and sings, trying to convince her to enter the bower and mate with him.

If he is successful, the female flies off after mating to build a nest close by, while the male promptly turns his attention to trying to find another female to mate with, playing no part in the upbringing of the offspring of any of his lovers.

Shiny coins, spoons, pieces of aluminium foil and even a glass eye have been used to entice birds to the bower. When building a new bower, a male will recycle an average of 30 per cent of the materials used to decorate the previous one.

Males who build the best bowers are very successful, as 75 per cent of females mate with the owner of the first bower they visit. Other males may never find a mate at all. The colour blue has been found to be particularly effective in attracting females. The reasons for this are unclear but one theory is that blue is the colour of the berries that are the females' favourite food. As well as shiny blue beads or pieces of broken glass and plastic, male birds have been seen painting their bowers blue with sticks that have crushed berries on their tips. The number of *Solanum* berries used in the decoration has been found to predict mating success.

In 2013, researchers who gave problem-solving tasks to bowerbirds in the wild concluded that mating success did not correlate with problem-solving ability.

BOWIE, David (1947–2016)

David Bowie began life on Elvis Presley's 12th birthday. Born David Robert Jones, he adopted the stage name David Bowie in honour of the American pioneer James Bowie who popularised the Bowie knife. His name change was mainly to avoid confusion with Davy Jones, who later became lead singer in the made-for-TV band The Monkees.

In 1999 he was made a Commander of the Ordre des Arts et des Lettres by the French government and was given an honorary doctorate by the Berklee College of Music in Boston, Massachusetts. He has also had a spider, *Heteropoda davidbowie*, and an asteroid, 342843, named after him, but in 2000 he turned down the offer of a CBE, and in 2003 he turned down a knighthood, saying that he seriously didn't know what it was for.

ARACHNOLOGY, HAIR

BOWLING

The triangular arrangement of the pins in tenpin bowling, with rows of four, three, two and one, is called a tetractys.

On Saturday 3 May 2008, Dale Davis of Alta, Iowa, made a perfect score of 300 in a bowling game with 12 consecutive strikes. Mr Davis was 78 years old and legally blind.

Ninepin bowling was very popular among the gambling underworld of America until 1841 when Connecticut banned ninepin bowling alleys, which is how tenpin bowling originated.

BOWLS, FIFTEEN, WHITE HOUSE

BOWLS

The great English cricketer W.G. Grace (1848–1915) also captained England at lawn bowls. In 1903, he became founder and first president of the English Bowling Association.

⚲ *MANGELWURZEL, MARY I, PARROT*

● BOXING

When Andy Bowen and Jack Burke fought a boxing match in New Orleans on 6 April 1893, it went on for 7 hours and 19 minutes: 110 rounds. The referee then ruled 'no contest' as he judged that both men were unable to continue. This was the longest gloved boxing match on record.

The same year saw a shorter but arguably even more dramatic fight between Harry Sharpe and Frank Crosby for the Missouri lightweight championship, which lasted 77 rounds. In the penultimate round, the men knocked each other down simultaneously. Crosby banged his head when he fell, got up dazed and was knocked out in the following round. Willie Green, the referee, had been taking nips of whisky for a cold and passed out in the 65th round after which the fight went on without a referee. The winner then gained the title, a $500 side bet, and an 11-month jail term for violating anti-prizefight laws.

⚲ *DOYLE, HOXHA*

● BOXING DAY

Boxing Day takes its name from the Christmas boxes given to servants when they returned to work after Christmas. The earliest reference to Boxing Day in the *Oxford Dictionary* dates back to 1743. The first references to a Christmas box are from 1711 and 1731.

In Ireland, Boxing Day is sometimes known as Wren Day, as this is also St Stephen's Day, and chattering wrens are supposed to have given away St Stephen's hiding place. Boxing Day was therefore said to be the only day of the year when killing a wren was not unlucky.

The words 'Good King Wenceslas looked out on the feast of Stephen' were written by the Anglican priest John Mason Neale in 1853. The good king this refers to was the 10th-century Duke of Bohemia Wenceslaus I, who was elevated to sainthood and posthumously declared a king after he was killed, probably by his brother and successor Boleslaus I.

A traditional meal for Boxing Day is St Stephen's Day pie, which is similar to cottage pie but made with left-over turkey or ham instead of beef.

Two American presidents died on Boxing Day: Harry S. Truman in 1972 and Gerald Ford in 2006. The only date that exceeds that number of presidential deaths is Independence Day, 4 July, which claimed three presidents.

'No man ever talked in poetry 'cept a beadle on boxin' day.' Charles Dickens, Pickwick Papers, *1836*

● BRADFORD

The University of Bradford is the only British university to have had a serving prime minister (Harold Wilson) as chancellor, a post he held from 1966 to 1985

⚲ *HULL*

● BRAHE, Tycho (1546–1601)

The 16th-century Danish astronomer Tycho Brahe wore an artificial nose attached with cement after he lost his own in a sword fight at the age of 19. The nose was reputedly made of gold and silver, but analysis of his body mould in 1901 suggested that it was actually copper. Brahe had a pet moose named Rix, which died after falling downstairs when drunk.

BRAHMS, Johannes (1833–97)

The great German composer Johannes Brahms developed a morbid fear of travelling by boat after a bad sea-going experience in a skiff. This led to his declining an honorary doctorate from Cambridge University in 1877, as the offer was conditional on his crossing the Channel to accept it in person.

'Brahms' (short for 'Brahms and Liszt') is cockney rhyming slang for inebriated or pissed.

In 1999, campus police at Pittsburgh University announced a plan to prevent students from becoming Brahms and Liszt by playing them Mozart during peak party times. Studies had shown that Mozart's music has a calming effect, and the plan was to play it at high volume over loudspeakers between 10pm and 2am from Thursday to Saturday.

BRAIN

Around 78 per cent of your brain is water. The average adult brain is 14 centimetres (5.5 inches) wide, 16.75 centimetres (6.6 inches) long, 9 centimetres (3.7 inches) high and weighs 1.4 kilograms (3 pounds) for men and 1.25 kilograms (2 pounds 11 ounces) for women. It contains 100 billion neurons.

Although it accounts for only 2 per cent of total body weight, the brain uses about 20 per cent of our total energy intake.

The Nobel Prize-winning author Anatole France was found after his death in 1924 to have one of the smallest human brains ever recorded.

The word 'brain' (or 'brains') does not occur at all in the King James Bible.

The only Shakespeare play to include the word 'brainless' is *Troilus and Cressida*.

'The brain is a wonderful organ. It starts working the moment you get up in the morning, and does not stop until you get into the office.' Robert Frost

♀ *BABBAGE, EINSTEIN, KOALA, LEMUR, LOVE*

BRANDING

Robbers, runaway slaves and criminals turned gladiators were branded on the forehead in ancient Rome. The Anglo-Saxons also adopted branding as a punishment, and this sentence was abolished only in 1879. Branding was done on the breast, cheeks or forehead, depending on the crime. In the 16th and 17th centuries, England employed branding as punishment for a variety of offenders including thieves, blasphemers, brawlers, gypsies and runaway slaves.

In North America, before the revolution, the English also branded petty criminals using letters according to their crime: A – Adultery; B – Blasphemy; D – Drunkenness or Desertion; F – Felony or Fray-making; M – Murder or Manslaughter; P – Perjury; R – Roguishness; S – Slave; SL – Seditious Libel; SS – Slave Stealer or Sower of Sedition; T – Thief.

In 1844, Jonathan Walker had the initials SS (for 'Slave Stealer') branded into his right palm for helping American slaves escape to the Bahamas. This was the last instance of branding as punishment in the USA.

♀ *CENSORSHIP*

BRASSIERE

The old French word *brassière* originally meant an upper-arm protector, then a bodice or child's vest, and later a lifejacket. The first garments similar to today's bras were worn by Minoan women on Crete around 2500 BC.

The first patent for a modern brassiere was obtained in the US by Mary Phelps Jacob in 1914. She has been widely praised as the inventor of the modern bra, but that honour seems better deserved by Marie Tucek of New York, whose 'Breast Supporter' came more than 20 years earlier in 1893. It comprised a plate 'made of sheet metal, cardboard or other suitable material and preferably covered with silk, canvas or other desirable fabric', bent to match the wearer's body and attached to cups to support the breasts. It was completed with a number of hooks and straps.

The 'Backless Brassiere' of Mary Phelps Jacob was less cumbersome, made essentially from two handker-chiefs, a ribbon and cord. Jacob, inci-dentally, was also a successful publisher who brought to the public some of the early works of Ernest Hemingway and Henry Miller. She also had a pet whippet called Clytoris.

In 1917, the US War Industries Board asked women to stop buying corsets in order to save metal. The resulting switch from corsets to bras was said to provide enough metal to build two battleships. The next significant development came when the A-to-D cup-sizing system was introduced by Warner Corset Company in 1935.

The world's biggest bra was made by Triumph International (Japan) in 1990 with a bust measurement of 28 metres (91 feet 10 inches).

In April 2001, the world's first combined brassiere and gun holster was invented by American personal security consultant Paxton Quigley. Designed to hold a .38 calibre snub-nose revolver on one side, and a pepper spray on the other, the garment was called the Super-Bra. The chest area was said to be a good place to conceal a weapon.

December 2001 saw another advance with the launch of the 'Frequent Flyer's Bra' by Triumph International (Japan). It was developed in response to reports that the metal parts of conventional bras had been setting off detectors at airports.

BRAZIL

The weight of coffee produced in Brazil is twice the weight of tea produced in India.

Half the people in South America live in Brazil, but Bolivia and Brazil produce about the same amount of Brazil nuts.

In 1964, a severe traffic jam was caused in Brazil when a couple kissed in a car and their dentures became inextri-cably locked together.

In 1969, some beetles were taken into custody in Brazil with a gang of Brazilian bus drivers who were charged with training the beetles to climb into fare boxes and take out coins.

In December 2001, Ellen Gracie Northfleet was sworn in as Brazil's first female Supreme Court judge, but the Supreme Federal Tribunal building had no women's toilet in the judges' cham-bers. 'If she has to go to the bathroom, she'll have to do it before the ceremony or wait until after it's over,' a spokesman explained.

In 2002, Brazilian weight-training instructor Edmar Freitas set a world record by doing 111,000 sit-ups in 24 hours. In the same year, scientists in São Paulo were reported to have cloned a bull accidentally. They were trying to clone a cow.

In Brazil, insurance policies on celebrity rear ends have become so common that insurers have a special term for them: 'bumbum policies'. In

2002 Brazilian model and actress Suzana Alves received an unusual insurance deal: in exchange for letting them put her image on its billboards, a company insured her buttocks, knees and ankles for $2 million.

In 2019, the bovine livestock in Brazil was estimated to number 214.7 million. The human population at the time was only 212.6 million, so we may conclude that there are slightly more cows than people in Brazil.

⚲ *COFFEE, COMPUTATION, EGGS, GOATS, PIZZA, SLAVERY*

● BREAD

The word 'lady' derives from an Old English expression for someone who kneads bread: 'hlaefdige', from hlaef (a loaf) and 'dig-' (to knead). The word for a worshipper of bread is 'artolater'.

According to an old Cornish superstition, a loaf with holes in it foretells a death in the family.

An equally old superstition, however, says that a loaf with holes in it is a sign that the woman who baked it is going to have a baby.

In 1984, the Tasmanian Supreme Court awarded £1,900 damages to a man who still vomited at the sight of bread four years after finding a dead mouse in a loaf.

⚲ *PUDDING, SMELL, STALE BREAD, TOAST*

● BREAKFAST

The earliest known breakfast food was a sort of porridge made in the late Stone Age by grinding grains with a large stone. The earliest known use of the word 'breakfast' in English was in 1463.

The average household in the UK has five packs of breakfast cereal, though the most popular breakfast in the UK is fried egg, bacon and sausage. Bacon sandwiches come second.

According to research by Quaker Oats, 25 per cent of people skip breakfast altogether. A survey by Weetabix in 2020 reported that the most passionate lovers eat peanut butter sandwiches for breakfast.

Joey Chestnut holds the record for eating hard-boiled eggs, 141 in eight minutes, set in 2013, but Matt Stonie holds the bacon record at 182 rashers in five minutes.

In 2015, J&D Foods in the US launched bacon-scented underwear, 'hand crafted to offer the support of briefs, the freedom of boxers and the smell of breakfast cooking in your pants'.

Breakfast At Tiffany's (1961) won two Oscars. It is the only film with 'breakfast' in its title to win an Oscar.

'Hope is a good breakfast but it is a bad supper.' Francis Bacon

'Only dull people are brilliant at breakfast.' Oscar Wilde

⚲ *BACON, CORNFLAKES, OYSTER*

● BREAST

In 2008, the size of a Japanese model's breasts helped her overturn a conviction for criminal damage. Serena Kozakura had been accused of kicking in her boyfriend's door and crawling inside, apparently because he was with another woman, but in her appeal, her lawyer held up a plate showing the size of the hole and pointed out that it was impossible for her to have squeezed through with her 43-inch bust.

⚲ *ANATOMY, CLEAVAGE, IMPLANT, NIPPLE*

BREASTFEEDING

In 1715, records show that there were four employment bureaus for wet nurses in Paris.

Queen Victoria considered breastfeeding 'animalistic' and most suited to women of low social class.

NUDITY

BRIDEGROOM

The bridegroom at a wedding in Turkey in August 2010 was arrested after he shot his father and two aunts dead during the celebrations. It is traditional in Turkey to fire a gun into the air in celebration at weddings or sporting victories, but the groom lost control over the weapon and accidentally fired at the guests. Eight other relatives were also wounded.

IRAN

BRITANNIA

The Roman-Celtic goddess Britannia first appears on Roman coinage in the second century. She was depicted in submissive pose, symbolic of Britain's conquest by the Romans. It was the Celtic worship of Britannia that led to the Romans naming the island 'Britannica'. It was not until the 16th or 17th century that Britannia was portrayed triumphant as a symbol of Britain's might.

Britannia's first appearance on a British coin in the post-Roman era was on a farthing in 1672. Until 1797, Britannia was always depicted carrying a spear. In that year, her weapon was changed to a trident, previously associated with Neptune.

'Rule Britannia' was written for a theatrical entertainment or masque called *Alfred* in 1740. The music was by Thomas Arne and the words were written by the Scottish poet James Thomson. The chorus begins 'Rule Britannia, Britannia rule [not 'rules'] the waves'. This is an exhortation to Britainnia to rule, not a statement that she does so. The original poem continued: 'Britons never will be slaves, but the Victorians changed 'will' (a prediction) to 'shall' (indicating determination).

BRITISH MUSEUM

The British Museum first opened to the public on 15 January 1759. It began with a bequest to the nation from the physician, collector and milk chocolate inventor Sir Hans Sloane, who died in 1753. Sloane's collection numbered about 71,000 items, including 40,000 books, but has now grown to 7 million, of which some 120,000 are on display. According to the British Museum database, it includes 1,941 mummies of which 74 are mummified cats. The British Museum Great Court, which opened in 2000, is the largest covered square in Europe.

BROCCOLI

The average person in the United States eats 2 kilograms (4.5 pounds) of broccoli a year.

Late on Christmas Eve or early on Christmas Day 2006 in the Chicago suburb of Villa Park, thieves stole a tractor trailer filled with broccoli that was valued at $50,000.

Research in 2007 showed that broccoli may prevent an inherited skin disorder in mice.

BUSH George Herbert Walker

BRONTË, Charlotte (1816–55)

Charlotte Brontë, author of *Jane Eyre*, was only 1.4 metres (4 feet 9 inches) tall. She was very short-sighted and could see better in the dark than in the light. She had a cat called Tiger.

♀ *PILLOW*

BRONTOSAURUS

Most dinosaurs died out around 65 million years ago, but the Brontosaurus was only officially expunged from natural history records in the 20th century, on the grounds that the Brontosaurus ('thunder lizard'), discovered and named by O.C. Marsh in 1879, was in fact only a grown-up Apatosaurus ('deceptive lizard'), which he had discovered and named two years earlier. The problem was partly caused by his attaching the wrong head to his Apatosaurus bones.

The error had been identified in 1903, after which, according to the rules of naming procedure, 'Apatosaurus', as the earlier term, took official precedence.

In 1970, the US Post Office was forced to apologise for calling an Apatosaurus a Brontosaurus on a series of dinosaur stamps.

BROOKLYN

According to the perfume company Bond No. 9, the New York borough of Brooklyn smells like grapefruit, cardamom, cypress, cedar and leather. Their 'Brooklyn' fragrance launched in 2009 was designed to capture the essential odours of Brooklyn.

♀ *BLAKE, MAFIA*

BROTHEL

In 2010, the Shady Lady Ranch became the first brothel in Nevada to hire a male prostitute. After it had secured state and county approval, the Shady Lady employed a man known as Markus whom it described as a 'prostidude'.

♀ *ENVIRONMENT, NIPPLE, PROSTITUTION*

BROWN

From auburn to zinnwaldite, there are 33 recognised shades of brown.

No film with 'brown' in the title has ever won a Best Picture Oscar, though Patricia Neal was voted Best Actress for her role as Alma Brown in the 1963 film *Hud*, and Daniel Day-Lewis won Best Actor in 1989 as Christy Brown in *My Left Foot*.

The word 'brown' occurs only four times in the King James Bible, all in Genesis 30.

The only vowel in the name of former UK Prime Minister Gordon Brown is 'O'. Every other British Prime Minister has had at least two different vowels. Gordon Brown's first name is James.

♀ *CASANOVA, FASHION*

BRUMMELL, George Bryan 'Beau' (1778–1840)

In 1797, trend-setter and dandy Beau Brummell abandoned a promising military career and resigned his commission when his regiment was sent from London to Manchester. He found Manchester's poor reputation and its lack of culture and civility more than he could bear.

Brummell never ate vegetables, on principle, but said that he once ate a pea. Byron considered Brummell to be the greatest man of the 19th century, ahead of Napoleon and himself.

♀ *PEAS*

BRUNEI

The Sultan of Brunei is the second richest royal in the world, behind only the King of Thailand. He has a 1,788-room palace, a collection of more than 5,000 cars including hundreds of Rolls-Royces, and is reported to have regular US$20,000 haircuts.

Brunei occupies two small parts of the island of Borneo with a total area of 5,765 square kilometres (2,226 square miles), which is about equal to that of Norfolk in the UK or Connecticut in the US. The population of Brunei is about 408,000, which is less than that of Leicester and less than that of any US State.

Brunei first participated at the Olympic Games in 1988, when their delegation comprised just one official and no athletes. Brunei have never won an Olympic medal or a Nobel Prize but their football team won the Malaysia Cup in 1999.

In Brunei it is considered impolite to point with one's index finger. The thumb is used instead. Traditionally Bruneians do not shake hands with people of the opposite sex.

The Belalong Tree Frog is a rare species of frog which is found only in Brunei.

According to the Roller Coaster Database, Brunei has only one rollercoaster.

♀ *INCOME TAX, MONARCHY*

BRUSSELS

The name of Brussels probably came from an old Dutch word meaning 'home in the marsh'. Brussels is the world's only capital city where a flea market is held every day of the year.

Brussels has many strange museums, including a Clockarium of ceramic clocks, a Sewers Museum, a Streetlight Museum and a Police Museum. It also used to have an Underwear Museum, which moved from Brussels to Lessines in 2016. There are 138 restaurants per square mile in Brussels.

As well as the famous Manneken Pis statue of a peeing boy, Brussels has statues of a peeing girl and a peeing dog.

In 2011, following complaints from Flemish-speaking Belgians, the operators of the Brussels metro stopped playing French songs at the stations. Experiments showed that 85 per cent of passengers were happy with a mixture of popular songs that were 70 per cent English and 15 per cent each Italian and Spanish.

♀ *BELGIUM, FRANKLIN, QUEUEING*

BRUSSELS SPROUTS

Brussels sprouts have been grown in Belgium since at least the 15th century. The term Brussels sprout however was first used in English only in 1796. The British eat more Brussels sprouts per head than any other country in Europe.

An analysis of whether young people liked or disliked Brussels sprouts was undertaken by John Trinkaus of New York and reported under the title 'Taste Preference For Brussels Sprouts: An Informal Look' in the journal *Psychological Reports* in December 1991. A survey of 442 business students revealed that about 50 per cent reported a dislike of sprouts, 10 per cent liked them and 40 per cent were indifferent. Older students were more likely to like them than younger ones.

However, according to research at the Royal Institution's L'Oreal Young Scientist Centre published in December 2011, Brussels sprouts are liked by more than twice as many people than had previously been thought. Their survey revealed that 60 per cent of people like sprouts, while another survey put the figure at 68 per cent. This is surprising, as earlier research indicated that 70 per cent of people ought to dislike sprouts. This is because 70 per cent of us have a gene known as TAS2R38 which responds to a chemical in sprouts, making them taste bitter.

In 2014, fundraiser Stuart Kettell, 49, rolled a Brussels sprout to the top of Snowdon using his nose. It took four days and 22 sprouts.

♀ SHOPPING TROLLEYS

BRUTUS

Marcus Junius Brutus was the best known of the assassins of Julius Caesar. His mother Servilia was said to be Caesar's favourite mistress for a period of 20 years.

♀ SHAKESPEARE

BUBBLE WRAP

The world record for the most people simultaneously popping Bubble Wrap is 366, set at a school in New Jersey in January 2013.

Hawthorne High School and the Sealed Air Corp., manufacturers of Bubble Wrap, confirmed that that number of people kept popping the product for two minutes to set the record on the 13th annual Bubble Wrap Appreciation Day, which is celebrated on the last Monday in January.

The company manufactures enough Bubble Wrap each year to stretch to the Moon and back.

BUCKINGHAM PALACE

Fourteen of the fifteen children of Queen Charlotte, wife of George III of England, were born in Buckingham Palace or 'The Queen's House' as it was then known. George III bought the property from the Duke of Buckingham in 1761 as a private residence for his queen.

The Palace has 40,000 lightbulbs, 760 windows and 1,514 doors. Its 775 rooms include 188 staff bedrooms, 78 bathrooms and 52 royal and guest bedrooms.

Edward VII is the only monarch who was born and died in Buckingham Palace.

♀ NETTLES, POSTCODE, ZEBRA

BUCKLAND, William (1784–1856)

William Buckland was not only Canon of Christ Church, Oxford, and later Dean of Westminster, but in 1819 also became the first person to find dinosaur fossils in Britain.

Buckland's passion for geology also incorporated a taste for the unusual – literally – and he was fascinated by the flavours of practically anything. In his opinion, the only thing that tasted worse than a mole was a bluebottle.

He claimed to have eaten his way through the animal kingdom, and on seeing an object that may or may not have been the embalmed heart of King Louis XIV of France, is reported to have said, 'I have eaten many strange things, but have never eaten the heart of a king before,' and promptly swallowed it. He also reputedly once identified his location when lost in the fog on the outskirts of London by kneeling down and licking the local earth, which he maintained with certainty was Uxbridge.

Quite apart from his sense of taste and pioneering work as a dinosaur hunter, Buckland also once stole Ben Jonson's heel bone from Westminster Abbey.

♀ DINOSAUR, JONSON

BUDGERIGAR

The budgerigar has been described as the third most popular pet in the world, behind dogs and cats. There are several theories concerning where the name 'budgerigar' comes from. The most likely is an Australian Aborigine dialect

BRUTUS | BUDGERIGAR

in which *boodgeri* means 'good' and *gar* is 'cockatoo'.

Research published in 1997 showed that male budgerigars are more likely to be unfaithful to their mates when their mates are not watching.

♀ STUDENT

BUFFALO

The world buffalo population is around 207 million, of which 97 per cent are in Asia, with India and Pakistan having the highest numbers.

The North American buffalo (*Bison bison*) is not, strictly speaking, a true buffalo at all but only a distant relative. Estimates of the number in North America 20,000 years ago vary between 30 million and 200 million. By the early 1900s, thanks to indiscriminate slaughter and poaching, the number had dwindled to little more than a hundred, but now it is back to around 200,000.

The Swamp buffalo (*Bubalus bubalis carabanesis*) has 48 chromosomes; the River buffalo (*Bubalus bubalis*) has 50.

Buffaloes are good swimmers, and so buoyant that their head, hump and tail remain above the water.

The mating ritual of male buffalo involves a display called 'flehmen', which consists of curling the lip back and extending the neck.

In January 2001, a three-day funeral was held in Thailand for Boonlert, a 32-year-old water buffalo which starred in the film *Bangrachan*, which was about an 18th-century battle between Thailand and Myanmar. Part of the film's success was credited to Boonlert's 3-metre (10-foot) long horns. At the funeral, a Thai opera was performed in front of the body of the buffalo to pay respect.

Buffalo milk has 25 per cent more protein than cow's milk.

The city of Buffalo is the second largest city (after New York itself) in the state of New York.

Buffalo wings, which are made of deep-fried chicken wings in a hot sauce, are so called because they originated in Buffalo.

♀ BADGER, HORN, PREGNANCY, THAILAND

BUGANDA

Buganda was a principality in what is now Uganda. From the 13th century until Uganda's independence in 1962, Buganda was a kingdom. This was then abolished until 1993, since when Muwenda Mutebi II has been recognised as the 36th Kabaka (or king) of Buganda. He was the son of the 35th Kabaka, who had been deposed by President Milton Obote. Commonly known in the non-Ugandan press as King Freddy, the 35th Kabaka was Sir Edward Frederick William David Walugembe Mutebi Luwangula Mutesa II. After completing his education at Magdalene College, Cambridge, King Freddy was commissioned as a captain in the Grenadier Guards.

The native language in Buganda is Luganda. The word for a second of time in Luganda is *tikitiki*.

BUGS BUNNY

Mel Blanc, who voiced the part of Bugs Bunny, could not stand the taste of carrots.

The character and nonchalant, fast-talking mannerisms of Bugs Bunny were said to have been modelled on Clark Gable and Groucho Marx.

♀ CARROT, GOOGLE, STAMPS

BULGARIA

Bulgarian yogurt has a unique taste thanks to the *Lactobacillus bulgaricus* bacterium which is found in the Bulgarian air. The yogurt is praised by many as a hangover cure and sunburn remedy.

Bulgaria is one of the few places on Earth where nodding your head means 'no' and shaking it means 'yes'.

According to an old Bulgarian peasant custom, coins are placed over the eyes of a corpse at a funeral before being washed in water. The liquid is then added to wine and given to men to make them blind to their wives' faults.

BULL

In April 2008, the Senate in the state of Florida passed a bill banning the display of imitation bulls' testicles in motor vehicles; a $60 fine was approved for anyone who did so, but the bill failed to pass the Florida House of Representatives. A similar bill had failed to get past the committee stage in the state of Virginia earlier in the same year.

The matter of 'truck nuts', as they were commonly known, became national news in 2011 when Virginia Tice, 65, of South Carolina was issued with a $445 ticket for refusing to remove a pair from her pickup truck when ordered to do so by a local police chief. The case went to trial and was seen as a contest between the state's obscenity laws and the matter of free speech. The police chief said that if the truck nuts were a matter of free speech, then 'I don't know what they would be trying to express'. The court case was postponed and resumed three times, but appears to have faded away with no verdict ever reached.

In Vietnam, a dish made of bulls' testicles is commonly called 'Ngầu pín'. It is supposed to increase men's sexual ability. In North America, a similar dish is referred to as 'Rocky Mountain Oysters'.

BRAZIL, EUROPE, NICARAGUA

BULLET

An Alphonsin is a three-pronged surgical appliance designed to remove bullets. It was invented in 1552 by Alphonso Ferri of Naples, after whom it was named.

No Alphonsin was ever used on William Lawlis Pace, who held the world record of 94 and a half years for living with a bullet in his head. Mr Pace was accidentally shot by his brother with their father's .22 calibre rifle in 1917; he died in 2012 at the age of 103. Doctors in Texas, where the accident happened, feared that attempts to remove the bullet might cause brain damage, so they left it there.

One of Mr Pace's eyes was damaged by the shooting, but he was still able to spend his working life as a cemetery custodian.

FASHION, GUATEMALA, LOBSTER

BULLOCK

The word 'taghairm' means inspiration sought by lying in a bullock's hide behind a waterfall. It was a divination method used in the Scottish Highlands. Sir Walter Scott uses the word in his 'Lady of the Lake' poem. Apparently, being sewn into the hide of a freshly killed ox concentrates the mind (or possibly summons up evil spirits) so well that it enables one to predict the future.

BIBLE

BUNGA BUNGA

The derivation and precise meaning of the term 'bunga bunga' became a matter of much speculation following its use in 2011 by the former Italian Prime Minister Silvio Berlusconi. According to one account, Berlusconi learned the term from Muammar Gaddafi and it was just a term for a high-class orgy.

The actress Sabina Began (originally Beganovic) claims that the term is a playful version of her name and that she organised some such events for Berlusconi.

The term 'bunga bunga', however, is much older than Berlusconi, having first attained some prominence around 1910 when a group of London hoaxers tricked their way onto the Royal Navy ship HMS *Dreadnought* by pretending to be the Prince of Abyssinia and his entourage. Whenever they were shown something impressive, they would look at each other, nod their heads approvingly and say 'bunga bunga'.

In the Philippines, 'bonggang-bongga' is slang for something fashionable, while in Indonesia it means 'a field of flowers'.

Bunga Bunga is also the name of a deity worshipped in the Far East, believed to take the form of a giant flower at the centre of the Milky Way Galaxy.

BUNKER, Chang and Eng (1811–74)

Chang and Eng, the original Siamese twins, were discovered by Robert Hunter, a Scottish merchant, who together with an American ship's captain named Abel Coffin brought them to the US when they were 17 years old. They adopted the surname Bunker in honour of the battle of Bunker Hill, during the American War of Independence. Joined at the breastbone by a 13-centimetre (5-inch) ligament, they were never separated and lived to the age of 62, dying within hours of each other.

Ten years of successful touring and a circus career left them well enough off to marry two sisters, buy their own property and live as farmers in North Carolina, taking American citizenship and even buying some slaves. Eng and his wife had 11 children, and Chang and his wife had 10. The children lived in two family houses with the twins spending three days at a time in each.

Later they resumed touring and signed a contract with P.T. Barnum, founder of the Barnum & Bailey Circus.

The Battle of Bunker Hill was actually fought on Breed's Hill in Massachusetts.

⚲ *SIAM, THAILAND*

BUNNY BOILERS

In January 2012, 17 rabbits were reported to have gone missing from a farm in Portland, Oregon, the night before the farmer was due to give a class on raising, slaughtering and cooking rabbits. The farmer said he suspected that political activists were behind the theft, but the rabbits were soon found at an adoption agency called Rabbit Advocates. By the time the police arrived, one of the rabbits had already been adopted.

A spokesman for the Portland Meat Collective said it was the first time this had ever happened.

BURGLARY

A candidate for Worst Burglar of 2011 was a man called John Finch who broke into a house in Delaware and couldn't find his way out. He stayed for five days, drank five bottles of spirits and was too drunk to climb out of the window he had entered by. He then called the police to help him escape.

⚲ *CAPITAL PUNISHMENT, HEDGEHOG, WHEELCHAIR*

BURIAL

At the burial of Humphrey Bogart in 1957, his wife Lauren Bacall dropped a small gold whistle into his grave in memory of the lines she spoke to him in the 1944 film *To Have and Have Not*: 'If you want me, just whistle. You know how to whistle, don't you? You just put your lips together and blow.'

Less romantically, Sir Walter Raleigh was buried with his favourite pipe and a tin of tobacco; Wild Bill Hickok was buried with his Sharps rifle; Rudolph Valentino was buried with a slave bracelet; and Bela Lugosi was buried in his black Dracula cape. Elvis Presley was buried wearing a white suit and blue shirt, with his trademark TCB (taking care of business) diamond ring.

CORTÉS, FERRARI, SAN FRANCISCO

BURKINA FASO

A priest from Burkina Faso was sent off in a church football tournament in Rome in 2008 for throwing his shirt at the referee. The incident led to the elimination of the Paul the Apostle's College team from the Clericus Cup.

BURMA

The Burmese word *ma* has many meanings according to pitch changes. One sentence composed entirely of *ma* repeated at different pitches can mean 'Get the horse, a mad dog is coming.'

BANANAS, MYANMAR, PEAS, UNDERWEAR

BURNS, Robert (1759–96)

Robert Burns' father William, who was a landscape gardener, spelt the name as 'Burnes' but Robert later adopted the spelling without the 'e'. The first ever Burns Supper was held on 29 January 1802, which was before Burns' correct date of birth was found to be 25 January.

In 1912, Burns was posthumously made an Honorary Chartered Surveyor by the Royal Institute of Chartered Surveyors, the only person ever to be so honoured.

In 2009, which was his 250th anniversary, Robert Burns became the first person to feature on a commemorative bottle of Coca-Cola.

Worldwide, there are around 60 statues and similar memorials to Robert Burns. It has been claimed that there are more statues of Robert Burns than any non-religious person other than Queen Victoria and Christopher Columbus. Shakespeare has only around 20.

The first country to issue a commemorative stamp for Robert Burns was the USSR in 1956.

Burns had a pet sheep called Poor Mailie and a dog named Luath. He fathered at least 12 children by four different women in his 37-year life. He was engaged to Mary Campbell, a dairymaid, fathered a child by Anne Park, a servant, and had twins by Jean Armour, whom he later married.

Burns was nearly sacked as an excise officer in Dumfries for selling cannons to the French. He died in 1796 of rheumatic fever, which he apparently caught after falling asleep in the open air following a drinking session.

Burns never wore a kilt. It was an outlawed form of dress after the Jacobite Rebellion.

BURNT FOOD

The Burnt Food Museum in Arlington, Massachusetts, is home to around 50,000 specimens of charred food, including over 2,000 items in the Hall of Burnt Toast. It was founded by Grammy-nominated harpist Deborah Henson-Conant after an accident in

1981 involving apple cider and a long telephone call. This inspired the collection, which celebrates culinary disasters.

It is a private museum, open to groups of up to nine people for private events.

BUS DRIVERS

Under the drivers' union contract with the New York Metropolitan Transportation Authority, being spat on is considered an assault, which entitles drivers to take paid leave. According to a 2010 report, of the 83 bus drivers who were spat on by passengers in the previous year, 51 took an average of 64 paid days off. One driver took 191 days of paid leave.

In 2021, all five district attorneys in New York City supported a plea by transport unions for legislation that would make spitting at a transit worker a misdemeanour punishable by up to a year in jail.

♀ *BRAZIL*

BUSH, George Herbert Walker (1924–2018)

On 18 March 1990, George H.W. Bush banned broccoli from being served on Air Force One, saying: 'I do not like broccoli and I haven't liked it since I was a little kid and my mother made me eat it. And I'm President of the United States and I'm not going to eat any more broccoli.'

Bush later added: 'My family is divided. For the broccoli vote out there: Barbara loves broccoli. She has tried to make me eat it. She eats it all the time herself. So she can go out and meet the caravan of broccoli that's coming in.'

In September 1990, when Bush arrived on Air Force One for the initial inspection of the brand new plane, there was a sign posted in the galley showing a bunch of broccoli with a slash through it and a note beneath it saying 'broccoli free zone'.

♀ *GUITAR, OPOSSUM, TWELFTH NIGHT*

BUSH, George W. (b. 1946)

In 2000, George Walker Bush became the first right-handed president since Jimmy Carter.

Reagan, Bush senior and Clinton were all left-handed. Barack Obama is also left-handed, but Donald Trump and Joe Biden are both right-handed.

George W. Bush was the second son of a president to become president himself. The first was John Quincy Adams, son of John Adams, second President of the United States.

George W. Bush's dog Spot was also the son of a former First Dog: its mother was Millie, Barbara Bush's dog. George W., however, is the only US President to be the father of twins.

After leaving office, he published two collections of his paintings, 'Portraits of Courage' (2017) and 'Out Of Many, One' (2020). A review of the second of these in *Art in America* magazine included the following assessment: 'Bush's painting style is inelegant: his subjects' eyes are often misaligned, his colors are sometimes muddied, and even though he attempts to create depth and shadow, the facial features ultimately fail to convey anything resembling human warmth.'

'I know the human being and fish can coexist peacefully.' George W. Bush, speaking in Michigan in September 2000

'They misunderestimated me.' George W. Bush, speaking in Arkansas in November 2000

♀ *TARTAN, UNITED STATES*

BUSH-CRICKET

A species of bush-cricket (also known as katydid) has the largest testicles in the animal kingdom relative to its size. In 2010, researchers at the University of Derby measured the testicles of 21 species of bush-crickets and found that testicle size varied greatly, but one species – *Platycleis affinis* – far surpassed previous records with testicles that accounted for 14 per cent of their body weight.

Despite their large testicles, the bush-crickets were found to release only a small amount of sperm at each mating compared with other species, but they also tended to mate with a larger number of females. This supports a theory that, in insects at any rate, large testicles correlate with promiscuity.

If a human's testicles were as large, proportionate to body size, as those of *Platycleis affinis*, they would weigh about 6 kilograms (14 pounds).

BUTCHELL, Martin van (1736–1814)

Said to be London's most expensive dentist, Martin van Butchell liked to ride through Hyde Park on a pony that had been painted with purple spots or black stripes, and he also carried a large white bone, probably the jawbone of an ass, with which to defend himself. His most valued possession, however, was the body of his late wife.

When Mary Butchell died on 14 January 1775, her will stipulated that her husband was entitled to a stipend from her fortune for as long as her body remained above ground. Butchell therefore had her body embalmed and put on display at his London home where he ran his dentistry practice. The body was dressed in a fine lace gown

and embedded in a thin layer of plaster of Paris and the embalming was finished with a pair of 'nicely matched glass eyes' before being placed in a glass-topped coffin with curtains.

Butchell introduced her to visitors as 'My dear departed' and allowed strangers to see her by appointment, 'any day between Nine and One, Sundays excepted'.

When Butchell remarried, his second wife, Elizabeth, was less than enthusiastic about the corpse and it was removed to the College of Surgeons, and after Martin's death to the Hunterian Museum, where it was later described as a 'repulsive-looking object'. Mary's body was finally destroyed by a German incendiary bomb in 1941.

BUTE, John Stuart, 3rd Earl of (1713–92)

In 1750, John Stuart, 3rd Earl of Bute, was appointed Gentleman of the Bedchamber to Frederick, Prince of Wales; in 1756, he became Groom of the Stole to Frederick's son, the future George III. He became Prime Minister in 1762. His father, the 2nd Earl of Bute, had been Lord of the Bedchamber to King George I from 1721 to 1723.

The duties of the Gentlemen and Lords of the Bedchamber included assisting the monarch with dressing, waiting on him when he ate, guarding access to his bedchamber and closet and providing companionship. The office of Groom of the Stole dates back to at least the 16th century when it was known as 'Groom of the Stool'. In either case, the role of Groom of the Stole was to carry the royal chamber pot on long journeys. On the accession of Queen Elizabeth I in 1558, the post was replaced by one called 'First Lady of the Bedchamber'.

The office was not filled during the reign of Queen Victoria and was finally discontinued formally when Edward VII became King in 1901.

BUTTERFLY

Despite frequent assertions to the contrary, the butterfly was never called the 'flutterby'. The name may derive from the butter-yellow colour of certain butterflies' wings or from its supposed habit of hovering over butter or eating it.

Butterflies have four wings and taste with their feet.

CALIFORNIA, CATERPILLAR, SEMICOLON, SWIMMING

BUTTOCKS

The word 'buttock' comes from the Old English 'buttuc', meaning a short ridge of land.

The *Oxford English Dictionary* lists 189 words that may be used to mean 'buttocks' or as adjectives describing buttocks. Among this buttock-related vocabulary are the following:

- Callipygous, or callipygian: fair-buttocked
- Cob: (nautical) to strike on the buttocks with a flat instrument
- Dasypygal: hairy-buttocked
- Nock: the cleft in the buttocks
- Steatopygous: fat-bottomed, especially as a medical condition

The first of these was originally applied to a statue of the Greek Goddess of Love, Aphrodite Kallipygos, which shows her raising her robes to reveal a shapely behind.

In 1998, a ferry in Seattle cut its maximum seating from 250 to 230 because US bottoms had become larger. 'Eighteen-inch butts are a thing of the past,' a spokesman said.

'It is like a barber's chair that fits all buttocks, the pin-buttock, the quatch-buttock, the brawn buttock, or any buttock.' William Shakespeare, All's Well That Ends Well, 1623 ('Quatch' means squat or plump.)

BRAZIL, DENVER, NUDITY, RENOIR

BYRON, Ada (1815–52)

Ada Byron was Countess of Lovelace and daughter of Lord Byron. Despite the fact that her father separated from Lady Byron a month after Ada was born, she named her two sons Byron and Gordon.

Her mother encouraged her to be educated in mathematics, which she hoped would protect her from the insanity her father had suffered.

Her studies led to a long collaboration with Charles Babbage and the two worked on his Difference Engine, which has been called the first computer. The programming language ADA was named after her.

She died at the age of 36, which was also the age at which her father Lord Byron had died.

COMPUTERS

BYRON, Lord George Gordon, 6th Baron Byron of Rochdale (1788–1824)

Byron was born lame and developed a club foot. Despite this, he played cricket at Harrow, using a runner, and was a fine swimmer. He kept a pet bear in his rooms at Trinity College, Cambridge, because he was not allowed a dog. He wore his hair in curlers at night.

When Byron was in his teens, a gardener presented him with a skull found buried in the grounds of a nearby former abbey. Saying that he fancied it had belonged 'to some jolly friar or monk', Byron had it made into a goblet from which he could drink claret. He even wrote a poem entitled 'Lines Inscribed Upon a Cup formed from a Skull'.

In 2017, an auction in Sherbourne, Dorset, included such a cup in a sale, which carried the words 'Skull Drinking Cup used by Lord Byron at Newstead Abbey' inscribed around its rim. Doubt was expressed that this was really Byron's skull cup, but it fetched £3,220 (including commission) compared with an estimate of £500–1,000.

Later the same year, another piece of Byron memorabilia was sold at auction, complete with documentation confirming that it was the damaged collar of his favourite Newfoundland dog, Boatswain. This included a note by the widow of Byron's gamekeeper confirming that the damage had been caused by 'A Bear which Lord Byron kept for his own amusement'. The collar sold for £14,000 compared with a pre-sale estimate of £3,000–5,000.

When Byron's coffin was opened in 1938, his lame right foot was found to be missing.

KNOWLEDGE, RUM, SWIMMING

BYZANTIUM

Nobody knows how Byzantium got its name, though there is an ancient Greek legend of a Greek king called Byzos, which means 'he-goat'.

Byzantium was the capital of the Roman Empire following Emperor Constantine's decision to move there from Rome in AD 324. He named the city Nova Roma (New Rome) but after his death it became known as Constantinople after him. In 1930, the city had its name officially changed to Istanbul. Its current population of 15.8 million is the highest of any city in Europe.

Possibly the greatest sporting riot in history occurred in Constantinople in 532 when two groups of chariot-racing fans joined forces in opposing taxation plans. The fans called themselves the Blues and the Greens, after the colours of their favourite teams, but they united in an insurrection called the Nika Riots. They took over the city's hippodrome from where they launched attacks in an attempt to replace Emperor Justinian. His troops then ambushed them and the resulting battle led to some 30,000 deaths.

CABBAGE

The word 'cabbage' only occurs once in the works of Shakespeare, in Act I, Scene I of *The Merry Wives of Windsor*, when Falstaff exclaims: 'Good worts! good cabbage. Slender, I broke your head: what matter have you against me?'

'Cabbaged' is the longest word in the *Oxford English Dictionary* that is spelled using only the letters from A to G, and is therefore the joint longest word, along with babbaged and debagged, that can be played on a musical instrument. 'Cabbaged' can mean pilfered, incapacitated by drugs or alcohol, or having cut off a deer's head just below the antlers.

'Cabbage: A familiar kitchen-garden vegetable about as large and wise as a man's head.' Ambrose Bierce, The Devil's Dictionary, 1906

⚲ BELGIUM, CAULIFLOWER, FEBRUARY, GERMANY

CAKE

According to the biography of former Dutch Prime Minister Dries van Agt, published in 2008, Queen Juliana of the Netherlands proposed a mass pardon for petty criminals when she left the throne in 1980.

When the Cabinet told the Queen such a pardon was impossible in the modern era, she had difficulty accepting it, and asked whether all prisoners could at least be served cakes instead.

⚲ BISCUITS, CUPCAKE, DONKEY, TWELFTH NIGHT

CALAIS

From 1347 until 1558, the city of Calais in France was owned by the English. It is still referred to by many as 'the most English city in France'.

⚲ CHANNEL, PYRAMID

CALENDAR

According to the International Organisation for Standardisation's ISO 8601, week 1 of any year is the week beginning on a Monday that includes 4 January. So if 1 January falls on a Friday, Saturday or Sunday, it is officially in week 52 or 53 of the previous year.

It is a curious consequence of the rules underlying the Gregorian calendar that the thirteenth of the month is more likely to fall on a Friday than any other day of the week. Those rules specify that the calendar operates on a 400-year cycle with a Leap Day added every fourth year, except for three out of every four century years. That results in 146,097 days every 400 years, which is equal to exactly 20,871 weeks. So, whatever the date is, you can be sure that date will fall on the same day of the week in 400 years' time.

Since there are 4,800 months in 400 years, there will be 4,800 thirteenths of the month, and whatever days of the week they fall on will be repeated during all subsequent 400-year cycles. When you work it out, it turns out that every 400 years, there are 685 Monday the thirteenths, 685 Tuesday the thirteenths, 687 Wednesday the thirteenths, 684 Thursday the thirteenths, 688 Friday the thirteenths, 684 Saturday the thirteenths and 687 Sunday the thirteenths.

🔎 *ETHIOPIA, FEBRUARY, IRAN, LEAP YEAR*

⬤ CALIFORNIA

If California were a country, it would, according to 2020 figures, have the seventh largest economy in the world, behind Germany but ahead of India.

On average, more than one Californian a day claims to have been abducted by aliens.

Anyone molesting a monarch butterfly in Pacific Drive, California, is liable to a $500 fine.

In 1972, the owner of an elephant named Bimbo was awarded $4,500 damages by the Californian Supreme Court after a road accident.

California can also be good for plants: a creosote bush called King Clone in the Mojave Desert may be the world's oldest living organism. Its age has been estimated as 11,700 years.

More turkeys are raised in California than in any other US state.

The state motto of California is Eureka! (Greek for 'I have found it!'), relating to the discovery of gold in the Sierra Nevada in the 1840s.

The music for the state anthem of California, 'I Love You California', was written around 1913 by Abraham Franckum Frankenstein, a cousin of the *San Francisco Chronicle*'s esteemed music and art critic Alfred V. Frankenstein.

On 30 July 1968, the Public Defender of California State, Don Jones, was fined for being too fat. His weight at the time was 108 kilograms (238 pounds).

In 2009, a Californian man was arrested on suspicion of human trafficking after reports that he had arranged to sell his 14-year-old daughter into marriage in exchange for 100 cases of beer, $16,000 and several boxes of meat. Police learned of the deal after the man asked them to get his daughter back because payment was not made as agreed.

🔎 *BOB*

⬤ CALIGULA (AD 12–41)

After Caligula's death in AD 41, his favourite horse, Incitatus, was deprived of its privileges. In his *Lives of the Twelve Caesars*, the Roman historian Suetonius wrote that Caligula made Incitatus both a consul and a priest, but that is not supported by other ancient writers, while modern historians suggest that any remarks Caligula may have made about such equine promotion would have been satirical and more indicative of his sense of humour than his madness.

⬤ CAMBODIA

In 2010, The Ministry of Information ordered the Cambodian Television Network to stop showing the series

Strange Lovers because it was 'totally opposite to good Cambodian tradition' and 'seriously affects the reputation and dignity of Cambodian women'. The plot concerned a beautiful, educated and successful Cambodian woman whose mother decides to auction her off as a bride to the highest bidder, starting at a price of 1 million dollars.

In 2004, the Cambodian government banned a pop song that showed scenes of a Buddhist monk hugging and kissing a girl while bathing in a pond near a pagoda, while in 2009, a proposed TV broadcast of the country's first rock opera, *Where Elephants Weep*, was cancelled after monks said it was insulting to see actors dressed as clergy breaking into song and dance and behaving immorally.

Cambodia's first transvestite beauty contest was held in 2001, when a 19-year-old dancer from Phnom Penh was crowned the country's most beautiful 'ladyboy' of the 30 entrants.

'We wanted to help the ladyboys be happy in society,' a spokesman from the sponsoring TV station said. No women were permitted in the contest, but contestants were required to be pretty, charming and similar to real women. The winner, Pop Pi, received a trophy, 500,000 riel (about £80) and a tiara.

In November 2002, a Cambodian woman was sentenced to 15 years' imprisonment after murdering her husband by hitting him repeatedly in the groin with an axe, then running off with her son-in-law. Passing sentence, the judge said, 'It is totally unacceptable in Cambodia that a wife should kill her husband by smashing his genitals.'

The price of rat meat was reported to have quadrupled in Cambodia in 2008 as inflation put other meat beyond the reach of poor people.

The Cambodian flag prominently features an outline of the Angkor Wat Temple. It is the only national flag to feature a building that is not part of an emblem or coat of arms.

♀ PROPERTY

CAMBRIDGE

According to research published in 2009, residents of Cambridge spend more per head on takeaway meals than any other town or city in Britain.

Of the 55 UK prime ministers, 28 went to Oxford and only 14 to Cambridge.

♀ *BYRON, CELIBACY, DARWIN, NOBEL PRIZE, UNIVERSITIES*

CAMEL

There are more camels in Somalia than any other country, but more wild camels in Australia, including the world's only herd of wild dromedaries. Camels were brought to Australia in the 19th century to aid exploration. The first one to arrive came from the Canary Islands and was the only one of a group to survive the voyage. It was named Harry.

At least 15,000 camels were brought to Australia between 1870 and 1900, most of which were dromedaries (one-humped). Many were left to roam wild when the motorcar increasingly replaced them as a means of travel.

The camel has no gall bladder and, despite the hump, the backbone of a camel is perfectly straight. A camel can drink 35 gallons of water in 10 minutes, but rats can survive longer than camels without water.

In 1995, Emir Sultan ibn Mohammad ibn Saud al-Kebir gave $500,000 in prize money to Saudi Arabia's first beauty contest for camels, called Miss

Dromedary. Saudi Arabia also opened the world's first commercial dromedary dairy in Riyadh in 1986 selling camel milk at £1.20 a litre.

In the village of Garissa, in north-east Kenya, in October 1987, an elderly man who got a schoolgirl pregnant while supposedly giving her private tuition was ordered by a court to pay four camels in compensation.

A cross between a camel and a llama is called a cama. Only two have ever been bred.

According to Alan Davidson's *Oxford Companion to Food*, 'It is generally considered that the best part of the camel for eating is the hump.' However, he mentions that the Greeks spoke of whole roast camels at banquets and the Roman Emperor Heliogabalus was particularly fond of camel's heel.

Recently, archaeologists and theologians have argued about camels: the Book of Genesis includes over 20 references to camels owned by Abraham and Isaac, but carbon dating has apparently shown that camels did not reach the Middle East until the 9th century BC, which was at least a millennium after the time of Genesis.

On 27 August 1997, a camel at Knowsley Safari Park on Merseyside was struck by lightning and killed. This is the only recorded case of a camel being killed by lightning in England.

⚲ *EYE, GADDAFI, LIBYA, OSTRICH, SOMALIA*

⬤ CAMEL URINE

According to a paper in the *Journal of Pharmacology and Toxicology* in 2010, camel urine is not harmful to humans. The paper, 'Dose escalation phase I study in healthy volunteers to evaluate the safety of a natural product PM701', by Khorshid et al, details the effects on healthy subjects of a product obtained from camel urine and says that no adverse effects were found on their kidney, liver or blood. 'Two patients only developed hyperacidity which was easily treated.'

They concluded that the product is safe and announced the intention to proceed to trials to determine whether it was effective as a treatment for some types of cancer.

Experts on Sharia law, however, are not agreed on whether camel urine is clean or unclean.

⬤ CAMP DAVID

The rural retreat of American presidents was originally a camp for federal government agents. It was opened in 1938 and was called Hi-Catoctin, as it is located in the Catoctin Mountain Park. In 1942, it became a presidential retreat and was called Shangri-La by President Roosevelt. The name of Camp David was finally given to it in 1953 by President Eisenhower after his grandson David.

⬤ CANADA

Canada not only has the longest coastline of any country, just ahead of Indonesia, but its area is also greater than that of Europe.

In terms of total area, Canada is the second largest country in the world after Russia, but if we are talking only about land area, it drops to fourth place, behind Russia, China and the United States.

The boundaries of Canada extend to the North Pole, even though there is no land there, only ice.

Vehicle licence plates in the Northwest Territories of Canada are in the shape of a polar bear.

In Canada, 0.3 per cent of all road accidents involve moose. Even if you have been involved in a collision with a moose, however, it is illegal to remove bandages in public in Canada.

There is a town in Newfoundland called Dildo.

In 1995, a survey reported that 38 per cent of Canadian women preferred chocolate to making love.

☞ *SHATNER, TARTAN, WOLF*

CANARY

The name of the Canary Islands is due not to canaries but to dogs. The Roman historian Pliny the Elder noted that the main island, now known as Gran Canaria, contained 'vast multitudes of dogs of very large size'. The ancient Romans therefore called them 'Insulae Canariae' – the islands of dogs. The bird known as 'canary' later took its name from the islands.

☞ *MOZART*

CANCAN

The entry on the cancan (or can-can) in the first edition of the *Oxford Companion to Music* in 1938 describes it as 'A boisterous and latterly indecorous dance of the quadrille order, exploited in Paris for the benefit of such British and American tourists as will pay well to be well shocked.' It ends with the words, 'Its exact nature is unknown to anyone connected with this Companion.'

CANNABIS

A caretaker at a zoo in Austria was sacked in September 2010 after it was discovered that he had been using a rhinoceros enclosure as a cannabis plantation. After a tip-off, police raided the rhino's quarters and found 30 cannabis plants growing in a part shut off to the public, to which only the caretaker had access.

☞ *MARIJUANA*

CANNES

The 'Palm Dog' (named by analogy with the Palme d'Or) is an unofficial prize awarded at the Cannes Film Festival each year, for the most memorable performance by a dog. The winners in 2021 were three dogs named Dora, Rosie and Snowbear from the film *The Souvenir Part II*. In 2020, no Palm Dog was awarded as the Cannes festival was cancelled, but in 2019 it was won by Sayuri the pitbull for her performance as Brandy in Quentin Tarantino's film *Once Upon a Time in… Hollywood*.

The strangest winner in the 20 years of the competition was when it was awarded to a chalk outline of a dog named Moses in the film *Dogville* by Denmark's Lars von Trier in 2003.

The trophy is a diamante collar with the words 'Palm Dog' stitched into it, which is presented at a ceremony at which the audience is customarily greeted with the words 'Ladies and gentlemen, dogs and bitches'.

CANOE

In 1998, Timothy Joseph Boomer fell into the Rifle River in Michigan after his canoe hit a rock and overturned. He surfaced, uttered a string of expletives, and was charged under an 1897 law that banned 'indecent, immoral, obscene, vulgar or insulting language in the presence or hearing of any woman or child'.

A jury convicted him and he was fined $75 and ordered to work four days in a child-care programme, but the sentence was put on hold pending an appeal. During the trial, District

Judge Allen Yenior ruled that the ban on cursing in front of women was unconstitutional, but its provision dealing with children was an acceptable control on freedom of speech. He ruled that while the phrases 'fucking bitches' and 'motherfucker' are not obscene as defined by the US Supreme Court, there was a 'compelling community and governmental interest in protecting the morality of our children'. In 2002, an appeals court overturned the conviction and ruled that the entire law was too vague, reasoning that it '... would require every person who speaks audibly where children are present to guess what a law enforcement officer might consider too indecent, immoral, or vulgar for a child's ears'. The mother of the children who had overheard Boomer's remarks expressed disappointment at the appeal court's ruling, saying that if she had wanted her children to hear such language she would have taken them to a bar.

♀ SHOES

CANTERBURY

Over 1,000 years ago, on 19 April 1012, the Archbishop of Canterbury, St Aelfheah (also known as Alphege), was killed by Viking raiders who had sacked Canterbury. Aelfheah was killed because he refused to allow a ransom to be paid.

Besides Aelfheah (which means 'elf-high'), two other Archbishops of Canterbury were murdered, another was burned at the stake and one beheaded. When Aelfheah became Archbishop, he brought the head of St Swithun with him from Winchester.

There is no evidence that Geoffrey Chaucer, author of *The Canterbury Tales*, ever visited Canterbury.

The word 'canter' came from 'Canter-

bury trot', the fast trot used by Pilgrims visiting Canterbury.

Some say the first 'nosey parker' was Matthew Parker, Archbishop of Canterbury from 1559 to 1575. Eighteen Archbishops of Canterbury have become saints, but none since the 13th century.

♀ CHAUCER, MARS

CAPITAL PUNISHMENT

In 1500, there were eight crimes for which a person could be hanged in Britain: treason, petty treason (killing of a husband by a wife), murder, larceny, robbery, burglary, rape and arson.

In 1671, after Sir John Coventry had had his nose slit when attacked in Covent Garden, an act was passed making it a capital crime to lie in wait with intent to put out an eye, disable the tongue or slit the nose. In 1699, shoplifting to the value of five shillings or more was added to the list.

The number of capital offences grew rapidly in the 18th century, including poaching, damage to forests and parks, cutting down an orchard, blacking the face, or using a disguise while committing a crime. By 1810, British law recognised 222 capital crimes.

Less serious crimes then began to be removed from the list and in 1861 the Criminal Law Consolidation Act reduced the number of capital crimes to four: murder, treason, mutiny and piracy.

It took another century before capital punishment was suspended, then in December 1969 Parliament confirmed its abolition for murder.

Important dates in the chronology of capital punishment in Britain:
- 23 June 1649: 23 men and one woman were hanged at Tyburn for burglary and robbery. This was probably the

largest number of ordinary criminals put to death in a single execution in Britain.

- 5 May 1760: Laurence Shirley, the 4th Earl of Ferrers, was hanged at Tyburn for the murder of a servant, the only Peer of the Realm ever to hang for murder.
- 18 March 1789: Christian Murphy, alias Bowman, was burned at the stake for counterfeiting.
- 2 April 1868: Last public hanging of a woman in England.
- 26 May 1868: Last public hanging in England.
- 3 January 1946: William Joyce – alias 'Lord Haw Haw' – was the last to be hanged for treason.
- 13 July 1955: Ruth Ellis became the last woman to hang.
- 13 August 1964: At 8am, Peter Allen (at Walton Prison, Liverpool) and Gwynne Evans (at Strangeways Prison, Manchester) were the last to be hanged.

  GUILLOTINE, SWEDEN

CAPONE, Alphonse Gabriel (1899–1947)

On his business card, Al Capone described himself as a used furniture dealer. His business earned his gang up to $100 million a year. Despite strong suspicions of his committing or at least ordering many murders, he was finally convicted only of tax evasion in 1931, for which he was sentenced to 11 years in Alcatraz. He was released in 1939 already suffering badly from syphilis. He died in 1947 of health complications including a stroke and pneumonia.

On 20 June 2000, his toenail clippers were sold for £5,000 at auction in San Francisco.

CARACAS

In Venezuela's capital, Caracas, the very low price of petrol has led to dangerous driving being seen almost as a basic human right. Indeed, when one Caracas mayor tried to tackle severe traffic jams in the city by banning driving for one day a week, the ban was overturned in court as an infringement of civil liberties.

In 2008, however, a law was passed making it possible for the courts to suspend a driver's licence. In 2011, the first such suspension was imposed on a bus driver who was speeding in an over-laden bus that was missing one of its rear wheels. The driver was suspended for one year. It would have been five years if he had killed someone.

CARBON

Despite being known in prehistoric times, carbon was only given its name, from *carbo*, the Latin word for coal, in 1788.

In 1772, the great French chemist Antoine Lavoisier showed that diamonds are a form of carbon.

  BODY, FART, FIZZY DRINKS, TREES

CARNIVAL

The word 'carnival' originally meant either 'a farewell to meat' or 'putting meat away', referring to the Christian tradition of giving up meat during Lent.

The carnival at Binche in Belgium has been officially recognised by UNESCO as a masterpiece of the oral and intangible heritage of humanity.

  SHROVE TUESDAY

CARNIVORE

The world's greatest carnivores are the Argentines, who each eat about 57 kilograms (125 pounds) of beef a year, which is about the weight of one human teenager. In the 19th century, they ate about three times as much.

⚲ BACULUM, COVID-19, TASMANIA

⬤ CARPENTRY

A woman from Bulawayo, Zimbabwe, filed for divorce in 2012 after consulting a carpenter over her broken marital bed.

The carpenter told her that 'judging by the way it was broken, something excessive might have been happening'.

The woman said that she had twice previously caught her husband having sex with other women and that her life had been 'a living hell' in her eight years of marriage. 'He broke the bed not having sex with me but another woman,' she said. 'I cannot take this anymore.'

She accordingly asked a magistrate to dissolve her marriage and make her husband pay $200 to mend the bed. Her husband said that the bottom line was that he had no money.

⚲ COFFIN, DARTS, FROG

⬤ CARPET

The oldest use of the word 'karpete' was in 1345, referring to a woollen tablecloth.

A carpet-bagger originally meant an itinerant who carried all his belongings in a bag made of old carpet. The term came to mean a political infiltrator, thanks to the success of itinerants from the southern states of America gaining influence in the north.

The world's largest carpet was unveiled in Iran in 2007. It covered an area equal to three football pitches.

Pericles, *Richard II*, *Twelfth Night* and *The Taming of the Shrew* are the only Shakespeare plays that mention carpets. There is no mention of carpets in the Bible.

'What if everything is an illusion and nothing exists? In that case, I definitely overpaid for my carpet.' Woody Allen

⚲ TURKMENISTAN

⬤ CARROLL, Lewis (Charles Lutwidge Dodgson), 1832–98

The original story that became *Alice's Adventures in Wonderland* was told by Carroll to amuse Alice Liddell and her sisters on a boat trip in Oxford on 4 July 1862.

The story has often been told that, after reading *Alice in Wonderland*, Queen Victoria requested a copy of Lewis Carroll's next book but was less than amused when it turned out to be *Syllabus of Plane Algebraical Geometry*. Sadly, this story has no basis in fact and was even denied by Carroll himself.

In the last 37 years of his life, Lewis Carroll wrote 98,721 letters to his friends, usually in black ink, though he preferred violet when writing to young girls.

Lewis Carroll was over 6 feet tall and never wore an overcoat.

⚲ MOZART, STAMMERING

⬤ CARROT

During the Second World War, the British Ministry of Agriculture launched a campaign to promote the eating of carrots to counter food shortages. A recipe for carrot fudge was included. The campaign included cartoons featuring Carroty George, Clara Carrot and Doctor Carrot. Eating carrots was said to improve people's ability to see during the blackouts, and pilots were told to eat carrots to improve their eyesight.

There is a carrot museum in the town of Berlotte in Belgium. It is an extremely small museum with no staff, no entry and consists only of a small factory window. But that window is 100 per cent dedicated to carrots. Only men are permitted to join the Carrot Club linked to the museum. They wear Carrot Club T-shirts and have carrot statues in their gardens.

Carrots originally came from Afghanistan and were purple, red, white or yellow. Orange carrots were bred by the Dutch in the 16th century to honour the royal House of Orange.

The ancient Greeks thought carrot an aphrodisiac. They called it *philtron*, meaning 'love charm'.

The record for the world's longest carrot, grown by Joe Atherton of Mansfield in 2016, was 6.245 metres (20 feet 5.86 inches) long.

The type of carrot with which Bugs Bunny is usually pictured is a species called Danvers.

The record for running the Arizona marathon dressed as a carrot is held by Jordan Maddox, 35, who finished the race in January 2022 in 2 hours 44 minutes and 12 seconds. He had run the same race in 2020 with a time of 2:41:27 while dressed as a banana.

 BUGS BUNNY, WEDDING RING

CARS

Since the first fatal car crash in 1899, 25 million people have died in car accidents.

There are more cars than people in Los Angeles, California.

Pound for pound, a new car is cheaper than a hamburger.

 LICENCE PLATES, NIGERIA, ROAD FATALITY

CARTER, James Earl (b. 1924)

Jimmy Carter is the only US President to hold a qualification in submarines. In 2005, a nuclear-powered, fast-attack Navy submarine was named after him. At least 11 other US Navy submarines are named after presidents, but over 150 have been named after species of fish.

 FLYING SAUCERS, UNITED STATES, WISDOM

CARTLAND, Barbara (1901–2000)

The novelist Barbara Cartland is the only woman in the *Dictionary of National Biography* whose entry includes the word 'penis'. Apparently 'more than one interviewer was surprised by her interest in the rumoured penis size of the Duke of Windsor'. In 1933, her first marriage to Alexander McCorquodale ended in a highly publicised divorce case when she sued him for adultery. He counter-sued, alleging that his cousin Hugh McCorquodale had visited her bedroom by day. Barbara answered this charge in court, explaining that this was because she wrote in bed. She married Hugh three years later. She wrote 723 books.

CARTOON

The first public performance of an animated cartoon was on 28 October 1892 in Paris. The cartoon was called *Pauvre Pierrot* (*Poor Pete*) and used to demonstrate the Theatre Optique system of Charles-Emile Reynaud.

Reynaud's animation system was overtaken by the Lumière brothers Cinematograph in 1895, driving him into bankruptcy and depression. Reynaud died penniless in a Paris hospice after throwing his animation equipment into the Seine.

'Cartoon' originally just meant a drawing on stout paper, from *carta*, the Italian for paper.

Beauty and the Beast (1991), *Up* (2009) and *Toy Story 3* (2010) are the only animated films to have been nominated for Best Picture Oscars.

MICKEY MOUSE, POPEYE, STAMPS

CARTWHEEL

From the 14th until the 19th century, the word 'cartwheel' was only used for the wheel of a cart. In the mid-19th century, it was used jokingly, in both the US and UK, to refer to a large coin, and around the same time the expression 'turning cartwheels' began to be used to describe types of somersault.

The most people performing cartwheels simultaneously is 2,256 and was achieved by members of the US Military Academy Corps of Cadets in West Point, New York, on 20 April 2017.

The most cartwheels in one minute is 67, set by Gaber Kahlwai Gaber Ali (Egypt) in Giza in 2015. The most cartwheels on rollerskates in one minute is 30, achieved by Tinuke Oyediran (UK) in London on 7 November 2020.

CARUSO, Enrico (1873–1921)

The great operatic tenor Enrico Caruso was convicted and fined $10 in 1906 for pinching a woman's bottom in the monkey house of New York Central Park Zoo. He was probably innocent. The charge against him was made by a policeman, and the woman he allegedly fondled did not turn up for the trial and was never found.

Caruso was the only one of his parents' seven children to survive infancy.

Caruso hung anchovies around his neck, which he believed helped prevent damage from smoking 40 cigarettes a day.

When his wife ran off with another man in 1908, he was quoted as saying: 'It was the very thing I desired.'

CASANOVA, Giacomo Girolamo (1725–98)

Seducer of an estimated 10,000 women, Casanova's handwritten memoirs in brown ink stretched to around 3,700 pages and were bought in 2010 by France's National Library for around 7 million euros. At the time, it was a record amount for the sale of a manuscript.

He is now best known for the affairs he recounts, of which there were about 120, but those account for only about a third of his memoirs, the remainder telling the story of a highly cultured traveller, translator, intellectual, mathematician and even spy. He also tells of meeting Benjamin Franklin in Paris in 1783 when they talked about hot-air balloons.

Casanova generally used a pig's bladder as a condom. He was awarded the Order of the Golden Spur by Pope Clement XIII.

OYSTER

CAT

Eighteen thousand mummified cats were sold at one auction in Liverpool in March 1890. They were expected to be used as fertiliser and sold for about 10 cats a penny.

In 1995, a survey showed that one in three British children believe that their mum prefers the cat to their dad.

In Bangkok, in October 1996, a wedding celebration costing £18,000 was held for two 'diamond-eye' cats called Phet and Ploy. Diamond-eye is a form of glaucoma that causes a thick blue film over the lens and is believed in Thailand to bring good luck. The cats were supplied with gold rings specially made for their paws, but the glaucoma had left both of them blind in one eye.

A cat needs three matings for ovulation to occur; an egg is produced 26 hours after the third mating.

The top three names for female cats in Britain in 2021 were Luna, Bella and Lily; the top three names for male cats were Oliver, Leo and Milo.

In 2020, New Zealand architects Brenda and Robert Vale calculated that a 3-kilogram (6.5-pound) cat has a heat output of 130 kilowatt hours per year, so a 150 square metre (1,600 square foot) house could have its heating requirements fulfilled by 18 cats. They also calculated that feeding the cats would cost around £2,160 a year.

Research by Susanne Schötz at Lund University in Sweden into cat–human interactions has revealed that sounds made by cats when communicating with humans are a great deal more than the purring and mewing that we usually recognise. She classified her recordings of cat sounds as purring, chirping, chattering, trilling, tweedling, murmuring, meowing, moaning, squeaking, hissing, growling, howling and yowling.

MATISSE, NEWTON, PIANO, TOES

CAT LITTER

In January 2012, a New York judge ruled against a company making cat litters, saying it must stop airing a commercial that unfairly seeks supremacy against a competitor. The judge said he found the claim in the advert for Clorox Pet Products – that 11 people on a panel would 'stick their noses in jars of excrement and report 44 independent times that they smelled nothing unpleasant' – to be 'highly implausible'. A spokesman for the Clorox company said they found the ruling disappointing and defended the advert's truthfulness.

CAT STEW

A businessman in China died in December 2011, and two business associates were sick, after they shared a meal of slow-boiled cat meat stew, which is a local delicacy in Guangdong province. The owner of the restaurant that prepared the meal was initially detained on suspicion of preparing unsanitary food, but later investigations revealed that the stew had been poisoned with a toxic herb called *Gelsemium elegans*. A local official with whom the victim had been in financial dispute was later arrested. One of the survivors of the meal said that the cat stew tasted more bitter than usual.

CATARACT

The first successful operation for removal of a cataract from the eye of a giant panda was performed in 1985 in China. The panda was 12 years old and female. She was named Xiaxia, or Blind One, because she had lost sight in both of her eyes. After the operation, her sight was restored in her left eye.

AIR HOSTESSES, EAGLE

CATERPILLAR

Some types of butterfly and moth lay eggs inside a species of bean. When these eggs hatch, it is the efforts of the trapped caterpillar trying to escape that make Mexican jumping beans jump.

BELGIUM, HEDGEHOG, NETTLES

CATFISH

On 25 June 1987, President Ronald Reagan established National Catfish Day in the US to recognise 'the value of farm-raised catfish'.

NOODLING

CATHERINE I, Empress of Russia (1684–1727)

She was born Martha Skavronsk, but rechristened Katarina Alexeyevna when she became the mistress of Peter the Great, whom she later married and became the Empress consort. When her husband died in 1725, she became Empress Regnant, the first woman to rule Imperial Russia.

She was the grandmother-in-law of Catherine the Great.

♀ ALCOHOL

CATTLE

Under the Metropolitan Streets Act of 1867, it is illegal to drive cattle through the streets of Britain between the hours of 10am and 7pm. Anyone who does so is liable to a fine of 10 shillings per head of cattle. According to the Act: 'The word "cattle" shall include bull, ox, cow, heifer, calf, sheep, goats, and swine, also horses, mules, and asses, when led in a string or loose.'

♀ COW, HAMMURABI, MOZAMBIQUE

CAULIFLOWER

Mark Twain described the cauliflower as a 'cabbage with a college education'.

CELERY

In 1996, Gillingham Football Club, playing in the second division of the English Football League, said any fans bringing celery into the ground would be banned for life. Club members had been bringing sticks of celery into the ground and throwing them at their goalkeeper. They were also said to wave sticks of celery around while singing a song containing the lines: 'Celery, celery, If she don't cum, I'll tickle her bum, With a lump of celery.'

In ancient Rome, celery was thought to be an aphrodisiac. Much later, celery was found to contain androsterone, a male sex hormone.

In ancient Greek sporting events, successful athletes were often presented with a bouquet of celery.

CELIBACY

The 11th-century preacher Robert of Arbrissel is said to have founded nunneries at which he slept with the nuns – chastely – in order to test himself. For similar reasons, St Swithun liked to sleep with two beautiful virgins, though he was criticised by St Brendan for the habit.

Until the late 19th century, dons at Oxford and Cambridge colleges were not permitted to marry, and between 1996 and 2018, the US Congress spent $2.1 billion on abstinence-only-until-marriage programmes.

Perhaps the most rational comments on the subject are found in the works of Samuel Johnson and his biographer. As Boswell succinctly put it: 'Even ill-assorted marriages are preferable to cheerless celibacy,' while Johnson claimed, with characteristic relish: 'Though marriage has many pains, celibacy has no pleasures. The unmarried are outlaws of human nature. They are peevish at home and malevolent abroad, a state more gloomy than solitude: it is not retreat but exclusion from mankind.'

CELLO

A condition called 'cello scrotum', which had been listed as a medical ailment since 1974, was revealed to be a hoax 34 years later when Baroness Murphy confessed that she had invented it as a joke in a letter to the *British Medical Journal*. Elaine Murphy and her husband John made up the supposed ailment in 1974 after reading about 'guitarist's nipple', a condition caused by the edge of the instrument rubbing against the breast. The letter, which they were surprised was published in the 11 May 1974 edition of the *British Medical Journal*, was as follows:

SIR,–Though I have not come across 'guitar nipple' as reported by Dr. P. Curtis (27 April, p. 226), I did once come across a case of 'cello scrotum' caused by irritation from the body of the cello. The patient in question was a professional musician and played in rehearsal, practice, or concert for several hours each day. I am, etc., J.M. Murphy.

⚲ STRADIVARIUS

⬤ CELLPHONE

According to the Global System for Mobile communication, in March 2021 there were over 10.36 billion mobile connections worldwide, which means there were 2.52 billion more mobile connections than people in the world. Worldwide, there are about 4.88 billion cellphone subscribers, which is about two cellphones for every three people on Earth. It is thought that the number of mobile phones on Earth overtook the number of people in 2011.

China has the most cellphone users with 1.3 billion, followed by India with 1.17 billion, the United States with 327 million and Brazil with 284 million.

In 2021, the average American spent 3 hours 35 minutes every day on their cellphone.

⚲ HANDBAG, MOBILE PHONE

⬤ CEMETERIES

Body bags, airlines, cemeteries and religious law came into conflict in 2001, when the Israeli airline El Al faced a request to allow some passengers to zip themselves into body bags when their plane flew directly over a cemetery. The problem stemmed from an Ultra-Orthodox Jewish law that forbade Jews descended from the biblical priests from entering a cemetery. A recent interpretation had clarified that ruling to cover the airspace above cemeteries, but the argument was that if they were in plastic body bags over the cemetery, they would no longer be deemed unclean.

El Al turned down the request, explaining to the religious authorities that zipping oneself into a body bag was not safe. Instead, they recommended an alternative solution of the Ultra-Orthodox Jews taking night flights from Tel Aviv, when noise pollution regulations forced the airlines to alter their usual flight path to one that avoided cemeteries.

⚲ ADDAMS, COFFIN, DEATH, FISH, SAN FRANCISCO

⬤ CENSORSHIP

The Hays Code, which controlled film standards in the US from 1930 to 1967, was named after William Harrison Hays, politician turned film Tsar. His 'Code To Govern The Making Of Motion And Talking Pictures' was based on three General Principles: that no picture should be produced that will lower moral standards; that correct standards of life … shall be presented; and that law, natural or human, should not be ridiculed.

Specifically, 11 items were banned, including anything containing the words 'God', 'Lord', 'Jesus' and 'Christ' (unless used reverently), 'hell' and 'damn'. 'Illegal drug traffic', venereal diseases and scenes of childbirth were also not allowed. A further 25 items demanded that 'special care be exercised'. These included: brutality, sympathy for criminals, lustful kissing, use of the American flag, and man and woman in bed together.

The last of these was generally interpreted to mean that when a man and a woman are shown on the same bed, each must have at least one foot on the ground.

The first film to be blocked by US Customs from entering the United States under this code was Hedy Lamarr's 1933 film *Ecstasy*.

♀ *CAMBODIA*

CENSUS

In the 1871 Census in Britain, the final question asked whether the people named were: 1) deaf and dumb; 2) blind; 3) imbecile or idiot; 4) lunatic.

This question remained unchanged in 1881, but in 1891 the last two sections were combined into a single section: 3) lunatic, imbecile or idiot.

In 1901 and 1911 the categories were again changed to: 3) lunatic; 4) imbecile or feeble-minded.

In 1911, the first two categories were expanded to: 1) deaf and dumb; 2) dumb only; 3) blind; while the remaining ones became: 4) imbecile or idiot; 5) lunatic. Returns revealed that there were 15,719 lunatics in Britain in 1911.

CENTAUR

According to the Roman poet and philosopher Lucretius (1st century BC), a cross between a man and a horse is impossible because their developments cannot be synchronised. A three-year-old horse is in its prime while a human of that age is still an infant 'and often even then gropes in sleep after the milky nipples of the breasts'. They also live to different ages, so the horse half would be dead when the man half was still in its prime.

CENTENARIANS

In 2009, Japan announced that, in order to cut costs, it was reducing the size of silver cups presented to those who reach the age of 100. In 1963, the year when the cups were first presented, a total of 153 were needed, but by 2008 the number had increased to 19,769, and in 2021 the number reached 86,510. Of all countries, Japan has the highest proportion of centenarians by population (0.06 per cent).

The number of centenarians in the UK in 2020 was estimated to be 15,120, while the number in the US is around 97,000.

♀ *JAPAN, LONGEVITY*

CENTIPEDE

The zoological name of the centipede is Chilopoda, from the Greek *kheilos*, meaning 'lip' or 'jaw' and *pous*, meaning 'foot'. The name refers to the poisonous fangs on its front legs.

All centipedes have an odd number of pairs of legs, so no centipede can have exactly 100 legs, as this would mean it had 50 pairs, an even number. Centipedes found in Britain may have anything between 15 and 101 pairs of legs.

Each leg of a centipede is slightly longer than the one in front, which helps them avoid tripping over their own legs.

♀ *EL SALVADOR*

CENTRAL AFRICAN REPUBLIC

In the 2019 Global Hunger Index, the Central African Republic was ranked 217 out of 217 countries and was the only one classified as falling into the 'extremely alarming' category. In 2021, the level of hunger in the Central African Republic had improved to merely 'alarming', in which category it was joined by Chad, the Democratic Republic of the Congo, Madagascar and Yemen, while Somalia had become the only country found to be 'extremely alarming'.

When Jean-Bédel Bokassa was crowned Emperor of the Central African Republic in 1977, only one of his 17 wives was permitted to attend the ceremony.

♀ NIGERIA

CÉZANNE, Paul (1839–1906)

It has been said that the painter Cézanne worked so slowly that the fruit in his still-life paintings usually went rotten long before he finished.

Nevertheless, his *Rideau, Cruchon et Compotier* (*Curtain, Earthenware-jug and Fruit-dish*), which sold at auction for $60.5 million in 1999, was the most expensive still life ever sold until overtaken by van Gogh's *Still Life, Vase with Daisies and Poppies* which fetched $61.8 million in 2014.

♀ PIGEON

CHAD

The flag of Chad consists of three vertical stripes – blue, yellow and red – the whole flag having a width-to-length ratio of 2:3. This is identical to the Romanian flag, except that the blue of Chad is officially indigo, while that of Romania is cobalt. The Romanians adopted their flag in 1989, which was 29 years after the Chad flag was adopted. In 1997, however, the Romanians registered worldwide copyright in their flag. In 2004, Chad referred the matter to the United Nations, but the President of Romania said they were not going to change their flag.

The country of Chad takes its name from Lake Chad, which is rather a tautological name as it comes from *tsad* which is the Arabic for 'lake'.

The country Chad has nothing to do with the 'hanging chads' on voting slips, which led to dispute in the US Presidential Election of 2000. Such chads are the bits of paper meant to be punched from voting papers. If not properly detached, they may be hanging chads (attached at one corner only), swinging chads (attached at two corners), tri-chads (attached at three corners), or pregnant chads (attached at all corners, but with indentation marks where the voting machine should have cut through the paper).

♀ NIGERIA, YEMEN

CHAIN

In 2006, Californian artist Trevor Corneliussen, 26, was reported to have hopped for 12 hours through the desert to get help after chaining his legs together to draw a picture of himself and losing the key. The accident happened while the artist was camping in an abandoned mine shaft about five miles north of Baker, San Bernardino. The Baker-area artist often sketched images inside mines in the Southwest.

'It took him over 12 hours because he had to hop through boulders and sand,' a Deputy Sheriff said. 'He did put on his shoes before hopping.' He was treated by paramedics and deputies with bolt cutters. When asked about the drawing, the Deputy Sheriff said: 'It was a pretty good depiction of how a chain would look wrapped around your legs.'

♀ POLAR BEAR, SHARJAH, TURING

CHAMOIS

The word 'chamois' is rather confusing. In Europe the chamois is a mountain antelope, but elsewhere it is more generally used for various species of antelope or goat. Chamois leather, however, does not nowadays come from goats or antelopes but sheep.

In the early 18th century, the French glove-making industry used true chamois, which was found to produce the ideal qualities of water absorption for their soft white gloves when the skin was tanned in cod oil from Biarritz. The word 'chamois' (pronounced 'shammy') then came to be used for the process of tanning in cod oil.

YODELLING

CHAMPAGNE

A relatively uncelebrated contributor to the history of Champagne was the English physician Christopher Merrett who, in 1662, showed that adding sugar to wine produces a bubble-producing secondary fermentation. Merrett also invented strengthened bottles to withstand the pressure of those bubbles.

Champagne itself is thought to have been invented by Dom Perignon, a monk at the Benedictine Abbey of Hautvillers in the region of Champagne, northern France. On sipping the first results of his doubly fermented brew he is said to have called out: 'Come quickly, brother. I am tasting the stars.' He was the cellar master at Hautvillers for 47 years until his death in 1715. The discovery is said to have been made on 4 August 1693.

It has been calculated that a bottle of champagne at room temperature contains about 49 million bubbles.

The Champagne house Pol Roger made a special one-pint bottle of champagne for Winston Churchill, to be served each day at 11am.

Marilyn Monroe is said to have once taken a champagne-filled bath. It took 350 bottles to fill the tub.

'Sabrage' is the name given to the art of opening a champagne bottle with a sabre. This was popularised by Napoleon's cavalry, who saw it as a way to celebrate victories.

'Too much of anything is bad, but too much Champagne is just right.' F. Scott Fitzgerald

BALLOON, COFFEE, ETIQUIETTE

CHANNEL

Until about 10,000 years ago, the English Channel did not exist. It was formed by melting waters at the end of an Ice Age, and the final land link between England and France from Dover to Calais was submerged about 8,000 years ago.

The first cross-Channel flight was made in 1785 by Jean Pierre Blanchard and Dr John Jeffries in a balloon. Blanchard, a French balloonist and the inventor of the parachute, did all he could to stop Jeffries, the American doctor who financed the trip, from sharing the glory with him. His tricks included wearing lead weights in his belt to try to convince Jeffries that the two of them were too heavy for the balloon. As they neared the French coast, the balloon lost height and the balloonists jettisoned everything, including their clothes, to keep it in the air. Neither of them could swim.

The first person to swim the Channel was a steamship captain called Matthew Webb, who coated himself in porpoise fat and swam across in 21 hours 45 minutes in 1875. The current fastest swim is 6 hours 55 minutes set by Trent Grimsey of Australia in 2012.

Australian Chloë McCardel has swum the Channel a record 44 times. No man has swum the Channel more than 34 times, a figure reached by Kevin Murphy of England. Altogether, 1,881 people have swum the Channel, of whom 63 per cent have been male. More than twice as many people have climbed Mount Everest.

The Channel was first swum by a grandmother in 1951, by a legless person in 1990, and first swum underwater in 1962. The first non-stop swim both ways was made by Antonio Abertondo of Argentina in 1961.

The first Channel crossing by hovercraft was made on 25 July 1959, 50 years to the day after Louis Blériot's historic first successful cross-Channel flight.

In July 2010, Jackie Cobell, 56, set a new record for the slowest ever Channel swim, covering about 105 kilometres (65 miles) when battling against tides, and finishing in 28 hours and 44 minutes. The previous record for the longest solo swim was 26 hours and 50 minutes set by Henry Sullivan in 1923.

AMPUTATION, BALLOON, EARTHQUAKE, EUROPE, SWIMMING

CHARLES, Prince of Wales (b.1948)

'To get the best results, you must talk to your vegetables … It's very important.'
Prince Charles, speaking in 1986

DIANA, SCILLY ISLES, WILLIAM IV

CHARLES I, King of England (1600–49)

Before he was beheaded, Charles I is said to have asked his executioner: 'Is my hair well?' Even before his head was removed, he was not very tall. Estimates vary between 1.4 and 1.7 metres (4 feet 7 inches and 5 feet 7 inches).

In 1661, on the 12th anniversary of Charles's execution, Oliver Cromwell, who had died of malaria in 1658, was exhumed and beheaded.

HUDSON, QUEEN MARY

CHARLES II, King of England (1630–85)

According to Samuel Pepys's diary, on 15 October 1666, Charles II became the first man to wear a waistcoat. He had apparently introduced the garment in England through royal proclamation eight days earlier.

Charles II was known to his lover Nell Gwyn as Charles the Third, because she had previously had two other lovers named Charles: the actor Charles Hart and Charles Sachville, Lord Buckhurst. Samuel Pepys called her 'pretty, witty Nell' and praised her as one of the finest actresses on the English stage.

Charles II kept King Charles spaniels as pets in his bedchamber. According to John Evelyn, they 'rendred it very offensive and indeede made the whole court nasty and stinking'.

ACTRESS, DIANA, MAYPOLE

CHATEAUNEUF DU PAPE

In 1308, Pope Clement V relocated the papacy to the town of Avignon in France. He was a great lover of burgundy wines, and Chateauneuf du Pape means 'the new castle of the Pope'.

Following a spate of alleged flying saucer sightings in France in 1954, the mayor of Chateauneuf du Pape issued the following decree:

Article 1. The overflight, the landing and the take-off of aircraft known as flying saucers or flying cigars, whatever their nationality, are prohibited on the territory of the community.

Article 2. Any aircraft, known as flying saucer or flying cigar, which should land on the territory of the community will be immediately held in custody.

Article 3. The forest officer and the city policeman are in charge, each one in his own jurisdiction, of the execution of this decree.

In 1984, the Bonny Doon vineyard in California launched a red wine inspired by Chateauneuf du Pape and called it Cigare Volant (flying cigar), which was the French term by which flying saucers were known.

● CHAUCER, Geoffrey (1340–1400)

It is said that Geoffrey Chaucer, author of *The Canterbury Tales*, owned 60 books, which was quite a large library in those days.

In 1360, he was captured at the siege of Rheims during the 100 Years War, and King Edward III paid £16 for his ransom. On St George's Day 1374, the King granted Chaucer 'a gallon of wine daily for the rest of his life'.

Chaucer's son Thomas was Chief Butler of England for 30 years and was elected as MP for Oxfordshire 15 times.

⚲ *CANTERBURY, MARS, NEWTON*

● CHEESE

The word 'cheese' occurs only twice in the King James Bible: once in 2 Samuel (17:29) and once in the Book of Job (10:10). As well as these, the plural 'cheeses' occurs once in 1 Samuel (17:17).

The Wisconsin Cheese Makers Association has hosted the biennial World Championship Cheese Contest since 1957. A Swiss Gruyère won in 2020 and 2022; a French Esquirrou won in 2018.

You cannot make cheese in Wisconsin without a cheese-maker's licence; Limburger cheese-makers require a master cheese-maker's licence.

According to a British study conducted for the British Cheese Board in 2003 by Dr Len Fisher of Bristol University, the optimum thickness of cheese to be put into a cheese sandwich varies according to the cheese: 7mm for Wensleydale; 5mm, Cheshire; 4.5mm, Caerphilly; 3mm, blue Stilton; 2.8mm, Cheddar; and 2.5mm for double Gloucester or red Leicester. His results were listed in a report entitled: 'Optimum Use of Cheese in a Cheese Sandwich'.

An Irish chieftain nicknamed Cheese-Guzzler O'Ruairc died of 'a surfeit of sex' in 1204.

In 1878, Thomas Nuttall built an 18-metre (60-foot) replica of Cleopatra's Needle out of 54 Stilton cheeses. Queen Victoria liked it so much she bought all the cheeses.

The first recorded sighting of the word 'cheeseburger' was on 23 December 1941 over a shop in Burbank, California.

'Cheese without a rind is like a maiden without shame.' Old Spanish proverb

⚲ *HOLES, MANSFIELD, PARMESAN, STILTON, WISCONSIN*

● CHEESECAKE

A world record cheesecake was made in Mexico City in January 2009 by a team of 55 chefs organised by the makers of Philadelphia Cream Cheese. It weighed 2,133.5 kilograms (4,703 pounds), had a diameter of 2.5 metres (8 feet 2 inches) and was 56 centimetres (1 foot 10 inches) high. The recipe included 800 kilograms (1,764 pounds) of Philadelphia cheese, 800 kilograms

(1,764 pounds) of yogurt, 350 kilograms (772 pounds) of cookies, 250 kilograms (551 pounds) of flour, 150 kilograms (330 pounds) of butter and 100 kilograms (220 pounds) of strawberries, among other ingredients.

In March 2012, Chandra Bahadur Dangi of Kathmandu, aged 72, who was 54.6 centimetres (1 foot 9.5 inches) tall was announced as the world's shortest man. So the world's shortest man was shorter than the world's tallest cheesecake.

The cheesecake record has improved greatly since then, and on 23 September 2017, a cheesecake created by Cheeseberry Company (Russian Federation) in Stavropol weighed in at 4,240 kilograms (9,347.60 pounds). This record was made and displayed on the main square in Stavropol for the city's 240th birthday.

● CHELSEA

Bill Clinton's daughter Chelsea is believed to have been named after the Joni Mitchell song 'Chelsea Morning'. The song has nothing to do with Chelsea in London, but refers to Chelsea on the outskirts of Boston, Massachusetts.

Chelsea Clinton was born on Elizabeth Taylor's 48th birthday: 27 February 1980.

Until around 1815, you could be hanged in Britain for imitating a Chelsea pensioner. You could also be hanged for damaging Westminster Bridge.

In 1998, Chelsea Football Club came only 67th in an unofficial table of the best away toilet facilities of league clubs.

♀ *WELLINGTON BOOTS*

● CHEQUE

The 350th anniversary of bankers' cheques was celebrated on 16 February 2009. Actually, it wasn't the 350th anniversary at all, but the 349th. The date on the very first cheque issued was '16th of February 1659', but before 1752 the year began on 25 March, so it was what we would now call 1660.

It was a cheque for £400 to Mr Delboe, drawn on Messrs Morris and Clayton, 'scriveners and bankers'. But it wasn't then called a 'cheque'. That word did not come into use until a 1706 Act of Parliament, and even then 'cheque' – or 'checque' as it was spelled – meant the counterfoil, not the money order.

Payment by cheque in the UK peaked in 1990 when 11 million were issued every day. If all those cheques were laid end-to-end, they would stretch 12 times around the world. According to the Oxford English Corpus, the adjective most likely to immediately precede the word 'cheque' is 'blank'.

● CHERRY

The Roman general Lucullus is said to have committed suicide in 56 BC when he realised he was running out of cherries. According to Pliny the Elder, Lucullus (full name Lucius Licinius Lucullus) introduced the sour cherry to Italy and brought a species of sweet cherry to Rome.

The official world record for spitting a cherry pip is 28.5 metres (93 feet 6.5 inches), set by Rick Krause of Michigan in 2004.

♀ *ICE CREAM, SPITTING, TURING*

● CHESS

According to followers of Freud, chess is a symptom of the Oedipus Complex: the object is to checkmate the enemy king (symbolic of killing the father) and the queen is the strongest piece (symbolic of loving one's mother).

In January 2004, the Russian Orthodox Church responded to a campaign led by a young churchgoer who had organised a petition claiming that chess is the work of the devil. Archbishop Wikenti from Yekaterinburg rejected the request and ruled that chess is not a sin. He pointed out that passionate and arousing games that cause confusion, anger and irritation are banned by the Church, but said that chess was 'a quiet, intelligent game that encourages people to think'.

The first official World Chess Champion, Wilhelm Steinitz, who held the title from 1886 to 1894, was the only holder of that title to be declared insane. Mikhail Tal, who won the World Championship in 1960, had only three fingers on his right hand.

In the 1978 World Championship, Viktor Korchnoi objected to the yogurt Anatoly Karpov was eating, claiming it might be a colour-coded secret message.

'[Chess is] as elaborate a waste of human intelligence as you can find anywhere outside an advertising agency.' Raymond Chandler

'It is a testy and cholericke game and very offensive to him that loseth the mate.' Robert Burton, 1626

'Chess is not a game that drives people mad; chess is something that keeps mad people sane.' William Hartston

BILLIARDS, BOGART, D'EON, TALIBAN, THAILAND

CHEWING GUM

The first commercially available chewing gum, State of Maine Pure Spruce Gum made by John Curtis, was introduced on 23 September 1848.

In 1997, a fine was imposed on Hong Kong businessman Leung Ka-Ching for chewing gum in court. He had the fine overturned on appeal, claiming that he had been chewing the gum to show respect for the court by having fresh breath.

In 2020, researchers from the University of Valencia in Spain published a paper in the journal *Scientific Reports*, based on genetic analysis of discarded chewing gum from five countries. Their results showed discarded chewing gum can be used to detect different strains of bacteria and identify oral infection trends.

BAR CODES, SINGAPORE

CHICAGO

According to a report by a US pest control company in January 2013, Chicago led the country in reports of bed bugs in 2012, followed by Detroit, Los Angeles, Denver and Cincinnati. The next five most bed-bug-rich cities in the US were reported to be Columbus, Ohio; Washington; Cleveland–Akron–Canton; Dallas–Fort Worth; and New York.

BLOOD, DIVORCE, GARLIC, PLAYBOY

CHICKEN

In 1975, experiments were conducted at the Atmospheric Sciences Research Center in New York to see if the observation of chickens could help in estimating tornado wind velocities. Chickens were placed in a wind tunnel and, by varying the conditions, the researchers would discover what wind speed was necessary to remove a chicken's feathers from their follicles.

Sadly, they discovered that the removal of chicken feathers in high winds operates according to complex and unpredictable rules depending on the condition of the chicken and various environmental factors as well as wind speed. They concluded that: 'Chicken plucking is of doubtful value as an index of tornado wind velocity.'

Analysis in 2008 of the DNA from a 68-million-year-old T Rex fossil concluded that the chicken is the closest living relative of Tyrannosaurus Rex. In 2021, analysis of fossil fragments found in Wales in the 1950s revealed that they were from a dinosaur distantly related to Tyrannosaurus Rex, but with a body the size of a chicken and a tail that took its length to about a metre. They had been kept in a drawer with crocodile bones for almost 70 years.

Chickens can travel at up to nine miles per hour, and will lay bigger and stronger eggs if you change the lighting in such a way as to make them think the day is 28 hours long.

There are four places in the United States with the word 'chicken' in their name: Chicken, Alaska; Chicken Bristle, in Illinois and Kentucky; and Chicken Town, Pennsylvania.

The largest chicken egg on record was nearly 340 grams (12 ounces) in weight and measured 31 centimetres (12.25 inches) at its widest circumference.

The greatest number of yolks in one chicken egg is nine.

The record for laying the most eggs is seven in one day.

The longest distance flown by any chicken is 91.9 metres (301.5 feet) and the longest flight lasted 13 seconds.

In Gainesville, Georgia – the chicken capital of the world – it is illegal to eat chicken with a fork.

On average, six chicken sandwiches are eaten every second in the UK. Since three Barbie dolls are sold every second worldwide, this means that every time anyone anywhere on earth buys a Barbie doll, two chicken sandwiches are eaten in Britain.

Jon-Stephen Fink's 1981 book *Cluck! The True History of Chickens in the Movies* lists 182 films in which chickens or their eggs have played a role.

A cross between a male chicken and a female turkey is called a churk.

'How often would I have gathered thy children together, even as a hen gathereth her chickens under her wings.' Matthew 23:37 (This is the only specific mention of chickens in the King James Bible.)

HENS, LAUGHFEST, SANDWICHES

CHICKEN POX

The term 'chicken pox' has nothing to do with chickens. It came from the Old English term 'gican pox', which means the itching pox.

CHICKEN SEXING

The art of chicken sexing was developed by the Japanese in 1924 and introduced to the West in 1927 at the World Poultry Congress in Ottawa. Before that, poultry farmers had to wait until chicks were five to six weeks old before being able to tell their sex. Since only the females were needed for egg production, this resulted in a good deal of wasted expense feeding male chicks. The new Japanese technique saved this expense by determining the sex of newborn chicks by examining their rear ends for a pimple-sized protuberance which is a degenerate penis. All males have this, but so do about 15 per cent of females, and the real skill in the job comes in assigning the sex of those 15 per cent.

In 1934, a team of Japanese chicken sexers went to Queensland to teach the Australians how to do it, and the top

Australian chicken sexers were later reported to be earning $400–700 a day telling the sex of 5,000–7,000 chicks.

In the 1950s, both the British and Japanese developed machines for testing the sex of chickens, the 'Keeler Optical' in Britain and the 'Chicktester' in Japan, but these seemed to demand as much skill in using as doing the job without them.

From the late 1960s onwards, genetic research and cross-breeding led to methods whereby the sex of a chick may be determined from its feathers within 48 hours of birth.

In the New Zealand Standard Classification of Occupations 1999 list, chicken sexer came between chicken processor and chief clerk.

The world record for correctly determining the sex of 100 chicks is 3 minutes 6 seconds; the record for most chicks sexed without mistakes in an hour is 1,682.

According to a Vancouver careers advisory service, chicken sexing is 'most compatible for people who enjoy following instruction and using their hands'.

CHILDREN

'Mummy' is the first word uttered by 30 per cent of English-speaking babies, while 45 per cent say 'Daddy' first.

'Childhood: the period of life intermediate between the idiocy of infancy and the folly of youth.' Ambrose Bierce, The Devil's Dictionary, *1906*

'You know your children are growing up when they stop asking you where they came from and refuse to tell you where they're going.' P.J. O'Rourke

CLOWNS, FORGERY, GOSSIP, HOMES, SANTA CLAUS, SHAKESPEARE

CHILE

On 28 November 1996, the former Chilean dictator Augusto Pinochet gave the following three pieces of advice to Chilean army officers: don't gossip about the military; watch your drink; and don't grow sideburns if you are visiting London.

The world's oldest mummy was found in Chile. It was a child, dated to around 5050 BC.

Chile also has the world's longest swimming pool. It is almost 1 kilometre (0.6 miles) in length and is in the private San Alfonso resort in Algarrobo.

CHURROS, FOG, MINT

CHILLI

In early civilisations such as the Incas, Mayans and Aztecs, chilli peppers were used as a currency. Aztec women believed in chilli as a cosmetic and beautified themselves with a skin cream made of chilli powder and urine. The Mexicans have eaten chillies since 7000 BC and cultivated them from 3500 BC.

African farmers attach chillies to fences to keep elephants away from their crops. Elephants hate the smell of chillies.

A chilli's hotness comes from chemicals known as capsaicins. The Scoville scale for measuring the heat of chillies was devised by Wilbur L. Scoville in 1912. Scoville ratings are worked out by diluting a chilli-containing sauce to the point at which a team of five expert tasters can no longer detect the heat. The level of dilution is given as the official heat of the pepper. Scoville ratings begin at zero Scoville units for the bell pepper, via 30,000–50,000 for Tabasco sauce, to 2.2 million for the Carolina Reaper, which is higher than police pepper spray.

Until 2008, the only other way to measure capsaicin content was by using high-pressure liquid chromatography, which was too expensive for practical purposes. In that year, however, Richard Compton, an Oxford chemist, devised a cheaper method using electrodes covered in carbon nanotubes. He tested his electrochemical device on a range of hot pepper sauces, including 'Mad Dog's Revenge', which has a Scoville rating of around 1 million. Compton's nanotube method gave a value of 991,700, confirming that the technique works.

The American rock band the Red Hot Chili Peppers began in 1983 as Tony Flow and the Miraculously Majestic Masters of Mayhem.

The world record for eating chilli con carne is 9.22 litres (2.438 US gallons) in six minutes by Carmen Cincotti, achieved at the Sixth Annual World Chili Eating Challenge in Florida in 2018.

♀ BOTTOM, CUPCAKE

CHIMNEY SWEEPS

Under the Chimney Sweepers Act 1894, it was an offence 'to solicit employment as a chimney sweep by knocking on doors, ringing bells or using any noisy instrument to the annoyance of any inhabitant'. This and earlier Chimney Sweepers Acts were repealed in 1938 following a debate in the British House of Commons in which it was asserted that the Acts were regarded by chimney sweepers, of whom there were only about 6,000 in England and Wales, as 'a slur upon their profession, for chimney sweepers are the only manual workers in the country who have to get an annual permit from the police in order to perform their duties'.

♀ FIRE-FIGHTING

CHIMPANZEE

The official name of the common chimpanzee is *Pan troglodytes*. Troglodyte means 'cave-dweller'. The word 'chimpanzee' derives from a Congolese Tshiluba language term *kivili-chimpenze* which translates as 'mock-man'.

Chimpanzees, despite their hairy appearance, have no more hair follicles than humans. Like humans, chimps go grey as they age. But unlike humans, both male and female chimps go bald.

The DNA of a Bonobo, or pygmy chimpanzee, is 98 per cent the same as that of a human.

In 2005, Ai Ai, a 27-year-old Chinese chimp, gave up smoking. She had taken to cigarettes after her mate died 16 years earlier.

According to a study in Arizona in 2004, chimps prefer composing their own music to listening to pre-recorded tracks.

In 1999, *New Scientist* magazine identified chimps in Madrid Zoo as the first non-humans seen to mash food simply because they prefer the taste and texture.

In November 2006, research established that male chimpanzees prefer older women. Female chimps remain fertile and do not experience a menopause.

One of Bill Clinton's last acts as US President was to sign into law on 20 December 2000 an act giving laboratory chimpanzees the right to a peaceful retirement.

♀ DNA, HANGOVER, YAWNING

CHINA

On average in China, 22.9 people are born and 19.0 people die every minute.

The Dog-Meat King restaurant in Beijing serves more than 50 dog dishes, including braised dog paws, stir-fried dog chops and boiled tail. In 2001, a petition signed by 11,000 dog breeders and owners was delivered to the Chinese urging an end to the breeding of St Bernards for their meat.

In China in the 10th century, eating goldfish was forbidden.

In 2001, Beijing announced a decision to raise the quality of its public lavatories to improve their chances of staging the 2008 Olympic Games. Toilets would be rated on a system which awarded between one and four stars, with four-star toilets having tissues, automatic flush, hand-washing facilities, hand dryers, granite floors, good lighting, lively music, and bathrooms specially designed for disabled and old people. According to one Beijing newspaper, this decision was taken because the Chinese capital still lagged far behind other cities in terms of its public toilets.

In preparation for the Beijing Olympics, China also reported that figures showed that its drive for better etiquette had led to cleaner streets, better queueing and less spitting. Results of a 2007 survey had shown that 2.5 per cent of people spat in public, down from 4.9 per cent in 2006; instances of queue jumping dropped to 1.5 per cent from 6 per cent; and littering fell to 2.9 per cent from 5.3 per cent.

℗ *DRAGON, GERBIL, GOLDFISH, NOODLE, TRANSVESTITES*

CHIPS

One in four of all potatoes consumed in Britain are cooked as chips. Around 7 per cent of the potatoes grown in the USA end up in McDonald's chip bags. The average Briton eats just over 3 kilograms (7 pounds) of chips a year; the average American eats 7.25 kilograms (16 pounds), although the Americans call chips 'French fries'. The verb 'to french', or 'to french cut', means 'to cut in thin lengthwise strips before cooking'. It was originally applied not to potatoes but to green beans. The Belgians call chips 'Belgian fries' and claim to have invented them.

One of the earliest references to 'chips' is in Charles Dickens's *A Tale Of Two Cities* (1859), where he mentions 'husky chips of potatoes, fried with some reluctant drops of oil'.

Scientists at Leeds University in 2009 announced the result of their investigation into the components that make up the smell of chips. They concluded that the smell includes butterscotch, cocoa, cheese and flowers.

In September 2010, Chris Verschueren, owner of a French fries business in the village of Kastel in Belgium, set a new world record for continuous chip-frying by spending 83 hours frying 1,500 kilograms (3,307 pounds) of chips, taking just one 100-minute break after 20 hours for a shower and a stretch. 'My fingers are burnt, my feet are sore and my wrist is painful,' he said after finally stopping, 'but it doesn't matter, I'm going to party now.'

℗ *CRISPS, FISH, RESTAURANTS*

CHOCOLATE

Archaeological evidence shows that cocoa beans were ground and enjoyed as a drink over 5,000 years ago in Central and South America, but it was 16th-century Aztec Emperor

Moctezuma II who started the myth about chocolate being an aphrodisiac. He reputedly drank 50 cups of chocolate a day as a cold drink out of a golden goblet to increase his libido. Aztec women were not allowed to drink it.

Among the Aztecs, cocoa beans were so valued that they became a form of currency: four beans for a rabbit or 100 for a slave. When Cortés conquered the Aztecs in 1520, he found that cocoa beans were prized even higher than gold. By the middle of the 16th century, cocoa had become a luxury drink at the Spanish court, but the word 'chocolate' was not recorded in English until 1604. England's first cup of chocolate was brewed at Balliol College, Oxford, by a student from Crete in 1647.

In 1842, Cadbury's were already offering 16 varieties of drinking chocolate. In 1847, J.S. Fry's of Bristol invented the chocolate bar, and in 1868 Cadbury's produced the first box of chocolates.

Among the Aztecs, only nobles, soldiers and sacrificial victims had been allowed chocolate; in Spain, it had been reserved as a luxury for state occasions; but in Britain, thanks to the Quakers, Fry and Cadbury, anyone could become a chocoholic.

Samuel Pepys drank his first cup of chocolate on 24 November 1664; he noted in his diary: 'To a Coffee-house, to drink jocolatte, very good.'

On New Year's Day 1900, Queen Victoria sent 100,000 boxes of chocolates as a personal gift to soldiers in the Boer War.

According to a survey at the end of 2019, around 59 per cent of Britons consider chocolate an essential part of their weekly shop and 46 per cent said they eat chocolate every day.

In 1982, researchers in New York discovered that falling in love correlated with high levels of phenethylamine (PEA) in the brain. Chocolate also contains PEA, which appeared to support Moctezuma's theory of chocolate as an aphrodisiac, or at least as an anti-depressant. Confusingly, a study in 1991 showed higher suicide and lower homicide rates in countries with the highest chocolate consumption.

Research in 2002, however, added another dimension when German psychologists correlated subjects' chocolate consumption with the type of film they had been watching. They concluded that men are more likely to reach for chocolate when they're happy than when they are sad. They suggested that people may divide into those who eat chocolate to avoid misery and those who eat it to get pleasure.

Under US regulations, chocolate may contain up to 60 insect fragments per 100 grams (3.5 ounces).

PENTAGON, SLOANE, SMARTIES

CHOPSTICKS

Thirty per cent of the world's population usually eat with chopsticks. Japanese and Chinese chopsticks, however, differ slightly in shape: Japanese chopsticks tend to be tapered or pointed at the eating end, while Chinese chopsticks tend to be longer with a blunt or square end.

According to research published in the journal *Applied Ergonomics* in 1996, the perfect chopstick is 240mm long (180mm for children) and tapers from 6mm to 4mm diameter, with a two-degree tip angle.

In 2004, physicists Dr Jim Al-Khalili and Dr Qiang Zhao at the University of Surrey produced a rather complex formula for the comfort of using chopsticks. Their conclusion, in non-scientific terms, was that slippery or crumbly food in small, heavy pieces brought slowly to your mouth is most difficult to eat with chopsticks, but you'll improve with practice.

The Kuaizi Museum in Shanghai contains over a thousand pairs of chopsticks. *Kuaizi* is the Chinese word for chopsticks, meaning 'quick little fellows'.

Fear of using chopsticks is called consecotaleophobia.

TABLE MANNERS

CHRISTIANITY

There are about 2.4 billion Christians in the world, half of whom are Catholics.

According to a survey in 1999, Queen Elizabeth II was only the fifth best-known Christian among Britons, but she was still two places higher than the Pope. The most famous Christian was Sir Cliff Richard.

CHRISTMAS

In AD 325, the Council of Nicaea, at which St Nicholas himself may have been present, fixed the date of Christmas as 25 December, but the earliest record of a celebration on that date was in AD 354.

According to the 16th-century mystic Godfridus, when Christmas falls on a Thursday, winter shall be good and 'He that falleth in his bed shall soon recover.'

In 1647, the English Parliament abolished Christmas Day as a feast day, but contrary to popular belief Cromwell did not make it illegal to eat mince pies.

On Christmas Day 1066, William the Conqueror was crowned King of England. On Christmas Day 1913, a New York couple were arrested and fined $15 for kissing in the street.

On Christmas Day 1989, President Ceausescu of Romania was executed.

'Jingle Bells' was composed by James Pierpont in 1857. Its original title was 'One Horse Open Sleigh' and it was written as a Thanksgiving celebration rather than Christmas.

Around £1 million a year is staked on snow falling in Britain on Christmas Day. Weather records suggest the odds against snow falling at any particular location is around eight to one, but there has been at least one snowflake seen falling somewhere in Britain on 39 of the last 53 years.

According to Norwegian scientist Arne Fjellberg, the average Christmas tree has about 30,000 bugs and insects on it. His microscopic examination of Christmas trees revealed midges, fleas, lice, parasitic wasps, spiders and beetles.

The total number of gifts given by 'My true love' in the song 'The Twelve Days of Christmas' adds up to 364.

The Taming of the Shrew and *Love's Labours Lost* are the only Shakespeare plays that mention Christmas.

'The Three Sisters' (a short story) and 'Sanditon' (an unfinished novel) are the only works by Jane Austen that do not mention Christmas.

FATHER CHRISTMAS, SANTA CLAUS, TWELFTH NIGHT

CHRISTMAS CARD

The first Christmas card, designed and sent in 1843, was the idea of Sir Henry Cole, founder of the Victoria and Albert Museum. He printed and sold, for a shilling (5p) each, 1,000 cards designed by the artist John Callcott Horsley. An original card sent by Sir Henry Cole in 1843 fetched a record £20,000 at auction in 2001.

Horsley had two other claims to

fame: he was the brother-in-law of Isambard Kingdom Brunel, and he conducted a campaign against artists' models posing in the nude, which led to him being referred to as 'clothes Horsley'.

In 2011, Royal Mail in the UK delivered around 2 billion items at Christmas, including 750 million cards. Deliveries were made using a million trays and 73,000 more containers than usual, carried by 38,000 trucks and vans and 64 flights.

CHRISTMAS, TALIBAN

CHRISTMAS EVE

The carol 'Silent Night' was first performed in 1818 at a church in Oberndorf, Bavaria, on Christmas Eve.

According to an old superstition, bread baked on Christmas Eve will never go mouldy.

According to an old Devonshire superstition, oxen in their stalls are to be seen kneeling at midnight on Christmas Eve.

In France, the traditional Christmas Eve midnight feast begins with oysters and champagne.

People born on Christmas Eve include actress Ava Gardner (1922), aviator/inventor Howard Hughes (1905), world chess champion Emanuel Lasker (1868) and King John of England (1166).

Portuguese explorer Vasco da Gama died on Christmas Eve 1524.

Pope Boniface VIII was elected to the papacy on Christmas Eve 1294, replacing Pope Celestine V, who had resigned, considering himself unworthy.

FATHER CHRISTMAS, JAPAN

CHROMOSOME

Humans have 46 chromosomes, peas have 14 and crayfish have 200.

A male jack jumper ant has only one chromosome; females have two.

BUFFALO, POTATO, SEX TEST

CHURCHILL, Winston (1874–1965)

It has often been maintained that Churchill's mother, Jennie Jerome, was one-eighth Iroquois Indian, and this belief has been described as a 'long-held family tradition', but the evidence for it is unconvincing and totally absent from genealogical records, tombstones or contemporary documents.

Winston Churchill's father and Al Capone's father both had syphilis. The French poet Charles Baudelaire also had syphilis, which he caught from a Jewish prostitute called Squint-Eyed Sarah (Sarah la Louchette).

CHAMPAGNE, DENTURES

CHURROS

A daily newspaper in Chile was ordered to pay a total of $125,000 damages to 13 readers who had suffered burns through following a recipe for churros, a snack made by frying dough in hot oil. The high court ruling was given in December 2011, seven years after the readers had burned themselves. Judges ruled that the newspaper failed to fully test the recipe which, if followed as printed, gave the churros a good chance of exploding.

CICADA

The male American cicada lives 17 years, mates only once and dies immediately afterwards. The female mates, lays about 500 eggs in tree branches, then dies.

CICERO, Marcus Tullius (106–43 BC)

When the Roman philosopher and statesman Marcus Tullius Cicero was assassinated in 43 BC, his last words are said to have been, 'There is nothing proper about what you are doing, soldier, but do try to kill me properly.' After his death, Fulvia, the wife of Mark Antony, whom Cicero had fervently opposed, is said to have pulled out Cicero's tongue and stabbed it repeatedly with her hairpin.

The early Catholic Church declared Cicero to be a 'righteous pagan' whose works could therefore be read and studied by believers.

♀ SLAVERY

CIGAR

In January 2005, Patricio Pena of Puerto Rico made a cigar 19 metres (62 feet) long. It took 9 kilograms (20 pounds) of tobacco and 100 leaves and is believed to be the world's longest cigar. That record was subsequently beaten several times by Jose Castelar Cairo, who was known to his fellow Cubans as 'Cueto'. In 2011, he rolled a monster cigar 81 metres (268 feet) long and in 2016 broke that record with an 87-metre (285-foot) cigar dedicated to Fidel Castro.

♀ PETER PAN, SMOKING, TOBACCO

CIGARETTE

The cigarette lighter was invented in 1823 by the German chemist Johann Wolfgang Döbereiner, which was three years before the British pharmacist John Walker invented the match.

♀ CHIMPANZEE, SMOKING

CINDERELLA

Part of the story of Cinderella dates back to an Egyptian legend of a girl named Rhodopis, who had one of her sandals snatched by an eagle. The bird flew away and dropped it in the lap of the

Pharaoh, who promptly sent soldiers to find the girl it belonged to so he could marry her.

The glass slippers in the modern version of the story were originally fur. The change came through confusion among translators between the medieval French vaire – 'fur' – and verre – 'glass'.

CINEMA

On 28 December 1895, the Lumière brothers held the first public screening of a motion picture to a paying audience, and the era of the cinema began. The programme featured 10 short films, starting with Workers Leaving the Lumière Factory and ending with Bathing in the Sea. Fishing for Goldfish was the fifth item shown. The word 'cinema' came from 'cinematograph', which was the word used for the device that made and projected the films.

The best year for UK cinema was 1946, when 1.64 billion tickets were sold. In 2019 it was 176 million.

On 16 September 1997, the state of Kelantan in Malaysia announced that lights would be kept on in cinemas in order to deter people from kissing and cuddling. 'If we can watch television at home with the lights on, then why not in cinemas?' a minister commented.

♀ ADVERTISEMENT, POPCORN

CIRCUMCISION

In 2018, a law was proposed in Iceland to ban male circumcision for non-medical reasons. The proposal was dropped in the face of considerable religious opposition.

In Israel, 97 per cent of Jewish male babies are circumcised. In the United States, the majority of male babies undergo circumcision, though from

1979 to 2010 the rate dropped from 64.5 per cent to 58.3 per cent.

Egyptian male mummies were all circumcised.

♀ *DIAGRAM*

CIRCUS

The history of the modern circus dates back to 9 January 1768, when Philip Astley performed a trick riding display in London.

The diameter of a traditional circus ring is 13 metres (42 feet), a distance fixed by Astley as the smallest around which a horse could gallop comfortably. Between horse-riding displays he brought in jugglers, acrobats and clowns, but he did not call his show a 'circus'. That term was coined by Astley's rival Charles Dibdin after the Roman circus of chariot races.

The patron saint of circus workers is St Julian the Hospitaller. According to legend, St Julian killed his own father and mother through a case of mistaken identity.

♀ *ALASKA, FLEAS, TURKMENISTAN*

CLEAVAGE

According to a survey by a cosmetic surgery company in 2010, four out of every 10 women admit that they are envious of a friend's cleavage and 46 per cent admit to having breast envy for a celebrity.

Other results from the survey:

14 per cent of men in Yorkshire wish their partners had bigger breasts.

51 per cent of UK women are unhappy with their breasts.

63 per cent of women want bigger breasts.

90 per cent of women check out other women's breasts at least seven times a day.

CLEOPATRA (69–30 BC)

The daughter of Ptolemy XII, the famous Egyptian queen was in fact Cleopatra VII. Very little is known of the first six Cleopatras. It has been suggested that Cleopatra VI was the mother of Cleopatra VII, though this may have been Cleopatra V, in which case Cleopatra VI would probably have been the elder sister of Cleopatra VII.

According to Plutarch, writing about Cleopatra VII early in the 2nd century AD: 'Her beauty was not of that incomparable kind which instantly captivates the beholder, but the charm of her presence was irresistible … it was delight merely to hear the sound of her voice.'

Plutarch also wrote of Cleopatra being smuggled one night into Julius Caesar's palace in a bedroll: 'It was by this device of Cleopatra's, it is said, that Caesar was first captivated, for she showed herself to be a bold coquette'.

A singer named Cleopatra represented Greece in the Eurovision Song Contest in 1992 and finished fifth.

♀ *BILLIARDS, CHEESE*

CLEVELAND, Grover (1837–1908)

Grover Cleveland is the only American president to have regained the presidency after being voted out of office. President from 1885 to 1889, he was defeated by Benjamin Harrison, but won again in 1893, thus becoming the 22nd and 24th President. That fact led to an error by Barack Obama in his inauguration speech in 2009. He stated that '44 Americans have now taken the presidential oath', but that was not so: the correct figure was 43, as two of the 44 Presidents from Washington to Obama were Grover Cleveland.

CLICK

In the !Xoo language of Botswana and Namibia, which is spoken by about 4,000 people, there are 112 distinct sounds (compared with about 40 in English).

About 70 per cent of words begin with one of 83 types of click, each of which is a variation on the five basic clicks in the !Xoo language.

⚲ MOTH

CLINTON, William Jefferson (b. 1946)

Clinton was born William Jefferson Blythe III. His biological father, William Jefferson Blythe Jr, was killed in a car accident three months before Clinton was born. His mother, Virginia Clinton Kelley, then married Roger Clinton, and Bill Clinton took his stepfather's surname.

William Jefferson Clinton and Richard Milhous Nixon are the only two presidents of the United States whose names contain all the letters needed to spell out the word 'criminal'.

⚲ LEWINSKY, SEXUAL HARASSMENT

CLITORIS

In 1559, the Italian anatomist Realdo Columbus (or Colombo) claimed to have discovered the clitoris. He was a lecturer in surgery at the University of Padua, and in that year published a book, *De Re Anatomica*, in which he described the 'seat of woman's delight'. He wrote that 'since no-one has discerned these projections and their workings, if it is permissible to give names to things discovered by me, it should be called the sweetness or love of Venus (*amor Veneris, vel dulcedo*).'

Columbus's successor at Padua was Gabriel Falloppio (Fallopius), who also claimed to have discovered the clitoris, but neither really deserves the credit as the ancient Greeks and Romans both knew about it. Hippocrates called it the *columella* (little column), Avicenna called it *albatra* or *virga* (rod), while Albucasis, an Arabic physician, called it *tentigo* (tension).

The word 'clitoris' first appeared in English in 1615 in a book by Helkiah Crooke called – inappropriately enough – *Mikrokosmographia: A Description of the Body of Man, Together With the Controversies and Figures Thereto Belonging*.

The derivation of the word, however, has never been clear. Some sources say it is from a Greek verb meaning 'to close', referring to the clitoris being obscured by the labia minora; some suggest a different verb meaning 'to touch or titillate lasciviously', while others say it is a diminutive of a word meaning a hill.

⚲ SLOTH

CLONE

The first dog to be cloned was born in South Korea on 24 April 2005 and was named Snuppy (from the initials of Seoul National University and the final letters of 'puppy'). He was created from a cell taken from the ear of an adult Afghan hound. Snuppy was named as *Time Magazine*'s 'Most Amazing Invention of 2005'.

In 2008, Snuppy also played his part in the birth of the first puppies from cloned parents when artificial insemination of his sperm in two female cloned dogs resulted in 10 puppies.

The team that produced Snuppy went on to create the world's first cloned sniffer dogs in 2007. The six dogs, all of whom were named 'Toppy' (short for

'Tomorrow's puppy'), started work for South Korea's customs service in 2009.

⚲ *BRAZIL, DOLLY, SNIFFING*

CLOONEY, George (b. 1961)

Actor George Clooney had a pet pot-bellied pig called Max, which he acquired some time around 1988. When Max died on 1 December 2006, Clooney commented, 'I was really surprised, because he's been a big part of my life.' He added that he had no plans to replace the pet. 'I think Max covered all my pig needs,' he said.

⚲ *IDES*

CLOWNS

Research at the University of Sheffield in 2008 reported the results of a survey on the decor preferred by children in hospital wards, which showed that all 250 patients, aged from four to 16, disliked the use of clowns. 'We found that clowns are universally disliked by children,' one of the researchers said.

Research in Israel published in the journal *PLoS One* in 2017, however, reported that 'clown-care reduces pain in children with cerebral palsy undergoing recurrent botulinum toxin injections', though they mention that 'one child requested that the clown remove his red nose'.

In Brazil's elections to Congress in 2010, the candidate who received most votes was Francisco Everardo Oliveira Silva, who was better known to the electorate by the name Tiririca, under which he performed as a clown.

He received more than twice as many votes as any other candidate in São Paulo state.

⚲ *CIRCUS*

COCKROACH

A cockroach can live for nine days without its head. In 1978, a paper entitled 'What does the headless cockroach remember?' was published in the journal *Animal Learning and Behaviour*, and included an account of an experiment in which a cockroach was decapitated and five of its legs removed, after which it was shown that the remaining leg could be trained to avoid electric shocks.

⚲ *OBAMA, HOPE*

COCOA

'Tea, although an oriental,
Is a gentleman at least.
Cocoa is a cad and bounder
Cocoa is a vulgar beast.'

G.K. Chesterton

It takes a cocoa tree five years to produce its first cocoa beans. The Ivory Coast produces more cocoa than any other country.

⚲ *CHOCOLATE, IVORY COAST, SLOANE*

COCONUT

'Coconut' comes from a Portuguese word 'coco', meaning a grinning face, or a witch with such a face.

More coconuts come from Indonesia than any other country. The next two countries in the coconut league are the Philippines and India.

According to the paper 'Injuries Due to Falling Coconuts' by Peter Barss in the *Journal of Trauma* in 1984, 'Falling coconuts can cause injury to the head, back, and shoulders', and an analysis of four years' admissions to a hospital in Papua New Guinea revealed that 2.5 per cent of injuries were due to the victims being struck by falling coconuts. Of four coconut-related case studies in his paper, two of the victims needed brain surgery. Two further cases were reported of falling coconuts causing instant death.

According to research published in 2001, 3.4 per cent of injuries requiring surgery in the Solomon Islands were coconut-palm related. Only 16 per cent of these were people hit by falling coconuts. The rest were people falling from trees.

The number of coconuts produced in the world every year is estimated to be 52 billion. The weight of coconuts produced in 2019 was around 62 million tonnes.

Coconut water contains most of the vitamins and minerals the body needs to sustain itself. You can therefore survive living only on coconuts. This must have been known in ancient times, since in Sanskrit, the coconut palm was called *kalpa vriksha* – the tree that provides all life's necessities.

When Barack Obama visited the Gandhi Museum in Mumbai, India, in 2010, security officials ordered that ripe coconuts be cut off the trees to prevent any accidental injury to the visitors. 'People do get hurt, or even killed, from falling coconuts. We had the ripe coconuts removed and some dried branches as well. Why take a chance?' an official explained.

On 23 April 2007, 5,567 people celebrated St George's Day in Trafalgar Square in London by setting a new record for the world's largest coconut orchestra. Led by Terry Jones and Terry Gilliam, they clip-clopped their coconut shells together in time to the Monty Python classic 'Always Look on the Bright Side of Life'. The previous record had been 1,789 coconut cloppers in New York the previous year.

📍 *MOUSTACHE, QUEENSLAND*

● COFFEE

Over 400 billion cups of coffee are drunk around the world every year, which means that the average person on Earth drinks about one cup of coffee every six days.

For many years, Kopi Luwak coffee from Indonesia had the reputation of being the world's most expensive, but it may recently have lost that title to a coffee from Brazil. Kopi Luwak is made from beans that have been eaten and excreted by the luak, or palm civet. The beans pass almost unchanged through the digestive system of the animal, and opinions differ on whether the unique flavour of the coffee is due to the civet's digestive juices or its ability to select the ripest beans.

The new drink on the scene is Jacu coffee, produced in a remarkably similar manner by the endangered jacu bird of South America. The jacu lives on coffee plantations and eats the ripest berries. Villagers collect the jacu's partially digested excrement and dry and clean it. The drink that results is said to have a clean, smooth taste with no bitterness. In 2021, it was available in London at £30 a cup.

In the late 15th century, Turkey took coffee very seriously, passing a law that made it possible for a woman to divorce her husband if he did not keep the coffee pot full.

It is said that coffee was introduced into Europe in 1683, when the Turkish army left sacks of coffee behind as they hurriedly retreated from the gates of Vienna.

Frederick the Great of Prussia took coffee made with champagne as a calming drink.

In 1920, the US National Coffee Roasters Association gave Professor

Samuel Cate Prescott $40,000 to research the perfect cup of coffee. His conclusion: one tablespoon of coffee per 225 grams (8 ounces) of water, just short of boiling, in glass or ceramic containers, never boiled, reheated, or reused.

Expenditure on coffee in Britain first overtook the amount spent on tea in 1998. Four years later, scientists discovered that sprinkling coffee grounds in the garden helps to deter snails and slugs.

♀ AMUSEMENT, FUEL, ITALY, MOSAIC, SUICIDE

COFFEE (decaffeinated)

Decaffeinated coffee was discovered by accident in 1903 when a batch of beans being delivered to German coffee importer Ludwig Roselius were found to have been spoiled by being accidentally soaked in seawater. Research showed that the beans had lost their caffeine content, and three years later Roselius patented the decaffeination process and launched Kaffee Handels-Aktiengesellschaft (Coffee Trading Company), commonly sold as Kaffee HAG.

COFFIN

Austrian carpenter Herbert Weber was presented with a certificate at the International Funeral Home and Cemetery Trade Fair in Salzburg in 2009 to mark his achievement in making 707,335 coffins over a 30-year career. Mr Weber claimed this to be a world record for coffin-making.

♀ BUTCHELL, GLADSTONE, PRAYER

COINS

The world's first coins were probably those minted in ancient Lydia (now western Turkey) around 700 BC.

One of the rarest British coins is the 1933 penny. Only six or seven were minted and three of them were buried under the foundation stones of buildings erected that year.

Decimal Day was 15 February 1971 in the UK. In 1983, the pound coin was introduced to replace the pound note. The £2 coin followed in 1986.

All of the 20p coins in circulation are worth more than all of the 50p coins.

The world's least valuable coin was probably the tiyin in Uzbekistan. About 2,000 were worth 1p when it ceased to be legal currency in 2000.

♀ EDWARD VIII, EURO, MONEY

COLOMBIA

The area of Colombia is 1.142 million square kilometres (440,930 square miles), which is identical to the areas of France, Spain and Austria combined.

The Kokoi frog, also known as the golden poison dart frog, is endemic to Colombia and is generally considered the most poisonous amphibian on the planet. One millionth of an ounce of its venom can kill a man.

Although best known as a producer of coffee and cocaine, Colombia is also the world's tenth biggest producer of bananas.

In 1996, the President of Colombia introduced a bill to make drunken walking illegal, and in 1998, officials in the capital, Bogota, introduced poetry reading on buses as a way to reduce stress levels.

There are 1,958 bird species to be seen in Colombia, which is more than any other country on Earth. Peru comes second with 1,832 bird species.

♀ HIPPOPOTAMUS, ROBBERY

COLON

In May 2011, the Benton Franklin Health District in Kennewick, Washington, reversed an earlier decision to endorse a colon cancer awareness campaign.

The reversal came after complaints about the campaign billboards, which posed the question 'What's Up Your Butt?'. The health authority accepted that this had been in bad taste.

⚲ *FREUD*

COLORADO

In 1992, the town of Avon, Colorado, held its first Bobfest for people named Bob. Bobs who go by the name 'Robert' were not allowed to participate. The event followed the building in 1991 of a new bridge over Eagle River in Avon. After a public contest, Avon Town Council voted to name the bridge 'Bob'.

The Bobfest was continued in 1993 and 1994, but in 1995 the series came to an end when its founder and organiser, Tom Britz, announced that he was tired of running it. 'I met one bad Bob,' he said, 'and it spoiled the bunch.'

In 1997, however, the event was held again with its name changed to BobSummerFest, which included activities like a Bob-BQ-cook-off and BobBall.

⚲ *PEANUT BUTTER*

COLT, Samuel (1814–62)

Samuel Colt, inventor of the first practical mass-produced revolver and founder of Colt's Patent Fire-Arms Manufacturing Company, died not in a gunfight but of gout.

His brother John killed a man who owed him money, not with a revolver but with an axe. He committed suicide on the day of his execution. Again, he didn't use a gun but stabbed himself through the heart.

⚲ *NIXON*

COLUMBUS, Christopher (1451–1506)

Christopher Columbus first reached the Americas on 12 October 1492. The date is celebrated as Columbus Day in the US on the second Monday in October.

Columbus is thought to have been born in Genoa in 1451 where he was known, in his native Ligurian dialect, as Cristòffa Cómbo. His father was a wool weaver who also owned a market cheese stand. Italians called him Cristoforo Colombo and the Spaniards called him Cristóbal Colón.

Like most educated people of his time, he knew the Earth was spherical but thought it was six parts land to one of water, as the Second Book of Esdras said: 'Upon the third day thou didst command that the waters should be gathered in the seventh part of the earth: six parts hast thou dried up.' That was why he underestimated the size of the Atlantic and thought it led to the east of India. Ancient Greeks knew the size of the Earth, but Columbus misunderstood their measurements. Until he died, he denied that he had found a new land, insisting that America was part of Asia.

He had two sons, one with his Portuguese wife, the other with his Spanish mistress.

Although Columbus had blonde hair in his youth, by the time he was 30, it had all turned white. He died in 1506 and was buried in Valladolid, Spain. His bones were moved to Seville in 1509, Cuba in 1795, and back to Seville in 1898.

His crew took smallpox, influenza and measles to the Americas, but brought back syphilis, which caused an epidemic in Barcelona in 1493.

AMERICA, CLITORIS, SYPHILIS

COMMON COLD

Research in the US has revealed that people are more likely to catch colds if they are undergoing stress that has lasted for a month or more, probably because stress generates a flow of steroid hormones that stifle the immune system.

Work-related stress, especially unemployment anxiety, made colds five times more likely, while stress in marriages or other relationships brought about a threefold increase. Money troubles in themselves seemed to have no effect on nasal infections.

Introverts were reported to be two and a half times more prone to colds than extraverts, while lack of sleep brought about a comparable increase in risk. Smokers were three times as likely to catch colds as non-smokers. On the other hand, the more 'social roles' people had, the less likely they were to catch a cold.

HANDSHAKING

COMMONWEALTH

The 54 member nations of the Commonwealth include 30 per cent of the world's population. Lesotho, Swaziland and Tonga are the only Commonwealth nations with their own king, but Brunei and Malaysia also have a king-like monarch. The smallest member of the Commonwealth is Tuvalu, with a population of 11,000.

The Commonwealth Games began as the Empire Games in 1930. They include netball, lawn bowls and rugby sevens, none of which are in the Olympics. The only teams to have competed at every Commonwealth Games are England, Scotland, Wales, New Zealand, Canada and Australia.

'It is easy enough to define what the Commonwealth is not. Indeed this is quite a popular pastime.' Queen Elizabeth II, speaking in 1977

ELIZABETH II

COMOROS

The Comoros island nation off the east coast of Africa supplies 80 per cent of the world's ylang-ylang, an oil obtained from tropical flowers. Ylang-ylang is a key ingredient of Chanel No.5 perfume and it takes 70,000 flowers to make 1 litre (34 fluid ounces) of the oil. Comoros gained independence in 1975, but has had around 35 changes of government through coups since then. In 2006, the Sunni Muslim cleric Ahmed Abdallah Sambi was elected President. He was a businessman who ran companies that produced perfumes and mattresses. During his presidency, he lived in a room above his premises, The House of Mattresses.

COMPACT DISC

It is said that the length of music that may be recorded on a standard CD was chosen to be 74 minutes, as that is just long enough to record a complete performance of Beethoven's Ninth Symphony. When Philips and Sony collaborated on developing CD technology, the prototype from Philips ran for 60 minutes, but it is said that Norio Ohga, the president of Sony, insisted that 60 minutes was too restrictive and it should be 74 minutes. Some accounts say this was because Ohga himself demanded that Beethoven's Ninth should be available on a single disc, others suggest that it was the favourite music of the wife of Sony chairman Akio Morita, while a third explanation is that the insistence came from Herbert von Karajan, conductor of the Berlin Philharmonic. None of these explanations has been confirmed officially.

COMPUTATION

A wolf bone found in France and dated back to the Paleolithic era around 30,000 BC shows 55 cuts arranged in groups of five, suggesting that we used our fingers for counting and possibly computation even then.

The Babylonians, in 3500 BC, had two separate number systems in use at the same time: a decimal system was used for everyday business, but sexadecimals (combining 60s and 10s) were used for complex mathematical and astronomical calculations. Dividing an hour into 60 minutes and a minute into 60 seconds have their origins in that system.

The ancient Romans, with their cumbersome system of letters such as M, D, C, X, L, V and I for numbers, put back calculation for centuries, though they had a good repertoire of calculational tricks to make things a little easier. They also developed a counting board, which could be seen as the first calculating machine and a precursor of the abacus. By the end of the 12th century, two-tone abacuses were seen, with black beads for positive numbers and red for negative – the origins of the modern bank statement and the expression 'in the red'.

Pythagoras believed that three was the first proper number, since it had a beginning, middle and end, unlike one and two. Some 2,000 years later, the Yancos tribe of the Amazon in Brazil were reported to stop their counting system at three, the word for which in their language was reported to be *poettarrarorincoaroac*.

Their near neighbours, the Pirahã people in Brazil, were found to have no words for precise numbers, even one and two. Words previously thought to mean 'one', 'two' and 'many', were found to mean 'few', 'some' and 'more'. Similarly, the Vedda, from the forests of old Ceylon, have been reported to have had no numbers at all in their language, while in 1972 a tribe of cave dwellers in the Philippines were found to be unable to count.

COMPUTERS

The origins of the modern computer may be traced back to Charles Babbage, a Cambridge mathematician who was the first to produce a blueprint for a calculating machine. In 1823, the Chancellor of the Exchequer personally agreed a grant of £1,500 from the Civil Contingencies Fund to support Babbage's Difference Engine, which would calculate mathematical tables. By 1842, it had cost £17,000 of public money and the project was abandoned, still incomplete. Babbage spent his final years an embittered man, with a particular grudge against organ-grinders, whom he blamed for wrecking a quarter of his entire working life through their audible nuisances.

If Babbage was the father of computing, its midwife was Ada Byron, Countess of Lovelace. A fearless horsewoman, mathematician and daughter of the sixth Baron Byron, she worked with Babbage and made notes on the potential of his machine. They were the first to introduce the concept of programmed calculation.

The first real computer bug, and the one that gave computer bugs their name, was a moth trapped in an early computer used by Grace Hopper at Harvard on 9 September 1947.

In 1996, the Japanese company Matsushita launched the first laptop computer built to survive coffee being spilled on its keyboard.

In 2011, Canada, the Netherlands and Switzerland were reported to be the only countries with more computers than people. There are currently over 2 billion personal computers in the world.

⚲ BABBAGE, BYRON Ada, TALIBAN

● CONCRETE

The Concrete Society makes annual awards for excellence in the use of concrete in the UK and Ireland. Projects deemed worthy of a Certificate of Commendation receive an A4 certificate; those deserving of a Certificate of Excellence get an A3 certificate; winners in each category receive a concrete plaque, while the overall winner receives a gold-concrete plaque. Glyndebourne Opera House in Sussex has an A4 certificate 'for outstanding excellence in the use of concrete'.

The theme of the Cement and Concrete Science Conference in 2019 was 'Innovation in Focus', while in 2018 the conference announced that topics to be covered would include 'hydration and microstructure of cement, alternative cementitious materials, low carbon cement, structural performance of concrete materials and sustainability'.

⚲ DIAGRAM, HULK, LINCOLN

● CONDOM

In 1995, the authorities in the Philippines threatened to ban fruit-flavoured condoms. A spokesman for the Bureau of Food and Drugs announced this decision, explaining: 'You only put a flavour in when it is something to eat.'

The musical condom, invented by Ferenc Kovacs, was launched in Hungary on 17 June 1996. While being unrolled, it played a tune, with users able to choose from a selection including a communist song, 'Arise Ye Worker'.

In 2012, The Original Condom Company was fined 10,000 euros for advertising its condoms as having come from the town of Condom on the River Baïse in south-west France, when in fact they were made in Malaysia.

The origin of the name 'condom' is unknown, but it was probably not named after the town of Condom. Many have claimed that it is named after a Dr Condom who publicised them, but no one has ever identified a doctor of that name who may have been responsible for it.

One of the earliest uses of the word, spelt as 'condon', was in a 1708 poem entitled 'Almonds for Parrots', with the subtitle 'A Soft Answer to a Scurrilous Satyr, call'd, St. James's Park. With a Word or two in Praise of Condons'. The last three and a half pages of the poem, which largely praises homosexuality, are devoted to condoms.

⚲ CASANOVA, NEW ZEALAND

● CONDUCTORS

The only confirmed fatal case of conducting happened to the French composer/conductor Jean-Baptiste Lully, who died in 1687 after stabbing himself in the foot with his conducting staff. The wound turned gangrenous and it killed him. He refused to have his leg amputated as this would stop him dancing. Despite this unfortunate incident, it was not until the 19th century that the baton became the favoured implement for conducting.

CONGO

The Republic of the Congo, formerly the French Congo, should not be confused with the Democratic Republic of the Congo, which used to be the Belgian Congo. The Republic of the Congo, often referred to as Congo-Brazzaville, is the only country where bonobo apes can be found in the wild.

The Congo River is the deepest river in the world.

CONNECTICUT

In 2007, a woman in Connecticut was charged with fourth-degree sexual assault and given two years' probation for groping Santa Claus in a shopping mall.

 FRISBEE, PYTHON

CONSENT

In England in 1576, 10-year-olds were allowed to marry. This is the lowest the age of consent has ever been in Britain.

It soon rose to 12, then in 1875 rose from 12 to 13; in 1885 it went up from 13 to 16, where it has stayed ever since. The current age of consent for sexual activity between a man and a woman varies around the world, from 12 in Mexico to 21 in Bahrain and Cameroon.

Vatican City is the only country in Europe in which sex outside marriage is banned. It is also banned in several Asian countries; the only other countries that ban it are Libya and Sudan.

CONSERVATIVE PARTY

The UK Conservative Party are also known as the Tories, a word that comes from the Irish *tóraidhe*, meaning a highwayman or brigand. It was adopted in the late 1670s as an abusive nickname for supporters of James, Duke of York, who later became James II.

Between 1809 and 1997, there were 22 Tory leaders, of whom only one did not become Prime Minister. He was Austen Chamberlain, who went on to win a Nobel Peace Prize.

Between 1997 and 2007, there were three Conservative leaders, none of whom either became Prime Minister or won a Nobel Prize.

'I never meant to say that the Conservatives are generally stupid. I meant to say that stupid people are generally Conservative. I believe that is so obviously and universally admitted a principle that I hardly think any gentleman will deny it.'
John Stuart Mill, 1866

CONTRACEPTION

Research at Duke University, California, in 2010 showed that male lemurs do not like the smell of female lemurs that have been injected with hormonal contraceptives. Previous research had already shown that males use scent cues to avoid mating with near relatives. Analysis of their odours now showed that females on contraceptives emit different chemicals, and that males are less interested in investigating the smells of contracepted females. 'The genital secretions of lemurs are extremely complex,' one researcher said.

 GERBIL, HIPPOPOTAMUS, LAUNDRY

COOK, Thomas (1808–92)

Thanks to the success of the trips to the Middle East organised by Thomas Cook and Son in the 1890s, John Mason Cook (Thomas Cook's son) was described as 'the second greatest man in Egypt [behind the country's ruler Tewfik Pasha]'.

TOURISM

COOLIDGE, (John) Calvin (1872–1933)

US President Coolidge was renowned for being a man of few words. His wife, Grace Goodhue Coolidge, once recounted that a young woman sitting next to Coolidge at a dinner party told him she had bet she could get at least three words of conversation from him. Without looking at her, he replied, 'You lose.'

When Dorothy Parker was informed in 1933 that Coolidge had died, she replied, 'How can they tell?'

INDEPENDENCE DAY

COPENHAGEN

Copenhagen's Strøget claims to be the longest pedestrian-only street in Europe. In 1967, for Denmark's 800th anniversary, Strøget was the scene of the world's longest coffee table.

In 2008, Copenhagen became the first city to be awarded the 'Bike City' label by the International Cycling Union.

MERMAID, STRIKE

COPERNICUS, Nicolaus (1473–1543)

After he died in 1543, Nicolaus Copernicus – the man who was first to put the Sun at the centre of the Solar System – was buried in Frombork Cathedral in Poland. The location of the grave remained lost for over 450 years

and his skull was only found and finally identified in November 2008.

COPYRIGHT

The word 'uncopyrightable' is one of the two longest English words that consist entirely of different letters. It shares first place with the less common 'dermatoglyphics', which means the study of fingerprints and similar ridge patterns on skin.

BIRTHDAY, TOILET PAPER

CORK

Cork is extracted from the bark of trees. Almost half the world's cork comes from Portugal. Around 60 per cent of all cork production is used to make stoppers for bottles. If all the corks from all the wine bottled in France in a year were laid end to end, they would go round the world three times.

Although the word 'cork' was first used for a bottle-stopper in 1530, the first mention of a corkscrew did not appear until 1720.

MOSAIC, PORTUGAL, TINS

CORNFLAKES

John Harvey Kellogg created the breakfast cereal known as cornflakes in 1894 for patients at the Battle Creek Sanitarium in Michigan where his brother Will Kellogg also worked. Cornflakes are said to have been conceived as therapy for mental patients at the sanitarium and as a means of curbing their sex drive. Originally, the flakes were made of toasted wheat rather than corn and known as 'Granose', but their 2895 patent for 'Flaked Cereals and Process of Preparing Same' left open the prospect of using other grains for the flakes. In 1906, Will Kellogg, who was the business manager at the sanitarium, decided to mass-market the product made of corn, and the Battle Creek Toasted Corn Flake Company was born. In 1928, the company brought another product to the breakfast food market: Rice Krispies.

A cornflake the shape of Illinois was sold on eBay in 2008 for $1,350. At first eBay rejected the item as it conflicted with their food policy, but the sellers changed it to a coupon redeemable for the cornflake.

CORONATION

Edward V (abducted) and Edward VIII (abdicated) were the only English monarchs who never had coronations. Coronation chicken was first made for the coronation of Elizabeth II.

'Coronation, n. The ceremony of investing a sovereign with the outward and visible signs of his divine right to be blown skyhigh with a dynamite bomb.' Ambrose Bierce, The Devil's Dictionary, *1906*

ϙ *EDWARD VII, GEORGE IV*

CORTÉS, Hernán Ferdinand (1485–1547)

In the 400 years after the death of Hernán Cortés, conqueror of the Aztecs, his bones were moved at least eight times, sometimes because the burial space was required for other purposes, sometimes to prevent desecration.

In 1836, they were moved to a secret location which was not revealed until 1843, when a secret burial act was filed with the Spanish Embassy in Mexico City. The act was considered a classified document and was guarded in the embassy's safe until it was finally revealed in 1946.

ϙ *CHOCOLATE, MONTEZUMA II*

COSMETICS

Isabeau of Bavaria became Queen of France on marrying Charles VI at the age of 15 or 16 in 1385. She bathed in milk and liked to paint her face with a concoction made of boar's brains, wolf's blood and crocodile glands.

In the Middle Ages, Japanese women painted their teeth black to look more beautiful.

The first martyr to modern cosmetics may have been the Irish beauty and London society hostess born Maria Gunning, who became Countess of Coventry on her marriage to the 6th Earl of Coventry in 1752. She died on 30 September 1760 from lead poisoning as a result of painting her face with white lead.

ϙ *CLEAVAGE, NOSE-PICKING, URINATION*

COSTA RICA

In 2021, the government of Costa Rica named the sloth, both two-toed and three-toed species, as their national animal and unanimously approved a project to declare sloths a national symbol.

The first World Conference of People in Contact with Extraterrestrials was held in July 1995 at Miramar de Puntarenas in Costa Rica. Delegates from 10 countries linked hands to form five concentric circles around three fires and chanted, hoping that their focused energy would attract extraterrestrials. After about 40 minutes, it poured with rain, which the organisers said was 'a sign from heaven'. Later it was claimed that four spaceships had appeared nearby, but most of the delegates did not see them or any extraterrestrial visitors.

Since 1987, all the baseballs used in the American major league have been made in a factory in the town of Turrialba in Costa Rica. The factory makes 2 million baseballs a year, each of which takes 15 minutes to hand-stitch.

SCORPION, SLOTH

COUCH POTATO

In 1976, Tom Iacino of Pasadena, California, coined the term 'couch potato' for a lazy TV-watcher. Previously they had been called 'boob tubers' after the TV tube. A potato is a tuber, hence the new name.

A couch potato's wife is called a 'couch tomato'.

COVID-19

'Coronavirus' is an anagram of 'carnivorous'. 'Omicron', the name given to a variant identified in 2021, is an anagram of 'moronic'.

By a remarkable coincidence, according to the *Oxford English Dictionary*, 2022 was the centenary of the interjection 'ohmigosh', which the dictionary said expressed 'excitement, surprise, dismay, fear, etc'. That's a century taken to move from ohmigosh to omicron, which one might also hold responsible for causing dismay, fear, etc.

In December 2021, it was reported that a man in Italy who held strong anti-vaccination views but wanted a vaccination certificate, wore a fake arm during a visit to health workers. The colour was realistic, but the silicone fooled no one.

One positive result of the Covid pandemic was reported in October 2021 by the National Zoo in Cuba where an unusually large number of baby animals had been born, especially of exotic and endangered species. Keepers attributed the increase in successful breeding to animals taking advantage of the peace and quiet brought about by low visitor numbers.

AMAZING, CRIME

COW

In Paris in 1740, a cow was hanged in public following its conviction for sorcery.

In Somerset in 1841, 737 cows were milked in order to make a 2.75-metre (9-foot) diameter cheese for Queen Victoria.

Under the Metropolitan Streets Act of 1867, cows may not be driven down a British roadway between 10am and 7pm unless there is prior approval from the commissioner of police.

In Switzerland in 1983, a Czechoslovakian was refused Swiss citizenship because his dislike of cowbells was taken as a sign that he had not assimilated successfully, despite having lived in the country for 14 years.

In 2008, a man from Pennsylvania who mailed a severed cow's head to his wife's lover was sentenced to probation and community service. The man's lawyer agreed that his client 'did step over the line' but said that he now 'understands that in a civilized society a person cannot send a severed cow's head to anybody'.

Research has shown that if you burst a paper bag near the ear of a Jersey cow, its milk flow will be interrupted for about 30 minutes. However, according to a British study published in 2009, cows with names such as Daisy, Gertrude or Buttercup produce more milk than their sisters with no names.

In Spain, experiments have shown that milk production can be improved by up to 60 per cent by fitting the cows with steel dentures, and research in Argentina in 2014 showed that fitting cows with dentures can increase the number of calves they produce and improve their overall longevity.

New Zealand scientists in 2021 showed that cows can be potty trained to urinate in a special pen known as a MooLoo. Furthermore, they pointed out that it took only 15 days to train the young calves, whereas many toddlers take much longer.

In Moscow circuses, cows have been trained to play football.

According to the *Oxford English Dictionary*, to 'leep' means to wash with cow-dung and water.

Cattle can be identified by their nose-prints.

A group of 12 or more cows is called a flink.

♀ *ANDORRA, HERACLEITUS, METHANE, NEPAL, SWEDEN*

CRAB

Launce's dog Crab, in *The Two Gentlemen of Verona*, is the only dog required to appear on stage in plays by Shakespeare. Launce describes the animal as 'the sourest-natured dog that lives'.

The crab peeler was patented by Harry M. Martin Sr in 1980.

'You will never make the crab walk straight,' Aristophanes, Peace, 422 BC

♀ *CRUSTACEAN, SEAL, TAIWAN*

CRANE

A derrick now means a type of crane, but its original meaning was a scaffold or gallows after the London hangman Thomas Derrick, who lived around 1600.

Derrick had himself been convicted of rape, but was pardoned by the Earl of Essex, on condition that he took the job of executioner at Tyburn. Among the more than 3,000 people he hanged in his subsequent career was the Earl of Essex himself.

Derrick's name was first used for a beam with pulley structure he invented to lift and support the hangman's noose, but was later adapted to refer to modern cranes.

♀ *ALASKA, BEETHOVEN*

CRASH TEST DUMMY

The first moose crash test dummy was designed by Magnus Gens of Sweden in a Master's thesis project begun in 1994 and published under the title 'Moose Crash Test Dummy' by the Swedish National Road and Transport Research Institute. He points out that 'In Sweden more than 13 moose collisions occur daily', but also mentions that in Australia kangaroo accidents are more common.

His dummy comprised four long legs, with a body and head made of rubber plates, all with roughly the same weight, shape and centre of gravity as a moose, to enable cars to be driven into it to simulate moose collisions.

Work began in Sweden in 2006 on developing the first female dummy for use in car safety tests. Until then, all crash test dummies had been based on how men's bodies react in collisions and other accidents. 'For neck injuries from rear-end collisions, or whiplash, the risk for women is twice as high as for men,' the National Road and Transport Research Institute said in a statement. In 1996, however, there had in fact been a US patent (number 5528943) issued for a 'Female crash test dummy having fetal insert' which was a crash test dummy with an abdominal cavity into which a crash test foetus could be placed to simulate pregnancy.

CREATION

According to Dr John Lightfoot of Cambridge University, writing in 1644, the world was created at 9am on Sunday 12 September 3928 BC. The date was recalculated in 1650 by the Archbishop of Armagh, James Ussher, who arrived at the date of 23 October 4004 BC. Both men agreed that the Creation took place on the day of the autumn equinox, which is in October, but Lightfoot had utilised information about the calendars in use at the time and incorporated the discrepancies between the Julian and Gregorian Calendars to give a September date.

Ussher's date was generally preferred because Ussher knew that King Herod had died in 4 BC, but had been alive when Christ was born. That placed the year of Christ's birth as 4 BC at the latest, and this made 4004 BC a convenient date for the Creation as it gave the millennially convenient period of precisely 4,000 years from the Creation that Christ was born. Ussher's calculation had been based on a combination of known dates and biblical references to produce the exact figure of 4,000 years from the Creation to Christ.

⚲ *TWENTY-TWO, VATICAN*

CREDIT CARDS

An unusual benefit of having credit cards was discovered in the city of Witten, Germany, in 2011 when a man who had been thrown out of a pub responded by stabbing the doorman in the chest four times. The doorman was saved from serious injury by the 20 plastic cards in the wallet in his inside pocket which stopped the blade piercing his body.

CREMATION

The first official cremation in Britain took place on 26 March 1885 at the newly built crematorium in Woking. The deceased was Jeanette Caroline Pickersgill of St John's Wood, who was described as a well-known person in literary and scientific circles, who had expressly asked to be cremated in her will. Cremation, however, remained a grey area under British law until the Cremation Act was passed in 1902.

There is one cremation every seven seconds in China.

⚲ *SRI LANKA*

CRESS

Around 14 grams (½ ounce) of cress boiled down will produce enough cyanide to kill a mouse.

⚲ *PARAPSYCHOLOGY, RYDER CUP*

CRICKET

For many years, the death in 1751 of the Prince of Wales was believed to have been caused by a blow from a cricket ball or possibly a real tennis ball. Modern opinion, however, tends to exonerate cricket and diagnoses a pulmonary embolism as the more likely cause of the death of Frederick Louis, who was the eldest son of George II and father of George III.

Another cricket-related fatality occurred in 1796 when an umpire in Pakistan was beaten to death with the stumps by fielders disputing his decisions.

Meanwhile, in Britain in the same year, at the Montpelier Tea Gardens in Walworth, a crowd of some 5,000 spectators saw a team of one-legged cricketers with wooden legs defeat a team of one-armed players by 103 runs. As one report put it, 'it soon became apparent that the timber-toes were the stronger team'.

The most auspicious date in cricket history is probably 11 June: on that day in 1907, Nottinghamshire were bowled out for 12, the lowest ever score in the County Championship; on 11 June 1952, Denis Compton made his 100th first-class century; on 11 June 1953, Len Hutton became the first professional cricketer to captain England.

You can calculate the temperature in degrees Fahrenheit by timing the chirps of an insect known as the temperature cricket:

$$F = C + 40$$

(where F is the temperature and C is the number of chirps in 15 seconds).

This is known as Dolbear's Law, formulated by the American physicist Amos Emerson Dolbear and published in 1897 in an article called 'The Cricket as a Thermometer'.

⚲ *DOYLE, FROG, FULHAM, NO BALLS, OLYMPIC GAMES, SPITTING.*

● CRIME

One in 136 people in the American population is in prison. This is the world's highest rate of prisoners, just ahead of Russia where one in 163 of the people are in jail. In Britain, the figure is one in 694.

In 2001, an Arizona woman was arrested after she phoned 'Guns For Hire' and asked if they could kill her husband. The company, which stages fights for films, gave her details to the police.

The number of crimes recorded by the police in England and Wales in 2019–20 was 6.08 million, but it dropped to 5.44 million in 2020–21. The decrease was attributed to the Covid-19 lockdown.

In January 2002, the website Convicts Reunited was started to help ex-jailbirds contact former cellmates.

According to a recent study, male scientists and criminals have similar career patterns: both achieve their best results before they get married. A study in 2018 also concluded that the three occupations with the most psychopaths are CEO, lawyer and media personality.

⚲ *BRANDING, CAPITAL PUNISHMENT, KOALA, MENSTRUATION, PIG*

● CRIPPEN, Dr Hawley Harvey (1862–1910)

Dr Hawley Harvey Crippen, who went down in history as the first criminal to be caught through the aid of wireless communication, was hanged for the murder of his wife on 23 November 1910.

The hangman was John Ellis, who committed suicide by cutting his own throat in 1932. He was said never to have recovered from the ordeal of executing Edith Thompson in 1923.

⚲ *EARTHQUAKE*

● CRISPS

What the British call crisps and the Americans call potato chips came into existence in the 1850s thanks to the combination of an irritable chef and a fussy diner. It happened at Moon's Lake House in Saratoga Springs, New York, where the chef was George Crum and the diner was probably business and shipping magnate Commodore Cornelius Vanderbilt.

The story goes that one evening, probably in 1853, a diner complained repeatedly that his French fries were not sliced thinly enough. Chef Crum became so annoyed that he sliced them as thinly as possible and fried them to a crisp. His intention had been to heap scorn on the diner but instead he found he had invented a delicious way of cooking potatoes. Soon after, Crum opened his own restaurant serving a bowl of 'potato crunches', as he called them, to each table. They became a favourite of diners and under the name 'Saratoga chips' spread throughout America.

George Crum may have invented potato crisps, but their success was secured by Laura Clough Scudder when in 1926 she started selling them in individual portions in sealed, waxed paper bags.

The world's largest bag of potato chips weighed 1,141 kilograms (2,515 pounds 7.59 ounces) and was made by Corkers Crisps (UK) in Pymoor, Cambridgeshire, on 13 September 2013.

Annual UK spending on crisps surpassed the billion-pound mark for the first time in 2021. For the 52 weeks ending 21 March 2021, approximately £1.2 billion worth of crisps were sold in Britain.

The world's largest collection of empty crisp packets went on display at the Hamaland Museum in Vreden, north-west Germany, in April 2008. They belonged to local resident Bernd Sikora and contained 1,428 different packets from 43 countries. The exhibition was entitled 'Snap! Towards the cultural history of a snack'. According to a report in 2020, this number has been greatly exceeded by Gary Key of East Yorkshire, but many of his 14,200 empty crisp packets are duplicates as he saved every packet his family ate.

PRINGLES, TELEVISION

CROATIA

The history of ties dates back to 17th-century Croatian soldiers who wore colourful scarves around their necks. When the fashion for such knotted neckwear reached Paris, the style became known as *à la Croate*, from which the word 'cravat' derived.

In 1936, King Edward VIII (before he abdicated) and Mrs Simpson obtained official permission to go bathing in the nude on the island of Rab in Croatia. To this day, a sizeable proportion of tourists to Croatia (some put the figure as high as 15 per cent) are nudists.

If you order the names of all the world's capital cities alphabetically, Croatia's capital, Zagreb, comes last.

ALEXANDRA, EDWARD VIII, TENNIS, TIES

CROCODILE

Crocodile wrestling was banned by Israel's Supreme Court on 23 June 1993. Alligator wrestling is also banned.

Artemidorus, the ancient Roman grammarian who lived around the 1st century BC, is said to have lost his wits when startled by a crocodile. As the early 17th-century clergyman and travel writer Edward Topsell wrote: 'It is reported that the famous Grammarian *Artemidorus* seeing a Crocodile lying upon the sands, he was so much touched and moved therewith, that he fell into an opinion that his left leg and hand were eaten off by that Serpent, and that thereby he lost the remembrance of all his great learning and knowledge of Arts.'

Despite such an example, it was not until July 1996 that the authorities in Queensland published their Workplace Health and Safety Guide, which included a warning not to 'place any part of one's body in the mouth of a crocodile'.

In 2008, an Australian farmhand was snatched by the arm by a crocodile while he was collecting crocodile eggs. He was rescued by a colleague who shot at the crocodile. Unfortunately, one of his shots hit the other man in the arm by accident. A police spokesman said the man's injuries were not life-threatening. 'He's going to be very sick and sorry and have a very good story to tell,' he said, adding that he had no information on the condition of the crocodile.

AQUARIUM, FRECKLES, REPTILES

CROSS-BREEDING

The mayor of a town in Kenya in 2004 ordered more than 500 pigs to be shot for mating with stray dogs. The Mayor of Nyahururu said the order was to prevent the outbreak of disease, but the pigs' owners protested that it was the result of collusion between the authorities and bacon traders to cut competition.

ZEBRA

CROSSWORD

The world's first crossword puzzle appeared in the *New York World* newspaper on 21 December 1913. It was composed by a journalist named Arthur Wynne, who had been born in Liverpool, England.

The original name for the puzzle was 'Word-Cross', but a typesetting error changed it to Cross-Word a few weeks later and the new name stuck.

The *Sunday Express* published the first crossword in a British newspaper in 1924.

The earliest recorded use of 'crossword' spelt as one word without a hyphen was in 1927.

In 1926, a Budapest coffee-house waiter left a crossword puzzle as a suicide note, saying that the answers gave his reasons for killing himself.

Crosswords were banned in Paris during the Second World War, to stop them being used by spies as a means of passing information.

A crossword-lover is known as a cruciverbalist. The study of crosswords is cruciverbalism.

Ambrose Bierce in his *Devil's Dictionary* (1906) defined egotism as: 'Doing the *New York Times* crossword puzzle with a pen.'

CRUSTACEAN

An annual 'Miss Crustacean' beauty pageant has been held in Ocean City, New Jersey, every year since 1976. Described as a 'symbol of crustacean comeliness', the Cucumber Rind Cup for decorated hermit crabs has been won by crabs with names such as Copa Crabana, Crabunzel, Santa Crab and Crabopatra. No painting is permitted on the crabs' shells.

Asked in 1996 to account for the longevity and success of the event, a spokesman for Ocean City said, 'This makes no sense, has no redeeming social value and offers no prize money.'

The beauty pageant is followed by the annual Hermit Crab Races, with the speediest crustaceans competing for the King of Klutz Award.

CUBA

Cuba is the largest island in the Caribbean. It was inhabited by the Taino (also known as Arawak) people before Columbus arrived in 1492. He claimed the island for Spain and named it Isla Juana after Juan, Prince of Asturias. The first Spanish settlement was set up in 1511, and by 1529 most of the native people had died from smallpox or measles brought by the Spanish.

The name of Cuba is thought to have come from a native language; however, nobody is sure exactly what it meant.

Christmas did not become an official holiday in Cuba until 1997, just in time for Pope John Paul II's visit to the island in 1998.

Government vehicles in Cuba are legally obliged to pick up hitch-hikers if passenger space is available.

When Fidel Castro took control in Cuba in 1959, he banned the game of Monopoly and ordered all sets to be destroyed. The tennis player John McEnroe was born on the day Fidel Castro seized power in Cuba.

The national bird is the brightly coloured Cuban trogon or tocororo. Its red, white and blue plumage mimics the colours of the Cuban flag.

Snow is only recorded to have fallen once in Cuba, on 12 March 1857.

֍ *COVID-19, HEALTH, LAMARR*

⬤ CUCUMBER

Cucumbers are mentioned only twice in the King James Bible, in Numbers 11:5 and Isaiah 1:8. The first of these verses also mentions melons, leeks, onions and 'garlick', in each case being the only reference to those foodstuffs in the Bible. There is also one mention of cucumbers in the Apocrypha in the Letter of Jeremiah 1:69, which tells us: 'For as a scarecrow in a garden of cucumbers keepeth nothing: so are their gods of wood, and laid over with silver and gold.'

The cucumber originated in Asia, spread to Europe, and was brought to the Americas by Columbus in 1494. The ancient Egyptians, however, enjoyed a drink made from fermented cucumbers. The Roman emperor Tiberius also enjoyed cucumbers, which he grew in carts that his slaves could wheel around so that the vegetables could catch the sun.

Cucumbers are about 95 per cent water. The skin is the most nutritious part.

The inside of a cucumber can be as much as 11°C (20°F) cooler than the outside temperature.

The word for 'cucumber shaped' is 'cucumiform', not to be confused with 'cuculliform', which means 'hood shaped'.

In September 1997, researchers threw 500 cucumbers into the Irish Sea to find out whether tidal currents were responsible for sheep droppings being washed up on English beaches. The cucumbers were painted five different colours for identification purposes. Cucumbers were selected for their hydrodynamic similarity to sheep droppings.

The world's longest cucumber was grown by Kathy Ffoulkes of Western Australia in 2020. It was 136 centimetres (53.5 inches) long. In 1998, Professor Dr S. Ramesh Babu set a vegetable cutting record by slicing a 28-centimetre (11-inch) cucumber into 120,060 pieces in 2 hours 52 minutes and 21 seconds.

In the 18th century, tailors used to refer to the summer months as 'cucumber-time', when cucumbers were in season and trade was slack.

In October 2021, there were 64 people in the US phone book with the surname Cucumber.

'A cucumber should be well-sliced, and dressed with pepper and vinegar, and then thrown out as good for nothing.'
Samuel Johnson, 1773

֍ *CRUSTACEAN, MARY I*

⬤ CUFFLINKS

In 2010, police in Leigh-on-Sea, Essex, asked the public to help in their search for a one-armed man who had stolen a single cufflink, in the shape of a boxing glove, from a jeweller. The gold cufflink was valued at £120 and had been taken by the man after he knocked over a tray of them. An assistant at the shop said, 'It wasn't until we watched the CCTV we saw he had an empty sleeve in his pocket.' A police spokesman said, 'A man fitting the same description was acting suspiciously in other shops, so jewellers in the area have been alerted. We hope members of the public will help us identify the man.'

A one-armed man was later charged.

⚲ *BOUNTY*

● CUPCAKE

Patrick Bertoletti set a world record in 2012 at the Isle Waterloo World Cupcake Eating Championship by eating 72 cupcakes in six minutes.

Other records recognised by the International Federation of Competitive Eating include deep-fried asparagus spears (5.69 kilograms/12 pounds 8.75 ounces in 10 minutes), boneless buffalo wings (4 kilograms/9 pounds in 10 minutes) and pickled jalapeno chillis (275 in eight minutes).

The Transportation Security Administration (TSA) in the US announced in December 2011 that it was reviewing the situation regarding cupcakes on aeroplanes after a woman had her cupcakes confiscated by a security officer at Las Vegas airport. The woman said that the officer claimed that the frosting on the top of the cupcake was sufficiently gel-like to violate TSA policy. A TSA spokesman, however, said that passengers are allowed to take cakes and cupcakes through checkpoints.

● CURRY

The word 'curry' comes from a Tamil word *karil*, meaning spices or sauteed vegetables. Portuguese traders used it in error for sauces served with rice, and the British army further changed the meaning. So curry, as we now know it, may be considered a British invention.

In 2008, Bath and North East Somerset Council in the west of England advised a man to sprinkle curry powder on his wife's grave to keep squirrels and deer away. The town of North Curry is in Somerset, but West Curry is in Cornwall.

There are more curry houses in London than in Mumbai. The first curry house in England was opened by Sake Dean Mahomet in 1810. It was not a success.

'Playwrights are like men who have been dining for a month in an Indian restaurant. After eating curry night after night, they deny the existence of asparagus.' Peter Ustinov

⚲ *KEATS, SPAGHETTI*

● CURTIS, Jamie Lee (b. 1958)

Jamie Lee Curtis is the daughter of actors Tony Curtis and Janet Leigh, and the godmother of actor Jake Gyllenhaal. Her godson and both her parents received Oscar nominations, which she has never done.

In both the 1994 film *True Lies* and the 2001 film *The Tailor of Panama*, Jamie Lee Curtis plays a character married to a man named Harry whom she doesn't know is a spy.

Jamie Lee Curtis was once engaged to a grandson of Marlene Dietrich. In 1996, she became Baroness Haden-Guest when her husband, Christopher

Guest, whom she had married in 1984, succeeded to the title of Baron Guest.

CUSTARD PIES

The World Custard Pie Championships have been held for more than 50 years, usually at Maidstone, Kent. Over 2,000 pies were thrown at the 2019 championship, with a team called The Minions beating I Love Marshmallows in the final. Some 30 teams took part, with names including French Tarts and Custard Spies. The 2020 event was cancelled because of Covid, but the event returned in 2021 and was won by a team called EF Girls, who beat Epic Dodgers in the final by 47 points to 27.

The rules specify four players to a team, who throw pies at their opponents. Six points are awarded for a pie in the face; three points from the shoulder up; and one point for any other part of the body. A player who misses three times has points deducted. Pies must be thrown left-handed at the opposing team, who stand 2.5 metres (8 feet) away.

The first event in the series was held in 1967 to raise funds to build a village hall. As the organisers pointed out, at the time the British ate 14,000 tons of custard a year.

⚲ *PIES*

CYBERSPACE

The first wedding in Cyberspace took place on St Valentine's Day in 1996. Joseph Perling, online at Venice Beach, California, married Victoria Vaughn, taking her vows at home in Hollywood, California, in a ceremony performed by the groom's father, the Reverend R. John Perling, from his church in Beverly Hills, California. Family and friends logged on as virtual guests.

According to the *Oxford English Dictionary*, the word 'cyberspace', meaning the world of virtual or electronic reality, was first used in 1982. In 1989, the name Cyberia was coined with the same meaning, but it does not seem to have caught on.

CYCLING

The only sport that causes more injuries than cycling in the US is basketball. Third to sixth places in the sports injuries league are taken by tennis, hiking, bowling and fishing.

⚲ *FISHING, MARCO POLO, VIOLIN*

CYPRUS

According to tradition, the Archbishop of Cyprus is the only person on the island allowed to write in purple ink. Since the 5th century, he has had the privilege of being allowed to sign his name on official documents in ink of imperial purple.

CZECH REPUBLIC

In November 2010, the Transport Minister of the Czech Republic was banned from driving for six months for using a fake licence plate on his car. A spokesman said the minister lost his licence plate on a dirt road while driving home from his wedding and had used a phony plate in its place. The minister, Vit Barta, said he accepted the punishment.

The Czech for 'a beautiful life', *krásný život*, sounds exactly the same as the Russian for 'a red stomach'.

⚲ *BEER, FORGERY, ROBOT, SPA*

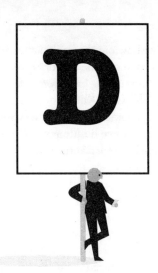

D'EON, Chevalier (1728–1810)

Charles Geneviève Louis Auguste André Timothée d'Eon de Beaumont was the most celebrated transvestite of his time. Diplomat, spy, dragoon officer, swordsman, lady-in-waiting, chess player and part-time nun, he/she was a celebrated figure in French and English circles of the 18th century, renowned for feats of swordsmanship (including fighting a duel dressed in a petticoat in front of an audience that included the Prince of Wales), international intrigue, and the fact that nobody was sure of his/her sex. Indeed, in the 1760s a total of around £120,000 was said to have been wagered on the matter.

A dispute over one such bet was, for legal purposes, resolved in court, with the judge ruling that d'Eon was definitely a woman. As a result, in royal circles d'Eon was ordered to always dress as a woman. On his/her demise in 1810, however, the doctor who certified the death pronounced him to be a 'fully-formed' male. The woman he had been living with for 20 years promptly fainted, and when the news was brought to George III it was said by some to have been the thing that finally drove the King irremediably mad.

The term 'eonism' was subsequently introduced by the early sexologist Havelock Ellis as a technical psychiatric term for transvestism.

DA VINCI, Leonardo (1452–1519)

Leonardo da Vinci was born in the village of Vinci in Italy, the illegitimate son of a lawyer and a peasant woman named Caterina. His friends described him as the most beautiful man who ever lived.

Da Vinci was a painter, polymath and scientist, and his notebooks show his contributions to a wide range of fields, including many less well-known inventions such as an alarm clock that woke the sleeper by gently rubbing their feet.

His most famous painting, the *Mona Lisa*, was not especially popular or even very highly regarded by the public until it was stolen from the Louvre Museum in Paris on 21 August 1911. It was not recovered for two years, but during that period it is said that more visitors to the Louvre turned up to stare at the empty space than had ever come to see the painting. Also, in the two years the *Mona Lisa* was missing, six Americans are known to have paid $300,000 each to conmen supposedly selling the painting.

The painting had been stolen by an Italian patriot who thought it belonged in his home country. He was finally caught when he attempted to sell it to someone representing the Uffizi Gallery in Florence.

📍 *PARACHUTE*

DAFT

In Old English, the word 'daft' meant 'mild' or 'meek'. The shift in meaning from mildness to stupidity may have contributed to the decline in the number of people in the UK with the surname Daft. According to research by Richard Webber, visiting Professor of Geography at King's College, London, the number of Dafts declined by 51 per cent between 1881 and 2008. However, this was outdone by the decline in people named Smellie, down by 70 per cent over the same period, while Gotobed went down by 42 per cent, Shufflebottom by 40 per cent, and Cockshott by 34 per cent. The number of people named Balls fell to 1,299 from 2,904, and the number of Deaths were reduced to 605 from 1,133. The biggest decline of all, however, was in people named Cock, who went down from 3,211 in 1881 to only 785 in 2008.

By contrast, the biggest increases between 1996 and 2008 were registered by the names Zhang, Wang and Yang. Zhang rose by 4,719 per cent, while Wang grew by 2,225 per cent.

DALI, Salvador (1904–89)

When the artist Salvador Dali was five years old, he was taken by his parents to his brother's grave and told that he was his brother's reincarnation.

His works include *Young Virgin*

Auto-Sodomized by the Horns of her Own Chastity (1954) and *Dream Caused by the Flight of a Bee around a Pomegranate a Second Before Awakening* (1944).

An Italian friar, Gabriele Maria Berardi, claimed that he performed an exorcism on Dali in France in 1947.

📍 *MOUSTACHE, PIZZA, SPEECH*

DALLAS

Nobody knows who Dallas is named after. George Mifflin Dallas, US Vice-President from 1845 to 1849, is possible but he had no link with the city. Other possibilities include George's brother Alexander, a Navy commodore, and their father, also Alexander, who was US Treasury Secretary. The founder of the town, John Neely Bryan, said he named it 'after my friend Dallas' but did not specify which Dallas he was referring to.

A report in 2011 named Dallas as the tenth most dangerous city for pedestrians in the US.

There are more shopping centres per head of population in Dallas than in any other US city.

A machine for making frozen margarita cocktails was invented in Dallas in 1971. The machine is in the National Museum of American History, where it's called 'a classic example of the American entrepreneurial spirit'.

There were 148 murders in Dallas in 2009, the lowest figure since 1967. In 2020, the figure had risen to 251, including two in the last hour of the year. This was the highest homicide figure in Dallas since at least 2004.

📍 *TATTOO*

DANCING

On 21 August 1923, the city of Kalamazoo, Michigan, passed a law forbidding dancers to stare into each other's eyes.

On 1 April 1990, the State of Oregon passed a bill making it illegal to be within two feet of a nude dancer.

In 2015, Japan finally lifted a 67-year ban on dancing in all places that did not have a dancing licence. Even places with such a licence had to stop at midnight.

HONEY, NICARAGUA, WATER SKIING

DANDELION

The English word 'dandelion' comes from the French '*dent de lion*' ('lion's tooth'), referring to the shape of the leaves.

Before the word 'dandelion' became popular, the English called the plant a 'pissabed', referring to its known qualities as a diuretic. The French for a dandelion is also *pissenlit*, and this property of dandelions was so well known that when apothecaries prescribed dandelion extract as an aid to urination, it was offered under the name Urinaria.

DANTE ALIGHIERI (1265–1321)

Following political ructions in Florence in 1301, Dante was condemned to perpetual exile, and if he returned to the city without paying a large fine, he could be burned at the stake. The city council of Florence finally rescinded Dante's sentence in June 2008.

GALILEI, THINKING

DARTS

The average speed with which a dart hits a dartboard in competition play is 64 km/h (40 mph). The now standard order of numbers around a dartboard was created by Brian Gamlin, a carpenter from Bury, Lancashire, who designed it that way in 1896 to minimise the role of luck in darts as a fairground game.

SKIING

DARWIN, Charles (1809–82)

Darwin was born on 12 February 1809, which is also celebrated as Abraham Lincoln's birthday in the USA, as the former president was also born on the same day and in the same year.

The first edition of Darwin's *On the Origin of Species* (1859) does not contain the word 'evolution'. Its very last word, however, is 'evolve', which occurs nowhere else in the book. The word 'pigeon' or 'pigeons' occurs 105 times in the book (excluding the index). No other animal is mentioned nearly as often. His publisher's chief editor, Whitwell Elwin, had advised him to write a lot about pigeons 'because everyone is interested in pigeons'.

Darwin was the grandson of the great potter Josiah Wedgwood. In 1839, Darwin married his first cousin, Emma Wedgwood, granddaughter of the potter. Before doing so he drew up lists of the pros and cons of marriage. Item three on his 'marry' list was: 'Object to be beloved and played with. Better than a dog anyhow.' One of the disadvantages was 'loss of time'. The last item on the 'not marry' list was: 'Perhaps my wife won't like London; then the sentence is banishment and degradation into indolent idle fool.'

When at Cambridge he founded the Gourmet Club, devoted to eating exotic animals 'which were before unknown to human palate'. He found brown owl inedible but described puma as 'remarkably like veal in its taste'.

Darwin pointed out that lice which move from Hawaiians to English sailors die within a week.

⚲ *MULE, OSTRICH, ZEBRA*

● DATE RAPE

The invention of an anti-date-rape straw was announced in 2011. It consists of a drinking straw impregnated with chemicals that detect date rape drugs and was invented in Israel by Fernando Patolsky and Michael Ioffe of Tel Aviv University.

▌ DAVIDSON, Harold Francis (1875–1937)

Ordained as a Church of England priest in 1903, Harold Davidson became Rector of Stiffkey and Morston in 1906, but extended his duties voluntarily to the West End of London, where he became chaplain to the Actors' Church Union, with a ministry comprising mainly showgirls and prostitutes. Calling himself the 'Prostitutes' Padre', he devoted himself to the rescue of young girls he thought were in danger of falling into vice. Naturally this role led to his befriending a large number of girls and finding himself in compromising situations that gained the attention of the Church. A complaint about his behaviour was sent to the Bishop of Norwich, and five charges of immoral conduct were brought against him in 1932. Two of these were 'making improper suggestions to waitresses' and 'embracing' a young woman in a Chinese restaurant. After an eventful trial (one report mentions him performing a tap dance in front of the judge) the Norwich Consistory Court found him guilty of disreputable association with women and Davidson was convicted and defrocked.

However, he continued to protest his innocence, even turning such protests into a lucrative sideshow. On one occasion he pleaded his case from inside a barrel on the Blackpool seafront. Another time, he went on a public fast inside a glass cabinet. Combining his defrocked rector act with that of lion-tamer, however, proved to be a fatal mistake, especially when it came to putting his head in the lion's mouth. On 28 July 1937, he was mauled in Skegness by a lion named Freddy and died two days later. His parishioners showed their loyalty by burying him in the village churchyard.

In his youth Davidson had been President of Oxford University Chess Club, in which role he cancelled their meeting on 2 February 1901 'out of respect to the memory of our late beloved Queen'.

● DAYLIGHT SAVING

The UK Parliament passed a bill to introduce Daylight Saving and British Summer Time in May 1916, but it was not without opposition at all levels of society. In an earlier debate, the former Prime Minister Lord Balfour had produced one of the most ingenious arguments against putting the clocks forwards an hour during the summer months. His reasoning referred to the autumn night when the clocks went back again: 'Supposing some unfortunate lady was confined with twins and one child was born ten minutes before one o'clock, the time of birth of the two children would be reversed. Such an alteration might conceivably affect the property and titles in that house.'

● DE NIRO, Robert (b. 1943)

The real-life character played by Robert de Niro in the film *Goodfellas* would have been eligible for parole in 2004 if he hadn't died in prison at the age of 69 in 1996. The character in the film was called James Conway and was based on James Burke, also known as 'Jimmy the Gent', who was convicted of conspiracy charges in 1982 and sentenced to 12 years in prison, thanks mainly to the evidence of Harry Hill (played by Ray Liotta in the film). While in prison, he was convicted of murder and sentenced to another 20 years.

'Robert de Niro' is an anagram of 'Error on bidet'.

♀ *MCENROE*

DE VERE, Edward, Earl of Oxford (1550–1604)

'This Earle of Oxford, making of his low obeisance to Queen Elizabeth, happened to let a Fart, at which he was so abashed and ashamed, that he went to Travell, 7 yeares. On his returne the Queen welcomed him home and sayd, "My Lord, I had forgott the Fart".' John Aubrey, Brief Lives, *written around 1698*

DEAFNESS

Inbreeding causes three out of every ten Dalmatian dogs to suffer from hearing disability.

It is thought that all large dinosaurs had limited hearing, according to German scientist Otto Gleich of the University of Regensburg, Germany. Tyrannosaurus Rex was practically deaf and certainly could not pick up high-pitched sounds. It would have been deaf to the sound of a human screaming, if humans had been around at the time.

♀ *CENSUS, ROBBERY, TORTOISE*

DEATHS

There are close to 40,000 deaths a year in the USA from traffic accidents, and 3,400 deaths a year from burns and fires (the second most common accidental cause). The most common fatal natural disaster is being struck by lightning – 49 deaths a year. Worldwide, an average of one person every 25 seconds is killed in a traffic accident.

In 2008, the cemetery in the village of Sarpourenx in south-west France became so full that Mayor Gerard Lalanne told the 260 residents of the village that 'all persons not having a plot in the cemetery and wishing to be buried in Sarpourenx are forbidden from dying in the parish'. His proclamation ended: 'Offenders will be severely punished.'

♀ *MALARIA, MEXICO, TELEVISION, VENEZUELA*

DEBT

On 8 October 2008, the National Debt Clock near Times Square in New York City ran out of digits as the US National debt exceeded $10 trillion. As a short-term fix, the $ sign at the beginning of the display was changed into the first digit of the new debt, and it was announced that two more digits would be added. The clock was put up in 1989 to draw attention to the debt, which was $2.7 trillion at the time. In 2022, the US National Debt was over $30 trillion and was growing at a rate of about $45,486 per second. The UK National Debt was above £2.6 trillion and growing at a rate of £5,170 per second.

♀ *GAMBIA, KAZAKHSTAN, MONET*

DECEMBER

December takes its name from the Latin for 'ten', *decem*, as it was the tenth month of the ancient Roman calendar.

According to a recent survey, people born in Britain in December are more likely to become dentists than those born in any other month.

Figures since the Second World War show that share prices are more likely to increase in December than any other month.

In the UK, more drivers are breathalysed during December than any other month. December is also the worst month for road deaths.

'In December, melancholy and phlegm much increase.' Richard Saunders, 1679

'Men are April when they woo, December when they wed.' William Shakespeare, As You Like It, 1623

♀ ACCIDENTS, AUSTRALIA, MOOSE, ONION, ROSES

DECENCY

Wearing sagging trousers is not a crime, a New York judge ruled in 2010, when he overturned a summons issued to a man exposing his underwear. The judge said it appeared to be an attempt by one police officer to show his displeasure with the style. He ruled that, although many may find the fashion for low-slung trousers distasteful, people can dress how they want as long as they do not offend public decency.

♀ GENITALS

DEER

Men of the Mocovi tribe of South America tie deer hoofs to their ankles and hands to help them run faster.

♀ CURRY, PIES, PREGNANCY, SANTA CLAUS, SINGAPORE

DEGREE

According to research at the University of Bristol published in 2010, people with university degrees are more likely to have cats than dogs as pets. The researchers suggest it is because longer working hours leave less time for looking after a dog.

♀ EDWARD VIII, FUNERALS, SLIPPERS

DEMOCRATIC REPUBLIC OF THE CONGO

From 1908 to 1960, the country now known as the Democratic Republic of the Congo was called the Belgian Congo. It covered an area 80 times as big as Belgium. In terms of total national earnings per person, the Democratic Republic of the Congo is the world's poorest country. Sharing borders with nine other countries, however, it does have more neighbours than any other country in Africa.

The Democratic Republic of the Congo is the only country in Africa split into two time zones.

Police in Kinshasa, capital of the Democratic Republic of the Congo, arrested 13 suspected sorcerers in 2008 accused of using black magic to steal or shrink men's penises. The accusations had led to mass panic and several attempted lynchings.

♀ MOZAMBIQUE, NIGERIA, OKAPI

DENGUE FEVER

Health experts in Thailand advised young women not to wear black leggings, to avoid attracting the attention of mosquitoes carrying dengue fever. The Deputy Health Minister explained that mosquitoes are attracted to dark clothing.

DENIM

The fabric known as denim has been in existence since 1695 and was first made in the French town of Nîmes, where it was known as 'serge de Nîmes'. The word 'jeans' comes from the French word for the Italian city of Genoa,

'Genes', where the earliest denim clothing was made from Nîmes cloth for the Italian Navy.

● DENMARK

According to the *Gesta Danorum* (*Deeds of the Danes*), a 13th-century manuscript by Saxo the Learned, Denmark was founded by two brothers named Dan and Angul. Angul later left to found the tribe known as the Angles, leaving Dan to name Denmark after himself. Angul and the Angles went on to conquer southern Britain and name it 'Angle-land'.

Not only is 14 January the anniversary of Queen Margrethe of Denmark acceding to the throne in 1972, but it is also the anniversary of the death of King Frederick V of Denmark in 1766. The date also saw the birth of Valdemar I of Denmark in 1131.

Every Danish monarch from 1513 to 1972 was named either Frederick or Christian. In fact, there was strict alternation between the two names.

The average age for men to get married in Denmark is 34.8, the highest in the world.

You are never more than 50 kilometres (31 miles) from the sea in Denmark.

Denmark has appeared three times as the top country in the World Happiness Report – in 2012, 2013 and 2016. Its record was overtaken in 2021 when Finland secured its fourth consecutive top place. The only other countries to have finished first are Switzerland (2015) and Norway (2017).

The Danish flag, a white cross on a red background, is the oldest national state flag still in use.

In 1989, Denmark became the first country to legalise same-sex unions. Same-sex marriage was not granted until 2012.

Danish pastries are called Viennese bread (*wienerbrød*) in Denmark.

In Germany, the Great Dane breed of dog is called Deutsche dogge (German mastiff).

Denmark introduced a tax on nuts in 1922. It was repealed in 2019.

When the film *King Kong* was screened in Denmark, it was called *Kong King*. '*Kong*' is the Danish for 'king'.

♀ GREENLAND, LEAP YEAR, VIKINGS

● DENTISTRY

In January 2005, an Iranian dentist and his assistant were arrested for extracting 15 teeth from an 18-year-old in an attempt to get him out of military service. The conscript had been mistakenly informed that the army did not take men who had lost 15 teeth, so he found a willing dental surgeon who took out 15 of his teeth in 10 days. The man's father filed a complaint and the dentist was arrested.

According to figures published in 2002, 29 per cent of British dentists have been involved in road accidents.

A Public Health England survey of dentists in 2018 reported that 1.1 per cent of men and 1 per cent of women attending dentists that year had none of their natural teeth.

Dental heroes:
1. In 1883, Queen Victoria's personal dentist Sir Edwin Saunders became the first dentist to be knighted. He was also dentist to Prince Albert and other members of the royal family. As well as these responsibilities, he invented a machine for sweeping city streets.
2. Mrs Hamilton, an English actress of the 18th century and a leading lady of

the English stage until, according to the *Dictionary of National Biography*, 'An accident to her false teeth as she played Lady Brumpton turned applause into ridicule.' She died in poverty and obscurity.

3. Edwin Thomas Truman, whose work on gutta-percha for insulating an Atlantic cable led to a patent in 1847 for gutta-percha tooth fillings. He was also famed for his surgical success at correcting a cleft palate.

⸸ *ANAESTHETICS, BUTCHELL, ORANGE*

DENTURES

A partial set of Winston Churchill's dentures was sold at auction for £15,200 in England in July 2010. The gold-mounted false teeth, specially designed to disguise Churchill's lisp, were sold by the son of the technician who made them. The buyer also owns the microphone with which Churchill announced the end of the war in Europe in 1945.

⸸ *BRAZIL, COW, FALSE TEETH, TEETH*

DENVER

A woman appeared in court in Denver, Colorado, in January 2012, charged with felony criminal mischief after punching and scratching a painting at the recently opened Clyfford Still Museum. She also rubbed her buttocks on it after pulling her pants down. In addition, Carmen Tisch was reported to have urinated after rubbing against the canvas, but tests had not confirmed whether urine had got on the painting.

Clyfford Still was an abstract impressionist who died in 1980. The painting that was the subject of the police report was called *1957-J No. 2* and had been valued at $30 million.

DESCARTES René (1596–1650)

The French philosopher/mathematician René Descartes found cross-eyed women particularly attractive.

He liked to get up around 11am.

DETROIT

In 2010, the city of Detroit announced plans to put up signs in buildings warning workers to avoid 'wearing scented products, including … colognes, aftershave lotions, perfumes, deodorants, body/face lotions …' and not to use 'scented candles, perfume samples from magazines, spray or solid air fresheners'. The move followed a $100,000 settlement in a federal lawsuit filed in 2008 by a city employee who complained that a colleague's perfume had made it challenging for her to do her job.

DIAGNOSIS

A doctor at the private Minsheng Hospital in Kaohsiung city in southern Taiwan was told to spend a little longer on each patient after an investigation in 2010 revealed that he took an average of only 84 seconds to reach a diagnosis. Dr Wu Ming-feng had been seeing 339 patients a day and had reached a total of 61,366 patients in the previous year. The doctor defended his record, saying that if the government wanted him to see fewer patients that was fine, but he felt it would be unfair not to see anyone who wanted to consult him.

DIAGRAM

The Diagram Prize is awarded each year at the Frankfurt Book Fair for the book judged to have the oddest title. The first winner, in 1978, was *Proceedings of the Second International Workshop on Nude Mice*. This was also given a special award for having the oddest title of the first 15 years of the Diagram Prize. A similar award for the oddest title in the first 30 years was given to the 1996 winner, *Greek Rural Postmen and their Cancellation Numbers.*

Other winners include the following:

- 1979: *The Madam as Entrepreneur: Career Management in House Prostitution*
- 1980: *The Joy of Chickens*
- 1985: *Natural Bust Enlargement with Total Power: How to Increase the Other 90 per cent of Your Mind to Increase the Size of Your Breasts*
- 1986: *Oral Sadism and the Vegetarian Personality*
- 1990: *Lesbian Sadomasochism Safety Manual*
- 1992: *How to Avoid Huge Ships*
- 2002: *Living With Crazy Buttocks*
- 2004: *Bulletproof Your Horse*
- 2005: *How People Who Don't Know They're Dead Attach Themselves to Unsuspecting Bystanders and What to Do About It*
- 2012: *Goblinproofing One's Chicken Coop*

The 2021 prize was awarded to Roy Schwarz for his book *Was Superman Circumcised?*, which was an exploration of Superman's Jewish origins. Accepting the prize, the winner said: 'The competition was stiff but I'm glad I was able to rise to the challenge.'

On two occasions no Diagram Prize was given because no title was considered odd enough to merit an award.

DIANA, Princess of Wales (1961–97)

When she married Prince Charles in 1981, Diana became the first English bride of an heir to the British throne since 1659. She was a direct descendant of the only sovereigns from whom Prince Charles was not descended: Charles II and James II.

In the 55-minute interview she gave to Martin Bashir, which was broadcast on BBC television in 1995 (on the Queen's 48th wedding anniversary, incidentally), she mentioned the name 'Charles' only twice.

ASCOT, FORTY-SEVEN, TELEVISION

DICKENS, Charles John Huffam (1812–70)

Charles Dickens's first job, which earned him six shillings a week, was labelling bottles at a warehouse of Warren's Blacking, a boot polish company. He was 12 years old.

His first wife was Catherine Thomson Hogarth, but he affectionately called her 'Pig' or 'Mouse'. She wrote on domestic management as well as compiling a cookery book entitled *What Shall we Have for Dinner? Satisfactorily Answered by Numerous Bills of Fare for from Two to Eighteen Persons.* They separated after 22 years of marriage and 10 children. Charles Dickens blamed her for the children, who gave him many financial worries.

Dickens combed his hair a great deal, was afraid of bats and hated the game of croquet. He always slept with his bed in a north–south position and had a pet raven called Grip.

David Copperfield is the only novel by Dickens that includes the word 'kangaroo'.

The *Oxford English Dictionary* lists 210 words, from 'abuzz' to 'yo-yoing', that first appeared in the works of Dickens. These include the nouns dustbin and fluffiness, and the use as verbs of the nouns apron, beeswax, corkscrew, manslaughter, mother-in-law and polka.

The earliest recorded use of the exclamation 'what the dickens?' was in 1599 so predated Charles Dickens by more than a century.

⚲ *BACON, CHIPS, POLAR BEAR, SPONTANEOUS COMBUSTION*

DIDEROT, Denis (1713–84)

After dinner on the evening of 30 July 1784, the French philosopher Denis Diderot is said to have reached for an apricot. His wife advised against it, but Diderot replied, 'How the devil do you think that will harm me?' Then he put the apricot in his mouth, rested his elbow on the table, and died. Whether he choked to death on the apricot stone, as some maintain, however, is open to question.

DIDGERIDOO

In 2005, the *British Medical Journal* published research detailing the effects of didgeridoo-playing on a group of people suffering from sleep disorders in Switzerland. The subjects, who suffered either daytime sleepiness or night-time disturbances caused by snoring and other breathing difficulties, were taught to play the didgeridoo for 25 minutes a day over a four-month period. The results showed that the group experienced improved breathing during the night and that their snoring had decreased. These improvements were attributed to the strengthening of their airways.

There are at least 45 different Aborigine words for the didgeridoo.

DIETRICH Marlene (1901–92)

In 2017, the American Film Institute named Marlene Dietrich the ninth greatest female star of all time.

⚲ *CURTIS, HOT DOGS, POPEYE*

DINGO

Until 1980, the Dingo Barrier Fence in Australia had strong claims to be the longest man-made structure on Earth. Constructed to protect sheep farms from wild dogs, it had a total length of 8,614 kilometres (5,352 miles), which according to general belief was longer than the Great Wall of China.

In 1980, however, the Dingo Barrier Fence was considered too long to be kept in a good state of repair and it was shortened by 3,000 kilometres (1,864 miles) to 5,614 kilometres (3,488 miles), which was still greater than the commonly given figure of 5,000 kilometres (3,107 miles) for the Great Wall.

A full architectural survey in 2009, however, established the total length of the Great Wall of China to be 8,815.8 kilometres (5,478 miles), which beats both the current Dingo Fence and the old longer one.

DINOSAUR

Dinosaurs became extinct before the Rockies or the Alps were formed. After roaming the Earth in the Mesozoic Era (between around 240 million and 65 million years ago), dinosaurs remained undiscovered until 1822 when Gideon Mantell found a few teeth and bones in Sussex. Mantell called them 'Iguanodon' ('iguana tooth'), but Reverend William Buckland called the teeth and bones he found near Oxford soon after 'Megalosaurus' ('great lizard'). The linguistic issue was resolved amicably in 1841 when Sir Richard Owen suggested the word 'dinosaur' from the Greek *deinos* ('terrible') and *sauros* ('lizard').

In 1938, fishermen off the coast of South Africa netted a coelacanth, thought to have been extinct for 70 million years.

In 1993, the Japanese sound specialist Matsumi Suzuki established that the sound made by a Tyrannosaurus probably resembled, in the words of one scientist, 'The sound made by a human stomach after a bad night in a cheap restaurant.' More recently, a 2016 study concluded that rather than roaring, as they generally do in films, a T Rex 'most probably cooed, hooted, and made deep-throated booming sounds like the modern-day emu'.

Tyrannosaurus babies were covered in a peach-like fuzz and were comparable in size to a small turkey.

On 14 October 1996, Australia's only known Stegosaurus footprint was stolen from Aborigine land north of Broome. It was recovered at the end of 1998.

The Stegosaurus ('plated lizard') had a brain that weighed in at 2.5 ounces, or half of one-thousandth of 1 per cent of its total body weight.

It has been suggested that no land animal bigger than a Seismosaurus (100 tonnes and 110 feet) could exist, because its legs would need to be so thick to hold it up, it could never move. After that theory was propounded, however, the Argentinosaurus was discovered, which may have been even bigger.

♀ *BRONTOSAURUS. BUCKLAND, CHICKEN, DEAFNESS, DUNG, LAMPREY*

● DIOGENES (c.412–323 BC)

The philosopher Diogenes of Sinope was described by Plato as 'A Socrates gone mad' and is said to have lived in a wooden tub or barrel outside Athens. A campaigner against social convention, he urinated on people who insulted him, defecated in the theatre and pointed at people with his middle finger. He also liked to live like a dog, and founded the philosophical school known as the Cynics, from the Greek word *kynos* for 'dog'.

There are several stories concerning the manner of his death: some say he died by holding his breath; others say he was poisoned by eating raw octopus; while another account claims that he died from an infected dog bite.

● DISNEYLAND

The first Disneyland opened in Anaheim, a suburb of Los Angeles, California, on 17 July 1955.

The first death at Disneyland happened in 1964 – apparently a suicide.

The first homicide in Disneyland was in 1981, when an 18-year-old was stabbed in a fight which apparently began when one youth touched another one's girlfriend.

♀ *EURO*

● DIVORCE

Researchers in Chicago in 2002 reported that unhappily married couples who divorce are just as likely to be unhappy five years later as unhappily married couples who stay together.

The country with the highest divorce rate is the Maldives, followed by Kazakhstan and Russia.

In the UK in 2019, there were 822 divorces among same-sex couples, of which 72 per cent were between female couples.

The patron saint of unhappy marriages is St Theodore of Sykeon, a 7th-century monk and bishop.

An Egyptian court in 1999 rejected a petition from a man who wanted his marriage annulled because his wife had only one breast. He accused her of deliberately misleading him by not telling him that she had been born with her right breast missing. He had only just discovered the error after 20 months of marriage.

Also in 1999, Californian couple Bonny and Michael Martin visited a psychiatrist for marital counselling. The session did not go smoothly. The problems began when Michael drew a gun, pointed it at Bonny and told her to shut up. She answered by shooting him in the shoulder, then everyone took shelter behind items of furniture while Michael and Bonny continued shooting. 'The only thing that kept them from killing each other was that they both ran out of ammunition,' the psychiatrist said later. He suggested that they might think about divorce, but Mrs Martin said, 'I can't. I really can't. It might sound crazy to you but I really love that man.'

In 1999, an Italian court heard a divorce case between a 94-year-old man and his third wife, who was 52. The court asked the man why he thought the marriage had broken down after five months and he said that it was probably because he wanted too much sex.

In Pueblo Indian communities of New Mexico and Arizona, a woman may traditionally divorce her husband by leaving his moccasins on the doorstep.

In 2009, an Australian senator announced that divorce contributed to global warming. Senator Steve Fielding told a Senate hearing in Canberra that staying married is better for the planet because divorce leads the newly single to live more wasteful lifestyles, thus making climate change worse.

♀ *IMPOTENCE, INFIDELITY, KIDNEY, LEPROSY, ZAMBIA*

DNA

We share 70 per cent of our DNA with a slug and 98.4 per cent with a chimpanzee.

The first time that DNA from an extinct species was used to induce a functional response in another living organism was in 2008 when genetic material from the Tasmanian tiger – officially declared extinct 70 years earlier – was inserted into mouse embryos, where it played a role in developing cartilage and future bone.

♀ *ECHIDNA, GOD, MOZART, PANDA*

DOCTORS

According to a survey published in the UK in 2008, in the previous year 76 per cent of doctors were given chocolates or other foodstuffs by grateful patients, while 66 per cent were handed bottles of alcoholic drink. Other gifts included washing up liquid, tights, a hamster and replicas of the Taj Mahal.

In 2017, NHS England published the following advice on gifts to doctors: 'Staff should not accept gifts that may affect, or be seen to affect, their professional judgement … Gifts valued at over £50 should be treated with caution and only be accepted on behalf of an organisation (i.e. to an organisation's charitable funds), not in a personal capacity. These should be declared by staff. Modest gifts accepted under a value of £50 do not need to be declared …' but 'Multiple gifts from the same source over a 12 month period should be treated in the same way as single gifts over £50 where the cumulative value exceeds £50.'

♀ *DOCTOR WHO, HEALTH, VIENNA*

DOCTOR WHO

As of the beginning of 2016, there was no Doctor Who on the UK Medical Register, but there were four doctors named Dr Hoo registered with a licence to practice, all male, and 18 named Hu, seven of whom are male and 11 female.

The first tribute song to *Doctor Who* was 'I'm Gonna Spend My Christmas with A Dalek' by The Go-Go's, a Christmas single in 1964.

Torchwood, another successful TV science fiction series, is an anagram of 'Doctor Who'.

In 2005, an original Dalek sold at auction for £36,000. That record price was beaten in 2016 when a Dalek fetched £38,000.

In 2011, the tenth Doctor, David Tennant, married Georgia Moffett, whose father was the fifth Doctor, Peter Davison.

In 2002, *Doctor Who* merchandisers won a battle against the Metropolitan Police for the right to patent the police phone box image of the Tardis.

● DODO

The last person to make a confirmed sighting of a dodo was the Dutch mariner Volkert Evertsz when he was shipwrecked on the island of Mauritius in 1662. The last previous sighting was 24 years earlier, though an escaped slave named Simon claimed to have seen one as late as 1674. Based on the dates of the last 10 confirmed dodo sightings, a statistical analysis published in the journal *Nature* in 2010 reported that the chance of the dodo not being extinct is 3.07 in a million.

● DOG

Around 1875 or 1880, a French engineer named Monsieur Huret invented a vehicle called a cynosphere, powered by dogs on treadmills. Basically, it was a tricycle with treadmills as its rear wheels, each containing a dog, with the driver seated between the wheels. It is said that early animal liberationists objected too strongly for it to gain popular acceptance, though it is not clear whether this ever even went into production.

The next great advance in dog transport came in 1957 when a Russian dog named Laika became the first mammal to orbit the Earth. No plans were made for its return trip and it burned up on re-entry. Three years later, in 1960, Belka and Strelka (Squirrel and Little Arrow) became the first dogs to return from space alive. Strelka later gave birth to six puppies, one of which was given by the Russians to President Kennedy.

Bothy Twisleton-Wykeham-Fiennes, a Jack Russell terrier, was the only dog to have been at both the North and South Poles, having visited both on expeditions with Sir Ranulph Twisleton-Wykeham-Fiennes.

Each day dogs deposit between 4 and 5 tons of excrement on London streets.

On 11 June 1991, Rodney H. Metts and Barry D. Thomas were granted US patent No. 5,023,850 for their invention of a Dog Watch, which they describe as 'A novelty clock, watch, and the like for keeping time at an animal's rate, defined in terms of a multiple of human rate by dividing the average lifetime of a particular animal into the average lifetime of a human being.' In other words, for dogs it multiplies time by seven, because humans live seven times as long as dogs. The first diagram accompanying the patent document shows 'a wristwatch worn by a typical dog'.

In January 2003, German inventor Stephan Licht was granted a patent for a 'harness for dog-wearing sunglasses'.

In 2005, an Italian court ordered a man to pay £694 a year maintenance to his ex-wife for their dog. The unnamed woman in the divorce case argued that the cost of keeping the dog was almost as expensive as raising a child.

In 2008, the German city of Dusseldorf introduced blue plastic shoes for its police dogs because of the high incidence of paw injuries when patrolling streets littered with broken bottles. A police spokesman commented: 'I'm not sure they like it, but they'll have to get used to it.'

The paper 'Effect of Alcohol on the Sexual Reflexes of Normal and Neurotic Male Dogs' (*Psychosomatic Medicine*, vol. 14), reported that regulated doses of alcohol may have a therapeutic effect on premature ejaculation in a neurotic dog.

The record for the largest dog litter was 24 puppies born to a mastiff in England in January 2005.

The top three female dogs' names in the UK according to a poll in 2020 were Bella, Luna and Poppy. The top three names for male dogs were Alfie, Charlie and Milo.

 CAT, DEGREE, FLEAS, MOON, MUSIC, POSTMEN, YAWNING

DOLLY (1996–2003)

Dolly the Sheep, the first mammal to be cloned from an adult cell, was born on 5 July 1996. She had been cloned from a cell taken from a mammary gland and, in the words of Ian Wilmut, leader of the project team at Edinburgh's Roslin Institute: 'Dolly is derived from a mammary gland cell and we couldn't think of a more impressive pair of glands than Dolly Parton's'. Dolly was mated with a Welsh mountain ram (name unknown) and subsequently gave birth to six lambs, Bonnie in 1998, Sally and Rosie in 1999, and Lucy, Darcy and Cotton in 2001. She then developed arthritis and died at the age of six.

She was stuffed and exhibited at the Museum of Edinburgh.

DOLPHIN

A dolphin has to be conscious to breathe, so only half its brain sleeps at any given time.

An average dolphin will eat 4–9 per cent of its body weight in fish every day. Despite having 80–100 teeth, dolphins swallow fish whole.

The US military is reported to have trained dolphins for attack-and-kill missions. In 2005, it was also announced that dolphins had been trained to sing the *Batman* TV theme tune.

Baby dolphins are born tail first.

On 13 December 2006, the baiji, or Chinese river dolphin, was declared to be 'functionally extinct'. Actually, no Chinese river dolphin had been seen since 2002, though a year after the extinction announcement a sighting was claimed in China.

In 1978, Californian vets faced the unusual problem of having to remove a piece of metal from the stomach of a dolphin which had inadvertently swallowed it. Their solution was to enlist the help of baseball player Clifford Ray, who reached inside the animal's stomach to retrieve the object. The appropriate qualification that made Mr Ray right for the job was an arm length of 1.1 metres (3 feet 9 inches).

'To the dolphin alone, beyond all other, nature has granted what the best philosophers seek: friendship for no advantage.' Plutarch, c.45–120

 HENRY VIII, MONGOLIA

DONALD DUCK

A US federal judge in 2011 heard a case brought by a woman who claimed that

Donald Duck groped her at Disney's Epcot theme park in Florida in 2008. He ruled that the case could go to court, and Disney must defend itself against April Magolon's charge that the Duck grabbed her breast as she held her child – and then joked about it. She says the encounter left her with post-traumatic stress in the form of nightmares, digestive problems and other permanent injuries

In 1995, asteroid 12410 was named after Donald Duck.

In 2017, it was pointed out that a picture of Donald Duck turned upside down looks uncannily like Donald Trump.

DONKEY

A jenny is a female donkey; a jack is a male.

Donkey is an 18th-century word, and originally rhymed with monkey.

Robert Louis Stevenson, in his *Travels with a Donkey*, reported that the word to encourage a donkey to move faster is 'Proot!'

In 2000, a Turkish man was reported to have tried to cure his sexual impotence by begging doctors on three occasions to transplant a penis from a donkey onto him. When he brought a donkey home for the third time, his family were so annoyed that the man's son shot him in the leg.

In 2008, a donkey named Monika was finally retired from the Mariinsky ballet in St Petersburg after having spent 19 years performing in the ballet *Don Quixote*. At her farewell party, Monika danced a waltz with one of the Mariinsky's ballerinas and was presented with retirement gifts of carrot cake, a pinafore and a kerchief.

In the same year, a donkey was jailed in southern Mexico for assault and battery after it bit and kicked two men near a ranch in Chiapas state. A police spokesman said the donkey would remain in jail until its owner agreed to pay the men's medical bills.

In 2009, Colchester Borough Council in England stopped giving out free recycling sacks after one was photographed being used as a saddlebag on a donkey in Spain.

It has often been claimed that more people are kicked to death by donkeys than die in aircraft accidents, but that is based entirely on a report issued by the US air force in 1947 which limited its donkey death statistics to a short period in one small area of the United States. There are no reliable figures for worldwide donkey-kick fatalities.

In 2018, the world donkey population was reported to be 50,451,887 and the mule population was 8,522,981. China had the most donkeys while Mexico had most mules.

BESTIALITY, MULES, WINE

DOODLE

The verb 'to doodle' originally meant 'to make a fool of'. The word 'doodle' to describe an aimless scrawl was first noted in 1937. 'To doodle' can also mean to play the bagpipes, which have been called a 'doodle-sack'. According to graphologists, people driven by emotions tend to draw rounded or curved doodles, while down-to-earth, practical types draw straight lines and angular and pointed shapes. Graphologists also say that outgoing people draw large, expansive doodles, while small compact doodles are the mark of observers rather than participators. The US comedian 'Doodles' Weaver was Sigourney Weaver's uncle.

'I know only two tunes: one of them is Yankee Doodle and the other isn't.'
President Ulysses S. Grant

HULL

DORSET

People from the village of Shitterton in Dorset had the name sign of their village stolen so often that in 2010 they decided to take action. So they clubbed together and raised £680 to have a new sign made in stone and set in concrete, weighing one and a half tonnes, which they hoped would be more difficult to steal. The name of the town derives from the Old English 'scite', meaning 'dung', and the whole name is said to mean 'farmstead on the stream used as an open sewer'.

DOUGHNUTS

The Dutch made the first doughnuts (or donuts) by dropping the leftovers from bread-making into boiling oil. They called them by the descriptive title *oly koeks* ('oil cakes').

The earliest use of the word 'doughnut' in print was in 1809 in Washington Irving's *History of New York*.

The first doughnut cutter was patented by John Blondell in 1872.

US sea captain Hanson Crockett Gregory is said to have invented the hole in doughnuts in 1847, and in 1947 a commemorative centenary plaque was put up on his house in Rockfort, Maine, to mark the event. The story is that he poked out the soggy centres of doughnuts in order to slip them over the spokes of a ship's wheel. A more plausible version is that the hole in the middle was added to ensure regular baking.

The International Federation of Competitive Eating record for glazed doughnuts is 55 in eight minutes by Joey Chestnut in 2017. Patrick Bertoletti holds the record for glazed and cream-filled doughnuts at 47 in five minutes in 2007. Joey Chestnut holds 46 world eating records, including 141 hard-boiled eggs in eight minutes, 76 hot dogs and buns in 10 minutes, 47 grilled cheese sandwiches in 10 minutes, and a whole 4.24-kilogram (9.35-pound) turkey in 10 minutes. Bertoletti's 32 records include 39 dozen oysters in eight minutes, 275 jalapeno chillis in eight minutes and 38 Mars Bars in five minutes

Ten billion doughnuts are made in the USA every year.

According to a study at Northwestern University in Chicago in 2008, two areas of the brain displayed activity when hungry volunteers were shown photos of Krispy Kreme doughnuts. The same response, however, did not occur after participants had previously stuffed themselves with up to eight Krispy Kremes. The paper, published in the journal *Cerebral Cortex*, was entitled 'The Spatial Attention Network Interacts with Limbic and Monoaminergic Systems to Modulate Motivation-Induced Attention Shifts'. Simply expressed, the conclusion was that we don't get so excited by pictures of doughnuts if we've eaten enough of them beforehand.

APATHY, PRESLEY

DOWNING STREET

Downing Street in London is named after the soldier and diplomat Sir George Downing. Though born in England in 1624, George Downing spent his teenage years in America where he became the second man to graduate from Harvard. A supporter of Oliver Cromwell, he spied on royalists first in Scotland and later in Holland, sending back coded messages. He rapidly changed allegiance when Charles II was restored to the throne. For this behaviour, Samuel Pepys called him a 'perfidious rogue'. In New England 'a George Downing' became an expression for a man who has betrayed one's trust.

On 22 September 1735, Sir Robert Walpole became the first British government leader to move in to Number 10 Downing Street.

The lace curtains at 10 Downing Street are bulletproof.

⚲ *LLOYD GEORGE, PRIME MINISTER, THATCHER*

DOYLE, Sir Arthur Conan (1859–1930)

Sir Arthur Conan Doyle, or Arthur Ignatius Conan Doyle, is best known as the creator of Sherlock Holmes, but he was also a ship's surgeon, a boxer, Deputy Lieutenant of Surrey, an occasional first-class cricketer and the man who popularised skiing in Switzerland.

His stint as a ship's surgeon was on board a Greenland whaler named *Hope* just after he had qualified as a doctor. Seen carrying boxing gloves onto the ship, he was promptly challenged to a boxing match by Jack Lamb, the ship's steward. After the fight, Lamb is reported to have said, 'So help me, he's the best surgeon we've had! He's blackened my eye.' By all accounts there was little for him to do as a surgeon during his time on the ship, and his main role seemed to be breaking up fights between other crew members.

He was knighted in 1902 and made Deputy Lieutenant of Surrey not for his Sherlock Holmes stories but primarily

for a pamphlet he wrote on the causes of the Boer War.

He played the occasional cricket match for the Marylebone Cricket Club, appearing in 10 first-class fixtures. His batting average was 19.25, with a highest score of 43. As an occasional bowler, he took only one wicket at a cost of 50 runs, but his victim was the great W.G. Grace.

His interest in skiing began in 1892 when he took his first wife to Switzerland for her health. He had seen skiing in Norway, so had a pair of skis sent so that he could take skiing up in Switzerland. He was taught to ski in Davos by two brothers named Branger who had already been skiing for a year when Conan Doyle arrived, but were viewed with such suspicion by the townsfolk when they did so that they tended to ski at night under cover of darkness. The contortions of an eccentric British author on eight-foot-long skis, however, was viewed first with amusement then admiration. Following his example, the Swiss took up the sport.

The English also started going to Switzerland for skiing after Conan Doyle wrote an article about it in *Strand Magazine* in 1894. 'The time will come,' he predicted, with uncanny accuracy, 'when hundreds of Englishmen will come to Switzerland for the skiing season.'

⚲ *LONDON, TEETH*

DRACULA

Before he became famous as the author of *Dracula* (1897), Bram Stoker was best known for being the personal assistant of the great actor Sir Henry Irving and the business manager of Irving's Lyceum Theatre in London. He was also the younger brother of Sir Thornley Stoker, President of the Royal College of Medicine in Ireland. Before creating Dracula, he wrote a rather less exciting book called *The Duties of Clerks of Petty Sessions in Ireland*.

Dracula is often linked to a 15th-century Romanian prince named Vlad the Impaler, though Vlad did not drink blood and there is no evidence that Bram Stoker had even heard of him. In modern Romanian, *drac* means 'devil' or 'Satan'.

When the Ministry of Tourism in Romania announced plans to build a Dracula theme park in 2001, they ran into problems on discovering that the rights to *Dracula* were held by Universal Studios.

Visitors to the Second World Dracula Congress in 1995 in the town of Poiana Brasov in Transylvania were all presented with miniature wooden coffins containing earth from beneath Castle Dracula.

When President Ceausescu was in charge of communist Romania, all mention of Dracula was banned.

♀ *GARLIC, STOKER, VAMPIRES*

DRAGON

The earliest known depictions of dragons date from China around the 16th century BC. While Chinese dragons were mainly benevolent, European dragons, which date back to around the 4th century, tend to be malevolent, though the Welsh red dragon, Y Ddraig Goch, is friendly.

The dragon is the only mythological animal that has a Chinese year assigned to it.

One of the myths that used to be associated with dragons is that wounds caused by swords dipped in dragons' blood would never heal.

There are 35 references to dragons in the King James Bible, 22 in the Old Testament and the other 13 all in the Book of Revelation, and there are 18 references to dragons in the plays of Shakespeare.

Water is said to have a calming effect on the fiery dragon temperament.

In Philippine legend, the Earth once had seven moons but six were eaten by Bakunawa dragons.

♀ *BLAKE, KOMODO, ST GEORGE*

DRAGONFLY

The state insect of Alaska is the four-spot skimmer dragonfly. This should not be confused with the official state fossil of Alaska, which is the woolly mammoth.

DRAMA

The French writer Georges Polti identified 36 Dramatic Situations covering everything that can possibly happen in a story: 1. Supplication; 2. Deliverance; 3. Crime pursued by vengeance; 4. Vengeance taken for kin upon kin; 5. Pursuit; 6. Disaster; 7. Falling prey to cruelty/misfortune; 8. Revolt; 9. Daring enterprise; 10. Abduction; 11. The enigma; 12. Obtaining; 13. Enmity of kin; 14. Rivalry of kin; 15. Murderous adultery; 16. Madness; 17. Fatal imprudence; 18. Involuntary crimes of love; 19. Slaying of kin unrecognised; 20. Self-sacrifice for an ideal; 21. Self-sacrifice for kin; 22. All sacrificed for passion; 23. Necessity of sacrificing loved ones; 24. Rivalry of superior vs. inferior; 25. Adultery; 26. Crimes of love; 27. Discovery of the dishonour of a loved one; 28. Obstacles to love; 29. An enemy loved; 30. Ambition; 31. Conflict with a god; 32. Mistaken jealousy; 33. Erroneous judgement; 34. Remorse; 35. Recovery of a lost one; 36. Loss of loved ones.

DREAM

On 28 August 1963, Martin Luther King uttered the phrase 'I have a dream' eight times in his famous 'I have a dream' speech.

Research shows that if you wake someone every time Rapid Eye Movement (REM) sleep begins, thus stopping them dreaming, it's almost as bad for them as not sleeping at all. Others who are woken just as frequently but allowed to dream do not suffer ill-effects. So it seems that it's dreaming we need far more than sleeping.

According to the British English Corpus, the adjective that most frequently precedes the word 'dream' is 'bad'. The next most common is 'American'.

The word 'dream' comes from an Old English word meaning 'mirth', 'joy', 'noise' or 'music'. The original meaning of 'nightmare' was 'a spirit of a hag on a horse (mare) that stifled the sleeping'. 'Dreamt' and 'undreamt' are the only common words in the English language ending in -mt. The only other such words in the *Oxford English Dictionary* are adreamt (visited by a dream) and crommt (made crooked).

⚲ *DALI, SHOES, TEETH*

DRESS

A woman was reported to have fatally shot her cousin during an argument in 2010 over proper dress at an Easter dinner. It started when one woman said she did not think the other was properly dressed when she arrived at the first woman's home in Columbus, Ohio, wearing a T-shirt and shorts. A fight ensued, then as the allegedly ill-dressed woman walked outside to leave, the other woman shot her in the head with a handgun.

⚲ *FANCY DRESS, FASHION, NUNS*

DRIVING

There are about 600,000 Heavy Goods Vehicle drivers in the UK of whom only about 1.2 per cent are women.

According to a survey conducted in 1997: 7 per cent of lorry drivers think of sex, food, drink and a night out while they are driving; 35 per cent think of their families; 16 per cent said they think of nothing at all.

⚲ *DRUNKEN DRIVING, GARDENING, GOLDFISH, SUPERSTITION, WAGNER*

DRUGS

In 2001, Jose Antonio Campos-Cloute was arrested at Melbourne airport after a lapse in concentration when filling out a Customs form: when asked whether he was carrying illicit substances, he absent-mindedly ticked the 'yes' box. The subsequent search revealed that he has answered honestly and was smuggling cocaine.

⚲ *GRAPEFRUIT, SNIFFING, WASP*

DRUNKEN DRIVING

On New Year's Eve 1997, a man identified as a chronic drunken driver was ordered by a judge in Ohio to move nearer a liquor store or face jail. Dennis Cayse, who had been convicted of drunken driving 18 times, was ordered to move within 'easy walking distance' of a liquor store within 30 days or face an 18-month jail sentence for drunken driving. He was also sentenced to spend the first week of each of the next five years in jail.

A cyclist who had modified his helmet to ensure that he did not have to stop drinking beer while on his bike was arrested by German police in July 2000. The man's helmet had a can of beer attached to each side and straws leading into his mouth. A blood test revealed that the cyclist had a blood alcohol level that could have cost him his driving licence if he had been driving a car. Police let him off with a warning and allowed him to keep the helmet – after he had promised to return it to its original design.

In 2000, a court in Munich imposed a three-month driving ban on a man who was arrested for being drunk in charge of his motorised wheelchair.

♀ *GARDENING, MOTORING*

DUBLIN

Between the hours of 5.30pm on a Friday and 3am the following Monday, Dubliners drink an average of 9,800 pints of beer an hour.

The O'Connell Bridge across the River Liffey in Dublin is 45 metres long (147 feet) and 50 metres (164 feet) wide. It is the only traffic bridge in Europe that is wider than it is long.

There are at least 15 places called Dublin in the USA.

Trinity College, Dublin, was founded by Queen Elizabeth I in 1592 and was officially known as the College of the Holy and Undivided Trinity of Queen Elizabeth near Dublin, but the city grew out to meet it.

♀ *QUIZ, UNIVERSITIES*

DUCK

According to hydrodynamic calculations, a duck, when swimming, is only a sixth as efficient as an average ship at utilising energy.

A statue of a drake was erected in 1953 at the Municipal Park in Freiburg as a memorial to world peace. The statue commemorates an incident in 1944 during the Second World War when a duck is said to have alerted the population of the town to an imminent air raid. According to expert opinion at a later noise abatement court case in Germany, 10 quacking ducks make as much noise as three motor lorries with trailers.

In 1970, Milutin Velkjovic set a new world record by living underground in a cave in Serbia for 463 days accompanied only by one cat, one dog, 10 chickens and five Canadian ducks.

In a storm in Arkansas in 1974, a sudden blast of cold air resulted in people being pelted by frozen ducks, killed in flight by the freezing wind.

The total number of ducks in the world was estimated in 2011 as 1,108,354,000, which is about one duck for every seven people. Around 6 per cent were in Vietnam, which was more than in any other country except China, which had two-thirds of the world's ducks.

There are 13.3 ducks per rood (53.3 ducks per acre) on the campus of York University, by far the highest density of ducks at any English university.

The first duck to receive a protection order in New York State's Suffolk County was a pet named Circles. The order was made by a court in 2008 after the duck was shot with a pellet gun by a neighbour.

Donald Duck's middle name is Fauntleroy, as was seen for the first time in the 1942 cartoon 'Donald gets Drafted' when the picture zooms in on Donald's draft papers. The name may have been suggested by the story of *Little Lord Fauntleroy* (published in 1886 by Frances Hodgson Burnett) who, like Donald, was always fond of wearing a sailor suit.

♀ *ARGENTINA, DONALD DUCK, ICELAND, MEMORY, PLATYPUS, SCOLD*

DUELLING

The Duke of Wellington fought a duel with Lord Winchelsea in Battersea Park in 1829. Wellington aimed at the legs and missed. Lord W. fired in the air and apologised. This was the only time a serving British prime minister fought a duel while in office. The Duke had issued the challenge to a duel in response to an alleged slur on his integrity over the religious crisis in Ireland. When the duel was over, Wellington returned calmly to Downing Street then went to Windsor to report the day's events to King George IV.

In 1809, George Canning (then Foreign Secretary, later Prime Minister) fought a duel with the War Minister Lord Castlereagh on Putney Heath on 21 September. The first bullets of both men missed, but Canning's second shot was deflected by a button on Castlereagh's coat and Canning was then wounded in the thigh. Canning was helped to limp away and both men resigned.

⚲ *HUDSON, IRELAND*

DUNG

In 2008, a pile of dinosaur dung was sold at auction in New York for $960 compared with a pre-sale estimate of $450. The fossilised dung from the Jurassic era was bought by the owner of a company that treats dog and cat waste. He said he bought the dung in the hope of motivating his employees. 'Poop is a big business in the pet industry,' he said.

⚲ *FRECKLES, GUANO, HERACLEITUS, YAK*

DURIAN

The durian fruit, loved by many but generally considered the smelliest food on earth, has an odour that was described by the American food

and travel writer Richard Sterling as 'pig-shit, turpentine and onions garnished with gym sock'. The French chef Anthony Bourdain said, 'Your breath will smell as if you have been French-kissing your dead grandmother.'

In Singapore, durian fruit is banned in public places including hotels.

The taste of the durian was much praised by the naturalist Alfred Russell Wallace, who described it as 'a rich butter-like custard highly flavoured with almonds', but his praise provoked a poem, published in *Horticulture* in 1973:

'The durian – neither Russell nor
  Darwin agreed on it,
Darwin said: "may your worst
  enemies be forced to feed on it."
Wallace cried "It's delicious,"
Darwin replied "I'm suspicious,
For the flavour is scented
Like papaya fermented,
After a fruit-eating bat has pee'd on
  it."'

DUVET

According to a survey in 2012, hogging the duvet is the greatest cause of arguments between couples in bed. The average couple were found to have bedroom arguments 167 times a year, with snoring coming second behind duvet-snatching in the list of most common causes.

The top five bedroom bickering reasons were found to be: 1. Hogging the duvet; 2. Snoring; 3. Being too hot; 4. Not being 'in the mood'; 5. Allowing the children to sleep in the bed.

⚲ *LONDON 2012*

DWARF

In October 1995, the 1.1-metre (3-foot-10-inch) tall Manuel Wackenheim petitioned the European Court of

Human Rights to take action against France for banning the pastime of dwarf-throwing. France's highest court, the State Council, had ruled that dwarf-throwing was degrading to human dignity, but Wackenheim pointed out that his human dignity was even more degraded if he was prevented from earning a living. In dwarf-throwing, the human projectile wears a crash helmet and padded clothes with handles on the back for ease of throwing, and the flights are generally about 6 feet long, ending on an inflatable mattress. Wackenheim's lawyer pointed out that his client had never been injured.

The case was argued in several courts over the next seven years, finally reaching the UN Human Rights Committee in September 2002, when a definitive decision ruled that: 'The ban on dwarf-tossing was not abusive but necessary in order to protect public order, including considerations of human dignity.' They also ruled that the ban 'did not amount to prohibited discrimination'.

Even before Wackenheim entered the legal fray, the ethics of dwarf-throwing had captured the minds of moral philosophers. In 1993, Robert W. McGee published a paper in the *American Journal of Jurisprudence* entitled 'If Dwarf-tossing is Outlawed, Only Outlaws Will Toss Dwarfs: is Dwarf-tossing a Victimless Crime?'. 'Dwarf tossing seems to be a win-win situation,' McGee argued. 'Everyone gains and no one loses. The dwarfs stand to earn substantial income, those who toss the dwarfs the farthest can win money plus gain the satisfaction of having won something, those who watch the tossing are entertained, and it is a source of income for promoters. No one loses, right?' McGee concluded that there are no valid arguments to justify outlawing or restricting the practice of dwarf-tossing.

Florida banned dwarf-throwing in 1989 and New York did so a year later. They remain the only US states in which dwarf-throwing is banned.

On 29 November 1995, a spokesman for the actors' union Equity explained the problems caused by 14 Christmas productions of *Snow White*: 'I think it's clear there are relatively few people who are physically suitable for this work,' he said. 'We have only 37 persons of restricted growth on our register.'

♀ *GNOME, HOBBITS, HUDSON, SNOW WHITE, WOLVERHAMPTON*

● DYNAMITE

The word 'dynamite' – from the Greek word for 'force' – was coined in 1867 by its inventor, Alfred Nobel.

♀ *CORONATION, MULES, NOBEL PRIZE*

EAGLE

The first golden eagle to be operated on for cataracts was named Electra; she was blinded when she crashed into overhead electricity cables while fleeing from an attack by crows in 2008. While being nursed for burns at a bird sanctuary in Craignure, Scotland, she was found to have developed the eye condition. The operation restored her sight in one eye, after which she joined the Wings Over Mull bird sanctuary and hospital where she was paired with a male eagle with a broken wing.

MOON, PHOENIX, YODELLING

EARS

In November 2012, Lasha Patraya of the Republic of Georgia set a record for the strongest ears by pulling an eight-ton truck 21.5 metres (70 feet) with his ears.

Spectacles were introduced in Italy in 1268 but arms to clip them round the ears were only added in 1727 by English optician Edward Scarlett.

An ancient Chinese belief is that long earlobes were associated with a person having a long life, while thick earlobes foretold great wealth.

Asians and American Indians have dry, flaky earwax, while Caucasians and Africans are more likely to have moist, brownish earwax.

'We have two ears and one mouth so that we can listen twice as much as we speak.'
Epictetus, Greek philosopher, c.AD 100

ADULTERY, GIRAFFE, TERMITE, TUATARA

EARTH

In May 2021, the US Space Surveillance Network reported over 27,000 pieces of orbital debris, or 'space junk', orbiting the Earth. As of September 2021, there were also 7,941 operational satellites in orbit. The figure for debris included only the objects large enough to be tracked. Additional objects included more than 128 million pieces of debris smaller than 1 centimetre in diameter, about 900,000 pieces of debris of 1–10 centimetres, and around 34,000 pieces larger than 10 centimetres.

The Earth's period of rotation slows by about 2 milliseconds a century. About a billion years ago, we had 481 days, each of 18 hours' duration, in a year.

Since the Earth is not a perfect sphere, the pull of gravity is not the same at all points of its surface. A person who

EAGLE | EARTH

weighs 68 kilograms (150 pounds) at the Equator would weigh 68.4 kilograms (151 pounds) at the North Pole.

The Earth weighs 5,974,000,000,000,000,000,000 tonnes.

℗ COLUMBUS, GALILEI, MARS, MOON, TEXAS, VENUS

EARTHQUAKE

According to an old African belief, earthquakes are caused by a wife calling the name of her mother-in-law.

And according to US geologist James Berkland, adverts for lost pets increase greatly before earthquakes.

On 6 April 1580, one of Britain's worst ever earthquakes was felt from London to York. Its epicentre is now thought to have been beneath the Channel. It caused a tidal wave that sank up to 150 ships and drowned 120 people in Dover. Fearing it was a sign of the wrath of God, the Privy Council wrote to the Archbishop of Canterbury (Edmund Grindal) to ask for spiritual guidance. He advised people to go without one meal a day, giving the money they saved as alms for the poor.

The only bigger British earthquake was on 7 June 1931 when the damage included the wax head of murderer Dr Crippen falling off at Madame Tussauds.

℗ PARMESAN

EARWIG

According to a paper by the Swiss zoologists Ralph Dobler and Mathias Kolliker published in the journal *Animal Behaviour* in 2011 under the title 'Influence of weight asymmetry and kinship on siblicidal and cannibalistic behaviour in earwigs', earwigs do take into account the weight of other earwigs and whether they are related to them before killing and eating them, but the interaction between weight and kinship recognition is complex and appears to depend on social factors.

The male *Diplatys flavicollis* earwig has two double-barrelled penises.

℗ HEDGEHOG

EASTER

Easter was declared a moveable feast by early Christians, who brought in rather complex rules. It does not sound too confusing when we read that Easter Day falls on the first Sunday after the first full moon that occurs on or after 21 March, but what makes it much worse is that the 'full moon' referred to is not the real Moon but a theoretical 'ecclesiastical full moon' that doesn't quite match the one in the sky. In 1928, the British House of Commons agreed to a bill fixing the date of Easter, subject to agreement by various Christian churches. We are still waiting for that agreement.

The name of 'Easter' was thought by the Venerable Bede to refer to Eostre, the pagan goddess of dawn, though there seems to be no evidence for that. Recent research even suggests that no such goddess existed and Eostre may have been the name of a season which was mistranslated by Bede in the 8th century.

The household accounts of Edward I of England for 1290 recorded an expenditure of 18 pence for 450 eggs to be gold-leafed and coloured as Easter gifts. The tradition of decorating eggs around Easter time, however, dates back much further. The ancient Egyptians and Persians used to dye eggs in spring colours and give them to friends as a symbol of renewed life.

Easter Island in the Pacific was discovered by the Dutch sailor Jacob

Roggeveen on Easter Day 1722.

The UK's first chocolate egg was produced in 1873 by Fry's of Bristol. Chocolate sales at Easter in the UK account for 10 per cent of the annual total. When eating a chocolate bunny rabbit, 76 per cent of people bite the ears off first.

⚲ *DRESS, LENT, SANTA CLAUS*

● EASTWOOD, Clint (b. 1930)

Clint Eastwood's birth name was Clinton Eastwood Jr. His father was Clinton Eastwood Sr.

Clint Eastwood's first film role was as a laboratory assistant named Jennings in the 1955 horror film *Revenge of the Creature*. He was also in the 1955 film *Tarantula*, playing the leader of the jet squadron that destroys the spider with napalm at the conclusion. He is not credited in either of these films.

'Clint Eastwood' is an anagram of 'Old west action'.

⚲ *MULES, ORANGUTAN*

● ECHIDNA

The echidna is a small marsupial of Australia. A baby echidna is called a puggle.

The male echidna does not use its penis to urinate and only brings it out of its body when mating. Its testicles are internal.

All animals carry genetic instructions on their DNA, but the echidna is the only one with DNA in its name.

⚲ *PLATYPUS, VAGINA*

● ECLIPSE

The word 'eclipse' comes from the Greek word *ekleipo*, meaning 'to vanish'. On 28 May in 585 BC, the Battle of the Eclipse between the Medes and the Athenians was brought to a sudden end by a solar eclipse. Both sides, baffled by the darkness, took it as a sign that the gods wanted them to stop fighting. A lunar eclipse in 413 BC caused trouble for the Athenians in the Peloponnesian War. They were so frantic that they delayed their retreat from Syracuse, and their commander Nicias was killed.

In 2134 BC, Chinese royal astronomers Hsi and Ho were beheaded for failing to predict an eclipse.

The longest time a total solar eclipse can last is about seven and a half minutes. There will be a 7-minute-20-second eclipse on 16 July 2186.

⚲ *LEAP YEAR*

● ECONOMICS

On 20 October 1995, Robert Lucas of the US was awarded the Nobel Prize for Economics, but the real winner was his ex-wife Rita, who had shown impressive economic judgement in 1989 when she had crafted their divorce agreement. According to a clause in that settlement, she would receive half his $1 million winnings if he won a Nobel Prize before 31 October 1995. Rarely if ever has economics made such an accurate or profitable prediction.

'The only function of economic forecasting is to make astrology look respectable.' John Kenneth Galbraith

● ECUADOR

The peak of the volcano Chimborazo in Ecuador is the point on the Earth's surface furthest away from the centre of the planet. Although Chimborazo is not as high above ground level as Everest, its top is further from the centre of the Earth as it is close to the bulge in the Earth around the Equator. The nearby Cayambe volcano is the only place on the Equator that is permanently covered by snow.

The best Panama hats are made in the town of Montecristi in Ecuador. They were given the name 'Panama' because they were marketed through Panama City and became very popular among workers on the Panama Canal.

♀ PANAMA

EDINBURGH

A penguin named Brigadier Sir Nils Olav III in Edinburgh Zoo is colonel-in-chief of the Norwegian King's Guard. The name 'Nils Olav' and various ranks have been passed down through three king penguins since 1972.

In 1824, Edinburgh became the first city in the world to have a municipal fire brigade.

The last public execution in Edinburgh took place in June 1864.

There are nine women for every eight men in Edinburgh.

The road known as the Royal Mile in Edinburgh is 1 mile and 107 yards in length.

♀ DOLLY, FLIGHT, PENGUIN, STATUE

EDISON, Thomas Alva (1847–1931)

According to an article in the *Fort Wayne Journal-Gazette* in 1906, Thomas Edison had claimed the credit for being the first to suggest the use of the word 'hello' to answer the phone, in place of 'Do I get you?' or 'Are you there?' which had formerly been used. In fact, in a letter to the journal *Antique Phonograph Monthly* in 1877, Edison had written, 'I do not think we shall need a call bell as Hello! can be heard 10 to 20 feet away.'

Starting with an Electrographic Vote-Recorder when he was 22, Edison patented 1,093 devices before his death

at the age of 84. That works out at about one patent every three weeks.

♀ BELL, LIGHT BULB

EDUCATION

'Education is what remains after one has forgotten what one has learned in school.' Albert Einstein

'Education with socialists, it's like sex: all right as long as you don't have to pay for it.' Alan Bennett

♀ CAULIFLOWER, ISOCRATES, SEX EDUCATION

EDWARD VII (1841–1910)

Edward VII was actually named Albert Edward and was known to his family as 'Bertie'. His coronation in 1901 had to be postponed to allow him to undergo an emergency appendectomy operation. When the ceremony finally took place two weeks late, the Archbishop of Canterbury placed the crown back to front on the royal head.

♀ ALEXANDRA, EDWARD VIII

EDWARD VIII (1894–1972)

King Edward VIII was christened Edward Albert Christian George Andrew Patrick David, the last four names being patron saints of the British Isles' countries. He went to Magdalen College, Oxford, but left after eight terms without a degree. On 20 January 1936, King George V died and Edward VIII acceded to the throne of the UK. He abdicated in the same year in order to marry divorcée Wallis Simpson. On 11 December 1936, his last act as King was to give Royal Assent to his own Declaration of Abdication Act.

When he flew to London from Sandringham to become King, he was the country's first monarch to take an aircraft. He was also the first British monarch with a pilot's licence, which he had gained around 1920. Living in France after his abdication, he was suspected of having Nazi sympathies. During the Second World War, he was appointed Governor of the Bahamas.

There were postage stamps in 1936 featuring the face of Edward VIII, but no coins were ever issued. In 1970, a sealed box at the Royal Mint was found to contain 59 coins of Edward VIII designed as pattern pieces. They are now in museums.

Until the abdication of Edward VIII, the direction in which a monarch's head faced on British coins had followed a strict alternating pattern from the time of Charles II. In the last two centuries: George IV faced left; his successor William IV faced right; Victoria faced left; Edward VII faced right; George V faced left, which would have resulted in Edward VIII facing right. So, when Edward abdicated and was replaced by his brother, the new coins had George VI facing left again to take account of the missing monarch. This avoided a potentially difficult problem. On the coins that had been minted, but never released, Edward VIII's head was facing left. Officially this was the wrong way, but the King always preferred to be viewed from that side.

Records show that Edward VIII had an extremely small head. His hat size was only six and three-quarters.

♀ *CROATIA, FASHION*

EGG

Security guards assigned to keep President Fernando Henrique Cardoso of Brazil safe in the late 1990s spent weeks studying the maximum distance an egg can be thrown. Their conclusion was

that the President would be perfectly safe from egg-throwing demonstrators, as long as he stood 60 metres (197 feet) away from them.

Hens in Europe produce 85 billion eggs a year.

The number of pleats in a chef's hat (known as a toque) are said to have originally signified the number of ways the wearer could cook an egg. A great chef was supposed to master up to 100 egg recipes.

'Is there any taste in the white of an egg?'
Job 6:6

♀ *CHICKEN, FLEAS, HENS, OSTRICH, PLATYPUS*

EGYPT

The Great Pyramid of Cheops at Giza was the tallest structure in the world for nearly four millennia. It was built in 2580 BC and its height of 147 metres (480.9 feet) was not overtaken until 1311 when Lincoln Cathedral's Central Tower was built.

A standard greeting in Egypt translates as 'How do you sweat?' Dry skin suggests fever; sweating shows health.

The *Egyptian Book of the Dead*, written about 1240 BC, comprises around 189 chapters of spells and incantations to ensure a smooth passage of the soul to the afterlife.

♀ *EMBALMING, HAT, MARS, PREGNANCY TEST*

EIFFEL TOWER

Because of thermal expansion, the Eiffel Tower is 15 centimetres (6 inches) taller in summer than in winter.

♀ *BLACKPOOL, TOOTHPICK*

EINSTEIN, Albert (1879–1955)

'Albert Einstein' is an anagram of 'Ten elite brains'.

Einstein's lowest grade in school examinations at the age of 17 was in French.

On first seeing him, Einstein's granny is said to have muttered, 'Much too fat, much too fat.'

The famous photo of Einstein with his tongue sticking out was taken on his 72nd birthday by Arthur Sasse. He was fed up after being asked so many times that day to smile for the camera.

In 1930, in collaboration with the physicist Leo Szilard, Einstein received a patent for a type of refrigerator they had invented. It never went into production and probably didn't work very well.

The chemical element einsteinium was discovered and named after Einstein in 1952. It has no known practical uses.

Einstein never wore socks and he never used shaving soap. He knew it was water, not soap, that softens the beard.

Einstein left his brain to science. After he died in 1955 it was removed without his family's permission and taken away in a jar by Thomas Stoltz Harvey, who conducted the autopsy. Harvey sent slices of the brain to various scientists to study, but in 1998, at the age of 85, tired of looking after what he saw as a holy relic, he handed it over to Princeton University.

According to a diary kept by Einstein's friend Johanna Fantova, he was given a parrot as a present for his 75th birthday. After diagnosing the parrot as suffering from depression, Einstein told it bad jokes to cheer it up.

'The hardest thing in the world to under-stand is the income tax.' Albert Einstein

⚲ *ATOMIC ENERGY, EDUCATION, GRAVITY, PI*

EISENHOWER, Dwight David (1890–1969)

After President Eisenhower suffered a heart attack in 1955, he was given a pair of red silk pyjamas by the White House Press Corps with the five stars of a general on them. The words 'Much Better Thanks' were embroidered on the left pocket. A sixth star was added for 'good conduct' by Dr Paul Dudley White, the cardiologist who looked after him.

⚲ *CAMP DAVID*

EL SALVADOR

When the Spanish conquistadors seized control of the South American nation known as Cuzcatlan in 1524, they renamed it La Provincia de Nuestra Senor Jesus Cristo, El Salvador del Mundo (The Province of Our Lord Jesus Christ, Saviour of the World). It was quickly abbreviated to El Salvador.

It has been reported that more people die of centipede bites in El Salvador than in any other country, but since the total number of deaths is no more than five, this may be open to dispute.

In 2017, a member of the US soccer team was bitten by an El Salvador player and also had his nipple twisted during a match which the US won 2–0.

⚲ *ABORTION, PRISONERS, VENEZUELA*

ELASTIC

During the Second World War, restrictions were placed on the making and purchasing of civilian clothing owing to severe shortages of many materials. These included rubber, as the Japanese had occupied the major rubber-producing areas in the Far East. As a result, the use of elastic was restricted to a very small number of garments, which included women's knickers. One of the results of this was a great increase in the use of braces by men to hold their trousers up.

Although clothes rationing in the UK was only finally abandoned in 1949, wartime restrictions on the use of elastic were reduced on 1 April 1946, specifically on its employment in the making of underwear, nightwear, overwear, hose, shirt armlets, identification bracelets, pocket books, pram covers and umbrellas. Restrictions remained in force on other items.

RUBBER BANDS

ELECTRIC CHAIR

Thomas Edison invented the electric chair in 1889, not as a means of execution but as a way of demonstrating the potential hazards of alternating current (AC) while he was trying to promote his own direct current (DC) system. Putting a positive spin on the dangers of the machine, however, the world's executioners were quick to include it in their repertoire, and its value as a warning of the risks of electricity was ignored.

Emperor Menelik II of Abyssinia (now Ethiopia) was one of the first outside America to be impressed by the new invention and ordered three of the chairs. Unfortunately, Abyssinia had no electricity at the time so Menelik had one of them converted into an imperial throne.

On 6 October 1941, two men were sent to the electric chair in Florida. Their names were Willburn and Frizzel.

ELEMENTS

According to a survey conducted at the University of Barcelona and published in 2008 in the *New Journal of Chemistry*, the most popular chemical elements in song lyrics are silver, gold, tin and oxygen, in that order. The paper also

reported that the composer Edgard Varese wrote a piece dedicated to platinum, called 'Density 21.5'. It is a solo piece written for the flautist Georges Barres to play on his new platinum flute.

BODY, FORTY-SEVEN, STEEL

ELEPHANT

In the Middle Ages, the manner of copulation in elephants was a matter for speculation. Back to back was one theory, suggested by the position of their genitals. Others thought that the male probably dug a pit or floated, to avoid crushing his mate.

King James I of England is said to have kept a menagerie in St James's Park, including an 'ellefant', which was given a gallon of wine every day.

The first elephant in the United States arrived in New York from India on 13 April 1796. It was described as 'the greatest natural curiosity ever presented to the public'. Visitors were charged 50 cents to see it but not many paid, so the price was lowered to 25 cents. Since then, 13 April has officially been celebrated in America as Elephant Day.

Between 1983 and 2000 the number of people killed by captive elephants in the US was 17.

On 17 July 1975, an elephant called Modoc died in California at the age of 78, the oldest known non-human land mammal. Exactly 22 years later, on 17 July 1997, the science journal *Nature* published a paper showing that the African golden mole is more closely related to the elephant than to the garden mole.

On 2 June 1971, the *Sun* newspaper in the UK reported that an elephant named Iris had been taught to play 'When the Saints Go Marching In' on a mouth organ.

The first dental filling on an elephant was performed in South Africa in 1981. A team of 17 doctors and dentists took part, using enough anaesthetic to kill 70 men.

A Boeing 747 Jumbo Jet weighs as much as 67 average African elephants.

The original Jumbo the Circus Elephant was killed in 1885 in a railway accident in Ontario. It took 160 men to remove his body from the tracks.

The gestation period of an African elephant is 660 days. The pulse of a healthy elephant is only 25 beats a minute. Its trunk contains about 40,000 muscles and no bones and can hold a pint and a half of water.

Elephants cannot jump, but the elephant is the only animal apart from man that has been taught to stand on its head.

The food eaten during the life of the average Westerner weighs as much as six fully grown African elephants.

ALASKA, BOTSWANA, IVORY COAST, PANGOLIN, SRI LANKA, TREADMILL

ELIZABETH

The world's largest gathering of Elizabeths is believed to have been held in the northern Illinois community of Elizabeth in 2008, when women with Elizabeth in any part of their name were invited to attend. The event drew around 400 Elizabeths from more than 20 US states, each showing a copy of her birth certificate or driver's licence. 'We did invite Queen Elizabeth II, but she politely declined,' said one of the organisers.

ELIZABETH I, Queen of England (1533–1603)

The *Dictionary of National Biography* entry on Queen Elizabeth I says: 'she swore, she spat upon a courtier's coat when it did not please her taste, she beat her gentlewomen soundly, she kissed whom she pleased'. She also had black teeth from eating too much sugar. But she clearly had a high regard for cleanliness as she took a bath once a month.

Queen Elizabeth's last words are said to have been, 'All my possessions for a moment of time.'

BACON Francis, DUBLIN, WIG

ELIZABETH II, Queen of England (b. 1926)

Queen Elizabeth's middle names are Alexandra Mary. She was born by Caesarean section at 17 Bruton Street, Mayfair.

Five years before she became Queen, Elizabeth married Prince Philip in Westminster Abbey on 20 November 1947; the 10-shilling note went out of circulation on 20 November 1970. General Franco of Spain died on 20 November 1975.

Queen Elizabeth II visited the Wimbledon tennis championships on 24 June 2010. Her most recent previous visit to the event had been in 1977, when she saw Britain's Virginia Wade win the Women's Singles.

In 2022, she celebrated her 70th year on the throne. No other living head of state had served for so long. During her reign there have been 14 UK prime ministers and 14 US presidents. She met all the US presidents except Lyndon B. Johnson, but she also met President Truman before she became Queen. Counting all the Commonwealth realms over which she has reigned, the Queen has had over 170 individuals serve as her prime ministers.

'The Queen looks after her gloves – she doesn't tend to leave them on buses like

the rest of us.' Genevieve Lawson, royal glove-maker *(Her Majesty takes size 7 gloves.)*

JELLY BEAN, LAMPREY, MOLE, PONY, VANUATU

EMAIL

The first email message was sent in 1971. Email was developed by Ray Tomlinson, who is also responsible for the choice of the @ symbol in email addresses, which he selected to show who was 'at' the computer. The first message he sent was 'qwertyuiop'. When asked why he had invented email, he said, 'because it seemed like a neat idea'.

Émail is the French for 'enamel'.

CARROT, INTERNET, LYING

EMBALMING

Powdered mummy was used as a medicinal drug from the 12th to the 17th centuries. Originally, this may have been due to a belief in the life-giving qualities of human bodies, but later the grounds shifted to a belief in the medicinal qualities of bitumen, which was thought to have been used in the embalming process in ancient Egypt. That was wrong too, as the Egyptians used resin, not bitumen.

EMERGENCY

Tokyo police responding to an early morning emergency call concerning a man driving the wrong way down a motorway in September 2010 apprehended the driver only after he had smashed through five police blockades and one tollgate. Explaining his actions, the man said, 'I was sad that my pet cat died and I wanted to do something crazy.'

AMNESIA, EDWARD VII, EXECUTION

EMU

An emu was shot on the German–Swiss border in 2007 after a chase involving the police of both nations. The bird was first reported in the German town of Grenzach-Wyhlen, but it evaded capture there, prompting an international operation. After being clocked running at 80 km/h (50 mph), dodging roadblocks and avoiding vets with tranquillisers, the emu was eventually shot by a hunter.

CONTRACEPTION, KANGAROO

ENEMA

The tobacco smoke enema, also known as rectal inflation, consisted of blowing tobacco smoke into the rectum and was a medical treatment employed in Europe from the 17th to the 19th century. It was a technique borrowed from North American Indians who were strong believers in the medical properties of tobacco, especially for colds, drowsiness and stomach pains.

The English royal physician Richard Mead was one of the first Western doctors to recommend tobacco smoke enemas to resuscitate victims of drowning, beginning in 1745 when he recommended it for patients who had inhaled water when being treated with immersion therapy. One of the earliest documented cases of resuscitation by rectally applied tobacco smoke was carried out in 1746 when an apparently drowned woman was treated. On the advice of a sailor, the woman's husband inserted the stem of the sailor's pipe into her rectum, covered the bowl with a piece of perforated paper, and 'blew hard', which led to the woman's revival.

By the 1780s, smoke enema kits were installed at various points along the River Thames by the Royal Humane Society, and by the beginning of the

19th century, tobacco smoke enemas had become an established practice in Western medicine, on a par with artificial respiration. The practice fell into decline in the 19th century when it was discovered that nicotine is poisonous.

An earlier account of a restorative enema was the case of Anne Greene, a woman hanged in 1650 for the supposed murder of her stillborn child. When her body was cut down, she was found by anatomists to be still alive and a variety of treatments were applied to revive her, including pouring hot cordial down her throat, rubbing her limbs and extremities, bleeding her, applying heating plasters and a 'heating odoriferous Clyster to be cast up in her body, to give heat and warmth to her bowels'. Finally, she was placed in a warm bed with another woman to keep her warm, after which she recovered fully and was pardoned.

ENGLISH

The longest word in the *Oxford English Dictionary* is a 45-letter lung disease: 'pneumonoultramicroscopicsilicovolcanoconiosis'. The longest word used by Shakespeare was 'honorificabilitudinitatibus', a 27-letter concoction which is found in *Love's Labours Lost*. It means 'the state of being able to receive honours'.

The eight-letter word 'Aegilops', which can mean either a genus of molluscs or an eye ulcer, is the longest word that has its letters in alphabetical order. 'Beefily' and 'billowy' share second place with seven letters each. The longest word with its letters in reverse alphabetical order is 'spoonfeed'.

The top three words in spoken English are 'I', 'you' and 'the'. In written English, they are 'the', 'of' and 'and'. The top three in the King James Bible are 'and', 'the'

and 'of'. In this encyclopaedia, they are 'the', 'in' and 'of'.

AZTEC, BUTTOCKS, EPONYM, FINGERS, GOOSE, KISSING

ENVIRONMENT

A brothel called the House of Desire in Berlin's red-light district announced in 2009 that it would be offering a discount to customers who cycled there. 'It is very difficult to find parking around here,' the brothel's owner said, 'and this option is better for the environment.'

BEIJING, YODELLING

EPONYM

A word that derived from a person's name. For example:

- Place names, such as: *Pennsylvania* (after William Penn) and *Monrovia* (named for US President James Monroe)
- Items of clothing, such as: *leotard* (after Jules Léotard, who gave his first performance in November 1859 as the daring young man on the flying trapeze at the Cirque Napoleon in Paris), *bloomers* (after Amelia Jenks Bloomer, the 19th-century social reformer who advocated wearing such things), and *cardigan,* named for James Brudenel, 7th Earl of Cardigan, who led the Charge of the Light Brigade
- Diseases, such as: *salmonella* (after the American surgeon Daniel Elmer Salmon) and *Asperger syndrome* (after Austrian paediatrician Hans Asperger)
- Culinary inventions, such as: *Caesar salad* (concocted by the Italian chef Caesar Cardini in the 1920s) and *Omelette Arnold Bennett* (made for the novelist Arnold Bennett at the Savoy Grill in London)

- Other human activities, such as: *boycott* (from Captain Charles Boycott, the Irish land agent whose high rents in 1880 angered the Irish Land League into having nothing to do with him), *mausoleum* (from King Mausolus, whose tomb was one of the Seven Wonders of the World), and *shrapnel* (after British army officer Lieutenant-General Henry Shrapnel, inventor of shrapnel shells)

Perhaps the most curious eponym in English, however, is *sideburns*, which seems to have been formed from the word *burnsides*, which was applied to a style of beard worn by the American General Ambrose Burnside, consisting of a moustache, whiskers and a clean-shaven chin, but 'burnsides' were often called 'side-whiskers' and then 'sideburns'.

… and do remember that, while 'tawdry' refers to shoddy goods bought at St Audrey's Fair in Ely, the word 'sleaze' comes from Silesia.

⚲ *HAT, LEGS*

◉ EQUALITY

The equals sign (=) was introduced by Robert Recorde in his 1557 publication *The Whetstone of Witte*. He chose the sign = because 'noe .2. thynges, can be moare equalle' than a pair of parallel lines.

The symbol = did not gain immediate popularity. The symbol || was used by some and ae (or oe), from the Latin 'aequalis' meaning equal, was widely used into the 1700s.

Robert Recorde's title of *The Whetstone of Witte* was an elaborate pun. Algebra, at the time, was known as the cossic art, from the habit of referring to the unknown as *cosa*, the Latin for 'thing'. Algebraists were called cossists and the first German algebra text, published in 1525, was called *Coss*. The word *cos* is Latin for whetstone, a stone for sharpening razors and tools. Hence the pun: it was an algebra book on which to sharpen one's mathematical wit.

The + and – signs were first used by Johann Widman in 1489.

⚲ *POTATO, WIMBLEDON*

◉ EQUINOX

The word 'equinox' means 'equal night' and is often seen as the days when day and night are each exactly 12 hours long. But that is wrong: such days are 'equiluxes' ('equal light') and occur a few days before or after the equinoxes. The reason is that daylight is from the first appearance of the Sun over the horizon to the end of its setting. On the equinox it is the centre of the Sun that is visible for exactly 12 hours. The equinoxes are the only days when the Sun rises directly due east and sets due west in the northern hemisphere.

An old myth was that eggs could be stood on their sharp ends only at the equinox. Supposedly that was because the gravitational pull of the Sun directly overhead exactly balanced that of the Earth. That is absolute nonsense.

⚲ *CREATION, GOOD FRIDAY, GROUNDHOG DAY, VATICAN*

◉ ESKIMO

The word 'Eskimo' comes from Algonquian Indian and means 'eater of raw flesh'.

⚲ *BUTTOCKS, SNOW*

◉ ESTONIA

When Estonia left the Soviet Union in 1991, life expectancy in that country was 69.2 years. By 2021 it had increased to 78.9.

There are only 53 Estonian men over 65 to every 100 women over 65, according to 2020 estimates. Russia and Belarus are worse, with 47 and 48 males respectively for every 100 females among the over-65s.

When Estonia became the 17th country to join the euro in 2011, its new coins were made in Finland.

BANANA, STOMACH, WIFE CARRYING

ETHIOPIA

Ethiopia has its own calendar, which has 13 months in a year. Twelve of those months have exactly 30 days, while the thirteenth is a shorter month of only five or six days. The six-day months only occur every fourth year, corresponding to the added leap day in our own calendar, though the Ethiopians add the leap day at the end of our August, which is six months later than our extra day. Also, their leap years do not omit three out of every four century years, so their calculations of the date are gradually moving ahead of ours. They also have a different way of calculating the birth of Jesus Christ, which results in Ethiopia calling the year that we know as 2022 as being 2014–15 in their calendar.

The Ethiopian method of telling the time is also unique but has a certain logic to it. The day begins with sunrise, which is called one o'clock, and sunset occurs at twelve o'clock, after which a night clock of another 12 hours takes over.

Emperor Menelik II of Ethiopia nibbled a few pages of the Bible whenever he became ill, believing in its curative powers. In December 1913 he ate the entire Book of Kings when convalescing after a stroke, and died.

BABOON, HONEY, LEPROSY

ETIQUETTE

According to a manual published around 1859 in England with the title *The Habits of Good Society: A Handbook of Etiquette for Ladies and Gentlemen,* a lady should accept only one glass of champagne when it is offered. Anything more or less would be improper.

The same book offers sound advice on carving dinner: 'Of a goose or a turkey we are told it is "vulgar" to cut more than the breast, but there can be no vulgarity in making a good dinner, and in the family circle you will be obliged to apply to the wings and legs. However, for company, slices of the breast suffice.'

The anonymous author also has some strong remarks to make on 'certain habits which are more or less annoying to your neighbours'. These include touching the ears and nose with your fingers, biting your nails, picking your teeth, or scratching the head or any part of the body. In Turkey, we are told, 'it is quite the fashion to scratch the bites of a little insect as common there as in certain London hotels, and it is even considered a delicate attention to catch the lively creatures as they perch on the dress or shoulders of your partner. Fortunately, we are not tempted to perform such attentions in this country; but, if you have the misfortune to be bitten or stung by any insect, you must endure the pain without scratching the bite in company. These same little insects being of very disagreeable origin, are not even spoken of with us.' And when blowing your nose, 'you must not make the noise of a trumpet, but do it gently and quietly; and, when you sneeze, use your handkerchief'.

CHINA, TABLE MANNERS

EURO

In 1994, the name of EuroDisney was changed to Disneyland Paris, as the prefix 'Euro' was found to have negative connotations for Europeans.

The first euro coin was made in France on 11 May 1998, but the launch of the euro on 1 January 2002 provoked a variety of reactions:

In Poland, two mathematicians demonstrated that Belgian euro coins were more likely to land heads than tails up when spun on a table. Their result, however, did not apply to tossed coins.

In Britain, the Magic Circle appealed for an increase in the size of euro coins, which they found to be too small for a number of tricks.

In Germany, tests showed that euro notes could survive being washed and spun-dry, but ironing ruined them. Meanwhile, replying to reports of toxicity in the ink, the European Central Bank stated that you would have to eat 400 banknotes to make yourself ill.

When the new currency was launched, 50 billion coins and 14.5 billion notes were brought into circulation. If all the one-euro coins had been put into a single pile, it would have been 49,000 miles high.

The initial letters of the 12 countries that joined the euro on its launch spell out the phrase 'baffling pigs'.

ESTONIA, LATVIA, TRICOLOUR

EUROPE

European civilisation began with a beef crisis: Zeus, head of the Greek gods, fell in love with Europa, daughter of the Phoenician King Agenor, and turned himself into a white bull in order to seduce her. Europa found him so sleek and gentle, she climbed on his back, whereupon he galloped into the sea and carried her off to Crete.

Europa's name comes either from the Greek for 'broad face' or a Semitic verb meaning 'to set' (symbolising her riding off into the setting sun on a bull). She gave her name to the continent, while the bull became identified with the constellation of Taurus.

The population of Europe is about 746 million, which is one-tenth of the world's population. Europe covers about 8 per cent of the Earth's land surface. The European part of Russia accounts for 40 per cent of Europe's land area.

Strictly speaking, Europe is not a continent but only a part of the Eurasian land mass. Its notional boundary with Asia began as a matter of convenience for the Greeks, who wanted a way to differentiate between the land on the two sides of the Hellespont (now Dardanelles). This confused the historian Herodotus, who wrote: 'As for Europe, nobody knows if it is surrounded by sea, or where it got its name from, or who gave it.'

The highest toilet in Europe is on Mont Blanc, nearly 4,270 metres (14,000) feet up.

The vast bulk of Europe, from the British Isles to the Urals, was formed between 570 million and 225 million years ago. Britain's insularity dates back only 6,000–10,000 years, when the seas rose to form the Channel and North Sea.

Man's ancestors, *Homo sapiens Neanderthalensis*, first appeared in Europe between 100,000 and 50,000 years ago – which is up to 100,000 years after the first hominids in Africa.

The earliest artefacts in Europe date back around 30,000 years, with the Willendorf Venus, dated at around

21,000 BC, the earliest known European sculpture of a female nude.

♀ *BED, DWARF, HIPPOPOTAMUS, MADRID, MEDICINE, RUBBISH*

● EUROVISION SONG CONTEST

Norway holds the record for scoring no points most often – a feat it has achieved on four occasions – but the country with most last places is Finland, with a total of eight.

In 1964, Germany came last with no points, despite having the longest ever title: 'Man Gewöhnt Sich So Schnell An Das Schöne' ('How quickly we get used to beautiful things').

The shortest titles have been 'Si' (Italy, 1974), 'El' (Spain, 1982), 'Hi' (Israel, 1983) and 'Go' (UK, 1988).

In 1968, the lyrics of the winning Spanish entry, 'La, La, La', included 138 occurrences of 'la'.

Ireland's Johnny Logan is the most successful Euro-contestant: he won as singer in 1980, singer and composer in 1987, and composer in 1992.

Vatican City is the only country in Europe that has never tried to enter the Eurovision Song Contest.

In addition, Kosovo and Liechtenstein applied to enter, but they were turned down as they were not members of the European Broadcasting Union at the time.

Of the 52 countries that have entered the contest since its inception in 1956, 27 have won it.

♀ *CLEOPATRA, IRELAND*

● EVEREST

Sir George Everest, after whom the world's tallest mountain was named in 1865, pronounced his surname with two syllables, Eve-rest, not three, as in E-ve-rest.

The Chinese called the mountain Qomolangma, after an earth goddess, in the mid-18th century. The British probably did not know that when their Great Trigonometrical Survey of 1852 confirmed Everest to be the world's highest peak.

The first people to climb Everest were Sir Edmund Hillary and Tenzing Norgay in 1953. In 1990, Peter Hillary, son of Sir Edmund Hillary, became the first son of an Everest climber to follow in his father's footsteps to the top of the mountain.

Since 1953, on average one person has climbed Everest every three weeks and one has died on its slopes every 12 weeks. Discounting the expeditions that end in neither death nor glory, the odds are therefore slightly worse than Russian roulette. Around 2,900 climbers have reached the top, including Nepalese mountaineer Apa Sherpa, 50, who retired in 2017 after doing so 22 times.

A record was set on 10 May 1993 when 40 climbers reached the summit, but since then many more have climbed Everest. On one weekend in May 2010, 216 did so, which did not include any who climbed from the Tibet side. On 23 May 2019, the record for the number of successful climbers in one day increased to 354.

On 25 May 2001, the American Erik Weihenmayer became the first blind man to conquer Everest.

Movement of the Earth's tectonic plates results in Everest growing at a rate of about 4mm a year.

♀ *ECUADOR, HILLARY, MOUNTAINEERING, TOKYO*

● EXAMINATIONS

St Joseph of Cupertino is the patron saint of examination-takers. He is also patron saint of air crews, air travellers, aircraft pilots, astronauts, aviators, flyers, paratroopers and students.

Various news items show that cheating in examinations is a worldwide phenomenon:

In 1995, schoolgirls in one area of Nigeria were instructed to remove their underwear before taking exams because so many had been smuggling in crib sheets in their undies.

In 1996, an Italian teacher was suspended for passing students answers hidden in salami sandwiches.

In 1999, thousands of Bangladeshi students were expelled for demanding the right to cheat in exams.

In 2022, a medical student in India was found to have had a Bluetooth device implanted in his ear to receive answers from another student who had been frisked to reveal a phone sewn into an inside pocket of his trousers.

Cheating would not have helped students in Uganda in 1998, when thousands of exam results were lost after rats chewed through computer cables at the National Examination Board.

Exam cheats can be sentenced to 10 years in jail in the Indian state of Andhra Pradesh.

♀ *HOMEWORK, SANDWICHES, SLIPPERS*

⬤ EXECUTION

According to Harold Hillman's classic report 'The Possible Pain Experienced During Execution by Different Methods' (*Perception*, 1993, vol. 22, pp. 745–53), stoning to death is probably the most painful way of being executed. As Hillman pointed out: 'Information about the physiology and pathology can be derived from observations on the condemned persons, postmortem examinations, physiological studies on animals undergoing similar procedures, and the literature on emergency medicine. It is difficult to know how much pain the person being executed feels or for how long, because many of the signs of pain are obscured by the procedure or by physical restraints, but one can identify those steps which are likely to be painful.'

On 15 March 2004, Utah became the last US state to give up executions by firing squad. Until then, their method had involved a five-man firing squad, one of whom was randomly allocated a blank cartridge so nobody would ever know who fired the fatal shot.

♀ *CAPITAL PUNISHMENT, CRANE, ELECTRIC CHAIR, GUILLOTINE, HANGING, KNICKERS*

⬤ EXORCISM

Exorcisms in the Church of England are carried out through the Deliverance Ministry, created in 1974 to ensure that every diocese included a team trained in both exorcism and psychiatry. This seems largely to have been influenced through the release of the film *The Exorcist* in 1973.

The International Association of Exorcists was founded in 1990 under the presidency of Father Gabriel Amorth, who was also chief exorcist of the Vatican and carried out more than 70,000 exorcisms in a career spanning 25 years. His favourite film is said to have been *The Exorcist*, and he spoke out against both Harry Potter and yoga, claiming that they 'lead to evil' because of their links with magic and spiritualism.

In 2006, he gave an interview to Vatican Radio in which he said that Adolf Hitler and Russian dictator Josef Stalin were both possessed by the Devil. He also said that, during the Second

World War, Pope Pius XII attempted a 'long distance exorcism' of Hitler but it failed to have any effect.

♀ AUCTION, DALI

EXPECTANT MOTHERS

The Sentence of Death (Expectant Mothers) Act 1931 prohibited the passing of a death sentence in English courts on an expectant mother. When a woman convicted of a capital offence claimed that she was expecting a child, the law specified that it was the duty of the jury that found her guilty to be responsible for deciding whether or not she was pregnant 'on such evidence as may be laid before them'. Although the death sentence was repealed in the UK in 1965, the Sentence of Death (Expectant Mothers) Act was not repealed until 1998.

EXTRATERRESTRIALS

It has been estimated that about 4 million Americans think they have been abducted by aliens.

♀ COSTA RICA, PHOENIX

EYE

Apart from being the word for an organ of sight, an 'eye', or a 'nye', is an obsolete word for a brood of pheasants.

Camels have three eyelids on each eye. Two have eyelashes while the third is a thin membrane that acts as a windscreen wiper in sandstorms.

On average we blink 12 times a minute. The average lifespan of a human eyelash is five months.

♀ CAT, CATARACT, GOLDFISH, ISLAM, MEMORY, SLUG, SQUID

EYEBALL

On 11 November 1911, the *British Medical Journal* published a paper entitled 'Removal of the Eyeball: A Quick and Easy Method'. Written by eye surgeon William Morrison, the account of the method begins with the words 'The patient is anaesthetised', which sounds like a good idea, and continues: 'Unless the surgeon be ambidextrous, to remove the right eyeball, he stands at the head of the table, and to remove the left at the patient's left side.' The necessary equipment consists of an eye speculum, a pair of toothed fixation forceps, a small pair of blunt-pointed scissors (straight or curved on the flat), and a curved needle threaded with fine iodised catgut.

♀ FROG

EYEBROW

In 2009, a 72-year-old man from Bloomington, Indiana, raised $1,600 for charity from people who paid to take turns trimming his out-of-control eyebrows, which had never been cut before. Si Burgher's eyebrows were reported to have been so long that he brushed them each morning. Some of the hairs cut off measured more than three inches long.

Since *cilium* was the Latin for eyelid or eyebrow, the word 'supercilious' refers to the haughty raising of one's eyebrows.

Leviticus 14:9 is the only verse in the King James Bible that uses the words 'eyebrow' or 'eyebrows': 'But it shall be on the seventh day, that he shall shave all his hair off his head and his beard and his eyebrows, even all his hair he shall shave off.'

A paper in the journal *Perception* in 2004 reported research at the Massachusetts Institute of Technology that revealed the importance of eyebrows in facial recognition. Apparently experiments showed that only about 46% of people recognised photos of celebrities when the eyebrows were removed.

The average person has about 250 hairs in each eyebrow and each such hair lasts only about four months before it falls out.

BODY, PIZZA

EYELASH

As long ago as 3500 BC, ancient Egyptian women were known to use methods to enhance the appearance of their eyelashes. The ancient Romans also sought to darken and lengthen their eyelashes after Pliny the Elder in 753 BC identified short lashes as a sign of ageing.

The invention of artificial false eyelashes, however, took much longer, and their invention is often attributed to film director D.W. Griffith for the 1916 film *Intolerance*, as false lashes were worn by Seena Owen. While that film certainly made them popular, the first US patent for false eyelashes was awarded in 1911 to Canadian Anna Taylor, who provided glue-on lashes said to be made of human hair.

Judy Garland's false eyelashes fetched $125 at auction in 1979 in Beverly Hills.

EYE, HAIR, OSTRICH

EZRA

'And I, even I, Artaxerxes the king, issue a decree to all the treasurers who are in the region beyond the River, that whatever Ezra the priest, the scribe of the Law of the God of heaven, may require of you, let it be done diligently.' Ezra 7:21, King James Bible

This verse from the Old Testament contains every letter of the alphabet except J, both in the King James and New English editions. At the time of King James, the letters I and J were the same; they only became distinct letters around 1700, so this verse has a good claim to be the only one in the Bible that includes every letter of the alphabet.

FA CUP

The first FA Cup Final was held at the Oval in London on 16 March 1872 with Wanderers beating Royal Engineers 1–0. The following year Wanderers retained the Cup by beating Oxford University.

The record score in an FA Cup tie was set when Preston North End defeated Hyde 26–0 in 1897.

Lord Kinnaird played in nine FA Cup Finals for Wanderers and Old Etonians, which is still a record. He celebrated his fifth Cup Final victory in 1882 by standing on his head in front of the pavilion.

In 1883, Blackburn Olympic became the first professional club to win the Cup, beating Old Etonians with a team full of English-only players.

Everton, Manchester United and Chelsea have each lost eight FA Cup Finals, just ahead of Newcastle United, Liverpool and Arsenal, who have lost seven each.

The first Football League and FA Cup double was achieved by Preston North End in 1888 when they won the league without losing a single match and the cup without conceding a goal.

The oldest existing version of the FA Cup itself, presented to winning teams from 1896 to 1910, was sold at auction in 2005 for £478,400. The very first trophy was stolen in 1895 and never seen again.

♀ *MANCHESTER UNITED*

FACEBOOK

An Israeli changed his name to Mark Zuckerberg in 2011 after he received what he said were threats to sue him from lawyers at Facebook. The man, under his former name of Rotem Guez, had launched an online business which offered free content to Facebook users who clicked 'like' on his company's Facebook profile. Facebook said this violated their terms of use. The entrepreneur formerly known as Rotem Guez responded by saying, 'If you want to sue me, you're going to have to sue Mark Zuckerberg.'

♀ *MOOSE, OIL, SWEDEN*

FALKLAND ISLANDS

According to their 2012 census, the resident population of the Falkland Islands is 2,840. There are also about 700,000 sheep in the Falklands, which is almost 275 sheep per person. In addition to the resident population, there are about 1,700 military personnel on the islands.

The islands are named after the Fifth Viscount Falkland, who sponsored an expedition there in 1690. The first human settlers on the islands were French sailors from the port of Saint-Malo in 1764 – which is why the Argentines call them the Malvinas. The Spanish bought the islands from the French, and later gave them to Argentina; the British took them by force from Argentina in 1833.

According to an official list of business opportunities in the Falklands, one opportunity is 'adding value to squid'.

Five species of penguin can be seen in the Falklands.

The Falklands' motto is 'Desire the right', which pays tribute to the ship *The Desire*, from which Thomas Cavendish discovered the islands in 1586.

● FALLOPPIO, Gabriele (1523–62)

The Italian anatomist Gabriele Falloppio, also known as Fallopius, after whom the fallopian tube is named, specialised not in the female reproductive system but in the human head. He was also a professor of botany and wrote a treatise on baths and thermal waters. In 1564, Falloppio wrote a treatise called *De Morbo Gallico* (*On the French Disease*). It was about syphilis.

♀ *GRÄFENBERG*

● FALSE TEETH

According to a survey by Düsseldorf University Hospital, false teeth are the third most likely item to cause problems by being swallowed accidentally. The only items that more often require medical treatment after accidental swallowing are chicken bones and fish bones.

In February 2012, a 74-year-old man named only as Chen died in New Taipei City after swallowing his false teeth during a session with a prostitute. The prostitute, who was 62, reported that at the end of the 30-minute session, Chen collapsed and fell back on the bed with his eyes open but without moving. She tried to wake him by shaking him, but called paramedics when this was unsuccessful. Medical staff rushed to the scene, but he was found to be dead on arrival at the hospital, where an examination revealed that his dentures were lodged in his throat.

♀ *DENTURES, LIECHTENSTEIN, TEETH*

● FAMILY

The word 'family' originally included not only relatives but also the servants of a household. It derives from the Latin *famulus*, meaning 'a servant'.

'Govern a family as you would cook a small fish – very gently.' Chinese proverb

♀ *BHUTAN, JAPAN, LOVE OBSTACLES, MUMMIFICATION*

● FANCY DRESS

The principal of a school in Perth, Western Australia, wrote to parents in September 2010 apologising for awarding a prize to a young boy dressed as Adolf Hitler in a costume parade. The boy had been judged 'best dressed' by the principal and other teachers. 'It's a one-off thing that in retrospect we'd do differently,' the principal told a local newspaper, but he also pointed out that Hitler 'was a fairly famous person'.

● FART

The average fart comprises 59 per cent nitrogen, 21 per cent hydrogen, 9 per cent carbon dioxide, 7 per cent methane and 4 per cent oxygen.

The 'hohi kenshutsuki' was claimed as the world's first fart detector when it was revealed in 2002 by Mitreben Laboratories, based in Osaka. Hideo Ueda, a member of the research team, explained: 'In hospitals, it is important for physicians to know if a post-operative patient has been farting. When a patient is coming out from under total anaesthesia, farting is an indication that the digestive tract is returning to normal. After major surgery, patients are still in a groggy state and aren't aware of this themselves. That is what led to the development of this device.'

⚲ DE VERE, FRANKLIN, GLOBAL WARMING, HERRING

● FASHION

'Fashion' originally referred to the process of making something, then the shape or appearance of something, and finally the current mode or the mode characteristic for a particular time. Shakespeare was one of the first to use it to imply something that is in vogue.

A fashion pre-dating Shakespeare's, however, came from Catherine de Medici, Queen of France, who in the 16th century decreed that all ladies at court must have 33-centimetre (13-inch) waists.

In 1994, the American designer Ed Kirko introduced a fashion by shooting holes through clothes. His bestseller was a Stetson hat with a bullet hole apparently going through the wearer's head.

On 1 March 1934, the Prince of Wales (later Edward VIII) said, 'I can see no reason why women should not wear shorts.'

On 11 September 1995, at a bridal fair fashion show in Harrogate, white wedding dresses for pregnant brides made their first appearance.

'Gentlemen never wear brown in London.' Lord Curzon

⚲ BIKINI, ROBOT, SHOES

● FEBRUARY

February is named after the purification ritual Februa, which was a sort of early Roman spring-cleaning festival. The month of February is said to have been invented by the legendary second King of Rome, Numa Pompilius, in 713 BC. Before then, the Roman calendar ended with December and did not begin again until March.

Before Julius Caesar reformed the calendar in 46 BC, February was the only month with an even number of days. Even after Caesar's calendar reform, which brought in leap years by giving February an extra day every four years, the last day of February was still always the 28th. The extra day was gained by counting the 24th twice. All the other months had either 29 or 31 days.

February frequently occurs in lists of the most commonly misspelt words in the English language. The Americans also have trouble with the word February. In 2015, a press release from the White House consistently spelled it as 'Feburary'.

Much Ado About Nothing is Shakespeare's only play that mentions February. 'You have such a February face, So full of frost, of storm and cloudiness.'

In Old English, February was called Solmonath (Mud month) or Kalemonath (Kale or cabbage month).

February is the only month that can pass with no full Moon. This happened in both 2009 and 2018.

LEAP YEAR, MARCH, ST VALENTINE

FEET

Research into shoe size has shown that people in the south of England have bigger feet on average than people in the north.

Nearly a quarter of all your bones are in your feet. Each foot has 26 bones, which is one less than the 27 in each hand.

On 17 November 1997, the Californian Supreme Court ruled that feet are not deadly weapons, as defined by the law of aggravated assault.

BUTTERFLY, MOLE, PENGUIN, POLAR BEAR, SHOES, SWAHILI

FENCING

Both meanings of 'fencing' owe their existence to the word 'defence'. A 'house of fence' was a fortified house; a 'man of fence' was a defender. Hence the word 'fence' came to be applied to the wooden structure marking the end of a property, and the man with a sword defending it.

The elephant is the only non-human animal ever to be taught to use a sword.

D'EON, OLYMPIC GAMES

FENG SHUI

According to a Filipino expert on Feng Shui, speaking in 1996, honeymooners must make sure the bathroom door does not open towards their bed and the TV set does not face them directly if they want to have good sex. Electrical wires lying about and radiation from the television can also disturb the energy field of the bed.

Merlina Merton advised that if newly married couples want to watch adult movies, the set should be angled to the bed, and added: 'But if you need to watch dirty movies while you're on a honeymoon, my God, the marriage is gone already.'

FERRARI

The funeral of Mrs Sandra West, a wealthy Beverly Hills socialite, was held on 19 May 1977 at the Alamo Masonic Cemetery in San Antonio. According to the terms of her will, she was to be laid to rest in the front seat of her Ferrari: 'next to my husband, in my lace night-gown … and in my Ferrari, with the seat slanted comfortably'. The car was a light-blue 1964 Ferrari 250GT and it was placed in a specially made concrete box before burial. Armed guards protected both the car and Mrs West's body at the funeral, which cost $17,000.

FERRET

The word 'ferret' comes from the Latin *furittus*, meaning 'little thief', probably referring to the ferret's practice of hiding away small objects. The verb 'to ferret out' referred to the old practice of using ferrets to hunt rabbits and rodents in their burrows.

A male ferret is a hob, a neutered male is a gib, a female is a jill, a spayed female is a sprite and a baby ferret is a kit. The collective noun for ferrets is a 'business' or 'fesnyng', which is an older term for a pack of ferrets. The chuckling sound made by happy ferrets is called 'dooking'.

FIFTEEN

FIDELITY

Italy's highest court, the Court of Cassation, ruled in 2008 that members of the Carabinieri paramilitary police must not have extra-marital affairs to avoid sullying the force's name. The ruling was made in a case in which one Carabinieri member was appealing against a lower court ruling sentencing him to four months in jail for insulting and threatening to throw a desk at his boss, who had asked the policeman to break off an affair with a married woman. The court agreed that any affair is a private matter, but noted that the military police were called to 'exemplary conduct and could not bring discredit to the armed forces with extra-marital relationships'. The motto of the Carabinieri is 'Faithful through the centuries'.

♀ *INFIDELITY*

FIDGETING

In 1993, Professor Leonard Storlien, from the Department of Biomedical Science at Wollongong University, Australia, discovered that fidgeting may be beneficial for its potential weight-loss benefits. The professor was conducting research on the Basal Metabolic Rate (BMR) of various humans. This is a measure of how much energy you need just to keep your body running while you're not exercising or doing anything energetic. Normal BMR is between 1,500 and 2,000 calories per day, but Storlein found that some people were burning up extra energy, varying from 200 calories per day to 1,200 calories per day depending on how much they fidgeted. As Professor Storlein said: 'A person would normally run 10 kilometres just to get rid of 300 calories.' So 1,200 calories is equivalent to a 33-kilometre (20-mile) run. Therefore a compulsive fidgeter could burn up as much energy as if he ran 33 kilometres (20 miles).

Later research showed a wide variance in the weight-loss consequences of fidgeting between individuals, as fidgeting itself may have differing effects on a person's BMR.

The scientific name for fidgeting, incidentally, is Non-Exercise Activity Thermogenesis (NEAT).

FIFTEEN

Fifteen is the minimum number of checkouts a supermarket needs to call itself a hypermarket.

When Mary, Queen of Scots was executed in 1587, it took the executioner 15 blows of the axe to sever her head.

The largest recorded litter of a ferret contained 15 babies.

The ring in a game of netball is 15 inches in diameter and a pin in tenpin bowling is 15 inches high.

Every 15 seconds, on average, someone, somewhere in Britain, starts to dig a hole in the road.

The pirates' sea shanty 'Fifteen men on a dead man's chest (Yo ho ho and a bottle of rum)' refers to the fate of a crew shipwrecked on the Dead Man's Chest, a reef close to the island of Tortola in the eastern Caribbean.

The Fifteen Years' War was fought between Austria and the Ottoman Turks between 1591 and 1606.

There are 15 letter 'O's in an Italian Scrabble set.

♀ *BUCKINGHAM PALACE*

FIJI

Fiji is an archipelago of 322 islands in the South Pacific, of which only 106 are permanently inhabited. The main island of Fiji is Viti Levu, which means Great Land. Tongans, on the neighbouring island, mispronounced the 'Viti' part as 'Fisi', which the Europeans wrote as 'Fiji'.

Captain James Cook described the Fijians as poor sailors, good shipbuilders, formidable warriors and ferocious cannibals.

The only beetle longer than the

15-centimetre (6-inch) giant Fijian long-horned is the South American *Titanus giganteus*.

The Fijian alphabet has no H, X or Z. In the Fijian language, nouns do not have just singular and plural forms; they also have ducal (for two of something) and paucal (for a few).

Fiji won the gold medal in the Men's Rugby Sevens event at the 2016 Olympics. It was their first Olympic medal and they took bronze in the same event in 2020, beating Great Britain in the third place play-off. Fiji has also won 15 medals at the Commonwealth Games: three gold, four silver and eight bronze.

⚲ *MERMAID, TOGO*

⬤ FINCH

In 2011, researchers in Australia reported that female finches with unattractive partners have stress hormone levels three to four times higher than those with attractive partners and are slower to reproduce. 'I would anticipate that we would find very similar things going on in humans,' said one of the researchers.

⚲ *BURGLARY, KATE, PECK*

⬤ FINGER LENGTH

Research has shown that top sprinters have long ring fingers. Specifically, it is the ratio of index finger to ring finger length that matters.

A study of finger length in a group of male traders in the City of London also showed that the earnings of men with relatively long ring fingers were up to six times higher than those of their colleagues.

The reason for both of these results may be connected with the presence of testosterone in the womb. At the period of growth when finger length is determined, the ring finger is believed to have more testosterone receptors, so high levels of testosterone, which are associated with competitiveness and aggression, also lead to longer ring fingers. The average ratio of index finger to ring finger in women is 1; in men it is 0.97, but in elite male runners the ratio may be as low as 0.9. Women athletes also have longer ring fingers than women non-athletes.

⚲ *PENIS, STATUE OF LIBERTY*

⬤ FINGERS

The *Oxford English Dictionary* lists several names for the second finger of your hand: it is the demonstrator, forefinger, index finger, insignitur, lickpot, teacher or weft finger. A small index finger has been called a pointling.

Your middle finger is your middling, your midsfinger or your nameless finger; the ring finger may also be called the leech finger, physician finger, goldfinger or wedding finger; and your little finger is the ear finger, mercurial finger or pinkie.

Your thumb is your pollex. Your big toe is your hallux.

⚲ *BOLEYN, GALILEI, GESTURE, MARRIAGE, SKULL, YETI*

⬤ FINLAND

Herkko Rosvo-Ronkainen was a legendary Finnish robber of the 18th century, said to have tested potential gang members by making them carry a heavy woman over an obstacle course. Or according to some stories, his band of raiders sometimes carried off the wives of victims on their backs. One of those practices is held as the origin of the annual wife-carrying championships in Sonkajaarvi, Finland.

When a hospital patient in Finland found the head of a mouse among the steamed vegetables on his plate one day in 2008, investigations concluded that it had most probably arrived in a bag of Belgian frozen vegetables. A hospital spokesman said that the body of the mouse had not been found, but 'being a Belgian mouse, the rest of it could be anywhere in Europe'.

⚲ DENMARK, PORONKUSEMA, WIFE CARRYING

● FIRE

Fires cause around 600 deaths and 18,600 non-fatal casualties every year in the UK, including about three-quarters of all accidental deaths occurring in dwellings.

Fires cost the UK over £7 billion a year in property loss.

Before England's Reform Act of 1832, only householders could vote in parliamentary elections. The test for this was whether the person had a separate fireplace on which his own pot was boiled. Voters were thus known as 'pot-wallopers'.

⚲ ALCHEMY, GUATEMALA, HANDEL, PARMESAN, SOLSTICE, UNDERWEAR

● FIRE-FIGHTING

There were an estimated 1,115,000 career and volunteer fire-fighters in the United States in 2018. Of the total number, 370,000 (33 per cent) were career fire-fighters and 745,000 (67 per cent) were volunteer fire-fighters, while 93,700 (8 per cent) were female.

US fire departments respond to about 2 million calls a year involving fires. That works out at an average of about 1.8 fires for every fire-fighter.

International Fire-fighters Day is celebrated on 4 May, as this is the Feast Day of St Florian, patron saint of fire-fighters. He is also patron saint of chimney sweeps, soap boilers and the city of Linz in Austria. St Florian, who died around AD 303, was a commander in the Roman Imperial army who was responsible for organising brigades of fire-fighters.

● FIREWORKS

An attempt to set a new record by setting off 110,000 fireworks in Dorset in 2006 suffered a mishap when the barge carrying them caught fire. They all then went off in about six seconds. One onlooker described it as 'a bit of a damp squib'.

The Pyrotechnics Guild International, for fireworks enthusiasts, was founded in 1969.

The British spend around £100 million on Guy Fawkes Night fireworks every year.

The West African state of Niger banned fireworks from their New Year 2001 festivities, saying they were making the public less attentive to the sound of real gunfire. The ban was ordered by the Interior Ministry after people had failed to report armed attacks by criminals, dismissing them as firecrackers.

The Ivory Coast also banned the use of fireworks, but for precisely the opposite reason: people there, who had been living through a bitter political crisis, tended to panic at the sound of fireworks, taking it to be gunfire. The wisdom of such a ban was seen on New Year's Day 2013 when at least 60 people were reported to have been killed and 200 injured in a stampede after fireworks celebrations in Abidjan, Ivory Coast.

⚲ BLACKBIRD, HANDEL, HENRY VII, IMPOTENCE

FIRST WORLD WAR

The first British shots of the First World War were fired in Belgium on 21 August 1914, by cavalrymen belonging to the 4th Dragoon Guards. It was the first military action by the British on European soil since the Battle of Waterloo.

By the end of 1914, 192 Old Etonians had been killed in the fighting. The Prime Minister, Herbert Asquith, Conservative leader Andrew Bonar Law and Labour leader Arthur Henderson all lost sons in the war.

In May 1917, the people of Guildford raised £396 in aid of sick and wounded horses.

Although the Armistice in 1918 ended the fighting, the Treaty of Versailles, which formally ended the war, was not signed until 28 June 1919, which is why the dates are sometimes seen as 1914–19.

A total of 633 Victoria Crosses were awarded during the war.

According to the *Oxford English Dictionary*, the earliest recorded use of the phrase 'First World War' was in 1931.

♀ *BRASSIERE, MALARIA, WRISTWATCH*

FISH

The first fish in space were South American guppies, which spent 48 days in orbit on the Russian Salyut 5 in 1976. Twenty years later, researchers at the University of New Brunswick published their findings that female guppy fish prefer brightly coloured males to drab ones. Whether going into space improves a male guppy's prospects with a female is not known.

A useful rule of thumb when pursuing or running from fish is that the top speed of a fish is generally equal to about ten times its own length per second.

In 2019, it was reported that the UK had imported 854,300 tons of fish and related products (worth $5 billion), which was more than twice the total in 1983. It exported 496,300 tons of fish and related products (worth $2.65 billion), which amounted to a trade deficit of $2.35 billion. It was estimated that between 60 and 80 per cent of all fish consumption in the UK was accounted for by five species: cod, haddock, tuna, salmon and prawns. Over 80 per cent of British fish exports to the US consisted of salmon.

According to 2022 figures from UK Fisheries, an average of 5.3 portions of fish and chips are consumed at fish and chip shops in Britain every second.

'School' – as in 'school of fish' – comes from the Middle Dutch *schole*, meaning a troop.

Aristotle recognised 117 species of fish.

♀ *ALCOHOL, GOLDFISH, GUPPY, NOODLING, SARDINE, TUNA*

FISHING

The most common fishing injuries are sticking a hook through your hand or straining a muscle getting out of a boat. According to a survey in 2020, in the league table of sporting injuries in the US, fishing comes sixth behind general exercise (such as jogging, exercising and aerobics), basketball, American football, cycling and soccer. Golf, tennis and badminton are equal with fishing with an annual injury rate of 1.8 persons per thousand.

In the UK, soccer accounted for most injuries but was well behind rugby union in injuries per participant.

On 19 August 1941, the US Patent Office issued patent No. 2253125 for a fishing hook with firing mechanism 'particularly for the catching of big fish' invented by H. Heineke and Walter Hauschild of Hamburg. The design is meant to ensure that, when the bait is taken, the gun fires, killing or at least stunning the fish. One such item, described as a 'Rare Heineke Patent Firing Fish Hook' was sold at auction in Rock Island, Illinois, in 2010 for $2,185.

It is illegal to use a crossbow to catch fish in Utah, other than carp.

CINEMA, PERU, POLAR BEAR

FIZZY DRINKS

The English chemist Joseph Priestley is well known as the discoverer of oxygen, but he is also the man who invented fizzy drinks in 1768 by bubbling carbon dioxide gas into water. Priestley wrote of the 'peculiar satisfaction' he felt at drinking the fizzy water, but evidently did not appreciate the commercial potential of his invention. Another four years went by before he published his paper 'Impregnating Water With Fixed Air', which he dedicated to the First Lord of the Admiralty, with a suggestion that fizzy water might be more healthy for men at sea. He ended the dedication by saying: 'If this discovery (though it doth not deserve that name) be of any use to my countrymen, and to mankind at large, I shall have my reward.'

The idea for marketing fizzy drinks was thus left to a German jeweller called Jacob Schweppe in 1794. Schweppe's Soda Water was originally promoted as treatment for 'Stone of the Bladder'. It then took more than a century before fizzy drinks began to be promoted for pleasure rather than for medicinal reasons.

Even Coca-Cola was first marketed as a 'brain and nerve tonic' and 'cure for all nervous affections' when it was created by Dr John Pemberton in 1886. It took its name from the coca leaf and kola nut among its ingredients.

Pepsi-Cola was created by Caleb Bradham in 1898. The name originally given to it was 'Brad's Drink'. 'Pepsi-Cola', incidentally, is an anagram of 'episcopal' and has been advertised by Britney Spears, which is an anagram of 'Presbyterians'.

Bib-Label Lithiated Lemon-Lime Sodas was the name of a drink launched in 1929. The title was soon changed to the more catchy 7-Up.

According to research published in 1999, the main appeal of fizzy drinks is not the fizz itself but a reaction between the drinker's saliva and carbon dioxide in the bubbles producing carbonic acid, which stimulates the mouth.

ASTRONAUTS, PEPPER, STRAW

FLAGS

The first known instance of a flag being flown at half-mast was on the English ship *Heart's Ease* in 1612 following the death of its master, James Hall, killed by Inuit in West Greenland. Some say the idea of flags at half-mast is to make space for the invisible 'flag of death', but it may be just an example of an old tradition of deliberately performing all tasks half-heartedly to show respect for the dead.

On 4 April 1818, the US Congress adopted the Stars and Stripes for its national flag. Nepal is the only country with a flag that is not rectangular. Its shape is two overlapping triangles. Belize has the only national flag with people displayed prominently on it.

In 1997, a model of the Malaysian flag was made from 10,430 floppy discs.

HAITI, LIBYA, NEPAL, TRICOLOUR

FLAMINGO

Flamingos are pink only because of the carotenoids in the algae and shrimps they eat. Other diets would likely make them a different colour.

There are six species of flamingo: lesser, greater, James's (or Puna), Caribbean, Chilean and Andean.

The first flamingo to be fitted with a plastic artificial leg was a bird known only as B9720, in Lincoln Park Zoo, Illinois. The operation was performed on 21 August 1997.

Flamingos can sleep standing on one leg. In fact research has shown that they expend more energy standing on two legs than on one.

A group of flamingos is called a 'flamboyance'.

FLEAS

A fossil flea found in Australia believed to be 200 million years old does not differ significantly from modern fleas. There are 2,200 species and sub-species of flea. Fleas can lay up to 1,500 eggs in a lifetime.

The cat flea and the dog flea are different species, distinguishable only under high magnification. The cat flea begins to lay eggs after its first meal of blood. Seventy-nine per cent of fleas found on dogs in the UK are cat fleas. Just one flea on your pet can become 1,000 fleas in only 21 days. According to the PDSA, every pet-owning household could have around 20,000 flea eggs at any one time. Britain's dogs may lose 2,200 gallons of blood every day to fleas.

The largest flea is *Hystrichopsylla schefferi*, a flea discovered in the nest of a mountain beaver in the US in 1913. The female can grow up to 1 centimetre long.

When a flea jumps, the rate of acceleration is 20 times that of the Space Shuttle during launch.

The term 'Flea Circus' was first seen in 1928 to describe 'Professor Heckler's Trained Fleas', which could be seen at Hubert's Museum in New York City, but performing fleas date back much further. In the 16th century, fleas with attached lock and chain were exhibited by watchmakers such as Mark Scaliot to demonstrate their miniaturisation skills. In the 1820s in London, the Italian impresario Louis Bertolotto demonstrated his *Extraordinary Exhibition of the Industrious Fleas* in Regent Street. Usually, fleas were trained to pull carriages or cannons on wheels, but more adventurous showmen would display them apparently playing musical instruments.

♀ *CAMEL, HEDGEHOG, SWEDEN, VIKINGS*

FLEMING, Ian (1908–64)

The author of the James Bond books, Ian Fleming, was the son of Valentine Fleming, the Conservative MP for Henley, and a step-cousin of the horror film actor Sir Christopher Lee. His illegitimate half-sister was the celebrated cellist Amaryllis Fleming. He once owned a passport that had belonged to the Italian dictator Benito Mussolini.

A keen bird-watcher, Fleming took the name of James Bond from a book on birds of the West Indies written by an ornithologist of that name. He wrote to the ornithologist's wife, explaining this decision: 'It struck me that this brief, unromantic, Anglo-Saxon and yet very masculine name was just what I needed, and so a second James Bond was born.' In a later interview with the *New Yorker*, he put it less politely: 'when I was casting around for a name for my protagonist I thought by God, [James Bond] is the dullest name I ever heard'.

♀ *JAMES BOND*

FLIES

A rather bizarre experiment in 2006 involved gluing a fruit fly to the wall of a sensory deprivation chamber in a way that allowed it to flap its wings and move its abdomen, legs and proboscis but not move otherwise. Its attempts to move, however, were recorded by tension devices attached to the fly. By measuring the time and size of such twitches, the researchers were able to see whether its attempts at movement were regular, random and in some way controlled. Their conclusion was that fruit flies have free will.

In 1994, Kathleen J. Spalding and Merrick W. Spalding of the US patented the musical fly swatter. Their 'Fly swatter with sound effects' had two sound circuits – one to play a tune at the flick of a switch, while the other was activated by the swatter hitting something.

⚑ *BEIJING, FRUIT FLY, GOD, PARAPSYCHOLOGY, SPIDER*

FLIGHT

On 15 June 1928, the Flying Scotsman train beat an aeroplane in a race from London to Edinburgh. The victory was not totally convincing for two reasons: first, the plane's flying time was actually much quicker but it had to stop twice to refuel; and second, the air passengers had arrived at Edinburgh's Turnhouse airport and were delayed by heavy traffic when making their way to Waverley Station to meet the train. They had landed some 15 minutes before the train had arrived, but only reached the station some four minutes after the train.

⚑ *AIR HOSTESSES, BALLOON, IN-FLIGHT CATERING, LINDBERGH, WRIGHT*

FLIRTING

New York State introduced a bill to outlaw flirting in public in January 1902. This old law specifically prohibits men from turning around on any city street and looking 'at a woman in that way'. The language of the bill was very vague, but Assemblyman Francis G. Landon who had proposed it made his intentions very clear to the *New York Morning Telegraph*: 'My bill is aimed at the flirters, gigglers, mashers and makers of goo-goo eyes in public. We have all been disgusted with them … so they must be brought to their senses.'

The verb 'to flirt' dates back to the mid-16th century. Its original meaning was to propel or flick away, often with a blow between fingernail and thumb. It came to refer to inconstant flitting from one thing to another, hence to play at courtship.

Shakespeare's only use of the word is found in *Romeo and Juliet* when Nurse condemns the bawdy words of Mercutio and says, 'I am none of his flirt-gills.'

In 1923, the Anti-Flirt Club was started in Washington to discourage young women from flirting and particularly from accepting lifts from men in cars. The first and only anti-flirt week began on 4 March 1923.

⚑ *INTELLIGENCE, PENGUIN, SAUDI ARABIA*

FLORIDA

In 2002, it was announced that Highway Patrol officers in Florida would lose their $500 bonuses if they were more than 7 kilograms (15 pounds) overweight.

⚑ *ALLIGATOR, BULL, DWARF, SKUNK*

FLOWERS

'Flowers are restful to look at. They have neither emotions nor conflicts.' Sigmund Freud

⚑ PLANTS, ROMANCE, VICTORIA

FLUTE

In 1996, an item described as a 'Neanderthal bone flute' made of bear bone and supposedly played more than 43,000 years ago was found in Slovenia. Later, doubts were cast on it as an example from the Stone Age, as the holes were thought more likely to have been made by animals gnawing rather than human musicians. A 35,000-year-old flute made from a vulture bone which was found in Germany in 2008 is now thought to be the world's oldest authenticated musical instrument.

⚑ ELEMENTS, ISOCRATES

FLYING SAUCERS

The term 'flying saucer' dates from 1947 when US pilot Kenneth Arnold reported seeing a disc-shaped craft moving at great speed.

US President Jimmy Carter thought he saw a flying saucer in 1973. Research suggests it was probably the planet Venus. However, Carter was far from alone. A poll in the USA in 1997 revealed that 92 per cent of respondents believed that space aliens are already living among us.

Project Sign, Project Grudge, Project Twinkle and Project Blue Book have all been names of official US investigations into flying saucers and, according to a 1995 report, as many as 5 million Americans may have been abducted by aliens. Pooling the data from those who claim to have been abducted, the details suggest that it takes on average six aliens to abduct one human.

You can insure against alien abduction with both British and American insurance companies. Over 40,000 people have taken out Alien All Risks insurance, but no successful claims have yet been made.

In October 2021, Mike St Lawrence of Altamonte Springs, Florida, told *Leader's Edge* magazine that he had been selling alien abduction insurance for 34 years and had close to 7,000 policy holders. For a one-off payment of $24.95 his policies offer a payout of $10 million for a subsequent abduction. To be successful, a claim must be counter-signed by an onboard alien. Another drawback is that the policy specified that the $10 million payout will be given at the rate of $1 a year for ten million years. Asked how he calculated the amount he charged for policies, he said: 'We started out with it being $9.95 in 1987, and then we increased it to $14.95 … if you price it too inexpensive, then people don't think it's worth anything. You have to be selling it for at least $19.95 for people to take it seriously.'

The first country to depict flying saucers on its postage stamps was Equatorial Guinea in 1975. The 'Flying Saucers' stamp was part of a series cele-brating USA–USSR space collaboration.

⚑ CHATEAUNEUF DU PAPE, SPACECRAFT, STAMPS, UFO

FOG

In very dry areas such as the Atacama Desert in Chile, fog can be a much-needed source of water. Large fog-catching nets can be used to capture the water droplets. Such nets are used to supply a Chilean brewery which creates 24,000 litres (6,340 US gallons) a year of its signature beer called Atrapaniebla, meaning 'Fog-Catcher'.

Argentia in Newfoundland has an average of 206 days of fog each year. It is said to be Canada's foggiest place.

FOOD

In a week, the average person in Britain spends £4.10 on buns, cakes and biscuits and £4.50 on fresh vegetables. Total consumer expenditure on food, drink and catering in the UK in 2019 was £234 billion.

In 2021, Americans spent $65.42 billion on ready meals. Since the population of the US is 329.5 million, that means the average American spends $198.50 a year on ready meals.

In the Scottish highlands, the word *giomlaireachd* means the habit of dropping in at mealtimes.

'Food is an important part of a balanced diet.' Fran Lebowitz

BURNT FOOD, CHOPSTICKS, MEERKAT, RESTAURANTS, SQUIRREL, TINS

FOOT-AND-MOUTH DISEASE

'Foot-and-Mouth Disease' is an anagram of 'Moo of death is sad tune' or 'Doomed site: fauna shot'.

PIG, REINDEER

FOOTBALL

The Romans called it *pila pedalis*, which the English translated as 'foteballe' or 'futball' and promptly banned. One of the first mentions of football listed in the *Oxford English Dictionary* was in 1424 in an Act of James I of Scotland: 'The king forbids that any man play at the fut ball under the pain of jail.'

Even so, James I was not the first British king to ban the game, as Edward III had already done so in Latin in 1349 because he thought football could distract men from archery practice.

By contrast, King James's objection to football was more a matter of principle, as he explained in his *Basilikon Doron*: 'From this court I debarre all rough and violent exercises, as the foot-ball, meeter for lameing than making able the users thereof.'

Even earlier, Edward II in 1314 had banned football in London because of the 'great noise in the city caused by hustling over large balls, from which many evils may arise which God forbid'.

Phillip Stubbes, in his *Anatomy of Abuses* (1583), called football: 'Rather a friendly kind of fight than a play or recreation, a bloody and murthering practise than a felowly sporte or pastime,' and the generally violent reputation of the game was confirmed by Joseph Strutt, in his *Games and Pastimes of the People of England* (1876). After mentioning that the game had 'fallen into disrepute, and is but little practised', he went on to explain: 'When the exercise becomes exceeding violent, the players kick each other's shins without the least ceremony, and some of them are overthrown at the hazard of their limbs.'

Other health risks of football are also well documented. On the day the Netherlands lost to France in a penalty shoot-out in the 1996 European Championship, 50 per cent more men died from heart attack or stroke in that country than on a normal day. Interestingly, no corresponding increase occurred in women.

In the UK around half a million people a year are treated in hospital for football injuries.

There are only two mentions of football in Shakespeare, both rather derogatory. In *The Comedy of Errors*, Dromio accuses Adriana: 'Am I so round with you, as you with me, That like a football you do spurn me thus?' While in *King Lear*, Kent calls Oswald a 'base football player' before tripping him up.

In 1885, the British Parliament legalised professional football. In 1890, football nets (invented by J.A. Brodie of Liverpool) were first used in goals, and in 1891 the first penalty kick in English league football was taken.

In 1994, Andres Escobar, playing for Colombia, was shot dead by fans for scoring the own goal that led to their elimination from the World Cup. In 2006, the Nigerian Football Association ruled that referees may accept bribes but should still judge matches fairly.

Soccer was on the programme for the first modern Olympics in 1896, but it was cancelled when no teams entered. Great Britain won the Olympic football in 1900, 1908 and 1912. In 1904, only three teams entered. Canada won ahead of two US teams.

ALGERIA, BHUTAN, CHELSEA, MANCHESTER UNITED, RED, RUGBY

FORD, Gerald (1913–2006)

Gerald Ford is the only person to have become both Vice-President and President of the USA without ever being elected to either post. When he was President, so many requests were received for autographs of his dog Patsy that a rubber stamp was made of its pawprint.

He became the longest-living US President on 12 November 2006 when he reached the age of 93 years and 121 days. The previous record of 93 years and 120 days had been held by Ronald Reagan. Ford died on Boxing Day, 2006, so the record then stood at 93 years 165 days. That was overtaken, however, on 16 March 2018, when Jimmy Carter attained the age of 93 years 166 days. Carter celebrated his 97th birthday on 1 October 2021.

FORESTS

A study in 2008 revealed that there are more than 800 definitions of forest used by various organisations, based on area, tree height and canopy cover. Generally, a forest is a large area of trees whose canopies cover at least 10 per cent of the sky. A wood's canopy covers 5–10 per cent of the sky. A rainforest is a forest of evergreens, with 2.5 metres (100 inches) of rain a year and whose canopies cover 100 per cent of the sky.

Forests cover 30 per cent of the Earth's land.

The Taiga region in the far north, covering much of Canada, Alaska, Scandinavia and Russia, is considered the world's largest forest. Around one-third of all the trees on earth are conifers in the Taiga.

The word forest comes from the Latin *foris*, meaning 'out of doors'. In the Middle Ages the word 'forest' was used for an area of land set aside for royal hunting.

The New Forest has not been 'new' since 1079, when it was created by William I.

'You can only go halfway into the darkest forest; then you are coming out the other side.' Chinese proverb

JUNGLE, MONKEY, PERU, TREES

FORGERY

In October 1997, police in the town of Jablonec in the Czech Republic announced that they had found a 1,000-crown note, which they described

177

as 'exceptionally well forged'. The only thing that gave it away was the fact that the words 'Forging of notes will be prosecuted in accordance with the law' had been replaced by a message saying: 'This note is a fake'.

A former policeman was arrested in Greece in 2011 for illegally claiming benefits for children he had invented. Using pictures from the Internet supported by forged birth certificates, the man was accused of making claims for 19 children over a period of 15 years. Police said that the forgeries were so expert that they suspected nothing until they noticed that he had more children than anyone else in the country. In fact he was divorced and had no children of his own.

⚑ ALCHEMY, CAPITAL PUNISHMENT

● FORNICATION

The word 'fornication' comes from the Latin *fornix*, which means a vault or arch. Since Roman prostitutes used to ply their trade under the arches of the Colosseum, the word became associated with extra-marital sex.

Fornication should not be confused with formication, which is an abnormal sensation, as of ants creeping over the skin.

⚑ CELIBACY, NOAH'S ARK, SWIMMING

● FORTUNE-TELLING

The *Oxford English Dictionary* lists over a hundred different words for ways of foretelling the future. Among them are the following:

- Armomancy: divination by the shoulders of beasts
- Belomancy: divination by arrows
- Capnomancy: divination by smoke
- Daphnomancy: divination by a laurel tree

- Enoptromancy: divination by means of a mirror
- Gyromancy: divination by walking in a circle until the subject falls over from dizziness
- Halomancy: divination by means of salt
- Ichthyomancy: divination by using the heads or entrails of fish
- Lecanomancy: divination by the inspection of water in a bowl
- Myomancy: divination by movements of mice
- Necromancy: divination by communicating with the dead
- Omphalomancy: divination by knots on the umbilical cord
- Pedomancy: divination by inspection of the soles of the feet
- Rhapsodomancy: divination by random selection of a line of poetry
- Spodomancy: divination by means of ashes
- Tyromancy: divination by cheese
- Uranomancy: divination by the stars
- Zoomancy: divination by observing the action of animals

⚑ MOLEOSOPHY, NIPPLE

● FORTY-SEVEN

In 1964, some mathematics students at Pomona College, California, noted with surprise that they encountered the number 47 surprisingly often. The college was reached by taking exit 47 from the freeway; there were 47 pipes in the top row of their organ, 47 letters in the motto on their founding plaque and 47 students in their first graduation class.

These and other such discoveries led them to form what was almost a cult worshipping the number 47 and celebrating 4–7 day each year on 7 April.

When Pomona graduate Joe Menosky became a writer on the TV show *Star*

Trek, he slipped the number 47 into scripts whenever a more or less random number was required. Messages were sent with replies expected in 47 hours; populations were destroyed leaving only 47 survivors; members of the Starship crew were rendered unconscious for 47 seconds. Even after Menosky left the show, others continued the practice to such an extent that, for many series of *Star Trek*, one can hardly watch an episode without hearing or seeing the number 47 somewhere.

If this is not enough to convert anyone to the cult, here are some more 47s:

In Japan, there are 47 regional prefectures, while the 47 Ronin were masterless Samurai who dramatically avenged their master's death at the end of 1702.

Furthermore, 47 piglets were used in making the film *Babe*; 47 members of the royal family were present at the funeral of Diana, Princess of Wales; there are 47 degrees of latitude between the tropics of Cancer and Capricorn and 47 strings on a concert harp; Osama bin Laden was his father's 47th child; and Pythagoras's Theorem is Proposition 47 in Euclid's *Elements*.

According to a popular but gruesome photo of the death of Mexican revolutionary Pancho Villa in1923, he was killed by 47 bullets. The picture is known as 'The Forty-Seven Wounds of Pancho Villa'.

The AK47 assault rifle takes its name from the year in which it was designed: 1947. Its successor was the AK74. The letters stand for Avtomat Kalashnikova – the Kalashnikov Automatic – after its designer Mikhail Timofeyevich Kalashnikov.

The English poet and humourist Thomas Hood wrote a poem entitled 'On Completing Forty-Seven'. Sadly, he didn't. He died 20 days before his 46th birthday in 1845.

FULHAM, PALINDROME, TIME

FOSSIL

In 1981, a fossilised peanut more than 100,000 years old was found in China, which is curious as peanuts arrived in Europe from South America where they have been cultivated for over 2,000 years.

BACULUM, BUCKLAND, DUNG, PANDA, TYRANNOSAURUS REX

FOX

Foxes have a long connection with medicine. In ancient Rome, many people believed that a headache could be cured by binding the genitals of a fox to the sufferer's forehead, while in the year 2000, a Scottish company began trials of a device in the form of a copper collar that was designed to treat arthritis in wild foxes.

People named Fox have also made their mark. In 1901, a pair of twin criminals from Hertfordshire called Fox played an important role in the introduction of fingerprinting in Britain. Other forms of identification could never tell them apart, but fingerprints secured a conviction. More recently, according to a 'Magnificent Mammaries' poll in a US film magazine in 1998, the English model Samantha Fox was assessed as having had the 43rd most beautiful breasts of all time.

Less successfully, the 1941 film *The Little Foxes* gained nine Oscar nominations but did not win any.

In November 2021, a family in Peru were worried when the cute puppy they had bought began to chase chickens and ducks and was reported to have eaten three guinea pigs. The 'cute puppy' turned out to be a fox.

The collective noun for a group of foxes is a 'leash'.

⚲ FOXTROT, GOOSE, GRAPES, ICELAND, RAVEN

● FOXTROT

The dance known as the foxtrot was invented by Harry Fox in 1914. The Japanese for 'foxtrot' is *fokkusutorotto*.

● FRANCE

At various times in the 9th century, Charles the Bald, Charles the Fat and Charles the Simple all ruled as Kings of France. Charles the Simple was the son of Louis the Stammerer.

Charles VIII of France had six toes on one foot. This deformity may have been behind his adoption of square-toed shoes in order to hide it. This royal approval greatly increased the popularity of such shoes.

The so-called Hundred Years War between Britain and France lasted 116 years, from 1337 to 1453.

The rules of the Miss France contest specify that the winner must be at least 1.70 metres (5 feet 7 inches) tall.

In July 1984, the Court of Cassation held that a French couple might not lawfully register their daughter under the name Manhattan. Under a law of 1803, only saints' names or names of well-known figures of ancient history are permissible.

There are more judges in Los Angeles than in the whole of France.

⚲ BAGUETTE, CHANNEL, GUILLOTINE, METRIC SYSTEM, NEW YORK, SHOES

● FRANKFURTER

The German city of Frankfurt-am-Mein celebrated the 500th birthday of the Frankfurter sausage in 1997.

⚲ HOT DOGS

● FRANKLIN, Benjamin (1706–90)

Benjamin Franklin rose early every morning and sat naked for half an hour or so either reading or writing, a practice he described as 'agreeable'. Sometimes he would then return to bed for an hour or two, saying this gave him 'the most pleasing sleep that can be imagined'.

Around 1781, when Franklin was American Ambassador to France, he wrote an essay entitled 'A Letter to the Royal Academy About Farting', which became commonly known as 'Fart Proudly'. This was his joking reply to a letter the Academy had sent to the country's best scientists to tell them which worthy projects they ought to be working on. Franklin's reply suggested that, above all their suggestions, research should be undertaken to develop a drug or tincture to add to food to render the resulting farts 'not only inoffensive, but agreeable as Perfumes', thus removing the offensiveness of a perfectly natural process.

Among other highly literate jokes perpetrated by Benjamin Franklin, perhaps the funniest was his 1745 'Advice to a Friend on Choosing a Mistress'. After recommending that the young friend should prefer marriage, he wrote: 'But if you will not take this Counsel … then I repeat my former Advice, that in all your Amours you should *prefer old Women to young ones*,' and gave a number of reasons in support of that advice. These included:

- Their conversation is more improving and agreeable as they have more Knowledge of the World.
- Older women study when they cease to be handsome and learn to do 1000 services small and great.
- There is no hazard of Children.

- Their experience makes them more prudent and discreet.
- With age, the upper part of the body deteriorates more greatly than the lower part 'and regarding only what is below the Girdle, it is impossible of two Women to know an old from a young one' making 'the Pleasure of corporal Enjoyment with an old Woman … at least equal, and frequently superior.

His list ends with the words: 'and Lastly, They are *so grateful!!*'

Benjamin Franklin was strongly against the use of the words 'notice', 'advocate' and 'progress' as verbs.

'Guests, like fish, begin to smell after three days.' Benjamin Franklin

⚲ *CASANOVA, GUNS, READING, RHUBARB, TAX*

FRECKLES

There are two kinds of freckles: ephelides, which are flat, light brown, and get darker in summer and lighter in winter; and lentigines, or age spots, which normally do not change according to the sunlight.

According to the ancient Greek philosopher–physician Galen, crocodile dung is a good treatment for freckles.

FREDERICK I BARBAROSSA

Holy Roman Emperor Frederick I Barbarossa, Duke of Swabia, King of Germany, King of Italy and King of Burgundy, died in 1190 by drowning in the River Saleph during the Third Crusade, after he had gone there to bathe. Attempts to preserve his body in vinegar failed so his flesh was interred in the Church of St Peter in Antiochia, his bones in the Cathedral of Tyre and his internal organs in Tarsus.

⚲ *UNIVERSITIES*

FRENCH

The French for 'French kiss' is *baiser amoreux* (love kiss). According to research published in 2006, French kissing many different partners can quadruple a teenager's chance of catching meningitis.

⚲ *CHIPS, CINDERELLA, DANDELION, EINSTEIN, EMAIL, GOLF*

FREUD, Sigmund (1856–1937)

The first paper by the founder of psychoanalysis was an account of his unsuccessful search for the testicles of the eel, despite dissecting hundreds of the creatures at a zoological research station in Trieste. The paper, published in 1877, was entitled 'Observations on the Form and Fine Structure of the Looped Organs of the Eel, Organs Considered as Testes'.

Explaining his lack of success in locating the eel testicles, Freud, in a letter to a friend, suggested, in humorous style, that all the eels he had dissected had been 'of the fairer sex'.

In July 2021, an unnamed man in Xinghua, China, was reported to have been hospitalised after he inserted a 20-centimetre (8-inch) eel into his anus to ease his constipation. The eel slithered into his colon and bit through it, entering his abdomen. Amazingly, the eel was still alive when it was surgically removed.

⚲ *CHESS, FLOWERS, TEETH*

FRIDAY

If you arrange the days of the week in alphabetical order in English, Friday comes first.

Friday takes its name from the Norse goddess of love, Freyja or Frigga. Fear of Fridays is called Friggaphobia.

Throughout history and around the world, certain events have occurred more often on Fridays than any other day of the week: crucifixions in ancient Rome, hangings in England, moving house in the UK, airline price rises and bank robberies in the USA are all events that happen or happened most frequently on Fridays. Friday is also the working day on which companies are least likely to hold board meetings, and the day on which an American is most likely to die.

♀ BOUNTY, CALENDAR, THIRTEEN

FRIDAY THE 13th

According to research in Finland in 2004, men are no more likely to die in traffic accidents on Friday the 13th than on other Fridays, but women are. Records showed that Finnish women have nearly a two-thirds greater chance of being killed in a crash on Friday the 13th than on an ordinary Friday. It was suggested this may be because women are more superstitious than men, which alters their behaviour.

♀ CALENDAR

FRIENDSHIP

The word 'friend' occurs 53 times in the King James Bible, with 'friends' 49 times and 'friendship' twice. But 'enemy', 'enemies' and 'enmity' occur 107, 266 and eight times respectively.

The opening shot of the TV series *Friends*, with the cast dancing around a fountain, was filmed at Warner Brothers in Los Angeles at five o'clock in the morning. The first line of dialogue in the pilot episode of *Friends* was: 'There's nothing to tell.'

'Outside of a dog, a book is man's best friend. Inside of a dog, it's too dark to read.' Groucho Marx

♀ DOLPHIN, TONGA

FRISBEE

The modern frisbee, as we now know it, first went into production on 13 January 1957. It is not clear who came up with the idea of a flying disc, but the credit is usually given to Los Angeles building inspector Walter Morrison. It is said to have begun with Morrison and his wife flinging pie tins to one another on the beach. The tins had the words Frisbie's Pies (from the Frisbie Baking Company) embossed on them. Morrison and his partner Warren Frascioni launched an improved plastic version of the pie tins which they sold as the Pluto Platter. Morrison was awarded a patent for the design which he sold to the Wham-O company who renamed it a frisbee.

The sport of disc golf, in which frisbees are thrown at targets, was invented in the early 1960s.

The official world record for throwing a flying disc is 263.20 metres (863 feet 6 inches) set by Simon Lizotte in the Nevada Desert in 2014.

In 2004, the journal *Psychological Science* published a paper with the title 'How Dogs Navigate To Catch Frisbees'. The world record for the longest frisbee throw caught by a dog is 122 metres (402 feet). The human record for a self-caught frisbee is 92.4 metres (303 feet) achieved on ice skates.

In 1968, the US Navy spent around $400,000 studying the motion of frisbees in wind tunnels.

'I'm more likely to be decapitated by a Frisbee.' Boris Johnson in 2010 on his chances of becoming prime minister

♀ SEX

FROG

The town of Vittel in France is headquarters to the Brotherhood of Frog Thigh Tasters and holds an annual Frog Eating Festival.

Thanks mainly to the culinary tastes of the French, the EU annually imports more than 6,000 tonnes of frogs' legs from Asia. The French eat 42 per cent of them, while Belgium and Luxembourg consume another 44 per cent between them. Depending on the size of frog, it takes between 10.8 and 18 kilograms of frogs to produce 450 grams (1 pound) of frogs' legs.

The great French chef Auguste Escoffier introduced frogs' legs to Britain in 1908 when he served them to Prince Albert Edward (who later became King Edward VII) under the name 'les cuisses de nymphes à l'aurore', or 'thighs of the dawn nymphs'.

Most frogs have four fingers (or toes) on each limb.

Frogs cannot eat with their eyes open. They use their eyeballs to push against the roof of the mouth to force food down into the stomach.

The carpenter frog is so-called because it has a croak that sounds like a hammer.

The correct word for a fear of frogs is ranidaphobia. Less accurate terms are bufonophobia, which is fear of toads, or batrachophobia, which is fear of amphibians.

The mating position adopted by frogs and toads, in which the male grabs the female around the waist or under the arms in a hug, is called 'amplexus'.

In 2008, a museum in Italy defied the Vatican by refusing to remove a sculpture of a crucified frog holding a beer mug, which had been declared blasphemous. The board of the Museion Museum in the city of Bolzano decided by a majority vote that the frog sculpture by the late German artist Martin Kippenberger was a work of art and would stay in place for the remainder of its exhibition.

According to research published in 2015 in the journal *Animal Cognition* under the title 'Numerical Discrimination by Frogs', frogs can discriminate between one and two objects, or between two and three, but cannot tell the difference between three and four.

⚲ *BRUNEI, COLOMBIA, IRELAND, MOZART, ZAMBIA*

⬤ FRUIT

On 10 May 1893, the US Supreme Court delivered its ruling that a tomato is a vegetable, not a fruit. Despite that ruling, the tomato is the state fruit of both Ohio and Tennessee and it is recognised as the state vegetable of New Jersey.

The 1893 decision was made in a case brought by tomato importers against the Port of New York in the hope of recovering duties they had been forced to pay under the 1883 Tariff Act.

In January 2022, more than 40,000 pounds of oranges, mandarins, lemons, grapefruits and tangelos were displayed at a supermarket in Louisiana to set a new record for the world's largest display of citrus fruits. Organisers said there were more than 100,000 individual fruits in the display.

⚲ *APPLE, BLACKBERRIES, DURIAN, GRAPE, GRAPEFRUIT, MANGO, STRAWBERRY*

⬤ FRUIT BAT

According to a paper entitled 'Fellatio by Fruit Bats Prolongs Copulation Time', published in October 2009, research in China had identified the fruit bat as the only creature other than the human in which the female uses oral stimulation of the male to prolong sexual activity.

The researchers comment that bonobo monkeys have been documented as indulging in oral sex, but usually as play behaviour among young males. By contrast, the female fruit bat licks the base of the male genitals while copulation takes place, and studies showed that licking had the result of prolonging the sexual encounter. In fact the length of time – C – that copulation lasted in seconds was given by the formula: $C = 101.24 + 6.22L$, where L was the number of seconds spent licking. In other words, copulation without licking lasted on average 101.24 seconds, but every second of licking prolonged the duration by just over six seconds.

● FRUITCAKE

Assumption Abbey in Ava, Missouri, in the Ozark Mountains, is the world's only Trappist monastery that sells fruitcakes on the Internet. The monastery's bakery is its main source of income and when it was set up the monks sought advice from Jean-Pierre Augé, who at one time served as chef to the Duke and Duchess of Windsor. His help, which included the donation of a recipe, established Assumption Abbey fruitcakes as the unrivalled leader in the Trappist fruitcake field.

In 1992, pollsters in America asked respondents what they thought was the most appropriate use of fruitcake: 38 per cent said 'a gift for someone else'; 13 per cent said 'a good doorstop'; and 4 per cent said 'landfill'.

♀ INVESTMENT, OYSTER

● FRUIT FLY

At the start of 2010, a problem about fruit flies that had mystified scientists for years was finally solved by a team from the University of California at Berkeley. The question related to the role of the bristles and hooks on the penis of the male fruit fly that could be seen only under a microscope. There were various theories: perhaps they stimulated the female; perhaps they had a penetrative function that aided conception; perhaps they served to destroy or remove the sperm of rival males. Their role could be discovered only by shaving them off and seeing what happened, but the bristles were too small for even the most microscopic instruments.

The new research, however, used a high-precision technique involving the removal of these bristles by laser. Some fruit flies were left unshaven, some had their penises shaved completely, some had only a third of each bristle shaved off. The results showed that partial shaving made no difference to their mating behaviour or success, but total shaving, while not changing their number of attempts at mating, cut the success rate to around 20 per cent of the unshaved rate.

Conclusion: The sole role of the bristles and hooks is to act as a natural Velcro, keeping the male and female together for the mating period.

'Time flies like an arrow; fruit flies like a banana.' Groucho Marx

♀ FLIES, GOD, SPACEFLIGHT

● FUEL

A car fuelled only by used coffee grounds made the 400-kilometre (250-mile) trip from London to Manchester in 2010, stopping every 96 kilometres (60 miles) to refuel. The 'car-puccino', as it was called, made the trip on the equivalent of 11,000 espressos.

♀ MARS, METHANE, SHEEP, SPACECRAFT, YAK

FULHAM

In 1835, a 'singular cricket match' between a team of married women and a team of unmarried women was reported in *The Times* newspaper to have aroused 'considerable amusement'. The match, which was played for a prize of ten shillings and a hot supper, took place at Parsons Green, Fulham. The married women, wearing light blue dresses, batted first and were all out for 47 runs, but their unmarried opponents, dressed in white, were bowled out for 29 runs. In their second innings, however, the single women fought back and eventually won by seven runs. Supper was provided by the White Horse on the Green.

FUNERALS

A new range of pendants was launched at the National Funeral Directors Convention in Cincinnati in 1996. Called the Heirloom Pendant Collection, it was designed to enable people to wear their loved one's ashes round their necks. The pendant came in three designs: Teardrop, Infinity and Love.

A survey in 2021 reported the top five most popular songs requested at UK funerals were as follows:

1. 'My Way' – Frank Sinatra
2. 'Time To Say Goodbye' – Sarah Brightman and Andrea Bocelli
3. 'We'll Meet Again' – Vera Lynn
4. 'Somewhere Over The Rainbow' – Eva Cassidy
5. 'The Wind Beneath My Wings' – Bette Midler

However, the Sun-Life survey pointed out that only 26 per cent of people indicate what music they would like for their funeral, so it is most often chosen by relatives or whoever is arranging the funeral. When the deceased have chosen their own music, the top three items are Eric Idle's 'Always Look on the Bright Side', John Lennon's 'Imagine' and 'You'll Never Walk Alone' by Gerry and the Pacemakers.

A poll conducted throughout Europe in 2005 by Music Choice of the songs people most wanted to be played at their own funerals reported the top five as follows:

1. 'The Show Must Go On' – Queen
2. 'Stairway to Heaven' – Led Zeppelin
3. 'Highway to Hell' – AC/DC
4. 'My Way' – Frank Sinatra
5. 'Requiem' – Mozart

In 2008, the University of Bath became Britain's first academic establishment to offer a degree course for funeral directors.

BUFFALO, FERRARI, GOLF, SANTA ANNA, SPORTS SONGS, TELEPHONE

GABON

In August 2006, an evangelist preacher in Gabon died while trying to demonstrate how Jesus walked on water. Franck Kabele, 35, told his congregation that he had had a revelation that if he had enough faith, he could walk on water like Jesus and he invited them out to a beach in the capital Libreville to watch him do it. He set off to walk across an estuary that is normally a 20-minute boat trip, but the waters closed over his head and he was never seen again.

GADDAFI, Muammar (1942–2011)

When Colonel Gaddafi was overthrown in 2011, he was the third-longest-serving head of state of any country behind Queen Elizabeth II of the UK and the King of Thailand.

He had a specially trained force of 'virgin bodyguards' comprising 40 selected women who had taken a vow of chastity before being enlisted. 'Women should be trained for combat,' Gaddafi said, 'so that they do not become easy prey for their enemies.'

On a visit to Paris in 2007, Gaddafi pitched his Bedouin tent, which he always took on foreign visits, in the grounds of a five-star hotel and also brought a camel with his 300-strong entourage.

In the same year, on a trip to Belgrade, he was awarded an honorary doctorate by the Megatrend private university for his scientific accomplishments in constructing a vast irrigation scheme in Libya.

📍 *LIBYA*

GALILEI, Galileo (1564–1642)

Galileo enrolled at the University of Pisa to read medicine but switched to studying mathematics and natural philosophy (as physics was known at the time). He dropped out of university and continued his studies on his own, and in 1589 he was appointed to the Chair of Mathematics in Pisa. Three years later, he moved to the University of Padua, where he taught geometry, mechanics and astronomy. As a mathematician, he calculated the height of Lucifer in Dante's 'Inferno' to be 2,000 arm lengths.

On 26 February 1616, Galileo was banned by the Roman Catholic Church from teaching or defending the view that the Earth orbits the Sun. In 1633, Galileo was found 'vehemently suspect of heresy' and was forced by the

Inquisition to sign a statement recanting his view that the Earth moved around the Sun and sentenced to house arrest for the rest of his life. It was not until 1992 that the Vatican formally cleared Galileo of any wrongdoing.

Galileo's father Vincenzo Galilei was a lute player, composer and music theorist who wrote the first published musical score in 1581.

Besides his scientific discoveries, Galileo invented an automatic tomato picker and a pocket comb that doubled as an eating utensil.

He had two illegitimate daughters and a son by a woman called Marina Gamba. Both of the daughters became nuns.

When Galileo's body was moved for reburial 100 years after he died, three of his fingers, a tooth and some vertebrae were stolen. The tooth and fingers are now on display at the Museum of the History of Science in Florence.

'To assert that the earth revolves around the sun is as erroneous as to claim that Jesus was not born of a virgin.' Cardinal Bellarmine, 1615, during the trial of Galileo

♀ *GRAVITY, HAWKING, LENNON, NEPTUNE, PASTEUR*

GAMBIA

A group of cryptozoologists from Britain went on an expedition to Gambia in 2006 in search of the Ninki Nanka, a legendary creature said to have a horse's head and the body of a crocodile but twice as long. The Ninki Nanka is said to be so fearsome that all who see it drop dead. Fortunately, none of the expedition members saw one.

GAMBLING

In 1996, a French gambler, annoyed at being charged 3.7 million francs tax on

his winnings, paid the debt in one-franc coins weighing 22 tonnes. The man turned up with three rented security vans containing 3,730,606 one-franc coins in 920 sacks. 'We were a bit surprised,' a tax collector in the town of Viarmes, north of Paris, commented, 'but we greeted him with a smile. He paid his taxes on time.'

♀ *BOWLING, LAOS, MARY I, POKER*

GAMING

In 2009, Swiss scientists announced the discovery of a disease they called 'PlayStation palmar hidradentitis', a skin disorder marked by painful lumps on the palms. They said this was caused by keeping too tight a grip on the console while playing video games and furiously pushing the buttons. The lesions were similar to those found on children's feet after taking part in heavy physical activity, they said.

♀ *BACCARAT, SANDWICH*

GARBAGE

In February 2011, a New Yorker who attempted suicide by jumping from a ninth-floor window was foiled when he landed on a heap of rubbish bags uncollected after blizzards the previous week. The 26-year-old was taken to hospital. His aunt told a local paper it was lucky the city had the snow and had not cleared the rubbish.

♀ *MOUNTAINEERING, PHOENIX, RUBBISH, TOKYO*

GARDENING

Not only was Jihae Hwang's 'Hae-woo-so' garden at the 2011 Chelsea Flower Show the first ever exhibited by a South Korean designer, it was also the first ever to be designed around a toilet. (The name *hae-woo-so* is a Korean term for a traditional toilet.) The designer was quoted as saying: 'I think gardens can contain any ideas, any places or any things from life. There's no limited number of topics you can make a garden from. Why not a toilet?'

The earliest known conviction for drunken driving while in charge of a lawnmower was in Norway in 1995. A 54-year-old man had been cutting grass in the south-western town of Hauge-sund when police caught him driving a small lawnmower from one garden to another. He was stopped as part of a spot check and his blood alcohol level was found to be well over the limit for motorised vehicles. He was fined and sentenced to 24 days in jail, but the sentence was suspended on the grounds that the lawnmower's top speed of 10 mph was too slow to do any harm.

HERON-ALLEN, KARLOFF

GARLIC

'Garlics, tho' used by the French, are better adapted to the uses of medicine than cookery,' wrote Amelia Simmons (*American Cookery*, 1796). On this evidence, it sounds as though Ms Simmons may have been an allium-phobe – the term for a garlic-hater.

Garlic is one of the world's oldest cultivated crops. It was fed to the builders of the Great Pyramid of Cheops in Egypt to give them strength.

The word 'garlic' occurs 21 times in Bram Stoker's *Dracula*, and only four times in the entire works of Shake-speare. There is only one mention of garlic in the King James Bible, in the Book of Numbers, Chapter 11.

Garlic attracts leeches. Experiments have shown that leeches take 14.9 seconds to attach themselves to a hand covered with garlic, but 44.9 seconds to suck blood from a clean one. One way to get the smell of garlic out of your hands is to rub them with salt and lemon juice, then rinse; to banish garlic breath, chew on fresh parsley or a coffee bean.

The city of Chicago is named after garlic: *chicagaoua* was a native Amer-ican word for wild garlic. The average American eats over 1.4 kilograms (3 pounds) of garlic a year.

The longest continuous string of garlic contained 1,600 garlic bulbs and was 36.5 metres long.

According to an old saying, 'Garlic is as good as ten mothers … for keeping the girls away.' Only the first half of this was taken as the title of Les Blank's 1980 film *Garlic is as Good as Ten Mothers*, in praise of garlic.

CUCUMBER, TAIWAN, UNDEAD, VAMPIRES

GATES, William Henry (b. 1955)

William Henry ('Bill') Gates III was the son of William Henry Gates II, who was the son of William Henry Gates I, who was a furniture store owner. Oddly enough, William Henry Gates I was also the son of a William Henry Gates, so perhaps the numbers after their names should all be increased by one.

The $124 billion at which Bill Gates's net worth was estimated in 2021 is about 10 per cent higher than that of all British banknotes then in circulation. If that were changed into dollar bills and put in a line, it would go to the Moon and back seven times.

GDANSK

Research at the University of Gdansk in Poland published in 2007 concluded that the perfect woman has a bust measurement equal to 49.3 per cent of her height. This was one result from a study of 19 vital statistics and 20 body features of the 24 finalists in a Miss Poland competition compared with 115 other women.

The ideal woman, they concluded, was 175 centimetres (5 feet 8 inches) tall, with a waist 76 per cent of her bust size and 70 per cent of the size of her hips. Shoulder width should be 20.9 per cent of height.

According to the Gdansk researchers, the woman who fitted this ideal best was Naomi Campbell.

⚲ *GUT*

GENETICS

The Human Genome Project (HGP) was formally launched in 1990, declared complete in 2003, frequently updated since then, and is still the subject of much dispute. The aim of the project was to identify all human genes, but estimates of how many there are differed hugely.

In 2000, leading geneticist Ewan Birney launched a contest called GeneSweep, in which he invited colleagues to estimate the number of genes they would find. Estimates varied from 312,000 to just under 26,000, with an average of about 40,000. In May 2003, the $3,000 prize was awarded for an estimate of 25,947 genes, which was the closest to the HGP finding of 24,847. By the end of 2003, however, the HGP estimate had dropped to around 21,000, and the latest precise count comes up with a figure of 21,306, but that is only for the genes that code proteins; the non-protein coding genes, which may include almost the same number again, are still a bit of a mystery.

The HGP project showed that the DNA of any two individuals are 99.6 per cent identical. The remaining 0.4 per cent is responsible for the differences between any two of us.

'Every dollar we invested to map the human genome returned $140 to the

economy – every dollar.' President Barack Obama, 2013 State of the Union address

GENITALS

Appearing before Teesside Crown Court in 2008, a man accused of being a flasher attempted to convince the jury that he was incapable of the offence because his genitals were too small and he was too ashamed to expose them. He produced photographs to support his claim but was still convicted on seven counts of outraging public decency.

⚲ *ART, ATTRACTIVENESS, CAMBODIA, HYENA, NUDITY, SYPHILIS*

GEORGE I, King of Great Britain and Ireland (1660–1727)

George I, who spent most of his reign in Hanover, was the last King of England who could not speak English at the start of his reign. When he needed to communicate with his Prime Minister, Robert Walpole, they spoke Latin.

⚲ *BUTE, PIGEON, WALPOLE*

GEORGE II, King of Great Britain and Ireland (1683–1760)

The victory of George II at the Battle of Dettingen in 1743 in the War of the Austrian Succession was the last battle commanded by a British king.

He died on 25 October 1760, five days before his 77th birthday, of a heart attack possibly brought on by chronic constipation. As his Prime Minister Robert Walpole wrote in his memoirs: 'He rose as usual at six, and drank his chocolate; for all his actions were invariably methodic. A quarter after seven he went into a little closet. His German *valet de chambre* in waiting heard a noise, and running in, found the King dead on the floor.'

⚲ *ASH WEDNESDAY, BARBER*

GEORGE III, King of Great Britain and Ireland (1738–1820)

King George III survived several assassination attempts, including one attempt to shoot him when he was in the royal box of the Drury Lane Theatre for the London premiere of Mozart's *Marriage of Figaro* in 1800.

When the film *The Madness of King George III* was released in the US, the title was shortened to *The Madness of King George* to avoid putting off people who might have thought it was the third part of a series of which they had missed the first two.

> BUCKINGHAM PALACE, BUTE, D'EON, PARKINSON, TINS, WIG

GEORGE IV, King of Great Britain (1762–1830)

When George IV met his cousin and future wife Caroline of Brunswick, his only words were, 'Harris, I am not well. Pray get me a glass of brandy.' The marriage was only consummated once, and Caroline, who is said to have been eccentric, promiscuous and stinking, was not allowed to be at her husband's coronation.

Having no living legitimate offspring when he died, George IV was succeeded by his brother, William IV.

> DUELLING, SHOES, WILLIAM IV

GEORGE V, King of Great Britain (1865–1936)

King George V had a pet African grey parrot called Charlotte, which he obtained in Port Said, Egypt. Charlotte is said to have perched on the King's shoulder during Privy Council meetings occasionally shouting, 'What about it?' in a powerful voice as the King was reading documents.

George V always made a point of falling asleep at precisely ten past eleven. His last words before dying were either 'How is the Empire?' or 'Bugger Bognor.'

> HOT DOGS, KIPLING, NEW DELHI, QUEEN MARY, VICTORIA CROSS

GEORGE VI, King of Great Britain (1895–1952)

King George VI was naturally left-handed but was forced to learn to write with his right hand. He played tennis left-handed. He played at Wimbledon in the men's doubles with Louis Greig in 1926, losing in the first round. His first name was not George but Albert; in fact, George was only his fourth name after Albert Frederick Arthur. His family knew him as 'Bertie'.

> SECOND WORLD WAR

GEORGIA, Republic of

The area of the Republic of Georgia, which gained independence from the former Soviet Union in 1991, is less than half the area of the US state of Georgia. Its capital, Tbilisi, takes its name from the word for 'warm' in the Georgian language. The Russians call Georgia 'Gruziya'; the Georgians call Georgia 'Sak'art'velo'.

The Georgian language seems to be unrelated to any other and uses a 38-letter alphabet, called Mxedruli.

Georgia includes the ancient land of Colchis from where, according to legend, Jason and the Argonauts brought back the golden fleece.

Georgia is one of the oldest wine-making regions in the world. Some 8,000 years ago Georgians discovered by accident that grape juice left underground over winter in earthenware pots fermented into wine. UNESCO lists the Georgian wine-making method in its Intangible Cultural Heritage of Humanity list.

From 1184 to 1213, Georgia was ruled by a queen known as the 'King-Woman Tamar', who was later made a saint in the Georgian Orthodox Church. When she died, she was buried in secret to prevent her enemies from dishonouring her grave. Her burial place has never been found.

♀ *HEALTH*

GEORGIA, US State

In 2007, football fans at the University of Georgia were asked not to flush the toilets at the football stadium after peeing during the first home game of the season. Signs were put up in bathrooms asking people not to flush 'if it's yellow', and to leave the task to attendants in order to conserve water during a drought.

♀ *CHICKEN, PEANUT, WATERMELON*

GERBIL

In 2008, the epidemic prevention division of the Changji city Forestry Bureau in China spent 80,000 yuan (about £7,000) on gerbil contraceptive pellets after a plague of gerbils was said to be threatening the region's fragile ecosystem. The state news agency explained that the pellets had little effect on other animals but could prevent pregnancy in gerbils and induce abortion in those already pregnant.

♀ *ADRENALINE, PARAPSYCHOLOGY*

GERMANY

According to an official report in 2008, Germany's young soldiers are fat, smoke too much and don't exercise enough. 'The public perception is that soldiers are slim, sporty and healthy. Unfortunately, the reality is very different,' Germany's army commissioner said as he presented the report. It revealed that around 40 per cent of soldiers between 18 and 29 are overweight compared to 35 per cent among Germany's civilian population. Both male and female young soldiers also smoked too much and failed to do enough sport.

In 2001, the British Advertising Standards Agency ruled that referring to Germans as 'krauts' is not offensive but is 'a lighthearted reference to a national stereotype unlikely to cause serious or widespread offence'. A German Embassy spokesman, however, disagreed with this ruling saying, 'It is offensive. If you were called cabbage, you would not like it. It is the same for us.'

♀ *BEER MATS, DUCK, GNOME, HOT DOGS*

GESTURE

In May 2011, the State Patrol in Colorado dropped a charge of harassment against a man who had extended his middle finger at a State Trooper. The American Civil Liberties Union had argued that while the gesture may have been rude, it amounted to protected free speech.

♀ *HELL'S ANGELS*

GHANA

The name Ghana means warrior king and harks back to the days of the Ghana Empire between the 9th and 13th centuries. The Ghana Empire was built on trade in salt and gold, which is why British merchants later called it the Gold Coast. It was also commonly referred to as the 'white man's grave' because of the prevalence of malaria and other fatal tropical diseases.

Lake Volta in Ghana is the largest artificial lake in the world by surface area, covering 8,482 square kilometres (3,275 square miles).

The only country that produces more cocoa than Ghana is the Ivory Coast.

In 1991, the Ghanaian athlete Ferdie Ato Adoboe set a world record of 13.6 seconds for running 100 metres backwards. That record was equalled by Roland Wegner (Germany) in 2007 but Adoboe still holds the sole record of 12.7 seconds for 100 yards backwards.

The only English word from the Ga language of Ghana is that of the wasting disease kwashiorkor.

The Greenwich Meridian goes through Ghana; the Equator misses Ghana by about 611 kilometres (380 miles).

♀ UNDERGARMENTS

● GHOSTS

In 1995, Swaziland Prime Minister Prince Bhekimpi was reported to have complained about ghosts terrorising his subjects in the mountainous northern region of Enkhaba. A family were said to have taken refuge with the Prince's household after ghosts invaded their own home, beat them, ordered them to cook food and stole their blankets. The Prince himself had also been verbally abused by the ghosts. Fortunately, the ghosts had not invaded the royal household because they were apparently afraid of the dogs. Having banned celebrations, political groups, love affairs with women under 21 and all alcohol except traditional beer, the Prince was reported to have said that he was determined to ban ghosts as well.

In October 1995, a woman on the Isle of Wight complained of a ghost that turned on lights and electrical equipment. A spokesman for Southern Electricity said it was the first time they had had a high bill blamed on a ghost.

The Chinese in Singapore celebrate a month-long 'Hungry Ghost' festival in August and September. In 1996, a power failure in Singapore was caused by too many people cooking for the Hungry Ghosts.

The sixth-century Irish saint Kevin was canonised for living as a hermit in a man-made cave cut into a hillside, and for putting up with the ghost of a woman he had murdered. Her name was Kathleen and he is said to have drowned her because of her persistent attempts to seduce him.

In 1998, three workers in a Havana museum resigned after seeing Ernest Hemingway's ghost.

The Royal Albert Hall in London is supposedly haunted by the ghost of a 19th-century organ-maker.

One paranormal almanac lists 58 types of ghost.

Because of the translucent legs and abdomen of the ant *Tapinoma melano-cephalum*, it is commonly known as 'ghost ant'.

♀ AUCTION, BABBAGE, LEMUR, QUEEN MARY, RAVEN, STATISTICS

● GIGGLE

The earliest recorded appearance of the verb 'to giggle' in the English language was in 1509 in a book *The Shyp of Folys of the Worlde* by the poet and clergyman Alexander Barclay who spelt it 'gyggyl'.

♀ FLIRTING

● GIN

Of the 7,217 examples of 'gin' in the first billion words in the Oxford English Corpus, 620 were gin and tonics. As this Corpus of modern English usage showed, 'tonic' is by far the most likely word to be found two words after 'gin'. The first citation in the *Oxford English Dictionary* of the abbreviation G&T for gin and tonic dates back to 1960.

Tonic water was patented by Erasmus Bond in London on 28 May 1858.

GIRAFFE

Giraffes cannot cough or swim, but they can clean their ears with their half-metre-long tongue.

The statue of Nelson Mandela in Johannesburg is 6 metres (19.5 feet) high, which is about 10 centimetres (4 inches) taller than the world's tallest giraffe.

It has frequently been said that giraffes are the only animals born with horns, but this is not strictly correct. Their 'horns' are not bone but ossified cartilage known as 'ossicones'. Giraffes have also been said to be the only mammals that do not yawn, but that too is arguable. The non-yawning comment seems to be based on research by psychologists Monica Greco in 1992 and Ronald Baenninger in 1997, who both report never seeing a giraffe yawn in their extensive research. So perhaps it is more accurate to say that giraffes never yawn when psychologists are watching them.

HOMOSEXUALITY, OKAPI

GIRL

Until the 16th century, the word 'girl' was used for a child of either sex. 'Boy' always meant a male child. The word 'girl' occurs only once in the King James Bible: Joel 3:3 refers to a girl sold for wine. The plural 'girls' also occurs only once, in Zechariah 8:5, mentioning 'boys and girls playing in the streets'.

Aristotle believed that unborn male babies lie on the right side of the womb, girls on the left.

Seventeen films with 'girl' in the title have won Oscars, which is six more than those with 'boy'.

'A girl should be two things: classy and fabulous.' Coco Chanel

BIBLE, CAMEL, JAMES BOND, KISSING, NOSE

GLADSTONE, William Ewart (1809–98)

William Gladstone is one of only two people to have had his coffin transported on the London tube. For his lying in state at Westminster Hall and funeral at Westminster Abbey, his body was taken by train from Broughton to Earl's Court, then transferred to the District Line from Earl's Court to Westminster. The other posthumous tube traveller was Dr Barnardo, whose body was transported on the Central Line in 1905, from Liverpool Street to Barkingside.

GLASS

The United Nations named 2022 as the International Year of Glass. It was also the International Year of Artisanal Fisheries and Aquaculture.

GLASSES

The Italian Salvino d'Armato introduced spectacles to Florence in 1268, but they were of a pince-nez style, designed to be held or balanced on the nose. Side arms to enable spectacles to be clipped to the head were introduced early in the 18th century. The first painting showing someone wearing glasses was by Tommaso da Modena in the middle of the 14th century.

ART, EARS, LEMON, MADRID, READING

GLOBAL WARMING

In December 2011, the Chilean government appealed to men to take off their ties as part of a campaign to save on air conditioning and cut down on energy use to help tackle global warming.

The earliest recorded use of the phrase 'global warming' was in 1952.

During the COP26 Climate Change Conference in Glasgow in 2021, US President Joe Biden is reported to have let out a huge fart during a conversation with Camilla, Duchess of Cornwall.

ALASKA, DIVORCE, WHISKERS

GNOME

The word 'gnomus' (plural 'gnomi') first appeared in the work of the Swiss alchemist Paracelsus in the 16th century. He may have been thinking of the Latin word *genomus*, meaning 'earth-dweller'. According to Paracelsus, a gnome is two spans long, a span being the distance from thumb to little fingertip on an outstretched human hand.

The phrase 'gnomes of Zurich' for Swiss financiers was invented by Harold Wilson in 1956. What he was actually referring to was 'the little gnomes in Zurich and other finance centres'.

Garden gnomes began as garden dwarfs in Germany in the 19th century. The first garden gnomes in the UK were introduced in 1847 by Sir Charles Isham. One of his original 21 gnomes still survives. It is called Lampy and is insured for £1 million. According to a recent estimate, there are 25 million garden gnomes in Germany.

'Gnome' was the codename of the Spanish communist Ramon Mercader, who assassinated Russian revolutionary Leon Trotsky in 1940.

GNU

The gnu is also known as the wildebeest (from the Dutch, meaning 'wild beast'). The word 'gnu' came to us from the language of the Khoekhoe people of south-west Africa, who also gave us 'quagga'.

'I like a man to be a clean, strong, upstanding Englishman who can look his gnu in the face and put an ounce of lead in it.' P.G. Wodehouse, Mr Mulliner Speaking, *1929*

GOAL

Research in 2010 concluded that soccer goalkeepers do better in penalty shoot-outs if they are wearing red jerseys. Researchers at the University of Chichester found that an average of 20 per cent more penalties were missed when the goalkeeper wore red. They put it down to evolutionary responses to the colour producing a subconscious perception of danger.

After red, the most successful colour for goalkeepers' jerseys was yellow, followed by blue and green.

AFGHANISTAN, FOOTBALL, KYRGYZSTAN

GOATS

Official figures reported that there were 157,361,699 goats in China in 2001. This figure had risen to 182,890,670 by 2013, which was 18.19 per cent of the total world goat population; 2013 was also said to be the year in which the world goat population rose above 1 billion.

In September 1996, a goat in Brazil was found dead after it had been registered to stand as a protest candidate for the post of mayor in a small town. Police were reported to be investigating allegations that the goat had been the victim of a political assassination. The goat's owner suspected that it had been poisoned.

A goat was arrested in Nigeria in 2009 on suspicion of attempted armed robbery after vigilantes had taken it to the police saying it was an armed robber who had used black magic to transform himself into a goat to escape arrest after trying to steal a Mazda car.

ITALY, NAVIES, QUEENSLAND, SURFING, THOR

GOD

The International Association for Divine Taxonomy was founded by the American conceptual artist Jonathon Keats, with the assistance of a group of scientists who helped him devise experiments to determine the genetic make-up of God. Since no sample of God's DNA was available to sequence its genome, Keats designed an experiment to attempt to see whether God was more like a bacterium or a fruit fly. Putting together evolutionary theory with the idea that God created life in his own image, it seemed reasonable to believe that God's DNA would resemble that of early life-forms.

Keats's method was to see which of bacterium or fruit fly would become more godlike when bombarded with godly material. He put one sample of blue-green algae under one bell-jar and 160 fruit flies under another, then played recordings of prayer from a number of religions at both samples for the biblical period of seven days and seven nights, after which period he measured which had become more godlike.

For that purpose, he took omnipresence as his measure of godliness, and saw which of the samples had reproduced more successfully, thus coming closer to omnipresence. His tentative results supported the view that God was more like a fruit fly than blue-green algae, but Keats said this was not definitive. Further research is clearly needed.

֍ *GUITAR, HOXHA, MEAT, MILKY WAY, NAVEL, OSTRICH*

⬤ GODIVA

Lady Godiva – or Godgifu – was the wife of Leofric, Earl of Mercia, and is said to have ridden naked through the town of Coventry in exchange for a promise from her husband to cut taxes. She is mentioned in the Domesday Book of 1086 as having inherited various estates from her husband, who died in 1057.

The story about the naked riding first appeared about 200 years after her death, and is almost certainly a myth. The embellishment of the story, which introduced the character of Peeping Tom, who was struck dead, or at least blind, for peeking at the naked horse-riding deeds of Lady Godiva, did not enter the tale until the 17th century. The horse is supposed to have been named Aethenoth, which means Noble Audacity.

⬤ GOLD

At August 2021 prices, all the gold in Fort Knox is worth about $470 billion. Since Jeff Bezos's net worth was estimated to be around $200 billion in 2021, he could have afforded to buy just under 43 per cent of all the gold in Fort Knox.

One-third of all the gold ever mined on Earth comes from the Witwatersrand Basin in South Africa.

During the Alaskan Klondike gold rush of 1897–98, potatoes were so valued for their vitamin C content that miners traded gold for bags of potatoes.

֍ *ALCHEMY, BRAHE, DENTURES, PURPLE, ST NICHOLAS, ZOG I*

⬤ GOLDFISH

In January 2022, Israeli researchers reported that goldfish have been taught to drive. The team at Ben-Gurion University developed an FOV – a fish-operated vehicle – fitted with remote sensing technology. 'Surprisingly, it doesn't take the fish a long time to learn how to drive the vehicle,' one of the researchers said. Six goldfish took part in the study and some showed that they are better drivers than others.

The Polish-born film director Sam Goldwyn was born Schmuel Gelbfisz in 1879. He anglicised his name to Samuel Goldfish after he came to England aged

15 and became Samuel Goldwyn at the age of 39.

In their natural state, goldfish are historically olive green. Domestic varieties result from breeding for colour. The domesticated goldfish was first documented in China in the 10th century. They were popular among the privileged classes and eating them was forbidden. The first book about goldfish was *Essay About the Goldfish*, written in China in 1596.

Goldfish have excellent hearing: they can distinguish between sounds one 150-millionth of a second apart.

Artificial waves can make a goldfish seasick.

An RSPCA inspector was commended in the 1970s for saving a goldfish from drowning. 'There are not many people who know that a fish could drown if it swallows too much water,' he said.

Contrary to popular belief, goldfish do not have short memory spans. Experiments have shown that goldfish can learn things and sometimes even retain the memory of what they have learned for at least six months.

In 1976, researchers showed that if you bung up a goldfish's nose so that it cannot smell, its sexual behaviour decreases significantly. In the same year, it was also reported that one-eyed goldfish swim as fast as two-eyed goldfish, but blind goldfish are slower.

Goldfish have been taught to swim on their tails, as if standing up in the water.

A pregnant goldfish is called a twit.

The only novel by Charles Dickens to mention goldfish is *Nicholas Nickleby*, in which he refers to an old gentleman who 'requested to be served with a fricassee of boot-tops and goldfish sauce'.

ALCOHOL, ART, CHINA, FISH, JAPAN, PARAPSYCHOLOGY

● GOLF

In 1456, King James II of Scotland decreed that 'futeball and the golfe be utterly cryit down' because they interfered with yeomen's archery practice. The ban lasted until the Treaty of Glasgow in 1502 between Scotland and England, giving archers more spare time. The first officially documented golf match was on 4 February 1504 between the Earl of Bothwell and James IV, who had signed the 1502 Treaty himself.

The diameter of a golf hole used to vary between 3 and 5 inches but was standardised in 1891 at 4.25 inches after a piece of drainpipe of that size was used to repair a hole at St Andrews. The 18-hole course also originated at St Andrews in 1764.

A golfer's caddie takes his name from the French word 'cadet', meaning a boy, or youngest son: he was the one who carried the bags. Another French contribution to golfing history happened on 7 February 1928, when golfers voted to sentence a blackbird to death for stealing 30 golf balls from the Saint-Germain course near Paris.

A snake in Australia that swallowed four golf balls in 2008 had a better outcome. A couple had placed the balls in their chicken shed at Nobbys Creek in New South Wales to encourage their hen to nest, but the snake swallowed them thinking they were chicken eggs. The snake's life was saved by emergency surgery and the golf balls were later sold for charity, raising £630 in an eBay auction.

In Ohio, 6 per cent of all deaths by lightning occur when the victim is playing golf.

Best golfing funeral: Mr Thomas J. Caradonia, 70, from Houston, was buried in August 1984 wearing full golfing regalia and holding a putter in his right hand.

On 6 February 1971, Alan Shepard became the first person to hit a golf ball on the Moon. He took two swipes with a 6-iron. He mis-hit the first, which went only about 30 metres (100 feet), but the second stayed in the air for 30 seconds and travelled a distance of 200 yards. The two golf balls have remained on the Moon since then, but Shepard brought his golf club back to Earth and in 1974, at the suggestion of Bing Crosby, donated it to the US Golf Association Museum in Liberty Corner, New Jersey.

'Excessive golfing dwarfs the intellect.' Sir Walter Simpson, The Art of Golf, *1887*

'Golf is a good walk spoiled.' Often attributed to Mark Twain, though the US novelist Harry Leon Wilson probably originated it

'I'm sure Jimmy would have wanted us to do that. He would have done the same.' Spoken at a golf club in Fife in September 1996 by a golfer who played on with three regular partners after a fourth, Jimmy Hogg, 77, had dropped dead at the first tee

HUMAN RIGHTS, KIPLING, RYDER CUP, SCROTUM, WOODS

GOOD FRIDAY

In AD 970, Good Friday falling on 25 March, the spring equinox, was seen by some as an omen that the world would end. It didn't.

GOOGLE

Google, the US multi-national grown from an Internet search engine, was founded as a private company by Larry Page and Sergey Brin on 4 September 1998.

The name 'Google' was in fact a misspelling of 'googol', which is the mathematical term for the number 1 followed by 100 zeros. The name was picked to symbolise the large amount of information Google hoped to provide.

Actually the word 'google' is much older than Google: the *Oxford English Dictionary* gives it as meaning 'to bowl a googly' in cricket from 1907.

The earliest listed use of the verb 'to Google', meaning to search the Internet, dates from 1999.

Google currently runs more than 3 billion searches every day. According to Google, the number of individual pages it has found on the Internet exceeded a trillion in 2008 and is now more than 130 trillion.

You can now conduct Google searches in 124 languages, including Klingon and the language it calls 'Ewmew Fudd', which is based on the speech defect of Bugs Bunny's hunter enemy, Elmer Fudd. On Google, the Ewmew Fudd language is achieved by replacing every 'r' or 'l' with a 'w', except, curiously enough, in the word 'Google', which presumably ought to be spelled 'Googwe'.

AARDVARK, INTERNET, RICHARD III

GOOSE

Traditionally, the earliest day for eating goose eggs is St Valentine's Day, 14 February.

'Goose', 'foot' and 'tooth' are the only common English words with plurals that change -oo to -ee. The only other word with a similar plural is 'swoose', a hybrid offspring of a swan and a goose.

When geese fly in a V-formation, the flap of each bird's wings creates an uplift easing the flight of the following birds. This has been estimated to improve their flying range by 71 per cent.

A group of geese on the ground is called a gaggle. A group flying in formation, however, is called a wedge or a skein.

Like the albatross and swan, geese are monogamous.

A goose produces about 680 grams (1.5 pounds) of droppings every day. An average-sized goose releases about 0.5 litres (1 pint) of fat when cooked.

Sacred geese in the Temple of Juno on the Capitoline Hill in Rome were said to have alerted the city to an attack by the Gauls in 390 BC.

Force-feeding geese to increase the size of their liver to make foie gras is a technique begun by the ancient Egyptians around 2,500 BC.

The Nottingham Goose Fair has been held on the first Thursday, Friday and Saturday in October since 1284.

There is no known connection between geese and gooseberries.

'Many wearing rapiers are afraid of goose-quills.' Hamlet (This was Shakespeare's way of saying, 'The pen is mightier than the sword'.)

♀ *ANIMAL NOISES, ETIQUETTE*

● GOOSEBERRY

What are now called kiwifruit used to be known as Chinese gooseberries. They were first brought to New Zealand in 1904, where they were grown and marketed without conspicuous success until 1959 when exporters to the US were told by American buyers that Chinese gooseberries needed a new name as their clients were not very fond of either China or gooseberries. The new name 'kiwifruit' was agreed upon and sales increased rapidly.

In January 2022, David Rush of Idaho set a record by breaking 52 Guinness World Records in a year. He said that one of the most difficult was the record for the most kiwifruits sliced in one minute using a Samurai sword while standing on a Swiss ball.

♀ *GOOSE*

● GORILLA

Gorillas were named in 1847 by US missionary Thomas Savage and naturalist Jeffries Wyman from the Greek *gorillai*, said to be 'a tribe of hairy women'. The first gorilla in Britain arrived at Liverpool Docks on 21 June 1876.

The correct scientific name of the subspecies Western Lowland gorilla is *Gorilla gorilla gorilla*. The Eastern Lowland gorilla is *Gorilla gorilla graueri*, and the Mountain gorilla is *Gorilla gorilla beringei*. In all cases the first name (Gorilla) is its Genus, the second (gorilla) is its species and the third is its sub-species. Gorillas never snore.

♀ *GORILLA SUITS, HAIR, MERMAID*

● GORILLA SUITS

31 January is, for fans of *Mad* magazine at least, National Gorilla Suit Day, when supporters dress in gorilla suits and knock on people's doors. National Gorilla Suit Day began in 1963 as a cartoon story in a collection by *Mad* illustrator Don Martin.

The first person to wear a gorilla suit in films was Hollywood make-up artist Carlos Cruz Gemora, who appeared as a gorilla in several films in the 1920s. Charles Gemora, as he was commonly known, was a Filipino who reached the US as a stowaway on a ship. He became known as 'the King of the Gorilla Men'.

GOSSIP

The word 'gossip' dates back to the 11th-century Old English word 'godsibb', meaning one who acts as a sponsor (or 'god sibling') at a baptism, and could also refer to a godmother or godfather. It then came to be applied to any close friend or acquaintance, then in the 17th century came to be used particularly for a person of trifling character or the talk such a person might indulge in.

Researchers in Michigan in 1995 reported that American children aged 9 to 12 gossip on average 18 times an hour.

⚲ *CHILE*

GRÄFENBERG, Ernst (1881–1957)

The highly sensitive area in a woman's vagina known as the G-spot is named after German gynaecologist Ernst Gräfenberg, who first suggested its existence in 1950, but the debate over whether it truly exists continued until 2008 when Italian researcher Emmanuele Jannini resolved the matter with ultrasound scans of the key vaginal area.

The existence or otherwise of the G-spot is important for ruling on whether or not the Italian anatomist Gabriele Falloppio, should be considered the only man to have a part of the female body – the fallopian tube – named after him.

GRAFFITI

The first major auction of work by graffiti artists was held in June 2000 in New York. Many of the items were withdrawn on failing to reach their reserve price, but a door from an apartment space above an art gallery, featuring art by various graffitists, was sold for over $25,000 to a telephone bidder.

In October 2021, Sotheby's in New York presented their first online auction of graffiti and street art under the title 'Public Intervention: Art of the Street'. Its 44 lots fetched a total of $1,770,552, of which 14 works by Richard Hambleton fetched $566,370. Hambleton was a Canadian artist known as the Godfather of Street Art. His middle name, appropriately enough, was Art.

GRAND NATIONAL

The Grand National horserace has been won more often by horses whose names begin with the letter R than any other letter of the alphabet.

In 2013, the initial letters of the first six horses to finish the race spelled out the word 'ACTORS', taking them in the order in which they finished. That coincidence was underlined by the fact that the fourth-place horse was Oscar Time.

No horse came third in 1928 because only two horses finished the course. The winner that year was 100–1 shot Tipperary Tim.

The jump known as Becher's Brook is named after jockey Captain Martin Becher, who took shelter in the water after being unseated and later commented: 'Water tastes disgusting without the benefits of whisky'.

⚲ *PECK, ROLLERCOASTER, SNAIL*

GRAPE

The wine business has made grape-growing the largest food industry in the world. There are more than 60 species and 8,000 varieties of grapes, and they are all suitable for making juice or wine. There are 25 million acres of grapes worldwide producing 72 million tons of grapes every year.

The grapes that we eat raw as fruit have a thin skin and very small seeds or no seeds at all. Wine grapes are smaller, with thicker skins and many seeds.

Botanically, grapes are not fruit but berries.

The expression 'sour grapes' derives from a story by Aesop, 'The Fox and the Grapes'. A fox repeatedly runs and jumps trying to get at a bunch of delicious ripe grapes hanging from a vine draped around a high branch of a tree, but fails every time. Then he walks away, asking himself why he was wearing himself out trying to get a bunch of sour grapes that were not worth the effort. The moral is: 'There are many who pretend to despise and belittle that which is beyond their reach.'

♀ HENRY III, POMEGRANATE, WINE

● GRAPEFRUIT

The grapefruit has been known by that name since 1814. It was given that name because it was seen growing in clusters like grapes. Previously, it had been known as a variety of shaddock and was sometimes called pampelmoes. The shaddock was said to have been named after a Captain Shaddock or Chaddock, commander of an East India ship who supposedly brought its seeds to Barbados and thence to England.

A grapefruit is 92 per cent water.

In 1995, medical researchers announced that grapefruit juice may boost anti-rejection drugs for transplants.

♀ BROOKLYN, FRUIT, SWEAT

● GRAVITY

Astronauts cannot belch – there is no gravity to separate liquid from gas in their stomachs.

Our understanding of gravity began with the work of Galileo at the end of the 16th century. Before that, everyone since Aristotle thought that heavy objects fell faster than lighter ones. Galileo showed that light ones fell more slowly because of air resistance, but the gravitational effect was the same on everything.

This led to Newton in 1687 showing that the force causing an apple to drop was the same as the force keeping the Moon in orbit around the Earth. A problem with Newton's theory was the orbit of Mercury, which his theory could not explain. In 1915, Einstein resolved the problem, presenting gravity as a consequence of space–time curvature. His theory of general relativity saw gravity not as a force but a warping of space caused by energy and mass.

The existence of gravitational waves was predicted by Einstein. Their confirmation won him the 2017 Nobel Prize for Physics.

The 2013 film *Gravity* won seven Oscars.

♀ APPLE, EARTH, SPACE FLIGHT

● GREAT WALL OF CHINA

China's first man in space, Yang Liwei, confirmed when he returned from his trip in 2004 that he could not see the Great Wall of China from space. The official in charge of teaching materials for China's schools was promptly told to stop printing the falsehood that the Great Wall could be seen from space in school textbooks.

♀ DINGO

● GREECE

The men's sailors' 100 metres freestyle swimming event in the 1896 Olympics was open only to members of the Greek Navy. So Greece won all the medals.

In 1856, Greece introduced a ban on

smoking in state buildings. In 2014, Greece had the highest rate of smoking in the EU, and this was confirmed in 2017 when a survey reported that 37 per cent of Greeks are smokers and only 44 per cent had never smoked a cigarette, the smallest percentage in the EU.

♀ *HUNGARY, LEPROSY, NIGHTINGALE*

GREENGAGE

The greengage was introduced into Britain in 1725 by Sir William Gage, 2nd Baronet of Hengrave, who probably brought it over from Paris. The French knew it as Grosse Reine Claude, after Queen Claude, Duchess of Brittany.

GREENLAND

The area of the European Economic Community (formerly known as the Common Market) was halved in 1981 when Greenland (until then part of Denmark) was granted full independence.

The population of Greenland in October 2021 was 56,899. It is the least densely populated country in the world. The population density is 0.14 people per square kilometre (or 7.2 square kilometres per person).

♀ *ART, BUTTOCKS, SANTA CLAUS*

GROUNDHOG

The groundhog is a 2-foot-long furry mammal also known as woodchuck, whistlepig or land beaver. It is a type of marmot. The name woodchuck has nothing to do with wood but comes from a Native American word for the animal, *wuchak*.

When alarmed, a groundhog emits a high-pitched whistle, hence the name whistlepig.

Groundhogs greet each other by touching their noses to the other one's mouth.

♀ *GROUNDHOG DAY, WIARTON WILLY*

GROUNDHOG DAY

The 2 February date of Groundhog Day is midway between the winter solstice and spring equinox. Its origins lie in the pagan festival of Imbolc and the Christian festival of Candlemas. The word 'Imbolc' comes from an Old Irish phrase meaning 'in the belly', which referred to the pregnancy of ewes.

The annual Groundhog Day weather forecast is made in the town of Punxsutawney by a groundhog named Punxsutawney Phil. According to folklore, groundhogs emerge from their burrow on this day. If they see their shadow they are said to dart back and winter will last six more weeks. Punxsutawney has celebrated Groundhog Day since 1887.

Groundhog Day celebrations in Punxsutawney are held at a place called Gobbler's Knob. Supporters of Punxsutawney Phil say that he always gets it right, but independent meteorological analyses suggest that Phil's forecasts are correct less than 40 per cent of the time.

In 2010, the animal rights group PETA said that the organisers of Pennsylvania's Groundhog Day should replace Punxsutawney Phil with a robotic stand-in. They protested at the animal's being kept in captivity and exposed to large crowds and bright lights. William Deeley, President of the Inner Circle of the Punxsutawney Groundhog Club, said, 'the animal is being treated better than the average child in Pennsylvania'.

There are two theories about how Gobbler's Knob got its name: one is that the area was once home to large groups of turkeys; the second is that the name comes from the practice of 'gobbling' up woodland creatures after a hunt.

The tradition of animals predicting the weather on this day began as a medieval Christian tradition involving hedgehogs.

Most of the film *Groundhog Day* was shot not in Punxsutawney but in Woodstock, Illinois.

♀ *WIARTON WILLY*

GROUSE

The courtship ritual of grouse involves a display known as lekking, in which the males compete to gain the attention of females.

According to the paper 'Non-random mating in classical lekking grouse species: seasonal and diurnal trends', published in 2000, 'Adult males and individuals occupying centrally located territories on the lek were found to have significantly larger testes than juveniles and peripheral individuals.'

In UK law, the Game Act 1831 declared 12 August as the beginning of the shooting season for red grouse. Since then, that date has been known as 'the glorious twelfth'. The red grouse is only one of 18 known species of grouse.

♀ *BLAKE, KANSAS*

GUANO

In 1856, the US Congress passed the Guano Islands Act, giving any US citizen the right to mine guano, or bird dung, on any uninhabited island. Guano was highly prized as a fertiliser. At the time, America bought vast quantities of guano from Peru, which was very rich in the stuff, thanks to large numbers of birds who fed off the shoals of anchovies near Peru's coast. The Incas appreciated the benefits of all these bird droppings and decreed that anyone who molested

the birds creating it should face the death penalty.

GUATEMALA

There are more than 30 volcanoes in Guatemala but only three of them are active.

Between 5 and 10 people are killed or injured in Guatemala by falling bullets every Christmas. In December 2001, police called on revellers not to fire pistols into the air to celebrate. 'Lots of people die when bullets fall on their heads,' a police spokesman said. 'This tradition of shooting in the air is a very dangerous practice.'

Many Guatemalans worship a Mayan deity called Maximon, a mythological character who promised to protect the men's wives when the men went to work, but slept with all the women instead.

♀ *BAR CODES*

GUILLOTINE

The Maiden, or Scottish Maiden, was an early form of guillotine used as a means of execution by beheading in Edinburgh. It was introduced in 1564 during the reign of Mary, Queen of Scots when the sword used for executions in Edinburgh was worn out. In February 1563, funds were needed to pay for the loan of a sword for a beheading, so the Provost and Magistrates of Edinburgh ordered the Maiden to be built. It consisted of a weighted blade, held up with a peg which, when removed, caused the blade to drop, guided by wedges in its wooden frame, to decapitate the victim. It remained in use for over 150 years until 1716.

The use of the guillotine in France began long after the Maiden, with a proposal submitted on 10 October 1789 by Dr Joseph Guillotin in an Assembly debate about the Penal Code. This included a recommendation that decapitation, without the accompaniment of torture, should become the sole form of capital punishment in France. The first guillotine execution in France was in 1792. The last public guillotining was in June 1939, and the last use of all was for the execution of convicted murderer Hamida Djandoubi on 10 September 1977.

One of the more gruesome accounts of a guillotining occurred in 1905 when Dr Beaurieux experimented with the head of Henri Languille, who was guillotined at 5.30am on 28 June. After waiting for the spasmodic twitching of the head to cease, the doctor clearly called out Languille's name in a loud voice. He reports that the eyelids lifted and 'Languille's eyes very definitely fixed themselves on mine and the pupils focused themselves.' When they had settled shut again, he repeated the name, with the same effect. A third call, however, elicited no movement. 'I have just recounted to you with rigorous exactness what I was able to observe,' he ended. 'The whole thing had lasted twenty-five to thirty seconds.'

♀ *HALIFAX, OYSTER, WAX*

● GUINEA

Until 1816, the guinea, worth 21 shillings (£1.05), was the main unit of currency in Britain. The name came from the fact that the gold from which guineas were struck came from West Africa, which was generally known as Guinea at the time. That name, in turn, came from a Moroccan word for 'black men' which was *aguinaw*.

Although the guinea has almost disappeared from common parlance,

apart from the names of horseraces such as the Ten Thousand Guineas, it is still common to auction rams for prices in guineas. The world's most expensive sheep sold at an auction in Lanark, Scotland, in August 2020 for 350,000 guineas.

♀ *BOWERBIRD, COCONUT, FLYING SAUCERS, GUINEA PIGS, NEW GUINEA, STAMPS*

● GUINEA PIGS

Guinea pigs are not pigs and do not come from Guinea. In fact they originated in the Andes.

There are various theories about the 'Guinea' part of their name: some say it was due to a confusion between Guinea in West Africa and Guyana in South America; others say it was because the first guinea pigs in Europe came on slave ships that went from Guinea via America to Europe; another theory is that it was a corruption of the word 'coney', the old term for a rabbit.

Guinea pigs get upset when left alone, so Swiss law prohibits owners from keeping a guinea pig on its own. This has resulted in Switzerland running the world's only rental agency for guinea pigs. Designed to cater for the needs of former owners of a pair of guinea pigs, one of which has died, the agency rents out guinea pigs to keep bereaved pets happy in their twilight years. In 2011, the price to rent a castrated male was quoted as 50 Swiss francs, and 60 francs for a female, with half this price returned when the animal was given back.

It is unclear how 'guinea pig' became an expression for any experimental animal or human who was trying something out for the first time. Guinea pigs are often used for experimentation, but not nearly as much as rats. Robert Koch's work on tuberculosis and Louis Pasteur's experiments on inoculation both used guinea pigs, and the high profile of those two men may have been responsible for guinea pigs gaining the experimental limelight.

♀ FOX

GUITAR

A five-string guitar was known in the 16th century, and a guitar with four double-strings existed in the 15th century. The guitar's sixth string was added in the late 18th century.

An inflammation called 'guitar nipple' was mentioned in the *British Medical Journal* in 1974. It is caused by rubbing from the guitar soundbox. Guitar-string dermatitis is another occupational hazard for guitarists.

In 1999, a Pennsylvania man tried to sue God for not giving him the skills to play the guitar. Presidents Reagan and Bush, as God's representatives on Earth, were named as co-defendants, together with a number of religious leaders and other politicians. The case was thrown out.

The smallest guitar in the world was made in 1997 at Cornell University in Ithaca, New York. It had six silicone strings, each about 100 atoms long, which is about one-twentieth the thickness of a human hair. It is strummed by a laser, played in a vacuum chamber, and emits a sound too high to hear.

David Gilmour's iconic black Stratocaster guitar became the world's most expensive guitar ever sold when it fetched $3.9 million at an auction in New York in June 2019. Gilmour had played this guitar in many of his most famous works with Pink Floyd.

The European Patent Office lists 2,388 guitar-related inventions. Patents include an electronic calculator for guitar scales, patented by two Californians in 1999.

The guitarfish is shaped like a guitar.

♀ CELLO, MOUTH ORGAN

GUNMAN

A gunman survived after being hit by at least 21 police bullets in New York in August 2010. Angel Alvarez had been involved in a gunfight with another man before being brought down by a hail of police gunfire. Forensic experts said he had probably set some sort of record by surviving so many hits.

♀ KENNEDY

GUNS

In February 1776, Benjamin Franklin wrote to a US major-general giving him six reasons why guns could never be as efficient as bows and arrows.

The first machine gun was patented in 1718 by London lawyer James Puckle. In 1913, John Steinocher patented a gun-firing scarecrow; and in 1916, Albert Pratt patented a gun that was part of a soldier's helmet. It also doubled as a cooking utensil. Fortunately it was never used as a gun as the recoil could well have killed the wearer.

In July 1998, a law was passed in Kentucky making it legal for ministers and church officers to carry a gun in church, as long as they have a permit for concealed weapons.

There were an estimated 393,347,000 guns in civilian possession in the US in 2017, and only 326,474,000 people. Around the same time, there were 263.6 million registered vehicles in the US, so there were more guns than cars too.

'All you need for a movie is a gun and a girl.' Jean-Luc Godard

'All you need for happiness is a good gun, a good horse and a good wife.' Daniel Boone

⚲ BRASSIERE, COLT, CRIME, DIVORCE, SCARE-CROW, SEX

GUPPY

Research on guppy fish published in the *Society Journal Proceedings B* in 2010 reported that uglier fish have better sperm. The findings were said to support 'sperm competition theory', where females mate with several males and the quality and swimming speed of the sperm determine which male fathers the offspring. Guppies are useful subjects in which to study this, because the males have two types of reproductive behaviour: courtship displays and non-consensual or 'sneak' mating. Highly attractive and orna-mented males perform well in court-ship displays, but after mating, their sperm was shown to be less effective at inseminating females than that of their uglier colleagues.

⚲ FISH

GUT

According to the *Oxford English Dictionary*, the word 'gut' may have its origins in prehistoric times. The dictionary also says that 'guts' was 'formerly, but not now, in dignified use with reference to man'. It is not known if the 'catgut' used for the strings of musical instruments was ever the gut of a cat. Usually it was sheep, but some-times horse or ass.

GUT may also stand for Grand Unified Theory (a theory to unify electro-magnetic force with the strong and weak nuclear forces), the Gdansk University of Technology (in Poland), or the genito-urinary tract.

'I am very proud to be called a pig. It stands for pride, integrity and guts.' Ronald Reagan

⚲ GUT BARGING, SHIRT, VIOLIN

GUT BARGING

The ancient sport of gut barging, in which two abdominally well-endowed men attempt to push each other over the edge of a 2.5 by 1.8 metre (8 feet by 6 feet) mat placed, traditionally, on a pub floor, burst upon the world on 30 April 1996, when Binkie Braithwaite, Gutfather of the World Gut Barging Federation, told the readers of *The Independent* newspaper the full history, rules, regulations, strategy, traditions and other sundry sordid details of a sport allegedly some two centuries old.

The basic rules are simple: each player tries to push his opponent off the mat, using only his beer gut. 'Anthro-pologically speaking,' Mr Braithwaite explained, 'one would have to place Barging somewhere between Sumo wrestling and the Peruvian territorial game of Dungwatt.'

He accepted that the concept of two fat men pushing each other across a mat gave it a superficial resemblance to Sumo, but insisted that its strategic delicacy owed more to the Peruvian game. Before each bout, he said, the players would lather themselves in engine oil and fling copious handfuls of Bombay mix over the mat.

Following the newspaper article, dozens of people wrote to Mr Braithwaite expressing a desire to participate, and gut barging suddenly became a reality.

Quite apart from having bouts staged on three continents, gut barging was demonstrated at the Royal Albert Hall in London during the interval of The Stranglers reunion concert in 1997,

GUPPY | GUT BARGING

and it even appeared in a script of the long-running BBC radio serial *The Archers*.

The cheerleader girls at gut barges are known as Gongoozlers, the referee is the Balou, and the world champion was Mad Maurice, the Belgian from Melksham who, Mr Braithwaite pointed out, was not mad, his name was not Maurice, and he did not, strictly speaking, come from Melksham. He was, however, admired by his fans for being 'the only man who can make his belly-button sneer'.

Binkie Braithwaite, known to few by his real name of Geoffrey Sargent, died in 2016. He is greatly missed by all who knew him, except those who believed everything he told them.

● GUYANA

Apart from being the country that hosted the world's largest ever cult mass-suicide, at Jonestown in 1978, when over 900 people killed themselves, Guyana was the birthplace and home of Sir Lionel Luckhoo, who has been described as the world's most successful lawyer.

Between 1940 and 1985, Luckhoo successfully acted in 245 consecutive cases in which his client was accused of murder, securing acquittals in all of them. He also owned several racehorses, an island and a hotel, and was a good amateur magician and a member of the Magic Circle. He was also the brother of the last Governor-General of Guyana, Sir Edward Luckhoo.

When Forbes Burnham became the first prime minister of an independent Guyana in 1966, one of his early acts was to ban the import of flour, split peas, cooking oil, butter, cheese, salted fish, pickled meats, preserved fruits, most canned items, and any food perceived as 'luxury'. This led to economic chaos and long food queues.

Burnham died in mysterious circumstances in 1985 and his body was flown to Moscow where it was pickled and preserved by a team led by Dr Debov, who also looked after the mummified body of Lenin. The body was sent back to Guyana, but with a change in policy following Burnham's death, the corpse was not put on display as intended, but had to be buried. 'It was a terrible waste,' said Debov.

♀ *GUINEA PIGS*

● GYMNASTICS

The gymnast Larisa Latynina holds the record for winning more Summer Olympics medals than any other woman. Competing for the USSR between 1956 and 1964, she won a total of 18 medals, comprising nine gold, five silver and four bronze.

Among both men and women, her total is beaten only by Michael Phelps, who won 28 medals of which 23 were gold, three silver and two bronze.

♀ *LATVIA, SPORT*

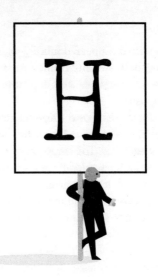

HACKER

On 9 September 1997, a Cincinnati woman was put on probation for child neglect after a court found that her children had been allowed to live in squalor while she spent 12 hours a day on the Internet. The woman's name was Hacker.

The use of the word 'hacker' to mean someone who tries to gain unauthorised access to a computer system dates back to 1963.

HAEMORRHOIDS

It is estimated that 4.4 per cent of Americans suffer from haemorrhoids (or hemorrhoids, as they more usually spell them). Haemorrhoids are graded on a four-point scale proposed by Banov in 1985.

⚲ *TOILET PAPER*

HAGGIS

Ancient Rome, Scotland, Scandinavia and France have all been claimed as inventors of the haggis. The sheep's heart, liver and lungs used in making haggis are known as the 'pluck'. The oldest known recipe for haggis is in a 1430 book from Lancashire called *Liber Cure Cocorum*.

HAIKU

A Japanese haiku has 17 syllables, as supposedly that is the ideal number to utter in one breath.

⚲ *POETRY, QUANTUM MECHANICS*

HAIL

The largest hailstone ever recorded weighed over 1 kilogram (2.2 pounds) and fell in Bangladesh in 1986.

⚲ *UGANDA*

HAIR

In Judaeo-Christian and Muslim tradition, gods tend to appear bearded to emphasise their manliness. In the 15th century BC, Queen Hatshepsut of Egypt often wore a beard for similar reasons.

'Women do not go bald,' said Aristotle, 'because their nature is like that of children.' Aristotle also claimed that the Libyan ostrich is the only bird with eyelashes, that man is the only animal with lashes on both upper and lower lids, and that castrated men never go bald. He was slightly wrong about birds on two counts: first, it could be maintained that since eyelashes are hairs, no birds have them, but what may appear to be eyelashes on an ostrich are in fact modified feathers. Secondly, Indian grey hornbills and blue-fronted Amazonian parrots also have what appear to be eyelashes.

There are around 100,000 hairs on the average human head, with about 50 lost each day. The empty follicle then rests for a few months before growing another hair. Each hair lives for about two years before falling out. Hair grows at a rate of 1 centimetre a month (beard hair slightly faster).

Men, women, chimpanzees and gorillas all have about the same number of hair follicles, though the hairs are less conspicuous in women and more conspicuous in apes.

Peter the Great of Russia imposed a beard tax in 1698, later adding a penalty of being shaved with a blunt razor or being plucked with pincers, one hair at a time. His anti-beard crusade began after a tour of Europe, which convinced him that Russia needed beardless Europeanisation. Holding a party on his return to Russia, he employed a court jester to rid nobles of their beards. Captain John Perry, an Englishman visiting Russia, wrote of the terror the courtiers had of having their beards 'pull'd out by the Roots, or sometimes taken so rough off, that some of the Skin went with them'.

On 22 May 1996, a court in Kassel, Germany, ruled that policemen may wear their hair in a plait if they wish. In 2005, however, a British court ruled that it is not sexual discrimination to sack a man for having long hair.

The Scottish Highlands have the world's highest proportion of redheads – around one in nine people.

The most expensive locks of hair ever sold at auction were: a lock of Marilyn Monroe's hair cut by her hairdresser Kenneth Battelle (aka Mr Kenneth) in 1959, which fetched $10,177 in Florida in 2016, and a lock of David Bowie's hair sold later the same year in Dallas, Texas, for $18,750. These greatly exceeded the amounts fetched by earlier locks of hair from Napoleon, the Duke of Wellington, Nelson and even Elvis Presley.

Historical footnote: in the 9th century, Charles the Bald was King of Germany and Wilfred the Hairy ruled Catalonia. The two men did not get on well, and fought a brief war in 878.

♀ *ANAESTHETICS, BEARD, LICE, MERKIN, POLAR BEAR, WOMBAT*

● HAIRCUT

A person who has never had a haircut is correctly referred to as asersecomic. The word comes from the classical Latin *acersecomes*, meaning a long-haired youth. This was not derogatory, as in ancient Greek and Roman times it was usual for youths to wear their hair long until they reached manhood.

♀ *BARBER, BRUNEI, HAIR, SAUDI ARABIA*

● HAITI

'The Lord's Prayer', as authorised by Francois 'Papa Doc' Duvalier, dictator of Haiti 1957–71, went like this:

Our Doc who art in the National
Palace for life, hallowed be Thy name
by present and future generations.
Thy will be done at Port-au-Prince
and in the provinces.
Give us this day our new Haiti and
never forgive the trespasses of the
enemies of the fatherland, who spit
every day on our country.
Let them succumb to temptation
and under the weight of their own
venom.
Deliver them not from any evil.
Amen.

Papa Doc Duvalier was excommunicated in 1961.

At the opening ceremony of the 1936 Olympics in Berlin, it was noticed that the flags of Haiti and Liechtenstein were identical, both consisting of a horizontal blue stripe above a red strip of equal size. Liechtenstein added a crown in the top left corner of its flag the following year to make it different.

FLAGS

HALIFAX

The Halifax Gibbet was an early type of guillotine that pre-dated the French version by well over a century. It consisted of an iron axe blade, lifted up by cord and pulley. Under the Gibbet Law, the device was kept by the Bailiff of the Lord of the Manor.

Summary execution was the punishment for crimes involving the theft of goods worth 13.5 pence or more. A jury of 16 men was promptly assembled to judge the accused and assess the value of the stolen goods. Execution after a guilty verdict was carried out immediately if it was a market day, otherwise saved until the next time they could expect a good crowd. If an ox, sheep, horse or other animal had been stolen, it was usual for the rope holding the axe to be attached to the beast. Freeing the animal would then cause the axe to fall.

A vagabonds' prayer of the 16th or early 17th century ran: 'From Hell, Hull and Halifax, Good Lord deliver us.' Hull was included because it was too strictly governed for beggars to make an acceptable living there. The inclusion of Halifax was a reference to the Gibbet.

TOWN CRIER

HALITOSIS

Mr White's Halitosis Detector was patented by George Starr White in 1925 and consisted of a small pair of hand-held bellows with an opening at one end of the barrel. The bellows were inflated by blowing into the straw-sized opening a few times, then the opening was placed at the nose and the bellows allowed to expel the breath to enable it to be sniffed.

George Starr White, incidentally, wrote on a number of alternative medicine therapies, generally employing his own recommendations for spelling reform. His biography was called 'My Biografy'.

In 1987, a considerably more sophisticated Device for Detecting Halitosis was invented and patented by a Japanese company, in which gas chromatography was among the scientific methods used 'for quantitative determination of the strength of the foul smell of human exhaled air'.

On 20 October 1997, the University of British Columbia announced a bad-breath-testing service including both scientific analysis for halitosis and assessment by a human nose.

LAVENDER

HALLOWE'EN

Hallowe'en, which refers to All Hallows' Eve, the evening before All Hallows' Day on 1 November, seems to have begun as the Celtic festival of Samhain, when the spirits of the dead were meant to return to haunt the living. Fear of Hallowe'en is thus called Samhainophobia.

Bobbing for apples at Hallowe'en has its origins in ancient Rome and the late-October Roman feast celebrating Pomona, the goddess of fruit and trees whose symbol was the apple.

HELL, PUMPKIN

HAM

In January 2010, Selfridges in London put on sale what was described as 'the world's most expensive ham'. Weighing 7 kilograms (15.4 pounds), the leg of ham was priced at £1,800.

In 2016, however, the top price for a leg of ham, was quoted as €4,100 (around £3,500) for Dehesa Maladúa ham from Huelva province in south-west Spain, and in 2020 a company on Osaka was reported to be selling a leg of Iberian bellota ham for the equivalent of £9,982.

The best Spanish hams come from specially bred pigs and are sold complete with their own DNA certificate as proof of authenticity.

BOXING DAY, PRINCESS, SANDWICHES

HAMBURGER

At the beginning of the 19th century, the Oxford English Dictionary defined 'Hamburg steak' as salt beef. Calling ground beef 'hamburger' dates from the invention of mechanical meat grinders in the 1860s.

The Hamburger Hall of Fame is located in Seymour, Wisconsin. Appropriately, in 1989 the world's biggest hamburger – a 5,520-pounder – was made in Wisconsin.

The biggest hamburger generally offered for sale is to be found at Denny's Beer Barrel Pub in Clearfield, Pennsylvania. It comprises a 6-pound hamburger, garnished with two whole tomatoes, half a head of lettuce, 12 slices of cheese, a cup of peppers, two onions, plus mayonnaise, ketchup and mustard. It is said that no one has ever finished one.

There are McDonald's restaurants in 118 countries and territories around the world. At the end of 2020, the total number of McDonald's restaurants in the world was close to 40,000. The total number of McDonald's hamburgers sold exceeded 100 billion some time in 1998. According to some estimates, the total worldwide is now over 300 billion.

CARS, UNDEAD, WISCONSIN

HAMILTON

The name of the Formula 1 World Motor Racing champion 'Lewis Hamilton' is an anagram of 'Oh, I'll win, mates'.

In 1971, Hamilton Academical became the first UK football club to sign players from Eastern Europe.

At least 25 of America's states have a town or city called Hamilton. Hamilton is also the largest inland city in New Zealand. It is named after John Charles Fane Hamilton, the captain of HMS Esk, who was killed in 1864 fighting the Maoris. His last words were 'Follow me, men!'

Alexander Hamilton was the first US Secretary of the Treasury. He was killed in 1804 in a duel with US Vice-President Aaron Burr. His eldest son, Philip, had also been killed in a duel at the age of 19, three years earlier.

Nelson's mistress, Lady Hamilton, was born Amy Lyon, worked under the name Emma Potts and changed her name to Emma Hart before marrying Sir William Hamilton, British envoy to Naples.

TEETH

HAMLET

The story of Shakespeare's Hamlet comes from a 13th-century manuscript called Gesta Danorum (Deeds of the Danes) by Saxo the Learned, which told of the Viking prince Amleth who killed his uncle to avenge his father's murder. In the original story, however, Hamlet travelled to Britain, married the Queen of Scotland and was killed in a battle with the King of Denmark.

⚲ *GOOSE, MOUSETRAP, TWENTY THREE, ULCER*

⬤ HAMMURABI

The Code of Hammurabi, formulated in ancient Babylon around 1760 BC, is the earliest known set of laws of any state. It comprises around 300 laws (282 in the most usual translation, but there is no numbering or separation of paragraphs in the original), including specifications of between 20 and 30 crimes that carry the death sentence. These include:

- Making a false accusation or an accusation of murder that one cannot prove.
- Stealing the property of a temple or the court.
- Stealing cattle or sheep, or an ass, or a pig or a goat, that belonged to a god or to the court and failing to pay 30 times its value when caught.
- Failing to produce witnesses in a dispute over property purchase.
- Holding escaped slaves in one's house;
- Hiring a mercenary to take one's place when ordered to go to war, and failing to pay him.
- Furthermore, anyone who steals property from a house he has entered in order to put out a fire, 'he shall be thrown into that self-same fire'.
- Finally, 'If the wife of one man on account of another man has their mates (her husband and the other man's wife) murdered, both of them shall be impaled' and 'If a man betroth a girl to his son, and his son have intercourse with her, but he (the father) afterward defile her, and be surprised, then he shall be bound and cast into the water.'

⚲ *SLAVERY*

⬤ HAMSTER

The golden (or Syrian) hamster was discovered in Aleppo in 1930 by Palestinian Professor Israel Aharoni, and the first group of their descendants was smuggled into the UK in 1932 in the pocket of a zoologist. It is often claimed that all domestic hamsters are descendants of these illegal immigrants, but that is by no means certain since other groups of Syrian hamsters were brought into the UK later.

Syrian hamsters were originally all short-haired, but breeding techniques have led to a classification of four types of fur today: short-haired, long-haired, satin and rex (curly, frizzy). Long-haired male hamsters have longer fur than long-haired female hamsters.

Experiments in 1996 at the University of Massachusetts showed that leaving an adolescent golden hamster in a cage for an hour each day with an aggressive adult hamster will cause the impressionable adolescent to grow up to be a bully. It will then pick fights with animals smaller than itself, but show fear for hamsters its own size.

Hamsters are the third most common animal to be used in experiments after mice and rats.

On 12 July 1992, the pet hamster in a South Glamorgan school died of a heart attack, believed to have been caused by the shock of hearing a starting pistol fired in a sports day rehearsal.

⚲ *DOCTORS, PREGNANCY*

⬤ HANDBAG

According to a study in 2004, most British women drastically underestimate the value of their handbag and its contents. According to the survey by Prudential Home Assurance, the average value was over £500, but was estimated by its owner to be £153.33. The average handbag itself was worth £50, and contained a cellphone worth £199, sunglasses worth £50, perfume worth £40 and house and car keys worth £100. This meant that British handbags altogether were worth £14 billion.

♀ *THATCHER*

HANDEL, George Frideric (1685–1759)

Handel's 'Music For The Royal Fireworks' was written to celebrate the end of the War of the Austrian Succession in 1748. Over 12,000 people attended its first performance in London's Green Park, causing a three-hour traffic jam. The wooden building housing the musicians caught fire, ending the performance early.

Handel is believed to have written more notes of music than any other composer.

♀ *SLOANE*

HANDKERCHIEF

The history of handkerchiefs has been linked to Marie Antoinette. One story is that she was irritated by their many shapes so persuaded her husband, King Louis XVI of France to decree that they must be square, which has remained the shape ever since.

It has even been maintained that Marie Antoinette invented the handkerchief from bits of lace torn from her clothes to wipe away the tears when leaving her home in Austria, but this tale is clearly wrong. More than 200 years earlier Shakespeare used the word 'handkerchief' at least 35 times, of which 25 are in *Othello* alone. Even earlier than that, in the 14th century, Richard II used to wipe his nose on square pieces of cloth, according to his courtiers.

♀ *BRASSIERE, ETIQUETTE*

HANDSHAKING

In April 1928, the authorities in Rome decided to ban handshaking on the grounds that it was unhygienic. Handshakes are a major route for spreading the common cold – more effectively even than kissing. Despite this, Irishman Brendan Morrissey claimed a world handshaking record in October 2003 by shaking hands with 14,169 people in eight hours.

Colorado entrepreneur Matt Holmes and his business partner Juan Diaz de Leon set a world record in Denver in 2016 for the longest two-person handshake at 43 hours and 35 minutes.

According to *The Power of Handshaking* by Robert E. Brown and Dorothea Johnson, there are 12 basic types of handshake. These range from the 'All-American' to the 'Water Pump' and 'Dead Fish'.

The Boy Scout tradition of shaking left hands stems from an Ashanti chieftain telling Baden-Powell that the bravest of the brave shake with the left hand.

The earliest known depiction of a handshake is a carving on a funerary slab dating back to around 500 BC of a priest and two soldiers shaking hands.

♀ *HYGIENE, TIBET, UZBEKISTAN*

HANGING

According to the Amnesty International report on death sentences in 2019, hanging was the preferred means of judicial execution in more countries (11) than any other method, with shooting (6 countries) in second place.

The first long-drop execution in England, with a calculated length of drop designed to break the neck rather than strangle the victim, was performed in 1871 by William

Marwood. According to Charles Duff in his *Handbook on Hanging* (1929), you should allow an 8-foot drop for a 14-stone person, adding two inches per half-stone less. James 'Hangman' Berry noted in his book *My Experiences as an Executioner* that he reduced drops by nearly half in the case of persons who had attempted suicide by slitting their throat.

In 1785, 90 per cent of people hanged in Britain were under 20 years of age.

In the 1940s and 1950s, the Home Office issued instructions for the proper preparations for a hanging. These began: 'Obtain a rope from Execution Box B making sure that the guttapercha covering the splice at each end is un-cracked by previous use.'

From 1800 to 1964, over 5,500 people are known to have suffered death by hanging in Britain.

♀ *CAPITAL PUNISHMENT, EXECUTION, FRIDAY, SWAZILAND*

HANGOVER

The word 'hangover' was first applied to describe the after-effects of alcohol in 1904, though the phrases 'morning-after' and 'hair of the dog' were both known in the 1880s.

Research has shown that cats, dogs, rats, monkeys and chimpanzees may all suffer symptoms similar to those of a human hangover after they are taken off a diet including alcohol, but in 2008 it was found that tree shrews do not suffer hangovers despite drinking alcoholic nectar.

Hangovers are estimated to cost British business about £3 billion a year.

According to the Oxford English Corpus, the adjectives that most frequently describe a hangover are 'bad', 'massive', 'worst', 'nasty' and 'terrible'.

In Mongolia, a traditional hangover cure is to eat a pickled sheep's eye in a glass of tomato juice. A simpler Puerto Rican alternative is to rub lemon under your arms.

The medical term for a hangover is 'veisalgia'. It comes from an Old Norse word meaning 'unease after debauchery' and the Greek word for pain. The term was first coined in 2000 in an article in *Annals of Internal Medicine*.

♀ *BULGARIA*

HAROLD II, King of England (c.1022–66)

King Harold II, most famous for having been killed at the Battle of Hastings, was crowned King of England on 6 January 1066, the first English king to be crowned in Westminster Abbey. He was described as 'very tall and handsome, remarkable for his physical strength, his courage and eloquence, his ready jests and acts of valour'. He had at least six illegitimate children by his mistress, Edith Swannesha.

Harold was born around 1022, the son of Godwin, Earl of Wessex. His mother, Gytha Thorkelsdottir, was sister-in-law of Cnut, King of Denmark and England. Two of Harold's six brothers, Gyrth and Leofwine, also died at the Battle of Hastings in 1066. His sister, Edith of Wessex, married English King Edward the Confessor.

Harold's marriage to Edith the Fair was not recognised or blessed by the Church.

Harold's dispute with William the Conqueror stemmed from his shipwreck off the coast of Normandy in 1064, when he is said to have pledged support for William's claim to England's throne. Another claimant was Harald Hardrada of Norway, whose invasion force was beaten by Harold at the Battle of Stamford Bridge in 1066.

The earliest account of the Battle of Hastings said that Harold had been killed and dismembered by four knights. The first report of Harold being shot in the eye with an arrow did not appear until 30 years later.

The Bayeux Tapestry illustration of the events at Hastings is not a tapestry but an embroidery. Tapestry is a heavy woven cloth; embroidery is a fabric ornamented by needlework.

⚲ *TATTOO*

● HARVESTMAN

The oldest fossilised penis may be that of a 400-million-year-old daddy longlegs or harvestman found near Aberdeen in Scotland in 2001. The male harvestman had a penis two-thirds the length of his body. 'I suppose it is to get past those long legs,' a researcher commented.

⚲ *SPIDER*

● HAT

The hat band has no functional purpose. It is a relic of ancient Egyptian head bands worn to keep hair in place while travelling.

At the time of Elizabeth I, everyone over the age of seven was legally obliged to wear a flat cap on Sundays and holidays. The only exceptions were lords, ladies and knights with an income of over 20 marks a year.

When John Hetherington donned a top hat in 1797, he was arrested for wearing 'a tall structure having a shining luster calculated to frighten timid people'.

Hat tax on men's hats was established in Britain in 1784 and abolished in 1811. The tax required retailers to display the sign 'Dealer in Hats by Retail'. They also had to pay for a hat retail licence costing £2 in London and five shillings elsewhere. Every man's hat they sold had to have a revenue stamp, with the amount of duty payable on it dependent on the cost of the hat. Anyone convicted of forging a hat-tax revenue stamp could face the death penalty.

The trilby is named after the eponymous heroine Trilby O'Ferrall of a George du Maurier novel.

The bowler hat was first tested and bought on 17 December 1849 by William Coke for 10 shillings. It was made by Thomas Bowler.

⚲ *ASCOT, EGG, FASHION, KENNEDY, LINCOLN, SWAT*

● HAWAII

Hawaii is the only US state with two official languages: English and Hawaiian. There are only 12 letters in the Hawaiian alphabet.

Mount Waialeale in Hawaii is the rainiest place on earth, with up to 350 rainy days a year.

⚲ *ALBATROSS, DARWIN, ICE CREAM, OBAMA, RAIN, WISCONSIN*

▌ HAWKING, Stephen William (1942–2018)

The physicist Stephen Hawking was born on 8 January 1942, exactly 300 years to the day after the death of Galileo. Interviewed before his 70th birthday in January 2012, Hawking was asked what he thought about most. His reply was: 'Women. They are a complete mystery.'

⚲ *DOCTOR WHO*

● HEADS

A two-headed albino rat snake was put on display at the World Aquarium in

St Louis, Missouri, in 1999. In 2006, it was offered for sale on eBay with an expected price of $150,000, but was soon withdrawn for contravening the site's policy against trading in live animals. The reptile, named We, died of natural causes in 2007 aged eight, which was said to be an astonishing life-span for a two-headed snake. Such creatures had been seen before, but most died within a week or two of their birth. Scientists said that one of the reasons it had been able to live so long was that both its heads were joined to the same stomach.

EUROPE, HAIR, MILK, OSTRICH, PUMPKIN, TERMITE, WIG

HEALTH

World Health Day is held each year on 7 April to celebrate the founding of the World Health Organisation on this date in 1948. The theme of World Health Day 2021 was 'Building a Fairer, Healthier World for Everyone'.

According to the World Bank, the countries with most doctors per capita are Cuba with (8.4 physicians per 1,000 people), Monaco (7.5) and Georgia (7.1). The figure for the UK is 2.8 and for the USA 2.6. Worldwide, there are 1.6 physicians per 1,000 people.

Around 6.6 million children under the age of five die each year worldwide.

In the UK, life expectancy at birth is 79.0 for men and 82.7 for women, and a man can expect to stay healthy for 64.2 years or 66.1 for women. Since 1990, average life expectancy worldwide has increased by six years.

According to the Bloomberg Health Index, which is based on life expectancy and health risk facts, the top five healthiest countries in the world in 2021 were Spain, Italy, Iceland, Japan and Switzerland.

The UK National Health Service is the third largest employer in the world after the Russian army and Indian railways.

The first health warning to appear on a bottle of alcoholic drink was in 1751.

'It is not healthy to swallow books without chewing.' German proverb

HYGIENE, PENGUIN, PLAGUE, RAGS, SOUTH KOREA, SPA

HEART

The human heart is not heart-shaped. A cow's heart is more heart-shaped than a human one.

The use of a heart shape in a logo to signify love was popularised by the graphic designer Milton Glaser in his 1977 'I ♥ New York' poster and T-shirt campaign.

According to the Oxford English Corpus, the adjectives most often used to qualify the noun 'heart' are 'coronary', 'sacred' and 'broken'.

BLOOD, BOLEYN, BUCKLAND, MARRIAGE, OCTOPUS, PLAYING CARDS

HEDGEHOG

A symbol of a hedgehog was common on ancient Egyptian amulets. Its hibernation and ability to survive outside fertile lands were seen as signs of rebirth and triumph over death. Pliny the Elder, in the 1st century, wrote of hedgehogs climbing apple trees, knocking the fruit down, then impaling apples on their spines to carry to their burrows. This is impossible. Hedgehogs can't climb trees.

Hedgehogs have 36 teeth and up to 5,000 spines. There is a record of one hedgehog eating 63 caterpillars, 22 earwigs, 75 beetles and many slugs, snails, millipedes and larvae in one sitting. The fleas on hedgehogs are 'hedgehog fleas' and cannot live on other animals or in houses.

'Erinaceous' means 'pertaining to the hedgehog'.

Baby hedgehogs are called hoglets or piglets.

In January 2002, eight policemen in New Zealand swooped on a house in Christchurch in response to a call about a burglary. The noise that had disturbed the residents was found to be not burglars but two hedgehogs mating. They snuffle very loudly when mating.

Hedgehogs are not considered to be weapons under New Zealand law. In 2008, a New Zealander was convicted of assault for throwing a hedgehog at a boy and wounding his leg. The more serious charge of assault with a weapon was dropped.

In 2009, authorities in Lawrence, Kansas, conceded that there was no reason to ban hedgehogs in the town. The decision brought to an end a two-year battle by an 11-year-old who wanted to keep a pet hedgehog but had been told it was against local laws.

GROUNDHOG DAY

HEELS

French footwear designer Christian Louboutin said in 2011 that he had been most impressed by something a fellow party guest had told him: 'She said that what is sexual in a high heel is the arch of the foot, because it is exactly the position of a woman's foot when she orgasms. So putting your foot in a heel, you are putting yourself in a possibly orgasmic situation.' Commenting on this, Kevan Wylie, a sexual medicine consultant, said that it is important to differentiate cause from effect: 'A woman's foot may be in this position during orgasm, but that does not mean

that putting her foot into this position under other circumstances will result in orgasm.'

SHOES, TUG OF WAR

HEIGHT

The tallest man who ever lived (for whom reliable measures were taken) was Robert Wadlow of Alton, Illinois, who died in 1940 at the age of 22. Eighteen days before his death, he was measured by doctors to be 2.7 metres (8 foot 11.1 inches) tall. Wadlow suffered from a disorder of his pituitary gland which caused him to continue growing all his life. He was a very popular American celebrity, and an estimated 40,000 people attended his funeral. He was buried in a half-ton coffin carried by 12 pallbearers. It was interred within a vault of solid concrete. Wadlow was born a normal-sized baby, but by the age of 13 was already 2.2 metres (7 feet 4 inches tall) and was acclaimed as the world's tallest boy scout.

BASKETBALL, GDANSK, HUDSON, MIDGET, NETHERLANDS, STALLONE

HELEN OF TROY

Dramatist Christopher Marlowe coined the phrase 'the face that launched a thousand ships' to describe the mythical Helen of Troy, whose abduction started the Trojan War. The line occurs in his play *Doctor Faustus*: 'Was this the face that launched a thousand ships, And burnt the topless towers of Ilium?'

Ilium was another name for the city of Troy. It is also the name of the largest part of the hip-bone.

BEAUTY

HELICOPTER

The word 'helicopter' was coined by the French aviation pioneer Gustave de

Ponton d'Amecourt, who built a small steam-driven model helicopter in 1863.

♀ *BODY ART, ISRAEL, PENGUIN*

● HELL

A couple from the town of Hell in Michigan won $115,001 on a Hallowe'en day lottery draw in 2007. In the same year, a Catholic school in Melbourne was reported to have refused a place to a boy because his surname was Hell.

♀ *BOSCH, HALIFAX, HOLES, LIBYA, NORWAY, PUMPKIN, THINKING*

● HELL'S ANGELS

The Hell's Angels Motorcycle Club was founded in 1948 and is said to be the world's largest such club. It was named after a 1930 Howard Hughes film about First World War fighter pilots.

A German student was arrested in the town of Allershausen in June 2010 after making a rude gesture at a group of Hell's Angels motorcyclists, then throwing a puppy at them and escaping on a stolen bulldozer. He later dumped the bulldozer, causing a 5-kilometre (3 mile) traffic jam.

Police said, 'What motivated him to throw a puppy at the Hell's Angels is currently unclear.'

● HEMINGWAY, Ernest (1899–1961)

When writing, Ernest Hemingway liked to eat rye crisps and peanut butter sandwiches. He could not pronounce the letter L. His father committed suicide by shooting himself in the right ear.

♀ *BRASSIERE, GHOSTS*

● HENRY II, King of England (1133–89)

Henry II was the first monarch to use the title 'King of England' rather than 'King of the English'. In 1155, Pope Adrian IV issued a Papal bull authorising King Henry II to conquer and rule Ireland.

♀ *UNIVERSITIES*

● HENRY III, King of England (1207–72)

The royal motto of Henry III was '*qui non dat quod habet non accipit ille quod optat*'. (He who does not give what he has, does not receive what he desires.)

His favourite wine was made with the Loire Valley red wine grape Pineau d'Aunis, which Henry himself introduced to England.

In 1231, Henry III wrote to the sheriffs and mayors of Oxford and Cambridge urging them to help in suppressing 'rebellious and incorrigible' students.

♀ *POLAR BEAR, UNIVERSITIES*

● HENRY III, King of France (1551–89)

King Henry III of France liked to walk the streets with a basket of puppies round his neck.

● HENRY V, King of England (1387–1422)

Although the Battle of Agincourt was won through the prowess of the English with the longbow, neither of the words 'longbow' or 'archer' appears in Shakespeare's *Henry V*. While the English army at Agincourt was under the command of Henry V, the French King Charles VI missed the battle as he was having one of his episodes of madness.

Mary de Bohun, mother of Henry V, was only 16 when she gave birth to him. He was her second child. She died at the age of 24, in childbirth with her seventh offspring.

♀ *SAUSAGES*

HENRY VII, King of England (1457–1509)

The first recorded use of fireworks in Britain was at the wedding of Henry VII in 1486.

♀ *BERWICK, JAMES I*

HENRY VIII, King of England (1491–1547)

At a dinner served in honour of the King of France, Henry VIII once served a feast including 2,000 fish, 1,000 sheep and a dolphin.

The armour of Henry VIII has the largest codpiece in the Tower of London.

♀ *BARBER, BEER, BOLEYN, SWAN, TWELFTH NIGHT, WRESTLING*

HENS

The highest number of eggs produced by one hen in a year is 371.

The Hen and Chicken Islands lie to the east of the North Auckland Peninsula off the coast of northern New Zealand. They were named by James Cook after the star cluster the Pleiades, which was also known as the Hen and Chickens. Originally owned by the Maori, the islands were sold to the New Zealand government in 1883.

The world's oldest known hen died of heart failure at the age of 16.

When being bred for meat, a pullet becomes a hen when it is one year old; when it is kept for eggs, however, it is considered a hen at 16–20 weeks.

♀ *EGG*

HERACLEITUS (c.535–475 BC)

The Greek philosopher Heracleitus was famed for pointing out that you cannot step into the same river twice. He died of suffocation after coating himself in cow dung, which he thought would cure him of dropsy.

HEROIN

Heroin, which is made from opium poppies, was first launched in 1895 as a children's cough medicine. Its name was created by Bayer Pharmaceuticals and derived from the German 'heroisch' (heroic), referring to its effectiveness.

♀ *AFGHANISTAN, PETER PAN*

HERON

There are 64 recognised species of heron. If stalked and surprised at close quarters, a heron will fall down in a kind of fit.

♀ *PHOENIX*

HERON-ALLEN, Edward (1861–1943)

The English writer, scientist, Persian scholar and authority on asparagus, palmistry and violins, Edward Heron-Allen always wore black and even gained permission from Lord Baden-Powell himself to have a black Scouts uniform.

His book on violin-making remained in print for over a century; his three-year tour of America lecturing on palmistry attracted good audiences; his guide 'Asparagus as a Hobby for Amateurs' attracted great interest from gardening societies; and his pornographic science fiction story *The Cheetah Girl* (written under the pseudonym Christopher Blayre) was included on the Vatican list of prohibited books.

HERRING

According to a study in 2003, herring may communicate at night in a manner that is close to breaking wind. Two teams, in the Atlantic and Pacific, monitored shoals of herring to find that they emitted a high-pitched noise accompanied by a stream of bubbles. The bubbles were found to be released through a duct close to the anus. On detecting the farts of other herring, the fish formed themselves into protective shoals, which suggests that the behaviour is a form of communication. It was later shown that the 'farting' was caused by swallowing air and forcing it through the anal duct. One scientist commented that the noise sounded like 'a high-pitched raspberry'.

The origin of the phrase 'red herring' is not completely clear. A common explanation is that it refers to the use of kippers, also known as 'red herrings', to train dogs to follow a trail by smell or to lure away dogs chasing escaped criminals. Yet there is no evidence this ever happened. The expression may have started in 1807, when William Cobbett wrote of a mistaken account in the press of the defeat of Napoleon. Cobbett claimed that he had once used a red herring to deflect hounds who were chasing a hare. He added: 'It was a mere transitory effect of the political red-herring; for, on the Saturday, the scent became as cold as a stone.' Cobbett's use of the phrase, and his repetition of the story, may have been responsible for others adopting it.

 ⚲ *AUGUST, LUTHER, MACKEREL, REMBRANDT, SWEDEN*

● HESITATION

According to research published in 2002, speakers of English say 'um' before a long pause and 'uh' before a short one. Another theory is that people use 'um' when they're trying to decide what to say, and 'er' when trying to decide how to say it. Recent research also suggests women and teenagers say 'um', while men and older people prefer 'er'. It has also been pointed out that Americans say 'uh' when the British say 'er'.

No US president between 1940 and 2021 uttered a single 'uh' or 'um' in his inaugural address. Harry S. Truman and Donald Trump are the only US presidents with 'um' in their names.

● HILLARY, Sir Edmund (1919–2008)

Apart from being the first person to reach the summit of Mount Everest, Sir Edmund Hillary was also the first to drive a tractor across Antarctica. In his native New Zealand, he was the son of a bee keeper. He worked with his father's bees in the summer, leaving the winter months free for mountaineering.

When he returned from Everest, he commissioned Michael Ayrton to cast a golden sculpture in the shape of a honeycomb in imitation of a wax process supposed to have been invented by Daedalus 3,000 years ago to produce the first man-made honeycomb structure. When completed, it was placed in Hillary's New Zealand garden, where his bees took it over as a hive and, according to Hillary, 'filled it with honey and their young'.

 ⚲ *EVEREST*

● HIPPOCRATES (c.460–377 BC)

The original Hippocratic oath, as written by Hippocrates, 'the father of Medicine', translates as follows:

I swear by Apollo, the healer, Asclepius, Hygieia, and Panacea, and I take to witness all the gods, all the goddesses, to keep according to my ability and my judgment, the following Oath and agreement:

To consider dear to me, as my parents, him who taught me this art; to live in common with him and, if necessary, to share my goods with him; To look upon his children as my own brothers, to teach them this art.

I will prescribe regimens for the good of my patients according to my ability and my judgment and never do harm to anyone.

I will not give a lethal drug to anyone if I am asked, nor will I advise such a plan; and similarly I will not give a woman a pessary to cause an abortion.

But I will preserve the purity of my life and my arts.

I will not cut for stone, even for patients in whom the disease is manifest; I will leave this operation to be performed by practitioners, specialists in this art.

In every house where I come I will enter only for the good of my patients, keeping myself far from all intentional ill-doing and all seduction and especially from the pleasures of love with women or with men, be they free or slaves.

All that may come to my knowledge in the exercise of my profession or in daily commerce with men, which ought not to be spread abroad, I will keep secret and will never reveal.

If I keep this oath faithfully, may I enjoy my life and practise my art, respected by all men and in all times; but if I swerve from it or violate it, may the reverse be my lot.

⚲ *CLITORIS, OREGANO, SEX, TAMPON*

⬤ HIPPOPOTAMUS

Britain's first hippopotamus, believed to be the first hippo in Europe since Roman times, arrived at London Zoo in Regent's Park on 25 May 1850. It was given the name Obaysch, after the island in the Nile where it was found.

Regent's Park Zoo opened in 1828. The first elephant arrived in 1831, a rhinoceros in 1834, the first giraffes in 1836, and a sloth in 1844, but none of these attained the superstar status of Obaysch the hippo. The number of visitors to the zoo doubled, and they rushed to buy hippo merchandise, including silver models of Obaysch. You could even buy sheet music for 'The Hippopotamus Polka'.

In 1854, a female, Adhela, joined him, but it was not until 1871 that Obaysch fathered London Zoo's first baby hippo, which sadly did not survive. The following year, two more were born, and the second of these, because of its 5 November birthday, was named Guy Fawkes, though it was subsequently discovered to be a female.

Obaysch remained a celebrity until his death in 1878, when *Punch* published a long memorial poem called 'hipposoliloquy', including these lines:

Urm'p! Urm'p! A feeble grunt! I fall apace
Old Hippo's mighty yet melodious bass
Sinks to a raucous whisper, short, not sweet!
Ah, well I've had my triumphs, and am yet Public Pet.

Hippopotamus flesh is said to be excellent to eat, closely resembling succulent pork or veal.

There are currently estimated to be between 125,000 and 148,000 hippos in the wild, with more in Zambia than any other country.

Hippos are estimated to kill around 500 people every year in Africa – more than any other mammal except humans.

In November 2021, the US donated 70 doses of a contraceptive to treat up to 90 hippos in Colombia, which had been imported by drug lord Pablo Escobar but had escaped and posed a dangerous threat, especially if they were allowed to breed.

ISRAEL, MOZAMBIQUE, NIGERIA

HIPS

Women with large hips and small waists perform better in intelligence tests than those with a larger waist/hip ratio. Their children also have higher intelligence scores. It has been suggested that this offers an explanation for men generally preferring women with low waist/hip ratios. Research in New York, however, has shown that it is not just a low waist/hip ratio that matters, but whether the hips sway when a woman walks. When subjects rated the attractiveness of women shown walking in videos and animations, they did tend to give higher ratings to those with low waist/hip ratios, but the attractiveness was rated higher if they waggled their hips while moving.

According to the World Record Academy, in 2013 the world's largest human hips were those of Mikel Ruffinelli, a 39-year-old model living in Los Angeles. Ruffinelli weighs 190.5 kilograms (420 pounds) and is 1.6 metres (5 feet 4 inches) tall, with a hip measurement of 2.44 metres (8 feet), though her waist is only 1.02 metres (40 inches). Her husband says he likes to tell people that he has a licence to work with heavy equipment.

BARBIE, GDANSK

HITLER, Adolf (1889–1945)

Adolf Hitler was named *Time Magazine*'s Man of the Year in 1938. Stalin was given the same honour in both 1939 and 1942.

In the Navajo language, the nickname for Hitler was 'Daghailchiih', meaning 'he smells his moustache'.

In 2012, an Indian who opened a shop called 'Hitler' in the city of Ahmadabad in Gujarat was told that the name was offensive to the Jewish community, who urged him to change it. The dot over the letter 'i' in the name was also in the shape of a swastika. The shop owner, Rajesh Shah, said he did not know the extent of Adolf Hitler's atrocities until people began to complain, but only knew that he was a strict man, much like the grandfather of his business partner who was also known as 'Hitler'.

Also in 2012, the Jewish community in Turkey protested at an advert that used old film footage of Hitler to advertise shampoo. It featured Hitler apparently saying, in Turkish: 'If you are not wearing women's dress, you shouldn't be using women's shampoo!' The Chief Rabbi's office in Turkey described it as unacceptable and demanded a public apology from the advertising company.

According to the 1945 edition of *Who's Who*, Hitler's address was Wilhelmstrasse 77, Berlin W.8 and his home phone number was Berlin 11 6191.

EXORCISM, FANCY DRESS, HITLERI, MERCEDES, MUSEUM

HITLERI

Two creatures, one extinct and one endangered, have been officially named after Adolf Hitler.

Roechlingia hitleri is a flying insect fossil, and *Anophthalmus hitleri* is a blind beetle found in caves in Slovenia. The beetle was discovered by entomologist Oscar Scheibel in 1933 and he named it after the recently elected German chancellor whom he greatly admired. Hitler was so pleased to have a blind beetle named after him that he personally wrote to Scheibel to express his thanks. *Anophthalmus hitleri* is about half a centimetre long and eats insect larvae. It is said to be in great demand among collectors of Nazi memorabilia.

HOBBITS

Tolkien claimed to have invented the word 'hobbit', but admitted that there were some old English words that had inspired it. However, he was not the first to use the word. Hobbit is included in a 19th-century list of folklore creatures alongside hobgoblins, hobhoulards and bugaboos. In the 17th century, a hobbit or hoppet was a word for a small hand-basket. In the 19th century, a hobbit or hobbet was used as a local measure equal to 2.5 bushels.

In 2015, a first edition of *The Hobbit*, inscribed in Elvish by Tolkien, fetched £137,000 at auction.

Hobbits, according to the prologue to *Lord of the Rings*, have hairy feet and have an average height of 3 feet 6 inches. Most cannot grow beards.

On 25 March every year is Tolkien Reading Day, as that was the date of the fall of Sauron in *Lord of the Rings*.

The first film in Peter Jackson's Hobbit trilogy has grossed over a billion dollars worldwide. Each dwarf in the film had eight wigs and six beards, made mainly from yak hair.

The ancient small hominins of the Indonesian island of Flores were named *Homo floresiensis*, but were informally called hobbits by their discoverers in 2004.

⚲ *OCTOBER*

HOLES

The deepest hole dug by humans is one on the Kola Peninsula near Murmansk in Russia, referred to as the 'Kola well'. It was drilled between 1970 and 1989 as part of a project to research the structure of the Earth's core. When the drilling stopped in 1989, the hole was a little over 12 kilometres (8 miles) deep. It was stopped when the drill struck liquid sulphur. According to an urban legend spread at the time, it was stopped because it had broken through to Hell and the tormented screams of the damned could be heard.

In 2001, the USA reduced the minimum size for holes in Emmental cheese from $^{11}/_{16}$ inch to $^{3}/_{8}$ inch.

⚲ *BREAD, FASHION, GOLF*

HOLLYWOOD

Hollywood was given its name by the real estate developer Hobart Johnstone Whitley while on his honeymoon in 1886.

In 1904, the voters of Hollywood decided, by a majority of 113 to 96, to banish the sale of alcohol in the town, except for medicinal purposes.

The first film to be made entirely in Hollywood was the 17-minute short *In Old California*, directed by D.W. Griffith and released in 1910.

The huge 'Hollywood' sign was put up in 1923 and originally spelled out the word 'Hollywoodland'. The letters were originally 15 metres (50 feet) high. The final four letters were removed in 1949 when the sign was rebuilt with 14-metre (45-foot) high letters. Originally intended to last only a year, the sign was declared a historical landmark in 1973.

In 1932, Broadway actress Peg Entwistle committed suicide by jumping off the letter 'H'.

⚲ *CYBERSPACE, GORILLA SUITS, VALENTINO*

HOMES

According to a survey in 1999, the top five reasons people hated their homes were as follows: 1. Too small; 2. Undesirable neighbourhood and area; 3. Too far from place of work; 4. Noisy neighbours; 5. In need of costly repairs.

HOMEWORK

A survey in 1999 reported the reasons most commonly given by 14–16-year-old schoolchildren for not doing their homework. The top five were as follows: 1. Not enough time; 2. I can't be bothered; 3. Lost my coursework; 4. Family funeral/sickness; 5. The pet ate my coursework. 'My House burned down' was in tenth place, offered as an excuse by 2 per cent of children.

A later survey conducted in Hong Kong in 2017 reported that over 70 per cent of children considered homework to be 'annoying' and 'boring', while over 70 per cent (probably the same children) thought that they should not be given homework during long holidays such as Christmas and the Chinese New Year.

BEER MATS, MOLOSSIAN, NAVIES, OCTOPUS, PIGEON

HOMOSEXUALITY

According to Bruce Bagemihl, whose 1999 book *Biological Exuberance* is a study of gay animals, over 50 per cent of male giraffes are homosexual. More recent studies have reported that 95 per cent of sexual interactions between giraffes are male-male, with 1 per cent female-female and 4 per cent male-female. Research has also shown that male walruses are almost exclusively homosexual before they reach sexual maturity around the age of four.

BLUE, CONDOM, LESBIANS

HONEY

The national drink of Ethiopia is Tej, a highly alcoholic honey-wine made with a species of buckthorn added to honey and water for flavouring and fermentation. Tej is traditionally drunk from a round flask called a berele.

Dancing with a berele of tej on one's head is also an Ethiopian custom.

Ethiopia is the world's tenth largest producer of honey and the third largest producer of beeswax, beaten only by Mexico and China. It is also a centre for apitherapy (treatment with honey or bee's venom).

BADGER, BEE, IRAN, POLAR BEAR, STRAW-BERRY

HONG KONG

In 2009, diners at the Mandarin Oriental Hotel in Hong Kong were served with what was claimed to be the world's first entirely synthetic gourmet dish. Created from the chemical components of a lemon, the first course resembled a jelly ball with a creamy filling and a crunchy coating. There were ten courses in all, costing £344 a head. The meal was created by Hervé This and Pierre Gagnaire.

BEAUTY, CHEWING GUM, LAVATORIES, MACAO, MICHELANGELO

HOPE

Nadezhda, which is the Russian for 'hope', was the name of the first creature to give birth after conceiving in space. Nadezhda was a cockroach who in October 2007 was reported to have given birth to 33 young after becoming pregnant on a flight the previous month. It was reported at the time that the space cockroaches were darker than usual, and later reports indicated that they grew up faster and stronger than their conceived-on-earth brothers.

In 1488, when Portuguese explorer Bartolomeu Dias became the first person in modern times to round the Cape, he called it Cabo das Tormentas (Cape of Storms). It is said to have been renamed Cape of Good Hope by the Portuguese King John II who saw it as a propitious sign that India could be reached by sea from Europe.

⚲ *BREAKFAST, DOYLE, JESUS CHRIST*

HORN

The traditional Horn Dance, which dates back at least to the Middle Ages, takes place annually in the village of Abbots Bromley in Staffordshire. It is performed by 12 dancers, six of whom carry reindeer antlers, which are housed in St Nicholas' Church in Abbots Bromley and have been carbon dated to around 1065. They probably came from Sweden.

The longest horns on a living animal belonged to a wild Asian water buffalo and measured 4.24 metres (13 feet 11 inches) from tip to tip.

The French horn originated in Germany. For that reason, the International Horn Society recommended in 1971 that the 'French horn' be called simply the 'horn'. The cor anglais, which means 'English horn' is neither English nor a horn. It is a double-reeded wood-wind instrument related to the oboe and originated in Silesia around 1720.

⚲ *BUFFALO, DALI, GIRAFFE, OWL, RHINOCEROS, UNICORN*

HORNBILL

The first two neck vertebrae of hornbills are fused together, which may make it easier for them to control their beaks. They are the only birds in which this happens.

⚲ *HAIR, OSTRICH*

HORSE

In 1875, road accidents, mostly involving horses, led to the deaths of 1,589 people in the UK. From 1921 to 1923 mortality among horse-riders in England and Wales was still more than 60 per cent higher than among motor-vehicle drivers.

A horseflesh dinner was served at the Langham Hotel in London on Leap Day, 29 February 1868. One diner, Frank Buckland, said that he 'gave it a fair trial, tasting every dish from soup to jelly' but he reported that he did not approve of any of it.

Horsemeat consumption worldwide declined from a 1979 peak of 628,300 tons to 567,400 tons in 1982, according to exporters at a 1984 international horsemeat forum in Tokyo. By 2018, it had overtaken the previous high figure and was up to 632,000 tons. The eight countries that consume the most horse meat consume about 4.3 million horses a year.

In March 2005, Wild Animal World in Changzhou, China, banned the practice of feeding live horses to lions and tigers in public. A spokesman said, 'The bloody scene could also have implanted violent tendencies in youngsters.' However, the zoo would continue to sell small birds for visitors to feed to the animals.

Useful horse word: 'jumentous', which means 'resembling horse urine'.

⚲ *CENTAUR, GRAND NATIONAL, MARS, MONGOLIA, ODIN, ROCKING HORSE.*

HORSE-RACING

A race at Monmouth Park track in Oceanport, New Jersey, in November 2010 ended in a duel down the straight between two horses named 'Mywifeno-sevrything' and 'Thewifedoesntknow'.

Mywifenosevrything, who won the race, was trained by a woman, while a man trained Thewifedoesntknow.

♀ ASCOT

● HORSERADISH

Bottled horseradish was the first product produced by Henry J. Heinz, who brought it to the market in 1869. The slogan '57 Varieties' was introduced in 1892, by which time Heinz was already producing over 60 different products.

Henry J. Heinz was second cousin twice removed of the 45th President of the United States, Donald Trump. The maiden name of Heinz's paternal grandmother was Charlotte Louisa Trump.

● HOSPITAL

The original meaning of 'hospital' (from around 1300) was a house or hostel for the reception of pilgrims, travellers and strangers. Hotel and hostel were versions of the same word. 'Hospital' only came to be used as a place for looking after the sick around 1600.

The earliest known reference to an operating theatre in a hospital was in 1824, though the word 'theatre' had been used since the 17th century for a large room in a hospital in which medical lectures were given to students.

♀ BOTTOM, CLOWNS, COCONUT, KUWAIT, PORTUGAL, UNITED STATES

● HOT DOGS

On 11 June 1939, at a party organised by President Franklin D. Roosevelt, King George V and Queen Elizabeth became the first British monarchs to eat hot dogs.

The origin of the Frankfurter, the first hot dog sausage, is a matter of dispute. In 1987, the German city of Frankfurt celebrated the 500th birthday of the hot dog. It is said that the Frankfurter was developed there in 1487. Another theory dates the origin to the 16th century when Johann Georghehner, a butcher of Coburg, invented the 'dachshund' sausage.

The first American hot dogs appeared in the 1860s and the earliest recorded use of the term 'hot dog' dates back to 1884. That casts doubt on another theory that the term was coined by a cartoonist called Tad Dorgan in the early 1900s when he was unable to spell 'dachshund'.

Marlene Dietrich once said her favourite meal was hot dogs and champagne.

Jayne Mansfield was National Hot Dog Girl and Miss Hot Dog Ambassador in 1950.

In January 2005, police on Long Island, New York, arrested two women hot dog vendors for allegedly selling sex alongside items from the usual menu. A police spokesman said: 'We've never seen hot dogs mixed with prostitution before.'

The World Hot Dog Eating Contest is traditionally held on 4 July at Nathan's in Coney Island, New York. On 4 July 2001, Takeru Kobayashi of Japan ate 50 hot dogs in 12 minutes, nearly doubling the previous world record to win the contest. Kobayashi favoured the 'Solomon method', which involves breaking each hot dog in half, then stuffing both halves simultaneously into the mouth. Other contestants preferred the 'Tokyo style', which is to eat sausage and roll separately. Kobayashi retained his title for the next five years, but was beaten in 2007 and 2008 by Joey Chestnut. The 2008 contest went to a five-dog eat-off after they tied at 59 hot dogs each in 10 minutes. The current record of 76 hot dogs in 10 minutes (the time was cut from 12 minutes in 2008) was set by Joey Chestnut in 2021.

'The noblest of all dogs is the hot-dog; it feeds the hand that bites it.' Lawrence J. Peter

♀ BASEBALL, DOUGHNUTS

HOUDINI, Harry (1874–1926)

The great escapologist's real name was Erich Weiss. He took his stage name from the French magician Jean-Eugène Robert-Houdin, who died in 1871.

♀ AUSTRALIA

HOUSEWIVES

The word 'hussy', meaning a promiscuous or immoral girl or woman, was originally a contraction of 'housewife' and had no negative connotations. The patron saint of housewives is Martha, the sister of Lazarus and Mary of Bethany and a friend of Jesus. She is also a patron saint of butlers, cooks, dietitians, domestic servants, home-makers, hotel-keepers, housemaids, housewives, inn-keepers, laundry workers, maids, manservants, servants, servers, single laywomen and travellers.

According to the UN Human Development Report 1995, the annual value of women's unwaged work worldwide was about $11 trillion. According to the *New York Times* in 2020, the figure was $10.9 trillion.

According to the latest available official figures, 13 per cent of British women between 16 and 59 are housewives. The average housewife has been calculated to walk 594 miles a year in the course of her housewifely duties.

In 1832, Joseph Thompson, a Carlisle farmer, sold his wife for 20 shillings and a Newfoundland dog. This was not as

unusual as it may seem. Between 1840 and 1880, 55 cases of wife-sale were recorded in Britain.

On 24 October 1975, 90 per cent of Icelandic women refused to cook, clean or look after children for a day. Men across the country responded by taking their children to work and overwhelming restaurants.

♀ ARGENTINA, PILLOW

HOXHA, Enver (1908–85)

When Enver Hoxha was dictator-for-life of Albania between 1945 and 1985, he banned jeans, miniskirts, lipstick, pre-marital sex, boxing and bananas, and declared Westerners, Yugoslavs, Russians, the Chinese and God unwelcome in his country. He declared beards illegal, and life imprisonment was the punishment for baptising one's children.

HUDSON, Jeffrey (1619–82)

Also known by the nickname 'Lord Minimus', Jeffrey Hudson quite literally sprang to fame at the age of seven when he jumped out of a pie on the dining room table of his boss, George Villiers, the first Duke of Buckingham. Dressed in full armour and waving a flag, Hudson then saluted King Charles I and his Queen, Henrietta Maria, who were there as Villiers' guests. The Queen was so impressed that she adopted Hudson as court dwarf. He was 46 centimetres (18 inches) tall at the time, a height he stayed at until the age of 30 (though he later shot up to 1.14 metres/3 feet 9 inches).

Hudson was born to parents of ordinary stature in 1619 in Oakham, the county town of Rutland, England's smallest county. His father, John, worked for the Duke of Buckingham as Keeper of the Baiting Bulls, a blood sport which involved pitting bulls against other animals, usually dogs.

Hudson's life was eventful: he took part in the English Civil War, after which he fled to France with the Queen, where he survived two duels, one against a turkey cock and the other with a man named Mr Crofts. In the latter, his opponent tried to make light of the matter and turned up for the duel with a water pistol, but Hudson insisted that the duel go ahead. He was put on a horse to get him level with Crofts, whom he promptly shot dead. As duelling was then illegal in France, Hudson was sent back to England.

He was later on a ship captured by Barbary pirates and was taken to be sold as a slave in North Africa where he remained for some 25 years until brought back to England by missionaries. He was imprisoned in London in 1678 as a papist plotter and died penniless soon after his release in 1680.

At the height of his fame, he appeared as a character in a novel by Sir Walter Scott and was also painted by Sir Anthony van Dyck.

HULA HOOP

An attempt at the world simultaneous hula-hooping record was made on Berrow beach in Somerset in 2009, but fell short of its target when only some 300 people turned up to hula hoop. The record they had hoped to break was 2,290 people. An organiser blamed the bad weather.

A new record was set in Thailand in 2013, however, when 4,483 people danced with hula hoops simultaneously for seven minutes without interruption. Almost 5,000 turned up for the record attempt, but around 500 dropped out after they failed to keep their hoops up.

HULK

According to calculations by Rhett Allain, Assistant Professor of Physics at Southeastern Louisiana University, when Dr Bruce Banner turns into the Incredible Hulk, he increases in bulk from about 70 kilograms (154 pounds) to almost 300 kilograms (661 pounds). Assuming that this extra mass has its source in energy, he calculated that it would take around 2.5 minutes of the total energy the Earth receives from the Sun in order to accomplish the transformation. He also calculates that in jumping some 122 metres (400 feet), as the Hulk does in one Avengers film, the force his feet would exert on the pavement when taking off would probably crack the concrete.

HIPPOPOTAMUS

HULL

Hull City is the only team in the English Football League whose name does not include any letters with an enclosed space that can be filled in by a doodler (such as a, b, d, e, o, etc.).

In 2015, Hull was identified by the UK Quality of Life Index as the second worst place to live in the UK. Only Bradford was considered worse. Hull is actually the name of a river; the proper name of the city on it is Kingston upon Hull.

BOUNTY, HALIFAX

HUMAN RIGHTS

The National Human Rights Commission in South Korea in 2010 upheld the right of a golf club to deny membership to a man because they did not like his tattoos. The applicant said the club was violating a human rights law which banned discrimination on the grounds of appearance. The commission, however, said the decision did not constitute 'unfair discrimination' but was within the club's right to reject membership for 'those who create a sense of incompatibility or give inconvenience to others'. They said there was a chance that other members may feel uncomfortable at glimpsing the tattooed skin, which covered the man's shoulders, chest, arms and back, when it became exposed while changing and showering at the club.

A court in Cologne in January 2011 ruled that it is not a disproportionate impairment of personal rights for an employer to insist that his female employees wear bras. Insisting on white or flesh-coloured bras is also reasonable. They may also determine permissible beard lengths for men and fingernail lengths for all.

⚲ *DWARF, MATCHMAKING, SAUDI ARABIA, UNDERWEAR, UNITED NATIONS*

⬤ HUMMINGBIRD

There are 361 known species of hummingbird. A flock of hummingbirds is most commonly called a 'charm', but 'bouquet', 'chattering', 'drum', 'glittering', 'hover', 'shimmer' and 'troubling' have also been used as collective nouns for hummingbirds, or perhaps best of all, considering the humming of their wings, a 'tune'.

Research has shown that the earliest training given to hummingbird chicks by their mother birds is to elevate their posteriors above the nest edge when defecating. Hummingbird nests are thus cleaner than those of other birds.

Hummingbirds cannot walk but are the only birds that can fly backwards.

⬤ HUNDRED

The word 'hundra' in Old Norse, from which our word 'hundred' derives, originally meant 120.

If your total weight is 70 kilograms (11 stone), then there will be 100 pounds of oxygen in your body.

The sum of the cubes of the first four integers equals 100.

You can spell out all the numbers below 100 without using the letter 'a'.

According to the Oxford English Corpus, the 100th most commonly used word in the English language is 'us'.

⚲ *FORTUNE-TELLING, FRANCE, MARRIAGE, MOTHERHOOD, SKIPPING*

⬤ HUNGARY

Hungary's first king, Stephen I, was crowned on Christmas Day 1000 with a crown sent by the Pope. He and his son Emeric were both made saints in 1083. The last king of Hungary was Charles IV, who was also the last king of Bohemia and Croatia.

Hungary has a higher proportion of smokers than any country other than Greece.

Hungarians won gold medals at every Summer Olympics except Antwerp 1920 and Los Angeles 1984, when they did not compete.

The word 'coach' derives from the name of the Hungarian town Kocs, where multi-passenger wheeled vehicles first appeared around 1500.

⚲ *BODYGUARD, CONDOM*

⬤ HUNTING

A hunting-lodge operator in Canada who shot his common-law wife because he mistook her for a bear was acquitted of second-degree murder in Quebec Superior Court in June 1984. The jury deliberated for nearly 10 hours.

⚲ *BOTSWANA, FOREST, SADDLE, SEAL, SNAIL, VERMONT*

HUTTON, Sir Leonard (1916–90)

Len Hutton was the first professional cricketer to captain England regularly. The 364 runs he scored in one innings against Australia in 1938 is still the highest score ever made by an England batsman in a test match.

Hutton made 129 centuries in his first-class career, which is the same as the number of mystery novels written by Erle Stanley Gardner. In 82 of those novels, Perry Mason solves a case.

CRICKET

HYDROGEN

The gas hydrogen was originally known as 'inflammable air'. The name of 'hydrogene' was given to it by Lavoisier, who discovered that it combined with 'oxygene' to form water. The earliest known use of the word 'hydrogene' in English was in 1791 by Erasmus Darwin, grandfather of Charles Darwin.

BODY, FART, SUN

HYENA

Baby hyenas are born with their eyes open and teeth and muscles ready for work.

Hyena mothers have been found to spend more energy on each cub than any other terrestrial carnivore.

The genitals of a female hyena can easily be mistaken for those of a male as they have a pseudopenis and pseudo-scrotum. Female hyenas are generally also more muscular and aggressive than males.

The hyena was excluded from Noah's ark in Raleigh's *History of the World* (1614) in the belief that it was a cross between a fox and a wolf: '... it was not needful to preserve them; seeing they might be generated again by others, as the mules, the hyenas and the like; the one begotten by asses and mares, the other by foxes and wolves'.

BACULUM, BERLIN, GENITALS

HYGIENE

The word 'hygiene' comes from the name of Hygeia, a Greek goddess of health and cleanliness, but 'hygiene' only came into the English language in the 1670s.

In April 1928, handshaking was denounced as bourgeois in Italy, and the Balilla fascist youth movement in Rome proposed to ban handshaking on the grounds that it was unhygienic. In 1938, handshaking was banned in Italian films and theatres, to be replaced by the straight-armed Nazi salute, and on 21 November 1938, the Ministry of Popular Culture issued orders banning the publishing of photographs showing people shaking hands.

CENSORSHIP, LAVATORIES, TOILET PAPER

HYPATIA OF ALEXANDRIA (c.360–415)

Philosopher, mathematician and astronomer, Hypatia was described as 'the wife of Isidore the Philosopher' but is said to have maintained her virginity. For this, she was praised by Christian authors as a model of virtue, though she was not a Christian herself.

Held responsible for creating religious discord, she was killed by a Christian mob who stripped her naked, dragged her through the streets, and had her skin peeled off with sharp oyster-shells before her body was thrown into a fire.

IBSEN, Henrik (1828–1906)

Apart from Shakespeare, Ibsen is the world's most often performed playwright. His early plays, written when he worked as a theatre director in his native Norway, were unremarkable and unperformed. It was only when he left Norway to live in Italy and Germany that he began to have success. After 27 years, he returned to Norway where he was made a knight, and was later raised to the level of commander and honoured with the Grand Cross of the Order of St Olav. In 1995, the asteroid 5696 Ibsen was named in his memory.

Ibsen kept a pet scorpion in a jar on his desk to remind him that his task was not to entertain but to sting his audience into thinking. When the scorpion was ill, he dropped soft fruit into its jar, which it would attack and sting. After expelling its venom into the fruit, the scorpion recovered.

After a series of strokes in 1900, Ibsen spent the final six years of his life an invalid. In 1906, when a nurse suggested to a visitor that his condition was improving, Ibsen snapped, *Tvärtemot!* ('On the contrary!') and promptly died.

♀ *TROUSERS*

ICE CREAM

At a rate of over 28.4 litres (7.5 gallons) per person every year, the average New Zealander eats more ice cream than any other nation. The USA (20.8 litres/5.5 gallons per capita) and Australia (18.4 litres/4.8 gallons) are the next highest. Remarkably, considering its comparatively cold climate, Finland (14.2 litres/3.75 gallons) comes fourth. The UK just squeezes into the top 10 ice-cream eating countries with 7.0 litres (1.8 gallons) per person.

The current global ice-cream market is estimated to be $89 billion. In 2018/19 in the UK, the average expenditure on ice-cream products was 22p per person per week. That figure had doubled since 2007.

When Ben Cohen and Jerry Greenfield went into business together, they opted for ice cream because bagel-making equipment was too expensive. Lovers of Ben & Jerry's ice cream have never regretted that decision.

On 13 June 1789, George Washington became the first US president to eat ice cream.

On 15 December 1903, Italo Marchioni of New York received Patent

No. 746,971 for his 'new and useful Improvements in Moulds', including 'apparatus for forming ice cream cups and the like' – and the age of the ice cream cone began.

In the USA, 25 per cent of Baskin Robbins' '31 flavours' ice-cream sales are for plain vanilla.

In the State of Kansas, it used to be illegal to serve ice-cream with cherry pie.

Hawaii and Wisconsin are the only states with laws governing ice-cream container size.

The last thing Elvis Presley ate was four scoops of ice-cream and six choco-late chip cookies.

♀ *ASTRONAUTS, OBAMA, SARDINE, TELEVISION*

ICE HOCKEY

In 2006, the organisers of the World Ice Hockey Championship in Riga, Latvia, dropped plans to include ice-skating polar bears in the opening ceremony. The costs of such a perfor-mance would be excessively high, the Latvian Education and Science Minister explained, and Latvia could not afford them.

ICEBERG

If an iceberg is measured to have a height of more than 75 metres (246 feet) above the sea, it is officially classified as 'Very large'. An iceberg with less than 1 metre (3.2 feet) above sea level is called a 'Growler'. From 1 to 5 metres (3.2–16.4 feet) high, it is called a 'Bergy bit'. Accumulations of floating fragments of ice each not more than 2 metres (6.5 feet) across are called 'Brash ice'.

♀ *ART*

ICELAND

When man first settled in Iceland in the 9th century, the Arctic fox was the only native mammal. There are now around 150 mammalian species, including the Icelandic field mouse, which is the largest field mouse in the world. There are no reptiles, amphibians or poisonous animals in the wild in Iceland.

Lake Myvatn in northern Iceland boasts 16 different species of nesting ducks, which is more than any other lake in the world. The official mascot of the lake is Barrow's goldeneye duck (*Bucephala islandica*). This duck is named after Sir John Barrow, who started his career as a mathematics tutor, then became a geographer, linguist, civil servant, and Second Secretary to the Admiralty in 1804.

The first armed robbery in Iceland's history took place in Reykjavik in 1984 when 2 million crowns (about £48,500) was taken from two messengers in the National Bank of Iceland. A man with dual Icelandic-American citizenship was later arrested.

Iceland has more chess grandmasters per head of population than any other country with more than two grand-masters. One in every 26,337 people in Iceland is a chess grandmaster.

The average Icelander goes to the cinema more often than any other nationality.

♀ *AMERICA, BLYTON, CIRCUMCISION, PENIS, ST KILDA, VIRGINITY*

ICICLES

Medical authorities in the region of Samara in central Russia reported that six people had been killed by icicles falling from buildings in three days in February 2008. This is only one fewer than the number of people killed in

Australia by wasp stings in the 22 years from 1979 to 1990.

IDAHO

A man walked into a police station in Jerome, Idaho, in 2011 and asked to be deported to Mexico. The police refused and told Guadalupe Cruz-Vasquez to go away, so he left the police station, broke a window of a police patrol car, and drove it away until he ran out of petrol. He was then arrested and deported to Mexico.

In January 2022, a pair of Idaho men broke a Guinness World Record by passing a beach ball between them 157 times in 1 minute. The same men had previously set the 30-second version of the same record with 84 passes.

GOOSEBERRY, MOSCOW

IDES OF MARCH

Julius Caesar was stabbed to death by a group of conspirators on the Ides of March in 44 BC. He died from the second of 23 stab wounds, according to a physician who examined the body and provided the earliest known post-mortem report.

Between them, the cast of the 2011 George Clooney film *The Ides of March* had 23 Golden Globe nominations when the film was released, one for each stab wound of Julius Caesar.

The ancient Romans did not number days of the month but counted back from the Nones (5th or 7th), Ides (13th or 15th) and Kalends (1st of the next month). 'In March, July, October, May, the Ides fall on the 15th day.' In other months, the Ides are on the 13th. The Ides of March often featured a military procession dedicated to Mars, the god of war.

Shakespeare's account of Caesar being warned by a soothsayer to 'beware the

Ides of March' came originally from the Greek historian Plutarch. According to the Roman biographer Suetonius, the seer was a fortune-teller named Spurinna, whose predictions were based on her examination of animal entrails. 'Beware the Ides of March' is an anagram of 'Caesar: few bothered him'.

St Nicholas, on whom the figure of Santa Claus was based, was born on the Ides of March in 270.

There is a US rock band called Ides of March, whose song 'Vehicle' was a hit in 1970.

The Ides of March is the earliest day on which Palm Sunday can fall. 15 March is also World Consumer Rights Day and the International Day Against Police Brutality.

The Ides of March is also the only date in the calendar on which a serving US president and British prime minister shared a birthday: from 1835 to 1837, the UK Prime Minister (Lord Melbourne) and US President (Andrew Jackson) both celebrated 15 March birthdays.

IDIOT

In January 2007, a bill was introduced in the Senate of New Jersey to remove the word 'idiot' from the state's constitution. The relevant section said that 'no idiot or insane person should enjoy the right of suffrage'. Instead, it was proposed that the law refer to 'a person who has been adjudged by a court of competent jurisdiction to lack the capacity to understand the act of voting'.

CENSUS, SCOUTING

ILLINOIS

The Eastern tiger salamander was voted official state amphibian of Illinois in January 2005, while the painted turtle was voted state reptile. More than 75,000 votes were cast and the Lieutenant Governor commended the candidates for a very strong, positive, educational campaign.

⚲ *CORNFLAKES, FLAMINGO, LINCOLN, PLUTO, PUMPKIN, SUPERMAN*

⬤ IMPLANT

A candidate in Venezuela's 2010 National Assembly elections held a fund-raising raffle in which the prize was a breast implant. 'We decided on breast implants because we wanted to target a specific public sector,' Gustavo Rojas said.

Around 30,000 breast implant procedures are carried out each year in Venezuela.

⬤ IMPOTENCE

In 2007, a German farmer sued three students for setting off fireworks which he said had so frightened his breeding ostrich that it was impotent for six months, thus causing him to lose a potential 14 ostrich offspring. The impotent ostrich's name was Gustav.

A woman was heavily fined by a court in India in July 2010 for citing her husband's impotence as grounds for divorce. The couple were married nine years previously but divorced after three months on the grounds that she 'could not have conjugal bliss' with her husband as he was impotent. The divorce was granted, but he then took her to court complaining that the impotence accusation 'rendered him unmarriageable and sullied his prestige'.

⚲ *DONKEY, ISRAEL, LAVENDER, MELBOURNE, SEX, TEETH*

⬤ IN-FLIGHT CATERING

It took only seven months for airlines to offer meals on their commercial flights. Regular air services began in March 1919, and by October 1919 passengers from London to Paris were offered packed lunches for 3 shillings extra. The first in-flight cooking took another eight years, and the first hot meals were served, again between London and Paris, on 1 May 1927 on Imperial Airways first-class flights. Time and space restrictions allowed only 18 such meals to be cooked on each flight in a galley at the rear of the plane.

⬤ INCEST

In 1984 in Charlotte, Tennessee, Mrs Mary Ann Bass, 43, was charged with incest when it was discovered she had been married for six years to her son, Danny, 26, who had been given up for adoption 23 years before. Both were given five-year suspended prison sentences and ordered to undergo psychiatric treatment at their own expense. Mary Ann Bass pleaded guilty to bigamy and no contest to incest and carnal knowledge charges. Her son pleaded guilty to perjury and no contest to incest and carnal knowledge charges. Pleading 'no contest' (*nolo contendere*) means acceptance of the charges and punishment without confessing guilt. Danny admitted he had lied to a grand jury when he said he did not know his wife was also his natural mother when they married in 1978.

⚲ *BORGIA, VOLTAIRE*

⬤ INCOME TAX

On 9 January 1799, William Pitt introduced 10 per cent income tax in the UK. It was brought in to help finance the Napoleonic Wars with France and ran from 1799 to 1801, then again from 1803 to 1816. Described as a temporary measure, it returned in 1842 and has remained ever since. An earlier income tax had been levied in 1404 but was so unpopular that all records of it were ordered to be destroyed.

The number of nations without income tax varies between nine and 23 countries depending on how one defines 'income tax'. Bermuda, for example, has no such specific tax but employers must pay a payroll tax which is very similar. Here are 12 countries strictly without such taxes: Andorra, Bahamas, Brunei, Bahrain, Kuwait, Maldives, Monaco, Nauru, Oman, Qatar, United Arab Emirates and Vanuatu.

Top rates of income tax were so high in Norway in the 1970s that some 2,000 people were listed as paying more than 100 per cent of their total income in tax.

♀ *EINSTEIN*

INDEPENDENCE

The number of soldiers killed in conflict in the American War of Independence was 4,435, which is less than the number now killed on America's roads on average every 43 days.

An escaped slave called Crispus Attucks is celebrated as the first person killed in the War of Independence.

♀ *GREENLAND, INDEPENDENCE DAY, LITHUANIA, MONTENEGRO*

INDEPENDENCE DAY

It has often been stated that on 4 July 1776, the date celebrated as US Independence Day, King George III of England wrote in his diary: 'Nothing of importance happened today.' This is a myth: George III never even kept a diary. The story is a version of a tale about King Louis XVI of France who, on

14 July 1789, when the storming of the Bastille began the French Revolution, wrote in his diary *rien* ('nothing'). Louis was apparently referring to an unsuccessful hunting trip he had been on that day.

Besides the USA, dogs also gained their independence on 4 July: that was the day in 1984 when the UK abolished dog licences.

4 July 1826 is the only day in history on which two US presidents died (John Adams and Thomas Jefferson); President James Monroe also died on 4 July 1931, On the plus side, President Calvin Coolidge was born on 4 July 1872, the only president born on the Fourth of July. King Taufa'ahau IV of Tonga was also born on 4 July in 1918.

♀ *BOXING DAY, BRUNEI, ST LUCIA, TEXAS*

INDIA

India has more post offices than any other country: in 2017, the number of post offices was given as 154,965.

Over 45 per cent of the world's individual visits to cinemas take place in India.

On 6 September 1987, military scientists in India announced the development of the world's first long-life chapati. The key ingredient was reported to be a preservative that kept the bread fresh for six months.

♀ *BANANA, KISSING, MOUSTACHE, PULSES, SILKWORM, SPYING.*

INDONESIA

Indonesia is the world's largest country comprised entirely of islands. According to the *CIA World Factbook*, there are 13,466 of them, of which 922 are permanently inhabited. It also has more volcanoes than any other country.

A £700 prize was offered in

Indonesia in 1985 for a song extolling the joys of planting soya beans. The director-general of food crops said he hoped the song would encourage farmers to plant more beans, thus slashing imports.

⚲ *COCONUT, COFFEE, KOMODO, MONACO, OBAMA, STALLONE*

● INFIDELITY

In December 2012, an Italian who was identified in court papers only as Antonio C, petitioned to divorce his wife, Rosa C, after finding love letters between her and another man in an old chest of drawers. What made the case noteworthy was that the letters were written in the 1940s and the couple had been married for 77 years. Antonio was 99 and his wife was 96. As far as is known, this set two records: at 99, Antonio was the oldest person ever to be divorced; and their marriage was the longest ever to end in divorce. In terms of their total joint age, however, they are narrowly beaten by a British couple, both aged 98, who divorced in 2009. But they had been married for only 36 years.

⚲ *BABOONS*

● INFLUENZA

Research published in 2010 revealed that male mice show increased resistance to the flu virus if they have sniffed the bedding of female mice.

⚲ *COLUMBUS, JERUSALEM*

● INSECT

The hawkmoth is the fastest insect flier, with a top speed measured at 53.6 km/h (33.3 mph).

⚲ *ETIQUETTE, HITLER!, SEMICOLON, SPIDER, STINGS, THATCHER*

● INSURANCE

The world's first insurance company was the Insurance Office, also known as the Fire Office, founded in 1667 by Nicholas Barbon. The idea was inspired by the damage caused by the Great Fire of London in 1666.

Nicholas Barbon was the son of a member of Oliver Cromwell's parliament, Isaac Praise-God Barebone, who, as one might guess from his name, was a fanatical preacher. He gave his son, born in 1640, the name Hath Christ Not Died for Thee Thou Wouldst Be Damned Barebone, but the son later changed it to the more conventional Nicholas Barbon.

⚲ *BRAZIL, LABRADOR, LOCH NESS, VAMPIRES, WIFE-CARRYING*

● INTELLIGENCE

Research in the Netherlands published in the *Journal of Experimental and Social Psychology* in 2009, showed that heterosexual males perform worse on memory tests if they have just been chatting up attractive women. Women's results, however, are not affected by flirtatious conversations with men beforehand. The researchers reported that 'men's cognitive functioning may temporarily decline after an interaction with an attractive woman'.

⚲ *CHESS, HIPS, PHOENIX*

● INTERNET

The Internet was created by Sir Tim Berners-Lee, who launched the idea worldwide on 30 April 1993. Thirty per cent of users are English-speaking, 14 per cent speak Chinese, and 9 per cent speak Spanish. In December 2020, the number of Internet users passed the 5 billion mark.

More books are sold on the Internet than any other product. Research has shown that South Koreans are most likely to buy books on the Internet, with 58 per cent having done so.

There are currently around 4.2 billion indexed websites on the Internet, but probably far more that have never been indexed by Google. It has been estimated that the Internet is growing at a rate of more than 80 pages every second.

Internet Addiction Disorder (or IAD) was first listed as a psychiatric complaint in 1995.

About 200 billion emails are sent over the Internet worldwide every day, of which an estimated 70 per cent are unsolicited junk.

Research in Germany in 2009 found that 84 per cent of respondents aged 19–29 said they would rather do without their current partner or an automobile than forgo their connection to the Internet.

FRUITCAKE, GOOGLE, PATERNITY, PIRACY, TWENTY-TWO, VATICAN

INVESTMENT

A fruitcake made in 1941 was auctioned for $525 by an Ohio company at the start of 2012. The anonymous buyer came from Arizona. The seller of the cake said that, although the cake was vacuum-packed and contained rum, which would act as a preservative, he considered it unlikely anyone would eat the cake and he thought it was more likely it had been bought as an investment.

TOOTH FAIRY

IOWA

Iowa is the only US state whose name begins with two vowels. It also has a higher ratio of syllables to letters in its name than any other state. It is the only state whose eastern and western borders are both formed by rivers.

Snake Alley in Burlington, Iowa, built in 1894, has the reputation of being the most crooked road in the world. It consists of five half-curves and two quarter-curves over a stretch of 84 metres (275 feet), rising 18 metres (59 feet) in the process. There is a legend that the town's fire department used this alley to test horses. If a horse could take the hairpin bends at a gallop and still be breathing when it reached the top, it was deemed fit to haul the city's fire wagons.

AIR HOSTESSES, SLEEP, STRAWBERRY

IPSWICH

Lord Nelson was appointed High Steward of Ipswich in 1800. Since 1557, only 23 men have been appointed to that post, including Nelson and Lord Kitchener. The duties of the High Steward are not officially defined, but once the position is granted, it is held for life.

BLOOD, LIGHT BULB, SARDINE

IRAN

The Iranian flag has the phrase 'Allahu Akbar' ('God is great') inscribed 22 times round its border, 11 in green and 11 in red. The number was chosen because the Islamic Revolution in Iran took place on the 22nd day of the 11th month in the Iranian calendar.

The Iranian calendar is based on the Zodiac, with the year beginning on 21 March.

Iran has no laws against money-laundering.

At Iranian weddings, the bride and groom traditionally lick honey off each other's fingers to ensure their life together starts sweetly. The opposite happened at a wedding in the city of Qazvin in December 2001, when a

28-year-old groom was reported to have choked to death on one of his new wife's false fingernails.

In 2008, an attempt in Iran to beat the record for the world's biggest sandwich failed when the impatient crowd ate the mega-snack before it was measured.

⚲ *CARPET, DENTISTRY*

● IRAQ

Formerly known as Mesopotamia.

In old Iraq, surgeons who lost the life of a gentleman patient paid for their ineptitude with the loss of a hand.

About half a million tons of dates are grown in Iraq every year.

⚲ *KUWAIT*

● IRELAND

Ireland used to be known as Greater Scotia, and Scotland is believed to take its name from the Scotti tribe of Ireland, who colonised it.

There are no snakes in Ireland; the only reptile is the common lizard and the only amphibians are a single species each of frog, newt and toad. The story of St Patrick standing on an Irish hillside and sending all the snakes slithering into the sea is not supported by the evidence; no snakes have been found in Ireland's fossil record.

Ireland has won the Eurovision Song Contest seven times, which is more than any other country. Sweden comes next with six wins.

Duelling was common in 18th-century Ireland, and most inn-keepers kept pistols behind the bar for their customers to use.

In 1996, a San Francisco bar and restaurant called the Bank of Ireland announced that it was changing its name to the Irish Bank after lawyers for the Bank of Ireland accused it of misappropriating its name. Papers filed in court pointed out that the bank had used the name 'Bank of Ireland' since 1783 and said that the bar's use of the name 'taints the bank's reputation'.

In March 2002, the Australian Quarantine Inspection Service used sniffer dogs to seize more than 60 four-leafed clovers sent from Ireland for St Patrick's Day.

⚲ *DRACULA, NUNS, ORGASM, ROBBERY, SHAMROCK, WHISKY*

● IRONING

In 2008, a group of 72 Austrian divers set a new record for ironing under water. They dived off a pier in Melbourne, Australia, with irons, ironing boards and linen to beat the previous record of 70 simultaneous underwater ironers that had also been set in Australia in 2005. 'It was cold and I think they were bloody crazy,' a local councillor commented.

In 2011, this record was more than doubled in the Netherlands by 173 members of a diving club who ironed under water for 10 minutes.

⚲ *EURO*

● ISLAM

In the Islamic religion, the colour blue is believed to protect against the evil eye. The reasons for this are rather obscure as the only reference to the colour blue in the Koran associates it with criminals or sinners. Blue clothes have always been frowned upon, and the reason for blue in the facades of buildings may be because it is thought to distract evil.

In Turkey in 2021, Islamic religious authorities denounced the wearing of eye-shaped blue glass amulets to ward off the evil eye.

⚲ *POLYGAMY, TOURISM*

● ISOCRATES (436–338 BC)

The Greek philosopher and teacher of rhetoric Isocrates believed that the role of education was to teach people to speak and make them well-rounded citizens. He owned slaves who were skilled in the art of flute-making and he lived to the age of 98.

'The root of education is bitter, but the fruits are sweet.' Isocrates

⚲ UNIVERSITIES

● ISRAEL

In 2008, the official magazine of the Israeli military reported that a drug used to treat impotence could help Israeli fighter pilots operate at high altitude. A study at Mount Kilimanjaro in Tanzania had revealed that tadalafil, the active ingredient in Cialis tablets, led to improvements in breathing in a thin atmosphere.

In 1989, a hotel in the Israeli holiday resort of Tiberias lost its kosher food licence for permitting a couple to have sex in a helicopter above its swimming pool.

In November 2009, it was reported that Israel has become the world's leading exporter of hippopotamuses. The Raman Gat Safari outside Tel Aviv had exported 14 hippos by air or sea to zoos in Kazakhstan, Russia, Turkey, Ukraine and Vietnam. The difficulty, a zoo spokesman explained, was in tran- quillising the animals. If a hippo is shot with a tranquillising dart when awake, it runs into the lake and is impossible to get out. So they wait for them to fall asleep, then tranquillise them and lift them out with a bulldozer.

⚲ BEAUTY, CROCODILE, MERMAID, ROBBERY, SADISM, YOM KIPPUR

● ITALY

Mussolini's government imposed a tax on goats in January 1927. In December of the same year, it brought in a tax on bachelors, to raise the growth rate of the population and encourage the young to work harder.

In 1996, an Italian court ruled that government workers have a statutory right to a morning coffee break.

According to a 1997 survey published in Italy, 70 per cent of 360 Italian men and women had confessed to telling between five and 10 lies every day. The most common lie was 'Don't worry about it. It's all been taken care of', while other frequent lies included 'That looks great on you', 'How nice to see you', and 'I'll always love you'. Forty-two per cent of respondents said they told lies to avoid conflict.

⚲ BEDROOM, NAPLES, PARMESAN, PASTA, PIZZA, RECESSION

● IVORY COAST

The French gave Ivory Coast its name after the trade in elephant tusks in that region of Africa.

About 90 per cent of Ivory Coast's foreign exchange earnings come from the sale of cocoa beans, of which it is by far the world's leading producer.

In 2009, research on chimpanzees in Ivory Coast showed that female chimps are more likely to have sex with males who share meat with them.

In 1985, the Ivory Coast government officially changed its name to Côte d'Ivoire. 'Ivory Coast' is an anagram of 'sooty vicar'; 'Côte d'Ivoire' is an anagram of 'erotic video'.

⚲ COCOA, FIREWORKS, JACKSON Michael

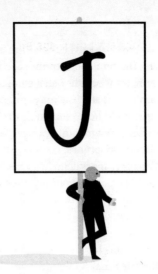

JACKSON, Michael (1958–2009)

Madame Tussauds in London made 13 wax figures of Michael Jackson during his career, more than anyone else except Queen Elizabeth II.

Jackson's pets included Bubbles the chimp, Ben the rat, a ram called Mr Tibbs, a python called Crusher and Louie the llama.

In the spring of 1986, the British Virgin Islands announced plans to release postage stamps featuring Michael Jackson after locals voted him the man they most admired. Shortly before their release, however, the stamps were cancelled owing to regulations stating that stamps bearing the likeness of living persons must be members of the Royal Family. The Caribbean island of St Vincent, however, did later issue stamps with Michael Jackson's face on them.

In 1992, Jackson was crowned King of Sanwi during impressive ceremonies held in the village of Krindjabo, located near Abidjan, Ivory Coast.

 ℗ MOSAIC

JACKSON, Thomas Jonathan 'Stonewall' (1824–63)

The left arm of US Confederate General Stonewall Jackson is buried at Fredericksburg, Virginia; the rest of his body is interred at Lexington, Virginia. His arm was shattered by fire from his own side during the Battle of Chancellorsville and was amputated the next day. He died a week later.

JAM

For the purposes of jam classification, carrots, sweet potatoes and pumpkins are fruits under EU regulations.

The Minaret of Jam in western Afghanistan is a UNESCO World Heritage site. It is under severe threat of erosion and has been on the World Heritage in Danger list since 2002.

 ℗ BAIRD, BISCUITS, BRAZIL

JAMAICA

The name 'Jamaica' comes from an Arawak Indian word meaning 'land of wood and water'.

In the 17th century, when Jamaica was a haven for pirates, Port Royal was known as the wickedest city in the world.

In 1988, Jamaica became the first West Indian nation to enter the Winter Olympics when they sent a bobsleigh team to Calgary. The only tropical countries to have entered the Winter Olympics before Jamaica were Senegal and the Philippines.

There are more churches per square mile in Jamaica than in any other country.

Noctilio leporinus, the Jamaican fish-eating bat, is found only in the Hellshire Hills in Jamaica.

Jamaicans have won the Miss World title four times. Only India and Venezuela have more Miss World victories, with six each.

⚲ BLUE, LEAP YEAR, OYSTER, RUM, SLOANE

JAMES BOND

James Bond was created by Ian Fleming in 1953. The first actor to play Bond was Barry Nelson in a 1954 US television adaptation of *Casino Royale*. Second to portray Bond was Bob Holness, who voiced the part in a South African radio adaptation of Moonraker in 1956. Holness went on to achieve celebrity as a quiz show host and died in 2012.

Of the 27 official Bond films, four have won Oscars: *Goldfinger* (Best Sound Effects), *Thunderball* (Best Visual Effects), *Skyfall* (both Best Sound Editing and Best Original Song) and *Spectre* (Best Original Song).

The only Bond girls played by actresses older than Bond were Honor Blackman and Diana Rigg, both of whom had also achieved success in the TV series *The Avengers*.

The first official image of James Bond was drawn by Ian Fleming himself as a guide for a *Daily Express* comic strip in 1957.

⚲ BACCARAT, FLEMING, MONTENEGRO, STAR WARS

JAMES I (1566–1625)

On 24 March 1603, Queen Elizabeth I died and King James VI of Scotland succeeded to the English throne as James I, uniting the Scottish and English crowns. He had succeeded to the Scottish throne at the age of 13 months on the abdication of his mother, Mary, Queen of Scots. He succeeded to the English throne as great-great-grandson of Henry VII.

Henri IV of France (or possibly his chief minister the Duc de Sully) called James 'the wisest fool in Christendom'.

In 1604, James I sponsored the Authorised Version of the Bible, also known as the King James Bible.

He did not speak until he was three years old, enjoyed bear baiting and cock fighting but disapproved of cutting trees down. In 1604 he wrote *A Counterblaste To Tobacco*, describing smoking as 'this filthie noveltie, a custome loathsome to the eye, hatefull to the nose, harmful to the braine, dangerous to the lungs'. He also wrote a treatise on witchcraft called *Daemonologie*. He believed in witches and took a personal interest in the torture and trial of alleged witches.

He generally took only one bath a year as water was thought to carry diseases.

He was buried in 1625 in Westminster Abbey, but the burial place was lost until his coffin was found in the 19th century in the vault of Henry VII.

When Guy Fawkes was arrested for attempting to blow up the Houses of Parliament, King James I gave special permission for him to be tortured – gently at first, then more severely.

⚲ ELEPHANT, FOOTBALL, MARY QUEEN OF SCOTS, UNION JACK

JANACEK, Leos (1854–1928)

On the opening night of Leos Janacek's opera *The Makropulos Case* at the Metropolitan Opera in New York in 1996, Richard Versalle suffered a heart attack after singing the line 'you can only live so long', then fell off a ladder onto the stage and died.

The debut album of the rock band Emerson, Lake and Palmer used an arrangement of the opening of Janacek's 'Sinfonietta' for the song 'Knife-Edge'.

JANUARY

January is the only month when on an average day the North Pole is colder than the South Pole.

The Latin name for this month, Ianuarius, comes from the word for door, *ianua* as it is seen as the door to a new year. The Anglo-Saxon for January was Wulf Monath (wolf month) or Aefterra Giola (after Yule). The Polish for January is Stycznia, from a word for joining: it joins the old year to the new.

Much Ado About Nothing and *A Winter's Tale* are the only Shakespeare plays that mention January.

According to census information, January was the 7,988th most popular name for a baby girl in the United States in 2020. January Suchodolski, however, was a male Polish painter and army officer. He was born in September 1797.

BLUE, BUBBLE WRAP, MARCH

JAPAN

National Foundation Day is on 11 February in Japan, marking the legendary founding of the nation by Emperor Jimmu on 11 February 660 BC. Jimmu is said to have been a direct descendant of the sun goddess Amaterasu and the storm god Susanoo.

Emperor Akihito of Japan is the world's only living emperor.

Japan has more people aged over 100 than any country other than the United States, but Japan has the highest number of centenarians per capita. It also has the world's highest life expectancy for women.

Tokyo has the world's largest fish market, handling over 2,000 tons every day.

The popular Japanese dish called Basashi is made of raw horsemeat with onions and ginger. The most popular pizza topping is squid. On Christmas Eve in Japan it has become traditional to eat Kentucky Fried Chicken.

More's Department Store in Kawasaki has the world's shortest escalator; it has five steps.

In 2016, Godzilla was officially made a citizen of Japan. He is also the tourism ambassador for the Shinjuku area of Tokyo.

Ninety-eight per cent of adoptions in Japan are of adult males, in order to have someone to bequeath a family business to and keep the family name.

In Japanese, the verb *tsujigiri* means 'trying out a sword on a chance passer-by'.

Lost property on public transport in Tokyo in 1979 included 17 goldfish bowls, complete with fish. No information is available on whether the owners of these were found, but in 2018 Tokyo Metropolitan Police returned to their owners over 545,000 ID cards (73 per cent of the total number of lost IDs) as well as 130,000 mobile phones (83 per cent) and 240,000 wallets (65 per cent).

BRASSIERE, CENTENARIANS, CHICKEN SEXING, MACAO, MOBILE PHONE, RICE

JEALOUSY

Researchers in the Netherlands and Spain in 2008 reported that short people are more jealous than tall people. Subjects were asked to list the qualities in a romantic competitor that were most likely to make them ill at ease. Men felt most nervous about attractive, rich and strong rivals, but feelings of jealousy were greater in short men.

⚲ *PHOBIAS*

JEFFERSON, Thomas (1743–1826)

In 1985, a bottle of 1787 Château Lafite that once belonged to Thomas Jefferson was sold for £105,000.

⚲ *INDEPENDENCE DAY, KANSAS, WHITE HOUSE*

JELLY

A million-dollar lawsuit filed by a New York student who broke his hip after wrestling a friend in jelly was thrown out by a judge in 2008. Avram Wisnia, who organised the event, sued his university for having agreed to the event and for having its food services office supply dustbins full of jelly, but the judge ruled he must have been aware of the potential for injury.

⚲ *HONG KONG, HORSE, JELLY BEAN, ROMNEY*

JELLY BEAN

A picture of Queen Elizabeth II made from 10,000 jelly beans was displayed at Fizziwigg's sweet shop in Brighton in 2010. Each bean in the display, which was called the Jelly Queen, was covered in lacquer. This is believed to be the first picture of the Queen made entirely from jelly beans.

'You can tell a lot about a fellow's character by the way he eats jelly beans.'
Ronald Reagan

JERUSALEM

Speaking in Jerusalem in 2009, an Israeli health minister said that the outbreak of swine flu should be renamed 'Mexican' influenza in deference to Muslim and Jewish sensitivities over pork.

⚲ *PRAYER*

JESUS CHRIST

In 2009, a sculpture of Christ was removed from St John's Church, Broadbridge Heath, West Sussex, after concerns had been expressed that it was scaring young children. The vicar said that the 3-metre (10-foot) high resin figure also failed to convey the message of hope of the resurrection of Christ.

'Jesus' was the 169th most popular name given to a baby boy in the United States in 2020. Its high point in popularity was reached in 2001 and 2002 when it was the 66th most popular name. Jesús was the 9th most popular name in Mexico in 2013.

⚲ *EL SALVADOR, ETHIOPIA, SWEARING*

JIFFY

The *Oxford English Dictionary* defines a 'jiffy' rather vaguely as 'a very short space of time' and identifies the earliest use of the word to have been in Erich Raspe's 1785 fantasy, *Baron Munchausen's Narrative of his Marvellous Travels and Campaigns in Russia*: 'Away we went, helter skelter, and in six jiffies I found myself and all my retinue safe and in good spirits just at the rock of Gibraltar.'

Later, however, jiffies became more precisely defined. In computer engineering, a jiffy is the length of one cycle, or tick, of the computer's system clock. Originally this was most frequently equal to one period of the alternating current powering the computer: 1/60 second in the USA and Canada, but 1/50 second elsewhere. More recently the jiffy became standardised as 1/100 second.

In chemistry and physics, however, a jiffy was defined around 1920 by Gilbert N. Lewis as equal to the time required for light to travel one centimetre (0.4 inch). This is about 33.3564 picoseconds. As there are a trillion picoseconds in a second, this means there are about 300 million chemists' jiffies in a computer engineer's jiffy.

JIGSAW

The jigsaw was invented by the English map-maker and geographer John Spilsbury in 1766. His first jigsaws were maps of the world pasted onto board and cut up as an educational aid to teach geography. Spilsbury had earlier been the apprentice to the Royal Geographer. He called his puzzles 'dissected maps'. The word 'jig-saw' did not come into use until 1873.

A jigsaw puzzle with 1,141,800 pieces was put together in five hours by more than 15,000 people in the southern German town of Ravensburg in 2008. It formed a 600-square-metre (6,458-square-foot) picture that nearly covered the town square.

JOAN OF ARC (c.1412–31)

Joan of Arc is said to have been born on 6 January 1412, though the evidence for that date is based only on a single letter. She was rather vague herself about how old she was, let alone the date of her birthday.

Her name is also unclear. 'Joan of Arc' is an anglicisation of the French 'Jeanne d'Arc', but her few known signatures use the spelling 'Jehanne'. As a child, she was known as Jeanne Romee (her mother's name) rather than Jeanne d'Arc (her father's).

She started seeing visions and hearing voices at the age of 13 and was put in charge of the French army fighting the English when she was only 17. Captured in 1430, she was sold to the English for 10,000 gold francs. Confirmed as a virgin, she was tried for heresy rather than witchcraft as virgins cannot be witches. Her guilty verdict was overturned by a Church court 25 years after she was burnt at the stake.

In 2007, relics kept in a French church alleged to be the remains of Joan of Arc were found to be from an Egyptian mummy.

She was beatified by Pope Pius X in 1909 and canonised by Pope Benedict XV in 1920.

A survey in 1997 reported that 12 per cent of US adults thought Joan of Arc was Noah's wife.

JOBS, Steve (1955–2011)

Steven Jobs, the co-founder of Apple Computers, was an adopted child. He only met his biological sister, Mona Simpson, when he was 31 years old. She married a man called Richard Appel, who was a scriptwriter on the TV series *The Simpsons*.

JOHN PAUL II, Pope (1920–2005)

The 27 years of John Paul II's papacy make him the second longest-serving Pope in history, after Pius IX (who was Pope for 31 years, 7 months, 23 days), or the third longest if you include St Peter, who was the first Pope and served for 37 years.

John Paul II conducted 100 foreign tours, on which he visited 129 countries. During his papacy, he canonised 482 new saints

When he visited the Philippines in 1995, an estimated 4 million people attended the Mass he celebrated in Manila, which is probably the largest crowd in history.

AZERBAIJAN, BASKETBALL, PAPAL SMOKE, POPES, ST GEORGE, WOLF

JOHNSON, Lyndon Baines (1908–73)

Lyndon Johnson, 36th President of the United States, was the first president to wear contact lenses. He married Claudia Alta Taylor, who had been known since infancy as 'Lady Bird'. They named their two daughters Lynda Bird Johnson and Luci Baines Johnson, so the President, First Lady and both their daughters had the initials LBJ.

ELIZABETH II, UNITED STATES

JOHNSON, Samuel (1709–84)

In his *Dictionary of the English Language*, Samuel Johnson defines 'lexicographer' as: 'A writer of dictionaries; a harmless drudge that busies himself in tracing the original, and detailing the signification of words.' He emphasises the point in his definition of 'dull': 'Not exhilarating [his spelling]; not delightful; as, to make dictionaries is dull work.'

Among words in Johnson's dictionary that have sadly become extinct are:

'Jobbernowl' – Loggerhead; blockhead

'Kickshaw' – A dish so changed by the cookery that it can scarcely be known.

The word 'kickshaw' was an English corruption of the French *quelquechose* ('something'). Shakespeare refers to 'kickshaws' in *Henry IV, Part 2* and to 'kickshawses' in *Twelfth Night*.

ALCOHOL, BOSWELL, CELIBACY, CUCUMBER, KNOWLEDGE, WEATHER

JOKE

According to a study reported in 2012, there is a great deal of difference in the joke-telling behaviour of senior male and female managers at meetings.

Dr Judith Baxter, a lecturer in applied linguistics, studied 14 senior managers, of whom seven were male and seven female. Not only were the men found to be three times as likely as the women to make jokes at meetings, but more than 80 per cent of jokes made by the women were met by silence, while 90 per cent of jokes made by men were greeted with laughter or approval. Furthermore, the women's jokes were often self-deprecatory and were viewed as 'contrived, defensive or just mean'.

Dr Baxter described joke-telling in such circumstances as 'part of leadership "tribe" behaviour which women find hard to join'.

CELLO, EINSTEIN, FRANKLIN, PALMERSTON, PIGGY BANKS, RESTAURANTS

JONSON, Ben (c.1572–1637)

The poet and playwright Ben Jonson was put on trial for manslaughter in 1598 after he killed an actor, but escaped the death penalty by claiming Benefit of Clergy, a handy loophole available to almost anyone who could read. This involved reading a verse from the Bible in Latin, known as the 'neck verse' for its ability to save a person's neck. In English, the verse says: 'For I acknowledge my transgressions: and my sin is ever before me.'

When Jonson was buried in Poets' Corner in Westminster Abbey, the plot allocated was found to be too small and he had to be buried in a sitting position. His heel bone was later stolen by William Buckland when the grave was disturbed in 1849, but turned up again in 1938 in an old furniture shop in Camden Town.

♀ *DINOSAUR, PLAYBOY, SEMICOLON*

● JUNE

According to an Internet-based analysis, if your name is June, you are 54 times more likely to be female than male.

Henry IV, Part 1 and *Antony and Cleopatra* are the only Shakespeare plays that mention the month of June.

♀ *NICARAGUA*

● JUNGLE

All rainforests are jungles but not all jungles are rainforests. Rainforests are tropical jungles with at least 80 inches of rainfall a year. Rainforests have canopies of thick vegetation shielding the ground from the sun. About 6 per cent of the Earth's land mass is classified as jungle.

It is estimated that 57 per cent of the species of plant and animal life on planet Earth live in jungles.

In the multi-billion-word British National Corpus, the descriptive term that most frequently precedes the word 'jungle' is 'concrete'.

The films *The Asphalt Jungle* (1950) and *The Blackboard Jungle* (1955) each received four Oscar nominations but neither won any. Walt Disney's *The Jungle Book* (1967) also received one Oscar nomination (for Best Original Song) and failed to win. The 2016 version of *The Jungle Book*, however, won an Academy Award for Visual Effects.

The word 'jungle' comes from a Sanskrit word meaning uncultivated land or desert.

♀ *PIZZA, WINNIE-THE-POOH, YOYO*

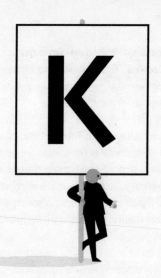

KANGAROO

In 2015, a group of scientists from St Petersburg State University published the results of their research into handedness in Australian marsupials. After studying numerous species, they concluded that two types of kangaroo and one wallaby all showed signs of left-handedness in common tasks such as grooming and feeding. Commenting on an earlier notion that handedness was a uniquely human characteristic, Dr Yegor Malashichev said: 'we are not alone in the Universe; we are two – humans and kangaroos'.

A fully grown kangaroo can jump 13 metres (42 feet). That is just over 4 metres (13 feet) longer than the human long jump world record. A kangaroo's means of locomotion is more efficient than running for speeds over 29 km/h (18 mph). Kangaroos and emus cannot walk backwards, which is why they were selected to appear on the Australian coat of arms.

Most male kangaroos have a bifurcated (two-pronged) penis, though the two largest species, the red kangaroo and the grey kangaroo, have only a single prong.

Kangaroo meat became legal for human consumption throughout all of Australia only in 1993. A diet that excludes all meat except that of kangaroo is called 'kangatarianism'.

⚲ ABORIGINE, AUSTRALIA, DICKENS, SCROTUM, VAGINA

KANSAS

Kansas has America's only gallery devoted to people who lost US presidential elections. Situated at the First State Bank in the town of Norton, the 'They Also Ran' gallery includes 59 drawings and photographs dating back to Thomas Jefferson, who lost to John Adams in 1796. The most recent additions were John McCain and Mitt Romney, added in 2009 and 2012 after they lost to Barack Obama.

The gallery, which is open during bank hours and free, gets about 100 visitors a year.

Kansas has the largest population of wild grouse (or prairie chicken, as the Americans call it) of any state in America. Three criminal teenagers in Kansas in 2011 had the promising idea of robbing motorists who were stuck in the snow. Unfortunately, they did not think it through properly and were arrested by the police and charged with armed robbery when they got stuck in a snowdrift themselves.

⚲ *BASEBALL, HEDGEHOG, ICE CREAM, STRING*

● KARAOKE

The word 'karaoke' comes from a Japanese phrase meaning 'empty orchestra'. In 2009, Kim Sun Ok, a South Korean housewife, claimed a world record after singing karaoke for 76 hours non-stop in a bar in Seoul. She said that she only stopped because her family were concerned about her health.

● KARLOFF, Boris (1887–1969)

The real name of horror film star Boris Karloff was William Henry Pratt. His brother, Sir John Thomas Pratt, was British Consul General in Shanghai. According to his daughter Sara, speaking in 1995: 'He loved playing cricket and gardening, and had a pet pig called Violet.' The pig weighed 181 kilograms (400 pounds).

For his role as Frankenstein's monster, Karloff needed five hours for his make-up to be applied.

● KATE

According to the *Oxford English Dictionary*, a 'kate' is 'a dialect name for several species of finches, as the brambling, hawfinch, and goldfinch'.

The name Katherine or Catherine, meaning 'pure and unsullied', was first recorded in English in 1196.

No woman named Kate, Katherine or Catherine has ever won a Nobel Prize, but Kate Winslet won the Best Actress Oscar in 2009, and Katharine Hepburn won it four times. Cate Blanchett won a Best Supporting Actress Oscar in 2005.

In the Middle Ages, the Catholic Church rated St Catherine among the 14 most helpful saints.

● KAZAKHSTAN

Kazakhstan is the world's ninth largest country, covering a greater area than all of Western Europe. However, there are on average only 15 people per square mile in Kazakhstan. The suffix '-stan' means 'land' or 'place of' in old Persian. 'Kazakh' means 'independent', 'a free spirit'.

According to UN data, the average Kazakhstani has a 31.6 per cent chance of not reaching the age of 60.

Kazakhstan's three jails are reported to be 18 per cent above full capacity.

In 2000, Kazakhstan became the first ex-Soviet republic to repay all its debt to the International Monetary Fund, seven years ahead of schedule.

In January 2007, a man was arrested in Kazakhstan for trying to smuggle 500 parrots. According to a Reuters news report, it was unclear how he managed to get the 500 birds into his Audi.

In July 2007, a chicken in Kazakhstan was reported to have laid an egg with the word 'Allah' on its shell.

In October 2007, the Kazakhstan central bank admitted that it had misspelled the word for 'bank' on its new banknotes.

The capital of Kazakhstan is Astana. The word *astana* means 'capital'.

⚲ *DIVORCE, KYRGYZSTAN, MADAGASCAR, UNICORN*

● KEATS, John (1795–1821)

Thomas Carlyle reviewed John Keats's poetry as 'fricassee of dead dog'. He described Monckton Milnes's biography of Keats as 'An attempt to make us eat *dead dog* by exquisite currying and cooking.'

KEBAB

In April 2008, a worker in a German fast-food restaurant lost her claim for damages after an angry customer threw a half-eaten kebab at her. The Munich court ruled that she was not entitled to compensation, as having a kebab thrown at you does not constitute a 'serious violation of human dignity and honour'.

⚲ *WRIST*

KENNEDY, John Fitzgerald (1917–63)

According to research published in 2001 in the *Journal of the Forensic Science Society*, there is a 93.6 per cent chance that John F. Kennedy's assassination was not the work of a lone gunman.

With a hat size of seven and five-eighths, John F. Kennedy had the second biggest head of any American president, exceeded only by William Taft at seven and three-quarters.

In a speech made in 1961, John F. Kennedy was recorded as speaking at 327 words per minute, the fastest known rate of public speaking in history.

⚲ *DOG*

KENYA

A prison inmate on death row in Kenya was operated on in December 2010 to remove a mobile phone from his large intestine. 'It's worrying the lengths inmates can go to smuggle things into prison,' the prison chief said. The phone was discovered in an X-ray. It had been there for a month.

⚲ *CAMEL, CROSS BREEDING, OBAMA*

KESTREL

In 1995, it was finally discovered how kestrels detect areas with high vole populations – their favourite food.

Although kestrels have very good sight, they seemed able to detect the presence of voles when they could not possibly see them. However, kestrels, like other birds, can see ultra-violet light, and vole urine and excrement can be seen under ultra-violet light. A group of researchers in Finland therefore decided to experiment to find out whether that was what was guiding the kestrels.

After watching the birds' behaviour in areas treated with vole urine but with no voles present, or areas with voles but no urine, they were able to show that kestrels find the voles from seeing the tracks left by their urine. Since voles urinate almost continuously, this makes them easy to spot.

⚲ *PIGEON*

KIDNEY

In snakes, the right kidney is closer to the head than the left kidney.

According to the Oxford English Corpus, the words most likely to follow 'kidney' are 'transplant(s)', 'pie', 'beans', 'failure' and 'disease'.

In 2003, doctors in Latvia reported a case of a man with four kidneys.

There is no general agreement on the precise value of a human kidney, but in 2009 a New York doctor demanded that his estranged wife pay him $1.5million to compensate him for the kidney he gave her while they were still happily married. He said he gave his kidney to his wife in June 2001. She filed for divorce in July 2005. In a 10-page judgement, the court rejected the doctor's request that it should consider his donated kidney as an item of property to be valued in the divorce suit.

⚲ *CAMEL URINE, SHATNER, TRANSPLANTA-TION*

KIPLING, Rudyard (1865–1936)

The youngest winner of a Nobel Prize for Literature was Rudyard Kipling in 1907 when he was 42. All other Nobel prizes have younger winners, except the prize for Economics of which the youngest winner was Esther Duflo in 2019 when she was 46.

Kipling wrote in violet ink, which he mixed himself. He also invented the game of snow golf, played in the snow with red balls.

Rudyard Kipling wrote the 1932 Christmas Day message that was delivered by King George V. It was the first ever royal Christmas message and began: 'Through one of the marvels of modern Science, I am enabled, this Christmas Day, to speak to all my peoples throughout the Empire.'

WINNIE-THE-POOH

KISSING

More germs are transferred when shaking hands than when kissing.

During the First World War, it was reported that: 'To kiss a girl in Hyde Park is an offence against the law for which a soldier is often fined the whole of the money he has in his pocket.'

The inhabitants of the South Pacific island of Mangia had never heard of kissing until the English arrived in the 1700s.

We know from Sanskrit texts that people have kissed in India since 1500 BC. In Europe, the Greeks seem to have been the first to do it, but the Romans, to judge by their language, added finesse to the art. They even had words for three different types of kiss: *osculum* was a peck-on-the-cheek; *basium* a more amorous kiss; and *saviolum* was a full-blooded snog.

The English language is now far richer in kissing words – baisemain: a kiss on the hand; beslobber: to kiss like a drivelling child; cataglottism: a lascivious kiss; deosculate: to kiss affectionately; exosculate: to give a big and hearty kiss; slummock (Scottish): to kiss amorously; suaviate: to kiss.

The latest addition to our spoken kissing repertoire, according to the dictionary, is the verb 'to mwah-mwah', which was first seen in 1993 and means to kiss in exaggerated fashion, especially on the cheek.

On 5 April 1910, kissing was banned on French railway platforms because it caused delays.

The science of kissing, including its evolutionary role in courtship behaviour, is called philematology. Fear of kissing is called philematophobia.

The world's longest kiss lasted 58 hours, 35 minutes 58 seconds between Ekkachai Tiranarat and Laksana Tiranarat at an event in Thailand, on 12–14 February 2013.

The world record for the longest underwater kiss is 20 minutes 11 seconds achieved by Nikolay Linder (Germany) in Freiburg, on 18 March 2012. He was given air through mouth-to-mouth kisses by a team of assistants.

The average person spends two weeks of their life kissing. Since a one-minute kiss has been calculated to burn 26 calories per person, that means the average person will burn off more than half-a-million calories in a lifetime's kissing.

BURMA, CHRISTMAS, DURIAN, FRENCH, MISTLETOE, POPES

KITE

Under the Town Police Clauses Act of 1847, any person in the UK who flies a kite, or who makes or uses any slide upon snow or ice, is liable to be fined or sentenced to up to 14 days in prison. This remained on the statute book until the Deregulation Act of 2015.

KIWI

The kiwi is the only bird with nostrils at the tip of its beak. Its egg may weigh as much as a quarter of its total body weight, the highest ratio of any bird. For the last few days before she lays the egg, the female kiwi has to fast as there is no room for food in her stomach.

⚲ *GOOSEBERRY*

KNEES

In 2009, a paper was published in the *International Journal of Biometrics* with the title 'Biometric Identification Using Knee X-rays'. Citing experimental results using X-rays that had been obtained in the diagnosis of clinical conditions in knee joints, the authors observed that 'knee X-rays can be used for the identification of individual persons' just as accurately as finger-prints, faces or irises.

In the Philippines in 1995, police were reported to be seeking a gang who had been stealing kneecaps from graves. The thieves were thought to be members of a sect which believed that grinding up kneecaps and scattering them around a house was a way of creating spiritual energy. Such spiritual power was believed to be concentrated in the knees because people kneel to pray.

The world's first knee transplant was performed by surgeons in southern Germany in April 1996, on a 17-year-old whose leg had been smashed in a motorcycle accident.

⚲ *MONGOLIA, YETI*

KNICKERS

Following the execution of Edith Thompson in 1923, at which a great deal of blood was spilled through internal haemorrhaging caused by the jolt of the noose, all women hanged in Britain were required to wear special knickers made of canvas. Only 17 women were hanged in the UK during the 20th century.

⚲ *ELASTIC, UNDEAD, UNDERWEAR*

KNIFE-THROWING

The motto of the International Knife-Throwers Hall of Fame is *Aut Sica Inherit, Aut Non Inherit* ('Either The Knife Sticks, Or It Doesn't').

KNIGHTHOOD

The word 'knight' came from the Old English 'cniht', which meant no more than a boy or servant. In the early Middle Ages, 'knight' was used to describe a soldier, especially one on horseback, who served the King. The first such military orders were the Knights Hospitaller founded at the First Crusade of 1099, and the Knights Templar, founded in 1119.

Knights of the Garter, founded around 1348, were among the first seen as orders of chivalry.

The Round Table on the wall of Winchester Castle bears the shields and names of 25 knights said to have served King Arthur, but Malory's Morte d'Arthur names around 120 Knights of the Round Table, which was said to seat 150, including various earls and kings.

Knighthoods may be removed on the advice of the honours forfeiture committee. The formal term for removal of a knighthood or other honour is 'debasement'.

Full knighthoods are only awarded to British subjects. Honorary knighthoods may be awarded to non-Britons, but they are not entitled to be addressed as 'Sir'. Romanian dictator Nicolae Ceausescu lost his honorary knighthood the day before his execution. Benito Mussolini had his honorary knighthood removed when Italy declared war on Britain.

💡 *BENNETT, BOWIE, VICTORIA CROSS, ZIMBABWE*

🔵 KNOWLEDGE

The New Oxford Thesaurus of English lists 36 synonyms for 'knowledgeable' but 90 for 'ignorant'. The Dutch scholar Desiderius Erasmus (1466–1536) is said to have been the last man to know everything there was to be known.

'Knowledge is of two kinds: we know a subject ourselves or we know where we can find information upon it.' Samuel Johnson, 1775

'Sorrow is knowledge.' Byron, 1817

💡 *BACON, CELIBACY, HIPPOCRATES, LEAP YEAR, PARROT, WORM*

🔵 KOALA

The koala gets its name from an Aborigine verb meaning 'no drink', because a koala gets all the moisture it needs from Eucalyptus leaves. Koalas communicate with a noise like a snore and then a belch, known as a 'bellow'. Koalas have two thumbs and three fingers on their front paws and sleep an average of 22 hours a day.

In their 1928 classic work *The Matrix of the Mind*, Frederick Wood Jones and Stanley D. Porteus described the koala's brain as 'ridiculously small'. Compared with the brains of other marsupials such as the wombat, they calculated that a koala's brain was only about 60 per cent of the size expected for its body size. One theory is that koala brains have

shrunk because of their diet of toxic eucalyptus leaves.

In 1996, Maciej Henneberg, a forensic scientist and biological anthropologist at Adelaide University, announced his discovery that koala fingerprints are very similar to human ones. 'Although it is extremely unlikely that koala prints would be found at the scene of a crime, police should at least be aware of the possibility,' he advised.

On 24 April 1997, Australia launched its first birth-control programme for koalas. In 2022, however, koalas were declared an endangered species along most of its east coast.

💡 *VAGINA*

🔵 KOMODO

The Komodo dragon of Indonesia was discovered only in 1910 and its existence not confirmed until 1912. Komodo dragons may be more than 3 metres (10 feet) long and are the world's largest lizards. Females outnumber males by four to one.

Komodo dragons can detect the smell of carrion over a distance of up to 9.6 kilometres (6 miles).

It takes a Komodo dragon between 15 and 20 minutes to swallow a goat.

The island of Komodo, Indonesia, quite apart from being the home of the Komodo dragon, contains more poisonous snakes per square metre than any equivalent area on Earth. These include the world's only blue viper.

The majority of people living on Komodo are descendants of former political prisoners and convicts who were exiled to the island in the 17th century.

🔵 KOOKABURRA

The headmaster of Lepage Primary School in Melbourne was reported to have admitted to being 'hypersensitive' when he changed the words of the traditional children's song 'Kookaburra Sits in the Old Gum Tree'. He had suggested to the children that instead of the chorus, 'Laugh, kookaburra, laugh, kookaburra, gay your life must be', they should sing the word 'fun' instead of 'gay'. The word 'gay', he said, was often used as a playground insult and he was trying to prevent disruption in the classroom. He had not intended to insult gay people.

KOREA

The last king to reign over Korea was King Gojong, who came to the throne in 1864 when he was 12 years old. He assumed direct royal rule in 1873 and in 1897 elevated his title to that of Emperor. When Korea was annexed by Japan in 1910, Emperor Gojong was forced to abdicate and was given the title of 'King emeritus'.

ARCHERY, NORTH KOREA, PAPER, SOUTH KOREA, TENNIS

KRILL

In terms of total biomass, the Antarctic krill is perhaps the most successful animal species on Earth. The total weight of these shrimps is about 380 megatonnes compared with about 350 megatonnes for humans. Both ants and termites outweigh krill or humans, but each of them comprises thousands of species.

SEAL

KU KLUX KLAN

The name of the Ku Klux Klan is thought to have been formed from the Greek *kyklos* ('circle') and the word 'clan', to suggest a brotherly organisation.

In 2011, an ice-cream shop in Ocala, Florida, had to get rid of a giant vanilla waffle cone that they had placed outside the shop to attract customers by waving at them; it had been found to lead to a drop in sales because people mistook the cone for a Ku Klux Klansman.

KUWAIT

In 1990, when Saddam Hussein declared Kuwait to be the '19th Province of Iraq', some dissidents started referring to it as 'Wimbledon', which, as SW19, might be considered the 19th province of south-west London.

By 2021, the Kuwaiti dinar had become the world's strongest circulating currency, with one Kuwaiti dinar equalling 3.32 US dollars, which put it just ahead of the Bahraini dinar.

On 31 July 1995, the *Al-Watan* newspaper in Kuwait reported the case of a man who had been rushed to hospital with severe exhaustion and back pain. Investigations quickly led to the conclusion that his condition had been caused by his having made love to his 17-year-old wife six times a day in the week following their wedding. 'He was pale and without energy and could not speak,' a neighbour was quoted as saying.

KYRGYZSTAN

If the name of Kyrgyzstan is spelled out in Scrabble tiles, their total value is 30, which is the same as Kazakhstan. The only single-word country name with a higher score is Mozambique, which adds up to 34. The next highest-scoring countries are Azerbaijan (28), Zimbabwe (26), Uzbekistan (25) and Switzerland (24). The lowest-scoring countries are Laos and Iran, scoring four points each.

A popular sport in Kyrgyzstan is Ulak Tartysh, in which two teams on horse-back fight for possession of the headless carcass of a goat, which they attempt to deliver across the opposition's goal line.

LABRADOR

An award for the most unusual pet insurance claim was given in 2010 to a Labrador named Ellie that ate a beehive full of pesticides and dead bees. Ellie, who is reported to have recovered from the meal, beat a Border Collie that ran through a window to attack a postman, and a terrier that bit a chainsaw.

⚲ *NEWFOUNDLAND*

LADYBIRD

The earliest known use of the word 'ladybird' is in Shakespeare's *Romeo and Juliet*, where Juliet's nurse exclaims: 'What lamb. What ladybird.'

The origin of the name is a little unclear but may be a reference to the Virgin Mary, who is often portrayed wearing a red cloak. The seven spots of the most common ladybird species may be seen as a reference to the Seven Sorrows of the Virgin.

There are about 140,000 ladybirds to the gallon.

LAMARR Hedy (1914–2000)

The actress Hedy Lamarr, whom the director Max Reinhardt called 'the most beautiful woman in Europe', not only featured in the first motion-picture orgasm (in the notorious 1933 film *Ecstasy*), but also collaborated with the avant-garde composer George Antheil in an invention that was far ahead of its time.

In 1942, they patented the idea of 'frequency hopping' using a piano roll to switch between 88 transmission frequencies to make radio-controlled torpedoes more difficult to jam.

The state of technology at the time made it impossible to put into practice, but the ideas behind it were used 20 years later in the US blockade of Cuba, and have more recently been used in the design of wireless phones and WiFi.

⚲ *CENSORSHIP*

LAMPREY

According to legend, King Henry I of England died in 1135 from 'a surfeit of lampreys'. Charles Dickens wrote: 'he died of an indigestion and fever, brought on by eating, when he was far from well, of a fish called Lamprey, against which he had often been cautioned by his physicians'.

Despite the sad end of Henry I, the eel-like lampreys were considered a delicacy throughout the Middle Ages. The City of Gloucester presented the monarch with a lamprey pie every Christmas. King John was particularly fond of lampreys and around 1200 levied a fine of 40 marks on the city of Gloucester for failing to 'pay him sufficient respect in the matter of his lampern'. As the lamprey became rare, however, this practice was discontinued in 1836, since when the traditional gifts of lamprey pie have only been given for coronations and significant anniversaries.

By 2012, the lamprey had become a protected species in Britain and 0.9 kilograms (2 pounds) of lampreys were sent from Lake Huron in North America to Gloucester in England to be used in a pie made to celebrate the Diamond Jubilee of Queen Elizabeth II.

Fossil remains show that lampreys evolved long before the dinosaurs. They have no jaws but instead have very primitive mouthparts surrounded by a large flexible lip that acts as a sucker. This feature provides the scientific name for the lamprey family, Petromyzonidae, which means 'stone suckers'.

● LAOS

A popular gambling pastime in Laos is rhinoceros beetle wrestling. Fights are staged between the beetles, and the crowd enthusiastically bet on which beetle they think will win. This also takes place in Thailand and Japan.

The last king of Laos was His Serene Majesty Savang Vatthana. He was deposed and sent to a re-education camp after the communist takeover in 1975.

The currency of Laos is the kip. There are 100 att in one kip.

⚲ *NAVIES, SNIFFING, KYRGYZSTAN*

● LATVIA

The currency unit in Latvia was the lat until it was replaced by the euro in 2014. The 500 lat note, which was worth about £550, had the reputation of being the world's most valuable banknote in circulation.

The highest point in Latvia is only 312 metres (1,023 feet) above sea level, which is about 70 metres (230 feet) lower than the top of the Empire State Building.

Latvia's first ever Olympic gold medal was won by Igors Vihrovs in the men's floor gymnastics event in Sydney 2000. At those Olympics, Latvia ended with a complete set of medals: one gold, one silver, one bronze.

In 1997, a team of doctors in the Latvian capital, Riga, wrote to Guinness World Records staking their claim for an entry on the grounds that they had sewn back four severed hands in five days.

In February 2008, the death was reported of Lisis, the pet rabbit of Latvian President Valdis Zatlers. The rabbit died less than a year after moving to the presidential home. It was reported to have apparently had trouble coming to terms with the move, despite being allowed to roam freely instead of being kept in a hutch.

Latvia's national liqueur is Riga Black Balsam, a sticky drink the consistency of crude oil. It is made from plants, flowers, buds, juices, roots, oils and berries.

⚲ *ICE HOCKEY, KIDNEY, POPCORN*

● LAUGHFEST

A world record was set at the Gilda's LaughFest event in Grand Rapids, Michigan, in 2013 when 1,544 people wore false moustaches at the same time.

The previous year, the LaughFest had set a world record for the greatest number of people wearing animal noses when 607 participants put on chicken beaks, and in 2011 they achieved the world's largest rubber chicken toss, with 935 rubber chickens thrown into the air.

In 2020, the LaughFest attempted a world record for the most people wearing unmatched socks, but achieved only 453 people when the record stood at 933.

Other achievements set at the LaughFest include a 2014 record for the greatest number of people wearing sunglasses in the dark.

● LAUGHTER

The scientific unit of laughter is the aH, which was developed by Yoji Kimura, a professor at Kansai University in Osaka. His measurements involved attaching sensors to the skin of a subject's stomach, particularly the diaphragm, to detect muscle movements. His researches showed that children laugh more freely, releasing 10 aH per second, which is twice as much as an adult.

Research shows that laughter helps manage pain, lowers blood pressure and lessens stress. Researchers have also shown that people in all cultures can tell true laughs from fake laughs, though some cultures are better at it than others. The Japanese are best at detecting fake laughter.

From 'arride' (to laugh in mockery) to 'yock' (laugh loudly) the *Oxford English Dictionary* lists 50 verbs with 'laugh' in their definition.

Plato, in the 4th century BC, said that comedy is a form of scorn, and guardians of the state should avoid laughter as it may provoke violence. The 17th-century philosopher Thomas

Hobbes said that laughter is a realisation of 'sudden glory' stemming from a feeling of superiority.

Research in 2014 showed that rats utter a high-pitched laugh when tickled.

♀ *JOKE, LINCOLN, PLATO, SMILING, WISDOM*

● LAUNDRY

The word 'laundry' was originally 'lavendry', from the Latin *lavanda*, meaning 'things to be washed'. A 'lavatory' meant simply 'a place to do washing'.

The scrubbing-board was invented in 1797; the first hand-operated washing machine with a revolving drum was invented in 1851; the first electric-powered washing machine was introduced in 1908; and Persil detergent was launched in the UK in 1909 as The Amazing Oxygen Washer. Persil is the French for 'parsley', but that has nothing to do with the detergent, which was named after two main ingredients: PERborate and SILicate.

In 2009, the official Vatican newspaper declared that the washing machine has done more to liberate women than the contraceptive pill or the right to work. The submission was made in a lengthy article titled 'The Washing Machine and the Liberation of Women – Put in the Detergent, Close the Lid and Relax'.

'Marriage is about the most expensive way for the average man to get laundry done.' Burt Reynolds

♀ *HOUSEWIVES, ROSSINI, ST CLARE*

● LAVATORIES

'Toilet' is the most popular word in Britain for the little boys' (or girls') room and is used by over half the population. 'Loo', on 33 per cent, comes second, though its derivation is obscure.

There is some evidence for a French connection, from *l'eau* (water) and the chambermaid's cry of *Gardez l'eau!* to warn that a chamber pot was about to be emptied from a window; or it could be from *lieux d'aisance* (places of ease). Others maintain a link via water closet and Waterloo, while yet another explanation suggests that the word is shortened from bourdaloue, an oblong chamber pot. The word 'lavatory' comes from the Latin *lavatorium*, which simply meant a place for washing.

The *Oxford English Dictionary* lists around 40 synonyms or euphemisms for lavatory, from Ajax to water closet, including bathroom, bog, cludgie, khazi and necessarium.

The earliest known lavatories – a hut built above a pig pen in China and an internal pit toilet in Mesopotamia – both date back to around 3000 BC.

The water closet was devised in 1589 by Sir John Harrington with flush, overflow pipe and cistern all part of his design. The invention failed to capture the public imagination, largely because insufficient sewers had been built to carry away the waste. Sir Thomas Crapper improved Harrington's design in the 1880s by inventing the boxed flush lavatory.

Among other lavatory pioneers, we may celebrate the following:

Arthur Ashwell of Herne Hill in south London, who in 1883 patented the Vacant/Engaged sign for public lavatories. The first public conveniences had been opened in London in 1852, on 2 February for men, and on 10 February for women.

John Nevil Maskelyne, stage magician and escapologist, who in 1892 invented a coin-operated lock for public lavatories that was used in England until the 1950s.

In 2011, Caltech engineer Michael Hoffman and his team received a $400,000 grant to develop a solar-powered toilet that can remove human waste for five cents per user per day. The following year, the toilet won the Gates Foundation's 2012 Reinvent the Toilet Challenge.

'Public Toilets should be the concern of every civilisation,' said Professor Wang Gung, at the opening of the 1995 International Symposium of Public Toilets in Hong Kong, 'because the cleanliness and standards of hygiene they do or do not set are truly a measure whereby the standards of a society can be gauged.'

The European Patent Office lists over 10,000 patents with the words 'lavatory' or 'toilet' in their titles. These include an 'Explosion-proof electrical incinerator toilet' (Germany, 1981); a 'Personal weighing device on toilet seat' (France, 1987) and 'Coreless toilet paper' (Japan, 1992).

⚲ BEIJING, CHINA, RAILWAY, RECRUITMENT, TURNSTILE, VENICE

● LAVENDER

Lavender has a long history of supposedly beneficial uses. The ancient Egyptians used it for perfume and in their mummification process. The Romans knew of its cleansing properties, as reflected in its name. which comes from the Latin *lavare*, to wash.

According to the 12th-century German nun Hildegard of Bingen, a good dose of strong drink mixed with lavender is a cure for migraine headaches.

In the 17th century, a bunch of lavender round your wrist was believed to protect you from the plague, and more recently lavender has been used as a herbal medicine to treat, among other things, muscular pains, cold sores, insect bites, head lice, halitosis and dandruff.

Spanish churches used to burn lavender in a ritual to keep away evil spirits. Lavender has also been claimed both as a way of repelling mice and a treatment for impotence in mice.

The smell of lavender has been shown chemically to consist of well over 100 ingredients, and according to a recent study by the Smell and Taste Research Foundation in Chicago, the most sexually exciting smell for a man is lavender and pumpkin pie.

LAWNMOWER

There was only one recorded case of a monk being killed by a runaway lawnmower in the UK in 2007. It happened in Milton Keynes.

GARDENING, REPTILES, TUESDAY

LAWYERS

Two-thirds of the world's lawyers live in the USA. One in every 268 people in the US is a lawyer.

'If there were no bad people, there would be no good lawyers.' Charles Dickens, The Old Curiosity Shop, 1840

AVOCADO, MAFIA, MOTHER TERESA, SCOLD, SWAT

LEAD

Lead pencils contain no lead. The writing material is graphite, but the results looked like those produced by lead wheels that were used to print straight lines on paper, so the implement became known as the lead pencil.

The wooden pencil first appeared in 1662, and the pencil eraser was invented by the Englishman Edward Naime in 1770, so it was over 100 years before pencil marks were erased by a rubber.

BEETHOVEN, CHANNEL, COSMETICS, GNU

LEADERSHIP

'Honcho' is a Japanese word meaning 'group leader' or 'squad leader', so the phrase 'head honcho' is tautological. It came into English in the 1940s from American soldiers who had been prisoners of war in Japan.

JOKE

LEAP YEAR

On 29 February 1504, there was a lunar eclipse. Christopher Columbus used his knowledge that this eclipse was about to happen in order to terrify the Jamaicans into feeding his crew.

Legally in the UK the age of anyone born on 29 February increases by a year on 28 February in non-leap years.

Pope Paul III was born on 29 February 1468. He was one of the few popes to have had children before his election.

Nikolai and Yuri Pimenov of Russia are the only pair of twins born on 29 February (in 1948) to have won silver medals in the Olympics, which they did in 1968, rowing in the coxless pairs.

In Denmark and Britain, women traditionally have the right to propose on Leap Day. Men who say no are expected to buy the woman 10 pairs of gloves.

The longest year in history was 1972, which not only had the usual extra Leap Day, but also had two extra leap seconds added to keep atomic time in line with the Earth's orbit round the Sun.

Julius Caesar introduced the leap year in 45 BC, adding an extra day to February once every four years. Before 45 BC the Roman calendar was a mess, with an extra month sometimes having to be added to make the year the right length. February then had 28 days in most years, but only 23 or 24 when an extra month was added. Caesar's calendar change gave an average year of 365.25 days, which was a few minutes longer than the true time of our orbit around the Sun. This discrepancy made the year gain one day every 128 years, which had become serious by 1582. The Gregorian calendar was then introduced, leaving century years out of the Leap Day rule unless the number before the 00 is divisible by 4.

The city of Anthony, Texas, 'the leap capital of the world', holds a huge party on 29 February.

⚲ *ETHIOPIA, FEBRUARY, JANUARY, ROSSINI*

LEFT-HANDEDNESS

At the time of the 1990 US census, Left was the 62,465th most common surname in the United States, but Lefthand was slightly more common, in 55,970th place.

⚲ *BUSH George Walker, CUSTARD PIE, KANGAROO, SCRATCHING, TROUSERS*

LEGO

Over 300 million Lego tyres are made every year, making Lego the world's biggest tyre manufacturer. The name 'Lego' comes from the contraction of a Danish phrase meaning 'play well'.

LEGS

It is a general rule among warm-blooded animals that those from cold climates have shorter legs than those from hot climates.

Research has shown that 23 per cent of people have legs that differ in length by a centimetre or more.

There is a memorial at Waterloo in Belgium to the leg of Lord Uxbridge,

blown off in the 1815 battle. The leg was originally buried there and became quite a tourist attraction. When Uxbridge died 39 years later, the leg was exhumed and buried with the rest of his body.

In 1942, the actress Betty Grable insured her legs for half a million dollars.

Police in Winchester once received a 999 call from a man whose wife had hidden his wooden leg.

The millipede *Illacme plenipes* has up to 750 legs, which is more than any other creature.

⚲ *FROG, LEMUR, OCTOPUS, TROUSERS, WORDSWORTH*

LEMUR

In the wild, lemurs live only on Mada-gascar and the nearby Comoro Islands. There are over 30 species ranging in size from the 28-gram (1-ounce) pygmy mouse lemur to the 6.8-kilogram (15-pound) Indri lemur. They have opposable thumbs and fingers and for grooming mainly use the second toe of their hind legs.

Lemurs form a matriarchal society with a dominant female in charge of each group. To resolve disputes, lemurs engage in 'stink fights' in which they rub their tails on sweat glands on their forearms and under their arms, then wave their tails around to waft the smell about, causing the enemy to run away.

Lemurs take their name from the Latin *lemures* (ghosts), which were exorcised during the Lemuria festival in ancient Rome. Linnaeus gave lemurs that name through an association with their mysterious and largely nocturnal lifestyles.

The Bemaraha woolly lemur (*Avahi cleesei*), also known as Cleese's woolly lemur, is named after John Cleese who has long been a great lemur fan.

⚲ *CONTRACEPTION*

LENNON, John (1940–80)

Christened John Winston Lennon, he changed his name to John Winston Ono Lennon after marrying Yoko Ono.

John Lennon failed all his GCE O-levels. Despite that, in 2002, a BBC poll ranked him the eighth greatest Briton of all time, behind Queen Elizabeth I but ahead of Lord Nelson, and in 2004, *Rolling Stone* magazine ranked the Beatles first and Lennon 38th on its list of 'The Immortals: The Fifty Greatest Artists of All Time'.

He shared an 9 October birthday with his son Sean Lennon, who was born on John's 35th birthday.

Lennon's hand-written lyrics for 'Give Peace A Chance' were sold at auction in 2008 for £421,350, while a pair of his glasses went for £39,650.

In 2008, the Vatican forgave John Lennon for saying, in 1966, 'The Beatles are more popular than Jesus.' This was 317 years quicker than it took the Vatican to forgive Galileo for saying that the Earth moved around the Sun.

♀ *FUNERALS, YOKO ONO*

LENT

The prescription of a 40-day fast for Lent was first set out at the Council of Nicaea in AD 325. In Western Christianity, Lent runs from Ash Wednesday to Easter Saturday. Its notional count of 40 days does not include the six Sundays in that period.

In the Eastern Orthodox Church, Sundays are included in the count, and the fast runs from Ash Monday to the Friday before Palm Sunday.

The word 'Lent' originally just meant 'spring'.

♀ *CARNIVAL, PANCAKE DAY, SHROVE TUESDAY*

LEPROSY

In 1612, Louis XIII of France forbade the marriage of persons with leprosy to anyone. This was far from being the first act against leprosy by a French king. In 757, King Pepin issued a decree making marriage illegal for anyone with the disease, which was also made grounds for divorce.

In Ethiopia, leprosy was grounds for divorce until 2000. In 2019, the Indian Parliament passed a law making leprosy no longer grounds for divorce. Leprosy was also grounds for divorce in Greece until the Divorce Law Reform of 1983.

♀ *ARMADILLO, POTATO*

LESBIANS

Inhabitants of the Greek island of Lesbos in 2008 took a gay organisation to court in an attempt to stop them using the word 'lesbian'. Lesbos was the birthplace of the ancient poet Sappho, who praised love between women, but one of the litigants said the Homosexual and Lesbian Community of Greece 'insults the identity' of the people of Lesbos, who are also known as Lesbians.

♀ *ALBATROSS, DIAGRAM*

LETTUCE

In 1493, Columbus brought lettuce seeds to America in order to test whether the soil was suitable for growing it.

On 28 August 1988, the Yantlee Polyclinic in Bangkok published a claim that you can get rid of hunger by pressing lettuce seeds into your ears 10 times before meals.

♀ *HAMBURGER*

LEWINSKY, Monica Samille (b. 1973)

'Monica Lewinsky' is an anagram of 'Yes, I lick man now'.

'President Clinton of the USA' is an anagram of 'To copulate, he finds interns'.

The only state with no letters in common with the name 'Lewinsky' is Utah. Durham is the only English county with no letters in common with the name 'Lewinsky'.

LIBRARY

In May 2010, New York's oldest library revealed that they were still waiting for the return of a book taken out by George Washington 221 years earlier. *The Law of Nations* by Emer de Vattel had been taken out of the New York Society Library by the President on 5 October 1789. According to a statement by a library spokesman, 'The book was not returned, nor any overdue book fine paid. This was a well-kept secret at the library for years.' The announcement was made at a ceremony when the book was replaced with another copy of the same edition donated by the library at Washington's family home in Mount Vernon, Virginia.

Under the UK Library Offences Act of 1898, it is illegal to gamble or bet in a library. Anyone convicted of doing so shall be liable to a penalty not exceeding 40 shillings. The Act does not apply in Scotland or Ireland.

𝒫 *CHAUCER, MAPS, MOBILE PHONE, ROBIN HOOD, SLEEP*

LIBYA

The official name of Libya is Great Socialist People's Libyan Arab Jama-hiriya, and its leader from 1969 until 2011 was Revolutionary Leader Colonel Muammar Abu Minyar al-Gaddafi (or Qadhafi), who held no official title but was de facto chief of state.

Colonel Gaddafi liked to drive around in his own small green Volkswagen Beetle, the same colour, incidentally, as the Libyan flag.

The flag that Gaddafi introduced was plain green, the world's only national flag that was a plain colour. Since his fall in 2011, no national flags have been just one colour.

Colonel Gaddafi's last book of short stories was called *Escape To Hell*.

In 1997, Gaddafi warned his people to fear the West. Among the possible reasons he listed for the West wanting to invade Libya were its camels, sand and watermelons.

For 90 years, the highest temperature ever recorded in the shade anywhere in the world was thought to be 57.8°C (136°F) at Al Aziziyah in Libya on 13 September 1922, but in July 2012, the World Meteorological Association published a report that reassessed the data and invalidated the record.

In 1951, Libya was officially the poorest country in the world.

𝒫 *AMMONIA, ATLANTIC, CONSENT*

LICE

In 2008, it was reported that investigation of the DNA of headlice taken from 1,000-year-old mummies in Peru supports the idea that the little creatures accompanied humans on their first migration out of Africa 100,000 years ago. The Peruvian lice were found to be nearly identical to strains that have been dated to when humans first began to colonize the rest of the world.

In the same year, seven young artists from Berlin staged an exhibit for three weeks in an Israeli museum by living with lice in their hair. 'Art is no longer just a painting on the wall,' Milana Gitzin-Adiram, chief curator of the Museum of Bat Yam near Tel Aviv, told

Reuters. 'Art is life, life is art.' The exhibit was inspired by a theme of 'hosts and guests' set by the museum.

♀ *DARWIN, LAVENDER, MERKIN*

● LICENCE PLATES

Registration plates for motor cars were introduced in Britain in the Motor Car Act 1903. The first such registrations consisted of a letter and a number. The A1 registration was issued in December 1903 by the London County Council to the second Earl Russell, though evidence suggests that other registrations had already been issued by other councils.

In October 2001, a Federal Appeals Court in the USA ruled that a Vermont car owner did not have the right to a car licence plate reading 'SHTHPNS'. Paula Perry had sued the Motor Vehicles Department saying she was a victim of 'viewpoint discrimination' when it revoked her specially requested plates that bore a shortened version of the phrase 'shit happens'. Arguing that plates saying 'POOPER' had not been objected to, she said the refusal for her plates was a denial of free speech. However, the court ruled that 'shit' is a profanity and 'pooper' is not.

♀ *CZECH REPUBLIC*

● LIECHTENSTEIN

Liechtenstein is the last survivor of the 343 states that once made up the Holy Roman Empire of German Nations. Its national anthem is sung to the same tune as 'God Save the Queen'.

Liechtenstein grew by nearly 1.3 square kilometres (half a square mile) in 2007, when some of the remote edges of its Alpine borders were found not to have been properly measured and a new survey showed the border to be 1.6 kilo-metres (1 mile) longer than previously thought. The extra area, equal to about 50 football pitches, means Liechtenstein now measures 258.2 square kilometres (99.7 square miles).

Liechtenstein is the world's largest exporter of false teeth, supplying about 20 per cent of the world's demand. Thanks largely to this dentures domination, Liechtenstein tops the world trade league for per capita exports with over $100,000 worth of goods per person each year. There are even two false teeth factories specialising in making dark brown teeth, for export to countries such as India where people chew tooth-blackening betel nut.

Johannes the Good, Prince of Liechtenstein from 1858 until 1929, was Europe's second longest-reigning monarch, exceeded only by Louis XIV of France. The current Prince of Liechtenstein is Hans-Adam II, who has ruled since 1989.

Liechtenstein won its first ever Olympic gold medal when Hanni Wenzel won the giant slalom in 1980. With ten Olympic medals in total since 1948 (all from the Winter Games in Alpine skiing) and a population just below 31,000, Liechtenstein is well ahead of any other nation in the league table of Olympic medals per capita. It is the smallest country, by both size and population, to have won an Olympic gold.

If the entire population of Liechtenstein went to the Millennium Stadium in Cardiff, Wales, there would be 39,500 empty seats.

Liechtenstein has no army, no coastline, no airport and only 22 policemen.

♀ *HAITI, PIGGY BANKS, UZBEKISTAN*

LIFE EXPECTANCY

In 1900, the average Western life span was just 47 years. This low figure was mainly caused by high rates of infant mortality.

In 2021, half the world's population were aged 31 or less.

⚲ BASEBALL, HEALTH, JAPAN, KAZAKHSTAN, NAVEL, NIGERIA

LIFETIME

In an average lifetime, a person will walk a distance equivalent to three times round the Equator; produce over 6,000 gallons of saliva; grow 2 metres (6.5 feet) of nose hair from each follicle; catch 140 colds; eat or drink the juice of about 12,000 oranges; create over 45,360 kilograms (100,000 pounds) of rubbish; spend five years dreaming; live for 2.6 billion seconds; enjoy about 3 billion heartbeats; spend 117 days having sex; and spend 7,709 days sitting down.

The average American will also visit McDonald's 1,811 times and spend six months waiting at red traffic lights.

⚲ BLOOD, HAIR, KISSING, SHARK, SKIN, TOILET

LIGHT BULB

The first street in the world to be lit by electric light bulbs was Mosley Street in Newcastle in 1879. The light bulbs used there were invented by Joseph Wilson Swan. Unfortunately, Swan was rather slow in filing for a patent and Edison got in first with a rather inferior version of the light bulb in January 1880. Nevertheless, it was early pictures of Edison with a light bulb that are thought to have led to the popular association of light bulbs with innovative ideas. The earliest use of the phrase 'light bulb moment' recorded in the *Oxford English Dictionary* was in 1974.

In January 2001, a light bulb in the men's toilet in a shop in Ipswich finally failed after giving nearly 70 years' good service. The shape of the bulb at the Martin and Newby electrical shop dated it back to the 1930s. This is believed to be a world record for a light bulb in constant use.

LIGHTNING

Every second around 100 lightning bolts strike the Earth.

Every year lightning kills around 1,000 people.

On 22 July 1918, in the Wasatch National Park in Utah, 504 sheep were killed by lightning.

⚲ CAMEL, DEATHS, GOLF, THOR

LINCOLN, Abraham (1809–65)

On 14 April 1865, Abraham Lincoln was shot by the actor John Wilkes Booth at Ford's Theatre in Washington. He died the following day. Booth is said to have waited for the line 'you sockdologizing old man-trap' before shooting the President. He hoped the laughter at that line would muffle the sound of the shot. The play Lincoln was watching when he was assassinated was Tom Taylor's *Our American Cousin*.

The President is said not to have liked the names Abraham or Abe, preferring to be called Lincoln.

After several attempts had been made to steal Lincoln's body and hold it for ransom, Lincoln's family had it exhumed in 1901 and reinterred in concrete several feet thick.

Lincoln was 1.9 metres (6 feet 4 inches) – the tallest US president ever. His hat size was seven-and-one-eighth, and his shoes were size 14.

When Lincoln, Illinois, was named in 1853, Lincoln said, 'Nothing named Lincoln ever amounted to much.'

Lincoln's celebrated Gettysburg Address was dismissed by the *Chicago Times* as 'silly, flat and dishwatery utterances'.

Challenged to a duel by a political opponent in 1842, Lincoln chose 'cavalry broadswords of the largest size' as the weapon. His opponent backed out when he saw the length of Lincoln's reach.

♀ *DARWIN, TREES, UNITED STATES*

LINDBERGH, Charles Augustus (1902–74)

When Charles Lindbergh made the first solo, non-stop flight across the Atlantic in 1927, he took with him five sandwiches, two canteens of water and 451 gallons of petrol as well as some maps. He took only a single bite from the sandwiches.

The flight won Lindbergh the Orteig Prize of $25,000, which had been offered by New York hotel owner Raymond Orteig for the first person to fly non-stop from New York to Paris or vice versa.

In 2002, Lindbergh's grandson Erik Lindbergh commemorated the 75th anniversary of the flight by making the same solo trip himself. He brought six sandwiches along for the journey and ate one and a half. 'I did it in half the time and ate twice as much,' he commented.

LINNAEUS, Carolus (1707–78)

Not only did the great Swedish botanist Carl Linnaeus arouse some scandal by writing about the sexual reproduction of plants, but he was the man who coined the term 'mammals', named after the mammary gland, for animals that nurse their young, and he also caused some scandal with a wedding portrait in which his shirt was unbuttoned, exposing some stomach flesh.

♀ *CHOCOLATE, LEMUR, WORM*

LION

The average weight of a lion is 180 kilograms for males and 130 kilograms for females.

A lion's roar can be heard 8 kilometres (5 miles) away.

There are about 20,000 lions in the wild in the world; a century ago there were 10 times as many.

Experiments in 2002 (as detailed in P.M. West and C. Packer's 'Sexual Selection, Temperature and the Lion's Mane' in *Science*, vol. 297) showed that lionesses prefer their men to be dark and hairy. Researchers at Serengeti National Park in Tanzania built four model male lions with clip-on manes made with tawny and dark brown hair, fashioned in clipped or bouffant style. Analysing the reaction of females to these dummies and taking infra-red measurements of their body temperature, the researchers were able to conclude that females prefer dark, hairy males.

According to a report in the *National Geographic*, in 1982 a pair of lions were observed to copulate 23 times in 5 hours 20 minutes. The lioness instigated all but one of the encounters.

The muzzle of a lion is like a fingerprint – no two lions have the same pattern of whiskers.

♀ *BIBLE, DANDELION, DAVIDSON, MADAGASCAR, PREGNANCY, ZEBRA*

LITERACY

It is estimated that one in five of the world's adults lacks minimum literacy skills.

UNESCO awards an annual King Sejong Literacy Prize, initiated by the government of South Korea and named after the 15th-century King Sejong the Great who created the Korean alphabet.

LITERATURE

Between 1912 and 1948, medals were awarded at the Olympic Games for Literature, and for Architecture, Music, Painting and Sculpture. Between 1928 and 1948, another of the events for which medals were awarded was Town Planning.

In 1928, there were even separate events and medals for Dramatic, Epic and Lyric Literature.

The winner of the gold medal for Literature in 1912 was Baron Pierre de Coubertin, who also happened to be the founder and president of the International Olympic Federation. He entered under the pseudonyms Georges Hohrod and Martin Eschbach. His winning entry was a poem entitled 'Ode to Sport'.

 BOOKS, KIPLING, NOBEL PRIZE

LITHUANIA

11 March is a national holiday in Lithuania, marking the day in 1990 when they regained their independence from the Soviet Union. Lithuania was the first country to break away when the USSR began to collapse.

Of all languages spoken today, Lithuanian is the closest to ancient Sanskrit.

The national sport of Lithuania is basketball. The Lithuanian women's basketball team won the European Championships in 1997.

Lithuania has been an EU member since 2004. After Lithuania joined the EU, its president, Dalia Grybauskaite, became an EU Commissioner. She was named Commissioner of the Year in a Europeans of the Year poll in 2005.

People of 154 nationalities live in Lithuania.

The 13th-century King Mindaugas was the only king Lithuania has ever had. For most of the Middle Ages its ruler was a Grand Duke.

Lithuania is the only country in the world with its own official scent, called, appropriately enough, the 'Scent of Lithuania'.

There are more hot-air balloons per head of population in Lithuania than in any other country.

The former British Foreign Secretary Sir Malcolm Rifkind is one of 15 British holders of the Order of the Lithuanian Grand Duke Gediminas.

 BASKETBALL, WIFE-CARRYING

LIVER

In the film *The Silence of the Lambs*, Hannibal Lecter spoke of eating a census-taker's liver 'with fava beans and a nice Chianti'. In Thomas Harris's novel on which the film is based, however, he drank not Chianti with the census-taker's liver but Amarone, which goes far better with liver.

The philosopher Pythagoras, active in the 6th century BC, would not let his followers eat fava beans: he believed they contained the souls of the dead.

A human liver weighs about 1.4 kilograms (3 pounds) and is the body's second largest organ after the skin.

 BEAVER, CAMEL URINE, CARROT, GOOSE, POLAR BEAR

LIVERPOOL

In 2003, Liverpool Council banned stallholders at fairs from giving goldfish as prizes.

The 'liver' in 'Liverpool' comes from the old English word 'lifer', meaning thick or muddy water.

 CAT, TUG OF WAR

LLAMA

There are about 7 million llamas in South America. They each have 32 teeth and can carry over a quarter of their body weight for several miles.

The Swiss footballer Alexander Frei sponsored a llama in Basel Zoo as an apology for spitting during Euro 2004. After Frei was found guilty of spitting at England midfielder Steven Gerrard, Swiss media branded him a 'llama', as it is an animal known for spitting. 'I have taken over sponsorship of a llama in Basel Zoo so that in future llamas do not spit,' Frei said.

♀ ALPACA, CAMEL, JACKSON Michael

LLOYD GEORGE, David (1863–1945)

Lloyd George was the first prime minister to have a bathroom during the whole of his residence at 10 Downing Street. It had been introduced by the wife of his predecessor Margot Asquith, though Disraeli (PM 1868 and 1874–1880) had had a bath with hot and cold water installed in the First Lord's Dressing Room for the sum of £150.3s.6d.

Disraeli described 10 Downing Street as 'dingy and decaying'; Lloyd George's wife Margaret found it 'cold and inhospitable'.

LOBSTER

A lobster that has lost one claw or has any missing appendage is called a cull. One that has lost two claws is called a bullet, dummy or log.

Lobsters urinate most when other lobsters behave aggressively towards them. After two lobsters have had a fight, they will recognise each other on any later encounter by the smell of each other's urine, and the loser of the original fight will back off.

♀ TALIBAN

LOCH NESS

The first sighting of the Loch Ness Monster is supposed to have been on 22 August 564 by St Columba. According to legend, he ordered the creature not to attack one of his followers.

In 2005, organisers of a major Triathlon competition in Scotland took out insurance for all contestants in case any were bitten by the Loch Ness Monster. 'With so many top athletes in the water of Loch Ness at one time, we couldn't take the risk of one of them being attacked by Nessie,' a spokesman said, explaining that a monster bite would be worth £1m. The event passed without incident.

♀ SCOTLAND

LONDON

The first escalator on the London Underground was installed at Earl's Court station in 1911. Initially, several members of the public were afraid of the new moving staircases, so the authorities are said to have employed a one-legged man known as William 'Bumper' Harris to ride up and down all day to show how easy they were to use. This was not a total success because some people became concerned that the escalator had been the cause of his losing his leg in the first place. Harris subsequently retired to Gloucester to make cider and violins.

There is considerable doubt, however, about whether this really happened. No reference has been found to any such one-legged man in contemporary newspaper accounts of the first escalator, though the escalator itself was much written about. According to one account, during the escalator's first week, nine dresses were torn, one finger pinched, and a lame passenger had fallen from his crutches. The addition of a guard rail eliminated further accidents over the next few weeks.

'I naturally gravitated to London, that great cesspool into which all the loungers and idlers of the Empire are irresistibly drained.' Arthur Conan Doyle, A Study in Scarlet, *1887*

♀ *HIPPOPOTAMUS, TAXI, TOWER OF LONDON, UMBRELLA, UNDERGROUND*

LONDON 2012

To prepare and build the Olympic Park in Stratford, East London, for the 2012 Games: 1.5 million cubic metres of soil had to be cleaned of oil, tar, arsenic and lead; 30,000 tonnes of silt, gravel and rubble had to be removed from the site; 16,000 beds, 22,000 duvets and 22,000 pillows had to be brought to the site; 4,000 trees were planted (as well as 350,000 wetland plants, 74,000 other plants and 60,000 bulbs); 2,000 newts had to be relocated; 220 buildings were demolished; and 160 cats and kittens were rescued from the site.

♀ *AFGHANISTAN, MONTENEGRO*

LONGEVITY

In 1999, the Health Ministry in Thailand announced that anyone wanting to live past 100 should brush their teeth and bathe twice a day, keep their homes tidy and clothes clean, eat three proper meals a day, take 30 minutes exercise three times a week, drink six to eight glasses of water a day, and have six to eight hours' rest. These 'secrets of longevity' were based on a study of 156 Thai centenarians.

♀ *COW, CRUSTACEAN*

LONGFELLOW, Henry Wadsworth (1807–82)

The Longfellow family from which the poet was descended came to America from Yorkshire in 1676. Longfellow's daughter Fanny was the first child in America to be delivered with the aid of anaesthetics.

Longfellow's bushy beard was the result of injuries to his face in a fire which made it too painful for him to shave. The fire, in which his wife died, was started by wax drippings used to seal locks of hair in envelopes.

Longfellow's first known work is a letter to his father asking for a toy drum and a bible for his sister.

'It takes less time to do a thing right than explain why you did it wrong.' Longfellow

♀ *LAVATORIES*

LOS ANGELES

In the 1850 census, the population of Los Angeles was 1,610. Oil was discovered in Los Angeles in 1891. By 1923, the area produced one-quarter of the world's oil, and by 2000, the population had grown to 3,694,820.

Los Angeles is home to people from more than 140 countries speaking 224 different languages.

According to the American Lung Association, Los Angeles is the most polluted city in the USA. The Chumash Indians called the region by a name that translates as 'valley of smoke'.

The original name of Los Angeles in 1781 was 'El Pueblo de Nuestra Señora Reina de los Ángeles sobre el Río Porciúncula' ('The Town of Our Lady Queen of the Angels on the Porciuncula River').

Public nudity, including naked sunbathing in a public park, is illegal in Los Angeles.

♀ *BASEBALL, BEDS, CARS, FRANCE, PROSTITUTION, ROBBERY*

LOTTERIES

On 11 January 1569, the winning numbers were drawn in Britain's first National Lottery. The price of a ticket was 10 shillings, which had the same purchasing power as £134 in today's money. The top prize was £5,000, which is well over £1 million at today's prices. Queen Elizabeth I had sanctioned the lottery as a way to raise money for the 'reparation of the havens [harbours] and strength of the Realme, and towardes such other publique good workes'.

In 1808, after investigating lotteries, a state commission in Britain ruled that 'Under no conditions can a lottery divest itself of evils and become a source of revenue'. Eighteen years later, parliament ruled that lotteries must end for ever. This decision was abided by until 1994.

According to a study in 2012 by UK National Lottery operator Camelot, about half the jackpot winners in the lottery move house within three months of their win. Apart from that, the Top 10 items purchased by lottery winners are as follows: 1. Someone to clean their house; 2. A hot tub; 3. A walk-in wardrobe; 4. Electric gates; 5. A games room; 6. A dog; 7. A snooker table; 8. A gym in the house; 9. A bar at home; 10. A cat.

'A lottery is a taxation, Upon all the fools in Creation.' Henry Fielding, 1732

♀ *HELL, MALAYSIA, PANAMA, RAT, SKIING, THIRTEEN*

LOUIS XIV, King of France (1638–1715)

The Sun King, Louis XIV, was born with two teeth. He permitted only his hairdresser to see him without his wig on.

He became king when still only four years old, but his mother acted as regent until 1661 when Louis began his personal reign. He was king for 72 years and outlived his son and grandsons.

Louis XIV was great-grandfather of Louis XV, who succeeded him, great-great-great-grandfather of Louis XVI, and great-great-great-great-grandfather of Louis XVII.

King Louis XIV only took three baths in his life but owned 413 beds and changed his linen three times a day.

♀ *BUCKLAND, LIECHTENSTEIN, SHOES, TABLE MANNERS, TEETH*

LOVE

According to the organisers of the First International Conference on Love and Attraction in Cardiff in 1990, love is 'the cognitive-affective state characterised by intrusive and obsessive fantasising concerning reciprocity of amorant feeling by the object of the amorance'.

In 1999, however, brain scanning techniques revealed that the sites in the brain that are most active when a person falls in love are generally much the same as those stimulated by cocaine. Italian scientists meanwhile reached the conclusion that love is a form of obsessive-compulsive behaviour.

According to a recent survey, when a man says 'I love you', the odds are four to one he's just saying it to get the person he's speaking to into bed.

The average British male learned about sex at school, lost his virginity just before he was 18, makes love 105 times a year, marries for the first time when he is 25.1 to a woman 2.3 years younger than himself and divorces at 31.5.

'Love, n: A temporary insanity curable by marriage.' Ambrose Bierce, The Devil's Dictionary, *1906*

ꝋ *BOWERBIRD, DRAMA, EUROPE, OBEDIENCE, ST VALENTINE*

LOVE OBSTACLES

'Obstacles to Love' is number 28 of the 36 Dramatic Situations identified by the French writer Georges Polti. For this situation to occur, he very reasonably identifies the elements it requires to be two lovers and an obstacle. He lists the following five variants:

- A: Inequality, which may be A1: Marriage prevented by inequality of rank; or A2: Inequality of fortune an impediment to marriage
- B: Marriage prevented by enemies and contingent obstacles
- C: Forbidden marriage, which may be C1: Marriage forbidden on account of the young woman's previous betrothal to another; or C2: Marriage forbidden on account of the young woman's previous betrothal to another, complicated by an imaginary marriage of the beloved object
- D: Family objections, which may be D1: Free union impeded by the opposition of relatives; or D2: Family affection disturbed by the parents-in-law
- E: Free union impeded by the incompatibility of temper of the lovers.

LOYALTY

According to a survey carried out by Santander in 2010, the average person in the UK says their longest relationship has lasted for 14.1 years, but they have stayed loyal to the bank that holds their current account for around 16.5 years.

ꝋ *DAVIDSON, LAMPREY*

LUCK

According to an old recipe found at the Musée de la Sorcellerie in Blancafort, France, a lucky bracelet to improve your fortune at games of chance can be made as follows:

Ingredients:
  An eel that died for lack of water
  Gall of a bull killed by fierce dogs
  Vulture blood
  A hanged man's rope
  Warm dung
  A fern picked on Midsummer's Eve
  A raven feather
  Your own blood.
Method:
Put the gall into the eel skin with a drachme of vulture blood. Tie the eel skin with hanged man's rope and leave in warm dung for 15 days. Dry in an oven heated with fern, then make a bracelet of it, writing the letters HYTV on it in your own blood using a raven's feather. With this bracelet on your arm, fortune will always smile on you.

In May 2010, the First Lady of Nigeria, Patience Jonathan, was named as the winner of a prize draw for a motorcycle organised by Union Bank for its customers. Patience Jonathan was the wife of President Goodluck Jonathan.

ꝋ *AARDVARK, BEANS, CAT, PEANUT, SOLSTICE, SUPERSTITION, TUESDAY*

LUCRETIUS (c.99–55 BC)

Very little is known about the Roman poet Lucretius except that he wrote a hugely influential work called *De Rerum Naturae* (*On the Nature of Things*).

According to one account, he was driven mad by a love potion and, after writing several books during periods of sanity, killed himself.

⚲ *CENTAUR*

⬤ LUGOSI, Bela (1882–1956)

The actor Bela Lugosi, famed for his roles in horror films and particularly his role as Dracula, was actually named Béla Ferenc Dezsö Blaskó, but took the name of Lugosi after the town of his birth, Lugos, in Austria–Hungary near the Transylvanian border.

⚲ *BURIAL*

⬤ LUNACY

On 11 September 1905, scientists blamed a rise in lunacy in Britain on the tedium of country life. On 17 September 1910, a London doctor warned that, if lunacy continued to increase at the same rate, there would be more insane people than sane by 1950.

⚲ *ASH WEDNESDAY*

⬤ LUNCH

A lunch with billionaire investor Warren Buffett was sold for $2.6 million (£1.76 million) in June 2010, to become the most expensive charity item ever sold on eBay. The winning bidder wanted to remain anonymous.

When the word 'luncheon' first appeared in English in the late 16th century, it meant a thick slice or a lump. It was not until the mid-17th century that it took on the meaning of a meal less substantial than dinner. Curiously, the word 'lunch' was also used in the late 16th century for a hunk or thick piece of anything, particularly bread, cheese or pork, but it also had an earlier meaning in the mid-15th century of the sound made by the fall of a soft, heavy body.

It was not until the 19th century that it began to be used exclusively for a whole meal.

⚲ *ASCOT, IN-FLIGHT CATERING, SANDWICHES*

⬤ LUNG

A school in Belgium in 2007 announced that it was allowing pupils aged over 16 to smoke on the premises, but only if they stood in a cage and wore a badge displaying an X-ray image of tobacco-damaged lungs.

'If this doesn't reduce the number of youngsters taking up the habit, I don't know what will,' a school director commented.

⚲ *ENGLISH, HAGGIS, JAMES I, SNAIL*

⬤ LUTHER, Martin (1483–1546)

The Church reformer and founder of Protestantism, Martin Luther, married a young nun, Katharina von Bora, whom he arranged to be smuggled out of a convent with some of her friends hidden among barrels of herring. He was 41 and she was 25 when they married and they had six children.

He believed that all aspects of life are God-given, so should not be thought of as unholy if not indulged in to excess, so reasoned that the sex drive was a divine force. 'Whoever is ashamed of marriage is ashamed of being human,' he said.

⬤ LUTON

According to a survey in 2010 by the Invertebrate Conservation Trust, Selbourne Road, Luton, is the most spider-rich street in the UK. In the course of their survey, there were 2,295 sightings of 143 species of spider in that street.

'Luton' (short for 'saluton') is a collo-quial way to say 'goodbye' in Esperanto.

LUXEMBOURG

Luxembourg was founded in AD 963 as the County of Luxembourg by Sigefroid, Count of the Ardennes, who built a fort there. The ancient Saxon name for the area was 'Lucilinburhuc', which meant 'little fortress'.

Luxembourg is the world's only Grand Duchy. The current ruler is the Grand Duke Henri. There have been nine grand dukes (including two ruling grand duchesses), of whom four have been called Wilhelm.

♀ FROG

LYCANTHROPY

Clinical lycanthropy is the unusual psychiatric delusion that one may transform into, or already has transformed into an animal, particularly a wolf. Tales of lycanthropy and werewolves date back at least to the seventh century and King James I/ VI in his 1597 *Daemonologie* identifies 'an excess of melancholy as the culprit which causes some men to believe that they are wolves'.

In the 1760s, there was an apparent werewolf epidemic in the South of France when 'The Beasts of Gevaudan' were blamed for well over a hundred killings and the French army was called out to kill the beasts which were described as wolf-like but bigger.

Although being bitten by a werewolf is by far the most common way for people to become werewolves in stories, some say that drinking rainwater from a wolf's footprint can also be responsible for the transition.

LYING

According to a survey by the Chartered Insurance Institute in 2018, the average Briton tells 657 lies a year. According to the Institute, emails are the favourite medium for lying, but social networks and mobile phones have also made it easier.

♀ CURTIS, ITALY

MACAO

Macao was the only region in mainland China ever to be a European colony, having been administered by the Portuguese from 1887 to 1999.

With a population density of 14,428 people per square kilometre, Macao has been described as the most densely populated region in the world. It also has one of the highest life expectancies in the world, currently standing at 84.4 years (81.3 for males and 87.2 for females) according to the World Health Organisation. Only Hong Kong and Japan have slightly higher figures.

MACKEREL

The only station on the London Underground system whose name has no letters in common with the word 'mackerel' is St John's Wood. The only station that has no letter in common with 'hare' is Pimlico. The only two tube stations which have all five vowels in them are Mansion House and South Ealing.

The only American state with no letters in common with the word 'mackerel' is Ohio.

There are no English counties whose names have no letters in common with the word 'mackerel', but Suffolk is the only county with no letters in common with the word 'herring'.

MADAGASCAR

The island of Madagascar is the fourth largest island in the world (excluding Australia), behind Greenland, New Guinea and Borneo.

Geologically speaking, Madagascar split from India some 80 million years ago. Its long isolation from neighbouring continents is responsible for its unique ecology. Of the 10,000 plants native to Madagascar, 90 per cent are found nowhere else in the world. Half of the 238 species of bird recorded on Madagascar have not been seen anywhere else.

The largest carnivorous mammal on Madagascar is the fossa, which has the body of a cat and the nose of a dog, but is most closely related to the mongoose.

The last monarch of Madagascar, Queen Ranavalona III, was deposed on 28 February 1897.

A traditional ritual in Madagascar involves removing relatives' bodies from tombs, rewrapping them, then burying them again.

In the animated film *Madagascar*, Alex the lion has 50,342 hairs in his mane.

Madagascar is the world's largest producer of vanilla.

The only vowel in 'Madagascar' is 'A'. It shares the record for the longest single-vowel name with Kazakhstan and Seychelles.

'If you cross in a crowd, the crocodile won't eat you.' Madagascan proverb

ANTIQUES, CENTRAL AFRICAN REPUBLIC, LEMUR

MADONNA (b. 1958)

Stage name of Madonna Louise Veronica Ciccone. In 1999, the rose-pink Lycra corset with satin conical cups worn by Madonna at a concert in Barcelona in 1990 fetched £12,650 at auction in London. In 2012, the same conical corset sold for £30,000 at another Christie's auction.

MADRID

The Palacio Real in Madrid has 2,800 rooms, which is more than any other palace in Europe.

When robbing a bank in Madrid in 1999, short-sighted Sanchez Fabres, 41, took off his glasses as a disguise. He then tripped over furniture and subsequently surrendered to police.

CHIMPANZEE, MARIJUANA, SYDNEY, VULTURE

MAFIA

In 2008, lawyers for US mafia boss Vincent Basciano asked for the judge in his trial to be replaced as they felt Brooklyn judge Nicholas Garaufis could not give him a fair hearing because Basciano had been accused of plotting to kill him. 'There is a serious question whether Garaufis has personal animosity towards a person who has allegedly sought to kill him,' a lawyer said.

RECESSION

MAINE

Maine is the only state in America whose name has only one syllable.

The town of Strong in Maine was once the toothpick capital of the world after the first wooden toothpick factory was set up there in the late 19th century. At one point they were making 75 billion toothpicks a year, including 95 per cent of America's toothpicks.

CHEWING GUM, DOUGHNUTS, MOOSE, OKLAHOMA, UMBRELLA

MALARIA

According to the World Health Organisation, there were an estimated 241 million cases of malaria worldwide in 2020 and about 627,000 deaths.

In the First World War, more soldiers died from malaria than were killed by weapons.

BODY ODOUR, BORGIA, GHANA, MEDICINE, PANAMA

MALAYSIA

In 1984 in Malaysia, a 16-year-old boy was beheaded and offered as a human sacrifice by a Chinese medium looking for the lucky number in a weekly lottery. The medium and three other men were arrested. Whether they were successful in the lottery is not known.

On 26 August 1997, a model of the Malaysian flag was exhibited, made out of 10,430 floppy disks. The country's deputy education minister said this was 'an event Malaysia can be proud of'.

In 2008, illegal betting syndicates in Malaysia announced that they were not taking any more bets on 1301 in a numbers game. That was the number of the room in which a former health minister was alleged to have been taped engaging in sexual acts with an unidentified woman. 'The last time we accepted bets after a particular set of numbers was published on the front page of a Chinese daily, we were badly hit and lost several million ringgit,' an unidentified bookie was quoted as saying.

CINEMA, CONDOM, POLYGAMY, SCRABBLE, SNAKE, VIRGINITY

MALDIVES

Until 2005, there were no political parties in the Maldives. In that year, the Maldivian parliament voted unanimously for the creation of a multi-party system to replace a system based on the election of individuals, rather than according to their party.

DIVORCE, INCOME TAX

MALI

In Mali there is one television set per 2,500 people, which is roughly 2,030 sets fewer than the average 2,500 Americans have.

NIGERIA

MAMMOTH

The record price achieved by a woolly mammoth skeleton at auction is €548,250 (£470,000), fetched by an example from Siberia at the Aguttes auction house in Lyon in December 2017.

ALCOHOL, DRAGONFLY

MANCHESTER

Central Manchester has been inhabited since at least AD 79 when the Romans built the fort Mamucium in the region.

On average, more than 1mm of rain falls in Manchester on 143 days a year.

Manchester University claims to be the world's only place to offer a degree in Mummy Studies.

BRUMMELL, CARROT, NEWTON, PANCAKE, PENALTY, TRANSPORT

MANCHESTER UNITED

Manchester United began life as the Newton Heath Lancashire and Yorkshire Railway Football Club. Its named was changed in 1902.

In a case in Leamington Spa in 1997, a woman cited her husband's 'obsession with football and Manchester United' as grounds for divorce. The husband said, 'I have to admit that nine times out of ten I would rather watch the Reds than have sex, but that's no disrespect to Emma.'

A case of 'Manchester United-induced Addisonian crisis' was reported in the *British Medical Journal* in 2011 as the first of its kind. Addisonian crisis happens when the adrenal glands do not produce enough stress-reducing cortisol, which can lead to a drop in blood pressure. The patient, a 58-year-old woman, was a Manchester United supporter who was reported to be 'having difficulty mounting an appropriate physiological cortisol response during the big games'. Symptoms included bouts of anxiety, palpitations, panic, light headedness, and a sense of impending doom towards the end of matches, but were said to be less serious when United was playing a lower-rated team at home. Treatment began at the start of the 2011/12 football season and the patient was reported to have attended all games at Old Trafford without adverse effects.

FA CUP

● MANDELA, Nelson (1918–2013)

Mandela's birth name was Rolihlahla, one meaning of which is 'troublemaker'. The name 'Nelson' was given to him by his teacher on his first day of elementary school.

In 2012, a prehistoric woodpecker was named after Mandela, *Australopicus Nelsonmandelai*. He has also had a species of spider, an American rescue dog, a tree, several sub-groups of flower, a nuclear particle and many racehorses named after him.

Mandela was voted 'Santa Claus of the Year' in December 1995 – the first recipient of that title awarded by the Santa Claus Foundation of Greenland.

'Nelson Mandela' is an anagram of 'Lean and solemn'.

ARACHNOLOGY, GIRAFFE

● MANGELWURZEL

The mangold, or mangelwurzel, is a vegetable related to the beetroot, mainly used as cattle food.

An annual Mangold Hurl is held in the village of Sherston, Wiltshire, under the auspices of the Mangold Hurling Association. The Mangold Hurl is conducted in similar way to the game of boules or lawn bowls, but with vegetables instead of balls, the object being to throw one's mangelwurzel so that it lands closest to a large leafless one. The large leafless mangold is called a 'Norman'.

The 2012 Mangold Hurl had to be called off because the organisers were unable to locate any mangelwurzels.

● MANGO

There are more than 400 varieties of mango.

According to the *Oxford English Dictionary*, besides being a fruit, 'mango' is also an obsolete and rare word for a dealer in slaves, especially prostitutes. It is also an old word in Ireland for a substance used in the bleaching of linen. The *Oxford English Dictionary* also lists the verb 'to mango', meaning to pickle, in the manner in which mangoes are pickled.

Ancient Sanskrit poets believed that chewing on mango buds helped to sweeten the voice.

The average length of a mango fruit is 13 centimetres (5 inches). Officially it is a drupe – a fleshy fruit growing around a long, flat seed, encased in a thick skin.

In 2020, India produced 24.7 million tonnes of mangoes, about 45 per cent of the world's total.

● MANILOW, Barry (b. 1943)

The singer Barry Manilow was born Barry Alan Pincus.

On 14 August 1995, the Independent Television Commission in Britain responded to a viewer's complaint as follows: 'One viewer who complained about a man wearing an artificial penis on his nose on *The Big Breakfast* was informed that this was not the case and the man was in fact doing an impression of Barry Manilow.'

● MANNEQUIN

In 2009, Iranian police warned shop-keepers not to use mannequins without headscarves or which exposed body curves. 'Using unusual mannequins exposing the body curves and with the heads without Hijabs (Muslim veil) are prohibited to be used in the shops,' the country's moral security police in charge of Islamic dress codes said in a statement.

MANSFIELD, Jayne (1933–67)

While at the University of Texas, the future sex symbol Jayne Mansfield won many beauty titles, including 'Miss Photoflash', 'Miss Magnesium Lamp' and 'Miss Fire Prevention Week'. She turned down the title of 'Miss Roquefort Cheese', because it 'just didn't sound right'.

֍ *HOT DOGS*

MAPS

The great Flemish map-maker Gerardus Mercator designed the 'Mercator Projection' in 1569, which has been the standard way of depicting the globe in maps ever since. Mercator's original surname was Kremer, which is the German for merchant. He changed it to Mercator, the Latin for merchant, when he went to university.

The Map Library of the British Library includes over 4.25 million atlases, maps, globes and books on cartography, from the 15th century to the present day. The oldest known maps were carved on Babylonian clay tablets and may date back to 3,500 BC.

On hearing of Napoleon's victory at Austerlitz in 1805, William Pitt the Younger said: 'Roll up that map [of Europe]; it will not be wanted these ten years.' It was an accurate prediction: Napoleon was finally defeated ten years later, at Waterloo in 1815.

In 1852, it was conjectured by mathematicians that four different colours are enough to colour any map, with adjacent countries never sharing the same colour. This 'four-colour theorem' was finally proved in 1976.

'The art of Biography is different from Geography: Geography is about Maps but Biography is about Chaps.' Edmund Clerihew Bentley

֍ *JIGSAW, LINDBERGH, WISCONSIN*

MARADONA, Diego Armando (1960–2020)

Before Diego Maradona went to South Africa as manager of the Argentine side in the 2010 World Cup, it was reported that the Argentine Football Association had sent a request for the bathroom at his accommodation to be fitted with new wash basins, toilet bowls, cisterns, taps and E-Bidet luxury heated toilet seats. 'They felt that the basins and toilet bowls were not up to Maradona's standards,' an organiser said. The E-Bidet, with heated seat, a warm air blow-dryer and front and rear bidet wands, is billed as 'the world's best toilet seat and electronic bidet'.

MARATHON

Abebe Bikila of Ethiopia is the only man to have won Olympic marathons both barefoot (in 1960) and in running shoes (in 1964).

A Greek runner who finished third in the first modern Olympic marathon in 1896 was disqualified for covering part of the distance in a horse-pulled vehicle.

The slowest London marathon was run – or rather walked – by Lloyd Scott in 2002, who completed the course in 5 days, 8 hours 29 minutes and 46 seconds in an antique deep-sea diving suit weighing 54 kilograms (120 pounds). Shortly afterwards, he completed the New York marathon in an even slower time.

The record for by far the slowest marathon, however, is held by the Japanese runner Shizo Kanakuri. In 1912, he was among the favourites to win the marathon at the Stockholm Olympics, but owing to the immense heat, he collapsed 27 kilometres (16.7 miles) into the race. He did not report his failure to finish to race officials and was consequently officially listed as missing. After 50 years, the Swedish authorities discovered he was alive and well and in 1967 invited him back to finish the race. Aged 75, Shizo crossed the finishing line more than 54 years after he started the race. Afterwards, he said: 'It was a long trip. Along the way, I got married, had six children and ten grandchildren.'

The world record for running a marathon backwards is 3 hours 43 minutes 39 seconds set by Xu Zhenjun of China in 2004.

⚲ *CARROT, SNAIL, TOWER BRIDGE, TURING*

● MARCH

March was the first month of the year in the ancient Roman calendar. January and February were thought too bleak to deserve names at all.

March was named Martius by the Romans after Mars, their god of war, as March was the start of the military campaigning season.

1 March is not only St David's Day but is also the Independence Day of Bosnia–Herzegovina.

The saying 'mad as a March hare' refers to the behaviour of hares in their March mating season.

The town of March in Cambridgeshire took its name from the marshes surrounding it before the fens were drained from the 17th century onwards. A traditional walk by Cambridge students takes place this month each year from March back to the university. It is known as the March March march.

March is the only month with three consecutive consonants in its name in English.

In Old English, March was called 'Hlyda', or 'Lide', meaning 'loud', referring to the loud March winds.

The actor Fredric March won two Best Actor Oscars, in 1932 and 1946. Born Frederick Bickel, he changed his name in a 1924 New Year's greeting to agents: 'This is 1924, I won't be Bickel any more, Fredric March is now my name, Wishing everyone the same, Happy New Year.'

'It was one of those March days when the sun shines hot and the wind blows cold.'
Charles Dickens, Great Expectations, *1861*

⚲ *FEBRUARY, IDES OF MARCH, SMOKING*

● MARCO POLO (1254–1324)

Marco Polo is the only person in history to have had an airport, a species of sheep, several ships, many hotels, a cycling team and a brand of tea all named after him.

The Polo mint, however, is not named after him but was given its name as the connection with the word 'polar' was thought to emphasise the crisp coolness of the mint. Around the world, 147 Polo mints are eaten every second.

⚲ *TOURISM*

● MARIE ANTOINETTE (1755–93)

Marie Antoinette married Louis-Auguste, Dauphin of France (who later became Louis XVI), when she was 14 and he was 15. The marriage was not consummated for another seven years.

⚲ *HANDKERCHIEF, POTATO, WHISTLING*

● MARIJUANA

When the first Madrid Marijuana Cup competition for cannabis growers was held in Spain in 1997, it attracted 51 entrants. One of the organisers was arrested and one woman passed out from the fumes and had to be helped out of the building.

Barcelona also holds an annual Cannabis Cup competition for cannabis growers. It takes place during a cannabis fair known as 'Spannabis'.

Marijuana was prescribed by the Chinese as a remedy for gout, rheumatism, malaria, beri-beri and forgetfulness.

Ŷ *TARANTINO*

🔘 MARQUESAS ISLANDS

The Marquesas Islands in French Polynesia are named after the Marquis of Cañete, Spanish Viceroy of Peru. There are only 15 letters and one glottal stop in the alphabet of the Marquesan language, and the only native word for a domestic animal in the language is the word for 'pig'. Goats are called 'pigs with teeth on their heads'.

The islands have a traditional pig-hunting dance and a massive weekly traditional pig roast known as Umu.

🔘 MARRIAGE

Research in the USA has shown that more than 10,000 marriages a year now begin with romances started during coffee breaks. Research has also shown that bachelors are three times more likely to go mad than married men.

Wedding rings are worn on the third finger of the left hand because the Romans believed that a nerve led directly from there to the heart. Senators in ancient Rome were forbidden to marry the daughter of an actor or actress.

The Priestess of Demeter was the only married woman allowed to watch the ancient Olympic Games. Any other married woman spectator was liable to be sentenced to death by being thrown from a cliff.

Around 1930, research on men born in England and Finland showed that for every extra kilogram they weighed at birth, they were 1.42 times more likely to marry. Every extra centimetre in length at birth increased the chance of walking down the aisle by a factor of 1.13. Even after social factors such as class and income were taken into account, shorter, lighter, thinner men were still significantly less likely to marry. That finding was confirmed in 2001 when figures published in the *British Medical Journal* showed that, even in old age, men who had stayed bachelors were 2.1 centimetres shorter than their married peers.

'There is not one in a hundred of either sex who is not taken in when they marry.'
Jane Austen, Mansfield Park, *1814*

Ŷ *CELIBACY, DARWIN, DIVORCE, FRANKLIN, LEPROSY, LOVE*

🔘 MARS

The red appearance of the planet Mars is caused by oxidised iron – basically, rust on its surface. The ancient Egyptians were the first to name it after its colour, as Har Decher, the Red One. The Assyrians called it the Shredder of Blood. The Greeks called it Ares and the Romans called it Mars – in both cases named after their gods of war.

The two moons of Mars were discovered by American astronomer Asaph Hall in 1877. Their names were suggested by Henry Madan, a science master at Eton, who called them Phobos (fear) and Deimos (panic), after the sons of Ares and Aphrodite that drove the chariot of Ares into war. Phobos is bigger than Deimos and closer to Mars, and it makes about four orbits for every one made by Deimos.

The association of Mars with men and Venus with women dates back at least to the 14th century. In Chaucer's *Canterbury Tales*, the Wife of Bath says (in modern English):

truly, I am all Venusian
In feeling, and my brain is Martian
Venus gave me my lust, my lickerishness,
And Mars gave me my sturdy hardiness.

Belief in intelligent life on Mars was started by a mistaken claim in 1877 by Italian astronomer Giovanni Schiaparelli that he had discovered canals on its surface.

The average temperature on Mars is -63°C (-81°F). A day on Mars lasts 24 hours 37 minutes – almost the same as an Earth day – but a year is 686.7 Earth days. Mars has the biggest volcano in the Solar System, Olympus Mons – large enough to cover Spain and three times the height of Everest.

If you weigh 68 kilograms (150 pounds) on Earth, you will weigh 26 kilograms (57 pounds) on Mars.

In a controlled experiment performed by psychologists in Cambridge in 1982, only one rat out of eight preferred a Mars Bar to Cheddar cheese.

Economists have used the 'Mars Bar Standard' to compare prices in terms of the number of Mars Bars something costs. A Rolls-Royce Silver Spirit was calculated in 2006 to cost 347,000 Mars bars. A more recent example calculated the price of Tolkien's *Lord of the Rings* when it was first published as equal to 151 Mars Bars, but in 2020 you could buy it for 42 Mars Bars, though the paper and binding of the early edition was superior.

♀ *NEPTUNE, STOMACH, SYPHILIS, TUESDAY*

MARSHMALLOW

The furthest a marshmallow has been blown out of one nostril and caught in the mouth of a catcher is 4.96 metres. Scott Jeckel of Illinois launched a marshmallow into the mouth of Ray Perisin on the set of American Guinness World Records on 13 August 1999. On catching the marshmallow, Perisin ate it.

♀ *CUSTARD PIES, PILLOW*

MARSTON, William Moulton (1893–1947)

William Moulton Marston is mainly remembered for his achievements in two apparently very different fields: he was the inventor of the polygraph lie detector, and he was also the creator of the first superheroine, Wonder Woman. What linked the two was his strong concern for truth and justice.

Marston's enthusiasm for the polygraph even led to his appearing in a 1938 Gillette razor blade advertisement that used a lie detector test to reveal men's 'true' feelings about various shaving methods. (The tests, incidentally, overwhelmingly confirmed that Gillette blades minimised the emotional disturbances caused by rival products.)

In 1941, under the pseudonym Charles Moulton, Marston created Wonder Woman. Unlike most academics, he encouraged parents to let their children read comics. 'It's too bad for us "literary" enthusiasts, but it's the truth nevertheless,' he said, 'pictures tell any story more effectively than words. If children will read comics, why isn't it advisable to give them some constructive comics to read?' In his own words, Wonder Woman was a 'distinctly feminist role model whose mission was to bring the Amazon ideals of love, peace, and sexual equality to a world torn by the hatred of men'.

MARY I, Queen of England (1516–58)

Mary I was the daughter of Henry VIII and his first wife, Catherine of Aragon. She was the first queen to rule England in her own right (excluding the disputed short reign of Lady Jane Grey). She was called Bloody Mary after having more than 280 Protestant dissenters burnt at the stake. Vodka and tomato juice was first called a Bloody Mary in 1939.

By the age of four and a half, Mary could play the virginals (similar to a harpsichord). By the age of nine, she could read and write Latin. When she married Prince Philip of Spain, he spoke Spanish while Mary replied in French.

Before becoming Queen, she liked spending her money on clothes and gambling at card games. In 1540, she made a bet on a game of bowls. Having no money on her, she wagered the next day's breakfast. She lost the game and the bet.

During Jane Seymour's pregnancy with the future Edward VI, Mary sent her cucumbers from her garden to satisfy Jane's pregnancy cravings. Her personal motto was *veritas temporis filia* ('Truth, the daughter of time').

One charge leading to Thomas Cromwell's beheading was that he had planned to marry Mary.

MARY, QUEEN OF SCOTS (1542–87)

Mary, Queen of Scots used to test her food for poison with a device said to be a piece of unicorn's horn.

The night before her execution, she wrote a letter to King Henri III of France, which she sealed with an intricate letterlocking system that involves folding the letter so that it forms its own envelope, then snipping a thread from the paper which remains attached to the rest of the letter but is threaded in a spiral through holes cut in the letter itself. This was a popular method from the 13th to 17th centuries to prevent letters being opened and read, which could not be done without destroying the snipped thread, which would make it obvious that it had been read by someone else when it reached the intended recipient. The details of Queen Mary's intricate letterlocking design were only revealed by computer tomography in 2021.

When she was beheaded at Fotheringay Castle in 1587, it took the executioner three blows of the axe (or two blows and one small cut according to some reports) to sever the head completely. She left an embroidered bedcover to her son, James I.

FIFTEEN, GUILLOTINE

MARY ROSE

The only female serving on Henry VIII's flagship the *Mary Rose*, which sank in 1545, was a dog named Hatch. The skeleton of the two-year-old dog was found near the sliding hatch door of the ship's carpenter's cabin. The dog is thought to have been on the ship as a ratter. The skeleton was displayed for the first time at Crufts Dog Show in 2010.

MATCH-MAKING

The National Human Rights Commission in South Korea upheld a complaint in 2010 against two match-making agencies by a man who had been refused membership because he was considered too short. 'The commission finds it an unreasonable act of discrimination for match-making agencies to reject male applicants because of their short height and urges their corrective action', it said in a statement, explaining that such discrimination amounted to a 'breach of human dignity'.

The complainant was 5 feet 2 inches tall and the agencies had refused membership to men shorter than 165 centimetres (5 feet 5 inches) on the grounds that brides prefer taller men.

MATHEMATICS

The record for most maths questions answered correctly in 48 hours is 182,455,169, set during World Maths Day in 2008. It was accomplished by about a million students at 20,000 schools in 150 countries.

According to the *Oxford English Dictionary*, the Americans called mathematics 'math' long before the British started calling it 'maths'. The US linguistic argument is that 'mathematics' is not a plural noun: we say 'mathematics is (not are) my favourite subject', so math should be singular, too.

The word 'mathematics' occurs three times in *The Taming of the Shrew*, which is the only Shakespeare play to use the word.

The last year that was a perfect square was 1936 (44×44). The next square year will be 2025 (45×45). The last year that was a perfect cube was 1728 (12×12×12); the next one will be 2197 (13×13×13).

⚑ *FORTY-SEVEN, GALILEI, ICELAND*

MATISSE, Henri (1869–1954)

The painter Matisse had three cats named Cousi, Minouche and La Puce, which he fed every morning with brioche bread.

When confined to bed in hospital in his later years, Matisse invented an art form called 'painting with scissors' in which he used scissors to cut shapes from paper which he then stuck in a collage on the wall, placing them with his walking stick.

On 3 December 1961, Henri Matisse's painting *Le Bateau* was finally put the right way up at New York's Museum of Modern Art after it had been hanging upside down for 46 days apparently without anyone noticing.

MAURITANIA

In 1981, Mauritania became the last country in Africa to officially abolish slavery. However, between 10 and 20 per cent of its population are still believed to live in slavery.

⚑ *BLUE*

MAY

The Romans named the month of May after Maia, a goddess of growth. She should not be confused (though even the Romans often did) with the Greek goddess Maia, the mother of Hermes.

In Old English, before we adopted a version of the Roman name, the month of May was called Thrimilce (three milks) – the season when you could milk cows three times between sunrise and evening. The Emperor Charlemagne, however, called May 'wunnimanoth' or 'joy-month'.

The priests of Vulcan in ancient Rome used to sacrifice a pregnant sow on 1 May. However, the Romans thought it unlucky to get married in May. According to the poet Ovid: 'Bad girls wed in May.'

According to old Cornish superstition, it is unlucky to buy a broom during the month of May, while according to a Greek superstition, May is an unlucky month altogether, especially if it begins on a Saturday.

Anthony Trollope wisely advised: 'Let no man boast himself that he has got through the perils of winter till at least the seventh of May.'

The proverbial saying 'Cast ne'er a clout till May be out' has nothing to do with clouts and may have little to do with the month of May. The first half means 'Don't give up your winter clothes', while it has been suggested that the closing words refer not to the end of the month of May but to the appearance of blossom on the hawthorn, or may-tree.

⚲ *MAYDAY, MAYFAIR, MAYPOLE*

● MAYDAY

According to superstition, washing your face in Mayday dew can restore faded or lost beauty.

'Mayday' was adopted as an international distress signal in 1923, replacing 'S.O.S.' owing to the difficulty in distinguishing the letter 'S' by telephone. The words 'may' and 'day' were chosen as the phonetic equivalent of the French *m'aidez*, meaning 'help me'.

● MAYFAIR

The area of London known as Mayfair is named after the May Fair that took place there every year from 1686 until 1764. It then moved to Bow in the East End of London because residents of Mayfair thought the fair lowered the tone of the neighbourhood.

⚲ *ELIZABETH II*

● MAYPOLE

In 1644, maypoles were banned by Parliament in England as a 'heathenish vanity'. Local officials who defiantly put them up could be fined 5 shillings a week.

A maypole 37.5 metres (123 feet) tall was put up in the Strand in London in 1661 to celebrate the return of Charles II. It was later bought by Isaac Newton as a telescope support.

● MAZE

The science journal *Nature* in 2000 reported that a slime mould has the ability to solve a simple maze. The amoeba-like mould *Physarum polycephalum* changes shape as it crawls over a gel, and if food is placed at different points it puts out pseudopodia to connect to the food sources. The experiment showed that the organism had the ability to find minimum-length solutions for the path to the food.

● MCDONALD'S

The only European countries without a branch of McDonald's are Albania, Armenia, Vatican City and Iceland, though Iceland had one until it closed for economic reasons in 2009.

⚲ *CHIPS, HAMBURGER, LIFETIME, MOSCOW, PYTHON*

● McENROE, John (b. 1959)

The former tennis champion John McEnroe owns an art gallery in Manhattan. In 2009, he was praised for his role in the arrest of alleged art fraudster Lawrence Salander, who was accused of scamming McEnroe out of $2 million.

Another of Salander's victims, to the tune of $1 million, was said to be the artist father of Robert de Niro.

⚲ *CUBA*

● MEAT

The total amount of meat eaten in the world in 2018 was estimated at 360 million tonnes. In that year, the USA led the world in meat consumption per head of population at 99 kilograms (219 pounds), followed by Australia at 92 kilograms (203 pounds) and Argentina at 90 kilograms (198 pounds). The British ate 44.9 kilograms (99 pounds). The total weight of poultry eaten in the world in 2010 was 98 million tons.

'If God did not intend for us to eat animals, then why did he make them out of meat?' John Cleese

'Heaven sends us good meat but the Devil sends cooks.' David Garrick

♀ *CARNIVAL, CAT STEW, CHINA, HAMBURGER, HORSE, PIES*

● MEDICINE

In modern Britain, doctors spend an average of 9.22 minutes seeing each patient in their surgeries. The European average is 10.7 minutes.

According to a survey published in the *British Medical Journal* in 2019, average times throughout the world varied from 48 seconds in Bangladesh to 22.5 minutes in Sweden.

In ancient Rome, barbers dressed cuts with spiders' webs soaked in vinegar.

'The art of medicine consists of amusing the patient while nature cures the disease.' Attributed to Voltaire

♀ *ENEMA, FOX, GARLIC, HEROIN, HIPPOCRATES, SYPHILIS*

● MEERKAT

Research in 2009 showed that adolescent meerkats stop begging for food from their parents because they have become unable to make effective begging calls. A paper in the journal *Animal Behavior* entitled 'Why Do Meerkat Pups Stop Begging' reported investigations into three possible explanations: 1. that adults stop feeding their young after a certain age; 2. that when the young meerkats have learned to forage for food on their own, they stop begging because it takes more effort; 3. that they lost the ability to make the right begging noises.

The first of these was shown to be false when adult meerkats were found to bring food to their adolescent children in response to the begging sounds of young meerkats. The second was shown to be wrong when provisions of food to meerkats was found to have no effect on their foraging or begging behaviour. The third was supported by evidence showing that adult meerkats stopped bringing food when recordings of adolescent meerkats were played.

● MELBOURNE

An impotence clinic in Melbourne was raided by burglars in 1996 who stole dozens of bottles of drugs that could cause five-day erections. 'We are looking for someone who is very embarrassed or very tired,' a police spokesman said.

♀ *PEACH, PENGUIN, PYTHON, SPORTS SONGS*

● MELON

In 1999, the supermarket chain Tesco reduced the size of their melons. This was in response to advice from a psychologist who pointed out that both men and women tend to think of breasts when buying melons: male shoppers buy melons most similar in size to the way they want their women's breasts to be; female buyers tend to pick varieties that match most closely their own bust shape and size.

Smaller breasts had recently become more fashionable and sales of large melons had decreased. This was confirmed when a Tesco spokesman reported that swapping 964 gram (2 pound 2 ounce) melons (DD cup size) for 510 gram (1 pound 2 ounce) melons (C cup size) led to sales of a million more melons.

⚲ CELIBACY, CUCUMBER

● MELVILLE, Herman (1819–91)

Herman Melville's novel *Moby Dick* was first published in three volumes in London on 18 October 1851 under the title 'The Whale'. Three weeks later, it appeared in New York with the title 'Moby-Dick or The Whale'.

The name of the whale was inspired by a real albino whale known as Mocha Dick, which had numerous skirmishes with whalers off the coast of Mocha Island in the Pacific in the early 19th century. Mocha Dick was said to have been responsible for the deaths of around 30 sailors before he was finally killed in 1838.

⚲ MOBY DICK

● MEMORY

Newborn ducks usually learn to remember who their mother is within a few minutes of first seeing her. Scientists at Oxford University in 2016, however, showed that if you show newly hatched ducklings a substitute mother object using only one eye, they do not recognise it when they have only the other eye available. Their experiments involved putting an eyepatch over one eye of the duckling, then presenting it with a red or blue duck decoy moving in a circle. The ducklings imprinted on the decoy and quickly learned to follow it. Three hours later, the ducklings were presented with two decoys, the red one and the blue one, while wearing the patch over the same eye, the other eye, or not having an eyepatch at all. When the patch had changed eyes, their choice of which decoy to follow showed no reliable preference.

Nobody has performed a similar experiment on human newborns, but researchers at the University of Wisconsin in 2002 showed that strong emotions may help us retain memories. Their studies involved people performing a memory task (remembering a list of words) then watching a video of a tooth extraction or a rabbit-processing factory. Such an experience led to them performing better at recalling the words than people who watched an emotionally neutral video or no video at all. The experiment was part of a study designed to show that emotional content helps us to remember, even if the emotion is of no personal relevance. One practical conclusion of the research was a recommendation that, immediately after a swotting session, students should watch a thriller or work out. 'Do something that'll get you excited,' a researcher said.

⚲ AMNESIA, GOLDFISH, INTELLIGENCE, SEA LION, WORM

● MEN

In the Arab state of Qatar in 2020, there were 302.4 males for every 100 females. In the 25–54 age range, the ratio is more than five men to every one woman. These are the highest male–female ratios in the world

According to surveys in 2008, 1 per cent of men in the UK have visited six or more lap-dancing clubs abroad; 28 per cent of men who own cats would rather change their partner than their cat; and 52 per cent of men have seduced a woman by impressing them with their cooking.

'Young men want to be faithful, and are not; old men want to be faithless, and

cannot: that is all one can say.' Oscar Wilde, The Picture of Dorian Gray, *1891*

ATTRACTIVENESS, MOUSTACHE, PENIS, SLAVERY, VOICE, WOMEN

MENSTRUATION

A survey at Holloway prison in 1945 showed that: 'Ninety-three per cent of female crimes are committed during the pre-menstrual phase.' There is also evidence that accidents in the home or on the road are more likely to happen to women in the days before menstruation.

MERCEDES-BENZ

The government of Nepal announced in September 2010 that it planned to repair, and use for tourist trips, a Mercedes-Benz that had been presented by Adolf Hitler to King Tribhuvan of Nepal in 1939. The car had been stored at an old palace garage for more than five years, after being abandoned by an engineering college which had been using it for classes. A Ministry of Culture official said that a sum equal to more than half a million dollars was being sought from the government to mend the damaged doors, seats and bonnet of the car and to restore a chariot once used by King Tribhuvan. 'The idea is to repair them so visitors can drive in the car and ride the royal chariot,' he said.

GENETICS

MERCURY

Mercury's day – sunrise to sunrise – is longer than its year.

Freddie Mercury, lead singer of Queen, had four extra teeth at the back of his mouth, which pushed those at the front forwards. He always refused to have them fixed, fearing it might affect his vocal ability.

GRAVITY, STALLION

MERKIN

The Oxford Companion to the Body dates the origin of the merkin, or pubic wig, back to 1450. Some women around that time shaved off their pubic hair as a measure against lice, then covered the area with an artificial hairpiece. Prostitutes also wore them, though their motivation was more often a desire to cover up signs of disease.

The same book also mentions a tale of one gentleman who acquired the infected merkin of a prostitute, dried it, combed it well, and then presented it to a cardinal, proudly telling him he was bringing him St Peter's beard.

MERMAID

The earliest known reference to a mermaid was in stories from Assyria around 1000 BC. The goddess Atargatis fell in love with a human shepherd but accidentally killed him. In shame, she jumped into a lake to live as a fish, taking the form of a half-fish, half-human mermaid.

In a later Greek legend, Thessaloniki, sister of Alexander the Great, turned into a mermaid when she died, living in the Aegean and making the waters calm or violent according to her mood.

In Chinese legend, the tears of mermaids turn to pearls.

The statue of Hans Andersen's Little Mermaid near Copenhagen harbour has twice had its head cut off by vandals, and once lost an arm. It has also been blown up once and several times coated in paint. The head of the statue was modelled by ballerina Ellen Price, but as she refused to pose in the nude, the body is that of the wife of sculptor Edvard Eriksen. The statue has always been a copy – the sculptor's heirs keep the original at an undisclosed location.

The 'Fiji Mermaid', displayed at P.T. Barnum circuses in the 19th century and allegedly the mummified body of a real mermaid, turned out, on closer examination, to be the head of a baboon sewn onto the body of a gorilla stuffed into the tail of a fish.

More recently, in August 2009, there were reports of a mermaid being sighted off the coast of Israel near the town of Kiryat Yam. The mermaid was said to have been seen leaping out of the water and doing dolphin-like aerial tricks before diving back. In 2009, the town offered a prize of $1 million for anyone who could produce conclusive evidence of the mermaid's existence, but it has yet to be paid out. Kiryat Yam is about 80 kilometres (50 miles) north of the city of Bat Yam, in the Tel Aviv district. 'Bat Yam' means 'Daughter of the sea' or 'mermaid'.

⚲ SWIMMING

METEOROLOGY

A remarkable event in the history of weather forecasting took place on 10 July 1997: a group of meteorologists in Belgium apologised for getting it wrong. The forecasters jointly issued an apology 'to the inhabitants of the centre of the country who could not enjoy the bright spells we forecast'.

METHANE

In 2008, the Swedish University for Agricultural Sciences in Uppsala received 3.8 million kronor (about £320,000) in research funds to measure the methane released when cows belch. The 20 cows in the study had different diets and wore a collar measuring the methane level in the air around them.

The belches of 10 cows are enough to heat a small house.

Bovine flatulence adds 85 million tons of methane to the atmosphere each year. Termites' eating habits add an estimated 150 million tons.

The flatulence of one sheep could provide enough methane to power a small lorry for 40 kilometres (25 miles) a day, according to research in New Zealand. Harnessing the methane output of 72 million sheep could solve the nation's fuel problems.

⚲ FART

METRIC SYSTEM

The metric system of measurements was devised in France after the 1789 revolution as the country was changing from monarchy to republic. In 1790, a group of scientists met Louis XVI, who gave approval to their ideas. The following day, the King tried to flee the country but was arrested and jailed. From jail he directed two engineers to determine the length of a metre, the first metric measure, which they had agreed should be one ten-millionth of the distance from the North Pole to the Equator on a line passing through Paris. The system was adopted in 1795, two years after Louis XVI was beheaded. The motto for the new egalitarian metric system was 'For all people, for all time'.

In 1963, the metre was redefined as equal to 1,650,763.73 wavelengths of the orange-red line of the emission spectrum of the krypton-86 atom. Twenty years later, in 1983, a slightly simpler definition was adopted and since then a metre has officially been the length of the path travelled by light in a vacuum during a time interval of 1/299,792,458 of a second.

The kilogram is the last remaining international SI unit that is still linked to a real object: a cylinder deposited in the International Bureau of Weights and Measures at Sèvres, France.

MEXICO

Mexico has more Spanish speakers than any other country.

According to the UN's figures, Mexico was the country with the fourth highest number of intentional homicide victims in 2018, behind only Nigeria, Brazil and India.

In 2008, the northern Mexican city of Torreon imposed fines of up to 346 pesos (about £17) for putting on make-up or shaving with an electric razor while driving. Other new offences included throwing rubbish out of a car window, and driving with another person or an animal on a motorist's lap.

The 2008 Olympics staged in Mexico City were the first to be held in South America and the first in a Spanish-speaking country. Mexico won three gold, three silver and three bronze medals. In the 1936 Olympics polo event, Mexico won the bronze medal despite losing the only game they played. There were only three contestants. Polo has not been held as an Olympic event since then.

Ten times as many people are killed from scorpion stings in Mexico as die from snake bites. Around 1,000 deaths from scorpion stings occur in Mexico per year.

CONSENT, DONKEY, IDAHO, RADISH, TEQUILA, WITCHCRAFT

MEXICO CITY

The 20 million inhabitants of Mexico City produce enough sewage to fill an Olympic swimming pool every minute.

CHEESECAKE, SANTA ANNA

MIAMI

In March 2009, Serena Williams played Rafael Nadal in what was billed as 'the first tennis match on water'. It was held in a Miami swimming pool, both players standing on acrylic sheets – Nadal at the deep end. The tennis court was built over a hotel rooftop swimming pool and took a week to construct.

AARDVARK, NEW YORK, WEATHER

MICHELANGELO (1475–1564)

Despite spending four years painting the ceiling of the Sistine Chapel, Michelangelo always thought of himself primarily as a sculptor and was irritated whenever he was described as a painter.

When the Teenage Mutant Ninja Turtles were created in 1983, and for all their early years, the name of Michelangelo was misspelled as 'Michaelangelo'. Since 2000, however, it has been corrected to be the same as that of the Italian artist.

On 1 August 1995, the High Court in Hong Kong ruled that Michelangelo's sculpture *David* is not obscene.

VATICAN

MICKEY MOUSE (b. 1928)

Mickey Mouse, Minnie Mouse and Donald Duck are the only Disney characters with official birthdays. Mickey and Minnie are said to have been born on 18 November 1928, which was the release date of *Steamboat Willie*, the first Disney cartoon with sound. In fact, that was Mickey's third appearance. He had previously been in two silent cartoons called *Plane Crazy* and *Gallopin' Gaucho*. Donald Duck's birthday is on 9 June. In 2022, Mickey Mouse attained the age of 94 while Donald Duck was a mere 88.

The name Walt Disney first chose for Mickey was 'Mortimer Mouse', but his wife Lillian thought Mortimer sounded pompous and suggested Mickey instead. The actor Mickey Rooney, however, always maintained that the character was named after him, following a visit he made as a five-year-old child star to Walt Disney.

Mickey Mouse is known as Michal Souris in France, Topolino in Italy, Mikki Ma-u-su in Japan, Raton Mickey in Mexico, Mikki Hirri in Finland and Miguel Ratoncito in Spain. His ears are always perfect circles whatever angle they are viewed from.

Italian dictator Benito Mussolini was a Mickey Mouse fan. He met Disney in Rome in 1935.

According to Swiss law professor Karl-Ludwig Kunz, Mickey Mouse committed seven criminal acts in his comics in 1952.

The first recorded use of the words 'Mickey Mouse' to mean worthless or ineffectual was in 1931. The verb 'to mickey mouse', meaning to fool around, first appeared in an Aviator's Guide in 1963.

♀ PARACHUTE, PARTON

● MIDGET

In September 2010, Edward Niño of Colombia was declared the smallest adult man on Earth by Guinness World Records. Nino, then 24, was 70.21 centimetres (27.64 inches) tall. According to his girlfriend Fanny, who is 1.6 metres (5 feet 3 inches) tall, he likes his women to be of normal size.

Unfortunately for Niño, Khagendra Thapa Magar of Nepal was 14 centimetres shorter and became eligible for the title in October 2010 when he turned 18. Khagendra Thapa Magar died aged 27 in 2020, since when Edward Niño has regained the title

of the world's shortest mobile man, according to Guinness World Records.

The shortest ever adult male whose height was verified was Chandra Bahadur Dangi, who was 54.6 centimetres (21.5 inches) tall.

In 2022, Marks and Spencer changed the name of their 'Midget Gems' sweets to 'Mini Gems' when concerns were pointed out to them that the word 'midget' was seen by some as offensive.

● MILK

In 1984, some cows in Sweden were fitted with plastic discs impregnated with insecticide to keep their heads fly-free in summer. Scientists monitoring the experiment said this improved milk yield.

♀ BUFFALO, CAMEL, COW, MAY, REINDEER, SARDINE, YAK

● MILKY WAY

In Babylonian mythology, the Milky Way was created from the severed tail of the primeval salt water dragoness Tiamat. It was added to the sky by Babylonian national god Marduk after he had slain her. In Greek mythology, the Milky Way was formed from the breast milk of Hera, Queen of the Gods, after she woke up to find the infant Heracles suckling at her breast while she was asleep.

If every star in the Milky Way were a grain of salt, they would fill an Olympic swimming pool.

♀ ASTRONOMY, BUNGA BUNGA, SUN

● MILNE, Alan Alexander (1882–1956)

The *Oxford English Dictionary* lists 'heffalump' and 'Pooh-sticks' as words A.A. Milne introduced in his Winnie-the-Pooh books, as well as the verbs 'to blip' and 'to tonk'.

In October 1928, Dorothy Parker, writing under her pen name Constant Reader, reviewed A. A. Milne's *The House at Pooh Corner* in *The New Yorker*, including the much-quoted line: '… And it is that word "hummy," my darlings, that marks the first place in The House at Pooh Corner at which Tonstant Weader fwowed up.' But she also admitted that 'To speak against Mr Milne puts one immediately in the ranks of those who set fire to orphanages.'

TUESDAY, WINNIE-THE-POOH

MINT

The managing director of Chile's mint was sacked in 2010 after releasing into circulation thousands of coins which had the country's name misspelled on them. The 50-peso coins were issued in 2008 and it was more than a year before it was noticed that they had 'CHIIE' on them.

COINS, EDWARD VIII, MARCO POLO, MONEY

MISTLETOE

Mistletoe (of which there are around 2,000 species) lives as a parasite off the tree to which it attaches itself and has no roots of its own. Its seeds are spread through the droppings of birds that eat the berries. The parasitic nature of mistletoe is reflected in the botanical name of the common American variety *Phoradendron*, which means 'thief of the tree'.

The Christmas habit of kissing beneath the mistletoe has its origins in an old Norse myth in which Baldur, god of the summer sun, was killed by Loki, god of evil, and restored to life by his mother Frigga, goddess of love. Her tears became the white berries on mistletoe and in her joy she is said to have kissed all who passed beneath.

Traditionally, one berry should be plucked for each kiss beneath the mistletoe; when the berries run out, no more kisses may be claimed.

A 'kissing ball' of decorated mistletoe was a popular decoration in 18th-century British homes. The ritual insisted that any girl standing under it could not refuse to be kissed, but if she stood under it and remained unkissed, it was a sign that she would not be married in the forthcoming year.

The Druids called mistletoe 'Allheal', believing it to be sacred and an antidote to poisons. According to a Treasury of Health compiled by Pope John XXI, 'Mistletoe laid to the head draweth out the corrupt humours'.

Titus Andronicus is the only Shakespeare play that mentions mistletoe, as Tamora, Queen of the Goths, refers to: 'The trees, though summer, yet forlorn and lean, O'ercome with moss and baleful mistletoe.'

MITTERRAND, Francois (1916–96)

On 31 December 1995, the former President of France, Francois Mitterrand, dying of prostate cancer, invited a few chosen friends round for a final meal. They began with 30 oysters each, followed by fois gras, capon and ending with ortolan, which is a tiny bird that is a rare delicacy as it is, and was at the time, illegal to sell or eat.

The traditional way of preparing an ortolan is to drown it in Armagnac, then pluck it, roast it and eat it all, including its bones and head, beneath a napkin in order to capture the delicate flavours and aroma. Mitterrand is reported to have eaten two of them, then neither ate again nor accepted any further medical treatment before he died eight days later.

MOBILE PHONE

The first call on a hand-held mobile phone was made on 3 April 1973 by Motorola researcher Martin Cooper to Dr Joel Engel, a rival of his at Bell telephone laboratories.

The first commercial city-wide mobile phone network was launched in Japan in 1977.

In 2021, there were almost 15 billion mobile phones in the world, and around 6.4 billion people, about 80.7 per cent of the world's population, subscribed to a mobile phone network.

The United Arab Emirates and the Seychelles top the league of cell-phone penetration, each having close to twice as many mobile phones as people.

Over 23 billion text messages are sent every day worldwide.

The 'SIM' in SIM card stands for Subscriber Identity Module.

Americans throw out around 416,000 mobile phones every day.

In 2008, Japan launched a new service that allowed fragrances to be downloaded on mobile phones.

AQUARIUM, CELLPHONE, LYING, QATAR, TELEPHONE, TITS

MOBY DICK

Herman Melville's great novel *Moby Dick* did not sell out its first printing of 3,000 copies during his lifetime and earned him only $556.37 in total.

In the novel, Melville tells us that whalers refer to the whale penis as a 'cassock' and that the skin of a whale penis can be used as an apron by a crewman to stay clean and tidy while slicing up the blubber.

MELVILLE

MODELLING

According to a poll taken in 2009, one in four American women would rather win *America's Next Top Model* than the Nobel Peace Prize.

MOLE

In 2002, Queen Elizabeth II appointed Victor Williamson to the post of Mole Controller. He had already served Her Majesty for ten years, keeping her estate at Sandringham as free as possible from moles. As royal molecatcher, he was not allowed to use poison to kill the moles, through fears that the royal corgis might eat it, so he mainly put his faith in traps.

The old name for a mole was mouldwarp or moldiwarp, literally meaning 'earth-thrower'. Moles are not quite as blind as they are often portrayed but have hairy skin covering their small eyes.

Moles locate worms underground by smell; their two nostrils operate independently so they can sniff in stereo.

The word 'mole' for a spot or blemish on the skin comes to us from Old English so is rather older than 'mole' the animal, which was first seen around 1400. The average human being has 25 moles on his or her body.

Moles' feet carried in a pocket are said to be a charm against cramp; moles' forefeet are said to cure aching arms, while the hind feet are supposed to be good for relieving pain in the legs.

The collective noun for moles is a 'labour' or 'company'.

On 8 March 1702, King William III died of complications after breaking his collarbone falling from his horse when it was startled by a mole. Jacobite opponents of the King promptly instituted a new toast – 'To the little gentleman in black velvet' – in honour of the mole.

🖑 *BUCKLAND, ELEPHANT, MOLEOSOPHY*

MOLEOSOPHY

Fortune-telling by the position of moles on the body is called moleosophy. Though it dates back to the ancient Greeks, moleosophy has never attained the popularity of other predictive methods such as palmistry, physiognomy or astrology. Its predictions include the following: generally a round mole signifies goodness, an oblong mole means a modest share of acquired wealth and an angular mole suggests both positive and negative characteristics; a mole on the right-hand side of the forehead is said to be predictive of talent and success; on the left it indicates stubbornness and an extravagant personality; a mole on the right knee predicts a happy marriage; a mole on the left knee means a bad temper. Moles on the buttocks indicate a lack of ambition; moles on the elbows indicate a desire to travel.

MOLOSSIAN

The Molossian were an ancient Greek tribe who gave their name to a breed of huge and vicious dog known as the Molossus, which is now extinct. Alexander III, 'the Great', King of Macedonia 336–23 BC, had a pet Molossus called 'Peritas', after which he named a town. It was one of the now-extinct Molossian breed, a sort of giant Rottweiler, bred for fighting, and is said to have won fights against a lion and an elephant. Alexander forbade his soldiers to wear beards, on the grounds that they were too easy to get hold of in a fight. He slept until noon and could not swim.

Mosaics have been found among the ruins of Pompeii depicting Molossians outside people's homes with the message '*cave canem*' ('beware of the dog').

MONACO

The area of Monaco is just under 2 square kilometres (0.77 square miles). You could fit about five and a half Monacos into the Royal Borough of Kensington and Chelsea in London; or you could cover the whole of Monaco with about 325 football pitches.

The flag of Monaco is two equal bands of red and white, with the red on top. The flag of Indonesia is identical in colour, but longer; the flag of Poland is the same, but with the white band on top.

The coat of arms of Monaco features two monks brandishing swords. This celebrates Francois Grimaldi seizing control in 1297 disguised as a monk.

Monaco is home to La Monegasque, a world leader in sales of anchovies.

A traditional dish in Monaco is pan bagnat, a roll drizzled with olive oil then stuffed with onion, green pepper, tomato, egg, olives and anchovies.

🖑 *HEALTH, NAURU, ROWING*

MONARCHY

The only absolute monarchies in the world, where the monarch has total power, are in Brunei, Oman, Qatar, Saudi Arabia and Swaziland. The Vatican may be added to this list if one considers the Pope to be a monarch.

🖑 *METRIC SYSTEM, TREASON*

MONDAY

'Monday' is the only day of the week in the English language that is an anagram of a single word: 'dynamo'.

The Russian for Monday is *ponedyelnik*, which means 'after do-nothing'.

Research has shown that Monday is

the most common day for heart attacks and other sudden deaths from psychological stress, and the least rainy day of the week on the east coast of America; this is probably due to the effect on weather patterns of daily changes in man-made pollution.

'The Monday Effect' is a theory held by many stock market investors that share prices on Monday will continue in the same direction they moved on the preceding Friday.

In the UK, there are fewer deaths from drug overdoses on Monday than any other day of the week.

BLUE, BUBBLEWRAP, OREGON, PSYCHOLOGY, SUICIDE

MONET, Oscar-Claude (1840–1926)

Monet's 1872 painting *Impression, Sunrise* is the one that gave rise to the term 'Impressionism'. The painting was compared by one critic to an unfinished sketch, or mere 'impression' of the subject matter. The term caught on and Impressionism was born.

In 1866, plagued by debt, Monet burned 200 of his own paintings to prevent them being seized by creditors. Two years later, he jumped into the Seine in an apparent suicide attempt.

'I would like to paint the way a bird sings.' Claude Monet

PIGEON

MONEY

The word 'money' derives from Moneta, one of the names of the goddess Juno. The Roman Mint where silver coins were made was close to her temple. Moneta became the personification of money and her name was associated with it.

The total value of all Bank of England banknotes in circulation at the end of February 2022 was £81,634 million. More than half this total was £20 notes. The coins in circulation added about another £3.1 billion to the total amount of money in circulation. In September 2021, the Royal Mint estimated the total number of coins in circulation to be approximately 29 billion. If all those coins were divided equally among the population of the UK, each person would end up with £65.70 each in loose change, weighing over 2.5 kilograms (5.5 pounds).

A £2 coin weighs exactly 12 grams; a £1 coin weighs 9.5 grams; a 50p coin weighs 8 grams; a 20p coin weighs 5 grams; a 10p coin weighs 6.5 grams; a 5p coin weighs 3.25 grams; a 2p coin weighs 7.12 grams; a 1p coin weighs 3.56 grams.

In the US, calling a dollar a 'buck' comes from a time when buckskin was used as currency. A dime has 118 ridges around its edge but a quarter has 119 ridges. The process of adding ridges to a coin is called 'reeding'.

'Money is better than poverty, if only for financial reasons.' Woody Allen

LOTTERIES, MARY I, MONOPOLY, PICASSO, ROBBERY, TOES

MONGOLIA

Mongolia is the most sparsely populated independent country in the world. If its people were spread equally over the land, they would be about a kilometre (0.6 miles) apart.

The independent state of Mongolia used to be called 'Outer Mongolia'. 'Inner Mongolia' is still an autonomous region of China. The name of Mongolia's capital, Ulan Bator, means 'Red Hero'.

The 40-metre (131-foot) high statue of Genghis Khan on a horse outside Ulan Bator is said to be the tallest statue of a horse in the world.

According to the Food and Agriculture Organisation of the United Nations, Mongolia has more than 70 million livestock comprising 32.3 million sheep, 29.3 million goats, 4.7 million cattle, 4.2 million horses and 0.5 million camels.

Mongolia won its first Olympic gold medals (in judo and boxing) at Beijing in 2008.

In 2007, the world's tallest man, Bao Xishun of Mongolia, who was 2.4 metres (7 feet 9 inches) tall, married a woman 68 centimetres (2 feet 3 inches) shorter than himself in a ceremony held at the tomb of Kubla Khan in Mongolia. The groom rode to the ceremony in a cart drawn by two camels but did not bow down before the bride's parents, as is traditional, because of arthritis in his knees. He had been in the news the previous year when he used his long arms to save two dolphins by pulling plastic out of their stomachs.

♀ BAR CODES, HANGOVER, YAK

● MONK

Traditionally, only two monks at any one time know the recipe for Chartreuse liqueur, which was given to the Carthusian brotherhood in 1605. An artillery marshal named François Hannibal d'Estrées, who was serving in the army of French King Henry IV, is said to have given an alchemical manuscript to the Carthusian monks at Vauvert, near Paris, containing a recipe for an elixir of life. The recipe reached the Carthusians' headquarters at the Grande Chartreuse monastery, north of Grenoble. It was said to include 130 herbs, plants and flowers as well as some secret ingredients, all combined in a wine alcohol base. For more than a century, the recipe was seen as an elixir or medicine, but in 1737 Brother Gérome Maubec improved it and the popular drink now known as Chartreuse was the result.

♀ BOSWELL, CHAMPAGNE, DIVORCE, LAWN-MOWER, ST ANDREW

● MONKEY

The word 'monkey', which was first recorded in English in 1530, may derive from a supposed similarity in appearance to a monk.

The smallest type of monkey is the pygmy marmoset which weighs only 113 grams (4 ounces).

For the Chinese Year of the Monkey celebrations in 2016, Taiwanese artist Chen Forng-shean produced the world's smallest sculpture of a monkey. Made from resin, it was only 1mm long and the monkey's head was described as smaller than a grain of sand.

When he was in his early 20s, Elvis Presley had a pet spider monkey called Jayhew.

Old World monkeys (species from Africa and Asia) have 32 teeth. New World monkeys (from the Americas) have 36. There are two more important differences between New World monkeys and Old World monkeys: if a monkey is swinging by its tail, it is probably from Central or South America. Monkeys from Africa and Asia do not generally have prehensile tails. Monkeys have tails; apes do not.

The howler monkey of America is the loudest land animal. Its howl can be heard 3.2 kilometres (2 miles) away in the forest or 4.8 kilometres (3 miles) in the open. The first animal to be launched into space was a rhesus monkey called Albert I on board a US-launched V2 rocket in 1948.

The nose of a proboscis monkey can be 10 centimetres (4 inches) long. Female proboscis monkeys seem to prefer males with long noses.

In October 1997, a monkey was arrested in the African state of Benin for stealing a television aerial. The street juggler who trained it was also arrested and jailed. The monkey was sent to a zoo.

In May 1998, the world's first overhead monkey crossing was built across a busy road in Taiwan. The result was proudly announced as 'fewer dead monkeys and damaged cars'.

Also in 1998, researchers in Washington established that monkeys can count up to nine.

Finally, in 2008, scientists in Singapore reported that monkeys are willing to 'pay' partners for sex. A study of 50 macaque monkeys revealed that male monkeys groom females to 'pay' for sex. Female monkeys increased their sexual activity from 1.5 times per hour on average to 3.5 times after being groomed. The study also found that market forces dictate how much a male has to 'pay' for sex. In an area with several females, a male could expect sex after eight minutes of grooming, but in areas with more males than females this rose to 16 minutes. This discovery contradicted previous evidence that market forces did not influence mating patterns in nature.

The marmoset and the tamarin are the only monkey species that are truly monogamous.

BABOONS, CARUSO, HANGOVER, ORGAN GRINDERS, SPACE FLIGHT

MONOPOLY

According to a statistical analysis of the game of Monopoly, the property most often landed on is Trafalgar Square (Illinois Avenue in the US version).

In 1975, twice as much Monopoly money as real money was printed in the USA.

Over 5 billion little green houses have been made for Monopoly since the game was launched in 1935.

CUBA

MONROE, Marilyn (1926–62)

Marilyn Monroe was born 41 days after Queen Elizabeth II.

'What do I wear in bed? Why, Chanel No 5, of course.' Marilyn Monroe

ARTICHOKE, CHAMPAGNE, HAIR, THATCHER

MONTENEGRO

After Montenegro gained independence from Yugoslavia in 2006, its Internet domain changed from .yu to .me. Its Internet addresses had in fact ended in cg.yu, with the cg coming from the Montenegrin name of the country, Crna Gora (which like Montenegro means 'black mountain').

The only Olympic medal so far won by Montenegro was silver in the women's handball at London 2012.

The high stakes poker game in the 2006 James Bond film *Casino Royale* was supposed to be taking place at the Casino Royale in Montenegro. In fact, it was filmed in the Czech Republic.

MONTEZUMA II (1466–1520)

Emperor of the Aztecs. According to Cortés, Montezuma, last King of the Aztecs, was very neat and clean, took a bath every afternoon, never wore the same clothes for two days in a row, had many mistresses and two wives, and was quite free from sodomy.

♀ *CHOCOLATE*

● MOON

Pliny the Elder (AD 23–79) believed that the Moon was larger than the Earth. In fact, it has a diameter of 3,474 kilometres (2,159 miles) and a mass of about 73,500,000,000,000,000,000 tonnes, which is about 1.2 per cent of the mass of the Earth.

Neil Armstrong's 'One small step' speech is often quoted as the first words broadcast from the Moon, but the first words broadcast were in fact, 'Houston, Tranquility Base here. The Eagle has landed.'

The first words spoken (rather than broadcast) from the Moon were Buzz Aldrin's: 'Contact light. OK, engine stop. ACA out of detent. Modes control both auto, descent engine command override, off. Engine arm, off. Four thirteen is in.'

The last words spoken on the Moon to date were: 'America's challenge of today has forged man's destiny of tomorrow,' by Eugene Cernan on 11 December 1972.

According to a paper in *Science* journal in 1970, seismological studies reveal that the structure of the Moon is closer to that of cheese than to rocks on Earth.

Research shows that people in the UK are most likely to be bitten by dogs when there is a full Moon.

Buzz Aldrin, the second man on the Moon, recorded the 37th best pole vault in the USA in 1951.

'You see one Earth, you've seen them all.' Jack Schmitt, from the Moon, December 1972

♀ *DRAGON, EASTER, GOLF, MARS, PHOTOGRAPHY, URANUS*

● MOOSE

The species known as a moose in North America is referred to as an elk in Europe. What the Americans call an elk is known as a wapiti in Europe. Although European elk can be found in North America, American moose do not exist in Europe.

The moose is believed to be a descendant of the Megaceros, which lived around 1 million BC. The Irish elk became extinct around 10,000 BC.

The scientific name for the moose is *Alces alces*.

Moose live from 15 to 25 years. Their hoofprints have tapered ends pointing in the direction of travel.

Only the male moose has antlers. The correct term for a spike on a moose's antlers is 'tine'. After the mating season, males knock off their antlers against trees in November or December. After shedding its antlers, a moose grows back a bigger pair the following year. The span of a moose's antlers may be almost 1.8 metres (6 feet). The term for the antler spread of a moose is 'rack'.

A fully grown moose weighs between 454 kilograms (1,000 pounds) and 726 kilograms (1,600 pounds). The world record for the biggest moose is 816 kilograms (1,800 pounds). Moose can run at up to 56 km/h (35 mph) and swim at 9.5 km/h (6 mph).

Before mating, a bull moose often digs a shallow pit with his paws, fills it with urine, then rolls around in it. The smell apparently attracts females. Male moose may get very bad-tempered during the mating season.

The gestation period of a moose is approximately eight months, after which the female moose usually gives birth to twins and often triplets.

An adult moose eats between 18 and

27 kilograms (40–60 pounds) of food a day and especially likes aquatic plants, which provide much-needed salt.

On one 50-kilometre (31-mile) stretch of railway in Alaska, 68 moose were once killed in a single night in collisions with trains. When a car hits a moose in America, the damage to the car usually exceeds $500.

The word 'moose' comes from an Algonquin Indian language and means 'twig-eater'.

ALASKA, BRAHE, CRASH TEST DUMMY, VERMONT

MORTGAGE

A 73-year-old man who was charged with robbing three banks in Florida in 2010 admitted the crimes but said he needed the money to pay his home mortgage, and he had planned to give the money back. The word 'mortgage' in English dates back to the 14th century and comes from the Latin *mortuum vadium*, meaning 'death pledge'.

MOSAIC

A mosaic by the Albanian artist Saimir Strati depicting five musicians broke the world record in 2011 for the largest mosaic made of coffee beans. Strati used 140 kilograms (309 pounds) of coffee beans, some roasted black, some averagely roasted and some not roasted at all, to create the image of a Brazilian dancer, a Japanese drummer, a US country music singer, a European accordionist and an African drummer. The size of the work was just over 25 square metres (269 square feet). Strati had also made a portrait of Leonardo Da Vinci with nails, a galloping horse out of toothpicks, the Mediterranean Sea with corks from wine bottles, Michael Jackson with paint brushes, and

the Greek poet Homer with industrial screws.

MOLLOSIAN

MOSCOW

Moscow was founded in 1147 by Prince Yuri Dolgoruky; his name means 'Yuri the long-armed'.

Until 2022 when McDonald's closed its Russian restaurants, Moscow had the world's busiest McDonald's (in Pushkin Square, where 40,000 people were served every day); it also has the world's biggest bell (the Tsar Kolokol in the Kremlin, which has never been rung because it was cracked before its installation), and sees the start of the world's longest train journey – 9,259 kilometres (5,753 miles) from Moscow to Vladivostok, taking between 144 and 166 hours.

Since 1800, 49 populated places in the United States have been named Moscow. Today, there are 27, only three of which are cities. By far the largest Moscow in the USA, with a population of around 24,000, is in Idaho. Nobody is sure how it got its name: some say it was founded by Russian immigrants, others suggest it came from a Native American tribe called 'Masco', while a third theory is that the name was chosen by an early settler who had come from Moscow, Pennsylvania.

ALCOHOL, COW, HAMBURGER, REGURGITATION, TWENTY-THREE

MOSQUITO

Mosquitoes prefer to bite people who have just eaten a banana. Mosquitoes have also been found to prefer biting people with smelly feet.

Mosquitoes are attracted to the colour blue twice as much as to any other colour.

Researchers at the University of Durham in 2000 found that pregnant women attract twice as many mosquitoes as non-pregnant ones.

⚲ *BODY ODOUR, DENGUE FEVER, UMBRELLA*

● MOTH

According to research published in 2002, female moths prefer to mate with larger males. The paper entitled 'Paternal inheritance of a female moth's mating preference' (*Nature*, vol. 419) reported their analysis of the mating preferences of female arctiid moths. Females with larger fathers showed the strongest preference for large mates, thus confirming that the female's mating preference is inherited from the male parent.

Some moths emit ultrasonic clicks which can jam the radar of insectivorous bats.

'Lay up for yourselves treasures in heaven, where neither moth nor rust doth corrupt.' Matthew, 6:20

⚲ *CARPET, CATERPILLAR, COMPUTERS, NABOKOV, SLOTH, VIRGINITY*

▍MOTHER TERESA (Agnes Gonxha Bojaxhiu, 1910–97)

In September 1996, an employee at the Bongo Java coffee shop in Nashville, Tennessee, was about to bite into a cinnamon bun when it struck him that the bun looked rather like Mother Teresa. So he put the bun aside and later started showing it to customers and staff to ask if they saw anything strange about it. More than half responded by saying that it looked rather like Mother Teresa.

Seeing a marketing opportunity, they put the bun in the fridge to preserve it and started selling similar buns under the name 'Immaculate Confection', which later became 'NunBun'.

Bob Bernstein, owner of the Bongo Java coffee shop, later received a letter from Mother Teresa and a phone call from her lawyers asking him to stop selling a cinnamon bun bearing her likeness. He immediately dropped Mother Teresa's name from his NunBun marketing materials and offered 15 per cent of the profits to her Sisters of Mercy charities.

According to Bob Bernstein, Mother Teresa herself was greatly amused by the bun, but thought that the name Immaculate Confection was unsuitable, but her American lawyer appeared to take it all very seriously.

On Christmas Eve 2005, there was a break-in at the Bongo Java. A thief took the front door off its hinges, broke into the coffee shop and stole the original NunBun and nothing else. A $5,000 reward was offered for its return, no questions asked, but it has not yet been seen again.

⚲ *ALBANIA, WISDOM*

● MOTHERHOOD

Eighteen per cent of women in the UK never become mothers. Of those women who do have children, the average age at which they first become mothers is 27.1 years.

In the US, Mother's Day is the most popular day to dine out at a restaurant.

'One hundred aunts is not the same as one mother.' Sierra Leone proverb

● MOTORCYCLING

In 2000, a Hertfordshire man was jailed for six weeks for speeding at 281.5 km/h (175 mph) on his Honda Fireblade motorcycle. This is Britain's fastest speeding conviction.

According to an analysis of insurance

claims in the UK, 5 April is the most likely date for motorcycle accidents to occur. Bikers named David are the most likely to make claims, followed by Paul and Andrew.

The risk of being killed or seriously injured when riding a motorcycle is about 54 times as great as in a car.

The first motorbikes were steam-powered velocipedes made in France in 1867.

BALLOON, BASTARD, KNEES, NORTH POLE, NOSE, PUMPKIN

MOTOR RACING

The only dead man to win the Formula 1 World Motor Racing Championship was Jochen Rindt, who was killed in practice for the Monza Grand Prix in 1970 while leading the world championship. Two races later, his title was confirmed.

HAMILTON

MOTORING

The Locomotive Act of 1865 in the UK specified that a person carrying a red flag must walk at least 60 yards ahead of any car travelling on the highway. In 1878, the red flag became optional, but the speed limit remained at 2 mph in towns and 4 mph in the country. Drunken driving became illegal in 1872.

The first person to be convicted of speeding in the UK was Walter Arnold of East Peckham, Kent, who on 28 January 1896 was fined 1 shilling plus costs for speeding at 8 mph in town. Also in 1896, however, the speed limit was increased to 14 mph by the Locomotives and Highways Act of 1896, which was celebrated by an 'Emancipation Run' from London to Brighton, which began with Lord Winchilsea tearing up a symbolic red flag.

There were an estimated 1,580 road deaths on British roads in the year ending June 2020, which included three months of the national lockdown. This was a decrease of 14 per cent compared to the previous year, but road traffic was also down by 14 per cent over the same period. In 2021, the World Health Organisation estimated that approximately 1.3 million people die of road traffic crashes each year. In 2020, the average Briton made 429 car journeys, which was about 30 per cent less than the previous year.

The total number of fines for speeding imposed in England and Wales in 2020 exceeded 2.3 million.

In August 2003, the Bureau of Transportation Statistics revealed that for the first time there were more vehicles than drivers in the USA.

CARS, HORSE, MOTORCYCLING, MOTORWAY, WAGNER

MOTORWAY

According to the Automobile Association, Britain's drivers covered more than 965.6 million kilometres (600 million miles) in 2009 in order to avoid motorways. Motorists used the AA's online route planner to find more than 5 million routes specifically designed to steer clear of motorways. The AA also reported that the question they are most frequently asked is how to avoid the M25 London Orbital Motorway.

EMERGENCY

MOUNTAINEERING

Noteworthy years in the history of mountaineering include the following:

- 1950: A four-month-old kitten followed a party of climbers in Switzerland and reached the top of the Matterhorn.

- 1974: A German team that had set out to climb Annapurna 4 reached the top of Annapurna 2 by mistake.
- 1984: Members of the Dining Out club, who are devoted to having dinner parties in strange places, held a black tie dinner at the 6,768-metre (22,204-foot) high summit of Huscara Mountain in Peru.
- 1988: On 27 June, Dave Hurst and Alan Matthews of Britain became the first blind climbers to scale Mont Blanc.
- 2000: An expedition to clean Mount Everest of previous climbers' garbage counted 632 discarded oxygen bottles among the rubbish removed.
- 2007: Europe's highest toilets were taken by helicopter to the top of Mont Blanc. Local mayor Jean-Marc Peillex was quoted as saying: 'This move was much needed. Our beautiful mountain's white peak was full of yellow and brown spots in summer.' A helicopter service operates daily in peak season to empty the toilet.

  EVEREST, HILLARY, ST BERNARD, YETI

MOUSE

In February 2008, it was announced that a team from Imperial College, London, had produced the first lab rodents that could catch a cold. Symptoms in the mice infected with rhinovirus included mucin secretion and airway inflammation.

When Douglas Engelbart invented the computer mouse in 1968, he called it an 'X-Y Position Indicator for a Display System'.

  BREAD, DICKENS, DNA, FINLAND, ICELAND, ST KILDA

MOUSETRAP

The world's longest-running theatre show, *The Mousetrap*, opened at the New Ambassadors Theatre in London's West End on 25 November 1952. It moved next door to St Martin's Theatre in 1974 and has clocked up over 27,500 performances. The play had its world premiere in Nottingham on 6 October 1952, in a pre-London tour, but 25 November is celebrated as its birthday. *The Mousetrap* began as a radio play, then a short story, both entitled 'Three Blind Mice'. Agatha Christie asked that the story not be published while the play was on in the West End. It has been published in the US but not in the UK.

The earliest patent for a spring-loaded mousetrap was issued to William C. Hooker of Illinois in 1894, but it was James Henry Atkinson from Leeds who made the first practical version called the 'Little Nipper' mousetrap in 1897. The European Patent Office lists 703 entries for 'mouse-trap' and 481 more for 'mousetrap'. The earliest known use of the term 'mousetrap' was in 1440. Before that it was a 'mousefall'.

A play called *The Mousetrap* is referred to in Shakespeare's *Hamlet*. That is the only reference to mousetraps in the works of Shakespeare.

MOUSTACHE

Eight types of moustache are recognised at the World Beard and Moustache Championships. These are called: Natural, English, Dali, Handlebar, Wild West, Fu Manchu, Imperial and Freestyle.

The world's longest moustache is believed to be a 3.5-metre (11 feet 6 inch) monster belonging to Ram Singh Chauhan of Rajastan, India, who regularly massages it with mustard and coconut oil to keep it healthy.

In 2004, it was announced that police in northern India would be paid an extra 30 rupees (40p) a month to grow a moustache. A spokesman for the Madhya Pradesh state police said that research showed police with moustaches were taken more seriously. However, he added, the shape and style of police moustaches would be monitored to ensure police officers did not start to look too mean.

United States marines are forbidden to have a moustache longer than half-an-inch.

The last US president to have a moustache was William Taft, who left office in 1913.

Researchers at Tel Aviv University in 1992 showed that men with thin moustaches have greater propensity to suffer from peptic ulcers.

According to research by Guinness, the average moustachioed Guinness drinker traps a pint and a half of the drink in his facial hair every year.

HAIR, HITLER, LAUGHFEST, OPERA, VIKINGS, WOODPECKER

MOUTH ORGAN

It has been claimed that the mouth organ, or harmonica, is the world's best-selling musical instrument, ahead of the guitar. Though the Chinese had an instrument based on similar principles around 3000 BC, the first European patent for a mouth organ was awarded to 16-year-old Christian Buschmann in 1821.

The fastest mouth-organ rendition of the song 'Oh Susanna' was 12.75 seconds set by Rich Beckman in 2007.

ELEPHANT

MOZAMBIQUE

In 2010, shortly after an old railway line had been reopened connecting the Indian Ocean port city of Beira to the interior of Mozambique, a train ran into a hippopotamus, killing it. Soon after, another train on a different line ran into a herd of cattle, killing 35 of them. Residents of the central Mozambican province of Sofala were reported to have claimed that the crashes were caused by angry ancestral spirits.

Mozambique is the only country with a one-word name that includes all five vowels, A, E, I, O, U. The only countries with multiple-word names that do so are Equatorial Guinea, Dominican Republic, Democratic Republic of the Congo and the United Kingdom of Great Britain and Northern Ireland.

KYRGYZSTAN, SNIFFING

MOZART, Wolfgang Amadeus (1756–91)

Wolfgang Amadeus Mozart was baptised Johannes Chrysostomus Wolfgangus Theophilus Mozart. The name Amadeus means love of God and is the Latin version of the Greek Theophilus.

While growing up, Mozart had a pet dog and a pet canary. For three years he kept a pet starling. His notebook includes a tune the starling sang which he modified slightly to use in his 17th piano concerto, K.453. When the starling died he buried it in his garden and wrote a poem in its memory.

Mozart was a very keen billiards player. When he died at the age of 35, a valuation of his estate included: 'One green cloth billiard table with five balls, 12 cues, one lantern and four lights'.

'Wolfgang Amadeus Mozart' is an anagram of 'A Famous German Waltz God'.

The species of frog *Eleutherodactylus amadeus* was named after Mozart in 1987.

Mozart wrote his first pieces for

piano at the age of five and composed his first opera, which was in Latin, at the age of 11. He had written eight operas by the aged of 16. When touring as a child prodigy, Mozart often took second billing to his sister Maria Anna (known as 'Nannerl'), but she was no longer allowed to perform in public on reaching marriageable age. When Mozart performed in London at the age of nine, some thought his playing was too good for a child and suspected him of being a dwarf.

There is a rare deformity of the ear known as 'Mozart ear', though whether Mozart himself suffered from it has long been a matter of debate. In all portraits of Mozart, his left ear is either covered by a wig or hidden from view.

Pope Clement XIV made the 14-year-old Mozart a Knight of the Order of the Golden Spur.

Mozart broke off his courtship of Constanze Weber for some time after she permitted her calves to be measured by a gentleman during a parlour game. She went on to bear Mozart six children, of whom only two survived infancy. Their fifth child, Anna Maria, was born and died on Christmas Day 1789. Neither of the Mozarts' surviving children married or had children. Before Mozart married Constanze, he had proposed to her older sister Aloysia Weber.

Nobody knows if the skull at the Mozarteum in Salzburg is really Mozart's. DNA tests performed in 2006 were inconclusive.

In his 30 years of composing, Mozart wrote 202 hours of music, which works out at one minute and six seconds of music every day.

Mozart was born on 27 January 1756; Verdi died on 27 January 1901.

One of the very few errors in Milos Forman's Oscar-winning film *Amadeus* on the life of Mozart was the inclusion of actresses wearing dresses that are clearly zipped up at the back. The modern zip, such as could be used on dresses, did not appear until Gideon Sundback's patent in 1913.

♀ BRAHMS, FUNERALS, GEORGE III, MUSIC, PIANO, WIG

MUBARAK, Hosni (1928–2020), 4th President of Egypt

'Hosni Mubarak' is an anagram of 'I ambush Koran'. 'Mubarak' means 'blessed' in Arabic.

MUGGING

According to a report in a Bangladesh newspaper in 1996, around 100 criminals attended the first conference of muggers, which was held in Dacca that year. They agreed that the city was rich enough to support a doubling of its daily rip-offs and set themselves a target of increasing the number from 60 to 120. The conference ended with the title of Master Hijacker being conferred on their leader Mohammad Rippon for his record 21 muggings in two hours.

MULES

In 2016, the BBC announced that the children's TV character Muffin the Mule was to celebrate his 70th birthday by appearing on his own YouTube channel. Actually Muffin was already 82. He was said to be 12 years old when he first appeared in 1946.

Muffin the Mule was the first character created for children's TV, appearing four years before Andy Pandy and six years before the Flowerpot Men. The presenter who played the piano while Muffin danced on it was Annette

Mills, who was the sister of actor Sir John Mills.

An animated version of *Muffin the Mule* was translated into Welsh in 2005 as *Myffin y Mul*.

A mule is the offspring of a male donkey and a female horse; the offspring of a male horse and female donkey is a hinny. Horses have 64 chromosomes, donkeys have 62, and mules and hinnies have 63.

Darwin saw the mule as an example of hybrid vigour. It is stronger and brighter than its parents.

Mules are generally sterile but about 0.1 per cent of them can reproduce.

In the film *Two Mules For Sister Sara*, Clint Eastwood uses dynamite, which was not available until a year or two after the time the film is set.

The earliest known use of the word mule to mean a drug courier was in 1922.

⚲ *CATTLE, DONKEY, WASHINGTON, ZEBRA*

⬤ MUMMIFICATION

Police in Tokyo in 2010 found that the person who was thought to be the city's oldest resident had in fact been dead for 30 years. Police found Sogen Kato's mummified body in bed, wearing underwear and pyjamas and covered with a blanket. They had been asked to investigate by welfare workers who had repeatedly tried to meet Kato, who was born in 1899, but family members chased them away, saying he did not want to see anyone.

⚲ *BENTHAM, BRITISH MUSEUM, CAT, EMBALMING, LAVENDER, LICE*

⬤ MUSEUM

In 1990, the Belgian artist Jan Bucquoy opened an Underwear Museum, the Musée du Slip, in Brussels. It was forced to close, through lack of funds, in 1992, but reopened as a celebrity underwear museum in 2009. The exhibits have been donated by celebrities, with the only condition being that they must have been worn at least once by the donor.

According to Bucquoy, framed underwear represents a utopian longing for an equal society. 'If I had portrayed Hitler in his underpants there would not have been a war. I think in this way you can contribute to a better world.'

There is also a History of Underwear Museum in Tompkins County, Ithaca, New York.

⚲ *CARROT, CHOPSTICKS, MUSHROOM, PARASITE, PENIS, POTATO*

⬤ MUSHROOM

A person who studies mushrooms and fungi is a mycologist; if you eat mushrooms, you are a mycophagist; if you like them, you're a mycophile.

Mushrooms differ from other plants in that they contain no chlorophyl. Because of this, some say they are not plants at all. The Italian mycologist Bruno Cetti published descriptions and pictures of 2,147 types of mushroom.

Most fatal cases of mushroom poisoning are caused by a variety called *Amanita phalloides*, or Death Cap. Roman Emperors Tiberius and Claudius, Tsar Alexander I of Russia, Pope Clement II and King Charles V of France are all thought to have died from mushroom poisoning.

The official state mushroom of Minnesota is the morel (*Morchella esculenta*). Oregon's state mushroom is the golden chanterelle (*Cantharellus formosus*). The state mushroom of Texas is *Chorioactis geaster*, commonly known as devil's cigar. These are the only states with an official state mushroom, though

Massachusetts, Missouri and Washington have also proposed to have one.

There is a mushroom museum in the borough of Kennett Square, Pennsylvania. It is open daily from 10am to 6pm. Kennett Square has held an annual Mushroom Festival for the past 36 years and considers itself the Mushroom Capital of the World.

The Tempest is the only Shakespeare play that mentions mushrooms.

⚲ *BOSCH, PHOBIAS, RHYME, SLUG*

● MUSIC

Beethoven had thick black hairs on the backs of his hands, according to the Austrian composer and pianist Carl Czerny, who had been Beethoven's student.

In 2006, an RSPCA rescue centre in Somerset reported that stressed dogs are calmed by the music of Mozart and Beethoven, but do not respond well to pop or dance music.

According to a survey of music-buying tastes in the UK, the further north you go, the faster the music gets.

⚲ *CONDOM, FLIES, MOZART, ROSSINI, SUICIDE, WAGNER*

● MUSSELS

Mature female mussels have orange flesh; white ones are male.

● MYANMAR

The British called the country Burma after the majority ethnic group the Bamar when they ruled it between 1824 and 1948, but after independence the new ruling group preferred to call it Myanmar. These are simply two different names for the country in Burmese dialects.

The standard way to get a waiter's attention in a restaurant in Burma, or indeed to get the attention of any particular person, is to look at the person and make a kissing sound.

The oldest known bee was found in amber from Myanmar. It was 100 million years old.

⚲ *BUFFALO, BURMA*

NABOKOV, Vladimir (1899–1977)

The author of *Lolita*, Vladimir Nabokov, had a number of genera and species of moth named after him, including *Eupithecia nabokovi*, commonly known as 'Nabokov's Pug'. Nabokov wrote that as a schoolboy he had dreamt of discovering an unknown pug, 'one of those delicate little creatures that cling in the daytime to speckled surfaces, with which their flat wings and turned-up abdomens blend'.

NAMES

In Sweden, babies' names must be approved by the Swedish Tax Agency within three months of birth. According to the law, 'First names shall not be approved if they can cause offence or can be supposed to cause discomfort for the one using it, or names which for some obvious reason are not suitable as a first name.' In June 1996, a Swedish woman finally won a nine-year-long battle to be allowed to name her son Christophpher rather than Christopher or Christoffer.

At the end of 2019, Christoffer was the 42nd most common name for a male in Sweden but was not in the top 100 names given to babies that year.

The top five house names in the UK in 2021 were: 1. The Cottage; 2. Rose Cottage; 3. The Bungalow; 4. The Coach House; 5. Orchard House.

🔎 *CAT, COW, DOG, OLIVE, PERU, SNOW WHITE, WALES*

NAPLES

In May 2010, Italian prosecutors revealed that 5,000 flowerpots had been stolen from a cemetery in Naples the previous year. They also said they believed that thousands of small, lower-end bakeries and pizza shops were using the wood from old coffins to keep their ovens burning. Italy's estimated 25,000 pizzerias employ around 150,000 people and account for an annual turnover of 5.3 billion euros.

🔎 *HAMILTON, NIGHTINGALE, PIZZA, TRANSPORT*

NAPOLEON BONAPARTE (1769–1821)

Napoleon's surgeon, Baron Dominique Larrey, could reputedly amputate a man's leg in 14 seconds. Larrey was responsible for some great innovations in military medicine, including improvised ambulances to treat the wounded at the Storming of the Bastille on 14 July 1789, the introduction of horse-drawn 'flying ambulances' during the Napoleonic Wars, and the use of dromedaries to transport wounded soldiers in the Egyptian Campaign of 1798.

Napoleon used about 3 kilograms (7 pounds) of snuff a month.

CHAMPAGNE, HAIR, MAPS, TEETH, TINS, WELLINGTON

NARWHAL

Narwhals, which are small Arctic whales, have only two teeth, both in the upper jaw, of which one, in most males, spirals straight outwards and develops into a long tusk. Around one in 500 males have two tusks but only 15 per cent of females have a tusk at all. The narwhal is the only animal with a straight tusk and in the case of two-tusked narwhals, it is unique in that the tusks spiral in the same direction unlike those of goats, for example, which spiral in opposite directions.

UNICORN

NAURU

With an area of 21 square kilometres (8 square miles) and a population of 10,824, the Republic of Nauru in the South Pacific (formerly Pleasant Island) is the world's smallest independent state in area apart from Vatican City and Monaco, but the population of Monaco is three times as large. This leaves Nauru the second least populated country behind Vatican City, with Tuvalu (population 11,792) in third place.

Nauru's economy is mainly based on phosphate mining, but the CIA lists it as a 'broad-based money-laundering centre' too.

INCOME TAX

NAVEL

In 1944, distribution to US soldiers of the 30-page booklet *The Races of Mankind* was opposed by a sub-committee of the House Military Affairs Committee of US Congress, partly because it depicted Adam and Eve with navels. They argued that Adam and Eve could not have had navels as they were not born from a woman, though others have argued that people were created perfect, and God would hardly have given all of us navels if He hadn't given them to Adam and Eve.

In 2002, Berlin psychologist Gerhard Reibmann's book *Centred: Understanding Yourself Through Your Navel* identified six different navel types and their associated personalities: a horizontal navel, he said, means you are emotional and will live on average for 68 years; a vertical navel signifies generosity, self-confidence and emotional stability, with a life expectancy of 75 years; while a protruding navel indicates optimism, enthusiasm and 72 years of life; and anyone with a concave navel will be gentle, loving, cautious, delicate, sensitive and prone to worrying but have the lowest life expectancy of only 65 years. An off-centre navel is a sign of being fun-loving with wide emotional swings and a 70-year life expectancy. Best of all, an evenly shaped, circular navel signifies modesty and an even temper with a quiet, retiring personality and 81 years of life.

In 2001 on an Australian radio science show, Dr Karl Kruszelnicki raised the question of why navel fluff, also known as belly-button lint or BBL, is so often blue.

This resulted in 4,799 people sending him their belly-button fluff to study. He concluded that the fluff is a combination of clothing fibres and skin cells that are led to the navel, via body hair, and that: 'Your typical generator of belly-button lint or fluff is a slightly overweight, middle-aged male with a hairy abdomen.' The question of why BBL is blue has never been satisfactorily resolved as many people who never wear blue clothes were found to have blue fluff.

For people troubled by BBL, the Stick-on Belly-button Cleaner has been designed in Japan. It is an adhesive pad which you apply 'over and into the offending area, and then remove it after 10 minutes (making sure you dispose of the evidence discreetly)'. They were sold in Hong Kong at a cost of HK$48 for six adhesive strips.

In 2010, Guinness revealed that Graham Barker, a 45-year-old librarian from Perth, Australia, was the world record holder for the most BBL. He had three and a quarter sweet jars (22.1 grams) filled with his belly-button fluff, which he said he had been harvesting every evening for 26 years.

● NAVIES

The five landlocked countries with the biggest navies are as follows:

1. Bolivia, with 5,000 men and 173 vessels; 2. Paraguay, with 2,800 men and 33 vessels; 3. Laos, with about 35 patrol boats; 4. Serbia. with one ship and about 15 support craft; 5. Switzerland, with 10 patrol boats.

In 2008, the British Ministry of Defence was reported to have begun a search to find foster homes for a herd of goats. They had been used in decompression sickness experiments to investigate the effect of pressure on Navy

crews. The trials helped Naval personnel to avoid decompression sickness if they had to exit a stricken submarine.

Ⴥ *BOLIVIA, CARTER, FRISBEE, NIGERIA, RUM, SWAZILAND*

● NEEDLE

The novel *The Eye of the Needle* was written by Ken Follett, and should not be confused with *The Needle's Eye*, which is by Margaret Drabble. To add to the potential confusion, both Follett and Drabble have birthdays on 5 June.

Ⴥ *CHEESE, ST CLARE, VIKINGS*

● NELSON, Horatio (1758–1805)

The statue of Nelson in Trafalgar Square (now National Heroes Square), Bridgetown, Barbados, is older than the one in Trafalgar Square in London.

When renovation work was done on Nelson's Column in 2005–6, its height was measured by laser for the first time and it was found to be shorter than had been thought. The correct height above street level was found to be just over 51.5 metres (169 feet), while previous 'official' heights had varied from 52.7 metres (173 feet) to 56.3 metres (185 feet).

There has been much dispute over Nelson's last words, with at least four contenders for that description: 'Kiss me, Hardy', 'Kismet, Hardy', 'Thank God I have done my duty', and 'Drink drink, fan fan, rub rub'. The second of those can definitely be ruled out as the word 'kismet' (Turkish for 'destiny') was not recorded in the English language until 1849, so this alleged quotation was probably a Victorian invention to avoid the implications of Nelson asking Hardy to kiss him.

Several witnesses to Nelson's death confirm that he did ask Hardy to kiss him, and Hardy did so, on the forehead, but these were unlikely to have been his last words. Alexander John Scott, who was Nelson's personal chaplain, reported the last words as 'Thank God I have done my duty,' but according to several accounts, he repeatedly uttered the refrain, 'Drink drink; fan, fan; rub rub', during his final hours as a plea for the three things that could ease the suffering from his wounds, and these may have been Nelson's real last words.

HAIR, IPSWICH, LENNON, RUM

NEPAL

The Himalayan kingdom of Nepal is the only country that does not have a quadrilateral flag. Its flag is shaped like two slightly overlapping triangles forming a double-pennon.

Most or all countries in South-East Asia used to have triangular flags, but while the others adopted the European design of rectangular flags, Nepal not only stuck with the tradition of triangles, but doubled it.

The national animal of Nepal is the cow, and slaughtering them is banned.

Nepal produces more mustard seeds than any other country.

BANKING, FLAGS, MERCEDES, MIDGET

NEPTUNE

The planet Neptune was first observed by Galileo on 28 December 1612. He saw it again on 27 January 1613, but on both occasions he thought it was a star, not a planet.

Its existence as a planet was only confirmed in 1846 by John Couch Adams (UK), Urbain Le Verrier (France) and Johann Galle (Germany), who all discovered it independently. It was Le Verrier who suggested calling it Neptune, though he later thought that 'Leverrier' might be a better name.

In Greece, the planet is called Poseidon, the Greek equivalent of the Roman god Neptune, who was god of water and the sea and also horses.

Neptune, Apollo and Mars were the only Roman gods to whom it was considered appropriate to sacrifice bulls.

Neptune was the furthest known planet from the Sun from 1846 until 1930, when Pluto was discovered. Neptune became the furthest planet again from 1979 to 1999, when its orbit moved outside that of Pluto, and has been the furthest planet again since 2006, when Pluto was reclassified as a dwarf planet by the International Astronomical Union.

ASTRONOMY, BRITANNIA

NERD

The word 'nerd' was first coined by Dr Seuss in *If I ran the Zoo* in 1950. He used it as the name of an animal who 'certainly doesn't look like the athletic type'.

NERO, Emperor of Rome (AD 37–68)

In AD 67, Nero took a fancy to a youth called Sporus whom he had castrated, then married. It is said that Sporus bore a strong resemblance to Nero's second wife Poppaea Sabina, whom Nero had kicked to death. Nero insisted that Sporus be addressed as 'Empress' but despite this, Sporus killed himself.

Nero's second wife, Poppaea, kept 500 asses to provide milk for her bath. Nero had had his first wife, Octavia, and his mother, Agrippina, put to death in AD 59.

NETHERLANDS

The hole in the centre of a CD was originally made to be the size of the smallest coin in Europe – a Dutch 10 cent coin. This coin was abolished when the Netherlands joined the euro.

The height of the average Dutchman increased by more than 3 centimetres (1.2 inches) from the start of the 1980s, to above 180 cm (71 inches) in 2000. But since then the increase has been marginal, and in 2021 government statisticians reported that men born in 2001 were slightly shorter than those born in 2020. Despite this, the Dutch are still the tallest nation with adult men measuring an average 182.9 centimetres (6 feet) and adult women 169.3 centi-metres (5.55 feet).

The entire population of the Neth-erlands was sentenced to death by the Spanish Inquisition in 1568.

The weight of fish landed in the Netherlands in a year is equal to 513 million kilograms, which oddly enough is equal to the weight of 54 billion British pound coins, which was the cost of refurbishment calculated in 2017 for the entire British rail network.

CAKE, CARTWHEEL, COMPUTERS, FOOTBALL, REMBRANDT, ROBBERY

NETTLES

Nettles sting through their poison-loaded hairs, which are hollow and stiffened with silica. They break when brushed against, leaving a sharp point which punctures the skin and delivers the venom. The world's most poisonous nettles are found in Java. Their sting can be fatal.

The 17th-century herbalist Nicholas Culpeper recommended nettles to 'consume the phlegmatic superfluities in the body of man'.

Mark Lane, the Buckingham Palace head gardener, says nettles play an important role in the gardens, providing a valuable food source for the Queen's caterpillars.

Dried and powdered nettle leaves have been used to treat small cuts and stop them bleeding.

The Latin name for nettles, *Urtica*, comes from the verb 'uro' meaning 'I burn'.

Nettles used to be hung in bunches in larders because of their fly-repellent properties.

'When people will not weed their own minds, they are apt to be overrun with nettles.' Horace Walpole

NEUTRON STAR

The density of a neutron star is so high that one teaspoon of it would weigh about 10 times as much as the total weight of all the people on Earth. Its gravitational pull is so strong that an object dropped from 1 metre (3.3 feet) above its surface would hit the ground in a millionth of a second at a speed of about 2,000 kilometres (1,243 miles) per second.

NEW DELHI

On 12 December 1911, King George V announced that the capital of India was to be moved from Calcutta to Delhi. On the same day in Delhi, the King and Queen were crowned Emperor and Empress of India.

Sir Edwin Lutyens designed the new capital, which was renamed New Delhi in 1927. The origin of Delhi's name is unknown. Ideas include a Persian word for gateway, a Hindi word for a loose pillar, or the name of an ancient king.

Delhi is the only city in India where women motorcyclists do not have to wear helmets. There are over 2 million bicycles in Delhi.

New Delhi is the only city in the world where the buses all run on compressed natural gas.

♀ *OBAMA, STATISTICS*

NEW GUINEA

New Guinea is the world's second largest island after Greenland. It was given its name by a 16th-century Spanish explorer, Yñigo Ortiz de Retez, because he thought the native inhabitants resembled the people of the Guinea region of Africa.

♀ *BOWERBIRD, COCONUT, SEX*

NEW YEAR'S EVE

It was reported in January 2011 that a man in Sicily had stolen sweets and chewing gum so that he could spend New Year's Eve in jail and avoid having to see his relatives.

♀ *DRUNKEN DRIVING*

NEW YORK

The Empire State Building in New York contains 60,000 tons of steel, 6,500 windows and is served by 73 lifts.

According to a survey in 2021, New York is the city that appears most in popular songs, featuring in 5,470 songs around the world. It is followed by Paris (3,226), Seoul (2,866), London (2,256) and Miami (1,505). France is the most sung about country, followed by Mexico and China.

♀ *BUS DRIVERS, FLIRTING, PENGUINS, POLAR BEAR, SNOW, STATUE OF LIBERTY*

NEW ZEALAND

The first sheep in New Zealand arrived with Captain James Cook in 1773. They now outnumber humans in New Zealand by a ratio of about 13 to 1.

In the Maori language of New Zealand, the word *konewa* means 'the habit of singing while near the house out of doors'. This is seen as a bad omen. The word *maori*, incidentally, means an ordinary or normal person.

In New Zealand, condoms, lubricants, gels, oils, lingerie, costumes, whipped cream and bubble bath all constitute deductible expenses for sex workers.

In 1893, New Zealand became the first country to give votes to women, but women did not have the right to stand for parliament until 1919.

Brewers in New Zealand decided to abolish barmaids on 18 January 1909.

♀ *GOOSEBERRY, HEDGEHOG, HILLARY, TUATARA, WIZARDRY*

NEWCASTLE

When Robert Curthose, eldest son of William the Conqueror, built a castle on his return into England from a raid into Scotland in 1080, he named it his Novum Castellum, or New Castle, and the name stuck for the castle and the region around it.

♀ *LIGHT BULB, TRANSPLANTATION*

NEWFOUNDLAND

The official dogs of the Canadian province of Newfoundland and Labrador are the Newfoundland dog and the Labrador Retriever, but the official animal is the caribou.

♀ *AMERICA, FOG, SWIMMING*

NEWTON, Isaac (1642–1727)

Isaac Newton has been credited with the invention of the cat-flap. He is said to have devised it as a means of allowing cats to enter his rooms in Cambridge without spoiling his optics experiments. This account is sometimes embellished with a story of Newton cutting a hole in the door for his cat, and later adding a smaller hole for kittens. The tale is dubious on at least two counts: first, it seems not to have been told until 1802; and second, there is an account of a cat-hole in a door in Chaucer's *Miller's Tale* which dates back to at least 1400, and there is also a cat-hole in Cheetham's Library in Manchester which was built in 1421.

From 1689 to 1690, Isaac Newton served as Member of Parliament for Cambridge University, but he is reported to have spoken only once, when he asked an usher to close a window because it was chilly.

There are 150 places called Newton in the UK.

⚲ *ALCHEMY, APPLE, GRAVITY, MAYPOLE, SLOANE*

● NEWTON-JOHN, Olivia (b. 1948)

Olivia Newton-John's father, Brinley Newton-John, was a Welsh Professor of German, who worked on the Enigma project at Bletchley Park during the Second World War and was the officer who took Rudolph Hess into custody. Her mother was the daughter of Nobel Prize-winning physicist Max Born.

⚲ *QUANTUM MECHANICS*

● NIAGARA FALLS

Niagara Falls resulted from glaciers melting at the end of the Ice Age around 12,000 years ago.

On 29 March 1848, an ice blockage in the Niagara River caused the Niagara Falls to run dry. They never ran dry again, before or since. The date is celebrated in the region as Niagara Falls Runs Dry Day.

The Niagara Falls are made up of three falls: the Horseshoe Falls (the largest) the American Falls and the Bridal Veil Falls (the smallest). The three waterfalls combine to produce the highest flow rate of any waterfall on Earth. On an average day, over 3,000 tons of water flow over the Falls every second.

It is not only dangerous but illegal to try to go over the Niagara Falls. In 1859, Charles Blondin became the first person to cross the Falls on a tightrope. When Nik Wallender did the same in 2012, he was required to carry his passport with him to show on the Canadian side.

In 1901, on her 63rd birthday, Annie Taylor was the first person to go over the Falls in a barrel.

Many fish are known to swim down the Falls. Around 90 per cent survive.

In 1883, Matthew Webb, who had been the first to swim the English Channel, drowned when trying to swim the rapids at the foot of Niagara.

⚲ *WATERFALL*

● NICARAGUA

Each year before Easter, the town of Masaya in Nicaragua celebrates the Festival of San Lazaro at the Santa Maria Magdalena Church, when people arrive with dogs dressed in ornate and elaborate costumes to give thanks to the patron saint of pets for keeping their animals in good health.

During June, the Pueblo Blancos of San Juan de Oriente, Diriá and Diriomo celebrate their fiestas with dancing warriors re-enacting battles by beating each other over the head with bulls' penises.

⚲ *ABORTION, BEANS, ORGASM*

● NIETZSCHE, Friedrich (1844–1900)

The German philosopher Friedrich Nietzsche has more consecutive consonants in his surname than any other major philosopher. In London, however, the street and underground railway station Knightsbridge has six consecutive consonants, which is one more than Nietzsche.

In 1889, Nietzsche suffered a breakdown in the streets of Turin, which caused a public disturbance. According to one account, he was upset by the sight of a horse being whipped, ran to the horse and threw his arms around its neck, then collapsed. Shortly after, he sent letters to colleagues and friends telling them that he had been crucified by German doctors and ordering the German Emperor to go to Rome in order to be shot.

NIGER

Niger has the world's highest fertility rate at 6.8 children per woman (2019 figures). Somalia is in second place with a figure of 6.0.

FIREWORKS, NIGERIA, UGANDA

NIGERIA

With 206 million people, Nigeria is the most populous country in Africa and has the seventh highest population in the world. It comes fourth from last in the world for life expectancy at birth, with an average of 55.75 years (2020 figures). Only Lesotho, Chad and the Central African Republic are worse.

In 2019, Nigeria had 1.8 million AIDS sufferers, which was the fourth highest in the world.

The serendipity berry, or Nigerian berry, *Dioscoreophyllum cumminsii*, which was discovered in Nigeria in the 1960s, is 1,500 times sweeter than sugar.

In the 1980s, it was reported that Nigeria's Navy included 20 ships whose names all meant 'hippopotamus' in various languages and dialects spoken in the country.

It is illegal to import green cars into Nigeria. Only the military may drive green cars.

ASH, EXAMINATIONS, GOAT, LUCK, PALINDROME, PUMPKIN

NIGHTINGALE, Florence (1820–1910)

Florence Nightingale was named after the city of her birth, Florence in Italy. Her older sister was called Parthenope, having been born in a Greek settlement of that name near Naples.

'Florence Nightingale' is an anagram of 'Flit on, cheering angel' or 'Reflecting on healing'.

In 2009, the Florence Nightingale Museum in London launched a campaign to raise £13,000 to buy her pet owl, Athena. Nightingale rescued the owl on a trip to the Acropolis in Greece where she saw it being tormented by a group of boys. Athena liked to sit on Florence's shoulder, or in her pocket, or in a specially made pouch, and became her constant companion. She had the owl stuffed shortly after its death in 1854.

NIPPLE

Mammarism, invented around 1940 by Patrick Cullen, is a form of divination from the crinkles around nipples. Cullen, who was an Irishman who operated on Brighton Pier, called himself a 'chest clairvoyant', claiming that he had developed the technique of nipple divination in the brothels of Shanghai during a 25-year career in the army, rising to the rank of regimental sergeant major.

His method involved daubing the client's breasts in paint, then pressing them against paper to obtain an imprint. In his later years, he took imprints of bottoms as well.

CELLO, CENTAUR, GUITAR, NUDITY, WITCH-CRAFT, WOMBAT

● NIXON, Richard Milhous (1913–94)

The item most frequently requested from the US National Archives is a photograph of Elvis Presley shaking hands with President Richard Nixon in 1970. When they met, Elvis gave Nixon a present of a Colt 45 pistol. Nixon gave Presley a Federal Bureau of Narcotics badge.

♀ *CLINTON, PRESLEY*

● NO-BALLS

In September 2010, Pakistani cricketers who had been accused of involvement in a betting scam involving the allegedly deliberate bowling of no-balls were urged to regain public respect by taking part in an advertisement for dog and cat neutering. The recommendation came from the US-based charity PETA (People for the Ethical Treatment of Animals), which issued a statement saying, 'No-balls may be a bad thing in cricket, but for dogs and cats, "no balls" are a lifesaver.'

● NOAH

According to the Book of Enoch in the Apocrypha, Noah was an albino. Describing Noah's birth, Enoch says that his mother, the wife of Lamech, 'brought forth a child, the flesh of which was white as snow, and red as a rose; the hair of whose head was white like wool, and long; and whose eyes were beautiful'. The implications of this passage were discussed in the *British Medical Journal* in 1958 in an article entitled 'Noah – An Albino' by Arnold Sorsby, a Research Professor in Ophthalmology.

♀ *NOAH'S ARK, JOAN OF ARC, RAIN, YEMEN*

● NOAH'S ARK

According to St Hippolytus, Noah's ark included Noah, his family, 14 birds of each species, 14 clean animals of each species, two unclean animals of each species, supplies of gold, frankincense and myrrh, and rows of sharp anti-fornication spikes to keep males and females apart.

♀ *HYENA, JOAN OF ARC, RAIN, RAVEN*

● NOBEL PRIZE

Alfred Nobel, who founded the prizes that bear his name, was the inventor of dynamite. His father, Immanuel Nobel, invented plywood.

Up to the end of 2021, 58 women had won a Nobel Prize. Since Marie Curie won it twice (once for Physics, once for Chemistry), a total of 59 Nobel Prizes have been awarded to women.

For the first 100 years of the Nobel Prize (1901–2000), more awards were made to men from Trinity College, Cambridge, than to women in the entire world, but since then the women have established a big lead. Trinity College still has only 34 Nobel Prizes.

Marie Curie (Chemistry and Physics) and Linus Pauling (Chemistry and Peace) are the only people to have won two Nobel Prizes in different disciplines. John Bardeen (Physics) and Frederick Sanger (Chemistry) each won two Nobels in the same discipline.

Only two people have turned down awards of Nobel Prizes: in 1964, Jean-Paul Sartre turned down the Literature prize on the grounds that such honours could interfere with a writer's responsibilities to his readers; and in 1974, Le Duc Tho, who had been offered a share of the Peace prize with Henry Kissinger for their work to end the Vietnam War, refused to accept it, saying that 'peace has not yet been established'.

28 February and 21 May have each been the birthdays of seven Nobel

Prize winners. No other dates have as many.

BOOKS, BRAIN, ECONOMICS, KIPLING, PHYSICS, WISDOM

NOISE

According to a study at University College London and Newcastle University in 2012 in which functional magnetic resonance imaging was used to examine how people's brains respond to unpleasant noises, the five worst sounds in the world are as follows: 1. Knife on a bottle; 2. Fork on a glass; 3. Chalk on a blackboard; 4. Ruler on a bottle; 5. Nails on a blackboard. All of those were declared to be worse than a female scream (sixth) or a baby crying (ninth).

DUCK, HEDGEHOG, HERRING, KOALA, OYSTER, SNORING

NOODLE

In 2005, the science journal *Nature* reported the find of a 4,000-year-old bowl of noodles in China. 'This is the earliest empirical evidence of noodles ever found,' said Houyuan Lu of the Institute of Geology and Geophysics at Beijing's Chinese Academy of Sciences. The noodles were made of two types of millet. Before this discovery of noodles at the Lajia archaeological site, the earliest record of noodles was in a book written during China's East Han Dynasty sometime between AD 25 and 220, Lu said.

The word 'noodle' was first used to refer to a thread of pasta in English in 1779, but 'noodle' meaning 'a stupid person or fool' was used in 1720, while 'noodle' as a slang term for the head appeared in 1762.

NOODLING

Noodling is currently legal in 19 US states. It was legalised in Texas by a vote in their Senate in May 2011, and West Virginia legalised it in 2018. Noodling is the old Southern tradition of catching catfish by hand. Until 2011, Texas noodlers faced a fine of up to $500.

The technique of noodling involves putting your hand into the hole in which a catfish lives, which makes the vicious fish try to bite it. The trick is to grab its jaws before it does so. Addressing the Senate, State Senator Bob Deuell, who represents the East Texas community of Greenville, said: 'I personally don't noodle, but I would defend to the death your right to do so.'

CATFISH, NOAH'S ARK

NORFOLK ISLAND

The name of the language spoken on Norfolk Island is Norfuk. It was listed as an endangered language by the United Nations in 2007. The name of the island in their language is 'Norfuk Ailen'. Their word for 'Europe' is 'Urup'.

The language spoken on nearby Pitcairn Island is Pitkern.

NORTH KOREA

In January 2005, North Korea stepped up its campaign against long hair, which, government spokesmen said, indicated a capitalist lifestyle. Long hair was also said to consume a good deal of nutrition and rob the brain of energy. Wearing blue jeans and practising a religion are illegal in North Korea.

NORTH POLE

The Geographic North Pole is a fixed point determined by the axis of the Earth's spin; the Magnetic North Pole slowly drifts across the Canadian Arctic.

It is currently moving north-west from Canada towards Siberia at about 55 kilometres (34 miles) a year. The Northern Pole of Inaccessibility is the point furthest from any land: it is at 84°03' N 174°51' W.

When Matthew Henson and Robert Peary became the first to reach the North Pole on 6 April 1909, their support team included 24 men, 19 sledges and 133 dogs.

The average temperature at the North Pole is -18°C (-0.4°F). At the South Pole it is -50°C (-58°F).

In magnetic terms, the Magnetic North Pole is a south pole – that is why the north pole of other magnets point to it.

On 20 April 1987, Fukashi Kazami of Japan became the first person to reach the North Pole on a motorcycle.

⚲ *CANADA, EARTH, JANUARY, METRIC SYSTEM, SANTA CLAUS, SOUTH POLE*

🔘 NORWAY

Norway was the first non-English speaking country to host the Golden Shears World Championship for sheep shearing. The 13th such championship was held in the village of Bjerkreim in 2008 and attracted around 28 shearers and some 2,700 sheep.

There is a town called Hell in Norway.

Statistics show that 22 per cent of Norwegians named August were born in August. The playwright August Strindberg was born in January.

⚲ *AA, BERGMAN, BOOKS, DOYLE, GARDENING, POLAR BEAR*

🔘 NOSE

Professor Lees Ray, of Wavertree near Liverpool, invented the Nose Improver in the 1890s. Made of pieces of brass, adjustable by screws, it was designed to press any unbeautiful nose into the desired shape 'from nez retroussé to nose Hebraic', as his advertising copy explained.

Prices ranged from nine shillings and sixpence to two and a half guineas and he was reported to do a good trade, selling 600 nose machines a year and treating an additional 2,500 people 'cursed with red or fiery noses'. He even had one request from a middle-aged man who wanted his nose put awry in order to induce the girl to whom he was engaged to give him up, as he had become engaged to another girl when away on a business trip. He apparently had faith that the device would restore the 'nasal status quo ante' after it bent his nose out of shape.

In 2014, plastic surgeons in the US asked a group of almost 4,000 men and women aged 18–25 to rank digital portraits of women from the same age range with noses that were 96, 101, 106, 111 and 116 degrees to their face. The survey concluded that the noses rated most beautiful were at 106 degrees to the face. They found that those of the Duchess of Cambridge, Scarlett Johansson, Kate Beckinsale and Jessica Biel best fitted that description.

In 2016, however, a leading cosmetic surgeon analysed the facial features requested by his patients over 10 years and reported that the perfect face combines Kate Middleton's nose, Angelina Jolie's cheeks, Keira Knightley's eyes and Miley Cyrus's forehead.

None of those mentioned above, however, had their noses insured for as much as leading European wine-maker and taster Ilja Gort who, in 2008, insured his nose for 5 million euros (£3.8 million). Under the terms of the policy, the Dutchman was not allowed to ride a motorcycle or be a boxer, knife thrower's assistant or fire-breather.

In January 2021, the *Ear, Nose and Throat Journal* published a paper 'Can Sex Improve Nasal Function? – An Exploration of the Link Between Sex and Nasal Function'. By measuring nasal breathing both before and at varying times after sexual climax, the researchers showed that sexual orgasms can be as effective as decongestant medicines in improving nasal breathing.

♀ *ADULTERY, BILLIARDS, BODY, BRAHE, PIZZA, WASP, WOMBAT*

● NOSE-PICKING

The technical term for compulsive nose-picking is rhinotillexomania.

In 2001, a study on nose-picking in schools in Bangalore reported that almost the entire sample of 200 admitted to nose-picking, with an average of 4 times per day: 7.6 per cent of the sample picked their noses over 20 times per day; nearly 17 per cent of subjects said they had a serious nose-picking problem; 25 per cent of subjects reported occasional nose bleeds interfering with their picking; 80 per cent used only their fingers while the rest were split, some choosing tweezers while others preferred pencils; 11 per cent claimed they did it for cosmetic reasons, and a similar number did it for pleasure; 4.5 per cent admitted they ate their nose-pickings.

● NOSTRIL

Research in 2002 showed that if a person is taught to recognise a particular smell through one nostril, he or she will recognise it through the other one as well. In 2020, however, a subtle twist on that result revealed that our two nostrils enable us to smell in stereo. Researchers in China gave subjects a visual test involving moving dots, then had them look at a fixed cross while applying smells to their nostrils, but giving a stronger concentration to one nostril than the other. The researchers found that participants consistently thought that they were moving in the direction of the stronger smell, despite being unable to tell which nostril had received the stronger concentration. 'The findings indicate that humans have a stereo sense of smell that subconsciously guides navigation,' the researchers said.

♀ *BODY, KIWI, MARSHMALLOW*

● NOVA SCOTIA

Nova Scotia was named in a 1621 Royal Charter granting the right to the Scottish courtier and poet Sir William Alexander to settle lands in Canada.

The first North American documented sighting of a UFO was on 12 October 1786 at New Minas, Nova Scotia.

Alexander Graham Bell, inventor of the telephone, is buried in Nova Scotia.

♀ *ST ANDREW*

● NOVEMBER

November is the Percussion Marketing Council's International Drum Month, as well as being National Pomegranate Month in the US.

In Old English, November was called 'Blotmonath', meaning 'sacrifice month'. The Welsh for November is Tachwedd, meaning 'slaughter', as it was time for slaughtering beasts. There is no mention of the month of November in any of Shakespeare's plays or sonnets.

2 November is the only date in the calendar that was the birthday of two US presidents: Warren Harding (1865) and James Polk (1795).

'If there's ice in November to bear a duck, there'll be nothing after but sludge and muck.' Old weather lore

♀ ACCIDENTS, MOOSE, OCTOBER

NUDISM

Although the adjective 'nude' dates back to 1493, the word 'nudism' was not seen until 1857, and 'nudist' first appeared in 1866 when it meant a painter of nude subjects.

Nudist Tomas Cameselle was fined a total of £65 in July 1982 in Pontevedra, Spain, £60 of which was for appearing naked in a public place (the beach) and £5 for failing to carry identity papers.

A Nudists' Conference was held at Whispering Pines resort in North Carolina in 1996. It was inaugurated by an owner of the resort, Carol Love, reading a poem she had composed specially for the event:

> Here we are sitting together in the
>   nude.
> Some folks in society would exclaim
>   to us, how rude!
> But we know we're all good people, we
>   came to praise the Lord.
> So let's all shout to Jesus and clap our
>   hands of one accord.

♀ CROATIA

NUDITY

Under the legal code of the state of Tennessee, 'nudity' means 'the showing of the human male or female genitals, pubic area, or buttocks with less than a fully opaque covering or the showing of the female breast with less than a fully opaque covering of any portion below the top of the nipple, or the depiction of covered male genitals in a discernibly turgid state'.

Breastfeeding, however, is explicitly stated not to be considered as nudity.

♀ CENSORSHIP, LOS ANGELES, PHOBIAS

NUMBER PLATE

A car number plate bearing only the number '1' sold for a record £7.1 million at a charity auction in the United Arab Emirates in February 2008. The record in the UK is £400,000, fetched by the number plate 25 O in November 2014.

♀ WALES

NUMBERS

'Forty' is the only number which, when spelled out in English, has its letters in alphabetical order. 'One' is the only number that has its letters in reverse alphabetical order.

None of the numbers from one to 99 contains the letter A.

The highest number that can be spelled out without using any letter more than once is 'five thousand'. The next highest is 'eighty-four'.

The only sums that can be spelled out without repeating a letter are: FOUR + SIX = TEN and variations on that, such as TEN – FOUR = SIX.

♀ ADDRESS, BENFORD'S LAW, COMPUTATION, DARTS, FORTY-SEVEN, ROULETTE

NUNS

A world record for the largest gathering of people dressed as nuns was set at a 'Nunday' event in Listowel, Ireland, on 30 June 2012, where 1,436 adults gathered in a sports field in nuns' attire. Adjudicators checked that they observed a strict dress code, including a habit, veil, black shoes and black socks or tights. In the early hours of the following morning, police entered a bar on two separate occasions and found 51 'nuns' on the premises. The publican was charged with serving alcoholic drinks to them after closing time.

♀ CELIBACY, GALILEI, RAVEN

NURSING

According to the *Oxford English Dictionary*, a 'nurse' originally meant specifically a wet nurse, then came to be used for a woman looking after children.

There are characters called Nurse in three Shakespeare plays: *Romeo and Juliet*, *Titus Andronicus* and *Henry VI, Part 3*.

♀ SEX

NYLON

On 16 February 1937, Wallace Carothers was granted a patent for his invention of the artificial fabric we now call nylon. Nylon's makers, du Pont, described nylon as 'synthetic fibre-forming polymeric amides having a protein-like chemical structure … and characterized by extreme toughness and strength'.

The word 'nylon' was not coined until 1938. A team at du Pont came up with a list of 400 possible names, all of which were rejected. One suggested name was 'no-run', but it was rejected on the grounds that nylon stockings might run just as silk ones did. The name of 'nylon' came from just playing around with 'no-run'. The claim that it signified New York and London has no basis in fact.

Wallace Carothers, who had long suffered from depression, killed himself by taking cyanide only months after the nylon patent was issued.

The first commercial nylon product was a toothbrush with nylon bristles in 1938.

♀ STOCKINGS

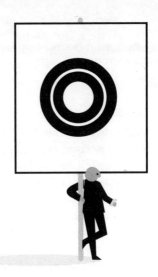

● OBAMA, Barack (b. 1961)

John McCain defeated Barack Obama in 2008, reaching the winning post before his opponent had left the starting line. The occasion was a race between two hissing cockroaches of those names, organised by the New Jersey Pest Management Association to publicise its trade show.

Meanwhile, in the presidential election between the cockroaches' namesakes, Barack Obama received help from an unlikely source in New Delhi, where a dozen priests were reported to have offered prayers to the Hindu monkey God Hanuman for an Obama victory. The businessman who organised the event said an Obama victory would be good for India.

According to Arnold Schwarzenegger, Barack Obama has 'skinny legs' and 'scrawny little arms'.

Until Barack Obama went to university, he was known as 'Barry'. He then switched to the full version of his name. His grandmother called him 'Bar'. His first name, Barack, means 'blessed' in Swahili.

He worked in a Baskin-Robbins ice cream shop as a teenager and now dislikes ice cream.

He is said to have applied to appear in a black pin-up calendar while at Harvard but was rejected by the all-female committee.

His shoes are size 11.

He kept a pet ape called Tata while living in Indonesia.

Obama's father, also named Barack, grew up as a goat herd in Kenya before studying economics in Hawaii. Obama's parents split up when he was two and his father lost both legs in a car crash in 1981.

While he was President, Obama had his hair cut once a week by his Chicago barber, Zariff.

'President Obama' is an anagram of both 'A most deep brain' and 'most pea-brained'.

♀ *BUSH George Walker, CLEVELAND, COCONUT, KANSAS, WINNIE-THE-POOH*

● OBEDIENCE

On 12 September 1922, the House of Bishops of the US Episcopal Church voted to delete the word 'obey' from the marriage vows. 'I swear to love, honour and obey,' became 'I swear to love and honour.'

'Disobedience is the true foundation of liberty. The obedient must be slaves.'
Henry David Thoreau

OBESITY

According to a report in July 2020, obesity can be taken as a sign of corruption. The paper 'Obesity of politicians and corruption in post-Soviet countries' by Pavlo Blavatskyy was based on the analysis of 299 facial images of cabinet ministers in former Soviet states, to estimate their body mass, which was then correlated with conventional measures of corruption. The author concludes: 'This result suggests that physical characteristics of politicians such as their body-mass index can be used as proxy variables for political corruption when the latter are not available.'

According to a report in 1999 entitled 'Reducing children's television viewing to prevent obesity', children who give up watching television for a week reduce their waist measurements by an average 2.3 centimetres (0.9 inches).

The people of the United States are overweight by a total of about 4 billion pounds.

In August 1996, a 'pot-bellies seminar' was held in India which 110 fat policemen were ordered to attend. A police chief commented, 'Photographs in the press of pot-bellied policemen have given the police a bad name.'

On 5 November 1997 in Wellington, New Zealand, William Dickie, 43, was sentenced to 12 months' house arrest because he was too big for prison clothing or a prison bed. Mr Dickie's weight was given as 305 kilograms (672 pounds).

♀ BOSTON, PENSIONER, SADDLE, TONGA

OCEAN

Seventy-one per cent of the Earth's surface is covered by the oceans, containing about 321 million cubic miles of water in which is dissolved about 47 million billion tons of salt, gases and other minerals. As all the oceans are connected, there is really just one ocean, though we have long divided it into four parts: the Atlantic, Pacific, Indian and Arctic Oceans. In 2001, the International Hydrographic Organization added a fifth: the Southern Ocean around Antarctica.

The ice in Antarctica contains almost as much water as the whole of the Atlantic. The number of water molecules in one teaspoon of water is roughly equal to the number of teaspoons of water in the Atlantic.

Mount Everest would be totally submerged if dropped into the Philippine Trench in the Pacific.

It would take over an hour for a heavy object to sink 10.8 kilometres (6.7 miles) down to the deepest part of the ocean, the Mariana Trench.

More than 100,000 cubic miles of water evaporate from the oceans every year, mostly returning as rain.

The top 3 metres (10 feet) of the ocean hold as much heat as the entire atmosphere.

Each year, three times as much rubbish is dumped into the world's oceans as the weight of fish caught.

Life began in the oceans more than 3 billion years ago. Life on land is a relative newcomer, having arrived only about 400 million years ago.

According to experts at the World Register of Marine Life, some 230,000 marine species have been identified, but the total may be over a million.

The word 'ocean' does not occur in

the King James Bible, but there are 425 instances of 'sea' or 'seas' and one of 'seafaring'.

The 2001 film *Ocean's Eleven* has cameo appearances by Angie Dickinson and Henry Silva, both of whom appeared in the original 1960 *Ocean's 11*.

⚲ *AMAZON, ATLANTIC, CRUSTACEAN, PANAMA, SUICIDE, YOKO ONO*

● OCTOBER

The Anglo-Saxons called October Winterfylleth (or Winterfilth, as Tolkien's hobbits preferred it), meaning the 'fullness' (rather than filth) of winter. The Welsh had a very different name for October: Hydref (originally Hyddfref), a word referring to the lowing of cattle.

In Catholic Europe in 1582, October had only 21 days. Because of the change from the Julian to the Gregorian calendar, the days from 5 to 14 October were omitted.

The 'October Revolution' in Russia in 1917 took place in November, but at the time Russians had not yet changed from the Julian calendar. Even when its anniversary had moved into November, they continued calling it the October Revolution.

According to a study in Italy published in the journal *Human Reproduction* in 2003, October is the best month for conceiving a boy. The research by Dr Angelo Cagnacci was based on an analysis of 14,310 births at the Policlinico of Modena in which the sex of the baby was compared with the month of conception. The results showed that for every thousand babies conceived in October, there were 535 males and 465 females, but when the baby was conceived in April, there were 487 males and 513 females. Dr Cagnacci suggested that this was nature's response to the fact

that male foetuses and newborns are more vulnerable than females. October is the month that offers the best conditions for conception happening, so more boy babies in that month compensates for their vulnerability.

⚲ *BOUNTY, COLUMBUS, GOOSE*

● OCTOPUS

According to a paper in the journal *Progress in Biophysics and Molecular Biology* in January 2022, octopuses may come from another planet. A team of 33 authors said that 'the possibility that cryopreserved squid and/or octopus eggs, arrived in icy bolides [very bright meteors] several hundred million years ago should not be discounted'. They also pointed out that the octopus has biological features that appear to suggest 'some type of pre-existence'.

Octopuses have blue blood and three hearts. Two of the hearts pump blood through the gills where it picks up oxygen, while the central third heart is responsible for circulating the oxygenated blood around the body.

An octopus brain is even weirder than its heart. Only about 10 per cent of its neurons are in the main central brain in its head; another 30 per cent are in its optic lobes and the other 60 per cent are shared by its eight legs, which lets the legs think and learn independently.

In July 1996, the Sealife Centre in Blackpool issued an urgent appeal for two unwanted Castlemaine XXXX beer bottles to serve as homes for their Australian blue-ringed octopuses. In the wild, they have been seen to choose such bottles for their nests: the neck is the right width for them to get in while keeping predators out.

The world's first hexapus – a six-legged version of an octopus – was found off the coast of North Wales in 2008. Experts said the missing legs were caused by a birth defect, not an accident. The hexapus was taken to Blackpool Sea Life Centre, where it was named Henry.

Strictly speaking, the plural of 'octopus' is 'octopuses'. Referring to them as 'octopi' is based on the misconception that the final -us comes from Latin, whereas the derivation is Greek. For that reason, the plural 'octopodes' is sometimes seen, though rather old-fashioned.

♀ BEER MATS, BLOOD, DIOGENES, QUEENSLAND

ODIN

The Norse god Odin was known as Woden in Old English; Wednesday (Woden's day) was named after him.

Odin had an eight-legged horse called Sleipnir, which had the job of conveying its rider to Valhalla or the Underworld. In modern times, the Bell Sleipnir™ Lift Device is a stretcher specially designed to be used by undertakers.

♀ RAVEN, THOR

OFFICE

The 1809 Sale of Offices Act was passed in haste as a result of a scandal involving the Duke of York and his mistress, an actress named Mrs Clarke. The Duke was commander-in-chief of the army, and for two months, the House of Commons examined witnesses who testified that Mrs Clarke had been selling military offices and promotions. It was also alleged that the Duke knew of the sales and even took some of the money himself.

Eventually, the House voted, by 278 to 196, that the Duke had not been guilty of personal corruption or connivance at corruption. Nevertheless, as he had clearly allowed his mistress to know too much of his official business, he was forced to resign his official appointments.

The Sale of Offices Act was then quickly passed by Spencer Perceval's government, making it a crime to sell public offices for money.

♀ BALLPOINT, BRAIN, UNEMPLOYMENT, WELSH, WINDOW

OIL

In 2020, five of the top eight highest-earning companies in the world were in the oil business: Sinopec (Chinese Oil and Petroleum), China National Petroleum, Royal Dutch Shell, Saudi Aramco and BP were in 2nd, 4th, 5th, 6th and 8th places in the Fortune 500. The only non-oil companies interrupting their dominance were Walmart (1st), the State Grid of China (3rd) and Volkswagen (7th). The top five most valuable global brands, however, were all computer or Internet-based: Apple, Google, Microsoft, Amazon and Facebook, all of which beat Coca-Cola into 6th place.

♀ DOUGHNUTS, GUT BARGING, LOS ANGELES, OLIVE, TALIBAN, WITCHCRAFT

OKAPI

The okapi, *Okapia johnstoni*, is the only known relative of the giraffe. It was discovered by British colonial administrator Sir Harry Johnston in 1901 after having been mentioned in the writings of Henry Morton Stanley a decade earlier. Unlike Stanley, who called the animal a 'donkey', Johnston shot one and sent its skin and skull back to England.

Okapi live in the Democratic Republic of the Congo and the People's Republic of the Congo and their tongues are long enough to wash their eyelids, clean out their ears, and even swat insects away from their necks. Their ears can rotate independently, which enables them to listen for sounds both in front and behind.

The first postage stamp to depict an okapi was issued by the Belgian Congo (now the Democratic Republic of the Congo) in 1932.

OKLAHOMA

In May 2000, the state of Oklahoma began a project to eliminate the word 'squaw' from its place names. 'Squaw' came from a native American word which originally meant a woman or wife, but was then used by trappers in a derogative way, finally becoming a slur understood as meaning a prostitute or a woman's genitalia. The Oklahoma legislature unanimously agreed to follow Montana, Maine and Minnesota in removing the word from all place names, beginning in the town of Red Rock, when a bridge over Squaw Creek was being replaced. After hearing appeals by members of the Otoe-Missouria tribe, Red Rock Mayor Geary Watson supported their viewpoint. 'If this creek's name was in its English equivalent,' he said, 'it would be considered an unprintable word.'

⚲ *SHOPPING TROLLEYS, WATERMELON*

OLIVE

The most popular names for boys and girls in England and Wales in 2020 were Oliver and Olivia. Both names are seen as referring to the olive tree as a symbol of peace. Remarkably, in the same year the girl's name Olive was 99th most popular, the first time it had broken into the top 100.

There are about 800 million olive trees in the world, of which about 20 million

are in China. Olive oil is mentioned 140 times in the Bible.

'Light that shines on olive leaves is like

a diamond and makes the painter lose focus.' Pierre Auguste Renoir

⚲ *MONACO, OLYMPIC GAMES, PENGUIN, POMEGRANATE, POPEYE, SPAIN*

OLYMPIC GAMES

Nobody knows when the first Olympic Games took place but they were certainly held every four years from 776 BC until AD 393 when the Roman emperor Theodosius banned the Games because they were showing increasing signs of competition for personal gain and glory, particularly in chariot races.

Held at Olympia in Greece, they were such a fixed part of the calendar that the Greeks calculated their calendar in 'Olympiads' – periods of four years between successive events. For that purpose, 776 BC was taken as the year of the first Olympiad, though the Games had definitely been held, if at irregular intervals, for some time before that.

The earliest known Olympic gold medallist (actually, winners received an olive wreath at the time, not a gold medal) was Coroebus of Elis, a cook who won a 200-yard race in 776 BC. This sprint down the length of the stadium was for a long time the only athletics event at the Games, though a second race, over twice the distance, was added at the 14th Olympics. There were also competitions in music, oratory and theatre. Only when the Spartans joined in during the 18th Olympics did the accent shift to physical prowess and a pentathlon of running, jumping, wrestling, the javelin and discus-throwing was included.

In 1896, Baron Pierre de Coubertin brought the Games back, with 13 countries competing in Athens. In 1900, the Olympics were a sideshow at the World Exhibition in Paris, dragging on for over five months. In 1904, the Americans squabbled so much over whether they should be held in Chicago or St Louis that most European nations stayed away. The Olympic movement was put back on track with the 'Intercalated Games' of 1906 in Athens, which set the scene for the London Olympics of 1908 at which the English protested about the Irish flag, the Russians complained about the Finnish flag, and everybody complained about the British judges and referees. Out of 110 events, Britain, which had by far the most contestants, won 56.

Events of which little has been seen in recent Olympics include cricket, at which Britain beat France – the only other team that entered – in Paris in 1900; and croquet, at which France won all the medals in 1900. There were women's archery events in 1904 and women's swimming in 1912, but no track and field events for women until 1928.

Greatest Olympian of all: Aladar Gerevich, the Hungarian fencer who won gold medals in six consecutive Olympic Games between 1932 and 1960.

♀ *BASKETBALL, BRUNEI, CHINA, LITERATURE, MARRIAGE, TUG-OF-WAR*

● OMAN

Around 4.8 per cent of the meteorites discovered in the world have been found in Oman. The most likely reason for this is that the central and southern deserts of Oman are very flat, which makes it easier for meteorite hunters to find them. Between 11 and 36 meteorites are found in Oman every year.

♀ *INCOME TAX, MONARCHY*

● ONION

Cheese and onion is the most popular crisp flavour among British schoolchildren.

To counter the 'melancholy and phlegm' brought on by December, Richard Saunders, writing in 1679, recommended eating cabbage, onion and roasted apples or pears after meat.

The world record for consecutive uses of the word 'onions' in a work of literature is held by Anthony Burgess, whose 1968 novel *Enderby Outside* includes this splendid sentence: 'Then, instead of expensive mouthwash, he had breathed on Hogg-Enderby, bafflingly (for no banquet would serve, because of the known redolence of onions, onions) onions. "Onions," said Hogg.'

♀ *BAUDELAIRE, CRISPS, DURIAN*

● OPERA

While singing in Boito's *Mefistofele* at the Casino Theatre, Vichy, in 1955, the Belgian tenor Jan Verbeek swallowed his false moustache. He continued singing, but high notes clearly gave him great difficulty, owing to irritation from hairs sticking to the back of his throat.

Much the same thing happened to the tenor Walter Midgley in *Rigoletto* at Covent Garden in 1953. The incident made newspaper headlines but it was very worrying. Midgley completed the first act, and some of the moustache was fished out of the back of his throat by Opera House staff during the interval, but an operation was needed the following day to remove the gauze.

♀ *BALLOON, CARUSO, CONCRETE, JANACEK, MOZART, ROSSINI*

● OPINION POLLS

The very first opinion poll was carried out in Delaware on 24 July 1824 and was designed to predict the result of the US presidential election contest between Andrew Jackson and John Quincy Adams. It predicted a win for Jackson, which turned out to be wrong, though the shares of the vote it predicted were fairly accurate for the area in which the poll was taken.

OPOSSUM

In 2007, the grey short-tailed opossum became the first marsupial to have its genome fully sequenced.

Strictly speaking, the opossum is a marsupial of North and South America. Possums are its Australian relatives, but opossums are known for short as possum in America. The name opossum comes from the Algonquin 'wapathemwa'. Australian possums were named after the American ones.

An opossum has 50 teeth.

When threatened or harmed, a possum may adopt the posture and smell of a dead animal. Hence the expression 'playing possum'.

There are at least five towns in the US called Possum Trot, but possums don't trot, they waddle.

There is also a dance called the Possum Trot, which made its debut in May 2006.

The Possum Growers & Breeders Association of America was founded in Alabama by Frank Basil Clark in 1971. Its motto is 'Eat More Possum'. Presidents George H.W. Bush, Jimmy Carter and Ronald Reagan were all proud to be members.

Newborn opossum pups have a remarkable ability to recover from severe spinal-cord injuries, which is why they are widely used in research on human diseases and were chosen for genetic sequencing.

♀ PREGNANCY, SNIFFING

ORANGUTAN

The orangutan gives a loud belch as a warning signal.

The orangutan that played Clint Eastwood's sidekick Clyde in the 1978 film *Every Which Way But Loose* was named Manis. By the time of the 1980 sequel, *Any Which Way You Can,* Manis had grown too much and two orangutans, Buddha and C.J. (short for Clyde Junior), shared the role.

♀ BERLIN

ORANGE

Brazil produces more oranges than any other country. In the year 2019–20, it produced 15.62 million tonnes, which was more than a third of the 46.05 million tonnes produced in the world. The second most prolific orange producer was China with 7.3 million tonnes, followed by the United States on 4.66 million. The total annual world orange production, if squeezed, would fill nearly 13,000 Olympic-sized swimming pools.

According to research published in Germany in 2001, the smell of oranges reduces fear and stress in women who are waiting to see a dentist, but has no effect on men in a similar situation.

In Spanish, the verb *anaranjear* means 'to kill a cock by throwing oranges at it'.

♀ BANANA, CARROT, PENGUIN, PERU, RHYME, SCISSORS

ORBISON, Roy (1936–88)

The singer Roy Orbison's middle name was Kelton.

'When you were trying to make a girl fall in love with you, it took roses, the Ferris wheel and Roy Orbison.' Tom Waits

♀ BEETLE

ORCHID

Orchids take their name from the Greek word *orchis*, which means 'testicle'. The reference is to the shape of the flower's roots. Before they were given the name 'orchid' they were sometimes known as 'ballocks stones'.

Surgical removal of one or both testicles is called 'orchidectomy'.

BHUTAN, RYDER CUP, TESTICLE

OREGANO

In ancient Greece, Hippocrates used oregano to treat respiratory and stomach ailments and as an antiseptic, while in Crete it has long been used to treat sore throats. More recently, the medicinal value of oregano was brought into doubt in 2005 when the US Trade Commission brought a legal action against a company which claimed that oil of oregano was good for colds and flu and for treating bacterial and viral infections.

In 2012, however, tests on the compound carvacrol, which is found in oregano, showed that it can kill cancer cells. Earlier studies had suggested that pizza may reduce cancer risk, which was attributed to the lycopene in tomatoes, but the new results suggest that the oregano seasoning may play a part.

OREGON

Following an appeal in 2011 by a man who had been convicted of first-degree assault after biting off another man's ear in a drunken fight, the Court of Appeals in Oregon ruled that teeth are not a dangerous weapon. The decision reduced his 90-month sentence for first-degree assault to 70 months for second-degree assault.

Teenage suicide attempts in Oregon are most common on Mondays in the spring.

CAT, DANCING, MUSHROOM, VASECTOMY

ORGAN

The organ was invented by Ctesibius of Alexandra in 246 BC. The instrument was called a hydraulis and was powered by water pressure. Ctesibius is also thought to have invented the instrumental keyboard, automatic doors and the bellows that operated his organ. His improvements to the water clock or clepsydra produced a clock that remained the world's most accurate for about 1,800 years. A crater on the Moon is named after Ctesibius.

FORTY-SEVEN, GHOSTS, MOUTH ORGAN, ORGAN-GRINDERS, PIPES

ORGAN-GRINDERS

'Never hold discussions with the monkey when the organ grinder is in the room.' This quotation is often attributed to Winston Churchill, but it is by no means clear that he ever said it.

On 16 May 1957 in the House of Commons, however, the then Shadow Foreign Secretary Aneurin Bevan, said the following: 'I am not going to spend any time whatsoever in attacking the Foreign Secretary … If we complain about the tune, there is no reason to attack the monkey when the organ grinder is present.' The 'monkey' and 'organ grinder' he was referring to at the time were Foreign Secretary Selwyn Lloyd and Prime Minister Anthony Eden.

BABBAGE, COMPUTERS

ORGASM

The earliest accounts of female orgasm refer to it as a hysterical condition caused by the womb gripping the windpipe and causing panting. Even the word 'hysteria' comes from the Greek for 'womb', *hysteros*. The Greek physician Galen believed that hysteria was caused by sexual deprivation which could be cured by massage to a state of 'paroxysm': 'Arising from the touch of the genital organs required by the treatment, there follows twitchings accompanied at the same time by pain and pleasure … from that time she is free of all the evil she felt,' Galen wrote.

AMNESIA, GRÄFENBERG, HEELS, LOVE, NOSE, PIG, VIBRATOR

OSCAR

The nickname 'Oscar' has been used for Academy Awards since 1934, five years after the Awards were instituted. It allegedly comes from a remark by Academy secretary Margaret Herrick, who said it looked like her uncle Oscar. The statuette, incidentally, is 34.3 centimetres (13.5 inches) high and weighs 3.8 kilograms (8.5 pounds).

If there were an Oscar for Greatest Disappointment, it would probably be shared by the films *The Turning Point* (1977) and *The Color Purple* (1985), each of which received 11 Oscar nominations without winning any.

Spencer Tracy (1938 and 1939) and Tom Hanks (1994 and 1995) are the only two men to have won two Best Actor Oscars in a row; Jason Robards was Best Supporting Actor in both 1977 and 1978. Katharine Hepburn won the Best Actress Oscar in 1968 and shared it with Barbra Streisand in 1969. Jack Nicholson (12 nominations and three Oscars) is said to use one of his Oscar trophies as a hat stand.

The only person named Oscar ever to have won an Oscar is Oscar Hammerstein, who received two awards for Best Original Song in 1941 and 1945.

ACTRESS, BROWN, FOX, JAMES BOND, JUNGLE, STORIES

OSTRICH

The ostrich is the largest living bird. It can be up to 8 feet tall, weigh 300 pounds, run at 45 mph and live for up to 68 years.

Ostrich eggs were much admired by the ancient Persians, who sent them as tributes to the Chinese emperors. The Spartans displayed the ostrich egg from which Castor and Pollux were supposed to have hatched. A cup made from an ostrich eggshell was found in a grave in Mesopotamia dating back to about 3000 BC.

The Bible is less kind to ostriches. Job 39:13–17 tells us: 'The wings of the ostrich flap joyfully, but cannot match the pinions and feathers of the stork. For she leaves her eggs on the ground and lets them warm in the sand. She forgets that a foot may crush them, or a wild animal may trample them. She treats her young harshly, as if not her own, with no concern that her labour was in vain. God hath deprived her of wisdom, neither hath He imparted to her understanding.' This is the only time the King James Bible mentions ostriches.

Pliny also commented on the stupidity of the ostrich, for believing that it could not be seen by a pursuer when it thrust its head into a bush. Diodorus praised the same behaviour as a sign of intelligence in realising that its head was its most vulnerable part.

According to F.J. Haskin, writing around 1920: 'the ostrich is abnormally finicky about mating. Some birds remain determined bachelors all their lives, and every one chooses his mate only with great delay and caution.' Once he has chosen, however, Haskin said: 'he is her devoted slave for life', and if she dies 'he remains a melancholy widower to the end of his days'.

The Romans liked to eat roast ostrich, particularly the wings. The Emperor Heliogabalus (r. AD 218–222) once served 600 ostrich heads at a banquet. The usurper Firmus, who rebelled against Aurelianus in Egypt, once ate a whole ostrich in a day.

An ostrich egg omelette will feed eight hungry persons, though the taste is said to be disappointing. Charles Darwin, however, spoke well of the ostrich dumplings he ate aboard the *Beagle*.

Remarkable pamphlet: *Ostrich Egg-shell Cups of Mesopotamia and the Ostrich in Ancient and Modern Times* by Berthold Laufer, Field Museum of Natural History, Chicago (1926).

⚲ HAIR

● OUTER SPACE

Space and outer space are the same, beginning 100 kilometres (62 miles) above Earth, known as the Kármán Line after Hungarian physicist Theodore von Kármán who, in 1957, showed the atmosphere is too thin to support aeronautical flight beyond that altitude. Space is 'only an hour's drive away if your car could go straight upwards' (Fred Hoyle, 1979).

The earliest known use of the phrase 'outer space' was in the poem 'Maiden of Moscow' by Lady Emmeline Wortley in 1842.

The United Nations passed its Outer Space Treaty in 1967, precluding any country from claiming sovereignty over anywhere in space.

The first film with outer space in its title was *It Came From Outer Space* in 1953.

The Voyager 1 spacecraft was 14.4 billion miles away from Earth in November 2021, a record for a man-made object.

The temperature of most of outer space is -270.45°C (-454.81°F), or 2.7 degrees above absolute zero.

The 1950s radio series *Journey Into Space* is said to be the last evening radio programme to attract a bigger audience than television.

Soviet cosmonaut Yuri Gagarin, who became the first man to go into space on 12 April 1961, died in 1968 in a plane crash when on a routine training flight.

● OWL

An owl has three eyelids: one for blinking, one for sleeping, and one for keeping the eye clean and healthy. A group of owls is called a 'parliament', 'wisdom' or 'study'.

The horned owl does not have horns. The bits that look like horns are tufts of feather.

⚲ DARWIN, NIGHTINGALE, TUESDAY

● OXEN

Only three words in English form their plurals in the old -en ending: oxen, children and brethren. An ox is a castrated bull.

There are more than 200 million oxen in the world. The ox is the fourth most common animal in the Old Testament, with more references than any other, apart from the sheep, lamb and lion.

Ash from burned ox hoofs was used by ancient Egyptians as an ingredient in their toothpaste.

The first letter of the Phoenician alphabet, 'aleph', means 'ox'. The symbol was inverted to form the Greek letter alpha.

In North America, the most common commands to an ox are get up (go), whoa (stop), back up (reverse), gee (turn right) and haw (turn left).

In 1880, a German named Johann

Ketzler set a record by eating a whole roast ox in just 42 days.

⚑ *CHRISTMAS EVE, OXFORD*

● OXFORD

Oxford was first occupied in Saxon times. It was originally known as 'Oxenaforda', meaning 'Ford of the Ox'.

⚑ *BALLIOL, CAMBRIDGE, CARROLL, CELIBACY, UNIVERSITIES*

● OXYGEN

The name *oxygène* was originally proposed in 1787 by its discoverer Antoine Lavoisier. It had previously been known as *l'air déphlogistiqué*. Phlogiston was the name given to the supposed hypothetical substance formerly thought to exist in all combustible bodies, and to be released in the process of combustion. Oxygen was therefore 'dephlogisticated air'.

⚑ *ELEMENTS, FART, FIZZY DRINKS, HUNDRED, MOUNTAINEERING, OCTOPUS*

● OYSTER

Oysters generally start life as males then change back and forth between the two sexes as their life progresses. They can even fertilise their own eggs.

In 1868, Maryland, USA, instituted a State Oyster Police Force to enforce oyster laws. Current Maryland regulations specify that the oyster season runs from 1 October to 31 March. A Maryland resident may take up to 100 oysters per day for personal, non-commercial use.

In Jamaica, one species of oyster can be found on the trees in mangrove swamps.

Oyster Day (also known as Old St James's Day) in the UK is 5 August. St James was the patron saint of oyster fishers and his saint's day is 25 July. In 1752, however, the year lost 11 days in changing from the Julian to Gregorian calendar and 25 July became 5 August. Oyster Day has been on that date ever since.

The last words of the Duc de Lanzon de Biron before he was guillotined in 1793 were: 'I beg a thousand pardons, my friend, but permit me to finish this last dozen of oysters.'

'Molly the Whistling Oyster' was a great success in 1840 at a tavern near London's Drury Lane Theatre. The place was renowned for its seafood, and on one occasion when the proprietor went to collect some oysters from a tank, a strange whistling noise was heard. The oyster making the noise was identified, and it was given its own tank and food and promptly became a celebrity. Nobody quite knew how the whistling sound was made, but it was conjectured that it came through water being ejected through a small hole in the shell. Such was the popularity of the mollusc that the tavern changed its name to The Whistling Oyster.

A baby oyster is called a spat.

In March 2005, Sonya Thomas set a new world record at the Acme Oyster House World Oyster Eating Competition by consuming 46 dozen oysters in 10 minutes. She set another record by eating 26 grilled cheese sandwiches in 10 minutes in 2006, and her record for eating fruitcake in 2003 has never been beaten.

The Roman Emperor Vitellius was reputed to have eaten 1,000 oysters in a day.

Casanova recommended eating 50 oysters for breakfast.

⚑ *BALZAC, BULL, CHRISTMAS EVE, HYPATIA, MITTERRAND*

PACIFIC

The Pacific Ocean was given its name 'Mar Pacifico' by Ferdinand Magellan in 1521 when he encountered favourable winds on reaching it during his circum-navigation of the world.

The Pacific Ocean covers 60 million square miles and holds just over half the world's oceanic water.

The point on Earth furthest from land is in the South Pacific, halfway between Pitcairn Island and Antarctica at 48°30'S, 120°30'W, where you would be 2,671 kilometres (1,660 miles) from the nearest land of any sort.

ATLANTIC, PANAMA, SAMOA, TOURISM

PAINTING

Staff at the National Museum in Wroclaw, Poland, took three days to notice that a young artist had hung his own work on the wall of one of their galleries in December 2011. Art student Andrzej Sobiepan said, 'I decided that I will not wait 30 or 40 years for my works to appear at a place like this. I want to benefit from them in the here and now.' The museum director said it revealed security breaches but was a witty artistic happening. The painting was kept on display before being sold at a charity auction.

ART, BLAKE, DA VINCI, GLASSES, MATISSE, PICASSO, PIGEON

PAKISTAN

According to a newspaper report in January 2010, Pakistani President Asif Ali Zardari had a black goat slaughtered at his house almost every day to ward off evil eyes and protect him from black magic.

A spokesman for the President said the goats were slaughtered as an act of Sadaqah – meaning 'voluntary charity', whereby one gives money or the meat of a slaughtered animal to the poor to stave off misfortune.

More than 120 people are bitten each day in Karachi by animals, mainly dogs but also horses, camels and donkeys.

CRICKET, NO BALLS, PULSES, SPYING, SWAT

PALINDROME

The longest one-word palindrome in English, according to the *Oxford English Dictionary*, is 'tattarrattat', coined by James Joyce in *Ulysses* to mean a knock on the door. This beats 'detartrated' (tartrates removed) by one letter.

The Finnish word *saippuakivikauppias* (a vendor of soapstone) is probably the world's longest single-word palindrome.

Illibilli in Sudan is the longest palindromic place name in Africa. Uburubu in Nigeria takes second place.

Joseph Haydn's Symphony No. 47 is nicknamed 'the Palindrome'. The third movement is a minuet and trio in which the second half of the minuet is the same as the first but backwards. The second half of the trio that follows is also a reflection of its first half, then the minuet is repeated.

♀ *PI*

PALMERSTON, Henry John Temple, 3rd Viscount (1784–1865)

Lord Palmerston must surely be the oldest British prime minister to be cited as co-respondent in a divorce case. He was 78 when it happened. He was named, in February 1864, in a divorce case brought by journalist Thaddeus O'Kane. Palmerston was said to have had an affair with O'Kane's wife, Johanna. Mrs O'Kane denied it and pointed out that since she and Thaddeus were never legally married it could not be classed as adultery anyway. The case was withdrawn and the judge said no stain should fall on Palmerston's character.

Benjamin Disraeli, leader of the Conservatives, wanted press coverage of the case suppressed as he feared it would increase Palmerston's popularity, while a popular joke in the music halls was the question: 'She may be Kane but is he Abel?'

Palmerston's last words are often quoted as: 'Die, my dear doctor? That's the last thing I shall do.' More reliable sources, however, give them as: 'That's article 98; now go on to the next.' It is believed he was reliving some incident during his time as foreign secretary.

♀ *BILLIARDS*

PANAMA

In 1593, Vasco Nunez de Balboa became the first European to discover that Panama was just a thin strip separating the Atlantic and Pacific oceans. The Panamanian currency is called the balboa after him, but US dollars are mainly used.

In 1990, a record 12,139 people bought Florida lottery tickets including the prison numbers of deposed Panamanian dictator Manuel Noriega. General Noriega was prisoner number 38699-079 at the Federal Metropolitan Correctional Center in Miami. In 2010, he was extradited to France to face money laundering charges but was sent back to Panama in 2011 to serve his sentence. He died in jail in 2017.

Panama has only ever won one Olympic gold medal, at Beijing 2008 for men's long jump. Panama sent only one person to the 1948 Olympics in London, but he won two bronze medals. This achievement by sprinter Lloyd LaBeach must be the record for medals per team member for any Olympic delegation.

When the French were the first to try to build a canal in Panama in the 1880s, nearly 20,000 workers died through landslides, malaria and yellow fever. The attempt was abandoned in 1893. The Canal was finally built by the Americans between 1904 and 1914 and cost $352 million. Five thousand workers lost their lives during its construction. Since the canal was opened in 1914, more than a million ships have passed through it.

The canal and its locks are wide enough to cope with 93 per cent of all seagoing vessels. It was controlled by the

US until 1999 and then finally transferred to Panama. It is now responsible for one-third of the country's economy. Total revenue of the canal in 2020 was $3.4 billion.

Panama hats are mainly made in Ecuador. They were called Panama hats because they were shipped from Ecuador to Panama before being exported worldwide.

Panama is the only place on Earth where you can watch the sun rise over the Pacific Ocean and set over the Atlantic.

⚲ CURTIS, ECUADOR, ROOSEVELT Theodore

PANCAKE

Aunt Jemima pancake flour was the first ready-mix food to be sold commercially. It was created in St Joseph, Missouri, and introduced in 1889.

In 2003, Stephen Wilkinson, a physicist at Leeds University, announced the secret of pancake tossing: $W = (g\sqrt{\pi})/4r$ where W is the angular velocity of the pancake, g is the acceleration due to gravity and r is the distance from the centre of pancake to the tosser's elbow.

Ralf Laue of Leipzig holds the record for the most tosses of a pancake in two minutes: 416. The official Guinness World Record, however, for the most tosses in one minute, is 140 achieved by Australian chef Brad Jolly in 2012, but the Guinness rules specified a larger pan and larger pancakes than Laue's.

There are two official world records for pancake eating: 50 × 3.25-ounce pancakes in 10 minutes by Patrick Bertoletti in 2012, and 113 × 1-ounce pancakes in 8 minutes by Matt Stonie in 2016.

In 1999, Mike Cuzzacrea ran the New York marathon in 3 hours, 2 minutes, 27 seconds, tossing a pancake all the way.

The expression 'as flat as a pancake' was first recorded in 1761, though 'as flat down as pancakes' dates back to at least 1611.

⚲ SHROVE TUESDAY, VOLLEYBALL

PANCAKE DAY

Shrove Tuesday, also known as Pancake Day, began as a week of confession and merriment before Lent. The Shrove Tuesday pancake race at Olney, Buckinghamshire, has been run since 1445. It is said to have started when a woman ran to church still holding a pan when her cooking was interrupted by the church's shriving bell.

Shakespeare uses the simile 'as fit as a pancake for Shrove Tuesday' in *All's Well That Ends Well*. The sales of Tate & Lyle golden syrup triple in the UK in the week of Shrove Tuesday.

If you do not like pancakes, another traditional Shrove Tuesday amusement in Britain was 'cock-throwing', in which things were thrown at a cockerel that was tied to a stake. This practice died out in the 18th century.

⚲ SHROVE TUESDAY

PANDA

In 1985, the Smithsonian Institute in Washington and the National Cancer Institute in Maryland announced that the giant panda is a bear. The lesser panda, however, is closer to a racoon.

After mating, male pandas leave the female to raise the cub and have no part in its upbringing.

Since 2010, pandas born in captivity in China have been looked after by researchers in panda suits to prepare the animals for life in the wild.

According to the World Wildlife Fund, there are only 1,864 pandas in the wild in China and about another 400 in zoos around the world. Officially, China owns all these pandas. Even those born outside China are technically on loan.

The male genitalia of the giant panda are small and pointed to the rear, unlike those of bears. Since a panda cub's external genitalia do not appear until it is several months old, the sex of a baby panda can only be determined by a DNA test.

Th giant panda has five fingers on each paw, plus a protrusion often called a 'sixth finger' that serves as a grasping thumb. It does not hibernate and bleats rather than roars.

When the red panda was first discovered by the Western world in the 1820s, it was known by a local name of 'wah' in imitation of its cry.

The scientific name of the giant panda is *Ailuropoda melanoleuca*, which means 'black and white cat-footed animal'. Fossil remains show that giant pandas have been around for at least 600,000 years.

⚲ *BEAR, CATARACT, PLATYPUS*

PANGOLIN

The pangolin is the only mammal with scales. It also has no teeth but is a very fussy eater, consuming only 19 of the world's many species of ants and termites. The pangolin gets its name from a Malay word meaning 'it rolls up', referring to the defensive posture it adopts when threatened. The technical term for rolling up defensively into a ball is 'volvation'.

According to an old Malay myth, the pangolin can defeat an elephant in a fight. It does so, it is said, by clinging remorselessly to the elephant's trunk. In some versions, this eventually asphyxiates the elephant (which sounds very implausible, as elephants do not breathe through their trunks), while in others this drives the elephant mad through its hopeless efforts to thrash around and dislodge the pangolin.

PAPAL SMOKE

The tradition of using smoke to signify the election of a pope dates back to the 19th century when the Vatican was in dispute with the Italian military government and came up with the idea of smoke to send messages to the Italian people. It was Pope Pius X who came up with the idea of burning the ballot papers after papal elections to maintain secrecy and produce the smoke.

This was first put into practice for the election of Pope Benedict XV on the death of Pius X in 1914, which was when the rule of black smoke for no decision and white smoke for a conclusive vote was instigated. The idea was that by burning the ballot papers with dry straw, white smoke would be produced, while burning them with wet straw would produce a darker smoke, but in practice, this was often less clear than the Cardinals would have liked.

During the 1958 conclave, white smoke emerged from the chimney after one vote. The crowd cheered, Vatican Radio announced that the Church had a pope, and then the smoke turned black. The fire had just needed some time to get going.

To avoid this sort of confusion, Pope John Paul II ruled that bells should ring to accompany the white smoke after a conclusive ballot.

In 2005, the Vatican introduced an 'auxiliary smoke-emitting device' that used chemical cartridges to produce clearly coloured smoke. It was not until 2013, however, that they revealed the

constituents of the papal smoke and
the technique of operating the machine
that emitted it. The ballot papers are still
burned in another stove.

PAPER

Paper was invented around the year AD
105 by a Chinese eunuch named Ts'ai
Lun, who was an official at the Imperial
Court. When he presented Emperor
Han Ho Ti with samples of his newly
invented paper, he was promoted by the
Emperor and became wealthy. Later he
was arrested on a charge unconnected
with paper and killed himself in prison
by taking poison.

For the next 500 years, the Chinese
succeeded in keeping paper a secret, but
the Koreans finally began making their
own paper early in the 7th century.

Another twelve and a half centuries
then passed before wrapping paper
began to be made. All the Christmas
gift-wrap used in the UK in one year
would cover 65 square kilometres (25
square miles), which is an area equal to
that of Guernsey.

The Paper Museum in Asukayama
Park, Tokyo, has 40,000 exhibits of
items relating to paper, while the
museum at the Research Institute
of Paper History and Technology in
Brookline, Massachusetts, claims to
have 'probably the largest collection of
handmade toilet paper in the world'.
The Tokyo museum opened in 1950 and
moved to its present location in 1998. It
has four floors of exhibits related to the
history of paper, including a kimono
made of paper, a teddy bear made of
paper and some paper made from
elephant faeces.

♀ CHAD, COW, CRISPS, SCISSORS, STRAW,
TOILET PAPER

PARACHUTE

An early version of the parachute as
we know it was invented in Italy in the
1470s. Leonardo da Vinci sketched an
improved version in 1485, but his design
was not successfully tested until 2000.

When Mickey Mouse tried to kiss
Minnie Mouse in his first on-screen
appearance in the silent animation *Plane
Crazy* in 1928, she parachuted out of the
plane to escape his embrace.

♀ CHANNEL, STOCKINGS, TOWER OF LONDON

PARAGUAY

Paraguay is the only country with a
national flag that is not the same on
both sides. Both front and back have,
from top to bottom, three horizontal
stripes of red, white and blue, but the
white stripe on the front bears the
National seal, while on the back it
displays the Treasury seal. This has been
the national flag since 1842, though it
has changed slightly to reflect changes
in the design of the seals.

♀ ASCENSION ISLAND, BOLIVIA, NAVIES

PARAPSYCHOLOGY

Research by Rupert Sheldrake in 1999
suggested that dogs can sense when
their owners are setting off for home,
even when departure times are varied
randomly. However, claims of possible
psychic links between animals and
humans are nothing new.

In 1983, the journal *Research in
Parapsychology* reported an experiment
in which a dog (a 'supposedly non-
psychic' dachshund) was rewarded with
a treat whenever a man guessed what
symbol was on a hidden card. The dog
was thus motivated to improve the man's
performance by thought transference.
The results showed that the man's results
did indeed improve, but the best results

were obtained when the dog performed the Extra-Sensory Perception test on its own. The conclusion was that further research was needed.

The Society for Psychical Research has investigated ghosts and telepathy and the possible existence of life after death since it was founded in 1882. In 1989, it published a paper entitled 'Two Tests of Survival After Death: Report on Negative Results'. This reported the attempts of two scientists to prove survival after death. One had encrypted messages for which only he knew the key word to break the code. The other had set a padlock with a combination only he knew. Both promised that after they died they would do their best to communicate the secrets to the living. They died in 1979 and 1984, but the passages have never been decoded nor the lock opened.

More positively, research in 1967 claimed to show that goldfish can tell if they are about to be fished out of a tank. The evidence for their precognition was increased movement when their numbers come up on dice thrown in another room.

In 1968, experiments appeared to show that the leaves of a philodendron plant react to the death of nearby shrimps. In 1970, a cat was claimed to be able to influence a heat lamp that was supposedly going on and off at random. In 1979, human willpower was shown to influence the activity levels of gerbils on a treadmill. In 1991, a healer supposedly demonstrated the ability to influence the growth of cress seeds, but in 1979, holy water was found to have no significant effect on the growth of radishes. In 1992, failure by 'spirit entities' to rearrange the playing cards in a sealed deck was put down to the 'conspicuous officiousness'

of the experimenters, causing the entity to withdraw its co-operation.

Further research is clearly needed.

PARASITE

The Meguro Parasitological Museum in Tokyo boasts 300 varieties of parasite on display, including a 30-foot tapeworm. In all, the museum is said to include over 45,000 immersed and prepared parasite specimens

♀ *MISTLETOE*

PARIS

Paris is the only EU capital city that bans the use of drones.

Dogs deposit 16 tonnes of excrement on Parisian streets and sidewalks every day.

♀ *ADDRESS, BIKINI, OLYMPIC GAMES, PORK, ROUSSEAU*

PARKER, Dorothy (1893–1967)

Writer and wit Dorothy Parker had a pet dog called Cliché and a pet parrot called Onan. The parrot's name came from the fact that it spilled its seed on the ground (see Genesis 38: 7–10).

Her own surname was that of her first husband. She was born Dorothy Rothschild and her uncle Martin Rothschild died at sea when the *Titanic* sank.

♀ *COOLIDGE, MILNE*

PARKING

In 2006, Darwin City Council in Australia reported that five of its parking wardens' helmets had been urinated into during a break-in at the council's compound. 'We're not quite sure whether or not it was someone who was a bit upset at getting a parking fine,' a council spokesman said.

♀ *ENVIRONMENT, MOOSE, SAUSAGES*

PARKINSON, James (1755–1824)

The English apothecary and surgeon James Parkinson, after whom Parkinson's disease is named, was born on 11 April 1755. On 11 April 1952, Parkinson's disease was successfully treated by surgery for the first time.

Besides his being the first to describe Parkinson's disease (which he called the Shaking Palsy), Parkinson was also involved in the first description of appendicitis. He was also involved in several secret political societies and was questioned by the Privy Council over an alleged plot to kill George III with a poisoned dart fired from a popgun.

His interest in palaeontology also led to his writing a three-volume work on fossils.

PARLIAMENT

According to Erskine May's official handbook entitled *Parliamentary Procedure*, the Speaker has the responsibility of ruling whether a particular expression is or is not allowed. More than a century of such decisions led to a glossary of unparliamentary language, but recent editions of Erskine May have abandoned the practice of listing banned words. The last such complete list was as follows: Blackguard; Blether; Cad or caddishness; Calumny, gross; Cheeky young pup; Corrupt or corruption; Coward; Criminal; Dishonest; Dog; Guttersnipe; Hooligan; Hypocrites; Impertinence; Impertinent puppy; Impudence; Jackass, behaving like an; Malignant attack; Malignant slander; Member returned by refuse of a large constituency; Murderer; Pecksniffian cant; Personal honour, not consonant with; Pharisees; Rat; Rude and vulgar interruptions; Ruffianism; Slanderer; Stool-pigeons; Swine; Traitor; Treason, charges of; Vicious and vulgar; Villains.

Recently the word 'sod' was added to the unwritten list. This happened on 12 November 1984 when the Member for Bolsover, Dennis Skinner, referred to Dr David Owen as 'this pompous sod'. The Speaker interrupted, saying, 'That, sir, is unparliamentary language. I demand you withdraw it.' Skinner thought it over, then replied, 'In deference to you, Mr Speaker, I withdraw "pompous".' The Speaker explained that it was the other word he objected to, and when Skinner refused to withdraw it, the Speaker, as the official report in Hansard put it: 'pursuant to Standing Order No. 24 (Disorderly conduct), ordered him to withdraw immediately from the House during the remainder of this day's sitting'.

In 2003, the Speaker wisely told MPs: 'There is no hard and fast list of unparliamentary words. Whether something said is a breach of order depends on the context,' and reminded them of Erskine May's advice that: 'good temper and moderation are the characteristics of parliamentary language'.

ARMOUR, CHRISTMAS, DAYLIGHT SAVING, LOTTERIES, MAYPOLE, THATCHER

PARMESAN

The greatest recorded loss of Parmesan cheese caused by an earthquake was in Italy in May 2012 when an estimated 300,000 wheels of Parmesan and Gran Padano cheeses were destroyed. The total value of the cheeses was about 250 million euros (£203 million).

A wheel of Parmesan or Grana Padano weighs up to 40 kilograms (88 pounds).

In 1666, when Samuel Pepys saw the Great Fire of London heading in the direction of his house, he dug a pit in the garden and put his wine and Parmesan cheese in it to keep it safe.

♀ UMBRELLA

PARROT

The German explorer Alexander von Humboldt reported meeting a talking bird in South America in 1800 with the sole knowledge of a dead language of an extinct tribe of Indians, the Atures. The parrot was female, but for some unknown reason was called Jacob.

There are 25 species of parrot fish in the seas around the Seychelles.

On 11 August 1995, in Leamington Spa, Warwickshire, the Avenue and Victoria bowls club banned Henry the parrot because its repeated shrieks of 'You're a yard short, a yard short,' were irritating contestants in the preliminary rounds of the English Women's Bowls Championship.

♀ EINSTEIN, FOOTBALL, GEORGE V, PARKER, TAXIDERMY, VICTORIA

PARSNIP

The world's longest parsnip ever grown was 6.55 metres (21 feet 5.87 inches long) and was displayed by Joe Atherton at the UK National Giant Vegetables Championships in Malvern in 2017.

Atherton has also held the records for the longest beetroot and carrot.

PARTON, Dolly (b. 1946)

Dolly Parton met her husband, Carl Thomas Dean, in 1964 at the Wishy-Washy launderette in Nashville. His first words to her were: 'Y'all gonna get sunburnt out there, little lady.' They married two years later.

When her theme park Dollywood in Pigeon Valley, Tennessee, won the Applause Award for the Best Theme Park of the Year in 2010, Dolly Parton

in her acceptance speech said: 'Walt Disney became successful because he had Mickey Mouse who has two big ears. So I figured I could be successful with Dollywood with my two big partners.'

♀ DOLLY

PASTA

There is much debate on how many types of pasta there are in Italy. Some say around 350, others say at least 600, but the question is complicated by different places using different words for the same shape.

According to purists, a perfect strip of tagliatelle should be 6mm wide.

♀ ART, NOODLE, SPAGHETTI

PASTEUR, Louis (1822–95)

When Michael H. Hart brought out his 1978 book, *The 100: A Ranking Of The Most Influential Persons in History*, Louis Pasteur was ranked number 12. In the revised edition of 1992, however, he rose to number 11, moving ahead of Karl Marx who dropped from 11th to 27th. Pasteur's position was just behind Einstein but ahead of Galileo.

♀ BEER, GUINEA PIGS

PATERNITY

In February 2008, a German court ruled that an unnamed woman had the right to know the identity of her child's father. Six different men had bid successfully in Internet auctions to have sex with the woman, and she wanted to know which one had made her pregnant, but she knew them only by their online aliases.

PATIENCE

Timon of Athens is the only Shakespeare play that does not include the word 'patience'. The Old Testament also does not mention 'patience', but it occurs 33 times in the New Testament.

Research shows that, when waiting for a lift, some people begin to get impatient after 15 seconds; most get impatient within 35 seconds.

'Patience: a minor form of despair disguised as virtue,' Ambrose Bierce, The Devil's Dictionary, 1906

PEACH

The scientific name of the peach is *persica*, from a mistaken belief that it came originally from Persia. In fact, the peach was cultivated in China around 1000 BC and brought first to Persia then Europe.

Peach Melba was created by the great French chef Auguste Escoffier for the Australian opera singer Dame Nellie Melba. Nellie Melba's real name was Helen Porter Mitchell. Her stage name 'Melba' was a contraction of her hometown of Melbourne. Besides peach Melba, Escoffier created Melba sauce and Melba garniture (tomatoes stuffed with chicken, truffles and mushrooms) for Dame Nellie.

'Peach' was first used to describe an attractive woman in 1710, and 'peaches and cream' was first used to describe an attractive complexion in 1893.

'In Hollywood, the women are all peaches. It makes one long for an apple occasionally.' Somerset Maugham

♀ *BASKETBALL, DINOSAUR*

PEACOCK

When a peacock displays its tail to a female, it ruffles the feathers to emit a low-frequency sound which humans cannot hear. The pitch of the sound changes according to how far away the female is. This sound and its function

were reported in a paper in the journal *Animal Behaviour* in 2015, in which the researchers concluded that 'The peacock's train display is a multimodal signal.'

The peacock can only hold its train high when its head is in the air; the tail drops if it looks down. Hence the myth that it is ashamed of its feet.

♀ *PHOENIX, SRI LANKA, TURKEY (BIRD)*

PEANUT

The peanut (also known as groundnut, earthnut, goober, goober pea, pinda, pinder, Manila nut or monkey nut) is the edible seed of the plant *Arachis hypogaea*. It is a member of the pea family and botanically the fruit is not a nut but a legume or pod.

Peanuts are the official state crop of Georgia where, in Turner County, you can see the 'World's Largest Peanut'. It is a 6-metre (20-foot) tall monument erected in honour of the importance of the peanut.

The Peanuts strip cartoon first appeared on 2 October 1950. Its creator, Charles Schulz, retired in December 1999 having written and drawn around 18,000 Peanuts strips. He died on 12 February 2000, the night before his last cartoon strip was published.

♀ *BODY ART, FOSSIL, HEMINGWAY, POLAR BEAR, SARDINE, SENEGAL*

PEANUT BUTTER

It takes about 550 peanuts to make a 340-gram (12-ounce) jar of creamy peanut butter. Fear of peanut butter sticking to the roof of your mouth is called arachibutyrophobia. The high protein content of peanut butter draws moisture from your mouth. That's why it sticks.

In the United States, around $800

million is spent annually on peanut butter. The average American eats 3 kilograms (7 pounds) of peanuts and peanut butter a year.

A bear got into an empty car in Denver, Colorado, in 2010, honked the horn, released the brake and sent it rolling 38 metres (125 feet) into a thicket, with the bear still inside. The owners say they had to get a new car, as the bear trashed the inside trying to get out after the door slammed shut. Police deputies responded to an emergency call and freed the bear by opening the door with a rope from a distance. The bear then ran into the woods. A peanut butter sandwich left on the back seat is thought to be what attracted the bear.

When astronaut Alan Shepard went to the Moon in 1971, he took a jar of peanut butter with him for good luck.

BEDROOM, ROMNEY, SANDWICHES

PEARS

The proper name of Sweet William pears is 'Williams' Bon Chrétien', ('Williams' good Christian'), as this variety seems to have its origins in the 15th century with the 'Bon Chrétien' pear in France. The 'Christian' referred to was Francis of Paola, a holy man who was called to the deathbed of King Louis XI to whom he gave a pear seed from his native Calabria. The seed was planted and the tree that grew was called 'Good Christian'. Much later, in the 18th century, a nurseryman named Williams introduced a version of the same pear to England, which became known as the Williams Pear. Still later, the Williams Bon Chrétien was found to be the same as the pear the Americans called the Bartlett.

The Williams pear, which is indeed sweet, should not be confused with the fragrant Sweet William flower, which is named for William, Duke of Cumberland, victor over the Scots at Culloden in 1746. The Scots, who saw the battle rather differently, retaliated by naming a distinctly less fragrant plant 'stinking Billy'.

The origin of the expression 'to go pear-shaped', meaning to go badly wrong, is obscure. Some say it is RAF slang from the 1940s, but no supporting evidence has been produced, though it has been suggested that it is related to the execution of looping-the-loop, which should see the plane going in a circle, but poor execution may result in its going pear-shaped.

BOURDALOUE, ONION

PEAS

Seventy-three per cent of the UK population say they love frozen peas. Trend-setter and dandy Beau Brummell never ate vegetables on principle, but did admit that he once ate a pea.

The oldest pea ever found has been carbon-dated to 9750 BC. It was discovered on the Burma–Thailand border.

The noun 'pease' was recorded in English around 1440, more than 200 years before the singular 'pea' developed from it.

In 1969, Birds Eye frozen peas became the first product to be advertised on colour television in the UK. There are on average 1,224 peas in a 450-gram (1-pound) pack of Birds Eye peas and the maximum diameter of each pea is 10.4mm.

Psychologists identify four types of pea-eater: the obsessive Stabber, who skewers them on a fork; the casual Scooper, who uses a spoon; the aggressive Squasher; and the random Shoveller. The average Briton stabs, scoops, squashes or shovels 8,568 peas a year.

♀ *CHROMOSOME, GUYANA, PULSES, VASECTOMY*

PECAN PIE

Thirty-five years of Secret Santa pie gifts came to an end at Christmas 2011 when a man in Columbus, Ohio, found a farewell note from the Pie Fairy. Willis Welch had received an anonymous pecan pie every year since 1976, but the last one came with a note saying, 'It has been a great ride.' It was signed 'Pie Fairy', and also explained, 'My wings are shorter now and I am a little too fat to fly anymore. But I still love you!!' Mr Welch, aged 87, said he never knew who was sending them.

PECK, Gregory (1916–2003)

Gregory Peck's original name was Eldred Gregory Peck, but he dropped the Eldred after graduating from university.

He was exempted from military service in the Second World War because of a back injury sustained during his actor training. His earliest movie memory was being scared by *Phantom of the Opera* when he was aged nine.

In the 1968 film *The Big Country*, Gregory Peck appears with his three sons Jonathan Peck, Carey Paul Peck and Stephen Peck. In 1969, he was awarded the Presidential Medal of Freedom, the highest civilian honour in the US. His racehorse Different Class finished third in the 1968 Grand National.

In 2003, his Oscar-winning portrayal of Atticus Finch in *To Kill a Mockingbird* (1962) was voted the 'Greatest Film Hero of the Past 100 years'. In 1983, he

was admitted to the International Best Dressed List Hall of Fame. His favourite drink was Guinness, which he had every day, even having a tap installed in his home. He was offered the role of Grandpa Joe in the 2005 film of *Charlie and the Chocolate Factory* but died before he could accept it.

PEDESTRIANS

Two Ig Nobel Prize awards were made in 2021 to different groups of researchers who had investigated the two sides of a vital pedestrian phenomenon. A group from Rome and California received the Physics prize for 'experiments to learn why pedestrians do not constantly collide with other pedestrians', while the Kinetics prize was awarded to scientists from Japan who conducted 'experiments to learn why pedestrians do sometimes collide with other pedestrians'.

A report published in 2011 ranked four cities in Florida at the top of a list of the most dangerous in America for pedestrians. The 'Dangerous by Design' report, produced by Transportation for America, ranked Orlando, Tampa, Jacksonville and Miami–Fort Lauderdale at the top of their list of hazardous cities for walkers, with Riverside (California), Las Vegas, Memphis, Phoenix, Houston and Dallas in fifth to tenth places, respectively. The best cities for pedestrians according to the same list were Boston, Cleveland, New York and Pittsburgh.

♀ *COPENHAGEN, DALLAS, SEXUAL DISCRIMINATION*

PEEING

In 1996, the villagers of Stigtomta, in southern Sweden, staged a Pee Outdoors Day in a symbolic environmental protest action. Some 2,000 men, women and children, including the village priest, joined in the mass public urination to draw attention to the dying ecosystem of their lake.

BOURDALOUE, BRUSSELS, GEORGIA

PELICAN

Under the London Royal and Other Parks and Gardens Regulations (1977), section 23, 'touching a pelican' is forbidden unless written permission has been obtained.

DINOSAUR, SAN FRANCISCO

PEN

A pen, according to San Diego Police, is indeed as mighty as a sword and can be a deadly weapon. A man was arrested at the Comic-Con convention in San Diego in 2010 for injuring another man with a pen. They were reported to have got into an argument over sitting too close to each other and one man struck the other with a pen, causing a minor cut around his eyelid. The man was arrested on suspicion of assault with a deadly weapon.

BALLPOINT, CROSSWORD, GOOSE

PENALTY

In 2009 in Manchester, a referee ordered a penalty to be retaken in a Sunday league football game between Chorlton Villa and International Manchester FC after an opposition player broke wind as the ball was kicked. The referee also gave the wind-breaking player a yellow card for the noise, which was classed as 'ungentlemanly conduct'.

ADULTERY, FOOTBALL, GOAL, HAT, JONSON, SENEGAL, WIFE-CARRYING

PENCIL

Although the first pencils, made by wrapping graphite in string, were produced in the 16th century, and the first wood pencils were invented in the 17th century, it was not until 1770 that the pencil eraser (rubber) was invented, and the pencil sharpener was not invented until 1847 when Therry des Estwaux of France came up with the idea.

In 1858, Hymen Lipman of Philadelphia received a patent for a pencil with an eraser at one end. This invention set the stage for a series of celebrated legal battles. In 1862, Joseph Reckendorfer of New York City refined Lipman's design. The original version had been a pencil which could be sharpened at both ends, one end producing the usual writing material and the other displaying a piece of India rubber. Reckendorfer instead moulded one end of the wood in a tapering fashion to form a receptacle for the rubber. This led to a series of patent law battles between the two inventors which were not resolved until 1875 when an appeal court ruled against both men. The crucial point the court made was that taking two inventions that already exist and sticking them together cannot, in itself, be considered a new invention.

'It may be more convenient,' the court ruled, 'to turn over the different ends of the same stick than to lay down one stick and take up another. This, however, is not invention within the patent law … We are of the opinion, that, for the reasons given, neither the patent of Lipman nor the improvement of Reckendorfer can be sustained.'

In other words, you can patent the widget that holds the rubber to the pencil, but you cannot patent the idea of a pencil with a rubber at one end.

LEAD, NOSE-PICKING, STRAW

PELICAN | PENCIL

PENGUIN

There are about 17 species of penguin in the world. Adélie penguins have pink feet; gentoo penguins' feet are orange; but gentoo penguins have pink excrement. Penguins can see very well under water but are generally extremely short-sighted on land.

In 1999, researchers in Antarctica found that flying a helicopter over baby penguins makes them flap their flippers or run away, but not, as had commonly been believed, fall over backwards. Two years later, a million-pound military project confirmed that penguins do not fall over when aeroplanes fly overhead.

In December 2000, scientists confirmed that waddling requires less energy from Emperor penguins than walking and is therefore their most efficient means of locomotion.

The most striking discovery about penguins, however, was revealed in 1998 in a paper with the title: 'Female Adélie Penguins Acquire Nest Material from Extrapair Males After Engaging in Extrapair Copulations'. This reported sightings of female Adélie penguins in Antarctica selling sex in exchange for gifts of rocks. Some birds even flirted with males until offered the rocks, which they then took without mating. One was seen to take 62 rocks from a gullible male without ever delivering on her apparent promises. This was the first known case of prostitution among birds.

In December 2003, the journal *Polar Biology* published a note entitled 'Pressures Produced When Penguins Pooh – Calculations on Avian Defaecation'. As the authors pointed out: 'Chinstrap and Adélie penguins generate considerable pressures to propel their faeces away from the edge of the nest.' They reported that 'the forces involved … are high, but

do not lead to an energetically wasteful turbulent flow'. They admitted that: 'Whether a bird chooses the direction into which it decides to expel its faeces, and what role the wind plays in this, remain unknown.'

In 1987, according to official figures, the New York Health Department treated 8,064 people for dog bites, 1,587 people bitten by other people, and one who'd been bitten by a penguin.

On 23 August 1997, Edinburgh Zoo applied suncream to its penguins because the unusually hot weather had been causing the birds to moult, leaving patches of bare skin that needed protection.

In February 2001, a baby penguin was treated for depression after it was found wandering the streets of Melbourne.

In 2002, a French researcher reported that penguins sleep more deeply in the afternoon than in the morning. His evidence for this was obtained by going round colonies of sleeping penguins seeing how many prods with a stick were needed to wake them up at different times of day. On average, five prods were enough in the morning, but nine were needed in the afternoon.

ANTARCTICA, EDINBURGH, FALKLAND ISLANDS, FEET, SEAL

PENIS

According to a 1995 survey, the average size of an erect penis is only 12.8 centimetres (5 inches), which is significantly smaller than most men believe. An Italian study in 2002 discovered that, of 67 men seeking enlargement operations, all had penises well within the normal size range.

Hospital records in America published in 2021 indicate that the most common cause of injury to the penis are getting it caught in a zipper. Around 2,000 cases of this are reported annually, which has been enough to give this type of injury its own name: ZIRPI, which stands for 'zipper related penile injury'.

The world's only museum of penises is the Phallological Museum in Reykjavik. Its collection boasts 282 specimens of penises or penis parts of 93 different animals, including 55 specimens belonging to 16 different kinds of whale. According to the museum's website: 'It should be noted that the museum has also been fortunate enough to receive legally-certified gift tokens for four specimens belonging to Homo sapiens.'

The Internet address of the museum is www.phallus.is. The apparently more appropriate address of www.pen.is was already used by a Reykjavik erotica shop.

According to research at the Naval and Veterans Hospital in Athens, the only part of the body of men under 40 which correlates significantly with penis length is the length of the index finger.

⚲ *BACULUM, BAGUETTE, DONKEY, FRUITFLY, HARVESTMAN, SQUID*

● PENSIONER

According to research published in 2010, overweight pensioners in Australia live longer than those who stay in shape. Health records of 9,200 men and women showed that a 70-year-old with a Body Mass Index that qualified them as 'overweight' had a 13 per cent greater chance of reaching the age of 80 than those in a 'normal weight range'. But people who were even fatter, with a BMI at the 'obese' level, could not look forward to a longer life.

⚲ *CHELSEA, SPONTANEOUS COMBUSTION*

● PENTAGON

The regulations of the Department of Food Procurement at the Pentagon take 20 pages to lay down the rules pertaining to hot chocolate.

● PEPPER

In 2010, the Indian military announced the development of a bhut jolokia pepper grenade to fight terrorism and immobilise crowds.

Until the 1950s the fizzy drink now known as 'Dr Pepper' had a dot after the Dr. The dot was then dropped.

⚲ *BOTTOM, BRASSIERE, CHILLI*

● PEPYS, Samuel (1633–1703)

The first time the diarist Samuel Pepys drank tea was on 25 September 1660 when he wrote in his diary that he had been discussing foreign affairs with some friends 'and afterwards did send for a Cupp of Tee (a China drink) of which I never drank before'.

⚲ *ASPARAGUS, CHARLES II, CHOCOLATE, PARMESAN*

● PERCEVAL, Spencer (1762–1812)

Spencer Perceval was the only British prime minister to be assassinated. He was shot by John Bellingham on 11 May 1812 on the steps of 10 Downing Street.

After his death, Bellingham, who had 12 children, was found to have only £106.5s.1d in the bank, so Parliament voted to give a grant of £50,000 to his six sons and six daughters and £2,000 a year to his widow. His eldest son, also called Spencer, was given £1,000 yearly. He also became a Member of Parliament.

⚲ *ADAMS, OFFICE*

● PERU

Peru is the only country whose name can be typed on a single row of letters on a typewriter. It is also the only country on Earth with place names that begin with a double-Q: Qquea, Qquec-querisca and Qquero are all places in Peru, the last of which, incidentally, can also be typed on the top row of letters on a typewriter. Peru is the world's second greatest fishing nation – its annual catch is exceeded only by China.

Since 1991, the currency of Peru has been the *nuevo sol*, a modern relic of the sun worship of the ancient Incas, though the sol was first introduced as the currency in the 1860s.

An unpopular decision by the referee at a Peru–Argentina match in the Peruvian capital, Lima, in 1964 resulted in the world's worst soccer riot. It ended with 300 fans killed and more than 500 injured.

In 1973, the Interior Ministry in Peru banned chilli sauce and hot spices from prison food because they might arouse sexual desires. The camu-camu fruit, which grows in the Peruvian rainforest, may arouse in a different way, as it has the highest vitamin C content of any food, around 60 times that of oranges.

⚲ *ALPACA, ASPARAGUS, COLOMBIA, FOX, GUANO, LICE*

PETER PAN

J.M. Barrie, the author of *Peter Pan*, was only 5 feet 2 inches tall (he stopped growing at the age of 15) and was impotent, but he could wiggle his ears. He smoked pipes or cigars constantly, and in 1921 was prescribed heroin by his doctor to treat the insomnia caused by his smoker's cough.

⚲ *BARRIE*

PETER the GREAT, Czar of Russia (1672–1725)

Peter the Great of Russia trained bears to serve alcoholic drinks to his guests. He married his first wife at the age of 17, and they had three children, but they never really got on and divorced after nine years of marriage, then he forced her to join a convent. She later took a lover but when Peter discovered, he sentenced him to death by impalement.

⚲ *ALCOHOL, CATHERINE I, HAIR, RHUBARB*

PETRARCH, Francesco (1304–74)

The Italian scholar and poet Petrarch (Francesco Petrarca) was crowned the first national Poet Laureate since ancient times in Rome in 1341. He has also been described as 'the first tourist' because he is said to have travelled just for pleasure.

⚲ *UNIVERSITIES*

PETS

There are more pet dogs, pet cats, pet fish and pet reptiles in the United States than in any other country, but China leads the world in pet birds. According to estimates made by the insurance industry in 2019, the figures for the US are: 89.7 million dogs, 94.2 million cats, 158.1 million fish, 9.4 million reptiles and 5.7 million birds. In 2017, the number of pet birds in China was estimated to be 73.5 million.

⚲ *ALASKA, BARCELONA, CHARLES II, EARTHQUAKE, GUINEA PIGS*

PHILIPPINES

In 1997, Marikina City, a suburb of the Philippine capital of Manila, passed a proposal to outlaw vomiting in public. Offenders would be fined and asked to clean up their mess. People who vomited because of sickness or from eating rotten food would be exempted from the ban.

In May 2006, a world record for simultaneous breast-feeding was set by 3,738 mothers in the Philippines. The following year, a new record was set, again in the Philippines, when 15,128 mothers fed their babies at the same time across 295 sites.

CONDOM, FENG SHUI, JOHN PAUL II, KNEES, YO-YO

PHOBIAS

Here are some of the lesser-known phobias, from A to Z:

- Atelophobia: fear of imperfection
- Barophobia: fear of gravity
- Clinophobia: fear of beds
- Dikephobia: fear of justice
- Eosophobia: fear of dawn
- Frigophobia: fear of getting cold
- Gymnophobia: fear of nudity
- Hedonophobia: fear of pleasure
- Iatrophobia: fear of doctors
- Japanophobia: fear of anything Japanese
- Koumpounophobia: fear of buttons
- Laliophobia: fear of stuttering
- Mageirocophobia: fear of cooking
- Nelophobia: fear of glass
- Octophobia: fear of the number eight
- Philematophobia: fear of kissing
- Quadrophobia: fear of things that come in fours
- Ranidaphobia: fear of frogs
- Selaphobia: fear of flashing lights
- Trypanophobia: fear of injections
- Uranophobia: fear of heaven
- Venustraphobia: fear of beautiful women
- Wiccaphobia: fear of witchcraft
- Xenophobia: fear of strangers
- Yotaphobia: fear of the letter Y
- Zelotypophobia: fear of jealousy

ANDERSEN, BARBER, CHOPSTICKS, HAIR, KISSING, SLIME, STRING

PHOENIX

The legend of the phoenix is thousands of years old and occurs in several mythologies, starting with ancient Egypt. The Egyptians thought it similar to a heron, while the Greeks and Romans compared it to a peacock or eagle. They all agree that there is only one of its kind, which lives for 350, 500, 1,461 or 12,954 years, according to which mythology you read. In the 5th century BC, the Greek historian Herodotus wrote about the phoenix but noted: 'I myself have never seen it.'

When the phoenix dies, it is said to be reborn from the ashes of its own funeral pyre, which is why in early Christian art the phoenix was often adopted as a symbol of resurrection.

According to the 3rd-century Roman author and teacher Aelian, the dawn song of the phoenix was 'so ravishingly beautiful, the rising sun reined in his horses to listen'.

In 1995, the world's most sensitive search for extraterrestrial intelligence was given the name Project Phoenix. In March 2004, a statement from the Project announced that they had examined the 800 stars on its list and failed to find any evidence of extraterrestrial signals. Their conclusion was that 'we live in a quiet neighbourhood'.

The name of Phoenix was suggested for the largest city in Arizona Territory, as it was a city born from the ruins of a former civilisation. The actor River Phoenix's real name was River Bottom.

In Phoenix, Arizona, it is illegal to bury a dead animal or place it in your garbage or recycling container. In 2022, a Phoenix man was arrested when 183 dead animals were found in his freezer.

ARIZONA, PEDESTRIANS, TRAFFIC

PHONE SEX

The earliest mention of phone sex recorded in the *Oxford English Dictionary* dates from 1982.

Thirty years later, in 2012, the Italian Supreme Court ruled that phone sex is not necessarily prostitution. The court overturned a lower court's conviction on a charge of sexual exploitation of a man from Milan who had paid a woman to talk dirty to him over the telephone. The high court ruled no crime had been committed since the man and the woman had no physical contact. According to the ruling, 'Verbally servicing an interlocutor for the purpose of sexual excitement does not constitute a sexual service, if it does not involve the bodily erogenous zones of the person who is getting paid for such a service.' The court, however, did remind the parties that Italian law says prostitution may well be carried out via telephone or Internet if the customer requests the vendor to perform a specific sex act.

PHOTOGRAPHY

An American farmer, Wilson A. Bentley, who died in 1931, devoted his life to taking 5,381 photographs of snowflakes.

On 4 September 1888, George Eastman received a patent for his roll film and registered the Kodak trademark, thus bringing photography to the masses. Eastman's invention of the name Kodak reflected his fondness for the letter K, which, he claimed, 'seems a strong, incisive sort of letter'. His suicide note in 1932 said simply: 'My work is done. Why wait?' He was aged 77 when he died.

The word 'photograph' comes from the Greek for 'light' and 'writing'. The word was coined by astronomer Sir John Herschel in 1839.

The first photograph of the Moon was taken in New York on 23 March 1840 by John William Draper.

The first book illustrated with photographs was *The Pencil of Nature* by William Fox Talbot in 1844.

Seventeen per cent of people say old photographs are the thing most likely to make them go on a diet.

⚲ *SILVER*

PHYSICS

Until Malala Yousafzai won the Nobel Peace Prize at the age of 17 in 2004, the five youngest winners of Nobel Prizes had all received their awards for Physics. The youngest before Malala was the British physicist William Lawrence Bragg, who was only 25 when he won the 1915 prize.

⚲ *GALILEI, GRAVITY, QUANTUM MECHANICS, TOILET PAPER*

PI

14 March is written 14.3 in the UK and 3.14 in the US, which is why it is celebrated in the US and by mathematicians worldwide as Pi Day, as it is the day closest to the mathematical constant pi (=3.1415926...). 14 March may be Pi Day, but the ultimate Pi Day was 14 March 1592, or 3.14.1592, as the Americans write it, which has the first seven digits of pi.

Appropriately, 31.4 trillion digits of pi were calculated by a Google employee in 2019 to set a new record. But pi goes on for ever without recurring.

Pi is not only the 16th letter of the Greek alphabet, but P is the 16th letter of our alphabet too.

The Welsh mathematician William Jones was the first to use pi to signify the ratio between a circle's circumference and its diameter in 1706. He chose the Greek for P as it was the first letter of 'periphery' or 'perimeter', which were the words then used for circumference.

If you write 3.14 on a piece of paper and hold it up to a mirror, it looks like 'PIE'.

Albert Einstein was born on Pi Day, 14 March 1879.

In 2015, Rajveer Meena of India set a world record by reciting the first 70,030 digits of pi from memory.

Pi Day in 2016 was special as (in the US) it was 3.14.16, which gives pi to four decimal places.

The sentence 'I prefer pi' reads the same backwards.

● PIANO

The piano was invented in 1726 by the Italian Bartolomeo Cristofori. Three pianos made by Cristofori still survive, in museums in New York, Rome and Leipzig.

In 1650, the German Jesuit scholar Athanasius Kircher described a 'Cat Piano' played by keys that stuck pins into the tails of cats which had been chosen for the different pitches at which they mewed.

The Trinidadian Charles Brunner holds the world record for continuous piano-playing, at 64 hours.

The French composer Erik Satie wrote a piano piece called 'Flabby Preludes for a Dog'. He also wrote a three-minute piece called 'Vexations', which includes the instruction 'to be repeated 840 times'. Its first complete performance was in 1963. It lasted 18 hours and was played by 10 pianists in two-hour shifts.

The 1993 film *The Piano*, written and directed by Jane Campion, was the last film Kurt Cobain watched before he shot himself.

♀ *ALCHEMY, BACH, BOSCH, LAMARR, MOZART, PORTER*

● PICASSO, Pablo (1881–1973)

The full name of Pablo Picasso was Pablo Diego Jose Francisco de Paula Juan Nepomuceno Maria de los Remedios Cipriano de la Santisima Trinidad Ruiz Picasso.

When Picasso's painting *Garcon à la Pipe* was sold for a record $104.1 million (£58 million) in New York in 2004, the price worked out at £46,474 per square inch.

'I'd like to live like a poor man with lots of money.' Pablo Picasso

♀ *PIGEON, PIPES, PIZZA*

● PICNIC

The word 'picnic' came from the French *pique-nique*, which is thought to have been formed from the verb *piquer*, to pick, and *nique*, nothing at all. Originally a picnic was an 18th-century social event at which each guest contributed something to eat.

The song 'The Teddy Bear's Two-Step' was composed by John W Bratton in 1907. It became 'The Teddy Bear's Picnic' in 1930 when Jimmy Kennedy added lyrics.

● PIES

Until the 14th century, the only meaning of pie in English was as a word for the magpie. The earliest reference to pie being used in relation to food was in 1301. In classical times, pies contained assortments of meat and fish.

Around £1 billion is spent on pies every year in Britain, of which pork pies contribute £145 million. According to a recent survey, 75 per cent of people enjoy a pie at least once a month.

The pastry crust of a pie used to be known as a 'coffyn' or 'coffyn of paste'. This was viewed as almost inedible and given to the poor or servants while the gentry ate the meat cooked inside it.

The expression 'to eat humble pie' comes from 'umble pie', which was a pie filled with the chopped or minced innards of an animal. 'Umble' came from 'numble', meaning a deer's innards.

'Pie in the sky' comes from a 1911 US folk song lyric: 'You'll get pie in the sky when you die', referring to heavenly reward for earthly suffering.

The only Oscar-winning film with pie in its title was the cartoon *Tweetie Pie* in 1947.

Pies filled with figs or dates are believed to have originated in ancient Egypt about 3,000 years ago, but the oldest known pie recipe – for a rye-crusted goat, cheese and honey pie – originated in ancient Rome about 2,000 years ago. Pies appeared in Britain in the 12th century, generally spelt 'pye' and containing meat. The base was a rectangular box of pastry. Fruit pies did not appear until the 16th century.

According to the Oxford English Corpus, the descriptive words most likely to precede 'pie' are 'apple', 'American', 'mince' and 'humble', with 'pumpkin' and 'meat' sharing fifth place.

'If you want to make an apple pie from scratch, you must first create the Universe.' Carl Sagan

♀ CHRISTMAS, CUSTARD PIES, FRISBEE

🔴 PIG

On 17 July 1408, a sow was hanged in the French town of Pont de l'Arche, having been convicted 'for the crime of having murdered and killed a young child'.

Pigs may oink in English, but in French they go 'groin, groin', in Polish they go 'chrum, chrum', and in Mandarin Chinese they go 'Hu-lu, hu-lu'.

In 2001, a pig race in Arklow, County Wicklow, had to be cancelled because of foot-and-mouth disease, so local councillors took the place of the pigs instead.

Fluorescent green pigs were first bred by Chinese scientists in 2006 by injecting fluorescent green protein into pig embryos. 'The mouth, trotters and tongue of the pigs are green under ultraviolet light,' a researcher explained.

A pig's orgasm lasts for 30 minutes.

♀ CLOONEY, GUINEA PIGS, KARLOFF, PORK, RICE, TALIBAN

🔴 PIGEON

The British royal family has kept racing pigeons since 1886 when King Leopold of Belgium presented some to the Prince of Wales, later Edward VII.

In the 17th century, King George I decreed all pigeon droppings to be the property of the Crown. This was because pigeon droppings were used in the manufacture of gunpowder.

Martha, the last known passenger pigeon in the world, died in Cincinnati Zoo on the first day of September in 1914.

Pigeon post was first used by the Sumerians in 776 BC, but it was not until 1946 that a pigeon called G.I. Joe was awarded the Dickin Medal for message-carrying services to the US army in the Second World War.

In 1995, Japanese psychologists reported that they had trained pigeons to tell the difference between paintings by Picasso and Monet, but they could not tell a Renoir from a Cézanne.

When the mayor of Venice banned food sellers from St Mark's Square in 2008, in an attempt to limit damage to buildings by pigeon droppings, licensed sellers of bird food demanded compensation of £75 for each day they were out of work.

ARCHERY, DARWIN, FOOTBALL, SPYING

PIGGY BANKS

Piggy banks get their name from a clay called pygg. Money was saved in pygg jars, which were then made in the shape of pigs and called piggy banks.

A company in Switzerland withdrew one of its products in 2010 and apologised after receiving complaints and heavy criticism from the state of Liechtenstein. The item that provoked the row was a piggy bank sold under the name 'Liechtenschwein'. Hans Buff & Co. said it had been intended as a joke and they were sorry it had caused offence.

PILLOW

International Pillow Fight Day was inaugurated by the Urban Playground Movement in 2008. In 2012, pillow fights were held on the streets of 115 cities in 39 countries.

Toronto has a Pillow Fight League for women. The world champion is Dinah Mite. Rules include no eye-gouging, biting, scratching, hair pulling or low blows, and no lewd behaviour.

Until the 16th century, pillows were used only by the rich and influential. Stone pillars were usual in ancient Egypt and China. In Tudor England, soft pillows were thought suitable only for weak men and pregnant women.

A 'standard' or 'continental' pillowcase is 51 centimetres (20 inches) wide and 66 centimetres (26 inches) long.

A 'housewife' pillowcase is one with a flap on one side of the open end to tuck the pillow into.

A 'dakimakura', also known as 'love pillow' or 'hug pillow', is a body-length Japanese pillow designed to be hugged.

The town of Pillow, Pennsylvania, is named after Gideon Pillow, a confederate general in the American Civil War.

'Last night I dreamt I ate a 10-pound marshmallow. When I woke up the pillow was gone.' Tommy Cooper

'A ruffled mind makes a restless pillow.' Charlotte Bronte

BEDS, LONDON 2012, SNORING, SOLSTICE, SPAIN, WALRUS

PINEAPPLE

There is no reference to pineapples in either the King James Bible or any of the plays of Shakespeare, but 'pine-apple rum' is referred to nine times in Charles Dickens's *Pickwick Papers* where it is the favourite drink of the Rev. Stiggins.

In Japan, bathing in coffee grounds mixed with pineapple pulp is supposed to remove wrinkles.

Anonaceous means 'pertaining to pineapples'.

PIPES

In 2010, Palestinian women in Gaza were banned from smoking water pipes, as it 'leads to divorce'.

Built around 1930, the organ at Boardwalk Hall Auditorium in Atlantic City, New Jersey, has 33,114 pipes, the most of any organ.

Piper is the name of a genus of pepper plants, a bird, or a New Zealand fish also known as garfish.

Much Ado About Nothing is the only Shakespeare play that mentions a piper or pipers.

FORTY-SEVEN, PETER PAN, SEA LION, SMOKING

PIRACY

Efforts by the music and film industries to fight against digital piracy were dealt a blow in April 2012 by a decision of the Swedish government to recognise as a religion the so-called 'church' of Kopimism. The central belief of Kopimism is that 'kopyacting' or sharing information across the Internet, is akin to a religious service. Its founder, 19-year-old philosophy student Isak Gerson, said that he hoped file-sharing would be given religious protection. 'For the Church of Kopimism, information is holy and copying is a sacrament,' he explained.

Members of the Kopimism Church are known as Kopimi. Their new status was secured only after they had applied for it three times.

On 28 April 2012, the Church of Kopimism held their first wedding. It took place in Belgrade between a Romanian bride and an Italian groom. The ceremony was conducted by a Kopimistic priest, known as an 'Op', who was wearing a Guy Fawkes mask, while a computer read aloud the vows and some central beliefs of Kopimism.

♀ CAPITAL PUNISHMENT

PISA

According to measurements by retired Dutch geometrician Jacob van Dijk, the Tower of Pisa lost its title of Europe's most leaning tower in 2008 to a 12th-century building in the northern Dutch town of Bedum. The 36-metre (118-foot) church tower of Walfridus leans at an angle of about 4.2 degrees, compared with the Tower of Pisa at about 4.1 degrees.

♀ GALILEI

PIUS

Pius is the name of 12 popes, including the only two to have become saints in the last 500 years: Pius V and Pius X.

The twelfth and last Pope Pius died in 1958, but the American-born Lucian Pulvermacher was elected Antipope Pius XIII in 1998 by a group who called themselves the True Catholic Church.

♀ EXORCISM, JOAN OF ARC, JOHN PAUL II, PAPAL SMOKE, ST BERNARD

PIZZA

The father of the modern pizza is generally considered to have been Rafaele Esposito of Naples who, in 1889, created the Pizza Margherita for King Umberto I and Queen Margherita of Italy. The colours of the tomato, mozzarella cheese and basil in Pizza Margherita were designed to match the red, white and green of the Italian flag.

The first pizza, however, dates back further, with similar flatbread dishes known and referred to as 'pizza' since at least AD 997.

The world's first real pizzeria, serving only pizzas, was the Antica Pizzeria Port' Alba in Naples. It opened in 1830 and still serves pizzas today.

Europe's first pizza convention, Pizzatec, was held in January 1997, not in Italy but in Berlin. It attracted 88 exhibitors from 12 countries and included in its displays copies of works by Dali, Picasso and Mondrian, painted on dough in tomato, cheese and olives.

The world's largest circular pizza was a 39.5-metre (130-foot) diameter pizza made in Rome in 2012. Its ingredients included 8,981 kilograms (19,800 pounds) of flour and 3,992 kilograms (8,800 pounds) of tomato sauce and the dough had to be baked in 5,234 batches over a period of 48 hours.

In 2001, inmates of the Dutra Ladeira Prison in Brazil made it the first jail in the world to run a pizza-delivery service. It operated both in and out of the jail.

The US Congress declared 4 June 1997 National Pizza Day to celebrate 100 years of American pizza. About 100 acres of pizza are eaten every day in the US – that's about 350 slices a second. In the UK, National Pizza Day is celebrated on 9 February.

Research in Britain shows that people with pierced noses, lips or eyebrows are 23 per cent more likely to ask for vegetarian toppings than meat toppings on pizzas.

According to a survey in 2004, 6 per cent of people say pizza is the food they would most miss if they were stranded in an Australian jungle.

On 19 August 1998, US clothing manufacturers VF Corporation ordered 13,386 pizzas for their 40,160 employees. Guinness World Records ranks it as the largest single order for pizza.

♀ *ASTRONAUTS, BERLUSCONI, JAPAN, NAPLES, OREGANO, SCRABBLE*

🌑 PLAGUE

Under the Public Health (Control of Disease) Act 1984, it is against British law to ride in a taxi if you are suffering from the plague. Smallpox, typhus and cholera are also forbidden in taxi-passengers.

♀ *GERBIL, LAVENDER*

🌑 PLANTS

A man was arrested in New York in August 2010 accused of being the 'bouquet bandit' who robbed a Manhattan bank holding fresh flowers and a note demanding money. Police

believed he was the same man as had previously robbed another bank while carrying a potted plant.

♀ *LINNAEUS, LONDON 2012, MADAGASCAR, SANTA CLAUS*

🌑 PLATINUM

From 1875 to 1960, the SI unit of length (the standard metre) was defined as the distance between two lines on a standard bar of an alloy of 90 per cent platinum and 10 per cent iridium, measured at 0° Celsius.

Although the word 'platinum' dates back to at least 1783, the term 'platinum blonde' was first recorded only in 1931.

♀ *ELEMENTS*

🌑 PLATO (c.427–347 BC)

Plato's given name was Aristocles, meaning 'the best' or 'most renowned'. He acquired the nickname of Plato, meaning 'wide', in his youth because of his wide shoulders.

Plato did not approve of humour and laughter as he thought they overrode self-control and had a detrimental impact on the ability to reason.

♀ *ALCHEMY, CELIBACY, DIOGENES, LAUGHTER, SMILING, UNIVERSITIES*

🌑 PLATYPUS

The platypus has a muzzle like a duck's bill, a tail like a beaver, lays eggs and suckles its young. A platypus has no teeth but has pads inside its mouth on which it grinds its food, which consists of insects, larvae, shellfish and worms scooped from underwater. This is often accompanied by gravel which helps with the grinding. A platypus is mostly silent but has been heard to make a sound that has been compared to the noise of a puppy growling or a brooding hen. It consumes about a quarter of its body weight daily and spends about half the day eating. Only the male duck-billed platypus can sting – through venomous spurs at the back of its hind legs.

When Europeans first reached Australia, they called the platypus duckbill, watermole or duckmole. In 1799 it was given the name of *Platypus anatinus*, which simply means a flat-footed animal of the duck family. Then the *Platypus* part of this name was changed to *Ornithorhynchus*, which means birdlike snout. Aborigines called the platypus mallangong, boondaburra or tambreet.

The platypus and two forms of echidna form the Monotremata – mammals that have a single orifice for both excretion and reproduction. The platypus and the echidna are also the only egg-laying mammals. The American public had their first sight of a duck-billed platypus on 15 July 1922 at New York Zoo.

In 2016, a survey of the most searched-for mammals on the Internet saw the duck-billed platypus just waddling flat-footedly into the Top 10 behind humans, elephants, lions, tigers, polar bears, killer whales, cougars, giant pandas and grey wolves.

⚲ *VAGINA*

● PLAYBOY

The Playboy Mansion in Chicago, once the home of Hugh Hefner, had a brass plate on the door with the Latin inscription, *Si Non Oscillas, Noli Tintinnare* ('If you don't swing, don't ring').

The original meaning of 'playboy', as used in Ben Jonson's play *Love Restored*, was a boy actor. It was not used to mean a man who leads a life of pleasure until 1829.

● PLAYING CARDS

The King of Hearts is the only playing card king without a moustache. Until the late 19th century, a playing card Jack was known as a Knave. In the game of All Fours, Jack was the name given to winning a trick containing the Jack of Trumps, so the name of Jack became associated with that card. Conveniently, When the letters K and Q became increasingly used for the King and Queen, calling the next card J avoided the awkward Kn double letter, so the term Jack gradually established itself.

In some circles, however, calling a Knave (which simply meant a servant) by the name of Jack was considered rather lower class, as seen in Dickens's *Great Expectations* when Estella speaks mockingly of Pip when playing cards: '"He calls the knaves Jacks, this boy!" said Estella with disdain.'

An experiment by psychologists in 2012 reported that when you ask people to name a card from a normal pack, over half of them choose one of four cards: the Ace of Spades (25 per cent), or the Queen (14 per cent), Ace (6 per cent) or King (6 per cent) of Hearts. However, if you ask them to *think* of a card, the popularity of the King of Hearts rises to 11 per cent.

⚲ *PARAPSYCHOLOGY, SHUFFLING*

● PLINY the Elder (c.AD23–79)

Scientific encyclopedist and historian Pliny the Elder was killed by the eruption of Mount Vesuvius while trying to rescue a friend in the city of Stabiae about 4.8 kilometres (3 miles) from the volcano.

⚲ *HEDGEHOG, MOON, OSTRICH, SEX, SHOES, UNICORN*

PLUM

The Australian billygoat plum contains 100 times more vitamin C than an orange.

♀ *PRUNE, TOMATO*

PLUTO

The US Dialect Society voted 'Plutoed' its Word of 2006 from the verb 'to Pluto', meaning to devalue or demote someone or something, after the planet Pluto was downgraded from full planetary status by the International Astronomical Union.

In 2009, the State Senate in Illinois voted to continue regarding Pluto as a planet, despite the fact that it had lost its planetary status three years earlier. The decision was apparently motivated by the fact that Pluto had been discovered by an Illinois man in 1930. The senate also voted for an annual 'Pluto Day' and declared that it had been 'unfairly downgraded'.

♀ *ASTRONOMY, NEPTUNE*

POE, Edgar Allan (1809–49)

Edgar Allan Poe was born in Boston, but his father left the family when he was one year old; his mother died the following year. Until that point, he had been simply Edgar Poe, but he was then looked after by John and Frances Allan of Richmond, Virginia, and although they never formally adopted him, they gave him Allan as a middle name. In 1836, Poe married his 13-year-old cousin Virginia Clemm.

In 1909, a silent film of Poe's life was directed by D.W. Griffith, but his middle name was misspelled in the title of the film: *Edgar Allen Poe*.

Every 19 January a mysterious visitor left three red roses and a half-bottle of Cognac at the grave of Edgar Allan Poe at Westminster Presbyterian Church in Baltimore on the anniversary of Poe's birthday. The visitor, dressed in black with a white scarf and wide-brimmed hat, would pour himself a glass and toast Poe's memory, then disappear into the night, leaving behind three roses in a distinctive arrangement and the rest of the bottle. Sporadic 'Poe Toaster' visits date back at least to 1950 and continued until 2010, since when they have not occurred. .

POETRY

According to the Japanese, the optimum length of human speech in a single breath is 17 syllables, hence the Haiku, a poem of 17 syllables. Actually it's a bit more complicated than that. Japanese poets did not talk of a 'syllable' but a 'mora', which was more a unit of speaking time than a phonetic measure, or time taken to say something. Only when it was taken into Western poetry did syllables start to count.

The next size up from a haiku is a 'tanka', which means 'short song' and has a length equal to 31 syllables.

♀ *BOXING DAY, COLOMBIA, KEATS, POLO, QUANTUM MECHANICS*

POISON

The nanny of a sex-toy entrepreneur appeared in court in London in January 2011 on a charge of 'administering poison with intent to annoy'. Allison Cox, 33, was accused of spiking her boss Jacqueline Gold's soup on three occasions with salt, sugar and windscreen wiper fluid. A toxicologist said the case was unusual because the substances used were unlikely to be harmful. Another expert said that possible side effects could depend on the brand of wiper fluid used. Ms Cox was sentenced to 12 months in prison.

COLOMBIA, MISTLETOE, MOLE, PAPER, TURING

POKER

Two pairs, aces and eights, is referred to as the 'dead man's hand', since the killing of Wild Bill Hickok in a poker game on 2 August 1876 as he held that hand, but while it is generally agreed that he held the two black aces and two black eights, there is considerable argument as to what his fifth card was. Saloon Number 10 in Deadwood, South Dakota, which is named after the bar where Hickok was shot, proudly displays the fifth card as the Nine of Diamonds, but the Lucky Nugget Gambling Hall, which includes the historic site of Saloon Number 10, shows the fifth card as the Jack of Diamonds. Another theory is that the fatal shooting took place after Hickok had discarded his fifth card in a game of draw poker, and had not yet been dealt a replacement when he was shot.

BACCARAT, MONTENEGRO

POLAND

There are 32 letters in the Polish alphabet. An unaccented 'Z' scores only one in Polish Scrabble. Two types of accented 'Z' score 5 and 7 respectively.

Augustus II of Poland, also known as Augustus the Strong, was a major porcelain collector in the early 18th century. He is even said to have sold a regiment of dragoons for 50 pieces of Ming porcelain. He is also said to have been able to break horseshoes with his bare hands. According to contemporary sources, he fathered either 365 or 382 illegitimate children, though this

may have referred to the number of nights he spent with his mistresses.

COPERNICUS, EURO, GDANSK, MONACO, PAINTING, TAX

POLAR BEAR

The first polar bear in Britain was given to Henry III by Haakon IV of Norway, who often gave polar bears to monarchs he liked. King Henry's polar bear was kept at the Tower of London and let out to swim in the Thames on the end of a rope. The King issued a writ 'directing the sheriffs of London to furnish six pence a day to support our White Bear in our Tower of London; and to provide a muzzle and iron chain to hold him when out of the water; and a long strong rope to hold him when he was fishing in the Thames'.

The name 'polar bear' only came into use after 1781. Until then it was simply 'white bear'. The first reference to a polar bear in literature was in Dickens's *Sketches by Boz*, where he describes some characters with the words: 'in their shaggy white coats they look just like Polar bears'.

The correct word to mean 'of or pertaining to the polar bear' is 'thalas-sarctine', from the Greek *arktos* ('bear') and *thalassa* ('sea'). The scientific name for the polar bear is *Thalarctos maritimus*.

When kept in zoos, many polar bears develop long rituals, called 'stereotypic behaviour', pacing up and down their cages or swimming round and round the same path. When Gus, a polar bear in Central Park Zoo, New York, developed stereotypic swimming behaviour in 1994, an animal psychiatrist was employed at a cost of $25,000 to devise a course of therapy. By delivering his food wrapped and at irregular times, and giving him playthings laced with peanuts and honey, the therapist was able to rekindle the bear's interest in life. After a year, his compulsive swimming behaviour was down by a third, he had stopped being mean to his female companions and was soon declared fully recovered. In the words of a zoo spokesman: 'He has done something that many New Yorkers find difficult to do. He has stopped seeing his therapist.'

In the 19th century, a team of Arctic explorers all died from a vitamin A overdose after they had eaten a polar bear liver; 450 grams (1 pound) of polar bear liver contains enough vitamin A to fulfil a human's requirements for 20 years.

A polar bear's gestation period is 39 weeks and results in between one and four cubs. Fully-grown, a cub may be up to 3.4 metres (11 feet) long and weigh almost 680 kilograms (1,500 pounds). Polar bears can run at 40 kilometres (25 miles) an hour and jump over 1.8 metres (6 feet) in the air.

It is often stated that all polar bears are left-handed, but this claim seems to be based on a single account by an Inuit elder and has never been verified by scientific observation, which suggests that polar bears use both paws equally.

The hair on the soles of their feet protects polar bears from slipping on ice.

In some Inuit communities, women do not comb their hair on a day when a polar bear is to be killed.

♀ *BACULUM, BEAR, ICE HOCKEY*

● POLO

The earliest known reference to the game of polo is in Persian poetry of the early 11th century. The name of 'polo',

however, comes from a Tibetan word for 'ball', which suggests that the game may have originated in China. It was first played in England in 1871, having been brought over by British army officers who had organised matches in India in the 1850s.

Polo neck pullovers were named in the 1960s after the small, round 'polo hat', which had been popular in the 1900s.

'Polo' is also a style of Flamenco music.

♀ *AFGHANISTAN, MARCO POLO, MEXICO, TIBET, YAK*

● POLYGAMY

A senior Malaysian politician was sentenced to a month in prison by an Islamic court in 2010 for taking a second wife without the permission of his first wife. Muslims are allowed to take up to four wives in Malaysia but must ask for permission from existing wives before taking another. Sentencing Bung Mokhtar, who was deputy president of the parliamentarians' club of the National Front coalition, the judge said, 'The accused had bad intentions and had toyed with the marriage solemnisation process and the rules of polygamy according to shariah law'. Bung's lawyers asked for a lesser sentence of just a fine, as it was his first offence.

♀ *LEMUR*

● POLYGRAPH

In 2003, a report from the National Academy of Sciences in the US found that the majority of research claiming validity in the use of the polygraph or lie-detector was 'Unreliable, Unscientific and Biased'. Despite this, polygraph evidence was admitted in 19 states in 2007. Montana is the only state in which polygraph evidence is banned under all circumstances.

♀ *MARSTON*

POMEGRANATE

Pomegranates are the fourth most frequently mentioned fruit in the King James Bible, with 34 references to them. Only olives (66 references), figs (61 references) and grapes (59 references) are mentioned more frequently.

Apples are the fifth most often mentioned fruit in the Bible, though the forbidden fruit that led to Adam and Eve's expulsion from the Garden of Eden is nowhere referred to specifically as an apple.

♀ *DALI, NOVEMBER*

POMPADOUR, Marquise de (1721–64)

During 1745–51, Madame de Pompadour was the official chief mistress of King Louis XV of France and was given a room in the Palace of Versailles directly above the King's. She was also the first person in France known to have a pet goldfish. Her original surname was Poisson, which is the French for 'fish'.

PONY

A 'pony' is any small horse, usually one less than 14.2 hands (56.8 inches) in height.

The world's smallest pony is thought to be a stallion called Einstein, born in New Hampshire in 2010 and only 51 centimetres (20 inches) high on his first birthday.

A 'pony' may also mean a small measure of alcohol or a small crib or study aid. Since the late 18th century, a 'pony' has been slang for £25 or 25 guineas. Nobody knows why.

My Little Pony toys were created in 1982 and the design was granted a patent in 1983.

Britain's last pit pony died at the age of 40 in 2011. It had retired from the Ellington pit in Northumberland in 1994. Its name was Tony.

The phrase 'one-trick pony' originated around 1900 and referred to ponies in travelling circuses that had been taught to perform only one trick.

The Pony Express mail service operated in the USA only in 1860–61. Its youngest rider was an 11-year-old named 'Bronco' Charlie Miller.

In 2012, Queen Elizabeth II banned tourists from riding on the ponies at Balmoral, after animal rights activists warned that the animals' health was being put at risk by carrying overweight riders.

♀ *BUTCHELL*

POPCORN

The science of popcorn was revealed in 2004 in the paper 'The Effects of Ingredients on Popcorn Popping Characteristics' by M. Ceylan and E. Karababa, in the *International Journal of Food Science and Technology*.

According to the Turkish researchers, popcorn popped in a microwave oven needs 1.5 grams of salt, 2 grams of vegetable oil and 6 grams of butter for every 25 grams of corn to get both the most expansion and the fewest unpopped kernels. On a stove top, however, only 1.1 gram of salt and 4.2 grams of butter will achieve optimum results. Adding about 0.3 grams of sodium bicarbonate can also enhance the popping. Microwave popping gives about 10 per cent less expansion than heating on top of the stove.

In February 2011, a man was arrested at a cinema in Latvia on suspicion of shooting another man dead for eating his popcorn too loudly during the film *Black Swan*.

ANCHOVY

POPES

Popes are always right-handed and tend to die in the job. The last popes to hand over the Papacy while still alive were Pope Benedict XVI, who resigned in 2013, and Gregory XII, who retired in 1415 to end a schism within the Church.

On the death of a pope, according to tradition, the Papal Chamberlain must call out his baptismal name three times and tap the head of the deceased with a silver hammer before he is officially declared dead.

Twenty-six popes are said to have been assassinated, though that number may include various violent deaths which were not technically assassination. Pope John XII, for example, was said to have been murdered in 964 by the jealous husband of the woman with whom he was in bed.

Once the death of a pope is established, his successor is elected by the College of Cardinals. All cardinals have a vote, except those over the age of 80.

In 897, Pope Steven VII had the body of his predecessor, Pope Formosus, who had died in 896, dug up, propped in a chair and put on trial for violating Church laws.

Because of an 11th-century miscount, there was a Pope John XIX and a Pope John XXI but no John XX.

Adrian IV (born Nicholas Breakspear), who was Pope from 1154 to 1159, was the only English pope. Very little is known about his early life except that he was probably born in Hertfordshire.

All the above popes would have been accustomed to having their toes kissed. From the 8th century until the 18th century, this was the traditional way to greet a pope. This custom is said to date back to AD 798 when 'a certain lewd woman' gave a pope's hand a squeeze when kissing it. The Pope, seeing the moral danger inherent in this act, cut his hand off and instituted toe-kissing.

In 1978, John Paul II became the first non-Italian pope since the death of Adrian VI in 1523.

LEAP YEAR, PIUS

POPEYE

Popeye the Sailor was the first cartoon character to have a statue put up in his honour. It was erected in Crystal City, Texas, as a gesture of thanks from the people in the city that calls itself the 'Spinach Capital of America'. The statue was unveiled on 26 March 1937.

Popeye himself first appeared in the daily comic strip *Thimble Theatre* on 17 January 1929. Originally, Popeye gained his strength by rubbing the head of the rare Whiffle Hen. Spinach only came into the story in 1932.

Sammy Lerner, who wrote the 'Popeye-the-sailor-man' theme song, also wrote the lyrics to 'Falling In Love Again', as sung by Marlene Dietrich in *The Blue Angel*.

There is a tourist attraction called Popeye Village in Malta, where the movie *Popeye* was filmed in 1980.

In 2004, the Empire State Building was lit up in spinach green to honour Popeye's 75th birthday.

In Spain, the name of Popeye's girlfriend Olive Oyl is seen as an insult to the olive tree, and she has been renamed Rosario. Olive Oyl had an elder brother called Castor Oyl.

POPULATION

Every 24 hours on average, some 385,000 people are born and 153,425 die. That is 4.5 births and 1.8 deaths every second.

In 1800, 2.8 per cent of the world's population was in the Americas, and 67 per cent in Asia. By 2000, 14 per cent was in the Americas and 58 per cent in Asia.

At the time of Christ, world population was about 250 million. In 1600, it was about 500 million (including 5 million in Britain). The figure is estimated to have reached 1 billion in 1804, 2 billion in 1927, 3 billion in 1960, 4 billion in 1974, 5 billion in 1987, 6 billion in 1999 and 7 billion in 2011.

If the present population of nearly 7.8 billion were shrunk to 100 people, keeping all categories in the same proportion, they would look like this: 59 Asians, 18 Africans, 10 Europeans, 8 South Americans and 5 North Americans; 52 would be female, 48 would be male. Six people would possess 59 per cent of the entire world's wealth, while 80 would live in substandard housing and 70 would be unable to read. 59 would be active Internet users; 50 would suffer from malnutrition and only one would have a college education.

According to American estimates, the world population reached 6 billion at 6.33pm on Monday, 9 August 1999. The UN suggested 31 October 2011 as the date on which 7 billion was reached, but the US Census Bureau claimed that the Day of Seven Billion was not reached until March 2012.

♀ *CHINA, DONKEY, EUROPE, GOATS, GREENLAND, JAPAN, MACAO*

PORK

In 2007, a French court ruled that it is not discriminatory to offer pork soup to the homeless. Police had banned the soup kitchen, on the grounds that the free soup discriminated against Jews and Muslims who do not eat pork on religious grounds. The administrative court said the distribution was 'clearly discriminatory', but could not be stopped because the organisers offered to feed anyone who asked for help. The Mayor of Paris condemned the ruling, which he said 'stinks of xenophobia'.

Addressing leaders of the pig farming industry in January 2010, Argentine president Cristina Fernandez said she had spent a satisfying weekend with her husband after eating barbecued pork. 'I've just been told something I didn't know: that eating pork improves your sex life,' she said. 'I'd say it's a lot nicer to eat a bit of grilled pork than to take Viagra.'

♀ *ANDERSEN, BACON, HIPPOPOTAMUS, PIES, TALIBAN*

PORONKUSEMA

In Finland, there is a traditional unit of distance called the poronkusema, which varies from 7.5 to 16 kilometres (4.5 to 10 miles) and is defined as the distance a reindeer can travel without needing a rest stop for urination. The variation depends on the age and condition of the reindeer, the size of its load, the terrain and the weather.

The word comes from two Finnish roots: *poro* ('reindeer'), *kus* (slang for 'urine' or 'piss').

PORTER, Cole (1891–1964)

Cole Porter was named after his maternal grandfather, James Omar Cole, who was said to be the richest man in Indiana.

After his first show, *See America First*, was a Broadway flop and lasted only 15 performances. Cole Porter is said to have joined the French Foreign Legion to fight in the First World War. There is some doubt as to whether this is true, but he was awarded the Croix de Guerre by the French government in 1917.

His legs were crushed in a riding accident in 1937 in which a horse rolled onto him. Doctors thought both his legs would have to be amputated, but he refused to agree and instead underwent surgical operations 34 times in the following 20 years. To continue his work, he had a piano built around his bed, but finally had to have his right leg ampu-tated in 1958. He then declared himself to be only 'half a man' and went into seclusion, never writing another song.

● PORTUGAL

When Pedro I was crowned King of Portugal in 1357, he proclaimed his lover, Ines de Castro, Queen, despite the fact that she had died in 1355.

In 1996, the Society for the Portu-guese Language set up a commission with the ambition of halving the influx of English words. Among those listed as particularly offensive were 'franchising', 'mall' and 'shopping centre'.

In 2019, Portugal was the world's biggest exporter of agglomerated cork, natural cork articles and hat forms (including headgear and parts thereof).

In February 2004, a hospital in Lisbon was reported to have asked a zoo to lend it X-ray equipment usually used on elephants, to enable it to treat over-weight patients.

The Portuguese eat more fish and shellfish per head of population than people in any other country except Iceland.

⚲ *BIKINI, SLAVERY*

● POST OFFICE

On 13 June 1920, the US Post Office declared that children may not be sent by parcel post.

The gum on an American postage stamp contains about one-tenth of a calorie.

Throughout the world in 2019, each person posted an average of 37 items. In 2016, the average American received 458 letters, the average Chinese only 16.

⚲ *DINOSAUR, INDIA, SANTA CLAUS*

● POSTCODE

The postcode for 10 Downing Street is SW1A 2AA. Number 11 is SW1A 2AB. Buckingham Palace is SW1A 1AA. The mailing address for the White House is 1600 Pennsylvania Avenue, NW Wash-ington, DC 20500.

● POSTMEN

In 2001, official figures showed that every year in Germany over 3,000 postmen are bitten by dogs, resulting in 2,255 pairs of torn trousers, 12,720 lost working days, £8 million of medical bills and 755 hospital stays. The German postal service promptly instituted training courses to teach dog psychology to postmen.

In February 2008, Australia's postal service increased the maximum weight for mailmen and women by 15 kilo-grams (33 pounds). Until then, Australia Post had a weight limit of 90 kilograms (198 pounds) for 'posties', because its motorcycles had a safe working limit of 130 kilograms (286 pounds), which was made up of 40 kilograms (88 pounds) for letters and up to 90 kilograms (198 pounds) for mailmen and women fully dressed. After talks with motorcycle manufacturer Honda, it was agreed the bikes could safely carry a person weighing 105 kilograms (231 pounds), carrying 25 kilograms (55 pounds) of mail.

⚲ *DIAGRAM, LABRADOR*

● POTATO

'Spud' originally meant a short knife or dagger. Nobody knows how the meaning transferred to a slang term for potato, which first happened in the 19th century.

Until the late 18th century, the French generally believed that potatoes caused leprosy. The vegetables overcame the hostility this created thanks largely to Marie Antoinette's habit of wearing potato blossoms in her hair.

The original Mr Potato Head dates back to 1946 when it consisted of plastic parts designed to be clipped onto a real potato. Its sales suffered because it led to too many rotting potatoes around owners' houses, but in 1951, rights to the product were bought by Hasbro, which added a plastic potato body and a big, child-friendly advertising campaign. In 1952, Mr Potato Head became the first toy to be advertised on American television and in the following year over a million were sold. In 2020, the title of 'Mr' before Potato Head was dropped in order to 'promote gender equality and inclusion'.

In October 1995, the potato became the first vegetable to be grown in space as part of a NASA project to develop ways to feed astronauts or future space colonies.

The world's top four potato-producing countries in 2016 were: China (99 million tonnes), India (43.8 million tonnes), Russia (31.1 million tonnes) and Ukraine (21.8 million tonnes). In terms of potato production per person, however, Belarus led the world, with Ukraine in second place.

The latest state-of-the-art technological improvement in the potato world is an industrial peeler that uses three laser beams to peel a potato in one second. Less technologically, Clark, which calls itself the 'Potato Capital of South Dakota', holds regular Mashed Potato Wrestling contests.

An old folk remedy recommends carrying potatoes in your pocket to cure or prevent rheumatism.

In the film *Close Encounters of the Third Kind*, dried potato flakes were used to represent snowflakes.

Prince Edward Island, Canada, is the location of the world's largest potato museum, which includes a Potato Hall of Fame, recognising those who have greatly contributed to the growth and development of the potato industry.

Jersey Royal New Potatoes were cultivated by Jersey farmer Hugh de la Haye, who cut up and planted a potato with 15 eyes just to see what happened.

The cultivated potato generally has 48 chromosomes in its genetic make-up. A human being has only 46.

On 15 June 1992, the US Vice President Dan Quayle misspelled 'potato' as 'potatoe'. It happened at a school in Trenton, New Jersey, when he was 'correcting' the already correct spelling of William Figueroa, 12, by adding an 'e' at the end.

⚲ *CHIPS, CRISPS, GOLD, SHAKESPEARE, SLUG, STAR WARS*

● POVERTY

Police in Taiwan took a collection to buy a bicycle for a bicycle thief in

September 2010 when they discovered how poor he was. The man explained that he had stolen the bike to save his daughter a 4.8-kilometre (3-mile) walk to the nearest bus stop to get to school each morning. When police discovered that he lived in a house with no water or electricity, they took pity on him.

♀ *MONEY, SENEGAL*

PRAT

An MP in the House of Commons was forced to withdraw a remark in which he had described Liberal Democrats as 'prats'. The MP, John Cryer, had already described the debate, before the summer recess, as a 'sort of whingeing gits day, so that we can get a few things off our chests', but while he was allowed the general description of members taking part in the debate as 'gits', calling the Lib Dems 'prats' was deemed to be going too far. Whereas a 'git' is defined in the *Oxford English Dictionary* as 'a worthless person', one slang meaning of 'prat' is 'a buttock'.

PRAYER

While driving through the countryside in Sweden in September 1996, Spanish businessman Edouardo Sierra stopped at a Catholic church. He found it empty except for a body lying in rest in a coffin. He stopped to pray for the deceased and signed a book of remembrance left by the coffin. His was the only signature in the book. Some weeks later, Sierra received a telephone call telling him he was a millionaire. The body was that of a Swede with no close relatives who had left his fortune 'to whoever prays for my soul first'. Never has the potential financial power of prayer been so well demonstrated.

In October 1996, the Internet company Virtual Jerusalem, which had recently been launched, announced that it was receiving between 15 and 20 prayers each day by email, which were printed out and placed on the Wailing Wall.

♀ *GOD, HAITI, HALIFAX, OBAMA*

PREGNANCY

Nobody knows who first discovered what causes pregnancy, but Aristotle definitely understood how babies were made: 'When a young couple are married, they naturally desire children; and therefore adopt the means that nature has appointed to that end.'

The sex of an unborn child, he maintained, could easily be determined by examining the mother: 'If it is a male, the right breast swells first, the right eye is brighter than the left. The face is high-coloured, because the colour is such as the blood is, and the male is conceived of purer blood and of more perfect seed than the female.'

Finer details of conception had to wait until the microscope was invented. The first person to see a sperm was the Dutch microscopist Anton van Leeuwenhoek in 1677; the first human egg was seen only in 1930. Egg and sperm were not introduced to each other in a laboratory until 1944.

Modern superstitions about the causes of pregnancy include the following: 'If you are in the company of two pregnant women, slap your backside three times or you too will become pregnant', County Tyrone (1972); 'If you sit in a chair recently occupied by a pregnant woman, you will soon get pregnant', Bedfordshire (1982).

Statistics show that childbirth generally takes place between 250 and 285 days after ovulation, with the majority between 266 and 270 days. In cases concerning the legitimacy of a child, an American court once accepted a 355-day pregnancy as legitimate, while British courts have accepted 331 and 346 days as within the bounds of possibility. There is only a 5 per cent chance that a baby will be born on its 'due' date, and a 25 per cent chance that it will be born within four days of its scheduled arrival. Only 5 per cent are more than a fortnight early or late.

Generally, larger animals have longer pregnancies than smaller ones, though the piglet (113 days) is slower to emerge than a tiger or lion cub (107 days each). The human period of about 268 days fits in between the fallow deer (250 days) and the buffalo (300 days) in the gestation league. At the more extreme ends, we have the Virginia opossum (12 to 13 days), golden hamster (16 days) and elephant (700 days).

The British Ministry of Defence placed its first order for maternity uniforms on 3 October 1995.

♀ GERBIL, GROUNDHOG DAY, MARY I, WOMEN

PREGNANCY TEST

In 2018, an ancient Egyptian papyrus dating back to around 1350 BC was translated and found to be a surprisingly early written record of a urine-based pregnancy test. The test involved getting a woman who was possibly pregnant to urinate on wheat and barley seeds. 'If the barley grows,' the papyrus told us, 'it means a male child. If the wheat grows, it means a female child. If both do not grow, she will not bear at all.' The test had been known for some time, but this was by far the earliest example. In 1963, research had found that, 70 per cent of the time, the urine of pregnant women did indeed promote growth in

wheat and/or barley, while the urine of non-pregnant women and men did not, but the results did not confirm the ancient Egyptian claims of forecasting the sex of the child.

Scientists believe that elevated levels of oestrogen in pregnant women's urine may be the key to the ancient Egyptian test. In the Middle Ages, similar tests were used by so-called 'piss prophets' to predict pregnancy, the sex of unborn children and various diseases, but they were mostly superstitious nonsense.

PREMATURE EJACULATION

According to a 2005 study of 491 couples in the USA and four European countries, the time between vaginal intromission and male ejaculation varies between 30 seconds and 44 minutes, with a mean of 5.4 minutes. The Turks were the fastest, with an average of 3.7 minutes, and the British the slowest at 7.6 minutes.

♀ DOG, SEX

PRENUPTIAL AGREEMENT

Details of a prenuptial agreement appeared among court records in a divorce case in Florida in 2006. When Sally Erickson and David Renzie married in 2001, Erickson, a mental-health counsellor, was reported to have agreed to cook breakfast a minimum of three times during the weekdays, and once on the weekends, according to the document. In return, her husband would not wake Sally up on her 'off days'. Renzie also agreed to rub Sally's back three times a week for five minutes, but if Sally used the F-word, she was sentenced to one hour of yard work. The agreement also specified that he had to pay $5 each time he complained, nagged or made 'a fuss about Sally's expenditures'. They separated after three and a half months and Erickson was served notice of the divorce suit six days later.

PRESBYTERIANISM

'Presbyterianism' is an anagram of 'Rise empty brains' or 'Ban priest misery'.

♀ SPEARS

PRESLEY, Elvis (1935–77)

The name Elvis derives from an Old Norse word meaning 'all wise'. Although Elvis's middle name on his birth certificate was 'Aron', his grave has it as 'Aaron', which was his own preferred spelling. Elvis had an identical twin brother, Jesse, who died at birth. Throughout his life, Elvis maintained that he could talk to his dead twin.

Elvis collected badges from police departments and had a pet chimp called Scatter, which enjoyed drinking Scotch whisky or bourbon.

Elvis's motto was TCB – 'Taking Care of Business' – and his last words were 'OK, I won't', spoken to his girlfriend, Ginger Alden.

Three tablespoons of water from a cup once used by Elvis Presley in 1977 fetched £237 on eBay in January 2005. Wade Jones of Belmont, North Carolina, had stored the cup in his freezer for 28 years after picking it up at an Elvis concert in Charlotte. He decided to sell it after seeing a cheese sandwich with a supposed image of the Virgin Mary sell for £14,600 on eBay. He said the winning bidder only got the water, because he was 'kind of attached to the cup'.

According to a CBS News Survey in 1989, 7 per cent of Americans believed that Elvis Presley was still alive.

A new record was set in 2007 when 147 Elvis Presley impersonators sang 'Love

Me Tender' in the Australian outback town of Parkes. The event included a chapel at which married couples could renew their vows before Dean Vegas, the only licensed Elvis-impersonating marriage celebrant in Australia.

Elvis's only TV commercial was for Southern Made Doughnuts in 1954. His sole line of dialogue was: 'You get 'em piping hot after 4am'.

The alphabet positions of the letters in 'Presley' add up to 100.

♀ BOWIE, BURIAL, HAIR, ICE CREAM, NIXON, STAMPS, TARTAN

PRIME MINISTER

The phrase 'prime minister' was originally a term of abuse. The title of Prime Minister was officially recognised in the UK only in 1937, though it has been in popular but often disparaging use since 1655. The brass plate outside 10 Downing Street still bears only the title 'First Lord of the Treasury'.

The Earl of Bath was officially Prime Minister for two days in 1746, but was unable to form an administration so gave up the post.

Of the 14 British prime ministers who have served under Queen Elizabeth II, Winston Churchill and Harold Wilson are the only ones she has dined with at 10 Downing Street.

According to the official history of Downing Street, James Callaghan, at 1.8 metres (6 feet 1 inch), was the tallest-ever PM, though some say Lord Salisbury was 1.9 metres (6 feet 4 inches).

Until 2020, Andrew Bonar Law (PM 1922–23), who was born in Canada, was the only British prime minister born outside the British Isles. He now shares that distinction with Boris Johnson, who was born in New York.

Alec Douglas-Home was the only British prime minister to have played first-class cricket.

Henry Campbell-Bannerman was the only British prime minister to have died at 10 Downing Street.

When Benjamin Disraeli moved into 10 Downing Street in 1877, he had a bath, with hot and cold water, installed at a cost of £150.3s.6d.

No prime minister has ever lived to the age of 100. The longest-lived was James Callaghan, who died one day before his 93rd birthday.

⚲ *BALFOUR, CONSERVATIVE PARTY, PERCEVAL, UNIVERSITIES, WILSON*

PRINCESS

Although the word 'prince' dates back to at least 1225, the word 'princess' did not appear in English until about 1385. In the Middle Ages, women of noble or royal families were called 'Lady', with no other specific titles except 'Queen'.

In the 19th century, the term 'princess' was given to a size of roofing slate. Such slates also came in sizes called 'queen', 'duchess' and 'lady'.

The verb 'to princess' refers to a way of dressing meat, such as lamb, with inlaid slices of ham, carrot and parsley.

In the Aarne-Thompson classification system for folktales, there are 16 plots involving princesses.

Andromeda in Greek mythology was the first princess to be saved from a monster by the hero.

⚲ *DIANA, DWARF, ROWING*

PRINGLES

When Fredric Baur of Cincinnati died aged 89 in 2008, his children honoured his request to bury him in a Pringles can by placing part of his cremated remains in one in his grave.

Mr Baur held the patent for the tubular container for Pringles and for the method of packaging the curved, stacked crisps in it.

The shape of Pringles is a hyperbolic paraboloid.

⚲ *CRISPS*

PRISON

The total UK government income from all forms of taxation in 1900 was £108,336,193. This is less than half the cost of running Scottish prisons in 2000.

⚲ *DE NIRO, KENYA, PANAMA, SALIVA, SEX-CHANGE, TAX*

PRISONERS

The United States hold more prisoners in their jails than any other country. The Top 5 countries for prison inmates are as follows (2020 figures):

1. United States, 2,094,000
2. China, 1,710,000
3. Brazil, 759,518
4. India, 478,600
5. Russia, 478,182

The US also heads the table of most prisoners per head of population with 639 per 100,000 in jail, followed by El Salvador with 572 and Turkmenistan with 552.

⚲ *ADRENALINE, BAIL, CAKE, SOUTH AFRICA*

PROFANITY

A spokesman for Guinness World Records in 2009 announced that *House of the Dead: Overkill* was the most profane video game ever and featured the word 'fuck' more than once every minute.

In total, there were 189 'fuck's, which accounted for 3 per cent of all the words spoken in the game.

⚲ *BASTARD, CENSORSHIP, LICENCE PLATES*

PROPERTY

Under the Foreign Ownership Property Law passed in Cambodia in 2010, foreigners may buy property in Cambodia provided it is at least one floor above the ground. The Cambodian National Assembly passed the law after a three-day debate.

♀ *HAMMURABI, JAPAN, KIDNEY, PIGEON*

PROSTITUTION

In 2008, South Korea introduced a new blue logo for its hot spring spas to remove any confusion about the types of services they offered. The new sign replaced a nearly century-old red icon of a circle with rising wisps of steam, which was being used by 'love motels' offering prostitution or short stays for couples having extramarital relations. The new logo depicts waves of water with two circles symbolising the heads of a father and son amid rising steam.

The Shady Lady Ranch, a brothel in Nevada, successfully won state and county approval to clear the way for hiring the state's first male prostitute in January 2010. The male prostitute, referred to as a 'prostidude' was known as 'Markus' and had a former brief career as a porn actor in Los Angeles.

♀ *HOT DOGS, PENGUIN. PHONE SEX, SEX WORK*

PRUNE

In 2001, the Food and Drug Administration in the US gave permission to plum-growers to start calling prunes 'dried plums' to avoid the negative connotations of the word 'prune'.

The word 'prune' occurs only twice in the King James Bible, both in Leviticus, but 'pruned' turns up in Isaiah and 'pruninghooks' occurs twice more in Isaiah plus once each in Joel and Micah.

Isaiah 2:4 says: 'And he shall judge among the nations, and shall rebuke many people: and they shall beat their swords into plowshares, and their spears into pruninghooks'; but Joel 3:10 says: 'Beat your plowshares into swords and your pruninghooks into spears: let the weak say, I am strong.'

♀ *WINE*

PSYCHOLOGY

Research has shown that sudden deaths from psychological stress are more likely to occur on Mondays than any other day of the week.

The US army's 18th Psychological Operations Batallion (18th PSYOP) has a Trojan horse on its coat of arms. The Trojan horse is identified with the use of subtlety and imagination in the accomplishment of military objectives and refers to the battalion's mission to conduct supporting psychological operations.

♀ *ALCHEMY, BABIES, INTELLIGENCE, MARSTON, POSTMEN, TOURISM*

PUCCINI, Giacomo (1858–1924)

Puccini's wife put bromide in his coffee, and when attractive women came to dinner, she soaked his trousers in camphor. This may have been justified as Puccini was known to have had numerous affairs.

PUDDING

A world record bread-and-butter pudding was made by British bread experts from Hovis in 2009. Made from more than 1,000 slices of bread, 70 apples and 56 eggs, it weighed 1,500 kilograms (3,300 pounds) and measured 2 by 1.5 metres (7 by 5 feet).

♀ *SWAT, TARTAN*

PUERTO RICO

The deepest point of the Atlantic Ocean is Milwaukee Deep in the Puerto Rico Trench, at a depth of 8,376 metres (27,480 feet). The first manned descent to this point was made in 2018.

♀ *CIGAR*

PULSES

2016 was designated the UN's International Year of Pulses, designed to spread awareness of their nutritional benefits. The UN defines pulses as crops harvested for their dried seeds. These include dried peas and beans, lentils and chickpeas. The word 'chickpea', incidentally, was an 18th-century error of Dr Johnson. Before that, it was 'chich pea'.

Legumes are plants whose seeds are enclosed in a pod. 'Pulse' refers only to the dried seed.

The word 'pulse' came from a Latin word for a sort of lentil soup, which in turn came from a Greek word for porridge. The word 'lens' came from the Latin word for 'lentil', because of its convex shape.

Evidence of pulse cultivation 5,000 years ago has been found in the Egyptian pyramids and India.

India is the largest producer and consumer of pulses, followed by Pakistan and Canada. Shakespeare used the word pulse (or pulses) 11 times in his works, but always referring to heartbeat. He doesn't mention lentils at all. The King James Bible, however, includes four mentions of 'lentiles'.

PUMPKIN

The world's biggest pumpkin weighed 1,226 kilograms (2,702.8 pounds) at the Big Pumpkin Festival in Peccioli, Italy, in 2021. It had been grown by an Italian named Stefano Cutrupi.

The furthest a pumpkin has ever been shot from a cannon is 1,368 metres (4,491 feet) at the Morton Pumpkin Festival, Illinois, in 1998.

The world's fastest time to carve a complete face, with mouth, nose, ears and eyes, into a pumpkin is 16.46 seconds by Stephen Clarke (USA), set on 31 October 2013 in New York.

The Hallowe'en practice of pumpkin-carving is based on an Irish folk tale about a drunkard named Jack who trapped the devil in an apple tree. When Jack died, this caused him to be denied entrance to either Heaven or Hell, so he roamed the earth, lighting his way with a hot coal in a pumpkin.

In 2009, it was reported that motorcyclists in Nigeria had taken to wearing dried pumpkin shells on their heads to get round new laws forcing them to wear helmets.

♀ *JAM, LAVENDER, PIES, WATERMELON*

PUPPETRY

World Puppetry Day has been celebrated on 21 March by the International Puppetry Association (UNIMA) since 2003. UNIMA (Union Internationale de la Marionette) was founded in Prague in 1929. UNIMA-USA, its American branch, was founded by Muppets creator Jim Henson in 1966.

Jim Henson's Muppets first appeared in US advertisements for Wilkins Coffee in 1957. Henson said that he chose the name 'muppets' simply because it sounded good. Others claim it was coined as a cross between marionettes (operated by strings) and puppets (worked by hand).

The *Oxford English Dictionary* also defines a muppet as 'A lure made to resemble a young squid, used in sea fishing'.

The earliest evidence of puppetry has been dated to around 2000 BC in Egypt. The oldest written record of puppetry is in the works of the Greek historian and philosopher Xenophon around 420 BC.

The word 'marionette' first described figures of the Virgin Mary in puppet morality plays. 'Marionette' meant 'little Mary'. When comedy was introduced into these shows, the Church banned puppetry.

⚲ *PUNCH AND JUDY*

⬤ PURPLE

The colour purple is named after a snail – the mucus glands of a tropical sea snail, to be precise. The Latin name for this snail is *purpura*; the English name is murex.

According to legend, the Phoenician god Heracles was walking with the nymph Tyrus when his dog bit into a murex shell. Its mouth immediately turned purple and Tyrus announced that she would sleep with Heracles if he dyed her a garment in the same shade. Heracles did so, and the highly valued Tyrian purple dye was created. Its expense was due to the fact that it took a quarter of a million snails to produce one ounce of dye, making Tyrian purple more expensive than gold.

Different species of murex produced different shades of purple, one of which, according to Pliny the Elder, was the colour of clotted blood.

By the 4th century AD, only the Roman Emperor was allowed to wear vestments coloured with the very best purple dye.

⚲ *BUTCHELL, CARROT, CYPRUS, RHYME, TOMATO, UNICORN*

⬤ PUNCH AND JUDY

The Punch and Judy show had its origins in the Italian Commedia dell'arte of the 16th century which had a stock character of Pulcinella. This name was anglicised to Punchinella when it arrived in England in the 1660s, and later abbreviated to Punch. The show developed its own vocabulary which included the following:

Punchman: the puppeteer, usually known as 'professor' who performs the show

Bottler: his assistant who gathers the audience and collects their money

Swazzle: the device that gives Mr Punch his kazoo-like squawking voice.

Traditionally, the original Italian show was performed with marionettes, but the British substituted glove puppets which allowed greater violence.

The phrase 'pleased as Punch' was first recorded in 1797 and is a reference to the self-satisfaction of Mr Punch.

Mr Punch's wife was originally named Joan.

⚲ *PUPPETRY*

PYRAMID

The Great Pyramid of Giza was the world's tallest structure when it was completed around 2500 BC, and it remained so for more than 3,800 years until surpassed by Lincoln Cathedral in AD 1300.

The stones and mortar in all the Egyptian pyramids would be enough to build a wall 3 metres (10 feet) high and 1.5 metres (5 feet) wide from Baghdad to Calais.

⚲ *ALCOHOL, EGYPT, GARLIC, PULSES*

⬤ PYTHAGORAS (c.570–500 BC)

According to the Roman historian Herodotus, Pythagoras was the son of a gem polisher named Mnesarchus, but according to modern historians of philosophy, he probably never existed at all, but was the fictional nominal leader of the group of philosopher/mathematicians who called themselves the Pythagoreans. If he lived at all, he had a deep philosophical dislike of beans, believing that they contained the souls of the dead. He is said to have allowed himself to be slaughtered rather than cross a field of beans.

COMPUTATION, FORTY-SEVEN, LIVER, SALT

PYTHON

In 2008, a man in Connecticut was arrested for ordering his pet python to attack two police officers. They had been called to his house after a report that he had been threatening his girlfriend with the 2.75-metre (9-foot) snake. As they arrived, he shouted 'Get them!' at the snake, but it took no notice.

Two men were arrested in Melbourne in September 2010 after they had been seen wrestling with a 1.5-metre (5-foot) long python in the carpark of a McDonald's restaurant. Police found that the python, whose name was Boris, had been stolen by the men earlier in the day from a Melbourne pet shop. A police spokesman said, 'In all honesty, it's just a case of dumb and dumber. Anyone who gets out there with a one-and-a-half metre python in a McDonald's carpark, they're pretty dumb.'

The python's owners said the snake had a very nice personality but was just upset at not being handled properly.

COCONUT, FUNERALS, JACKSON Michael

Q

The *Oxford English Dictionary* lists entries for 14 words beginning with Q in which the second letter is not 'u'. The best known of these must be qwerty and qwertyuiop, referring to standard keyboard design, followed by the Chinese life force qi and the related philosophical technique qigong. Others are artistic, such as qawwali, which is a style of Muslim devotional music, and qawwal, which is someone who performs it, perhaps even on the seven-stringed Chinese zither called a qin.

We also have qasida, which is a form of Arabic or Persian poem; qila, a fort or fortress; qipao, a traditional Chinese dress; qivint, which is just the word you need when talking about the underwool of a musk ox; and qindar and qindarka, which were monetary units in Albania.

Most indispensable, however, is qinghaosu, which is defined as 'a sesquiterpene lactone, originally isolated in China from the annual mugwort'. Apparently it is used to treat malaria.

The word 'qat' (a chewable shrub or narcotic drug), though allowed in Scrabble, does not have an entry of its own in the *OED* but is mentioned in various citations given under the alternative spelling 'khat'. Neither 'qin' nor 'qila' is accepted in Scrabble, but 'qis' is allowed as the plural of 'qi'.

QATAR

Qatar had only four recorded robberies in 2000.

According to the Numbeo Crime Index, Qatar was the safest country in the world in 2017, 2019 and 2020. It also had the least crime in mid-2022.

The mobile phone number 666 6666 fetched £1.5 million in a charity auction in Qatar in 2007.

INCOME TAX, MEN, MONARCHY

QUACKING

In 2004, the police were called when people in the town of Wiesbaden, Germany, saw a distressed mother duck quacking after two of her ducklings had fallen through a manhole cover and become trapped in a sewage pipe. Two officers succeeded in leading the ducklings to safety by imitating duck noises. Apparently, their quacking was more convincing to the ducklings than that of the mother duck.

DUCK

QUAGGA

Related to the zebra, the quagga had stripes extending down head, neck and chest, but its back half was plain brown. Only one quagga was ever photographed alive; five pictures exist of a London Zoo quagga taken around 1870.

The last quagga in the world died in an Amsterdam zoo on 12 August 1883. It was not realised at the time that she was the last of her species.

♀ *GNU*

QUANTUM MECHANICS

Max Born, co-winner of the 1954 Nobel Prize for Physics, and the man who coined the term 'quantum mechanics', was the grandfather of the singer/actress Olivia Newton-John.

In 2002, the 'text artist and poet' Valerie Laws spray painted words onto sheep which were then allowed to graze to see what poems they came up with as they rearranged the words. The project was given the name 'Haik-Ewe', though the total number of syllables on the sheep's backs was 19 rather than the traditional 17 of the haiku. Ms Laws explained, 'I decided to explore randomness and some of the principles of quantum mechanics through poetry, using the medium of sheep.'

The project was supported by a grant from Northern Arts.

QUEEN MARY

Henry IV, William III and George V all married women called Mary. The State of Maryland in the USA is named for Queen Henrietta Maria, wife of Charles I, who was generally called 'Mary' in England.

The liner *Queen Mary* was launched on 26 September 1934 by Queen Mary, wife of George V. The 28 words used by the Queen when she launched the ship were her only recorded public utterance. The ship is said to have received its name after Cunard went to George V asking for permission to name the ship after 'England's greatest queen' – meaning Victoria. The King said that his wife would be delighted, so the name became *Queen Mary*.

The ship retired in 1967 from passenger service after 1,001 Atlantic crossings, but can now be visited at Long Beach, California. It is said to be haunted and reports include alleged sightings of women in vintage swimsuits. According to paranormal researchers, the first-class swimming pool is a vortex that allows ghosts from other realms to enter.

The *Queen Mary 2* was launched in 2004. It is called the *Queen Mary 2* rather than 'Queen Mary II' because the numeral refers to the second ship rather than the second Queen Mary. The whistle on the *Queen Mary 2* can be heard for 10 miles. It was originally on the *Queen Mary*.

QUEENSLAND

The 'Queen' in the Australian State of Queensland was Victoria, who signed the order creating the State of Queensland in 1859. The first European to sight Queensland was the Dutch explorer Willem Jansz in 1606. The area of Queensland is roughly seven times that of the United Kingdom, or a sixth of all of Europe.

There are 120 species of snake in Queensland. Most are venomous, 20 are classed as 'dangerous' and 16 are 'potentially fatal'.

Since 1883, the box jellyfish has been responsible for at least 70 recorded deaths in Australia, with Queensland having the highest number. When visiting Queensland, you can also be killed by the Irukandji jellyfish, stonefish, blue octopus, sharks, crocodiles or a wide variety of venomous spiders and insects.

These are not the only natural hazards. In 2002, Queensland announced plans to replace its coconut trees following increased litigation by tourists hit or even killed by falling coconuts. This resulted in the uprooting of over 2,000 coconut trees. In 2015, however, Port Douglas Shire Council in Queensland reported that it had located 8,929 active coconut trees which could pose a threat to members of the public and pointed out that worldwide around 150 people a year are killed by falling coconuts. Also, nearby Whitsundays Council recommended demolition of 975 coconut trees within their jurisdiction.

There is a town called Coconuts in Queensland. According to the 2016 census, it had a population of 224.

Aborigines were finally given the vote in Queensland in 1965.

In 2006, researchers at the University of Queensland reported tests showing that wild goats can be frightened off by the smell of tiger excrement.

CROCODILE, SARDINE, TEA, TOWN CRIER, WELLINGTON BOOTS

QUEUEING

Most dictionaries agree that 'queueing' and 'queuing' are both acceptable spellings of the present participle of the verb 'to queue'. The latter is most often seen in America, while 'queueing' is more frequent in Britain. The British spelling would make 'queueing' the most common word in English with five consecutive vowels. Some sources, however, mention the mediaeval musical term 'euouae', which is connected with plainchant, as having six consecutive

vowels, but this word is not in the *Oxford English Dictionary*. Other sources go even further with the word 'uoiauai', which is said to be an Old English word for 'twin', but that is also not in the *OED*.

A world record for the longest queue for a toilet was set in 2009 by 756 people in Brussels. The toilet queue was organised by UNICEF on World Water Day to raise awareness of the need for clean water.

CHINA, VOWELS

QUINCE

In the Balkans, when a baby is born, a quince tree is planted as a symbol of love, life and fertility. Aristophanes and other ancient Greek poets, however, used quinces as a mildly rude term for teenage breasts, while in Turkey, the expression *ayvayi yemek*, meaning literally 'to eat the quince', is a derogatory term indicating any unpleasant situation to avoid.

QUIZ

According to an old story, the word 'quiz' was invented by Dublin theatre manager Richard Daly in 1791 in connection with a bet he made that he could introduce a nonsense word that within 24 hours (some say 48 hours) would be the talk of everyone in the city. He supposedly then asked his employees to scrawl the word 'quiz' on walls around the city during the night, and the next day everyone was indeed talking about it and asking what it meant.

There are three main problems with this story: first, that there is no evidence for it; second, that it seems to have appeared first in 1835, which is more than 40 years after the events it supposedly recounts; and third, that the words 'quiz' and 'quoz' were already used around 1780 to mean an odd or eccentric person.

BENNETT, JAMES BOND

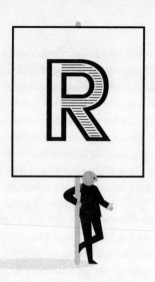

RABBIT

The word 'rabbit' was originally used only to refer to a young rabbit. Adult rabbits were called coneys. But the word 'coney' originally rhymed with 'money' and went out of fashion because it sounded too much like a swear word.

In parts of northern Canada, a group of rabbits is called a 'fluffle'.

When a rabbit is extremely joyful it jumps in the air and twists its body and head in opposite directions. This jump is known as a 'binky'.

ARMADILLO, BUNNY BOILERS, EASTER, LATVIA, MEMORY, SANTA CLAUS

RABIES

More than 70 per cent of US rabies cases from 1980 to 2018 were caused by vampire bat bites.

SERBIA, VAMPIRES

RADISH

In the town of Oaxaca, Mexico, the radish is celebrated in a festival called Noche de los Rabanos (Night of the Radishes) on 23 December as a part of Christmas festivities.

ADULTERY, APHRODISIAC, PARAPSYCHOLOGY

RAGS

According to the Public Health (Control Disease) Act 1984, anybody in the UK who collects or deals in rags, old clothes or similar articles, or anybody assisting or acting on behalf of any such person, may not, while engaged in collecting such articles, sell or deliver, whether gratuitously or not, any food or drink to any person, or anything at all to any person under the age of 14.

RAILWAY

The longest stretch of completely straight railway track in the world is part of the Trans-Australian Railway crossing the Nullarbor between Western Australia and South Australia for 478 kilometres (297 miles), never straying from its straight path.

'National Rail Timetables' is an anagram of 'All trains aim to be late in'.

British trains were first fitted with lavatories on 2 April 1873, but only in sleeping-cars. In 1988, two German inventors patented the 'toilet chute for railway carriages'.

It was recently reported that 4 per cent of complaints made to British rail operating companies concern the way they handle complaints.

There is an urban myth that the 4-foot-8.5-inch gauge of the tracks on British and US rail is equal to the distance between the wheels of a Roman chariot, but there seems to be no evidence for this. In both countries, early rails were put in the ruts on roads left by wagon wheels, and the distance between these was determined by the distance between the two horses that pulled a wagon. The strange 4-foot 8.5-inch standard was determined by George Stephenson in England as the best distance to have between the inside edges of such ruts.

ALASKA, HEALTH, KISSING, STEPHENSON, TRAINS, TRANSPORT

RAIN

The rainiest place in the world is Mount Waiale'ale in Hawaii, which has 335 rainy days a year.

Raindrops are about one-fifth of an inch in diameter; drizzle is about one-fiftieth of an inch. Including drizzle, the total weight of rain falling on the British Isles in a year has been calculated as around 115 billion tons. The maximum speed of rain is 29 km/h (18 mph).

Weather forecasters use a number of expressions which have precise definitions that most of us do not know. For example: a 'shower' is officially 'precipitation from a convective cloud' (that's a bubble-type broken cloud); 'rain' is precipitation from 'layered cloud'. If a shower lasts more than 20 minutes, it's probably rain; 'scattered showers' means around a one-in-10 chance of any particular place having a shower.

To reproduce the biblical description of Noah's flood, one inch of rain would have to fall every second for 40 days without any evaporation.

Useful rain word: 'ombrifuge' – a place or device that provides shelter from the rain.

HAWAII, SARDINE, SHAKESPEARE, ST SWITHUN, UGANDA, UMBRELLA

RAINCOAT

The waterproofing method that led to the creation of the raincoat was invented by the Scottish chemist Charles Macintosh. Nobody knows why the garment named after him, the mackintosh, has an extra letter 'k' added to its name. Macintosh patented his waterproofing system on 17 June 1823. The earliest known example of a 'k' being added to the name of the garment was in 1835, but that rapidly became the standard spelling.

The first waterproof mac(k)intosh was sold in Glasgow on 12 October 1823.

RALEIGH, Sir Walter (c.1552–1618)

Sir Walter Raleigh never spelled his surname that way. Until 1581, he used the spellings Rauley or Rauleygh. He then changed it to Ralegh, still without the 'i'. He founded Virginia and named it after Queen Elizabeth, the Virgin Queen.

After he was beheaded, his widow is said to have taken his head in a bag to be embalmed and she kept it by her side until she died 29 years later. The head was then moved to a cupboard under the stairs at the family residence in West Horsley, Surrey, but was finally buried in 1660 with the bodies of three of his grandchildren who died in an epidemic.

BURIAL, HYENA, SMOKING

RAMBLING

In May 2010, a court in Switzerland overturned a fine imposed on a rambler for hiking in the nude. The fine had been imposed after a woman had complained to the authorities about the hiker's 'indecent behaviour'. The nudist's lawyer, however, argued that his client was not behaving in an indecent manner, and that the woman must have followed him to observe his actions. He also pointed out that there was no law against naked hiking. The court waived the 100 franc fine on the nudist and instead ordered the state to cover legal costs of 2,000 francs.

RAPE

In English law, prior to the commencement of the Sexual Offences Act on 20 September 1993, only boys over 14 could rape; there was no such limitation in Scotland.

Twenty countries, including Russia, Thailand and Venezuela, allow men to have rape convictions overturned if they marry the women or girls they have assaulted.

♀ *CAPITAL PUNISHMENT, CRANE, DATE RAPE, URANUS, YETI*

RAT

The rat population in Taipei doubled in 1984 (the Chinese Year of the Rat) and they now outnumber the 2.6 million humans by about four to one. Fried wild rat with basil is a popular dish among native Taiwanese people.

Mainland China killed 526 million rats in 1984. A lottery was run in Shanghai that year with a dead rat as the price of a ticket.

In 2005, Spanish researchers showed that rats can be trained to distinguish spoken Japanese from spoken Dutch. No application of this ability has yet been found.

According to research in 2012, rats enjoy being tickled and remember which humans have tickled and played with them. They will then prefer to spend time with those people.

In 2019, it was reported that scientists in Germany had succeeded in training rats to play hide-and-seek with humans.

Rattus rattus is black; *Rattus norvegicus* is brown.

♀ *CAMEL, GUINEA PIGS, HAMSTER, HANGOVER, LAUGHTER, SNIFFING*

RAVEN

The raven is the largest bird of the crow family. This family is called Corvidae and an old word for a raven was 'corbie'.

In mythology, the raven is often connected with death, which is why Poe chose it for his poem 'The Raven'. In Irish myth, the raven's book was a list of the dead or soon to die. To be in the raven's book meant fated to die soon.

In French myth, ravens were seen as the souls of wicked priests. Wicked nuns' souls became crows.

In Norse mythology, the most powerful god Odin possessed two ravens named Hugin and Munin, which reported to him all they saw or heard.

In Swedish mythology, ravens are the ghosts of murdered people.

In Genesis 8:7, a raven was the first creature to leave Noah's ark after the flood.

The origin of the ravens at the Tower of London is unknown, but seven or eight birds are always kept there, six for show and one or two reserves. The person in charge of the ravens is called the Ravenmaster, a post held by Chris Skaife since 2011.

In 2013, an urban fox killed two of the Tower of London ravens. They were immediately replaced.

♀ *BANGLADESH, CAMBODIA, CAMEL, EXAMINATIONS, HAMSTER, HANGOVER, JACKSON Michael, MARS, PARLIAMENT*

READING

Around one in eight of the world's population cannot read or write.

The average person reads at a speed of about 200 words a minute.

In the UK, one new book title is published every four minutes.

In the 1780s, Benjamin Franklin invented bifocals by having his reading glasses cut in half and fused with his distance glasses. The earliest recorded use of the term 'reading glasses' is from Charles Dickens's *Bleak House* (1853).

⚲ BOOKS, FRANKLIN, LITERACY, NUDISM, SUNGLASSES

REAGAN, Ronald (1911–2004)

Until Donald Trump was elected to the White House, Ronald Reagan was the only US president to have been divorced. His middle name was Wilson, which along with 'Johnson' have the honour of being the only surnames shared by a US president and a British prime minister.

According to his wife Nancy, Ronald Reagan did not like Brussels sprouts or tomatoes.

⚲ ASTROLOGY, CATFISH, FORD, JELLY BEAN, UNITED STATES, ZOG I

RECESSION

According to a report published in 2010 by a small business and shopkeepers association in Italy, the Mafia bucked the recession in 2009, raising profits by almost 8 per cent. 'Mafia Inc. is reinforcing its position as the number one Italian company,' the report said.

RECRUITMENT

According to the experience of Swedish furniture chain Ikea in 2000, lavatory walls may be a good place for recruitment advertising. In that year, they began an innovative recruitment drive with job advertisements handwritten on lavatory walls. 'In the toilet people are more relaxed and receptive to our message,' a spokesman said.

From a financial perspective, the walls of the restaurant lavatories in Malmo were very cost-effective. They cost one-tenth the amount charged by newspapers and the response was encouraging. After the adverts had been up for only four days, 60 applications had been received, which was four or five times as many as had usually been received previously through a normal newspaper advertisement.

RED

According to research at the Universities of Plymouth and Durham, published in the *Journal of Sports Sciences* in 2008, football teams wearing red shirts have an advantage thanks to our deep-rooted biological response to the colour.

⚲ ATTRACTIVENESS, BEE, GOAL, MARS, UNION JACK

REGURGITATION

Following complaints in Australia in September 2010, the Moscow circus which was performing there announced the cancellation of an act in which a performer swallowed a live fish then regurgitated it. According to animal rights activists, the act, which was called 'the fountain' was described as 'educational'. A spokesman for the circus said that live fish would not be used in the act in future.

REINDEER

In 2001, Harrods department store in London was unable to use a reindeer and sleigh for its Christmas festivities. Santa's traditional mode of transport had to be replaced by a horse and carriage because the movement of reindeer in Britain was severely limited by an outbreak of foot-and-mouth disease. 'This is the first time in living memory Harrods has not used a reindeer,' a spokesman for the store said.

Reindeer milk is very rich and nutritious, containing 22 per cent butterfat and 10 per cent protein. The richest cow's milk has only 5 per cent butterfat and 3.5 per cent protein.

In its natural habitat, duck droppings are a reindeer's favourite food.

BERLUSCONI, HORN, PORONKUSEMA, SANTA CLAUS

RELIGION

In 2004, a 67-year-old woman was killed when a 3-metre (10-foot) tall metal crucifix fell on her head in the small southern Italian town of Sant'Onofrio. The crucifix was part of an annual religious festival being set up in the town square.

ADOLESCENCE, GOD, ISLAM, NORTH KOREA, PIRACY, RUM

REMBRANDT Harmenszoon van Rijn (1606–69)

Originally named 'Rembrant', the Dutch painter added the penultimate letter 'd' in 1633. His reason for doing so is not known. However one spells it, this was his first name, not his surname. The middle name 'Harmenszoon' just means that his father was called Harmen, and the 'van Rijn' at the end indicated that his family lived near the River Rhine. Despite gaining international fame, he never ventured outside the Netherlands.

Rembrandt's favourite meal was simply bread and cheese or pickled herring. He was profligate in his spending and was declared bankrupt in

1656, when he even had to sell his wife's grave. He died penniless in 1669.

Including paintings, etchings and drawings, Rembrandt is known to have composed at least 40 and possibly as many as 90 self-portraits.

The theme song of the popular sitcom *Friends* was written and performed by a band called The Rembrandts.

RENOIR, Pierre-Auguste (1841–1919)

The painter Pierre-August Renoir was the father of actor Pierre Renoir, film-maker Jean Renoir and ceramic artist Claude Renoir, and the grandfather of the film-maker Claude Renoir.

Renoir said, 'A painter who has the feel for breasts and buttocks is saved.' He also said: 'When I've painted a woman's bottom so that I want to touch it, then [the painting] is finished.'

OLIVE, PIGEON

REPTILES

A crocodile named Elvis seized a lawnmower at a reptile park in Sydney in December 2011, and dragged it into the water, causing two workers at the park to run for their lives. Elvis already had a reputation for volatile behaviour, having previous eaten two of his girl-friends at another park. The Operations Manager at the Australian Reptile Park at Gosford said that Elvis had previously been known to chase workers around, and the lawnmower had become a vital piece of equipment. 'We have a golden rule – keep the mower between you and the croc,' he was quoted as saying.

HEADS, ICELAND, ILLINOIS, PETS, SALAMANDER, TUATARA

RESTAURANTS

According to a survey in 1999, the top five causes of arguments when dining out are: 1. Pinching your partner's chips; 2. Eyeing up other diners; 3. Loud and messy eating habits; 4. Arguing over who pays the bill; 5. Speaking too loudly.

In February 2008, a group of diners at an Italian restaurant in Lichfield, Staffordshire, were reported to have been outraged by some 'absolutely disgusting language' which appeared on their bill after they had complained about the food and quality of service. The restaurant said it was a kitchen joke that had misfired. A later report clarified the nature of the complaint by saying that the words 'Suck my dick, fuck face £0.00' had appeared on the bill between the fish cakes and the cabernet sauvignon.

⚘ *ALCHEMY, BRUSSELS, CAT STEW, KEBAB, SINGAPORE, TOKYO*

REVOLVING DOORS

On 7 August 1888, Theophilus van Kannel of Philadelphia patented the Van Kannel Revolving Storm Door, the world's first successful revolving door. The very first such patent, however, had been obtained more than six years earlier by H. Bockhacker of Berlin for his Tür ohne Luftzug (door without draft of air). Apparently nobody was sufficiently impressed by Bockhacker's invention to go ahead and make one, so the first revolving door to be installed was at a restaurant called Rector's in Times Square, New York.

Van Kannel's invention impressed for a number of reasons: it was silent; it kept out rain, snow and dust; it kept heat in; it let people go in and out at the same time without bumping into each other. The original slogan for the door was 'always closed'. Some also suggested that van Kannel's motivation came at least in part from his intense dislike of the chivalry of men being expected to hold doors open for women.

The International Revolving Door Association was established in 1991. It is based in California.

RHINOCEROS

The word 'rhinoceros' comes from two Greek words for 'nose' and 'horn'. Apart from 'rhinoceroses', the *Oxford English Dictionary* lists 'rhinocerons', 'rhinocerotes', 'rhinocerontes' and 'rhinoceri' among the recorded plurals of the word.

There are five species of rhinoceros: black, white, Indian, Javan and Sumatran. The Indian and Javan rhinoceroses have one horn; the other species have two.

The white rhino is a dirty grey colour. Its name is a mistranslation or a mishearing from the Afrikaans 'weit', meaning 'wide' – it has a wider face and body than the more common black rhino. In courtship, the female partner is the active one.

The total number of Indian greater one-horned rhinos in the world is estimated to be only 3,588. There are around 18,000 white rhinos, 5,500 black rhinos, fewer than 80 Sumatran rhinos and only 75 Javan rhinos.

A fully grown rhino may eat half a ton of grass a day.

Unlike most animal horns, which have a bony core, rhino horn is entirely keratin, which is what hair and fingernails are made of.

The collective noun for rhinoceroses is a 'crash' or a 'herd'.

Macbeth is the only Shakespeare play that mentions a rhinoceros.

⚘ *BOSWELL, CAMBODIA, CANNABIS, HIPPOPOTAMUS, WOMBAT*

RHUBARB

The use of the word 'rhubarb' often repeatedly, to indicate mumbling or pointless prattle, dates back only to the 1950s, when actors in a crowd scene were reported to be saying 'rhubarb, rhubarb' to sound as though they were murmuring in the background.

Rhubarb first became known in England in the 16th century for its medicinal properties, though much earlier it was used medicinally in China. It did not begin to appear as an ingredient in cookery books until the beginning of the 19th century. Botanically, rhubarb is a vegetable, but in 1947 the US Customs Court ruled it to be a fruit, since that is how it is normally eaten.

Russia dominated rhubarb trade during the time of the tsars, having obtained it from China, grown it themselves and imposed a strict ban on its export. Two Scottish physicians, Thomas Garvine and James Mounsey, who worked at the court of Peter the Great and Catherine II in the 18th century, at great personal risk smuggled out some rhubarb seeds and grew them in Ayrshire. Mounsey even slept with a loaded gun by his bed in case any Russian agents arrived to punish him.

On 11 January 1770, Benjamin Franklin sent a consignment of rhubarb from London to John Bartram in Philadelphia. This was the first rhubarb in the United States.

Macbeth is the only Shakespeare play that mentions rhubarb. Macbeth himself asks: 'What rhubarb, cyme, or what purgative drug, Would scour these English hence?' (Cyme is another term for the laxative senna.)

⚲ SEX

RHYME

It is often asserted that there are no English words that rhyme with purple, orange, silver or month. These are all untrue:

- A curple is a strap on a horse's saddle (also known as a crupper), or a slang term for the buttocks. To hirple is to walk with a limp. To turple is to fall or tumble or, in the case of animals, to die.
- A sporange is a spore-containing sac in mushrooms (which also leads to the compounds hypnosporange, macrosporange, megasporange, microsporange, prozoosporange and tetrasporange).
- A chilver is a ewe-lamb.
- Grunth (or Granth) is a sacred Hindu scripture.

'Take a simple name like "Nicholas": you can rhyme it with "ridiculous". If you aren't too meticulous. You know, every word's rhymable.' Sammy Cahn

⚲ DONKEY, RABBIT, SPORTS SONGS

RICE

Dakigokochi is the Japanese name for a rice-filled bag shaped like a bundled baby and printed with the newborn's face and name. These were marketed at the start of 2008 by a small rice shop in Fukuoka, southern Japan, which was then swamped with orders from parents of new babies to send to their friends and relatives. Each rice bag is tailor-made to weigh as much as the baby and shaped so the rice fills the bag up. Holding the round-edged bag would feel like holding a real newborn.

On 13 August 1997, the Laotian news agency reported that farmers had successfully completed trials using pig manure as a snail repellent on rice crops.

♀ CHOPSTICKS, CURRY, SARDINE

● RICE, Sir Tim (b. 1944)

The full name of the lyricist generally known as Tim Rice is Sir Timothy Miles Bindon Rice. The first night of the musical *Blondel* on 8 September 1983, which Rice wrote with Stephen Oliver, saw the earliest recorded appearance in public of a denim codpiece.

● RICHARD II (1367–1400)

King Richard II's favourite greyhound was named Mathe. Jean Froissart, in his *Chronicles* compiled in the 14th century, wrote: 'King Richard had a greyhound called Mathe, who was in the constant practice of attending the king, and he would not follow any other person; for whenever the king did ride, the person who had the charge of keeping the said greyhound would always let him loose, and he would run directly to the king, and leap with his forefeet upon his majesty's shoulders.'

♀ CARPET, HANDKERCHIEF

● RICHARD III (1452–85)

Richard III, despite his reputation as a tyrant, introduced both bail and legal aid to our courts. Although Shakespeare and others portrayed him as a hunchback with a limp, there is no contemporary written evidence of such deformity.

At the age of 11, Richard became Commissioner of Array for the Western Counties, in charge of mustering forces for the Wars of the Roses.

'Now is the winter of our discontent', from *Richard III*, is the eighth most quoted line from Shakespeare according to number of Google hits. A camping and outdoor goods shop once advertised a December sale with the line: 'Now is the winter of our discount tents'.

'A horse, a horse, my kingdom for a horse' from *Richard III* also features in Shakespeare's top 20 lines.

Richard married Anne Neville, who was both his first cousin once removed and his sister-in-law. Technically, this marriage was invalid on the grounds of their close affinity.

After being killed at the Battle of Bosworth Field by the forces of Henry Tudor, Richard's body was hanged in public. It was later buried, dug up, reburied and lost. In 2012, archaeologists found what are thought to be his bones in a grave under a car park in Leicester. DNA from Richard's 17th-generation grand-nephew was compared with the remains and appeared to confirm this identity.

♀ TEETH

● ROAD FATALITY

The first person to be killed in a road accident in Britain was Bridget Driscoll, who was run down by a car at Crystal Palace, London, on 17 August 1896. At the time, there were only at most 20 petrol-driven cars in Britain, and Mrs Driscoll stood transfixed as it moved towards her. Witnesses said the car was going 'like a fire engine' or 'as fast as a good horse could gallop', but tests showed that the car, driven by Arthur Edsall, was incapable of speeds above 4 mph. The driver said he had rung his bell and shouted 'stand back' but she seemed 'bewildered'. At the inquest, the coroner said he hoped this would be the last death in this sort of accident.

Bridget Driscoll, who died in this accident, should not be confused with Bridget O'Driscoll who survived a different accident in 1912: she was a passenger on the maiden voyage of the *Titanic*, but was rescued when the ship sank. She lived until 1976 when she died at the age of 91.

ROBBERY

Here are brief details of some remarkably unsuccessful robberies around the world:

- Ireland: in January 2022, two men walked into a post office and said they'd come to collect the pension of a third man who was propped up between them. The third man turned out to be dead. When this was confirmed, the two men dropped the body and fled. The dead man was identified and evidence was later found that he had been alive earlier that same day. A post-mortem ruled out foul play and it was not known whether the two men who had fled knew he was dead.
- Israel: a bank robber in Tel Aviv in 1995 fled in embarrassment after his plans were foiled by a deaf cashier. When he whispered 'this is a hold-up', the cashier asked him to speak up as she could not hear what he was saying.
- Florida, USA: a patient bank robber waited in line for 20 minutes in 1995 for a cashier to bring him a bag of money. By then, the police had arrived and he was arrested as he left the bank.
- Netherlands: also in 1995, a Dutch would-be robber gave a shopkeeper a note demanding cash but fled when handed a reply saying: 'Sod off'.
- Los Angeles: in 1996, a 71-year-old grandmother appeared in court on a charge of armed robbery. She pleaded not guilty, saying she had been driven insane by the Internal Revenue Service.
- Colombia: a blood bank was robbed in Colombia in 1996.
- Canada: a man was charged in 1997 after threatening to kill a racoon if people didn't hand over their money.
- South Africa: in 2002, a thief at a South African zoo made a fatal mistake: he attempted to make his getaway via the tiger's cage. The tigers clearly disapproved and the robber died of a broken neck and a fractured skull.

The first time a getaway car was used in a robbery was on 27 October 1901 in Paris.

⚲ *APRIL FOOLS, CAPITAL PUNISHMENT, GOATS, ICELAND, KANSAS*

ROBIN HOOD

According to a manuscript discovered in the library of Eton College in 2009, Robin Hood may not have been as 'loved by the good' as myth and song celebrate him. Dr Julian Luxford, a lecturer in art history at St Andrews University in Scotland, found a note dating back around 550 years written by an unknown monk in the margin of a manuscript called the 'Polychronicon', which itself dates back to the late 1340s. The note, written in Latin, said: 'Around this time, according to popular opinion, a certain outlaw named Robin Hood, with his accomplices, infested Sherwood and other law-abiding areas of England with continuous robberies.' It is the only historical record of Hood's life written in England and places him at the time of Edward I.

⚲ *ARCHERY*

ROBOT

The word 'robot' was introduced by the Czech playwright Karel Capek in 1920 in his play *R.U.R.: Rossum's Universal Robots*. The word comes from the Czech *robota*, meaning 'work', especially of a tedious, repetitive type.

Ninety per cent of all robots work in factories and more than half make cars.

A robot fashion model took to the catwalk at the 2009 Japan Fashion Week in Tokyo, but it was generally agreed, even by her designers, that HRP-4C needed more work.

⚲ *GROUNDHOG DAY*

ROCKING HORSE

According to EU Safety Standard EN71 part 8, rocking horses' saddles should be no more than 60 centimetres (23.6 inches) above the ground. Rocking-horse makers may make bigger horses, but should seek approval before doing so.

ROLLERCOASTER

A world record was set in March 2019 when 195 naked people rode the Grand National rollercoaster at Blackpool Pleasure Beach in England at the same time. This was a record for the most naked people on a theme park ride.

ROMANCE

In 2010, a German woman was reported to have called the police when she heard the sound of someone climbing up to her balcony. Police discovered that it was her boyfriend paying her a surprise visit carrying flowers and a bottle of wine. After confirming his identity, they arrested him as he was wanted on an outstanding warrant.

⚲ *MARRIAGE, ST VALENTINE*

ROMANIA

In January 2005, the Bucharest daily newspaper *Libertatea* carried a report that a local couple had named their baby Yahoo after the Internet website that had brought them together. A week later, the same paper reported that the journalist responsible had been sacked, because the story had been invented. 'If it were real, it would have been a good story indeed,' *Libertatea*'s deputy editor-in-chief, Simona Ionescu, commented.

⚲ *BALLET, CHAD, DRACULA, PIRACY, RUGBY, SAUSAGES*

ROMNEY, Mitt (b. 1947)

Senator Mitt Romney's middle name is 'Mitt'. His first name is Willard.

His favourite snack is reported to be a peanut butter and jelly sandwich with a glass of chocolate milk.

⚲ *KANSAS*

ROOF

Under the Town Police Clauses Act of 1847 it was 'illegal to throw anything other than snow from the roof of a building in the UK, and snow may only be thrown so as not to fall on any passers-by'. This clause, and many others, however, were omitted when the Deregulation Act of 2015 was enacted.

⚲ *PRINCESS, TUNISIA*

ROOSEVELT, Franklin D. (1882–1945)

Franklin D. Roosevelt became the first serving US president to fly in an aeroplane when he flew to Casablanca to discuss the war with Winston Churchill on 14 January 1943.

⚲ *CAMP DAVID, HOT DOGS, SHAKESPEARE*

ROOSEVELT, Theodore (1858–1919)

When asked permission to lend his name to the 'teddy' bear, President Roosevelt replied, 'I don't think my name is likely to be worth much in the bear business but you are welcome to use it.' The request came following a hunting trip in 1902 in which Roosevelt, unlike other hunters in the group, had failed to locate and shoot a bear. His colleagues then captured one and tied it to a tree for the President to shoot, but Roosevelt thought it unsporting and refused to do so.

In November 1906, President Roosevelt began a visit to Panama, thus becoming the first US president to travel outside the United States on official business.

ROSES

The average American buys 4.67 roses a year.

'God gave us memory so that we might have roses in December.' J.M. Barrie

POE, RICHARD III, SAUDI ARABIA, ST VALENTINE

ROSSINI, Gioachino Antonio (1792–1868)

Rossini was born on 29 February 1792. As 1800 was not a leap year, the second true anniversary of his birthday occurred in 1808 when he was 12 years old.

He wrote 36 operas, most of which were hugely successful, then retired at the age of 37. His last 40 years were devoted mainly to eating and food, and he invented several great dishes. The best known is tournedos Rossini, which Rossini designed and had cooked for him by the master chef Marie-Antoine Carême.

The word 'tournedos' comes from the French for 'turn the back', which some say was Rossini's reply to a head waiter who said the dish was 'unpresentable'. A more likely explanation is that the chef finished his presentation of the dish behind Rossini's back rather than on the table, to keep his methods secret.

At its premiere, Rossini's *Barber of Seville* was jeered, probably by friends of the composer Paisiello, who wrote an opera with the same story.

Rossini is said to have served as an altar boy as a child, in order to get at the communion wine.

'Appetite is for the stomach what love is for the heart. The stomach is the conductor, who rules the grand orchestra of our passion. The bassoon or the piccolo, grumbling its discontent or shrilling its longing, personify the empty stomach. Eating, loving, singing, and digesting are, in truth, the four acts of the comic opera known as life.' Rossini

'Give me a laundry list and I'll set it to music.' Rossini

ROULETTE

If you add together all the numbers on a standard roulette wheel, the result is 666, the Number of the Beast in the Book of Revelation.

There is a township in Pennsylvania called Roulette, not after the game but after a land agent named John Roulette.

EVEREST

ROUSSEAU, Jean-Jacques (1712–78)

On 24 October 1776, the philosopher Jean-Jacques Rousseau was knocked down by a Great Dane while walking through the streets of Paris. He fell hard on the cobbled street and was knocked unconscious and bleeding badly but was helped by passers-by. Rousseau later forgave the dog, though some say the concussion he suffered hastened his death two years later.

♀ BOSWELL

ROWING

In the single sculls event at the 1928 Olympics in Amsterdam, Australian rower Henry Pearce stopped for a moment in his quarter-final to let a family of ducks pass safely in front of his boat. He went on to win the heat and took the gold medal in the final.

The actress Grace Kelly, who later became Princess Grace of Monaco, was the daughter of John B. Kelly Sr, who won three Olympic gold medals for the US in sculling. He was the first person to win three rowing golds.

♀ LEAP YEAR, VENICE

RUBBER BANDS

The first elastic bands were patented by Stephen Perry & Co. of London on 17 March 1845. The world's biggest rubber band ball was made between 2004 and 2008 by Joel Waul of Florida out of 700,000 rubber bands. It stood 2 metres (6 feet 8 inches) high and weighed 4,097 kilograms (9,032 pounds).

In 2003, a rubber band ball weighing 1,179 kilograms (2,600 pounds) and having a circumference of 4.5 metres (14 feet 8 inches) was dropped from an aeroplane at a height of 1.6 kilometres (1 mile) above the Mojave Desert in Arizona to see how high it would bounce. Sadly, it didn't bounce at all but made a huge crater and a cloud of dust that rose an estimated 4.5–6 metres (15–20 feet).

RUBBISH

America produces 215 million tons of solid garbage every year. The average European household produces 2 tonnes of rubbish a year, of which half is packaging, and Americans produce more than three times as much.

♀ GARBAGE, LIFETIME, MEXICO, MOUNTAINEERING, OCEAN

RUBIK, Erno (b. 1944)

The world record for solving a Rubik Cube is 11.13 seconds, set by Californian Leyan Lo in January 2006.

In November 2021, however, Canadian student Jesse Bradford, 17, set a different world record by solving 300 Rubik's Cube puzzles in 2 hours 13 minutes while balanced on a unicycle.

RUGBY

Rugby football is said to have been invented at Rugby School in 1823 when William Webb Ellis, aged 16, picked up the ball and ran with it in a soccer game. A stone at the school bears the inscription: 'This stone commemorates the exploit of William Webb Ellis who with a fine disregard for the rules of football, as played in his time, first took the ball in his arms and ran with it, thus originating the distinctive features of the rugby game A.D. 1823.' This story, however, first appeared some 50 years later and has never been verified by a first-hand account.

William Webb Ellis went on to Oxford University, where he won a blue not for rugby but for cricket. He went on to become an Anglican clergyman.

Rugby was included in the Olympics of 1900, 1908, 1920 and 1924. The United States are the reigning Olympic champions, having beaten France in the final in 1924 (Romania was the only other entrant). Britain's Olympic rugby record reads: played two, lost two. Despite this, they won bronze in 1900 (last of three entrants) and silver in 1908 (two entrants).

The Seventh Underwater Rugby World Championship was held in Denmark in 2003 and won by Sweden. Later winners have been Finland (2007), Norway (2011 and 2015) and Colombia (2019).

The Zulu for 'scrum half' is *iskramuhhafu*.

♀ COMMONWEALTH, FIJI, FISHING

RUM

The British Royal Navy's association with rum began in 1655 when Jamaica was captured by the British and their sailors' daily dose was changed from brandy to rum. From 1740, the Navy began watering down the rum to reduce drunkenness, with the watered-down drink becoming known as 'grog'. Admiral Edward Vernon, who ordered it, became known as Edward 'Grog' Vernon. The daily rum dose was referred to as 'tapping the admiral', probably through a mistaken belief that Nelson's body was brought back in a barrel of rum; the modern view is that brandy was probably used to preserve Nelson's body.

There are more than 140 rum producers around the world, mostly in South America and the Caribbean, but also in India, Australia and Newfoundland.

In the 1800s, rum was considered excellent for cleaning hair and strengthening its roots.

Older terms for rum include Kill-Devil and rumbullion, which also meant a tumult or uproar.

'Rum, n. Generically, fiery liquors that produce madness in total abstainers.'
Ambrose Bierce, The Devil's Dictionary, 1906

'There's nought no doubt so much the spirit calms as rum and true religion.'
Lord Byron

♀ INVESTMENT, PINEAPPLE

RUSEDSKI, Greg (b. 1973)

Former British number one tennis player and finalist in the 1997 US Open, 'Greg Rusedski' is an anagram of 'Rugged kisser'.

RUSSIA

About one-fifth of the world's trees are in Russia.

A kick-boxing school specifically for nannies opened in St Petersburg in 1997 in response to the growing problem of child-kidnapping.

The Hermitage Museum in St Petersburg is home to over 70 cats. This continues a tradition begun in 1745 when Empress Elizabeth of Russia introduced cats at the Hermitage to keep down the number of mice.

♀ ALASKA, ALCOHOL, CATHERINE I, EUROPE, HAIR, POTATO

RWANDA

At the start of 2009, Rwanda was the only democratic country in the world with more women members of parliament than men. Its 2008 elections led to 45 women members from a total of 80.

Rwanda has a higher proportion of female members of parliament than any other country. In their 2018 election, 49 female deputies were elected out of a total of 80, making it one of only three countries in the world in which women held a parliamentary majority. The other two are Bolivia and Cuba, but Rwanda's parliament had a higher proportion of women than either of these, despite the fact that their number went down from 51 in the previous election in 2013.

As well as 61% of its MPs being female, Rwanda has about the same percentage of the world's mountain gorillas.

Since 2008, there has been a ban on plastic bags in Rwanda. This is part of its policy for clean and healthy living which also includes a car-free day every month.

With 551 people per square kilometre, Rwanda is the most densely populated country in mainland Africa.

No Rwandan has ever won an Olympic medal, though Jean de Dieu Nkundabera took bronze in the 2004 Paralympics in Athens in the T46 men's 800 metres.

♀ *UNDERGARMENTS*

● **RYDER CUP**

The golfing trophy, the Ryder Cup, was donated by Samuel Ryder in 1927. He was a seed merchant who made his fortune from the idea of selling garden seeds in small packets. Ryder's seeds sold under the slogan 'Everything a penny, from orchids to mustard and cress'.

Born in 1858, Ryder became Mayor of St Albans in 1906. He took up golf for the fresh air and light exercise it offered when he became ill through overwork.

The figure depicted at the top of the Ryder Cup is Abe Mitchell, the British professional whom Samuel Ryder employed as his personal golf tutor. Abe Mitchell missed the first Ryder Cup. He was on the train taking the British team to the boat but was taken off with acute appendicitis.

When Samuel Ryder died in 1936, his favourite 5-iron was placed in his coffin.

SADDLE

In 2012, it was reported that ranches and hunting camps in the American Rockies were adding supersized saddles and heavyweight horses to cope with the growing obesity issues of visitors. 'We call them big-butt saddles,' a ranch spokesman said. 'I've got a 22-inch saddle, which is basically unheard of, and I've got people who will overflow all sides of it.'

Over the past 30 years, the size of the largest commercially available saddles has grown from 42 centimetres (16.5 inches) to over 46 centimetres (18 inches). 'We have to seat 400 fat people every summer,' said another ranch owner.

⚲ *HUNTING, OBESITY, RHYME, ROCKING HORSE*

SADISM

A species of spider discovered in Israel in 2010 has been named *Harpactea sadistica*, because of the brutality of its mating behaviour. Most spider males deliver sperm that is deposited onto a small web and manually inserted using a pair of appendages on their undersides known as pedipalps. The sperm are then held by the female until she produces an egg. This is a bit of a reproductive gamble for the male, as the receptacle in which the sperm is stored operates on what has been termed a 'last in first out' principle – so if any other male mates with the same female, it pushes the original male's sperm back in the queue. The *Harpactea sadistica*, however, gets round this problem by injecting its sperm directly into the female's ovaries. To accomplish this, it subdues the female, wraps itself around her, then bores holes into the female's abdomen in two neat rows through which the sperm is introduced. This technique is known as 'traumatic insemination'.

SAILORS

'Mallemaroking' means 'the carousing of seamen on an icebound ship'. According to the *Oxford English Dictionary*, the word is 'a borrowing from the Dutch' where *mallemerok* was a term for a silly woman or fool.

⚲ *DARWIN, FIJI, GREECE, RUM, WEATHER*

SALAMANDER

Asbestos was originally believed to be the wool of the salamander.

Monkton Conservation Commission in Vermont in 2010 was awarded a

£99,000 grant to install culverts under a stretch of road to protect salamanders, other amphibians, reptiles and small mammals which needed to cross between a swampy area and the uplands. This is believed to be the first official salamander crossing in the United States.

A research project at Hope College, Michigan, in 1971 included a mysterious case of an axolotl, for no clear reason, shedding its skin several times, changing the shape of its head, losing its gills, slimming its tail, changing its colour and turning into a tiger salamander. The researcher said he was at a loss to explain why the change happened, but he thought it may have happened before.

⚲ *ILLINOIS*

🔵 SALIVA

According to a court ruling in New York in 2007, saliva can be a 'dangerous instrument'. The ruling came in a case in which an HIV-positive man was sentenced to prison for 10 years for aggravated assault after he had bitten another man. Under the law, aggravated assault is a felony which requires the use of a 'dangerous instrument', which is 'any instrument, article or substance which, under the circumstances in which it is used or attempted or threatened to be used, is capable of causing death or serious physical injury'. Gay rights groups have campaigned to have the conviction overturned.

⚲ *FIZZY DRINKS, LIFETIME, PRISON, STRESS*

🔵 SALT

Nowadays when we use the word 'salt' we are referring to sodium chloride used as a condiment, but in the 16th and 17th centuries, according to the *Oxford English Dictionary*, salt also meant 'Sexual desire or excitement (usually, of a bitch)'.

The word 'salary' comes from the Latin for salt, as some Roman soldiers used to be paid in salt.

Only 7 per cent of the world's salt production is eaten by people. The rest is used by the chemical and manufacturing industries, and for gritting roads. More than 2 million tons of salt are spread on to UK roads each year.

The recommended daily intake of salt is 6 grams. The average daily intake by UK males is 8.1 grams, having dropped by about 15 per cent in the last decade.

'Salt is born of the purest of parents: the sun and the sea.' Pythagoras

'Thou hadst better eat salt with the Philosophers of Greece, than sugar with the Courtiers of Italy.' Benjamin Franklin

⚲ *MILKY WAY, MOOSE, OCEAN, POPCORN, SAUSAGES*

🔵 SALT LAKE CITY

The Great Salt Lake in northern Utah, after which Salt Lake City is named, is the largest saltwater lake in the western hemisphere.

A woman was arrested in Salt Lake City in 2012 for robbing her neighbours of thousands of dollars while wearing a very large man's suit and a false moustache. The woman was trapped by a couple who installed security cameras and left money as bait. They recognised the woman on the pictures, despite her suit, moustache and a beanie hat. According to one report: 'Pretty much the only thing she wasn't doing in the video was twirling the fake mustache in sinister fashion while standing next to a set of train tracks.'

⚲ *TRAFFIC LIGHTS*

SAMOA

There were only 364 days in Samoa in 2011, when the island nation decided to change its side of the International Dateline. As a result, it skipped Friday 30 December and moved straight from Thursday 29 December to Saturday 31 December.

The Dateline zigzags down the Pacific Ocean, and countries near the line of zero longitude have traditionally been able to choose which side of it they consider themselves to be on. The change was thought advisable as this brought Samoa in line with Australia and New Zealand, which are its main trading partners. To gain public support, the government ruled that employers must still pay workers for the missing Friday, but banks would not be allowed to charge interest for the lost day. Seventh Day Adventists in Samoa were reported to be divided on the change, over whether they should now celebrate the Sabbath on Saturday or Sunday.

The former New Zealand dependency of Tokelau, which has its administration in Samoa's capital Apia, also changed sides of the Dateline, but nearby American Samoa decided to remain on the original side, in common with the USA.

TATTOO

SAMURAI

Samurai swords used to be tested on the bodies and bones of corpses and condemned criminals.

The divided skirt/pants worn by Samurai are called hakama.

FORTY-SEVEN, GOOSEBERRY

SAN FRANCISCO

In 1848, San Francisco had 469 residents. The population in 2021 was estimated to be 875,114.

The Chinese fortune cookie is said to have been invented at the Japanese Tea Garden in San Francisco around 1900.

Burials have been banned in San Francisco since 1901 because the cemeteries were full, burial was considered a health hazard and, perhaps most important of all, graveyards were on prime real estate land. From 1912 onwards, more than 150,000 bodies were moved from San Francisco to the town of Colma, which in 2016 was reported to have 1,600 living residents plus 1.5 million dead ones.

Alcatraz Island in San Francisco, site of the former notorious prison, was once a fort and took its name from an old Spanish word for 'pelican'.

BRASSIERE, CAPONE, CEMETERIES, LUNCH, TOOTHPICK

SANDCASTLE

On 18 June 1997, physicists at the University of Notre Dame, Indiana, published their discovery of the 'sandcastle effect'. This solved the mystery of why sandcastles do not collapse when the water in them has dried out. Later research concluded that a mixture of 99 per cent sand and only 1 per cent water provides the best cohesion for making the tallest sandcastles.

SANDWICH, Earl of (1718–92)

The sandwich is named after John Montagu, the 4th Earl of Sandwich, who started a craze for eating beef between two slices of toast.

The year 1762 saw the earliest recorded use of the word 'Sandwich' to mean a type of food, by Edward Gibbon writing of dining at the Cocoa-Tree Coffee House in London: 'That respectable body, of which I have the honour of being a member, affords every evening a sight truly English. Twenty or thirty, perhaps, of the first men in the kingdom in point of fashion and fortune supping at little tables covered with a napkin, in the middle of a coffee-room, upon a bit of cold meat, or a Sandwich, and drinking a glass of punch.'

Almost 300 years earlier, in the late 15th century, however, the word 'sandwich' had been used to refer to a type of cord that had connections with the town of Sandwich in Kent.

The account of Lord Sandwich inventing the sandwich as a way of staying at the gaming tables first appeared in a 1770 book by the French travel writer Pierre-Jean Grosley.

◦ *BACON, CHEESE, IRAN, LUNCH, PEANUT BUTTER, PRESLEY*

SANDWICHES

According to a poll among British schoolchildren in 2019, the five sandwich fillings children most liked to find in their lunchboxes were: 1. Ham; 2. Cheese; 3. Chocolate spread; 4. Sliced chicken; 5. Jam. An earlier survey had revealed the five most hated sandwich fillings to be: 1. Egg mayonnaise; 2. Salad; 3. Pate; 4. Salami; 5. Marmite.

If you eat a sandwich for breakfast, lunch and dinner, the amount of bread produced from one bushel of wheat will last for 168 days.

◦ *BEDROOM, BREAKFAST, CHICKEN, HEMINGWAY, LINDBERGH, WIMBLEDON*

SANTA ANNA, Antonio López de (c.1795–1876)

President Santa Anna of Mexico led the siege of the Alamo in 1836. His left leg was blown off at the Battle of Vera Cruz in 1838. He kept the leg at his hacienda near Veracruz, but when he became

President in 1842, it was given a state funeral. The leg was stolen from the Pantheon of Saint Paula in Mexico City and dragged on a rope through the city during the 1844 riot that toppled him.

He was then fitted with an artificial leg made of cork and wood, but in 1847, during the Battle of Cerro Gordo in the war between the USA and Mexico, he had to flee hastily from the 4th Illinois Cavalry and left his leg behind. It can still be seen at the Illinois State Military Museum.

SANTA CLAUS

In 1927, a Finnish radio programme identified Santa's home location as being on Lapland's Korvatunturi, or 'Ear Mountain'. The mountain area resembles a rabbit's ears, from which it was said Santa can hear if children are being naughty or nice.

In June 1995, a not very jolly New Zealand Santa Claus was sentenced to six months' detention for smashing the security glass at a petrol station the previous Christmas when they would not give him a free ice cream. On a happier note, 1995 was also the year when the Canadian post office gave Santa his own postcode: H0H 0H0.

The 32nd World Santa Claus Conference in Copenhagen in 1995, however, was marked by a huge dispute. The Finnish Santa, claiming to be the only true one, refused to attend unless the others acknowledged his uniqueness. 'This is the last straw,' a conference organiser said. 'We had invited the Finnish Santa to attend and explain himself at this year's conference. Now we're going to strip him of his white beard and red robe and excommunicate him once and for all.'

In 1998, a man appeared in court

in Finland after driving his car into a reindeer-drawn Santa sleigh. Although he was drunk, the jury recommended leniency on the grounds of his understandable surprise.

In Great Yarmouth in 2000, a street trader dressed as Santa was arrested for brawling. A police spokesman said, 'It was extremely upsetting for the young children to see Santa being nicked and handcuffed.'

In 2001, a Mother Christmas sued a store in America for $100,000 because she was sacked for having breasts. In the same year, two banks in Switzerland banned entry to anyone in Santa Claus costume for fear of robberies.

Santa's reputation took another blow at Christmas 2003, when Professor John Trinkaus in New York classified the expressions on the faces of 300 children visiting Santa in department stores. He reported that one was 'exhilarated', two were 'happy', 247 were 'indifferent', 47 were 'hesitant', none were 'sad', and three were 'terrified'.

It has been calculated that Santa would need 200,000 reindeer flying at 200,000 times the speed of sound in order to deliver presents to every child on Earth on Christmas Eve.

According to tradition, Santa's reindeer will eat 360 different plants, but not carrots.

♀ *CONNECTICUT, IDES OF MARCH, MANDELA, ST NICHOLAS*

● SARDINE

In 1998, a spokesman for the European Patent Office said that their most frequently requested patent document was the one for sardine-flavoured ice cream. 'No one believes that it actually exists until they've called it up and seen it themselves,' patent examiner Bernard Delporte said. The patent he referred to is numbered JP6233654 and was granted to Sato Shigeaki on 23 August 1994. According to the patent application, the purpose of the invention is: 'To obtain a delicious ice cream and to promote industries by expanding consumption of fishes by thoroughly removing a fish-like smell so as to make children who dislike fishes eat fishes.'

The constitution of the product is given as follows: 'Miso (fermented soybean paste) and Welsh onion are put on ground sardine meat, steamed with sake (rice wine), boiled with milk and alcohol, mixed with paste of walnut, paste of almond and paste of peanut and boiled. The cooked sardine is mixed with an ice cream base of chocolate taste and cooled to produce the objective ice cream of sardine.'

In 1989 it rained sardines over the town of Ipswich in Queensland.

● SATELLITE TV

In 2011, a store in Montana was reported to be offering customers a voucher for a free gun (subject to the usual background checks) if they signed up for a satellite TV package. Customers who did not want a gun could have a Pizza Hut voucher instead.

♀ *AZERBAIJAN*

● SAUDI ARABIA

In recent years, Saudi Arabia has beheaded more convicted criminals than any other country. At least 158 people were beheaded in 2015, at least 154 in 2016, at least 146 in 2017, and 149 in 2018. In 2019, Saudi Arabia beheaded a record 184 people, but the figure dropped to only 27 in 2020.

This was attributed at least partly to Covid-19, when the government carried out no executions from February to April because of a lockdown. In 2021, the figure rose again to 67 beheadings by trained swordsmen and on 12 March 2022, 81 executions took place, a record for a single day. On rare occasions when no swordsman is available, execution by firing squad takes place. Recently, however, it has been reported that more swordsmen have been hired to avoid the need for firing squads.

In early 2008, shortly before Valentine's Day, the Commission for the Promotion for Virtue and Prevention of Vice in Saudi Arabia banned red roses and ordered florists and gift shop owners in Riyadh to remove any items coloured scarlet, which is widely seen as symbolising love and encouraging relations between men and women outside marriage. Later the same year, it was announced that men who flirt publicly with women in northern Saudi Arabia were to be punished by being given haircuts. Police were ordered to administer the trims after a group of men with long hair had been seen pestering female students as they left school in the town of Skaka.

⚲ *AUSTRALIA, CAMEL, MONARCHY, TEA*

⬤ SAUNA

The finals of the 2010 World Sauna Championships were halted when Vladimir Ladyzhensky, a Russian amateur wrestler said to be in his 60s, collapsed alongside reigning champion Timo Kaukonen of Finland after about six minutes. Both men were bleeding from severe burns and Ladyzhensky was pronounced dead. The organisers said the competition, which had over 130 participants from 15 countries, would never be held again.

⬤ SAUSAGES

The earliest known mention of sausages is in a play by Aristophanes dating back to the 5th century BC. Even earlier, however, the Sicilian playwright Epicharmus is said to have written a play called *The Sausage*, sadly now lost, and the ancient Sumerians are thought to have eaten something like sausages 5,000 years ago.

The word 'sausage' comes from the Latin *salscius*, meaning 'prepared by salting'.

In the 4th century, the Catholic Church banned the eating of sausages as a sin as they were associated with pagan festivals.

Sausage-eating has a long tradition in Britain. King Henry V is quoted as saying: 'War without fire is like sausages without mustard.' The British spend around half a billion pounds on sausages in a year, eating over quarter of a million tonnes of them.

Research in the UK shows that 6.8 per cent of people eat sausages 'because they are convenient'; 13.4 per cent eat them 'for a change'; 8.4 per cent 'for a treat'; and 30 per cent because 'they are my favourite meal'.

The British Sausage Appreciation Society has over 6,000 members and sausages are the third most popular foodstuff taken on holiday by Britons when travelling abroad.

The world's longest sausage was 62.75 kilometres (38.99 miles) long. It was made in a tent in a parking lot in Romania in 2014. The record for sausage-eating is 3.75 kilograms (8.31 pounds) of Vienna sausage in 10 minutes, set by Sonya Thomas in 2005.

Sausages were first divided into links during the reign of Charles I in the 17th century.

The phrase 'not a sausage' meaning 'nothing at all' dates back only to the 1930s.

'To retain respect for sausages and laws, one must not watch them in the making.' German chancellor Otto von Bismarck

'The dog's kennel is no place to keep a sausage.' Danish proverb

BREAKFAST, FRANKFURTER, HOT DOGS, SANDWICHES, SPAGHETTI

SCARECROW

When the word 'scarecrow' entered the English language around 1550, it meant a person who scares off birds in farms or gardens. It took another 50 years before someone realised that a scruffy statue offered an easier way to do the job.

A gun-firing scarecrow was patented in 1913 (US patent 1056602) by John Steinocher of West Texas 'for scaring off birds, animals and such like as tend to prey upon or devastate crops, stock or like property'.

CUCUMBER, GUNS

SCENT

Three London tube stations introduced a fragrance called 'Madeleine' on 23 March 2001 in the hope that it would make the tube smell better. The experiment was quickly terminated on 24 March 2001 as it was making people feel sick.

CONTRACEPTION, DETROIT, HERRING, LITHUANIA, ST VALENTINE, SINGAPORE

SCHILLER, Friedrich von (1759–1805)

The German poet, historian and dramatist Schiller used to work with a bowl of rotting apples on his desk. He believed that the smell stimulated his creativity.

In 1826, the mayor of Weimar had 23 skulls dug up from the mass grave in which Schiller had been buried 21 years earlier in order to determine which had belonged to the poet. Informed opinion at the time narrowed the choice to two, but debate continued over which of these was Schiller's true skull. Finally, in 2008, after a two-year project which involved exhuming the skulls of members of Schiller's family and comparing their DNA with that of the candidate Schiller skulls, experts finally gave the answer: neither of them was the authentic Schiller skull.

SCILLY ISLES

Since 1986, Prince Charles has received one daffodil a year as rent from the Isles of Scilly Wildlife Trust for land on the Isles.

SCISSORS

The World Rock Paper Scissors Society hosted professional tournaments in the game (which is also known as 'Scissors-Paper-Stone' or 'Rochambeau') from 2002 to 2009, but since 2015, such tournaments have been organised by the World Rock Paper Scissors Association.

The first open international championship was held in Toronto in November 2002 and was won by Canadian website operator Pete Lovering. Over 250 people took part and the top prize was $1,200, a video game system and a gold medal. Lovering said the secret to winning is maintaining a clear mind and judging each opponent individually.

Knowledge of the game is also useful in the evolution and mate-selection of the common side-blotched lizard, of which the blotches come in three colours: orange, yellow and blue. When males are competing for the attention of a female, the three colours have different strategies, and it has been noted that orange beats blue, blue beats yellow and yellow beats orange. Research has shown that changes in the distribution of the three colours reflect the optimal strategies for the equivalent Rock Paper Scissors game.

♀ *EYEBALL, MATISSE*

SCOLD

Although the ancient offence of being a 'common scold' was described as 'obsolete' by the British Director of Public Prosecutions in 1962, it was not formally abolished until 1967 when the Criminal Law Act removed it from the statute book, along with the crimes of champerty, barratry, challenging to fight and eavesdropping.

A common scold was a troublesome woman who habitually disturbed the peace by picking arguments and quarrelling with her neighbours, and anyone convicted was liable to be punished either by having to wear a 'scold's bridle', which was a metal mask strapped over her face, with a piece of metal going into the mouth to stop her tongue moving, or being placed in something called the 'cucking stool'. This may have been the same as the 'ducking stool', in which troublesome people (usually women) were strapped and ducked in a river or pond, but others have identified it as a chair on which a person is strapped in a manner that exposes their buttocks. That explanation is supported by the fact that 'to cuck' was an old verb meaning 'to pass waste from the bowels'.

The offence of being a common scold was exported to America with the early colonists, where the punishment, possibly through a confusion between cucking and ducking, was the ducking stool.

In 1829, a woman named Anne Royall was convicted in Washington of being a common scold, but the court ruled that the ducking stool was obsolete and fined her $10 instead.

The last prosecution for being a common scold was in 1972 when the state of New Jersey prosecuted a woman named Marion Palendrano. She was charged with various offences that included being 'a common scold and disturber of the peace of the neighborhood and of all good and quiet people of this State to the common nuisance of the people of this State'. The judge ruled that the offence of being a common scold was defined too vaguely to be considered valid, and in any case, since all definitions appeared to imply that only women can be scolds, it violated the Equal Protection Clause of the 14th Amendment of the US Constitution.

Champerty and barratry, incidentally, both relate to the practice of lawyers or organisations encouraging others to start litigation, with the idea of sharing any profits that may result. The abolition of these offences opened the doors for 'no win, no fee' deals.

♀ *XANTHIPPE*

SCORPION

In 2007, a scorpion stung a man on an American Airways flight from Miami to Toronto. The man was returning from a camping trip in Costa Rica where the creature was thought to have crawled into his rucksack. 'This is rare,' said a spokesman for the airline. 'I'm not aware of a scorpion stinging a person on any of our flights before.'

♀ *IBSEN, MEXICO*

SCOTLAND

The name of Scotland seems to have come from an Irish tribe whom the Romans, in the early fourth century, called the Scoti. By the 5th and 6th centuries, the Scoti had established communities in northern Britain, which the Romans referred to as the Land of the Scoti, or Scot-Land.

St Columba is not only credited with being the man who brought Christianity to Scotland, he is also thought to be the first person to claim a sighting of the Loch Ness Monster in AD 565.

BERWICK, BOSWELL, IRELAND, ST ANDREW, TARTAN, UNION JACK

SCOTT, Sir Walter (1771–1832)

Walter Scott took up fiction writing at the age of 42, having spent his professional life before that as a lawyer, playwright and poet. His first novel, *Waverley*, came out in 1814 and in that year sold more copies than all the other novels in the UK put together.

'Ivanhoe by Sir Walter Scott' is an anagram of 'A novel by a Scottish writer'.

BLAKE, BULLOCK, HUDSON, YODELLING

SCOUTING

Robert Baden-Powell was persuaded, despite his great reluctance, to remove a section entitled 'Continence' from his *Scouting for Boys*. 'You all know what it is,' he wrote, 'to have at times a pleasant feeling in your private parts.' The excised section that followed was a warning of what could happen to a boy who gave way to the temptations associated with that feeling: 'The practice is called "self-abuse". And the result of self-abuse is always – mind you, always – that the boy after a time becomes weak and nervous and shy, he gets headaches and probably palpitation of the heart, and if he still carries it on too far he very often goes out of his mind and becomes an idiot. A very large number of the lunatics in our asylums have made themselves ill by indulging in this vice although at the time they were sensible cheery boys like any one of you.'

SCRABBLE

The game of Scrabble was invented by Alfred Butts in 1921, first called 'Criss-Cross-Words' then simply 'It'. It was not popular until 1948 when the name was changed to 'Scrabble'. Since then about 150 million Scrabble sets have been sold in 121 countries in around 30 official languages. Alfred Butts also produced another game, marketed under the title 'Alfred's Other Game'. It was not a great success.

British Scrabble organisers were taken to court in 1995 by a player who complained that he was allowed insufficient time to go to the lavatory between games.

Leicester Police once received a call from a five-year-old boy complaining that his sister was cheating at Scrabble.

There are 124 permissible two-letter words in international Scrabble competition, from AA to ZO, using every letter except V. One of the most recent such words to be added is ZA, which is a colloquial abbreviation for a pizza.

The only number (in English) that scores its own value when played on a Scrabble board (excluding bonus squares) is TWELVE. No numbers score their own value in French Scrabble, but both ACHT (8) and SECHSUNDZWANZIG (26) do so in German Scrabble.

There are 19 'A's in a Malaysian Scrabble set, the highest number of any single letter in any language. In Finnish Scrabble, the letter D is worth seven, which no single letter scores in English.

In one episode of *The Simpsons*, Bart played the fake word KWYJIBO in a Scrabble game, defining it as a 'balding North American ape with a small chin'.

⚲ *AA, FIFTEEN, KYRGYZSTAN, POLAND, Q, VOWELS, WALES*

⬤ SCRATCHING

Studies have shown that right-handed people tend to scratch with their left hand and left-handed people with their right.

The phrase 'up to scratch' comes from either boxing or cricket. In the former, the two contestants in a boxing match began each round by standing at a scratch mark on the ground to see if they were fit enough to stand up, in which case the contest could proceed. In cricket, the scratch was an early word for the crease, and batsmen were encouraged to place their bats up to the scratch to face a ball. It is not clear which sport was the first to use the phrase.

⚲ *ACNESTIS, DENVER, ETIQUETTE, PILLOW*

⬤ SCROTUM

The Scrotum Gift Shop based in Cronulla, New South Wales, sells purses, pouches and golf ball holders made from kangaroo scrotums. Embossed corporate scrotum pouches are also available. Their most recent additions include a limited number of 'unusually sexy shaped kangaroo scrotum pouches'.

⚲ *CELLO, HYENA, VERMONT*

⬤ SCULPTURE

Konstantinos Dimitriadis won a gold medal for sculpture for Greece at the 1924 Olympic Games. This was the only time Greece won an Olympic gold medal in any of the arts categories, which ran from the start of the modern Olympics until 1948.

There was only one category in the sculpture class until 1928, when separate competitions were held, one for statues, the other for reliefs and medals. In 1936, reliefs and medals were each given their own category.

⚲ *EUROPE, FROG, JESUS CHRIST, MICHELANGELO, TESTICLE, YAK*

⬤ SEA LION

One way to tell a sea lion from a seal is that a sea lion has ear-flaps, whereas a seal does not. Here are some more distinguishing features: sea lions have no distinguishable nails on their front flippers, whereas seals have claw-like nails; seals have nails on all digits of their hind flippers, but sea lions have nails only on the middle three digits; sea lion flippers are usually hairless, unlike those of seals; the front flippers of a sea lion are long and wing-like, the front flippers of a seal are short and blunt. Another way to tell a seal from a sea lion is that a sea lion's hind flippers can turn round to aid propulsion when moving on land, while a seal's cannot.

Research published in 2004 showed that a sea lion could remember things it had learned 10 years previously, the longest memory interval ever recorded in a non-human mammal.

The Chinese used to use sea lion whiskers to clean opium pipes.

Sea lions are unable to see the colour red; they cannot distinguish it from grey.

Sea lions can suffer from epilepsy.

⚲ *BACULUM*

SEAL

Under old laws of Newfoundland, seal-hunting ships were obliged to serve soup on a Saturday.

In 2008, researchers on Marion Island in the southern Indian Ocean reported seeing an Antarctic fur seal attempting to mate with a king penguin. The seal was male; the penguin's sex was unknown. It was described as the most unusual case of mammal mating behaviour yet known. The seal's efforts to copulate, however, were unsuccessful and after 45 minutes it gave up, swam into the water and then completely ignored the bird it had just assaulted. The incident was put down to the youthfulness and sexual inexperience of the male seal.

The crabeater seal doesn't eat crabs. Its favourite food is the small shrimp-like creatures called krill. French explorers gave it the name of 'crabeater' in error.

Allowing your pet seal to swim in the Trevi Fountain in Rome is not allowed. In 1951, two Italian journalists were fined for this.

The collective noun for a group of seals is a 'herd' or a 'pod'.

The term for a breathing hole made in ice by a seal is an 'aglu'.

The study of signet rings and seals (not the maritime mammal) is called sphragistics.

♀ AUGUSTUS, DINOSAUR, SEA LION

SEAWEED

The colouring in blue Smarties comes from a seaweed called spirulina. This was introduced in 2008 after a drive to rid Smarties of artificial colouring had caused blue ones to be dropped two years earlier.

♀ SWIMMING

SECOND

A second of time was originally the ancient Roman *pars minutia secunda* (second small part) of an hour, the *pars minutia prima*, or first small part, being what we now call the minute. The pars minutia was not just any small part but very specifically one-sixtieth. The Romans borrowed this system from the ancient Babylonians.

Until 1960, a second was defined as 1/86,400 of a mean solar day (the average period of rotation of the Earth on its axis relative to the Sun). In that year, however, the General Conference of Weights and Measures adopted a more precise definition of 1/31556925.9747 of a tropical year, thus changing the definition from one based on the Earth's rotation to one based on its orbit round the Sun. For all its accuracy, that new definition only lasted seven such orbits, for in 1967, following the development of atomic clocks, another definition was adopted. Since then, a second has been equal to '9,192,631,770 oscillations of the electromagnetic radiation corresponding to a particular quantum change in the superfine energy level of the ground state of the caesium-133 atom'. Thanks to this, a caesium clock is accurate to within one second in 316,000 years.

♀ BIRTH, BUGANDA, CHICKEN, STREETS, SUN, TIME

SECOND WORLD WAR

In 1939, the British Ministry of Information commissioned a number of propaganda posters to be displayed in the event of war and invasion by Germany. The idea was to send a message from King George VI to his people as reassurance if Britain was invaded.

One such poster, which was never officially issued, consisted simply of the royal crown and beneath it the words 'Keep Calm and Carry On'. It was rarely displayed in public and had been almost forgotten when a copy was found in a bookshop in Northumberland in 2000. The slogan was subsequently used in a wide variety of products.

BERLIN, CARROT, CROSSWORD, DUCK, EXORCISM, SPIRITUALISM

SEDUCTION

According to a law listed during the reign of King Aethelbert of Kent around AD 600, any man who seduced a maiden of the King's household had to pay 50 shillings in compensation.

In 2008, scientists reported that female voices are most seductive when women are at their most fertile. Researchers recorded women counting from one to 10 at different times in their menstrual cycle, then played the voices back randomly to a group of students. Both males and females judged the voices to be most attractive when they were recorded at periods of peak fertility.

CENSORSHIP, HIPPOCRATES, TUESDAY

SEMICOLON

There is a North American flying insect called the semicolon butterfly named for a pale mark resembling a semicolon on the underside of its lower wings.

The modern punctuational semi-colon first appeared in 1494 in the first edition of Pietro Bembo's *De Aetna*. Similar-looking marks had been used by the Romans, but the convention of using them to signify something stronger than a comma, but less than a full stop, was the idea of the printer Aldus Manutius the Elder and Francesco Griffi, his punch-cutter. Griffi went on to design the first italic type in 1500.

The earliest recorded use of the word 'semicolon' in English was in Ben Jonson's *English Grammar* (published around 1637), where he describes it as 'a distinction of an imperfect Sentence, wherein with somewhat a longer Breath, the Sentence following is included'.

SENEGAL

Senegal is placed 168th on the United Nations Human Development Index for 2019, making it the 22nd least desirable country on Earth to live in, one place ahead of Afghanistan.

The average annual income is about £300, and 54 per cent of the population live below the poverty line.

Only 39.1 per cent of the adult population can read and write, and the average Senegalese woman gives birth to 5.03 children.

The official language is French, but the Senegalese also speak local languages, including Wolof, Pulaar, Jola and Mandinka.

The highest point in Senegal is only 581 metres (1,909 feet) above sea level, which is so unremarkable that it does not even have a name.

Fish and peanuts are two of Senegal's major exports.

In a four-nation football tournament in Senegal in 1991, both semi-finals, the final and the third-place play-off all ended in penalty shoot-outs.

Medicine men in Senegal treat dizziness and madness with the roots of the wild custard apple.

In 1997, the whole of Senegal was in darkness for four hours after a sparrow hawk collided with a high tension power line, short-circuiting the National Grid.

BABOONS, JAMAICA, STEEL

SEPTEMBER

September is the only month with the same number of letters in its name in English as the number of the month. It is also the only month in which share prices are more likely to fall than rise. According to the US Census Bureau, September is the 4,110th most common female name in the US, just behind Shandi but ahead of Saran. Despite that, Shakespeare did not mention September in any of his plays.

⚲ BATMAN

SERBIA

According to a survey in 2010, the average Serbian citizen spends 363 minutes a day watching television, which was 38 minutes more than in 2009. This trend changed greatly over the next decade and a survey in September 2020 reported that Serbian citizens spend only 77 minutes a day watching TV, but 104 minutes on social media, 81 minutes listening to the radio, and 23 minutes reading newspapers and magazines.

Serbia is the only country whose name is an anagram of both a disease of dogs (rabies) and a means of cooking (braise).

⚲ DUCK, NAVIES

SERVANTS

According to the Servants' Characters Act in British law of 1792, it was an offence to give a false character reference for a servant or to imper-sonate a master or mistress. In 2008, the House of Lords began a process to repeal this and some 260 other obsolete laws.

Under the 1861 Offences Against the Person Act, however, 'Not providing apprentices or servants with food,

&c. whereby life is endangered' is still against the law.

⚲ BOURDALOUE, BOXING DAY, FAMILY, HOUSEWIVES, PIES, TENNIS

SEX

Perhaps the only society that has never shown any interest in sex is the Dani tribe of Grand Valley, New Guinea. They were first discovered by Europeans in 1909 and further expeditions in the 1920s and 30s confirmed the unusual nature of their lives. Males and females sleep in separate areas, weddings take place only on special pigfeasts, which are held every four to six years, sexual intercourse is prohibited until two years after marriage, sex is also banned for several years after any birth, and they seem to show no particular interest in sexual matters.

Meanwhile, in the rest of the world, people enjoyed sex to the point of obsession but there were many areas they did not understand properly, particularly on the question of having babies. The Egyptians and most ancient Greeks believed that the father alone provided the seed from which a person grew; the mother at best provided only warmth and nourishment. Aristotle challenged that view, accepting that women played more than a nursing role.

Among the secrets of nature that Aristotle divulged was that the womb is divided into two halves, the right side for boy babies, the left for girls. He recommended that if a woman wants to have a girl baby, she should lie on her left side at the time of conception and think strongly of a female. That was because he believed that babies tend to look like whatever the woman was thinking about at the time of conception.

Hippocrates had similar ideas: 'If, in

a woman pregnant with twins, either of her breasts lose its fullness, she will part with one of her children; and if it be the right breast which becomes slender, it will be the male child, or if the left, the female.' Pliny the Elder believed that sexual intercourse is a good remedy for pains in the loins, dimness of sight, insanity and melancholia.

In 1824, Sir Astley Cooper's 'Surgical Lectures', in the *Lancet*, were doubtful that turpentine and rhubarb did any good for the treatment of premature ejaculation, and blamed impotence on 'general torpor' and 'sluggishness of constitution'.

More recently, an analysis of sexual activity concluded that one act of love-making expends the same energy as 45 minutes of frisbee-throwing, 1.5 hours of card-playing or 7.5 hours standing around at cocktail parties.

In 2008, Italy's Supreme Court ruled that it is not illegal to record secret videos of yourself having sex with your partner, as long as you do not distribute them to other people. The court acquitted a man who had been sentenced to four months in jail for not telling his girlfriend that their sessions were being recorded.

♀ *BEDROOM, CELIBACY, CENSORSHIP, CHEESE, MONKEY, PENGUIN*

SEX-CHANGE

The first case of a prisoner in a UK jail undergoing a sex-change operation was that of an inmate of Gartree Prison in Leicestershire, who underwent sex-change operations in 1999 and 2001, paid for by the National Health Service. The prisoner was then transferred to Holloway women's prison but in 2006 decided that she wanted to revert to being a man. She grew a beard while still in Holloway, and had surgery to revert to her original sex after 10 years as a woman.

According to a survey in 2008, 68 per cent of women who play computer games online have chosen male characters, while more than half of the male players have chosen female persona.

SEX EDUCATION

In north-east Kenya, in October 1987, an elderly man in the town of Garissa who got a schoolgirl pregnant while pretending to give her private tuition, was ordered in court to pay four camels in compensation.

SEX TEST

The first sporting disqualification as a result of a sex test was of the Polish sprinter Ewa Klobukowska in 1967. The record she had helped set when winning Olympic gold in the sprint relay in 1964 was struck from the record books. She had been ruled ineligible for female athletic events because she had an extra chromosome. This, however, did not prevent her from becoming pregnant a few years later and the mother of a healthy baby. The test that identified her ineligibility was later ruled inadequate.

SEX WORK

According to a survey in 2011, one in three university students in Berlin would consider sex work as a means to finance their education, compared with only 29.2 per cent in Paris and 18.5 per cent in Kiev. The study found some 4 per cent of the 3,200 Berlin students surveyed said they had already done some form of sex work, including prostitution, erotic dancing and Internet shows.

♀ *NEW ZEALAND*

● SEXUAL DISCRIMINATION

In 2008, the Swedish government ordered the National Road Administration to design a female alternative to the walking-man signs found at the Scandinavian nation's pedestrian crossings. The new sign would show a woman instead of a man crossing the street, giving more gender balance to Swedish road signs.

♀ *HAIR*

● SEXUAL HARASSMENT

In 2001, David Joyner, who was serving 14 years in a Texas prison for robbery and assault, sued *Penthouse* magazine for publishing what he described as a 'disappointing layout' of Paula Jones, a woman who had previously accused President Clinton of sexual harassment. The lawsuit alleged that the photos of Jones were not sufficiently revealing and caused the plaintiff to be 'very mentally hurt and angered'. He sought $500,000 in damages. District Judge Sam Sparks dismissed the suit and fined Joyner $250 for filing a frivolous legal motion. His judgement was accompanied by a 12-line poem which began: "Twas the night before Christmas and all through the prison, inmates were planning their new porno mission."

● SHAKESPEARE, William (1564–1616)

'William Shakespeare' is an anagram of 'I am a weakish speller'. He had red hair and in his will he left his second-best bed to his widow.

The only world heavyweight boxing champion to have lectured on Shakespeare at Yale University was Gene Tunney.

Here are some of Shakespeare's rare mistakes:

- In *Julius Caesar*, Act II, Scene I, Brutus says, 'Peace, count the clock,' and Trebonius replies, 'The clock hath stricken three.' But the chiming clock was not invented until some 1,400 years after Julius Caesar's time.
- In *The Winter's Tale*, Act III, Scene III, Bohemia is described as 'a desert country near the sea', but Bohemia was landlocked and about 160 miles from the sea at its closest point.
- In *The Merry Wives of Windsor*, Act V, Scene V, Falstaff says, 'Let the sky rain potatoes', but the first potatoes reached Britain in 1586 and the play is set in the early 15th century.
- In *Henry IV, Part 1*, Act II, Scene II, First Carrier exclaims, 'God's body, the turkeys in my pannier are quite starv'd.' But the play takes place almost a century before the discovery of America, which was the source of the first European turkeys.

St George's Day – 23 April – is often given as the date of both the birth and death of Shakespeare, but while the death date has been confirmed, all that is known about his birth is that he was baptised on 26 April. People who definitely did die on their birthdays, however, include Ingrid Bergman, Franklin D. Roosevelt, King Mongkut of Thailand, Telly Savalas and Louis Armstrong.

Shakespeare's *Romeo and Juliet* contains the first known use in English of the word 'butterfly'.

♀ *BIBLE, RHUBARB, RICHARD III, SHATNER, STARLING, TWELFTH NIGHT*

● SHAMROCK

Technically, there is no such thing as a shamrock. It's just a word used to refer to several varieties of clover, mainly *Trifolium repens*.

In the 5th century, St Patrick is said

to have used the clover to illustrate the concept of the Trinity: three leaves on one stem.

The word 'shamrock' comes from the Irish *seamróg* or *seamairóg*, meaning 'little clover'. The word 'shamrock' was first seen in English only in the late 16th century.

The shamrock was originally associated with the mythical Celtic goddess Ana (or Anu) of Ireland. Ana was worshipped in the three aspects of her life, maiden, mother and crone, corresponding to the three leaves of the shamrock.

In 2002, Australia classified shamrock as a weed and banned it as a possible carrier of foot-and-mouth disease. It is still illegal to send shamrock plants and seeds by mail to Australia.

The official callsign for the Irish airline Aer Lingus is 'shamrock'.

Around one in 10,000 clovers has four leaves, but the record is 56, discovered in 2009 in Japan.

SHARJAH

In March 2013, workers at the manufacturing firm MSSL Mideast in Sharjah in the United Arab Emirates submitted four world records to Guinness World Records for verification. These were for the most people wearing paper hats, the largest barefoot race, the longest high-five chain and the largest hopping race. The company hoped to add the records to the four they already held: most people polishing shoes, most people opening bottles simultaneously, longest balloon train and longest conga dance line.

SHARK

Sharks continue growing new teeth to replace old ones throughout their lifetimes. A 10-year-old shark may well have gnawed and bitten its way through about 24,000 teeth. Curiously, the biggest shark species has the smallest teeth. The 12-metre (39-foot) long whale shark has more than 4,000 teeth, each only 3mm long.

Steven Spielberg named the shark in *Jaws* 'Bruce' after his lawyer.

♀ FISH, QUEENSLAND, SNIFFING, WEDDING

SHATNER, William (b. 1931)

William Shatner was born in Montreal. He trained as a Shakespearean actor and performed at the Stratford Shakespeare Festival in Stratford, Ontario, from 1954.

He speaks fluent French and Esperanto. In 1965 he starred in *Incubus*, a horror film made entirely in Esperanto.

His first film role was in 1958 in *The Brothers Karamazov*, where he played Yul Brynner's younger brother, Alexey Karamazov.

He came top of a poll in 2000 for the man most people would like to see as King of Canada. The verb 'to shatnerize' has been coined to mean: 'To deliberately produce something so bad it's good'. It is not yet in the *Oxford English Dictionary*.

The original *Star Trek*, in which Shatner played Captain James T. Kirk, ran for only three series in 1966–69. It became cult viewing when it was repeated after the 1969 Moon landing. After the first series was cancelled, Shatner was out of work and had to live in a camper van.

In 2006 he had a kidney stone removed and auctioned it for charity. It fetched $25,000. 'William Shatner' is an anagram of 'Slim alien wrath' or 'Will is Earthman'.

On 13 October 2021, at the age of 90, William Shatner became the oldest person ever to go into space. He was born one year to the day after Stephen Sondheim.

The middle initial in James T. Kirk stands for 'Tiberius'.

SHAVING

In 2008, the northern Mexican city of Torreon imposed fines of up to 346 pesos (about £20) for putting on make-up or shaving with an electric razor while driving.

EINSTEIN, FRUITFLY, HAIR, MARSTON, MEXICO

SHEEP

Sheep are the most frequently occurring animals in the Bible. Lambs come next.

You could be hanged for sheep-stealing in Britain until 1818. The last woman to be hanged for sheep-stealing was Ann Baker, who went to the gallows in Oakham, Rutland, on 3 August 1801. The last man so punished was James Poulter at Horsemonger Lane Jail in Surrey in 1819. Presumably the crime had been committed when sheep-stealing was still a capital offence.

The fat from an average lamb can be used to make half a gallon of diesel fuel. In 1986 a test fleet of 40 New Zealand lorries averaged 10 miles per lamb.

In 2001, a team of five Cambridge psychologists conducted experiments showing that sheep can remember the faces of 50 other sheep for over two years.

On 25 June 1911, Sir John Throckmorton won a bet of 1,000 guineas (£1,050) that a woollen coat could be made between sunrise and sunset starting with the shearing of the sheep.

The dwarf blue sheep is found only in Tibet.

BALLOON, BIBLE, CUCUMBER, HAGGIS, METHANE, QUANTUM MECHANICS

SHIRT

Men of the British army's 70th Regiment were ordered in 1788 to have four good shirts.

The shirt Pele wore in the final of the 1970 Football World Cup sold for a record £157,750 in 2002. The previous record of £91,750 was set by the shirt Sir Geoff Hurst wore in the 1966 World Cup Final. The Bayern Munich shirt is the one that is most expensive for a sponsor to get his name on.

The world record for a vintage band t-shirt is $19,300, which a yellow Grateful Dead shirt dating back to 1967 fetched at a Sotheby's auction in New York in October 2021. Designed by Hell's Angel artist Allan 'Gut' Terkel, it was billed as the earliest official mass-produced Grateful Dead t-shirt.

The Bonzo Dog Band recorded a track called 'Shirt' consisting mainly of interviews with passers-by in Willesden who were asked their views on shirts by Viv Stanshall.

RED, SUPERSTITION, UNITED STATES

SHOES

'Shoe' and 'canoe' (and their derivatives) are the only common English words in which 'oe' is pronounced 'oo', though according to the *Oxford English Dictionary* the hoopoe bird may be pronounced either as 'hoop-oo' or 'hoop-oh'.

Pliny, in his *Natural History* in AD 77, recommended spitting into your right shoe before putting it on, as a defence against evil spells.

In AD 396, St Augustine of Hippo mentioned the belief that you should go back to bed if anyone sneezes while you are putting your shoes on.

The feet of two kings played vital roles in the development of the modern shoe. Louis XIV of France was the first person to wear high-heeled shoes; and George IV of Britain was said to be the first to wear a pair of shoes individually tailored for his right and left feet. Most common folk, however, had to wait until about 1850 before they stopped wearing a pair of identical shoes that were equally uncomfortable on either foot. In 1978, after years of research. the Goodyear Rubber Company reported that right shoes wear out faster than left shoes.

In 14th-century France, long shoes called poulaines were fashionable, which also acted as status symbols according to length. Noblemen and princes wore shoes up to 0.6 metres (2 feet) in length. At the Battle of Nicopolis in 1396, French Crusaders had to hack off the tips of their shoes to give themselves a better chance of escape when they ran away.

According to a study in 2008, foot injuries caused by wearing high heels cost the UK £29 million a year to put right. It has also been found that, on average, high heels increase bottom protrusion by 25 per cent.

One organisation that specialises in finding single shoes for people with only one leg or with feet of different sizes is the National Odd Shoe Exchange of Chandler, Arizona, which goes by the curiously inappropriate acronym N.O.S.E.

AUGUSTUS, FRANCE, LINCOLN, SHARJAH, SUPERSTITION, WOMEN

SHOOTING

Hungary's best pistol shooter at the time of the 1936 Olympics was probably Károly Takács, but he was a serving soldier and was denied a place in the team as he was only a sergeant and not an officer. The ban was later lifted, but by then, his right hand, in which he held the gun, had been badly maimed by a grenade exploding as he held it. Not letting a little thing like that put him off, he learned to shoot left-handed and took gold at the Olympics in 1948 and 1952.

APRIL FOOLS, BULLET, DIVORCE, FASHION, HANGING, POPCORN

SHOPLIFTING

An elderly German man who attempted to steal a suit from a shop in 2008 by hiding it under his clothes was detected because he forgot to remove the suit from its hanger, which was bulging out as he tried to leave. 'Only a sign saying "stop me, I'm a thief!" would have made the thief look more unprofessional,' a police statement said.

CAPITAL PUNISHMENT, SHOPPING

SHOPPING

In 1699, you could be sentenced to death in Britain for shoplifting to the value of 5 shillings (25p) or more.

In 1996, a Portuguese language commission listed 'shopping centre' as a particularly offensive phrase in its fight against the influx of English words.

The number of shops in the UK fell from about 400,000 in 1955 to 306,985 in 2020, of which 208,795 were VAT registered.

Mr John Moore, a trader of Clapham High Street, was banned in the High Court in December 1984 from calling his shop 'Sellfridges' because he sold fridges. In November he had been banned from calling it 'Harrodds'.

🔎 *BANGLADESH, CONNECTICUT, DALLAS, PORTUGAL, TOURISM*

● SHOPPING TROLLEYS

The world's first shopping trolley arrived in the aisles of a supermarket in Oklahoma on 4 June 1937.

According to research in 1999, people in supermarkets were using the contents of other people's trolleys to assess their potential merits as romantic partners. Up to 11 per cent of single under-25s were believed to use this 'love-coding' (also known as 'trolley-snooping') to aid their judgements about others. A long list of foods identified as sending out clear signals included asparagus, which supposedly meant 'I am a sensual lover who loves exotic holidays'; chocolate fudge cake ('Let's have a wild time doing whatever pleases us'); cocktail cherries ('I am rather shallow and pretentious'); fish fingers ('I'm unadventurous between the sheets'); and stir-fry vegetables ('I love to experiment').

Around £35 million worth of shopping trolleys go missing from UK supermarkets every year. Many of these end up in rivers, but British Waterways have deliberately put trolleys into the Forth and Clyde canal to protect Bennett's pond weed, a rare water plant.

On 26 August 1996, a man in Sweden became the first person to be charged with being drunk in charge of a shopping trolley. He was stopped by police after hurtling downhill at 48 km/h (30 mph), after which his trolley collided with a car. A police prosecutor said, 'He was certainly careless, but I suppose it's debatable whether he was driving. But he was rather drunk and his trolley wasn't showing proper lights.'

The album *Abandoned Shopping Trolley Hotline* was released by the rock group Gomez in 2000. According to one review it was 'far better than most such discs'.

Physiotherapists have listed uncooperative shopping trolleys as a major cause of back pain.

● SHRIMP

The mantis shrimp from the Great Barrier Reef can recognise 11 or 12 primary colours, compared with a human's ability to detect only three, and can also see colours far beyond those of the human spectrum, ranging from ultraviolet to infrared.

🔎 *FLAMINGO, KRILL, PARAPSYCHOLOGY, SEAL*

● SHROVE TUESDAY

The word 'shrove' is the past tense of the verb 'to shrive', which means to confess and do penance for one's sins. The expression 'short shrift' also comes from this verb, originally referring to the short confession and penance of a condemned man before his execution.

The tradition of eating pancakes on Shrove Tuesday originated as a way of using up the flour and lard that were forbidden during Lent.

The Irish call Shrove Tuesday 'Maírt na Smut' – Sulky Tuesday – from the sulkiness of girls who have not found a husband before Lent.

It is also the last day of the Venice Carnival, where it is known as Fat Tuesday.

🔎 *BELGIUM, PANCAKE DAY*

● SHUFFLING

Although the verb 'to shuffle' first appeared in English in 1532, 'reshuffle' arrived only in 1802. The earliest use of 'shuffle' for a redistribution of government posts was in Australia in 1897. In Harold Macmillan's notorious 'Night of the long knives' reshuffle of 1962, seven members of the Cabinet were sacked.

The game of shuffleboard, in which a coin is propelled across a polished surface, was first called shove-board or shovel-board in the 1530s.

Apart from the usual riffle or overhand shuffles for playing cards, there are also shuffles called Pile, Hindu, Corgi, Mondean, Weave and Mexican Spiral. A riffle shuffle, interleaving two halves of the pack, is an out-shuffle or in-shuffle, according to whether the top card stays on top or not. Fifty-two perfect in-shuffles restore the original order of the cards, but you only need eight perfect out-shuffles to bring back the original order.

Shuffle-wing is an old name for hedge sparrows.

SIAM

The original Siamese twins, Chang and Eng Bunker, were born in Siam on 11 May 1811. On 11 May 1949, Siam changed its name to Thailand (which it had previously done in 1929, only to revert to Siam in 1945). The name 'Siam' may come from a Sanskrit word meaning 'dark' or 'brown', while 'Thailand' means 'land of the free'.

King Bhumibol Adulyadej came to the throne of Thailand in 1946 and was the world's longest-serving head of state when he died in 2016. Only Louis XIV of France reigned for longer, though Bhumibol's reign was overtaken by that of Queen Elizabeth II in 2022.

⚲ BUNKER, THAILAND

SIGN LANGUAGE

In the 5th century BC, in his dialogue *Cratylus*, Plato has Socrates say: 'If we hadn't a voice or a tongue, and wanted to express things to one another, wouldn't we try to make signs by moving our hands, head, and the rest of our body, just as dumb people do now?' Yet it was not until 1620 that the Spanish priest Juan Pablo Bonet produced the first sign language alphabet in his *Reducción de las letras y arte para enseñar a hablar a los mudos* (*Reduction of letters and art for teaching mute people to speak*).

According to research in Tennessee published in 2001, people who use sign language are five times more likely to suffer hand and wrist injuries than people who don't use sign language.

In Utah in 2005, a one-year-old child who had been taught American Sign Language was seen signing the word 'Help' when he was seated on Santa's lap in a shopping mall.

SILKWORM

More than half the world's production of silk from silkworms comes from India. The next two major silkworm-producing countries, a long way behind, are Uzbekistan and Brazil.

SILVER

An English pound was originally the value of one Troy pound of sterling silver, hence the name: Pound Sterling.

Gold medals at the Olympics are only about 6 per cent gold. Most of the rest is silver.

Before the advent of digital photography, half the silver mined in the world was used in photographic applications. Now the figure is under 20 per cent.

⚲ BRAHE, ELEMENTS, HIPPOPOTAMUS, POPES, RHYME, TUNA

SINGAPORE

The mascot and symbol of Singapore is the Merlion, a supposedly mythical creature that is half man, half fish. Unlike most mythical creatures, the Merlion is not very old; it was designed by the British ichthyologist Alec Fraser-Brunner in 1962 for the Singapore Tourist Board.

Since 1992, it has been illegal to import chewing gum into Singapore. Their war against chewing gum had by then already been raging for a decade. In 1982, Singapore spent £50,000 on removing chewing gum from floors and walls of government buildings.

In 1996, Singapore passed a law against appearing nude in a public place, or a private place exposed to public view. The penalty was a fine of about £1,000 or a three-month jail term, or both. In the same year, the Prime Minister of Singapore announced two markers of a gracious society: appreciation of music and clean public toilets.

Singapore law imposes heavy fines on people caught urinating in lifts. Many lifts are equipped with CCTV and 'Urine Detection Devices' that identify the scent of urine, setting off an alarm and closing the doors until the police arrive to arrest the offender. Thanks to these, only 14 people were convicted of urinating in lifts in Singapore in 1996, down from 40 in the previous year.

In 2002, Singapore's Changi Airport launched the world's first live airport game show.

In 2017, the Imperial Herbal Restaurant in Singapore was reported to be serving dried deer penis soup. It was said to be the only place you'd find deer penis soup in Singapore.

♀ DURIAN, GHOSTS, TOILET

SIX-PACK

The term 'six-pack' for six bottles or cans of drink was first used in 1961, and a 'six-pack' of abdominal muscles in 1992.

SKATES

The first recorded appearance of roller skates was a disaster. They were worn by Joseph Mervin, a Belgian entertainer, who appeared on them playing a violin at a party in Carlisle House, London, in April 1760. Unfortunately, he lost control and crashed into a mirror, injuring himself and causing some £500 worth of damage.

♀ CARTWHEEL, FRISBEE

SKIING

The oldest known depictions of people skiing are Norwegian rock carvings dating back to 2500 BC. A Siberian rock carving of roughly the same time shows a man on skis apparently trying to have sex with an elk.

By 1721, however, the Norwegians led the world in skiing. In that year, the Norwegian army became the first to have a specialised ski unit and Norwegian army skis were the first to have leather straps on the heel as well as toe straps. Two centuries before that, in 1521, the earliest known stretchers were used to carry away wounded soldiers during a conflict between Denmark and Sweden. They were made by stretching a piece of canvas between two skis.

Figures published in 2009 revealed that, in the EU region, there are roughly 300,000 snow-sport related injuries each year that require hospital treatment, including 170,000 ski injuries and 90,000 snowboard injuries.

In 2011, research in the US reported that snowboarding is less deadly than skiing. Snowboarders, it said, were more likely to suffer ankle and head injuries than skiers, but less likely to be killed in an accident. Your chance of winning the jackpot in the British National Lottery if you have only one ticket is about the same as your chance of being killed during six minutes' skiing.

Statistics on sports injuries in Britain in 2018 revealed that footballers are most likely to be injured, with 71 per cent of those surveyed having suffered injury at some time, closely followed by basketball (69 per cent) and hockey (68 per cent). Only 44 per cent of skiers had been injured, but the safest sport of all was found to be darts (18 per cent).

DOYLE, LIECHTENSTEIN, YAK

SKIN

The skin of the average adult, at any given time, weighs 2.7 kilograms (6 pounds). In total, each person sheds 18 kilograms (40 pounds) of skin in his or her lifetime. Every night each human sheds about 3 grams of skin particles.

There are more living organisms on the skin of each human than there are humans on the surface of the Earth.

BEAUTY, EGYPT, GAMING, MOLE, NAVEL, STRAWBERRY

SKIPPING

The origin of skipping ropes is unknown but they are thought to have started among rope-makers in ancient Egypt and China. The ancient Chinese are known to have played a game called 'hundred rope jumping' as part of their New Year festival.

Although Europeans are known to have been skipping in around 1600, the earliest known use of the term 'skipping rope' in English was in 1802. In the United States, they refer to skipping ropes as jump ropes.

A skipping activity in which the skipper jumps over two ropes turned in opposite directions by others is called 'double dutch'. Other skipping techniques are called 'elephant', 'toad', 'inverse toad' and 'egg beater'.

Skipping is a competitive sport in about 40 countries.

Skipping for an hour at a moderate pace can burn off more than 700 calories for a 70-kilogram (155-pound) person. The most skips made in 30 seconds is 108; the record for one hour is 12,702.

The Song of Solomon is the only book of the King James Bible that contains the word skipping: 'The voice of my beloved! behold, he cometh leaping upon the mountains, skipping upon the hills.' Solomon 2:8

SKUA

There are seven species of the skua seabird, which form the genus Stercorarius, which is the Latin word for 'dung'. This name was given to them through a slightly mistaken belief that they ate the excrement of other birds. It was only later observed that the skua dives at its victims and eats the food they sick up in fright, often even catching the food before it hits the ground.

SKULL

Part of the skull of St Andrew, together with his little finger, is kept in a special tomb in the Church of St Andrew at Patras in Greece.

BENTHAM, COPERNICUS, MOZART, OKAPI, SCHILLER, UNICORN

SKUNK

A skunk can spray the pungent liquid from its anal glands a distance of 4.5 metres (15 feet). Its smell can be detected a mile and a half away.

Skunks eat wasps and honeybees and are immune to snake venom. It is legal to kill a skunk at any time of year in Florida.

SLAVERY

The word 'slave' comes originally from a Greek word meaning the Slavic people, who were once captured by the Vikings and sold into slavery. Much earlier, however, the Code of Hammurabi, written around 1760 BC, mentioned slavery as an established institution.

Aristotle thought that some men are born to be slaves by nature.

In 1452, Pope Nicholas V gave the King of Portugal the right to take any Saracens or pagans into slavery.

Around 1800, it is estimated that the slave trade comprised 5 per cent of the British economy.

'Do not obtain your slaves from Britain,' Cicero advised, 'because they are so stupid and so utterly incapable of being taught, that they are not fit to form part of the household of Athens.'

Before the abolition of slavery, Brazil had more slaves than any other country in North or South America. With over 3 million slaves imported from Africa to work on Brazilian sugar plantations, some Brazilian slaves even had slaves of their own.

⚲ CENSORSHIP, HUDSON, MAURITANIA

SLEEP

Although Yuri Gagarin became the first man in space on 12 April 1961, the first person to sleep in space was the Russian cosmonaut Gherman Titov on 6 August of the same year.

In January 2013, the Board of Trustees of Iowa City Public Library began to debate the vexed question of whether visitors to the library should be banned from sleeping there. The director of the library stressed the importance of being sensitive to homeless people while also ensuring that the library's limited space is used for its intended purpose. She pointed out that not everyone caught sleeping at the library is homeless and any sleeping ban had to be applied equally to all. 'If it's a 20-year-old sitting there with a textbook in front of them and they're asleep, you treat them the same way as someone who is dressed in a less put-together kind of way, is slumped down in their chair and has their coat over their head,' she said. 'So if you have a rule, it has to be enforced for everybody, and that's only fair.'

⚲ ALASKA, BEDS, DIDGERIDOO, DOLPHIN, KOALA, WALRUS

SLIME

Sanditon is the only novel by Jane Austen that includes the word 'slime'. It is also her only work containing the word 'slimy', which occurs twice.

Blennophobia is an irrational fear of slime.

⚲ MAZE, SNAIL, WORM

SLIPPERS

In 1995, Britain's most successful examination taker, Francis Thomason, gave credit to his warm slippers when explaining how he had managed to pass 70 O-levels, 16 A-levels, one S-level and gain an Open University degree. 'It is important to have comfortable feet,' he said.

King John and *Taming of the Shrew* are the only Shakespeare plays that mention slippers.

'For every ailing foot, there is a slipper.'
Brazilian proverb

♀ *CINDERELLA*

● SLOANE, Sir Hans (1660–1753)

Hans Sloane was a physician who worked on slave plantations in Jamaica. After returning to England, he set up a private practice, through which he promoted inoculation against smallpox and the health benefits of drinking chocolate. Having been introduced to cocoa in the West Indies, his innovation was to drink it with milk and sugar and he is therefore praised as the inventor of milk chocolate.

He succeeded Sir Isaac Newton as President of the Royal Society, and left his private collection of more than 71,000 objects to the nation to form the basis for the British Museum. Both Sloane Square and Hans Crescent in London's Knightsbridge are named after him. He is said to have become enraged at the composer Handel for putting a buttered muffin down on one of his manuscripts.

♀ *BRITISH MUSEUM*

● SLOGAN

In September 2010, the Taiwanese government announced the winners of a competition to write a slogan encouraging people to have children in order to boost birth rates. The winner was 'Children – our best heirloom' followed by 'Happiness is very easy, baby one, two, three' and 'It's good to have a child'. In 2009, the number of babies born in Taiwan was 191,310, which was a rate of 8.29 births per 1,000 people compared with a global average of over 20. The number of births rose to about 229,480 in 2012 but had dropped to 165,250 in 2020,

suggesting that the slogans did not have a lasting effect.

♀ *HORSERADISH, REVOLVING DOORS, RYDER CUP, SECOND WORLD WAR*

● SLOTH

The maximum ground speed of a sloth is about 2 metres (6.5 feet) a minute, which works out at 1.6 kilometres (1 mile) in about nine hours. But a sloth can swim twice as fast as it can run – 1.6 kilometres (1 mile) in four hours. A sloth may spend about 20 hours a day motionless, though it is unclear how much of this time it is asleep. One recent study on sloths in the wild reported that they sleep for only 10 hours a day.

The main diet of a sloth is leaves, from which it extracts very little energy, very slowly. A sloth takes a month to digest a meal, and only defecates and urinates once a week. It does this by leaving its usual place on the branch of a tree and climbing down to the ground to deposit its waste products, always in the same place. Up to two-thirds of the body weight of a fully fed sloth may consist of the food in its stomach.

Whereas almost all other mammals have seven cervical vertebrae (neck bones), the two-toed sloth has six and the three-toed sloth has nine.

The greenish appearance of a sloth's coat is created by algae living in its fur. Moths may also live in a sloth's fur, and 120 moths were once counted in the fur of a single sloth.

The world's only sloth orphanage is in Costa Rica. Its sick quarters are called the 'slothpital'.

In 1832, the US naturalist Richard Harlan showed great sensitivity when writing *Observations on the Anatomy of the Sloth*. After beginning one paragraph with the words 'The reproductive organs of this animal are singularly anomalous,' he then protected any easily offended readers by continuing in Latin in which he gave many details, including the observation that the female sloth has a clitoris.

The eighth World Correspondence Chess Championship took five years to finish and ran from 1975 to 1980. The winner of this slow event was a Dane named Jørn Sloth.

⚲ *BEAR, COSTA RICA, HIPPOPOTAMUS*

SLOVENIA

The Slatina spring in Slovenia is alleged to have been discovered by the mythological winged horse Pegasus. Slovenia is the only country with 'love' in its name. By coincidence, the name of its capital, Ljubljana, is thought to derive from the Slavic prefix *ljub-*, meaning love or like.

⚲ *FLUTE, HITLER!*

SLUG

Slugs have thousands of tiny teeth. Their two eyes, which are at the end of retractable tentacles, operate independently so they can keep an eye on two moving objects simultaneously. Slugs eat 36,000 tonnes of potatoes each year in Britain.

Slugs are hermaphrodites. Vitamin B stunts their growth, shortens their lives, and inclines them towards cannibalism.

The record speed for a slug is 0.32 km/h (8.9 centimetres per second). A slug can smell a mushroom up to 2 metres (6.5 feet) away. At the above record speed, it can cover that distance in just under 23 seconds.

The words 'slug' and 'slugs' do not appear in the King James Bible, but six verses in Proverbs refer to 'sluggards'.

Lazy people have been called slugs since the 15th century; the word was only applied to slimy gastropods some

300 years later. Shakespeare, in *Romeo and Juliet*, has the first recorded use of the insult 'slug-a-bed'.

⚲ *COFFEE, DNA, HEDGEHOG, POTATO*

SMARTIES

After making a product called 'Chocolate Beans' for over 50 years, Rowntree's of York changed the name to 'Smarties Chocolate Beans' in 1937. They then dropped the words 'Chocolate Beans' in 1977 when trading standards officers said the use of the word 'beans' was misleading.

In 1988, the brown Smartie was replaced by a blue Smartie, but the blue Smartie was dropped in the UK in 2006 when the company declared a ban on artificial colourings. Blue came back in 2008, when a natural colouring agent was found.

⚲ *SEAWEED*

SMELL

According to a survey in 2015, the top five favourite smells in the UK are: 1. Freshly baked bread; 2. Frying bacon; 3. Cut grass; 4. Coffee; 5. Baking cakes.

The five most disliked household odours were found to be: 1. Refuse bins; 2. Drains; 3. Body odour; 4. Sewage; 5. Vomit.

⚲ *BABIES, LEMUR, MOLE, NOSTRIL, ORANGE, SCENT, SLUG*

SMILING

The advice that smiling is to be preferred to frowning because 'it takes more muscles to frown than to smile' is dubious. A genuine (technically known as 'zygomatic') smile uses the following muscles: zygomaticus major, zygomaticus minor, orbicularis oculi, levator labii superioris, levator anguli oris, risorius. There is one of each of these on each side of the face, giving a total of 12 muscles. To frown, you need the orbicularis oculi, platysma, depressor anguli oris and corrugator supercilii, of which there is again one on each side of the face, plus the procerus, orbicularis oris and mentalis, which are all single muscles, giving a total of 11.

However, the smiling muscles may well be better exercised for most people than the frowning ones, so using them may take less energy.

The insincere smile is the most energy-efficient and can be accomplished with the use of only the two *risorius* muscles.

The word for someone who never smiles is 'agelast' or 'agelastic'.

Plato was deeply suspicious of laughter, which he saw as often malicious or otherwise morally harmful, but he had no strong objections to smiling.

⚲ *ALBANIA, STATUE, TENNIS*

⬤ SMOKING

No Smoking Day is held on the second Wednesday in March each year. Appropriately enough, the first was on Ash Wednesday in 1984.

Tobacco and hallucinogenic drugs have been smoked in the Americas since at least 5000 BC.

The Aztec goddess Cihuacoatl was said to have had a body consisting of tobacco.

Nicotine is named after the Frenchman Jean Nicot who introduced tobacco to France in 1660. Walter Raleigh brought tobacco from Virginia to England on 27 July 1586, though the French and Spanish had brought it there when he was a child.

The word 'cigar' first appeared in English in 1735 and 'cigarette' in 1842.

Pipes for smoking tobacco were first mentioned in English by Thomas Hariot in 1588.

An estimated 120,000 people die each year in the UK from diseases caused by smoking.

In the UK, 14.1 per cent of adults smoke cigarettes (2019 figures). That adds up to about 6.9 million smokers. The proportion of smokers has dropped from 27 per cent in 1993.

In January 2001, the University of Tokyo introduced a service for people who had made a New Year's Resolution to give up smoking: when the urge to light up became too strong, they could press a button on their mobile phone and receive a message encouraging them not to give up giving up. The price of the new service was designed to be the same as the cost of a packet of cigarettes.

'Giving up smoking is the easiest thing in the world. I know because I've done it thousands of times.' Mark Twain

⚲ *CARUSO, CHIMPANZEE, JAMES I, PIPES, SUNGLASSES, TURKMENISTAN*

⬤ SMURFS

When Sony Pictures filmed a Smurf movie in the village of Juzcar in Andalucia, they used around 1,000 gallons of paint to turn all the houses blue. They promised that, at the end of filming, they would repaint all the houses back to their original white, but the townsfolk, in a referendum in 2011, voted to keep them blue as they had boosted tourism to the village from 300 a year to about 80,000. 'Thanks to being painted blue we are known throughout the world,' Mayor David Fernandez said.

● SNAIL

Historically, snails have had a number of surprising medical uses. Oribasius, a 5th-century physician from Byzantium, used to treat wounds with an ointment made from crushed snails and flour. If he ran out of snails, he used earthworms instead. In the 19th century, a treatment for tuberculosis involved snail-slime and sugar, while research in Italy in 2018 confirmed that snail-slime can speed up the healing of skin wounds.

Bristol glassblowers, in the years before the First World War, used to eat snails to improve their lung power. By contrast, snail-hunting is illegal in the Swiss canton of Valais.

In 1996, a Nottingham professor discovered that sexual activity among tropical snails could be increased by feeding them porridge.

Thanks to the sticky carpet they exude, snails can crawl along the edge of a razor blade without injuring themselves. Sadly, they cannot crawl fast enough to escape the French, who eat 40,000 tonnes of snails every year.

The World Snail Racing Championship takes place annually at the Cricket Field in Congham, Norfolk. The world record for the 33-centimetre (13-inch) course was set by a snail called Archie who won in 1995 in a time of two minutes. L'Escargot (which is French for 'the snail') won the Grand National in 1975.

A snail can have up to 25,600 teeth. The giant African land snail can grow to a size of 39 centimetres (15.4 inches) from head to tail.

⚲ *COFFEE, HEDGEHOG, PURPLE, RICE, TOBACCO*

● SNAKE

In March 2006, a Malaysian set a world record by kissing a poisonous snake 51 times in three minutes. In the same year another snake-kissing record was set by a Thai snake-charmer named Khum Chaibuddee who kissed 19 different cobras. According to one report of this feat, 'The kisses were full-lipped, but otherwise chaste, with no tongues involved.'

The mortality rate if bitten by a Black Mamba snake is over 95 per cent.

⚲ *AUSTRALIA, GOLD, HEADS, IRELAND, KIDNEY, KOMODO, PYTHON*

● SNIFFING

The makers of the Dario glucose monitoring meter (mydario.co.uk) have released the amazing story of Katie Gregson, 13, who has Type 1 diabetes and has trained her sheepdog Pip to sniff out changes in her blood sugar.

Research in 2014 put humans in 13th place in a list of animals with the most genes for smelling. Surprisingly, the African elephant came top of the list, followed by rats and opossums, but bears have a third of their brains devoted to smelling, and sharks have two-thirds. A shark can detect a single drop of blood in the water from about 1.6 kilometres (1 mile) away.

Research has shown that dogs can be trained to sniff out cancer or Covid-19, and rats can sniff tuberculosis. Teams of rats have been used in Angola, Mozambique, Cambodia, Thailand, Vietnam and Laos to sniff out landmines and ammunition.

In 2015, expert British cheese-sniffer Nigel Pooley had his nose insured for £5 million.

In 2009, South Korea said it was deploying the 'world's first cloned sniffer dogs' to check for drugs at its main airport and border crossings. Wasps and bees (known as 'bomblebees') have also been trained to detect plastic explosives.

♀ *ADRENALINE*

● SNOOKER

Under the official rules of snooker, the referee shall, if a player is colour blind, tell him the colour of a ball if requested.

A score of more than 147 can be made in a snooker frame only if a player is snookered after a foul shot with all the balls on the table. The player may then take any ball as a red, then continue as usual. This led to the highest recorded break in competition of 151 for Wally West in a club match in Hounslow. The highest ever break in a professional competition was 148 for Jamie Burnett of Scotland in a UK championship qualifier in 2004.

♀ *LOTTERIES, TWENTY-TWO*

● SNORING

Around a quarter of all people in the UK are believed to snore habitually and about 45 per cent snore sometimes.

Over 2,000 devices and appliances to help prevent snoring are registered at the European Patent Office with the word 'snoring' in their title. A typically ingenious anti-snoring patent was the one taken out in 1955 consisting of a hinged board beneath the pillow which would shake the sleeper awake when a microphone positioned above his nose detected snoring noises.

There is also an abundance of folk remedies for snoring. One claims that the best way to stop it is to pinch the snorer's big toe, while another theory recommends hanging a gold coin around your neck. This method is said to work on dogs, too.

In Massachusetts, snoring is prohibited unless all bedroom windows are closed and securely locked. This apparently is an old law which has never been repealed.

The noise of a really rasping snore can register 69 decibels – a pneumatic drill is 70–90 decibels.

According to Mark Twain (in *Tom Sawyer Abroad*, 1894): 'There ain't no way to find out why a snorer can't hear himself snore.'

♀ *DIDGERIDOO, DUVET, TENNIS*

● SNOW

According to Geoffrey Pullum's highly entertaining paper 'The Great Eskimo Vocabulary Hoax' published in 1989, the misleading story about Eskimo snow began in 1911 when the German/American anthropologist Franz Boas cited four Inuit (Eskimo) words for different types of snow. Snow, he argued, is important to Eskimos, so they develop a wide range words for different conditions. This topic was taken up in 1940 by the amateur linguist Benjamin Lee Whorf, who was a fire prevention officer in Connecticut and who had probably never met an Eskimo. Writing in a popular science journal, he borrowed Boas's example but upped his four to seven different types of snow, for which he asserted that Eskimos had different words, though he did not say what those words were. This article was picked up in all sorts of places, and the Eskimo verbal snowmobile gathered speed.

Whorf's claim of seven Eskimo snow words was outbid in a 1984 trivia encyclopedia, where the number was asserted to be nine. Not to be outbid, a *New York Times* editorial in the same year gave the number as 100, which was confidently increased to 200 in a

Cleveland weather forecast.

So how many Eskimo words for 'snow' are there? As so often with such questions, it all depends what you mean by 'word'. Are 'snow', 'snowman', 'snowflake' and 'snowdrift' four words, or just four versions of the same word 'snow'? And what do we mean by 'Eskimo' anyway? There are, after all, a number of different Inuit dialects, each of which may have its own snow vocabulary.

Pullum, however, offers a good piece of advice to anyone subjected to ill-informed assertions regarding Eskimo snow. After mentioning his own behaviour of cringing and creeping away when such things happen, he says: 'Don't be a coward like me. Stand up and tell the speaker this: C.W. Schultz-Lorentzen's *Dictionary of the West Greenlandic Eskimo Language* (1927) gives just two possibly relevant roots: *qanik*, meaning "snow in the air" or "snowflake"; and *aput*, meaning "snow on the ground". Then add that you would be interested to know if the speaker can cite any more.'

Snowballs, however, appear to be easier to count than snow words. After a massive snowstorm over Britain on 2 February 2009, it was reported that enough snow fell for everyone in the country to make 251,800 snowballs.

♀ *BUTTOCKS, CHRISTMAS, CUBA, ECUADOR, KIPLING, YETI*

SNOW WHITE

In the original tale of *Snow White and the Seven Dwarfs*, as it appeared in the collection by the brothers Grimm, the dwarfs had no names. They were first given names in a 1912 Broadway play of *Snow White and the Seven Dwarfs* written and produced by Winthrop

Ames, who called them Blick, Flick, Glick, Snick, Plick, Which and Quee. When Walt Disney made his animated film of the story in 1937, his names for the dwarfs were selected from a list of over 50. The names that did not make it were as follows: Silly, Sappy, Scrappy, Snappy, Snoopy, Goopy, Gloomy, Gaspy, Gabby, Blabby, Flabby, Crabby, Cranky, Lazy, Dizzy, Dippy, Dumpy, Dirty, Deafy, Daffy, Doleful, Woeful, Wistful, Soulful, Helpful, Awful, Graceful, Tearful, Tubby, Weepy, Wheezy, Sneezy-Wheezy, Sniffy, Puffy, Stuffy, Strutty, Shorty, Shifty, Thrifty, Nifty, Neurtsy, Hotsy, Hungry, Hickey, Hoppy, Jumpy, Jaunty, Chesty, Busy, Burpy, Baldy, Biggy-Wiggy, Biggo-Ego.

♀ *DWARF, STORIES, TURING, WOLVERHAMPTON*

SNOWFLAKE

In 1951, the International Commission on Snow and Ice listed seven types of snowflake: plates, stellar crystals, columns, needles, spatial dendrites, capped columns and irregular. A more detailed classification by C.W. Lee and C. Magono in 1966 listed 80 different snow-crystal types.

The word 'snow' dates back to the 9th century, but 'snowball' arrived in 1400, 'snowflake' in 1734, and 'snowman' only in 1827.

The use of the word 'snowflake' as a derogatory term mocking a person characterised as overly sensitive or easily offended is dated back to 1983 by the *Oxford English Dictionary*, originally alluding to the notion that no two snowflakes are identical, but later used to refer to their pristine or fragile condition.

♀ *CHRISTMAS, PHOTOGRAPHY, POTATO, SNOW*

SOAP OPERAS

The Christmas 1997 issue of the *British Medical Journal* carried a warning to characters in soap operas: they had a considerably higher mortality rate than almost any professional group. Furthermore, they were three times more likely than the average person to die violently. 'Death Rates of Characters in Soap Operas on British Television: is a Government Health Warning Required?' by Tim Crayford, Richard Hooper and Sarah Evans was, as its authors emphasised, 'a hard-hitting analysis of mortality in British television soap operas'. According to their findings, a character under 30 years of age in *Coronation Street*, for example, had a 10 per cent chance of dying within five years of being introduced into the series. The figure for the general population is 0.3 per cent. Indeed, being a character in *Coronation Street* was more hazardous than being an oil-rig diver or bomb-disposal expert. Only Formula 1 drivers had a greater chance of dying, and even they were better off than *EastEnders* characters. 'Characters in these serials,' the writers conclude, 'would be advised to wear good protective clothing ... and to receive regular counselling for the psychological impact of living in an environment akin to a war zone.'

SOCIALISM

In 1961, the Russian premier Nikita Khrushchev declared rubber wellington boots to be socialist footwear, while leather wellingtons were the capitalist style. Stalin wore leather ones.

 EDUCATION

SOCKS

In January 2013, the Russian army started to wear socks for the first time.

Since the 17th century, Russian soldiers had wrapped their feet in squares of cloth – cotton in summer, flannel in winter – called *portyanki*. These had definite advantages: they were easier to make than socks, and quicker to wash, dry and mend. Under army regulations, they were changed once a week and boiled clean.

Announcing the end of *portyanki*, the Russian Defence Minister ordered that by the end of 2013, 'we need to finally, fully reject this concept in our armed forces'.

The Russian for 'sock' is *nosok* (носок).

 ALCHEMY, EINSTEIN, LAUGHFEST, NUNS, SUPERSTITION, TROUSERS

SOLSTICE

The winter solstice is the shortest day of the year between sunrise and sunset. It is also the day when the Sun, at its highest point, is lower than on any other day of the year. Places on the Arctic Circle see the Sun on the horizon at midday on the winter solstice.

In Greek mythology, the gods and goddesses met on the days of the solstices.

The face of Stonehenge's Great Trilithon faces the rising Sun on the day of the winter solstice.

The winter solstice is celebrated in Brighton in a ceremony called Burning of the Clocks. It was cancelled in 2009 in the 'interests of public safety' because melting snow had made the streets slippery.

In the Middle Ages, fires were lit on the summer solstice to enhance the Sun's power. These were the original bonfires, or 'bone-fires', as animal bones were used for fuel.

According to an old Swedish

superstition, the night of the summer solstice was auspicious to female lovers, who were advised to pick seven wild flowers, walk home backwards and leave them under their pillows to dream of their future husbands.

According to an old Celtic superstition, when you wake up on the day of the summer solstice, you should rotate three times clockwise before rising, for good luck.

GROUNDHOG DAY

SOMALIA

Somalia has the longest coastline of any country in mainland Africa. In Somalia, there are about 200 times as many camels as cars.

CAMEL, CENTRAL AFRICAN REPUBLIC, NIGER, NIGERIA

SONGS

According to the American Society of Composers, Authors and Publishers, the Top 5 most performed songs of the 20th century were: 1. 'Happy Birthday'; 2. 'Tea For Two'; 3. 'Moon River'; 4. 'Over The Rainbow'; 5. 'White Christmas'.

Blue was found to be the most musical colour, with 'Blue Moon' in 8th place and 'Rhapsody In Blue' in 9th.

BOWERBIRD, BRUSSELS, EUROVISION SONG CONTEST, FUNERALS, NEW YORK

SOUP

In 2020, the global soup market was worth $17 billion, of which 50 per cent was spent on tinned soups. In the UK, the fresh soup market is worth £137 million a year and is increasing by about £6 million every year.

Cream of tomato was the first Heinz soup when it was launched in 1910. Chicken, mulligatawny, Scotch broth, beef broth and others quickly followed.

Heinz makes over 32 million tins of cream of tomato soup a year and uses enough tomatoes to fill an Olympic size swimming pool every day to produce all its tomato-based products.

HORSE, PORK, SEAL, SINGAPORE, SWAT, WEDDING

SOUTH AFRICA

There are 11 official languages in South Africa: Afrikaans, English, Ndebele, Pedi, Sotho, Swazi, Tsonga, Tswana, Venda, Xhosa and Zulu. No other country has as many.

According to the *CIA World Factbook*, there are 96,972,500 mobile phone subscriptions in South Africa, which works out at 1.66 per person.

There are 407 airports in South Africa, of which 130 have paved runways.

Every year, thanks to movement of the Earth's tectonic plates, South Africa moves about 5 centimetres (2 inches) further away from South America.

In 2020, there were 235 prisons in South Africa with an official capacity of 118,572 prisoners, though the total number of inmates was 147,922.

ELEPHANT, GOLD, HIPPOPOTAMUS, OSTRICH, PIZZA, ROBBERY

SOUTH DAKOTA

The capital of South Dakota is Pierre. It is the only US state capital whose name has no letters in common with the name of the state.

The state bird of South Dakota is the ring-necked pheasant, and the state insect is the honeybee.

POKER, POTATO

SOUTH KOREA

The South Korean delicacy known as *poshintang* (literally: 'body preservation stew') is considered very good for your health. The main ingredient is dog meat.

The first woman to appear on a South Korean banknote was Shin Saim-dang, whose face was shown on the 50,000 won (about £30) note that appeared in 2009. Shin Saim-dang was an artist who died in 1551.

There are 501 heliports in South Korea. This places it in 6th place on a list of countries with most heliports. Only the USA, Russia, India, the United Arab Emirates and Brazil have more.

CLONE, HUMAN RIGHTS, KARAOKE, MATCH-MAKING, SNIFFING, YOGURT

SOUTH POLE

In December 1911, the Norwegian explorer Roald Amundsen led his team of five to become the first people to reach the South Pole. Amundsen's diary entry for the day read simply: 'So we arrived and were able to plant our flag at the geographical South Pole. God be thanked!'

Robert Falcon Scott's team reached the South Pole 33 or 34 days later, realising only when they arrived that Amundsen had beaten them to it.

The average temperature at the South Pole is -50°C (-58°F). At the North Pole it is -18°C (-10.4°F).

Because of wobbles in the Earth's rotation, the location of the South Pole moves about 33 feet a year.

In October 2020, the geographic South Pole was about 2,858 kilometres (1,776 miles) from the Magnetic South Pole, whose location moves with the Earth's magnetic field.

Until 1956, only 17 men had visited the South Pole. The first women there were an all-female team led by US geologist Lois Jones in 1969.

Since the Amundsen–Scott station was built in 1957, 1,633 people have spent all winter at the Pole.

ANTARCTICA, DOG, JANUARY, NORTH POLE

SOVIET UNION

The word 'Soviet' in 'Soviet Union' is Russian for 'Council' and came from a verb meaning 'to give advice'. The Soviet Union was seen as a union of the various regional councils in the country.

A Moscow restaurant called 'Anti-Soviet' changed its name in 2009 under pressure from local authorities who said it offended Russia's older generation. The 'Anti-Sovetskaya' was renamed 'Sovetskaya'.

AFGHANISTAN, ESTONIA, LITHUANIA, UKRAINE

SPA

The word 'spa' for a health resort with hot or cold springs comes from the town of Spa in Belgium, where the supposed health-giving properties of the waters were known in ancient Roman times.

The Czech spa of Chodova Plana is best known today for the 'Original Beer Spa' run by its brewery. Guests can soak in a mix of dark lager/mineral water/hops and other herbs blended in copper tubs. The beer soak spa treatment is said to have medicinal benefits. Iceland, Austria, Japan, Hungary and the United States have since copied the idea and opened their own beer spas.

MANCHESTER UNITED, TENNIS

SPACE FLIGHT

The first animals to be sent into space were fruit flies in 1947. A monkey known as Albert II became the first mammal to go into space on a V2 rocket launched by the US in 1949.

More dogs. monkeys and mice went into space before the first manned flight took place in 1961. The first tortoise in space was in 1968.

In 1973, two spiders named Arabella and Anita on Skylab became the first to spin webs in space. They were part of an experiment to test the effect of zero gravity on a spider's web-building ability.

♀ *SPACECRAFT*

● SPACECRAFT

The first docking of two spacecraft happened on 16 March 1966 when the US Gemini 8 craft docked with an unmanned target vehicle. The commander of Gemini 8 on that occasion was Neil Armstrong.

One form of docking involves two craft of different designs known as male and female. Two ships of the same gender cannot dock. Another form, known as androgynous, involves the docking of two ships of identical design.

The first recorded use of the word 'spacecraft' was in 1929. 'Spaceship' was first used in 1880. The term 'flying saucer' was coined in 1947; 'UFO' (Unidentified Flying Object) followed in 1953.

In 1903, the Russian mathematician Konstantin Tsiolkovsky published a paper showing that liquid fuels and multi-stage rockets could attain lift-off for a spacecraft. His formulae are still in use.

While in orbit, spacecraft travel around Earth at a speed of about 28,164 km/h (17,500 mph).

The first Space Shuttle was launched on 12 April 1981, the 20th anniversary of the very first manned space flight by Yuri Gagarin. From 1981 to 2011, the five US Space Shuttle craft flew half a billion miles on their 135 flights. The Space Shuttle programme then ended.

♀ *OUTER SPACE*

● SPAGHETTI

According to a survey by Hotpoint in 2010, spaghetti bolognaise is the most frequently home-cooked meal in the UK. The Top 10 home-cooked meals were found to be as follows: 1. Spaghetti bolognaise; 2. Roast dinner; 3. Indian/curry; 4. Chinese/stir-fry; 5. Lasagne; 6. Mexican wraps/fajitas; 7. Jacket potato; 8. Shepherd's pie; 9. Sausage and mash; 10. Chilli.

♀ *CURRY*

● SPAIN

Spain produces by far the most olive oil of any country. The next three biggest olive oil producers are Portugal, Tunisia and Greece, but Spain produces more than all three combined.

There are 47 UNESCO World Heritage sites in Spain. Only Italy, China and Germany have more.

Spanish children do not believe in the tooth fairy. Instead, they leave shed teeth under their pillows to be collected and paid for by a magical mouse called Ratoncito Pérez.

In 1995, the Spanish village of Bérchules in Granada celebrated the New Year on 5 August. The village had been hit by a power cut lasting 13 hours on the previous 31 December and had had to cancel their festivities. So they rescheduled them for 5 August, when the church bells sounded 12 times at noon to ring in the New Year, in a very un-Christmassy temperature of 39°C (102.2°F). Villagers then danced around Christmas trees while artificial snow made of white mousse fell around them.

♀ *ARTICHOKE, CHOCOLATE, HEALTH, MARIJUANA*

SPEARS, Britney (b. 1981)

As we have already mentioned, 'Britney Spears' is an anagram of 'Presbyterians'. 'Britney Jean Spears', which is her full name, is an anagram of 'Japanese berry tins'.

♀ FIZZY DRINKS, WITCHCRAFT

SPECTACLES

Spectacles to improve the wearer's sight date back to the 13th century in Italy when the frames were made of wood or leather. Until 1902, however, soldiers in the British army were not permitted to wear spectacles off duty.

♀ EARS, GLASSES

SPEECH

A world record for the longest speech was set by Frenchman Lluis Colet in 2009, who talked non-stop for 124 hours about Spanish painter Salvador Dali, Catalan culture and other topics. The 62-year-old local government worker spoke non-stop for over five straight days to set the record in Perpignan. The previous record was held by an Indian who gave a 120-hour speech.

♀ DREAM, GOOGLE, KENNEDY, LICENCE PLATES, MOON

SPEED LIMIT

Between 1865 and 1896, the speed limit for a steam-driven car in the UK was 2 mph. In 1896, the speed limit was increased to 14 mph and increased again by the Motor Car Act 1903 to 20 mph. This limit became increasingly ignored and it was abolished in 1930. Six years later, the 1936 Road Traffic Act introduced a 30 mph limit in built-up areas, which were defined as places having street lamps no more than 183 metres (200 yards) apart.

♀ MOTORING

SPELLING

The correct spelling of Lake Chargoggagoggmanchauggagoggchaubunagungamaugg, the place with the longest name in the US, was discovered only in 2009 after signs to the lake in Webster, Massachusetts, had for years carried a misplaced 'o' instead of a 'u' at letter 20, and an 'h' at letter 38 which should be an 'n'. When a local newspaper unearthed the correct spelling, it was announced that the signs would be changed.

According to a survey in 2020, the word most commonly misspelled in English is 'separate', well ahead of 'questionnaire', 'potato' and 'diarrhoea'. An earlier survey in 2009, however, listed the top three words most frequently misspelled as 'definitely', 'sacrilegious' and 'indict'. The methodology was unclear for both polls, but the words suggest that the first was based only on a count of the number of misspellings, while the second also took into account the times the words were spelled correctly, so was based on the proportion of times people got it wrong.

♀ AARDVARK, BURNS, GOOGLE, POTATO, PRESLEY, ST SWITHUN

SPERM

The first person to see human sperm was Antonie van Leeuwenhoek who, after making love to his wife, collected a sample of them from her and viewed them through his microscope. He wrote about the tiny 'animalcules' he saw in a letter to the Royal Society in London in November 1677 entitled 'de Natis e semine genital Animalculis'.

Healthy fertile males produce 86 million sperm cells each day, which is about 1,000 every second.

♀ BUSH-CRICKET, FRUIT FLY, GUPPY, PREGNANCY, SADISM, SQUID

SPIDER

The Greek poet Ovid wrote of a woman named Arachne who boasted she could spin better than the goddess Athena, which is why Athena turned her into a spider and spiders are called arachnids.

Each acre of land in Britain contains approximately 2 million spiders, which adds up to about 120,000 billion spiders in Britain alone. The total weight of insects eaten each year by spiders has been estimated to be greater than the weight of all the humans on earth.

The harvestman spider may distract predators by detaching one of its own legs. The sacrificed limb twitches to keep the predator interested, while its former owner scuttles away on the other seven.

In 1994, Edward Doughney patented a latex ladder to enable spiders to climb out of baths.

In 1996, it was reported that US army trials showed that silk from the golden orb weaver spider is twice as strong as the current US army body armour, Kevlar. This discovery led to a decade-long project to see if spider genes could be transferred to goats in order to produce goat milk containing the protein that gives spider thread its strength. Sadly, a sticky milk plasma was the best ever produced from a transgenic spider-goat.

A spider's web consists of thick threads forming the radii and a thin spiral weaving them together. Only the spiral threads are sticky. The spider walks on the radii to eat flies caught in the web. That is why it doesn't get stuck itself.

The smallest spider is a mygalomorph spider from Borneo. It is no bigger than a pinhead. The Goliath bird-eating spider is the world's biggest, reaching up to 27.9 centimetres (11 inches) across. When threatened, a Goliath spider makes a hissing sound by rubbing its legs together.

'The spider taketh hold with her hands, and is in kings' palaces.' Proverbs 30 (This is the only mention of spiders in the King James Bible.)

♀ BOWIE, LUTON, MANDELA, MEDICINE, SADISM, SPACE FLIGHT

SPIRITUALISM

In 1942 the American National Association of Spiritualists patriotically resolved that, while the Second World War continued, no medium should ask the spirit of a departed serviceman any question whose answer might furnish military information to any enemy agents who could be in the audience.

♀ EXORCISM

SPITTING

The town of Eau Claire in Michigan is known as the Cherry Pip Spitting Capital of the world. At the inaugural cricket-spitting contest in the town of Marshfield, Wisconsin, in 2009, Brian Johnsrud spat a dead cricket 7 metres (22 feet 8 inches). His son Jared Johnsrud then managed 3.1 metres (10 feet 5 inches) to win the 9–11 age division. Mr Johnsrud said the key was to pick the biggest insect and take a deep breath before putting it in your mouth to avoid swallowing it.

A 2007 survey in Beijing showed that the city is making progress, with only 2.5 per cent of people spitting in public, down from 4.9 per cent in 2006.

♀ BUS DRIVER, CHINA, LLAMA, SHOES, WILLIAM IV

● SPONTANEOUS COMBUSTION

In September 2011, a coroner in Ireland investigating a case in which pensioner Murdo Macleod was found burned to death at his home reported: 'This fire was thoroughly investigated and I'm left with the conclusion that this fits into the category of spontaneous human combustion, for which there is no adequate explanation.'

Spontaneous Human Combustion (SHC) first caught the imagination in 1725 when a French woman called Nicole Millet was found burned to death in an unburned chair. Her husband was accused of murder, but a young surgeon, Nicholas le Cat, convinced the court that her death had been caused by SHC.

In 1763, French author Jonas Dupont published a 25-page book *De Incendiis Corporis Humani Spontaneis*, in which he collected together all reports of SHC in history.

In *Bleak House*, Charles Dickens describes vividly the death of rag-and-bone dealer Mr Krook by SHC, and strongly defended himself against critics who said that such things do not happen.

One scientific theory is based on the 'wick effect', through which subcutaneous fat is released into the clothing, making it act like a wick in a burning candle. An initial flame could cause a split in the skin through which the fat is released, yet no convincing explanation has ever been offered of what would cause that initial flame.

In the case of Murdo Macleod, the body was found next to a burning fire, yet the coroner appeared to rule out any suggestion that the fire had ignited the body.

● SPOON

One of the books shortlisted for the 2010 Diagram Prize for oddly titled publications was *Collectible Spoons of the Third Reich* by James A. Yannes. It is considered to be the definitive work for Nazi spoon hunters. This was not the only Diagram Prize nomination featuring spoons, for in 2006, one of the favourites for the prize was Robert Chenciner's *Tattooed Mountain Women and Spoon Boxes of Daghestan*. Sadly, and in the opinion of many unjustly, it lost out to *The Stray Shopping Carts of Eastern North America: A Guide to Field Identification*.

At the age of 17, while still at school, Chenciner had also written a treatise on 'Swedish Padlock Keyhole Covers' which won him a scholarship to Cambridge. He died in November 2021, which was a great loss to the study of tattooed mountain women, spoon boxes, Daghestan and Swedish padlocks.

The record for balancing spoons on one's own body is held by Abolfazl Saber Mokhtari, 50, of Iran, who balanced 85 spoons in various locations on his body. He said the secret to his ability was focus but that he had been developing his spoon-balancing talent since he was a child.

♀ *BOWERBIRD, PARAPSYCHOLOGY, PEAS*

● SPORT

On 11 June 1906, Britain's first woman stunt parachutist, 21-year-old Elizabeth Mary 'Lily' Cove, fell to her death from a gas-filled balloon at a gala event in Haworth near Bradford. Her death led to a strong backlash against women's sports, with questions even being asked in the House of Commons about a possible ban.

Concern spread to America also, where, for example, Dr Dudley Sargent,

Physical Director at Harvard University attacked the new trend for hockey, lacrosse and netball in women's colleges and cautioned women against playing contact sports: 'Let women rather confine herself to the lighter and more graceful forms of gymnastics and athletics, and make herself supreme along these lines as she has already done in aesthetic dancing. Let her know enough about the rougher sports to be the sympathetic admirer of men and boys in their efforts to be strong, vigorous, and heroic.'

♀ ALBANIA, FOOTBALL, HAMSTER, TUG-OF-WAR, URINATION, YAK

SPORTS SONGS

In September 2010, the Archbishop of Melbourne banned sports songs and popular tunes from funerals after a study found the signature song for Australian Rules Football team Collingwood was one of the top requests at Melbourne funerals. The Archbishop said that sports songs were not appropriate for a service which emphasises the solemn nature of death and is not designed as a celebration of the deceased's life. Nursery rhymes and sentimental secular songs were also banned as 'inappropriate because these may intensify grief'.

SPRINTING

According to research published in 2008, sprinters in lanes nearest the starting pistol have an advantage over those in lanes further out, even when the starting gun is simultaneously broadcast to all athletes through loud-speakers behind their starting blocks.

Research at the 2004 Olympics showed that the average reaction time in lane one was 160 milliseconds, compared with 171 milliseconds in

lane two. Oddly, lane seven of the eight was slowest with a reaction time of 185 milliseconds.

♀ FINGER LENGTH, OLYMPIC GAMES, SEX TEST

SPYING

In May 2010, a pigeon was reported to be under armed guard in India under suspicion of having been on a spying mission for Pakistan. The pigeon had a ring around its foot and a Pakistani phone number and address stamped on its body in red ink. A police spokesman said they suspected that the pigeon had flown from Pakistan with a message, although no trace of a note was found.

♀ CROSSWORD, CURTIS, D'EON, TROJAN HORSE

SQUID

At 38 centimetres (15 inches) in diameter, the eyes of giant squid are the largest on Earth.

According to a paper in the *Journal of Molluscan Studies* in 2010, the erect penis of a giant squid can be as long as its entire body. This was discovered while examining a giant squid caught during a deep-water research cruise, which surprised researchers by having an erection during the examination. This finding threw light on the mystery of how giant squid mate. All cephalopods have problems mating, as the male's mating organ is enclosed within the large hood, known as a mantle, through which water is forcibly passed for propulsion. Shallow water cephalopods have evolved a special limb to act as a sperm carrier to inseminate females. Giant squid, however, do not have this arm but inject sperm directly into the female, though how they do it is still a mystery as giant squid mating has never been observed. The penis of a male giant squid, however, may be around 2 metres (7 feet) long. 'Obviously a strongly elongated penis is the solution,' said Dr Arkhipin, leader of the research team.

♀ *EYE, FALKLAND ISLANDS, JAPAN, OCTOPUS, PUPPETRY*

⬤ SQUIRREL

Of the 265 species of squirrel, 44 are 'flying squirrels', which glide through the air using a membrane that stretches from fingers to ankles.

In 1946, when wartime shortages were still affecting British food supplies, the UK Food Ministry issued a recipe for squirrel pie and another recipe for squirrel tail soup.

Squirrels twitch their tails to alert other squirrels to possible danger.

The African pygmy squirrel is only 10 centimetres (4 inches) long; the Indian giant squirrel may reach a length of 0.9 metres (3 feet).

In the winter, squirrels can smell food buried under a foot of snow.

A squirrel's nest is called a drey (or dray). A group of squirrels is a scurry.

Squirrels do not recognise themselves in mirrors and are liable to attack the image.

Squirrels can rotate their ankles 180 degrees. This is how they can go head-first down trees.

Research in 2009 showed that squirrels are very good at learning from others, particularly in regard to methods of stealing food.

According to research published in September 2010, male squirrels in Namibia masturbate as a form of 'genital grooming', which may have a cleansing effect and reduce the chance of sexually transmitted infection.

♀ *ALE, CURRY, DOG*

⬤ SRI LANKA

In ancient times, the island of Sri Lanka was known to the Arabs as 'Serendib' or 'Serendip', which means, according to whom you read, 'Island of rubies' or 'Island where lions live'. In the period of British rule from 1815 to 1948, the island was known as Ceylon. From 1948 to 1972, Ceylon was a dominion within the British Commonwealth. Its name was changed to Sri Lanka on full independence in 1972.

The southern Expressway in the Sri Lankan coastal city of Matara displays signs warning: 'Danger Peacocks Ahead'.

The Temple of the Tooth, in the city of Kandy in Sri Lanka, houses the sacred relic of a tooth of Gautama Buddha, founder of Buddhism. According to legend, the tooth, a left canine, remained after Buddha's cremation.

In Sri Lanka, shaking one's head from side to side with a slight wiggle means 'yes'.

There are nearly 4,000 elephants and two elephant orphanages in Sri Lanka.

In 1960, Sri Lanka (when it was still Ceylon) became the first country in the world to have a woman prime minister.

Sri Lanka has one of the world's lowest divorce rates, but possibly the highest suicide rate.

♀ *TRANSVESTITES*

⬤ ST ANDREW

Andrew, the patron saint of Scotland, is also patron saint of Greece, Russia, Amalfi (Italy), fishmongers, fishermen, gout, spinsters, singers and sore throats. He was the son of Jonah (according to St Matthew) or John (according to St John) and was a fisherman.

He was crucified in the city of Patras in Greece on 30 November AD 60 by order of the Roman governor Aegeas or

Aegeates. Paintings of Andrew's death often depict him bound to an X-shaped (or decussate) cross, but that tradition apparently began in the 14th century and was the reason the cross of St Andrew is X-shaped.

His relics were taken to Constantinople about AD 357 and moved to the Cathedral at Amalfi in the 13th century, where most of them still remain.

According to legend, a Greek monk called St Rule was directed by an angel in AD 357 to take what remains of St Andrew he could carry to the 'ends of the earth' for safekeeping. So he took them to Scotland. The place where St Rule came ashore later became known as St Andrews.

St Andrews University has no apostrophe in its name because it is the University of the town of St Andrews (without an apostrophe) rather than the University belonging to St Andrew.

St Andrews in Nova Scotia does not have an apostrophe, but St Andrew's in Newfoundland does. The apostrophe only came into European languages in the early 16th century, so places named before then do not have them.

♀ *GOLF, SKULL, TIE KNOTS, UNION JACK, WORM*

ST APOLLONIA

St Apollonia is the patron saint of toothache sufferers and dentists. Her qualification for this is that her martyrdom by the Romans in AD 249 is said to have included having her teeth knocked out. She is depicted in artworks with a pair of pincers in which a tooth is gripped.

In the Middle Ages, relics claimed to be Apollonia's teeth were peddled as cures for toothache. During the reign

of Henry VI in the 15th century, several tons of her alleged teeth were collected in a bid to stop the scam.

ST BERNARD of Montjoux (c.923–1008)

St Bernard of Montjoux, after whom the St Bernard dog is named, is the patron saint of Alpinists, mountaineers, backpackers, snowboarders and skiers and should not be confused with St Bernard of Clairvaux, who is patron saint of bee keepers, bees, candle-makers, chandlers, Gibraltar, Queens College Cambridge, wax melters and wax refiners.

St Bernard of Montjoux founded hospices for climbers and organised patrols to rid the Alps of robbers. He was named patron saint of the Alps by Pope Pius XI in 1923.

♀ *CHINA*

ST CLARE of Assisi (c.1194–1253)

A follower of St Francis of Assisi, St Clare once saw a vision as though it were projected onto her bedroom wall. For that televisual miracle, she was declared patron saint of television in 1958.

She is also patron saint of embroiderers, eye disease, eyes, gilders, goldsmiths, gold workers, good weather, laundry workers, needle workers, telegraphs, telephones and television writers.

ST GEORGE

St George replaced Edward the Confessor as patron saint of England in the 14th century. He is also patron saint of Catalonia, the Greek army, knights, archers, boy scouts and sufferers from syphilis, though nobody is sure whether he ever existed.

Some say he was martyred in the 4th

century, but no connection was made between St George and his legendary feat of slaying a dragon until the 12th or 13th century. In any case, the story of a saintly, spear-wielding dragon-slayer was first applied not to St George but to St Theodore Tiron in the 9th and 10th centuries. Also some say the 'dragon' may not have been a dragon at all, but just an allusion to the tyrant Emperor Diocletian, who persecuted the Christians.

Because of the uncertainty surrounding his existence, St George was demoted to 'optional worship' by Pope Paul VI in 1969, but Pope John Paul II reinstated him to full membership of the calendar of saints in 2000.

The poets Shakespeare, Wordsworth and Rupert Brooke all died on St George's Day, 23 April.

⚲ *COCONUT, SHAKESPEARE, TOWN CRIER, UNION JACK, YEMEN*

● ST KILDA

Despite the fact that a Scottish island group and a suburb of Melbourne, Australia, are named after her or him, there never was a St Kilda. There are numerous theories about how the island got its name, including the suggestion that it is from an old Icelandic word, *skildar*, meaning shields, referring to the shape of the island. This name may have been mistranscribed by a 16th-century cartographer as St Kilda, which was then taken to refer to a saint.

In 2010, the National Trust for Scotland, which owns St Kilda, announced plans to build the islands' first public lavatory to accommodate the needs of the growing number of visitors on cruise ships. In the same year, plans were also announced to recruit a mouse-catcher for St Kilda in order to assist an Edinburgh University study into the St Kilda field mouse, which is unique to the islands and nearly twice the weight of its relatives on the mainland.

● ST KITTS and NEVIS

The Federation of St Kitts and Nevis (formerly the Federation of St Christopher and Nevis) comprises two islands in the eastern Caribbean: St Kitts and Nevis. St Kitts is shaped like a baseball bat and Nevis has the shape of a ball. The inhabitants are known as Kittitian or Nevisian, depending on which island they come from.

The population of the islands is 53,192, including one World Athletics Championship gold medallist, Kim Collins, who is a Kittitian.

● ST LUCIA

The earliest inhabitants of St Lucia were probably Arawaks from South America who called it Iouanalao, meaning 'land of the iguanas'. In the 17th and 18th centuries, the island changed hands between the British and the French 14 times.

The French were first to colonise St Lucia and they named it after St Lucy of Syracuse. St Lucia is the only country in the world named after a woman.

The British ruled St Lucia from 1815 to 1979. The British Queen is still its head of state.

St Lucia has more Nobel Prize winners per head of population than any other country. The island's two Nobel laureates from a population of only 183,629 are Arthur Lewis (1979, Economics) and Derek Walcott (1992, Literature).

The national dish of St Lucia is *fig vét é lanmowi* (green figs and saltfish).

The 'figs' in the name are in fact unripe bananas.

Tourism and bananas are the main foreign currency earners for St Lucia.

'Saint Lucia' is an anagram of 'is nautical' or 'is a lunatic'.

● ST MATTHEW

In 2001, the Russian Orthodox Church named the apostle Matthew patron saint of Russia's tax police. St Matthew himself was a tax collector, before giving up the profession to follow Jesus. A spokesman for the tax police said, 'We are not planning to make our heavenly protection into a cult. It simply means that tax police will have another holiday on 29 November, St Matthew's Day.'

To judge from this, Russia's tax police were readers of the New International Version of the Bible, where Matthew 10:3 refers to 'Matthew the tax collector'. In the King James version, however, Matthew is referred to as a publican. The anomaly was due to the translation of a Greek word that probably meant someone who dealt with public money, so the tax police may have been right in welcoming Matthew as one of their own.

♀ *ST ANDREW*

● ST NICHOLAS

The only facts that seem certain about St Nicholas is that he was Bishop of Myra in Asia Minor and died on 6 December in the year 345 or 352. He is said to have been present at the Council of Nicaea when the early Christian Church fixed the date of Christmas but his name is not on any official list. His relics are still preserved in the church of San Nicola in Bari. An oily substance known as 'Manna of St Nicholas', with powerful medicinal properties, is said to be exuded from these relics.

The legend of St Nicholas as gift-giver stems from stories of him leaving bags of gold in the stockings of poor children. That story gave rise to the tradition of Christmas stockings.

Apart from being patron saint of children, St Nicholas is also patron of more than 100 other groups including butchers, bakers, candle-makers, embalmers, lovers, virgins, the infertile, robbers, thieves, murderers, prostitutes, unmarried men, spice-dealers and military intelligence.

In March 2005, the town of Demre in Turkey decided to remove a bronze statue of St Nicholas, who had lived and worked in the town in the 4th century, and replace it with a brightly coloured model of Santa Claus.

The mayor of Demre insisted that he and the town council respected Saint Nicholas but Santa Claus had wider popular appeal.

♀ *CHRISTMAS, HORN, IDES OF MARCH*

● ST PAUL'S CATHEDRAL

The first cathedral dedicated to St Paul was said to have been built on the site of the present St Paul's Cathedral in London in 604 by Mellitus, Bishop of the East Saxons. It burnt down and was rebuilt in 962. The present St Paul's is the fifth cathedral built on the site. Following Christopher Wren's design, work began on the cathedral in 1675. It was not completed until 1710.

A violent protest was attempted at St Paul's in 1913, when suffragettes left a bomb under the bishop's throne in the choir. Luckily, it was defused in time.

After his death at the Battle of Trafalgar in 1804, Lord Nelson was buried in the centre of the crypt directly beneath the crossing and dome.

At 111 metres (365 feet) in height, St

Paul's was the tallest building in London from 1710 until 1962. There are 528 steps up to the Golden Gallery, the highest accessible point of the cathedral.

The only British monarch ever buried at St Paul's was Ethelred the Unready in 1016.

The weight of the dome of St Paul's is about 65,000 tons. The lantern on its top weighs 850 tons.

ST SWITHUN (or Swithin, c.800–862)

'St Swithin's Day, if thou dost rain, For forty days it will remain; St Swithin's Day, if thou be fair, For forty days 'twill rain na mair.'

The legend connecting St Swithin's Day with the weather dates back to 15 July 971, when the bones of St Swithun, Bishop of Winchester (the *Dictionary of National Biography* firmly castigates 'Swithin' as a misspelling), were scheduled to be moved from an unmarked grave outside his church to a consecrated site within the walls of the building. On that day, however, it is said to have poured with rain, and continued to do so for the next 40 days, which was taken as a sign that his bones preferred to remain where they were.

That story, however, seems to be a piece of 16th-century romanticism at variance with contemporary accounts of the event. Back in the 10th century, it was generally thought that Swithun had been overjoyed at having his bones reburied, and he was credited with hundreds of miracles supposedly performed in gratitude.

The long-range weather forecast associated with Swithun also fails to stand up to scrutiny. An analysis was published in 1894 calculating the number of rainy days in the 40-day period following 15 July. After a wet St Swithun's Day, there were an average of 18.5 rainy days, while for a dry 15 July, the rainy score was slightly higher at 19.25.

Whatever the statistics show, St Swithun did give Britain its own meteorological saint's day to match those of St Medard (8 June) in France, St Godelieve (6 July) in Belgium, and the Day of the Seven Sleepers (27 June) in Germany, all of which carry a similar tradition of 40-day, long-range weather forecasts. And none of those work either. In fact, records suggest that it has not rained incessantly for 40 days since the Great Flood.

♀ CANTERBURY, CELIBACY

ST VALENTINE

There are at least 13 saints named Valentine, of whom two have feast days on 14 February. Both of those Valentines were Romans, one a priest and physician who was beheaded on 14 February 269, the other a bishop who was martyred around the same time. Or it may have been a few years later. Or they may both have been the same person. Nobody is at all sure, and it's unclear how much either had to do with courtship, but the romantic side is tied in with two other mid-February rituals.

The first is an old British belief, mentioned by Chaucer, that 14 February is the day birds choose their mates. The second is the Roman festival of Lupercalia, celebrated on 15 February, at which young men, clad in wolf-masks and loincloths, would run through the city hitting people with strips of goat skin. According to tradition, women who wanted to become pregnant could improve their chances by being hit by goat hide. The romantic celebrations of St Valentine's Day were officially instigated as the Christian answer to Lupercalia by Pope Gelasius in AD 496.

Besides the similar dates, an unlikely connection between Lupercalia and Valentine's Day was suggested in a letter to the *New England Journal of Medicine* in 1987. It pointed out that the disease brucellosis may be transmitted to humans by contact with freshly killed goat skins and its symptoms include depression, dizziness, loss of weight, insomnia and general malaise. As the writer observed, these are precisely the symptoms of lovesickness. He concluded that the Valentine's/ Lupercalian tradition of lovesick young men in mid-February was nothing more than an annual outbreak of brucellosis caused by close contact with goat skins.

The world's earliest known Valentine message was sent by a Norfolk woman, Margery Brews, to her fiancé John Paston in 1477. Her letter 'unto my right well-beloved Valentine' was lost for centuries but was rediscovered at the British Library in 1999.

Thailand issued the world's first rose-scented stamps in February 2002 for Valentine's Day.

In Mexico, 14 February is a day of national mourning.

♀ CYBERSPACE, GOOSE, WOLF

STALE BREAD

An employee tribunal in Leipzig, Germany, in 2010 ruled that taking stale bread home to eat is not grounds for dismissal from a supermarket chain. A woman employee of the supermarket had been given some bread that was no longer fit for sale and told to put it in a bio-waste container. When the bread was found in her bag the next day, she was sacked. The woman argued that she had intended to throw the bread away as instructed, but her employer had believed she intended to take it home and eat it. However, the Leipzig court ruled that even if she had taken it home, it was not grounds for dismissal as the bread no longer had any monetary value for her employers.

STALLION

The following extract is the official summary of UK Patent No. 2073 from 1897, granted to E. de Pass. It is accompanied by a picture of a horse wearing an appliance with various numbered parts:

'Self-abuse, preventing, by administering electricity. An appliance to be worn by stallions for preventing masturbation consists of a surcingle 1, carrying a battery 2 and an induction coil 3, the secondary terminals of which are connected, one to the bit 10, and the other to an insulated contact-plate 15, attached to the body of the animal. When the penis is erected, it makes contact with the plate 15 and completes the secondary circuit of the induction coil. To prevent current passing when the animal is lying down, an automatic mercury switch is arranged in the primary circuit.'

This patent is only one of many similar inventions, as Paul Mountjoy of Western Michigan University shows in his paper 'Some Early Attempts to Modify Penile Erection in Horse and Human: An Historical Analysis' (*The Psychological Record*, 1974). In his opening words, he tells us: 'Between 1856 and 1919 Letters Patent were granted by the U.S. Patent Office for 49 antimasturbatory devices; 35 were designed for application to *Equus caballus* [stallions], while 14 were intended for *Homo sapiens*.'

🔑 *PONY*

● STALLONE, Sylvester (b. 1946)

The average wingspan of the Indonesian fruitbat is equal to the height of film-star Sylvester Stallone. His full name is Michael Sylvester Gardenzio Stallone and he was born in the New York neigh-bourhood known as Hell's Kitchen, which was named after a notorious 19th-century motorcycle gang.

In December 2021, the Osthaus Museum in Hagen, Germany, opened a retrospective exhibition of more than 50 paintings by Sylvester Stallone.

● STAMMERING

Famous stammerers include Lewis Carroll, the Emperor Claudius and possibly Moses. Notker the Stammerer (840–912) was a poet, musician, author and Benedictine monk at the Abbey of Saint Gall in modern Switzerland. Louis the Stammerer was a 9th-century French king, son of Charles the Bald.

It is not known whether any of those followed the advice of Geronimo Mercuriali (1530–1606), who recommended reduced love-making as a cure for male stammerers.

Michael Palin based his stammering role in *A Fish Called Wanda* on his father, who stammered all his life.

🔑 *FRANCE*

● STAMPS

Britain introduced postage stamps in 1840 with a standard rate of one penny for up to half an ounce. As the originator of stamps, Britain has kept the distinction of never putting the country's name on them.

The first non-royal person displayed on a British stamp was William Shakespeare in 1964, which was the 400th anniversary of his birth. In 1997, Bugs Bunny became the first cartoon character to appear on a stamp. The stamps were designed to promote stamp collecting among America's youth. In 2020 more Bugs Bunny stamps were issued to celebrate the 80th anniversary of the rabbit's first appearance in 1940. However, the most popular US stamp ever released was in 1993 and bore a picture not of Bugs Bunny but of Elvis Presley. It sold 120 million copies.

In 2013, the United Arab Emirates introduced the world's biggest postage stamp. It was 1.36 by 1.77 metres (4.46 by 5.8 feet) in size.

The record for most stamps licked and stuck in one minute is 70 and was achieved by Deepak Sharma Bajagain (Nepal) on 6 August 2010. One envelope was disqualified as the stamp fell off before counting began.

According to the US Postal Union, the gum on an average stamp contains about one-tenth of a calorie.

By weight and size, the most valuable man-made item ever sold is the British Guiana 1c Magenta (1856) stamp, dubbed the 'Mona Lisa of the stamp world'. Gram for gram, it is worth around 2.5 million times more than 24-carat gold, according to leading dealer Stanley Gibbons, which bought the stamp for $8.3 million (£6.2 million) at auction in June 2021.

In 2020, according to the Universal Postal Union, 121 billion items were posted in the US.

🔑 *DINOSAUR, FLYING SAUCERS, JACKSON Michael, TRISTAN DA CUNHA, ST VALENTINE*

● STAR TREK

In 2010, the Jenolan Caves in Australia announced that they would be offering tours spoken in Klingon, in addition to the eight languages already on offer. 'We will now be the first tourist attraction on this planet at least to have a Klingon tour,' a spokesman said. The idea stemmed from the *Star Trek Next Generation* episode 'Relics,' which included the naming of a 'Sydney Class' Starship as the USS Jenolan.

֍ *AMAZON, ASH, FORTY-SEVEN*

● STAR WARS

Star Wars Day is May 4, when fans of the films greet each other with the words 'May the fourth be with you'. Those words were actually first seen in a newspaper headline greeting Margaret Thatcher's election as UK Prime Minister on 4 May 1979.

The first official Star Wars Day celebration was in 2011 in Toronto, Canada, though Los Angeles City Council had declared 25 May to be Star Wars Day 34 years earlier in 1977 which was the day when the first Star Wars movie was released.

25 May was later expanded into Geek Pride Day, adding the works of authors Douglas Adams and Terry Pratchett to the celebrations.

In early drafts of the first Star Wars film, Luke Skywalker was called Luke Skykiller.

In 1996, 37 per cent of the toys sold in the USA are said to have been Star Wars products.

In one scene of *The Empire Strikes Back*, one of the deadly asteroids is actually a potato.

The total box office revenue generated by the Star Wars films is around $10.3 billion (£8.6 billion). The only series that has made more money is the Marvel Cinematic Universe franchise.

Denis Lawson, who plays Wedge Antilles in *Star Wars IV, V* and *VI*, has his first name misspelled as 'Dennis' in the credits of the first two of those.

֍ *BEETLE, YODA*

● STARLING

In the early 1890s, about 100 European starlings were released in New York City's Central Park by a group dedicated to bringing to America every bird ever mentioned by Shakespeare. The starling is mentioned in the third scene of Act 1 of *Henry IV, Part 1*, when Hotspur says: 'I'll have a starling shall be taught to speak/ Nothing but "Mortimer," and give it him/ To keep his anger still in motion.' Thanks to this single mention of the bird, there are now some 200 million European starlings in North America. Federal aviation officials say they have caused $4 million in damage between 1990 and 2009.

'Starlings' and 'Startling' are the two longest common English words from which one letter may repeatedly be deleted, each time leaving another word, ending up with one letter: Starlings, Starling, Staring, String, Sting, Sing, Sin, In, I. The longest word of all which conforms to this pattern is 'austringers', a Miltonian form of 'astringers', both of which mean 'keepers of goshawks'. The one-letter-at-a-time reduction goes: Austringers, Astringers, Stringers, Stingers, Singers, Singes, Singe, Sing, Sin, In, I.

● STATISTICS

The Indian Statistical Institute in New Delhi was forced to close for some time in 2004 because of reports from students that the ghost of a dead classmate had knocked on doors, jostled them on staircases and left traces of aftershave lotion and cigarette smoke. Students linked the aftershave smell to a first-year student who had died the previous month of a rare heart condition. 'A fear psychosis had gripped some students,' the head of the Institute said. 'We thought it was best to allow them to go home if they wanted to.'

BARBIE, BENFORD'S LAW, GDANSK, NORWAY, SKIING, TATTOO

STATUE

Plans were announced in January 2012 to erect a statue in honour of a bear named Wojtek, which was officially drafted as a private in the Polish army during the Second World War. Originally adopted as a mascot by the Polish Second Corps, he lived with other soldiers in their tents, except when travelling in a crate, and helped at the Battle of Monte Cassino in Italy by transporting ammunition. After the war, Wojtek, which means smiling warrior, retired to Edinburgh Zoo where he would wave at visitors who spoke to him in Polish. He died aged 22 in 1963, and the Wojtek Memorial Trust erected a bronze statue in his memory in Princes Street, Edinburgh in 2015.

DUCK, MERMAID, NELSON, POPEYE, ST NICHOLAS, SUPERMAN

STATUE OF LIBERTY

On 5 August 1884, the cornerstone of the Statue of Liberty was laid on Bedloe's Island in New York Harbour. Actually, it's not called the Statue of Liberty at all. The proper name is 'Liberty Enlightening The World'.

The statue was a gift from the people of France to America to celebrate the centenary of the US Declaration of Independence. The original idea was to present the statue on the date of that centenary – 4 July 1876 – but with various delays and lack of money it was finally completed 10 years late. The statue was shipped from France to New York in 350 pieces packed in 214 crates. It was sculpted by Frédéric Auguste Bartholdi, who obtained a US patent for the design.

The length of the nose on the statue is 1.37 metres (4 feet 6 inches), her index finger is 2.4 metres (8 feet) long; she is 10.5 metres (35 feet) thick at the waist and each of her fingernails weighs about 1.5 kilograms (3.5 pounds). The internal engineering of the statue was done by Alexandre Gustave Eiffel, better known for his tower in Paris. The statue itself is 46 metres (151 feet) tall, but including the pedestal, its height is 93 metres (305 feet).

In 1956, an Act of Congress was passed changing the official name of Bedloe's Island to Liberty Island.

In a high wind, the statue may sway 7.5 centimetres (3 inches) and the torch may move 12.5 centimetres (5 inches).

FORTY-SEVEN

STEEL

Steel is an alloy of iron with small amounts of other elements, most commonly carbon. The earliest known examples of steel were in weapons and ironware dating back to 1800 BC. Steel can be 1,000 times as strong as iron.

The amount of steel in use in the world today is equal to about 227 kilograms (500 pounds) per person on Earth. The weight of crude steel made in the world in 2020 was about equal to 180,000 Eiffel Towers. An average household appliance is about 65 per cent steel. An average computer is about 25 per cent steel.

Stainless steel contains at least 11 per cent chromium, often combined with nickel, to resist corrosion. It was developed on an industrial scale in Sheffield by Harry Brearley over 100 years ago.

The earliest known use of the phrase 'steel band' in a musical sense was in the late 1940s.

Steel is the second biggest industry in the world after oil and gas. Its annual turnover is about £637 billion.

Sixty per cent of the cans in the world's grocery stores are made of steel.

'If you had teeth of steel, you could eat iron coconuts.' Senegalese proverb

COW, NEW YORK, SYDNEY, TUG-OF-WAR

STEEPLECHASE

The longest 3,000 metres steeplechase ever was at the 1932 Olympics when the runners did an extra lap of the track, putting the distance up to 3,460 metres, owing to a mistake in lap counting by one of the officials.

The official lap counter in fact was looking the wrong way when he should have rung the bell for the final lap, as his attention was firmly on the decathlon pole vault at the time.

The winner of the steeplechase was Volmari Iso-Hollo of Finland, who would probably have set a new world record had the race stopped at the right time.

STEPHENSON, George (1781–1848)

Neither of the parents of the great railway pioneer George Stephenson could read or write.

In 1825, Stephenson assured a parliamentary inquiry that trains would never go faster than 25 mph.

On 15 September 1830, the first fatal rail accident occurred at the opening of the Manchester–Liverpool Railway. The train had stopped to take on water, and several passengers, including William Huskisson, President of the Board of Trade, took the chance to get off and walk around chatting. When the train restarted, most of them got out of the way but, in the words of one witness: 'Poor Mr Huskisson, less active from the effects of age and ill-health, bewildered, too, by the frantic cries of "Stop the engine! Clear the track!" that resounded on all sides, completely lost his head, looked helplessly to the right and left, and was instantaneously prostrated by the fatal machine, which dashed down like a thunderbolt upon him, and passed over his leg, smashing and mangling it in the most horrible way.'

Another contemporary account recalled: 'His first words, on being raised, were, "I have met my death," which unhappily proved true, for he expired that same evening in the parsonage of Eccles.'

STEVENSON, Robert Louis (1850–94)

Stevenson's famous book about a man with a split personality originally appeared under the title *Strange Case of Dr Jekyll and Mr Hyde*. Later publishers found this odd and added the word 'The' at the start of the title, thus removing some of the strangeness of Stevenson's original intention.

DONKEY

STEWART, James Maitland (1908–97)

The real name of the English actor Stewart Granger was James Stewart. He had to change it because Jimmy Stewart (whose real name was James Maitland Stewart) was already acting under that name. Granger was the maiden name of Stewart Granger's Scottish grandmother.

♀ *YETI*

● STILTON

The earliest known recipe for Stilton cheese was published by Richard Bradley in 1723.

It takes 78 litres of milk to make an 8 kilogram (17.5-pound) Stilton.

In 1996, the Stilton Cheese Makers' Association (SCMA) achieved Protected Designation of Origin status for Blue Stilton from the European Commission. Since then, the name 'Stilton' may only be used by cheeses made in the counties of Leicester, Derby and Nottingham by members of the SCMA. Since the village of Stilton is in Cambridgeshire, Stilton cheese can no longer be made there.

It was sales of the cheese at the Bell Inn in Stilton that were mainly responsible for its becoming known as 'Stilton cheese'.

♀ *CHEESE*

● STINGS

The Schmidt sting pain index was devised by Arizona entomologist Justin O. Schmidt in 1983 to compare the effects of different insects' and spiders' stings on humans. It consists of a five-point scale, rating stings from 0 (completely ineffective) to 4 (which Schmidt described as 'pure, intense, brilliant pain ... like walking over flaming charcoal with a three-inch nail embedded in your heel'.) Most wasps and bees and many ants have sting level 2.

♀ *IBSEN, ICICLES, MEXICO, NETTLES, PLATYPUS*

● STOCKINGS

Until nylon was invented, women's stockings were made of silk and were worn only by the rich. The first pair of experimental nylon stockings was made by Union Hosiery Company for Du Pont in 1937. When they came on the market in 1940, 5 million pairs were sold on their first day.

When America entered the Second World War, nylon production was mainly restricted to parachute fabric and cord, though American soldiers who brought pairs of nylon stockings over with them to Britain were said to be especially popular with local women. When nylon stockings returned to US stores in 1945, the huge demand resulted in 'Nylon Riots'.

On 7 July 1942, the Vatican allowed bare-legged women to enter St Peter's in Rome for the first time.

♀ *NYLON, ST NICHOLAS*

● STOKER, Bram (1847–1912)

Before settling on the title *Dracula*, Bram Stoker called the book first 'The Dead Un-Dead' and later just 'The Un-Dead'. He also changed the name of the main character from Count Wampyr to Dracula. He took the name from the Transylvanian-born Vlad III Dracula of Wallachia. The name 'Dracula' comes from the 'Order of Dracul' (dragon) to which Vlad II (father of Vlad III) had been admitted in the 15th century.

The only fictional character to appear in more major film roles than Dracula is Sherlock Holmes.

♀ *DRACULA, VAMPIRES*

● STOMACH

Tripe, made from a cow's stomach, was voted Britain's most hated dish in a poll in 2006. Jellied eels came second, followed by deep-fried Mars bars in third place.

'To an empty stomach, white bread tastes like brown.' Estonian proverb

COW, DINOSAUR, DOLPHIN, FROG, LAUGHTER, NAVEL, SLOTH

STONE

The pastime of skimming a stone across the surface of water has been known since the time of the ancient Greeks and a world record of 38 bounces was achieved by J. Coleman-McGhee in 1992. Valuable scientific advice to stone-skippers had to wait until 2004 when Clanet, Hersen and Bocquet published a paper in *Nature* on the subject. Their conclusion, based on monitoring the collision of a spinning disc with water, was this: 'An angle of about 20 degrees between the stone and the water's surface is optimal with respect to the throwing conditions and yields the maximum possible number of bounces.' The leading edge of the stone should also be 20 degrees above its trailing edge and it should be thrown at 40 feet per second with a flick of the wrist giving it approximately 14 rotations per second.

ALCHEMY, DORSET, FIZZY DRINKS, PYRAMID, RUGBY, SHATNER

STORIES

Originally, in the 14th century, the word 'story' was used to refer only to true or supposedly historical events. The earliest use of 'story' to mean a fictional anecdote was in 1425.

Very little is known about the author of *Aesop's Fables* except that he was a storyteller and slave who lived in Ancient Greece around 500 BC. *Aesop's Fables* was first translated into English

and published by William Caxton in 1484.

The brothers Jacob and Wilhelm Grimm first published their collection of folk tales in 1812. This included 'Snow White', 'Hansel and Gretel', 'Sleeping Beauty' and 'Cinderella', among others. Twenty-three films with the word 'story' or 'stories' in their titles have won Oscars. *West Side Story* in 1961 was the most successful of those, winning 10 Oscars.

In 1995, *Toy Story* won a Special Achievement Academy Award for being the First Feature-Length Computer-Animated Film. *Toy Story*, *Toy Story 3* and *Toy Story 4* all won Oscars. *Toy Story 2* won a Golden Globe for Best Musical or Comedy and was nominated for an Oscar for Best Original Song, but did not win.

The earliest known reference to short stories was in 1877. A reference to love story was first seen in 1594.

The Arne-Thompson classification system for folk tales lists 2,399 categories for story plots, beginning with 'AT1: The Theft of Fish'.

BLYTON, DOYLE, LIBYA, MERMAID, WELLS

STRADIVARIUS

One of the most valuable and famous musical instruments made by Antonio Stradivari is a cello known as the Duport Stradivarius, named after Jean-Pierre Duport, who played it in the early 19th century. The instrument, which was later owned by the great Russian cellist Mstislav Rostropovich, has a small dent in it, said to have been made by Napoleon Bonaparte in 1812 when he insisted that Duport let him try to play it.

STRAW

Paper drinking straws were patented by Marvin C. Stone of Washington DC on 3 January 1888. The ideal straw, he maintained, was 22 centimetres (8.5 inches) long, with a diameter just narrow enough to stop lemon pips being sucked up. Before Marvin Stone's invention, people used to suck up drinks through blades of rye grass. The Sumerians drank beer through natural straws more than 5,000 years ago. Stone experimented with tubes of paper wrapped round a pencil, then perfected his invention by using paraffin-coated manila paper.

Marvin Stone's father, Chester Stone, was also an inventor, holding patents for a 'self-acting cheese press' and a clothes rack. The first paper straws were made by Marvin Stone's company, which had previously made paper cigarette holders. Stone's patent for spiral-wound tubing was later employed on non-paper products including the first mass-produced radios. The flexible drinking straw was invented by Joseph B. Friedman in 1937.

Research in 2005 reported that drinking fizzy drinks through a straw can reduce tooth decay.

DATE RAPE, DRUNKEN DRIVING, PAPAL SMOKE, STRAWBERRY

STRAWBERRY

Nobody knows for sure why they are called 'strawberries'. The name comes from the Old English 'streawberige', where 'streaw' may refer to the straw-like runners sent out by the plant, or it may have been a reference to the seeds 'strewn' round the fruit.

Grown on every continent except Antarctica, the strawberry is technically a 'false fruit'. Strictly speaking, each of the seeds on its outside is a fruit in its own right. On average, there are 200 seeds on every strawberry, so it could be said that each strawberry is 200 fruits.

The Musée de la Fraise or Strawberry Museum may be visited in the town of Wépion, Belgium, where it tells the history of strawberry production in the region and explains its importance to the economy and culture of Wépion.

The 'World's Largest Strawberry' can be seen atop City Hall in Strawberry Point, Iowa.

In 1995 the Nebraska Supreme Court ruled that strawberries may be sold either by weight or volume, but not both by the same store at the same time.

Strawberry juice combined with honey is said to be a good treatment for sunburn: rub it into the skin and rinse with warm water and lemon juice. Pregnant women, however, used to avoid strawberries, for fear their babies would have strawberry birthmarks.

'Doubtless God could have made a better berry, but doubtless God never did.'
William Butler, physician, writing in praise of the strawberry around 1600

CHEESECAKE, CHICKEN, WIMBLEDON

STREETS

The UK Internet map site streetmap.co.uk lists 11 streets with the name 'Second Street' but only 10 named 'First Street'.

There are three First Streets which do not have a matching Second Street, four Second Streets which do not have a First Street, and seven places with both a First Street and a Second Street. The reason for this is that in some places, the first street was named 'Main Street' or something similar, and the next one became Second Street without a First Street on the town map.

⚲ *BABBAGE, CATTLE, COW, DOG, PARIS, PILLOW, UKRAINE*

STRESS

According to research in 2006, visiting an art gallery can be very beneficial to people suffering from stress. A group of 28 highly stressed City of London high-fliers were studied by psychologists at the University of Westminster as they visited the Guildhall Art Gallery during their lunch hour. After 40 minutes wandering round the Gallery, their self-reported stress levels fell by 45 per cent. Saliva samples from the men and women were also found to contain 32 per cent less cortisol stress hormone than they did before the visit.

⚲ *BALLET, COLOMBIA, COMMON COLD, MONDAY, MUSIC, ORANGE*

STRIKE

The longest strike in history is believed to be that of apprentice barbers in Copenhagen. It began in 1938 and was finally called off on 4 January 1961.

⚲ *MICKEY MOUSE*

STRING

The correct word for a fear of string is linonophobia. Sufferers would be well advised to steer clear of Cawker City, Kansas, where there is a ball of string said to be the largest in the world. Started by Kansas farmer Frank Stroeber in 1953, its initial objective was simply to clear his yard of string once used to hold stray bales together, but as the years went by, the ball grew bigger and bigger until he eventually presented it to the city as a tourist attraction. The ball now weighs over 9,000 kilograms (20,000 pounds), is around 13 metres (42 feet) in circumference and contains close to 2,575 kilometres (1,600 miles) of string. And every August, a String-a-thon is held at which people may bring more string to add to it.

⚲ *ARCHERY, FORTY-SEVEN, GARLIC, GUITAR, TAMPON, VIOLIN*

STRIPTEASE

The scientific term for a striptease artiste is 'ecdysiast'. The word was suggested in 1940 by H.L. Mencken, who wrote: 'It might be a good idea to relate strip-teasing in some way ... to the associated zoölogical phenomenon of moulting ... A resort to the scientific name for moulting, which is *ecdysis*, produces both *ecdysist* and *ecdysiast*.'

⚲ *BUNGA BUNGA*

STUDENT

According to a report by British student accommodation providers Unite, the three most common items left behind by students when they leave their digs are 1. Mobile phone chargers; 2. Textbooks; 3. iPods.

Other items left behind included: a six-foot snake; a pole-dancing pole; a life-sized skeleton; a pair of budgerigars; a giant white pet rabbit; a 10-foot inflatable rubber pool full of water; frozen chicken feet; a whip, together with a copy of the Kama Sutra; a scuba-diving kit with air tank and flippers; a full-size air hockey table.

⚲ *BRAHMS, FORTY-SEVEN, HENRY III, SEX WORK, TROUSERS, UNIVERSITIES*

STURGEON

Under the Wreck of the Sea, Whales and Sturgeons Act of Edward II, passed in 1317, any whale or great sturgeon washing up on British shores is the property of the monarch.

SUDAN

In 2009, senior Muslim clerics in Sudan urged youngsters to boycott Valentine's Day, saying it is a Western institution that could lead couples astray. Members of the Sudan Ulema Authority, an influential body of religious leaders, called on young men and women to ignore the event on 14 February and resist the temptation to mark it by taking romantic strolls in parks.

⚲ *ALGERIA, CONSENT, PALINDROME*

SUICIDE

In 1985 in New York, a man filed a $20 million suit against the estate of a banker's widow who landed on him in a suicide leap from her 19th-floor apartment. He said he was 'violently struck by Mildred T. Walker' who jumped 'without regard for human safety' and he suffered 'severe and serious neurological and psychological injuries'.

The case was settled for $500,000 in 1988 but again led to legal proceedings when the man, angry at the testimony given by a doctor who had treated him, went to pound on the locked door of the doctor's office. According to police, he then punched through a glass door and began pounding on another door. The doctor retreated to a conference room and when the man broke in, the doctor shot him in the left side. 'I didn't want to kill him. I just wanted to stop him,' the doctor said. Police charged the doctor with illegal weapon possession, as he was licensed to carry his handgun in New Jersey but not in New York.

In 1991, a study revealed that countries with high chocolate consumption have more suicides but fewer murders than non-chocoholic nations. In 1996, suicide rates in different regions of the United States were shown to correlate with the amount of country music being played on the radio: the more country music, the higher the suicide rate. Also in 1996, women who drink coffee were found to be less likely to commit suicide than those who do not.

In 1989, David Lester found that suicide rates by drowning were higher in American states that bordered on oceans or the Great Lakes. In 1993, however, he found no correlation between suicide rates in 27 different nations and the lengths of their coastlines.

On 13 June 1995, an unsuccessful novelist in Taiwan, 38-year-old Huang Chia-yuan, attacked six cars with a hammer in the hope that their owners would kill him. Apparently he got the idea from a publication called *The Complete Suicide Book*. He had already unsuccessfully tried other methods it recommended. This one failed too: he was rescued from the irate car-owners by police and taken to hospital with severe bruising.

The worst day for suicides in the UK in recent years was 1 January 2000. In general, more suicides take place on Mondays than any other day of the week, but 1 January 2000 was a Saturday.

⚲ *CHERRY, CHOCOLATE, GARBAGE, GUYANA, HANGING, TOWER BRIDGE*

SUMATRA

The titan arum flower or corpse flower of Sumatra is 3 metres (10 feet) tall and smells of dead flesh. Its botanical name is *Amorphophallus titanum*, which means giant misshapen phallus.

⚲ *BUNGA BUNGA, RHINOCEROS*

SUN

The Sun is around 93,000,000 miles away and weighs 332,946 times as much as the Earth. Its mass is 99.87 per cent of the entire Solar System and its light takes 499 seconds (8 minutes 19 seconds) to reach us. It is about 75 per cent hydrogen and 25 per cent helium but about 700,000,000 tons of hydrogen are converted to helium in nuclear reactions every second. That means it has enough fuel to continue burning for about another 5 billion years. The Sun is already about 4.5 billion years old.

The temperature at the centre of the Sun is thought to be about 15 million degrees Celsius.

The Sun is one of about 100 billion stars in the Milky Way galaxy. It orbits the centre of the galaxy at a speed of about 220 kilometres (137 miles) per second, and completes an orbit about once every 225 million years.

⚲ ASTRONOMY, EQUINOX, GALILEI, PANAMA, PERU, URANUS, VENUS

SUNGLASSES

In 2011, police in Vietnam were banned from wearing black sunglasses, chatting, smoking and putting their hands in their pockets while they are on duty in public places.

New, tough rules on behaviour also banned them from hiding behind trees to ambush people with fines, reading books, making or answering non-work related phone calls, drinking alcohol or eating at restaurants that illegally encroach onto pavements.

More sunglasses were used filming 'The Matrix' trilogy than any other motion pictures.

⚲ DOG, HANDBAG, LAUGHFEST, VIETNAM

SUNTAN

Every year, about 1,500 tons of suntan lotion washes into the Caribbean Sea off the bodies of tourists.

SUPERMAN

A statue of Superman's girlfriend Lois Lane was unveiled in Metropolis, Illinois, which already boasts a 4.5-metre (15-foot) bronze statue of Superman in Superman Square. The Lois Lane statue is modelled on actress Noel Neill, who played the part in films and on television in the 1940s and 1950s.

⚲ DIAGRAM

SUPERSTITION

According to a recent survey, shoes, trainers, necklace, t-shirts, socks and football shirts, in that order, are the most popular items worn for good luck during driving tests. Other items worn for luck included a tutu, clean Y-fronts and a silk G-string.

Another survey revealed that young drivers aged 18–24 were the most likely to be superstitious, with 60 per cent adopting such measures as lucky pants (7 per cent), lucky charm (6 per cent) or herbal remedies (9 per cent) before their driving test.

⚲ BREAD, HAIR, PREGNANCY, SHOES, UNDERWEAR, VIRGINITY

SURFING

Since 2006, the dog surfing season in the US has begun with the Loews Coronado Resort Surf Dog competition at Imperial Beach, San Diego. Each dog is given 10 minutes to catch his or her best wave and is judged on confidence level, length of ride and overall ability to 'grip it and rip it'.

Before the 2010 event, at which about 60 dogs were expected, one of the main judges commented: 'I personally look for attire, whether they come dressed seriously with board shorts on, what's going on with their tails, whether they're wagging them or sitting on them. For me that means they're having fun and that's what this is all about.'

The first time two goats shared a surfboard was in July 2012 when goat owner Dana McGregor of Pismo Beach, California, succeeded in getting two of his goats to share a tandem surfboard. An onlooker described it at 'one of the oddest and coolest things I've ever seen on the beach'. Mr McGregor said it was 'easier than surfing with the wife.'

SURNAME

The most common surname in the UK, the USA and Australia is Smith, with Jones coming second in the UK and Australia, and Johnson second in the US. In Germany, however, Schmidt is only the second most common surname, behind Müller.

DAFT, EVEREST, HELL, POMPADOUR, RALEIGH, WALES

SWAHILI

Swahili (the word means 'coasts') was originally a language of the coastal people of Africa. The *Oxford English Dictionary* lists 77 words which have come into English from Swahili, the most common of which is probably 'safari', which was originally a journey or expedition.

Useful phrases in Swahili include:

Hakuna matata (the catchphrase of Timon and Pumba in Disney's *The Lion King*): 'No worries.'

Shikamoo!: literally meaning 'I touch your feet'; this is the respectful greeting from a young person to an old one.

Wapi choo: 'Where are the toilets?'

'Wednesday' in Swahili is *Jumatamo*, which means fifth day of the week. Confusingly, the word for 'Thursday' is *Alhamisi*, which is Arabic for fifth day of the week.

'When two elephants fight it's the grass that gets hurt.' Swahili proverb

OBAMA

SWAN

In 1993, the British royal appointment of Keeper of the King's Swans was split into two roles as Warden of the Swans and Marker of the Swans.

At some of King Henry VIII's banquets, swans were served with burning cotton placed in the beak to look as if they were breathing fire.

GOOSE, POPCORN, SWAN-UPPING, WINNIE-THE-POOH

SWAN-UPPING

The object of Swan-Upping is to count the number of young cygnets each year on the River Thames and ensure that the swan population (currently about 30,000) is maintained.

The ceremony is presided over by the Queen's Marker of the Swans, a post held since 1993 by David Barber. Traditionally, the swan marker dresses in a scarlet jacket, white trousers and a white peaked cap topped with a swan's feather.

On sighting a brood of swans, the swan marker shouts 'All Up' as a signal for his team to start their work. It is called 'Swan-Upping' because the swans are chased up onto the river bank. Swan-Upping dates back to the 12th century when the Crown claimed ownership of all mute swans, which were considered an important food source. In the 15th century, ownership of such Thames swans was extended to the Vintners' and Dyers' Companies.

Since 1993, the Warden of the Swans has been Professor Christopher Perrins of Oxford, who assists the Swan-Upping by giving the swans a health check.

The greatest threats to swans are vandalism, discarded fishing tackle and attacks by wild mink.

● SWAT

Swat is a principality on the North-West Frontier, which has been a part of Pakistan since 1969. The principality was ruled by the Wali of Swat (great-grandson of the Akond of Swat who was the subject of a nonsense verse by Edward Lear) until 1969 when Swat ceased to be a Princely State of Pakistan and became part of the North-West Frontier Province. He kept the courtesy title of Wali, however, until his death in 1987. Wali Miangul Jahan Zeb always wore a felt hat and an English suit. As king, religious leader, chief minister, commander-in-chief, chief exchequer and head qazi (magistrate) he kept Swat free from practising lawyers (up to 80 cases a day were decided by personal audience), and ate three-course meals, always starting with mulligatawny soup and ending with apple pudding.

♀ *FLIES*

● SWAYING

To 'wintle' or to 'showd' is to sway gently from side to side. To 'shoogle' is to rock back and forth with small rapid movements or from side to side.

♀ *BEETHOVEN*

● SWAZILAND

When a king of Swaziland dies, his successor is chosen from among his younger sons and must be a right-handed man with no full brother.

The current monarch of Swaziland is King Mswati III, who has reigned since 1986. He has 15 wives and 36 children. The King's mother is known as The Great She-Elephant.

In 1985, a Swaziland MP said that anyone found possessing human flesh or bones without reasonable cause should be hanged in public. He claimed that the practice of human sacrifice was harming Swaziland's reputation.

In 1998, Swaziland was reported to be having difficulty finding a hangman. The country's previous hangman was reported to have 'disappeared without trace' in the mid-1980s and adverts from the Ministry of Justice for a 'brave young man who has what it takes' had not found a replacement. In 2002, however, the method of execution was changed from hanging to lethal injection which the Justice Minister said 'does not have to be administered by a specialist but only by a qualified medical practitioner'. The last execution in Swaziland was in 1983.

In 2002, Swaziland lost track of its only ship. The Transport Minister was quoted as saying, 'Our nation's merchant navy is perfectly safe. We just don't know where it is; that's all.' He went on to say, 'We believe it is in a sea somewhere.'

On 6 November 1995, a group of Swaziland MPs called for new laws to protect men and boys from being raped by women. They argued that the current rape laws were sexually discriminatory.

Swaziland competed at the 1972 Olympics and every Summer Olympics since 1984 but has yet to win a medal. Swaziland's only representative at a Winter Olympics was Keith Fraser, who was born in Scotland. He came

63rd in the Giant Slalom in 1992. He is now reported to be a ski instructor in Colorado and is known affectionately as 'Swaz'.

📍 *AIDS, COMMONWEALTH, GHOSTS, MONARCHY*

⬤ SWEARING

A hearing in Cincinnati in 1996 upheld the right of a local high school to suspend a student for violating a ban against swearing by saying 'Jesus Christ!' in class. The boy's mother had said that his constitutional rights had been violated. Describing herself as a non-Christian, she said, 'We do not consider saying "Jesus Christ" any more of a curse word than saying "red sneakers".'

⬤ SWEAT

According to research in 2009 by a company in Geneva specialising in flavours and smells for the food and perfume industries, men's underarm sweat contains a substance smelling like cheese, while women's has a substance smelling like grapefruit or onion.

📍 *EGYPT, LEMUR*

⬤ SWEDEN

In January 2022, the Swedish village of Fucke applied to the government to change its name. Residents were reported to be tired of being censored when mentioning their village on Facebook.

Sweden is the only country where the consumption of Coca-Cola drops at Christmas. This is due to production of a local festive drink called Julmust.

In the Middle Ages, the Swedish town of Hurdenburg elected its mayor by seeing which candidate's beard was selected by a louse.

In the 17th century, Queen Christina of Sweden had a miniature cannon made, which she used for firing tiny cannonballs at fleas.

The town of Ystad in Sweden hosts a game of Cow Bingo every year at which visitors place bets on which of 81 squares in a field a cow will first drop a cow pat on.

The Swedes drink more coffee per head than any other nation and spend more per head on tomato ketchup.

A man was fined £9 for striking his 11-year-old son in Gallivare, Sweden, in 1984. The child had taken a bicycle ride in defiance of his father. It was the first conviction under an anti-child-spanking law of 1979.

On 8 May 1921, Sweden abolished capital punishment. Twelve years later, to the day, on 8 May 1933, the USA first used a gas chamber to carry out a death sentence.

Anyone born in Sweden on the last day of February in 1712 never had another true birthday. As the country dithered between Julian and Gregorian calendars, February had 30 days in both Sweden and Finland that year.

📍 *ANORAK, CRASH TEST DUMMY, LEAP YEAR, MILK, NAMES, PEEING*

⬤ SWEETS

British forces in Afghanistan ate 923,583 bags of Haribo sweets in 2009 according to a survey by NAAFI. The survey also revealed that fizzy drinks and chocolate were servicemen's and women's favourite treats.

📍 *JELLY BEAN, MIDGET, NEW YEAR'S EVE*

⬤ SWIMMING

Fornication avec l'onde was how the French poet Paul Valéry described swimming, and humans have been fornicating with the waves for as long as history records. 'And he shall spread out his hands in the midst of them as he that swimmeth spreadeth forth his hands out to swim,' says Isaiah 25:10.

In Greek mythology, the lovelorn Leander drowned in his attempt to swim against the strong currents of the Hellespont in order to be with his girlfriend Hero. Byron swam it in an hour and 10 minutes on 3 May 1810 and wrote, when he had dried himself off: 'I plume myself on this achievement more than I could possibly do any kind of glory, political, poetical, rhetorical.'

As the quotation from Isaiah suggests, early swimmers used the breaststroke. The 'overarm' stroke was considered effective only over short distances. In 1902, however, J.A. Jarvis wrote: 'I am firmly convinced that the present records at all distances will be wiped out and fresh ones put in their place by trudgers.' Trudgers were practitioners of the trudgen (or trudgeon), a cumbersome overarm stroke introduced into Britain by John Trudgen, who had been taught it by swimmers in Buenos Aires in 1863. In the same year that Jarvis made his prediction, however, Richard Cavill, an Australian, demonstrated the front crawl, and trudging vanished forever.

The next major improvement came with the invention of the butterfly stroke by the German Eric Rademacher, in 1926. Nobody took much notice, however, until 1933, when an American, Henry Myers, used it as a means of legal cheating in breaststroke races. It took the authorities until 1953 before the laws were sorted out and butterfly was recognised as a distinct stroke.

In 1875, Matthew Webb became the first man to swim the Channel, but earlier he had won a wager that he could remain in the sea longer than a Newfoundland dog. After Webb had remained in the water for an hour and a half, it was reported that 'the poor brute [the dog, presumably] was nearly drowned'.

DUCK, GREECE, GUPPY, ISRAEL, POLAR BEAR, TITANIC

SWITZERLAND

Switzerland has held first place in the World Intellectual Property Organization's Global Innovation Index for every year from 2011 to 2021. It is the fifth best country to live in, according to the Social Progress Index, behind Finland, Canada, Denmark and Australia.

On 16 July 1661, Switzerland became the first country in Europe to issue banknotes.

Genetically modified chocolate is illegal in Switzerland.

COW, DIDGERIDOO, DOYLE, GUINEA PIGS, RAMBLING, VIOLENCE

SWORD

A world record for sword swallowing was set in Australia in 2010 by Chayne Hultgren, also known as the Space Cowboy, who swallowed 18 swords, each 72 centimetres (28.35 inches) long simultaneously. He described it as one of his greatest achievements and stressed that it needed a lot of practice. 'I stretch my throat with hoses and use a few different techniques to basically enable me to do what, until now, has been impossible. I don't just straightaway grab 18 blades and shove them down my throat – you've got to practise a lot and build up to it,' he said.

BRAHE, D'EON, FENCING, GOOSEBERRY, GUILLOTINE, SAMURAI

SYDNEY

Sydney, Australia, was named after the British Home Secretary, Thomas Townshend, Lord Sydney, who set up the charter establishing a penal colony there. Sydney in Canada is also named after him, though Lord Sydney never visited either Canada or Australia.

Tokyo and Madrid are the only cities in the world to have larger fish markets than that of Sydney.

The total cost of building Sydney Harbour Bridge, which was opened in 1932, was double the original quote. It was not fully paid off until 1988. Sixteen men died during the building. The only one to survive a fall from the bridge into the water was Vincent Kelly, who was given a medal for 'Preserving His Own Life'.

Sydney Harbour Bridge may rise or fall up to 17 centimetres (7 inches) as the steel expands or contracts in hot or cold weather.

The oldest person to take part in the Sydney Harbour Bridge Climb was Mrs Chris Muller, who accomplished the ascent at the age of 100. It consists of a guided climb up the arches of the bridge.

AUSTRALIA, NAVEL, REPTILES

SYPHILIS

'Syphilis' was originally the title of a 1530 poem written in Latin by Fracastoro, concerning a hero named Syphilis who has syphilis.

In the 16th century, astrologers believed that syphilis was caused by the conjunction of Saturn, Jupiter and Mars in Cancer, which corrupted the air. Petrus Maynardus, who taught medicine at Padua, said that only men born under the sign of Scorpio are prone to catch syphilis. He further predicted – sadly incorrectly – that syphilis would vanish after another conjunction in 1584.

Before it became generally known as syphilis, the Dutch called it the Spanish disease, the Russians called it the Polish disease, the Turks called it the Christian disease, and in Tahiti it was known as the British disease. In 2008, researchers in the US reported that a genetic analysis of syphilis supported the theory that syphilis was brought to Europe by Christopher Columbus's crew.

BAUDELAIRE, CHURCHILL, COLUMBUS, FALLOPPIO, ST GEORGE

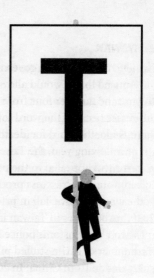

TABLE MANNERS

Louis XIV of France ordered that table knives must have rounded, not pointed ends, to stop them being used as daggers during mealtime arguments.

Japanese etiquette forbids licking the ends of chopsticks, a piece of rudeness known as *neburibashi*. Other chopstick taboos include waving them indecisively over your food (*mayoibashi*) and stuffing food into an already full mouth (*komibashi*).

TABLE TENNIS

When the game began as an improvised after-dinner amusement in England in the 1880s, it was known first as 'table tennis', then as 'whiff-whaff', 'ping-pong' or 'gossima'. The name 'ping-pong' was trademarked by John Jacques and Son in 1900.

The man usually credited with inventing the modern game was James Gibb, who introduced the celluloid ball to ping-pong in 1900. The other main innovator was E.C. Goode, who introduced the modern racket with a pimpled surface. The first official organisation was created in 1921, with the founding of the Table Tennis Association in England. Five years later, the International Table Tennis Federation came into existence. In 1988, the game was included in the Olympics.

A ball, when dropped from 30 centimetres (11.8 inches), should, by international rules, bounce to a height of 23 centimetres (9 inches). It should weigh 2.7 grams and have a diameter of 40mm. The table is 2.75 by 1.5 metres (9 by 5 feet), and 76 centimetres (30 inches) high.

In 1929, the World Table Tennis Championship was won by lawn tennis champion Fred Perry. From 1930 to 1950, table tennis was banned in the USSR as it was considered bad for the eyesight.

TABLOID

The word 'tabloid' was first coined and registered on 14 March 1884 as a trademark by Henry Solomon Wellcome; at the time it was a proprietary brand name for pills, medicine chests, food, tea and publications. The phrases 'tabloid newspaper' and 'tabloid journalism' were first used in 1901.

TAIWAN

In 1995, the Taiwanese government announced that it would allow people to omit the number four from their addresses because the word for 'four' sounds like the word for 'death'.

The following year, the Taiwanese government appealed to the people to eat more garlic. Excess production had caused a drastic fall in prices. In 2020, garlic prices in Taiwan increased massively and customs police seized a container of garlic-stuffed pillows smuggled in from China. In 2021, a 'garlic grinder' machine was invented in Taiwan to trim the roots of newly picked garlic bulbs and greatly reduce the workload for garlic farmers.

The first nude wedding in Taiwan was held on 19 October 1997. The bride was a stripper and former parliamentary candidate.

In August 2010, servicemen in Taiwan were banned from taking naps, or closing their eyes to rest, while on public transport. The Defence Ministry announced the ban 'to maintain the image of the armed forces'.

In 2010, motorists in Southern Taiwan were urged to give land crabs right of way as the animals make their way to the spawning grounds. 'It's shocking to hear the loud sounds of crabs being crushed under the cars and see their smashed bodies scattered all along the highway,' a national park official said.

DIAGNOSIS, FALSE TEETH, MONKEY, POVERTY, RAT, SLOGAN

TAJ MAHAL

The Taj Mahal took 22 years to build, by an estimated 20,000 workers using about 1,000 elephants to move the construction materials. The building is a cenotaph built by Shah Jahan in honour of his wife Mumtaz Mahal, who died while giving birth to their fourteenth child.

DOCTORS

TAJIKISTAN

In 2009, the Central Asian state of Tajikistan banned mobile phones from all schools and universities. 'This measure has been taken in order to improve the quality of teaching at schools,' a government spokesman said.

UZBEKISTAN

TALIBAN

When the Taliban were in control in Afghanistan between 1996 and 2001, a list of 'unclean' items banned by their Ministry of Virtue and Prevention of Vice included the following: pork, pig, pig oil, anything made from human hair, satellite dishes, cinematography, any equipment that produces the joy of music, pool tables, chess, masks, alcohol, tapes, computers, VCRs, television, anything that propagates sex and is full of music, wine, lobster, nail polish, firecrackers, statues, sewing catalogues, pictures and Christmas cards.

TAMPON

The first disposable tampons were invented by the ancient Egyptians and made from softened papyrus. The ancient Greeks invented tampons made from lint wrapped around a small piece of wood. Hippocrates wrote of these in the 5th century BC.

Other materials used for early tampons included: wool, paper, vegetable fibres including grass, and later cotton.

In 1929, the modern tampon (with applicator) was invented and patented by the Denver general practitioner Earle Haas, who had been motivated by the desire to offer a mass-produced tampon for his patients. Haas filed for his first tampon patent on 19 November 1931 and the patent was issued on 12 September 1933. He entitled his invention a 'catamenial device', derived from the Greek word for monthly. He later trademarked Tampax as the brandname for his product.

In 2012, the celebrated chef Heston Blumenthal pointed out that sucking on a tampon can enhance one's appreciation of the flavour of foods: 'If you have a spoonful of ice-cream then put a tampon on the tongue for a couple of minutes, when you eat the ice-cream again the taste will be richer,' he said, though he did add that it can be quite funny 'sitting there with the little string coming out of your mouth'.

TANZANIA

Following a survey in 2008, the height of Mount Kilimanjaro in Tanzania was determined as 5,891.8 metres (19,330 feet), which is was just over 3 metres (10 feet) shorter than the official height of 5,895 metres (19,340 feet) which had been thought since 1952.

♀ *BOTSWANA, ISRAEL, LION, WASP*

TAPEWORM

Human tapeworms can grow to a length of up to 22.9 metres (75 feet). An adult tapeworm consists of a head, neck and chain of segments called proglottids. Each proglottid contains a complete sexually mature reproductive system.

♀ *PARASITE*

TARANTINO, Quentin (b. 1963)

It is often stated that all of the clocks on the wall in *Pulp Fiction* are stuck at 4:20. This is very much an exaggeration. Many of the clocks, especially in the pawn shop scene, display that time but certainly not all of them, even in that particular scene. The time of 4.20 may be a reference to a common time of meeting for Californian marijuana smokers, which became so much a coded term for the drug itself that 20 April, or 4.20 as Americans called it, became a slang reference for dope.

The word 'fuck' occurs 155 times in Quentin Tarantino's *Pulp Fiction* and 177 times in *Reservoir Dogs*.

♀ *ANCHOVY, BASTARD, CANNES*

TARTAN

The oldest known tartan design is the Falkirk tartan, which dates to around AD 245 and was discovered in a jar of coins near Falkirk.

6 April is Tartan Day, celebrating the Declaration of Arbroath, signed on 6 April 1320, declaring Scotland's independence. In the US in 2008, an annual 6 April Tartan Day was proclaimed by President George W. Bush. Australia and some other countries celebrate Tartan Day on 1 July, the anniversary of the repeal in 1782 of the 1746 UK Act banning the wearing of tartan. The ban on tartan was part of an attempt to bring warring tribes under government control.

Every province and territory in Canada, except Nunavut in the north, has its own official tartan.

The first colour photograph, taken in 1861 by James Clerk Maxwell, was of a tartan ribbon.

The only tartan to have been to the Moon was a piece of MacBean tartan, taken there in 1969 by Alan Bean, the fourth man to walk on the Moon.

There are officially three tartans that honour Elvis Presley. The Presley of Lonmay Tartan, in blue, grey, green and yellow, was designed in 2004 to mark the alleged roots of the Presley family in Lonmay in Aberdeenshire. This was designed by kilt-maker Mike King, who also designed a tartan called Presley of Lonmay Modern in 2007.

The Scottish Register of Tartans also lists the 'Presley of Memphis' tartan, designed by Brian Wilton in 2004, which it says is based on the 'America' tartan in the colours of the US flag, but 'discretely introduces Elvis Presley's favourite colour pink plus a gold band to represent his legendary number of Gold Discs'. Further technical details are that the white thread count is 42, which was Elvis's age when he died, while the eight narrow white threads represent the day of the month in which he was born and the eight blue threads represent the month of the year in which he died.

⚲ BILLIARDS

TASMANIA

On 24 November 1642, the Dutch navigator Abel Tasman became the first European to see Tasmania. He named the island Antonie Van Diemen's Land after his sponsor, Antonie van Diemen, governor-general of the Dutch East Indies. The name was shortened to Van Diemen's Land and renamed Tasmania, after its discoverer, in 1856.

Tasmania is home to the Mountain Ash, also known as the Tasmanian Oak, which, attaining heights of over 100 metres (328 feet), is the world's tallest flowering plant.

The Tasmanian Tiger is not a tiger but a dog-like marsupial. The last known example died in 1936. The Tasmanian Devil is the largest carnivorous marsupial in the world. Until recently, it was found only in Tasmania, but a small breeding population has been introduced to New South Wales.

The Australian state of Tasmania consists of the island of Tasmania plus 333 far smaller islands.

The actor Errol Flynn was born in Tasmania in 1909. His father was professor of biology at the University of Tasmania.

Hobart, the capital of Tasmania, was named after Robert Hobart, 4th Earl of Buckinghamshire and Britain's colonial secretary.

⚲ BREAD, DNA, VAGINA

TATTOO

The first tattoos were carried out by the ancient Egyptians, possibly as early as 4000 BC. The word 'tattoo' (signifying body-art) comes from a Samoan word *ta-tau*. News of this was first brought to the British by Captain Cook in his journal in 1769, where he wrote of the Samoan 'method of Tattowing' in the following words: 'As this is a painful operation especially the tattowing their buttocks it is perform'd but once in their life times.'

This has nothing to do with 'tattoo' meaning a military drum or bugle signal, which comes from the Dutch *taptoe* – to close the tap of a wine cask. The idea of closing off a tap was carried over to be used for a drum or bugle call for soldiers to return to barracks.

During the Second World War, statistics show that a tattooed American was one and a half times more likely to be rejected for military service than an untattooed one, and a man with a tattoo of a naked woman was more likely to be rejected than a man whose tattoo showed a flag or landscape. The traditional view among New Zealand Maoris, however, is to regard a tattooed chin as a sign of high rank.

King Harold II of England, who was killed at the Battle of Hastings in 1066, had the words 'Edith and England' tattooed over his heart. This was presumably a reference to his first wife Edith the Fair, also known as Edith Swan-Neck.

The world record for tattooing is held by Oliver Peck of Elm Street Tattoo in Dallas, who applied tattoos of the number 13 on 415 people in a 24-hour marathon tattooing session in 2008.

The record for being tattooed, however, is held by performance artist Lucky Diamond Rich (Gregory Paul McLaren), whose skin is 100 per cent tattooed including the insides of his eyelids, mouth, ears and foreskin.

'Bookkeeper', 'bookkeeping' and 'tattooee' are the only English words with three consecutive pairs of double letters – but despite gaining nearly half a million hits on a Google search, tattooee is not in the *Oxford English Dictionary*.

First-time receivers of a tattoo are known to tattooers as 'freshcuts'.

♀ *BODY ART, HUMAN RIGHTS, SPOON, VOLLEYBALL*

● TAX

The Greek grammarian Julius Pollux listed 33 terms of abuse for tax collectors in his Onomasticon thesaurus.

In 1986, Polish police hunting the killers of a taxman whose dismembered body was found in two suitcases arrested a man and a woman he visited on the day he disappeared. They owed more than 12,000 zlotys (£50) in arrears.

In 2006, the Australian tax office ruled that sex toys are tax deductible for prostitutes.

'In this world, nothing can be said to be certain except death and taxes.' Benjamin Franklin

'Avoidance of taxes is the only intellectual pursuit that carries any reward.' John Maynard Keynes

'The difference between tax avoidance and tax evasion is the thickness of a prison wall.' Denis Healey

♀ *ALBANIA, GODIVA, HAIR, HAT, INCOME TAX, OSTRICH, ST MATTHEW*

● TAXI

The word 'taxi' was originally an abbreviation of 'taxameter' or 'taximeter', a device to measure distance travelled and used to calculate fares. The first reference to a 'taxi' in the UK was in 1907. Before that, they were known as Hansom cabs or Hackney carriages. The horse-drawn Hansom cabs were patented by architect Joseph Aloysius Hansom in 1834, while Hackney carriages took their name not from a part of London but from an old French word for a horse.

Taxis were banned from driving through London's Hyde Park from 1685–7 after some women had behaved in an unruly manner in a Hackney carriage, and the ban was reinstated from 1711–1924.

Until 1976, when the London Hackney Carriage Act of 1831 was finally repealed, London taxi drivers were liable to be fined 20 shillings for blocking the road by feeding horses 'save only with Corn out of a Bag, or with Hay which he shall hold or deliver with his Hands'. That original act was the source of an oft-repeated myth that taxi drivers had to keep a bale of hay in their cabs.

♀ *PLAGUE, SEX-CHANGE*

TAXIDERMY

The oldest stuffed bird in existence is believed to be a parrot which was the companion of Frances Teresa, Duchess of Richmond, who was maid of honour to Catherine of Braganza, queen of Charles II. The African grey parrot, which lived with Frances Teresa for 40 years, can be seen at Westminster Abbey proudly perched on a stand next to a wax effigy of her.

   WIARTON WILLY

TEA

According to legend, tea was discovered by the Chinese emperor Shen Nung in 2737 BC. This mythological ruler is also hailed as the man who introduced acupuncture.

Since the Japanese Way of Tea was established in the 16th century, there have been only 16 grand masters of tea. The principles underlying the tea ceremony are *Wa Kei Sei Jaku*, or Harmony, Respect, Purity, Tranquility.

Iced tea was first served during a heatwave at the St Louis World Fair in 1904, which was also the year the banana split and the paper plate were invented.

In 1784, the tax on tea in the UK was cut from 119 per cent to 12.5 per cent to discourage smuggling.

The world's biggest tea bag weighed 250 kilograms (551 pounds 2.56 ounces) and was made in Jeddah, Saudi Arabia, on 20 September 2014 by the Rabea Tea company. This broke a record set the previous year in Queensland, where the Planet Organic company made a tea bag weighing 151 kilograms (333 pounds) and standing 3 metres (10 feet) high. Its makers said it contained enough organic green tea to make 100,000 cups, but they were not ready to pour boiling water on it as they did not have a cup big enough to hold it.

'A hasty person drinks tea with a fork.'
Chinese proverb

   BEER, BRAZIL, COFFEE, PEPYS, UMBRELLA, YAK, ZAMBIA

TEACHING

The first evidence of a non-human 'teacher–pupil' relationship was identified in 2006 in ants. Research indicated that some ant species adopt a technique known as 'tandem running', by which one ant leads another from the nest to a food source. These findings were cited as evidence that teaching does not necessarily require a big brain.

   ADMIRALTY ISLANDS, GREAT WALL OF CHINA, UNIVERSITIES

TEETH

Richard III, Napoleon Bonaparte, Louis XIV and Julius Caesar were all born with teeth, though that happens to only about one in 2,000 babies.

George Washington had several sets of dentures, in which elephant tusks, lead, cow teeth, hippo teeth, human teeth and possibly a walrus tusk all played their part. He soaked his dentures overnight in port to improve their taste.

A world simultaneous toothbrushing record was set in 2019 by the Indian Association of Public Health Dentistry when 26,382 people brushed their teeth at the same time in Bhubaneswar in the state of Odisha.

The numbat, a west Australian marsupial, has 52 permanent teeth, the most of any land mammal. It doesn't use them, but swallows ants and termites whole.

The common expression 'By the skin of my teeth' is a misquote from the Book of Job. The original (Job 19:20) said: 'My bone cleaveth to my skin and to my flesh, and I am escaped *with* the skin of my teeth.'

Aristotle, in his *History of Animals,* asserted that: 'males have more teeth than females in the case of men, sheep, goats and swine'. As Bertrand Russell pointed out, Aristotle could have avoided the error by the simple expedient of 'asking Mrs Aristotle to open her mouth'.

'The husband was a teetotaller, there was no other woman, and the conduct complained of was that he drifted into the habit of winding up every meal by taking out his false teeth and hurling them at his wife.' Arthur Conan Doyle, 'A Case of Identity', 1891

⚲ LIECHTENSTEIN, MONKEY, PANGOLIN, PLATYPUS, SLUG, SNAIL

⬤ TELEPHONE

On 10 March 1876, Alexander Graham Bell made the first telephone call, saying to his assistant in another room, 'Mr Watson, come here. I want to see you.' Watson later explained that Bell's reason for the call was that he had spilt some battery acid on his trousers.

There is an indie-rock band in the US midwest called 'Come Here Watson'.

The Nokia ringtone for text messages is the Morse Code for the letters SMS which stands for Short Message Service.

The word frigensophobia has been coined to mean a fear that mobile phones can damage the brain. Frigensophobia actually means fear of frying.

On the day of Alexander Graham Bell's funeral, US phones were stopped from ringing for a minute.

There are over a billion telephone lines in the world. Worldwide, the equivalent of over $1.5 trillion was spent on telecommunications in 2019, which works out at around $200 for every man, woman and child on the planet.

⚲ BELL, BURNT FOOD, MAYDAY, MOBILE PHONE, PHONE SEX, ST CLARE

⬤ TELEVISION

The 1966 World Cup Final in which England defeated West Germany was watched by 32.3 million TV viewers, which is the highest audience ever in Britain. Just behind, at 31.1 million viewers, was the funeral of Diana, Princess of Wales, in 1997.

In 2004, the number of television sets in the UK overtook the number of people. In 2019, the average person in the UK spent 182.95 minutes a day watching television. This figure has been declining since 2010 when the average was 242 minutes.

The average American sees 13,000 deaths on television between the ages of five and 14. Including the murders, the crimes committed on-screen in an average week's viewing would merit 6,000 years in prison. Despite this, a survey in the 1980s reported that 44 per cent of American children prefer the television to Daddy.

According to a survey of 1,000 adults in 2017, 96 per cent of Americans say they're likely to snack when tuning in to their favourite programmes, and a third of them believe that certain snacks taste better when paired with different TV shows. For emotionally-rich shows, ice cream and chocolate were recommended, while crisps were best for watching reality shows. The survey also found that 38 per cent of people want to eat something both sweet and salty while watching TV. More than half share snacks with whoever is watching with them.

According to a poll in the UK in 2001, the Top 5 favourite snacks to eat while watching TV are crisps, chocolate bars, fresh fruit, sandwiches and ice cream, in that order.

The first UK television advert was for Gibbs SR toothpaste on 22 September 1955.

There are about 219,000,000 TV sets in the US, which works out at an average of about 1.8 per household. Around 3 per cent of households do not have a TV set, though they can still access television programmes on other devices such as computers or phones.

'You know the really great thing about television? If something important happens – anywhere in the world – night or day – you can always change the channel.' Christopher Lloyd in Taxi

> BAIRD, BEDROOM, BHUTAN, MONKEY, OBESITY, SOAP OPERAS

TEMPERATURE

It was long claimed that the highest temperature ever recorded in the shade was 57.8°C (136°F) in Libya on 13 September 1922, but in 2012 this was reassessed by the World Meteorological Organisation which has invalidated it. According to the WMO, the highest temperature ever recorded was 56.7°C (134.1°F) on 10 July 1913 in Furnace Creek, California, but that too is considered by some to be exaggerated. Other possible record-holders include China, Tunisia and Israel.

> CRICKET, CUCUMBER, MARS, NORTH POLE, SOUTH POLE, SUN

TENNESSEE

After previous failed attempts, the Tennessee state legislature finally succeeded in March 2012 in passing a bill to stop children from wearing their trousers too low. Unlike a previous attempt that specified a $250 fine on students who wore their trousers a specific distance below the waist, the new bill leaves it to the discretion of teachers to judge whether trousers are too low and baggy, and also to decide the appropriate punishment. Other US authorities passed similar ordinances later, including Alabama, Georgia and Missouri.

> FRUIT, INCEST, NUDITY, PARTON, SIGN LANGUAGE, WISCONSIN

TENNIS

The word 'tennis' probably comes from the French *tenez* ('take' or 'receive'), a warning shouted by the server.

Although the first lawn tennis club was founded in Leamington Spa in 1872 by businessmen and sportsmen Major Harry Gem and Augurio Perera, the game of lawn tennis was patented under the name 'Sphairistike' by Major Walter Wingfield in 1874, though it grew out of the much older game of real (or royal) tennis, which was played indoors in long, narrow rooms.

Wingfield's game was in many ways as we know it today, but played on an hour-glass-shaped court, 9 metres (30 feet) across at its widest but only 6 metres (20 feet) at the net. He sold Sphairistike sets, comprising ball, four racquets and netting to mark out the court, for five guineas (£5.25).

The rectangular court became the norm in 1875 when the All England Croquet Club at Wimbledon decided to add tennis (as it was by then being called) to its repertoire. Twenty-two players paid a guinea (£1.05) each to enter the first tournament, and Spencer Gore, who also played first-class cricket for Surrey, became the first Wimbledon champion. He said he didn't think this new game would catch on.

When lawn tennis was introduced by the British to the King and Queen of Korea in 1892, Queen Min is said to have commented, 'These Englishmen are becoming very hot. Why do they not have their servants do it?'

Goran Ivanisevic is the only Wimbledon champion whose entire name is a strict alternation of consonants and vowels.

Amélie Mauresmo (2006 Ladies Champion) is the only Wimbledon singles champion, male or female, whose first name and surname between them include all five vowels.

Sewing a tennis ball into the back of a person's pyjamas is a recommended remedy for snoring.

Charles VIII of France died in 1498 when he was only 17, after hitting his head on a lintel above a door when on his way to watch a real tennis game. When returning home from the game, he fell into a sudden coma and died nine hours later.

According to research published in 1998, drinking caffeine-rich fluids between points improves the accuracy and results of women tennis players but has no effect on men.

   ♀ *ALBANIA, BALFOUR, ENGLISH, TABLE TENNIS, TIE-BREAK, WIMBLEDON*

● TENNYSON, Alfred Lord (1809–92)

Commenting on the tempestuous marriage between the Scottish historian Thomas Carlyle and Jane Baillie Welsh (who was the subject of Leigh Hunt's poem 'Jenny Kissed Me'), Tennyson approved of the matrimony, saying: 'By any other arrangement, four people would have been unhappy instead of two.'

Tennyson's last words, spoken on 6 October 1892, were: 'I have opened it.' Nobody knows what he was talking about.

   ♀ *BABBAGE, TWELFTH NIGHT*

● TEQUILA

The drink Tequila is named after the Mexican town of Tequila. In 1999, a company in Mexico was fined around $27,500 and told to withdraw a drink they had called 'Tequila Cabron' from supermarket shelves after officials at the Federal Consumer Protection Agency had ruled that the word 'cabron' was too profane for the country's national drink.

'Cabron' means 'male goat' in Spanish, but when used in anger in Mexico, the nearest English equivalent would be 'bastard'. Between friends, however, it is used to mean a boss or figure of authority.

● TERMITE

Termites have no ears. Soldier termites send alarm messages through a colony by banging their heads on tunnel walls, making a great noise and setting up vibrations that are picked up by other termites through sensory organs on their legs. Different species of termite bang their heads at different rates.

   ♀ *AARDVARK, KRILL, METHANE, PANGOLIN, TEETH*

● TERRAPIN

The name of the terrapin comes from an Algonquin Indian word meaning 'edible'. According to an article in the *New York Times* in 1988, the diamond-backed terrapin is to many connoisseurs the best-tasting turtle in the world. The genus *Terrapene* consists of box turtles. These are not terrapins.

♀ *TURTLE*

TESTICLE

The science journal *Nature* in 1976 carried a short paper entitled 'Scrotal Asymmetry in Man and in Ancient Sculpture', in which Chris McManus pointed out that the left testicles in Greek statues are always larger and lower than their companions. As he pointed out, however, in humans it is the smaller testicles that are lower, not the bigger ones. Furthermore, the right testicle tends to be higher in right-handed subjects, whereas the converse is true in left-handers. So the Greeks were wrong about the left being larger in the majority, and it is the smaller right testicles which are lower.

The scientific instrument for gauging the size of testicles is called an orchidometer.

♀ *ABORTION, AVOCADO, BEAVER, BULL, BUSH-CRICKET, FREUD, ORCHID*

TEXAS

Texas is the only state in the USA that was a country in its own right. It is commonly believed that because of this, the Texan state flag is the only one permitted by federal law to be flown at the same height as the Stars and Stripes. However, no such specification exists in the US flag code. Under the Texas flag code, the Texas flag should be flown below that of the USA if they are on the same pole, but level with it if they are on separate poles.

2 March is celebrated as Independence Day in Texas, marking the state's separation from Mexico in 1836. The Republic of Texas then maintained its independence for almost 10 years before being incorporated into the United States in 1845. The area of Texas is almost three times that of the UK.

Texas accounts for 7.4 per cent of the land area of the USA. It was 8.8 per cent until Alaska joined.

In 1987, the lightning whelk *Busycon perversum pulleyi* was named official state shell of Texas. The armadillo is the official state mammal of Texas. The state flower is the bluebonnet.

'Texas' is an anagram of the word 'taxes'. The only other US state which has a common one-word anagram of its name is 'Minnesota' in the midwest ('nominates'). 'Utah' is an anagram of the obsolete word 'haut', meaning 'high'.

Since 1976, when the US Supreme Court brought back judicial execution, 40 per cent of all executions in the US have taken place in Texas.

There used to be a law in Texas specifically making it illegal to milk another person's cow.

There is a town called Earth in Texas. It is said to be the only place on Earth called Earth.

The third line of the Texas state song is: 'Boldest and grandest, withstanding every test.' The first word was changed from 'Largest' to 'Boldest' when Alaska became a state in 1959.

♀ *MUSHROOM, NOODLING, POPEYE, SEXUAL HARASSMENT, TIES*

TEXTING

A world record was set by Portugal's Pedro Matias at the LG Mobile World Cup Championship in New York City in January 2010, for typing a set text, comprising 264 characters and 54 spaces, in 1 minute 59 seconds. This beat the previous record by 23 seconds.

The team title was won by South Korea.

The set text was this: 'The telephone was invented by Alexander Graham Bell (UK) who filed his patent for the telephone on 14 February 1876 at the New York Patent Office, USA.'

THACKERAY, William Makepeace (1811–63)

The novelist William Thackeray had a brain that weighed 1,658 grams (58.5 ounces). Despite this, he once gambled away £1,500 in one night as a student. He had a pet cat called Louisa.

♀ *DONKEY*

THAILAND

Thailand is the only country in south-east Asia that has never been colonised by Europeans.

The official name of its capital, Bangkok, is 'Krung Thep Maha Nakhon Amon Rattanakosin Mahinthara Yutthaya Mahadilokphop Noppharat Ratchathani Burirom Udom Ratchaniwet Maha Sathan Amon Phiman Awatan Sathit Sakkathattiya Witsanukam Prasit' (usually abbreviated to 'Krung Thep'). Loosely translated, this means 'The City of Angels, the Great City, the Residence of the Emerald Buddha, the Capital of the World Endowed with Nine Precious Gems, the Happy City Abounding in Enormous Royal Palaces which Resemble the Heavenly Abode wherein Dwell the Reincarnated Gods, a City Given by Indra and Built by Witsanukam'. Unsurprisingly, this name is generally accepted as the longest name of any capital city in the world, though there is debate about precisely how many letters it has, because it is a transliteration from the Thai alphabet and several different versions are in circulation. The one used above has 169 letters; other sources suggest a total of 167.

A Monkey Buffet is held every year in front of the Pra Prang Sam Yot Temple in Thailand's Lopburi province, where around 600 monkeys are encouraged to feast on over 2 tonnes of grilled sausage, fresh fruit, ice cream and other treats. It is the local villagers' way of thanking the monkeys for being there and attracting so many tourists.

The song 'One Night in Bangkok', from the musical *Chess*, was banned in May 1985 from a TV channel and government radio station in Thailand because the lyrics could 'cause misunderstanding about Thai society'.

A world record for vasectomies was claimed in Bangkok in December 1983 when 50 doctors held a nine-hour state-sponsored vasectomarathon session that attracted 1,190 patients.

Thailand, appropriately enough, unveiled what was then the world's longest tie on 15 May 1995. It was 99.6 metres (327 feet) long and 6 metres (19.5 feet) wide, and was made to honour King Bhumibol's 50 years on the throne of Thailand. This record stood until 2003.

♀ *BUFFALO, CAT, DENGUE FEVER, HULA HOOP, SIAM, ST VALENTINE*

THAMES

The Debris Clearance Operation of the Port of London Authority removes around 1,000 tonnes of litter every year from the Thames. It used to be much worse. In 1858, sewage in the Thames was so bad that it was known as the year of the Great Stink. Recent cleaning of the river has led to 119 species of fish being found in the Thames. Despite this improvement, a report in 2002 revealed that more than 2 billion litres of raw sewage were dumped in the River Thames over just two days.

There are around 400 sewage works along the Thames, cleaning the sewage and returning the water to the river. This is necessary because a drop of rain falling into the Thames at its source may have been drunk by as many as eight people before it reaches the sea.

⚲ *ENEMA, POLAR BEAR, SWAN-UPPING, TOWER BRIDGE, UNIVERSITIES*

THATCHER, Margaret Hilda (1925–2013)

'Margaret Thatcher' is an anagram of 'That great charmer'.

Margaret Thatcher was born six months before Queen Elizabeth II and seven months before Marilyn Monroe.

She had an intense dislike of insects and a near phobia of snakes.

According to an interview she gave in 1975, her favourite colour was turquoise.

In both her first two parliamentary elections, in 1950 and 1951, Margaret Thatcher (then Roberts) came second to Labour candidate Norman Dodds. In his victory speech in 1951, Dodds congratulated his opponent on her engagement to Denis Thatcher and wished them both well.

Writing in 1995, Margaret Thatcher paid tribute to Dodds as 'a genuine and extremely chivalrous socialist of the old school'. Shortly after, Dodds gained some notoriety when he came to Parliament with pyjamas, a pillow and a car rug, allowing him to catch some sleep during all-night sittings.

The first person to describe Margaret Thatcher as the 'Iron Lady' was Soviet journalist Yuri Gavrilov in the Red Star army newspaper in 1976.

Her first recorded words in the House of Commons in 1960 were: 'I beg to move that the Bill be now read a second time.' It was a bill about press access to official meetings.

The word 'Thatcherite' was first seen in 1976, 'Thatcherism' in 1977 and 'Thatcheresque' in 1979.

She once described her handbag as 'the only safe place in Downing Street'.

'In politics, if you want something said, ask a man; if you want something done, ask a woman.' Margaret Thatcher, 1975

'It will be years – and not in my time – before a woman will lead the party or become Prime Minister.' Margaret Thatcher, 1974

⚲ *STAR WARS*

THEATRE

The word 'theatre' comes from the Greek *theatron*, meaning 'something to behold'. Actors are known as thespians after Thespis, a Greek actor of the 6th century BC. Not only was Thespis the earliest-known actor, but he was the first to use stage make-up.

The first proper theatre in London was called, appropriately enough, 'The Theatre' and was built in Shoreditch in 1576.

The Kremlhof Theater in Villach, Austria, is said to be the world's smallest permanent professional theatre. It has a maximum capacity of eight seats.

⚲ *ACTRESS, DIOGENES, TWELFTH NIGHT, WOLVERHAMPTON*

THERBLIG

Around 1920, American psychologists Frank and Lillian Gilbreth introduced the therblig as the basic unit of operational efficiency and named it by approximately reversing their own name. Their studies identified 18 standard components of work that constitute the various types of therblig.

The complete list is as follows: search, find, select, grasp, hold, position, assemble, use, disassemble, inspect, transport loaded, transport unloaded, pre-position for next operation, release load, unavoidably delay, avoidably delay, plan, and rest for overcoming fatigue. Every operation, according to the Gilbreths, is a combination of these basic components and the number of them is its rating in therbligs.

● THINKING

Rodin's sculpture *The Thinker* was originally called 'The Poet'. The statue was intended to depict Dante at the Gates of Hell pondering his epic poem 'The Inferno'.

'Nobody is hanged for thinking.'
Hungarian proverb

'I think that I think, therefore I think that I am.' Ambrose Bierce, The Devil's Dictionary, *1906*

'Thinking is the most unhealthy thing in the world, and people die of it just as they die of any other disease.' Oscar Wilde

♀ *CELIBACY, FRANKLIN, GNOME. GOLF, IBSEN*

● THIRTEEN

Fear of the number 13 (known as triskaidekaphobia) was common to both ancient Babylonian and Old Norse myths. Norse mythology contains the story of a banquet that ended in disaster after Loki, the god of mischief, arrived as the 13th guest. For the Babylonians the fear was linked to a belief that the Sun needed to be kept separate from the 12 Zodiac signs. This was connected with a numerological belief that 12 was a good number because of its divisibility by 2, 3, 4 and 6, but adding one resulted in 13 which totally ruined the divisibility.

According to the 1894 edition of *Brewer's Phrase and Fable*: 'The Turks so disliked the number 13 the word is almost expunged from their vocabulary.'

In Christian tradition, fear of Friday the 13th (called paraskevidekatriaphobia) combines the day of the Crucifixion (Friday) and the number at the Last Supper (13), but despite these origins, a Friday the 13th superstition was first recorded only in the Middle Ages.

No more than three Friday the 13ths can occur in a single year. This happened in 2012 and 2015; the next time will be 2026. The longest period that can pass without a Friday the 13th is 14 months, as happened between Friday 13 July 2018 and Friday 13 September 2019.

Louis XIII of France was so attracted to the number 13 that he married 13-year-old Anne of Austria in 1615. By the 19th century, however, the number had become so feared that a society of French aristocrats was formed called the *quatorziennes* (14ths), who were available to come at short notice to dinners where 13 had turned up.

Even in today's supposedly enlightened age, it has been estimated that fear of the number 13 costs the US economy a billion dollars a year in absenteeism, cancellations and reduced commerce on the 13th days of the months.

Anyone seeking supporting evidence for the superstition, however, need look no further than the British National Lottery, where the number 13 has been picked less frequently than any other of the 49 original lottery numbers.

The wedding anniversary corresponding to 13 years' marriage is called a Lace Wedding.

The spoil from digging the Channel Tunnel between England and France would have filled Wembley Stadium 13 times.

CALENDAR, FRIDAY THE 13TH

THOR

The Norse god Thor, the eldest son of Odin, was the powerful and bad-tempered god of thunder, strength, agriculture, farmers, free men, rain and fertility. His most-feared weapon was a hammer called Mjöllnir, which he used both as a weapon and an instrument to deliver blessings. After Thor had thrown it and it had done its damage, Mjöllnir returned boomerang-like to his hand. This hammer, which was forged for Thor by dwarfs, is a symbol of fertility and a model of it is placed in the lap of the bride in traditional wedding ceremonies in Nordic countries. Thor couldn't throw his hammer without the aid of Megingjardir, his magic girdle which doubled his power.

Alone among the Norse Gods, Thor was not allowed to cross Bifrost, the bridge connecting Midgard, the world of men, with Asgard, the realm of the gods. It was feared that his lightning, or the very heat of his presence, might destroy it.

Thor rode in a chariot drawn by two fierce billygoats named Tanngnjóstr ('Toothgnasher') and Tanngrisnir ('Toothgrinder'). These goats could be killed and eaten, and they would be revived, good as new, the next day. The rolling of the wheels of Thor's goat-drawn chariot is said to create thunder.

In the great end-of-the-world battle at Ragnarok, Thor fights the Wyrm of Midgard, a serpent whose body encircles the whole world. Both are killed.

THUNDER

If you want to hear the sound of thunder, the best place to go is Tororo, Uganda, which has the reputation of being the most thundery place on Earth, where thunder can be heard on 251 days a year.

BHUTAN, DINOSAUR, HIPPOPOTAMUS, THOR, WEATHER

TIBET

The words 'polo' (the sport), 'yak' (the animal), 'zho' (a yak–cow hybrid) and 'Shangri-la' (an earthly paradise) all came into the English language from Tibetan. A female zho is called a zhomo.

Bumping foreheads is part of a traditional handshake in Tibet.

EVEREST, POLO, SHEEP, YAK, YETI

TIE-BREAK

The tie-break in tennis was invented by the American James van Alen in 1965. On the day of van Alen's death in 1991, Stefan Edberg lost at Wimbledon to Michael Stich 4-6, 7-6, 7-6, 7-6 without ever losing serve in the match. On hearing of the death, Edberg said: 'If he hadn't lived, we might still be out there playing.'

TIE KNOTS

According to the Cambridge physicists Thomas Fink and Yong Mao, there are 85 possible ways to knot a conventional tie, but only 13 of them are aesthetically pleasing from a balanced and symmetric point of view. Those found to pass the aesthetic tests are the knots which they call the Oriental, the Four-in-Hand, the Kelvin, the Nicky, the Victoria, the half-Windsor, the St Andrew, the Plattsburgh, the Cavendish, the Windsor, the Grantchester, the Hanover, and the Balthus. The Pratt and the Christensen are excluded from the list as they are less well-balanced than knots of comparable complexity.

Style-setter Beau Brummell is said to have spent hours perfecting the art of knotting, pleating, folding and arranging his cravat, and various authors tried to outdo each other in listing different knotting methods. *Neckclothitania,* published in 1818, offered 12 styles, *L'Art de se mettre sa cravate* described 32, and *L'Art de la toilette,* which came out in 1830, outlined 72.

'A well-tied tie is the first serious step in life.' Oscar Wilde, 1891

TIES

The oldest known tie was found in the mausoleum of Chinese Emperor Shih Huang Ti (259–210 BC). Ties were first worn in Europe by Croatian soldiers in the 17th century. Thailand's record for the world's longest tie was beaten by a tie exhibited in Croatia in 2003. It was 700 metres (2,300 feet) long and 25 metres (82 feet) wide. Displayed in the open, the tie was defended by a 2-metre (7 foot) model owl to stop seagulls using it as a toilet.

Wearing a tie is banned on the Texas holiday island of South Padre, where wearing a tie was ruled by the Board of Aldermen in 1997 to be 'detrimental to the welfare' of the island and its visitors. Police officers would issue a warning to first offenders but subsequent tie-wearing would lead to a fine equal to the price of a 'fine silk tie' and destruction of the offending neckwear.

'There is no time, sir, at which ties do not matter.' Jeeves to Bertie Wooster in P.G. Wodehouse's Jeeves and the Impending Doom, *1926*

♀ CROATIA, GLOBAL WARMING, TIE KNOTS, WHISKERS

TIGER

The tiger not only has striped fur, its skin is striped too. Every tiger has its own pattern of stripes, identifying it uniquely, like human fingerprints.

In December 1995, during a period of bad weather, the Isle of Wight Zoo announced that they would be giving special training to their Siberian tigers because they had never seen snow before.

♀ BRONTE, DNA, QUEENSLAND, ROBBERY, TASMANIA, WOODS

TIME

According to John of Trevisa's 1398 translation of Bartholomeus's *De Proprietatibus Rerum* (*Of the Properties of Things*), an ounce of time contains 47 atoms. An 'atom' was the smallest of all medieval measures of time, being equal to 15 ninety-fourths of a modern second.

According to an ancient French encyclopedia, there are five points in an hour, two ancient minutes in a point, four moments in an ancient minute, one and a half ostents in a moment and eight ounces in an ostent. By this reckoning, if anyone says, 'I'll be with you in a moment' or 'It'll only take a moment', they should keep you waiting one and a half modern minutes.

♀ CALENDAR, JIFFY, SECOND, WEDDING RING, WELLS

TIN

Tin is the 50th most abundant element in the Earth's crust, just ahead of europium but behind bromine. The Atomic number of tin is also 50.

> ⚲ *BISCUITS, BURIAL, ELEMENTS, FRISBEE, SOUP, TINS*

TINS

Tinned food originated with a prize offered by Napoleon Bonaparte in 1795 for a method of food preservation to feed his armies on long campaigns. The prize was won by a scientist named Nicolas Appert who preserved food by putting it in glass jars, sealing them with cork and sealing wax then placing them in boiling water. Modern tinned food came a step closer in 1810 when a merchant named Peter Durand received British Patent No. 3373 from King George III for a food preservation method similar to that of Appert, but widening the range of food containers to include pottery and tin.

Despite this, the modern tin-opener was not invented until 1870 and tinned food had to be opened with a hammer and chisel. The worldwide database of the European Patent Office lists 143 types of tin-opener among its patents.

> ⚲ *BISCUITS, FOOD, NAPOLEON BONAPARTE, SHOPPING TROLLEYS*

TITANIC

A ticket for the *Titanic*'s doomed maiden voyage was sold at auction for £33,000 in Devizes, Wiltshire, in 2008. Only four such tickets exist.

The *Titanic* was the first sailing vessel to be equipped with a heated swimming pool.

Only 306 bodies were ever recovered of the 1,517 who died when the *Titanic* sank. Only two of the many dogs on board survived the sinking: a Pekingese and a Pomeranian.

The last surviving passenger on the *Titanic* was Elizabeth Gladys Dean, who died aged 97 in 2009.

> ⚲ *BISCUITS, CARROT, PARKER, ROAD FATALITY, YEARS*

TITS

According to research published in 2009, great tits have different accents according to the part of the country they come from. Researchers from Aberystwyth recorded the song of great tits at 20 different locations around Britain and found that the birds from rural locations sang at a lower pitch than those from towns and cities. They conjectured that the higher pitched sounds had evolved to make themselves heard above the noise of traffic and mobile phones.

TOAST

According to research at Leeds University in 2003, to produce a perfect slice of buttered toast, the bread needs to be heated to at least 120°C (248°F), and the butter should be used straight from the fridge and spread unevenly within 2 minutes of the bread coming out of the toaster. The amount of butter should be about one-seventeenth the thickness of the bread.

Their research also showed that only 27 per cent of toast-eaters liked their butter to be completely melted, while the other 73 per cent preferred the 'mouthfeel' of partly melted butter.

A world record for the highest popping toaster was claimed at the Royal College of Art graduate show in 2008, when Freddie Yauner, 26, sent a slice of toast 2.6 metres (8 feet 6 inches) into the air.

'I never had a piece of toast
Particularly long and wide
But fell upon the sanded floor
And always on the buttered side.'

James Payn

ⓟ *BURNT FOOD, MOLE, POE, SANDWICH,*
VIBRATOR

TOBAGO

Christopher Columbus gave the name
'Belaforme' to Tobago 'because from
a distance it seemed beautiful'. The
mainland Caribs called it 'Urupina',
which was their word for a big snail,
while the island Caribs called it 'Alou-
baéra', because it bore a resemblance to a
giant snake known as 'alloüebéra', which
was said to live in a cave on Dominica.
In 1511, a royal order in Spain called
it 'Tabaco', a name suggested by a
supposed resemblance to a big cigar.

ⓟ *BEAVER, BURIAL, ENEMA, JAMES I, LUNG,*
SMOKING

TOES

A cat with 26 toes raised $125,000 in
six weeks for the Milwaukee Animal
Rescue Center in 2011. In urgent need
of money after the rent was raised, the
owner of the Center placed the cat at the
head of an appeal for donations of $26,
one dollar for each toe.

ⓟ *ALFRED THE GREAT, ALLIGATOR, COSTA*
RICA, FRANCE, POPES

TOGO

Togo, Fiji and Peru are the only four-
letter countries whose capital cities also
have four letters: Lomé, Suva and Lima.
In 1984, the Togo Cabinet passed a law
forbidding sexual relations with schoolgirls because of the growing number of
teenage pregnancies.

TOILET

The first World Toilet Summit of the
World Toilet Organisation was held in
Singapore in 2001 and attracted around
200 delegates from Asia, Europe and
North America. In 2013, the United
Nations declared that 19 November
every year would be the official UN
World Toilet Day.

According to a poll in 2008, the
average Briton spends more than three
months of his or her lifetime sitting on
the toilet. They spend more than a year
and a half of their lives in the bathroom,
including six months in the bath or
shower and 62 days to dry off. Women
use the bathroom the most, with showering, teeth brushing and using the loo
adding up to one year, seven months
and 18 days.

ⓟ *BEIJING, BRAZIL, CHELSEA, GARDENING,*
LAVATORIES, LIGHT BULB

TOILET PAPER

Between 1963 and 1981, the British
government was involved in a long
quest for the best toilet paper. It
began when Sir John Pilcher, British
Ambassador to Austria, was examined
by a physician who said that the hard,
shiny government lavatory paper was
bad for his haemorrhoids. Her Majesty's
Stationery Office, which was responsible
for all the government's paper requirements, then became involved in long
correspondence with, among others,
staff unions, the School of Hygiene and
Tropical Medicine (which approved of
the hard, shiny paper) and the Treasury
typing pool. In 1980, a team of epidemi-
ologists reported that soft paper was
more hygienic, and the following year,
soft paper made its first appearance in
government lavatories.

In April 1997, a writ was served

against Kimberley-Clark Ltd for using a copyright design for a Kleenex brand of toilet tissue. The design used a pattern known as Penrose tiling after its creator the physicist/mathematician Sir Roger Penrose. Penrose tiling solved a geometric problem involving the creation of the smallest number of shapes that can be used to cover a plane in a non-repeating manner. This was first achieved with over 100 shapes, but Penrose reduced it first to single figures, then to just two. The application to quilted toilet paper involved the potential clumping and rumpling of the paper as it forms a roll. A non-repeating, non-periodic design is what is needed to avoid this happening, and the Penrose tiling was perfect. But Sir Roger had assigned the rights to develop products based on his design to a company called Pentaplex, and David Bradley, the director of that company, succinctly explained what they felt of Kimberley-Clark using the design: 'When it comes to the population of Great Britain being invited by a multi-national to wipe their bottoms on the work of a Knight of the Realm without his permission then a last stand must be made!' The offending toilet paper was soon withdrawn from the market. In 2020, Sir Roger Penrose was awarded the Nobel Prize in Physics, not for his work on toilet paper but his discoveries concerning black holes.

♀ *LAVATORIES, PAPER, UNITED NATIONS*

TOKYO

Twelve restaurants in Tokyo have three Michelin stars, which is more than any other city in the world. Including the two-star and one-star restaurants, Tokyo in 2021 had 203 Michelin-starred restaurants with 268 stars between them, which was far more Michelin stars overall than any other city in the world.

If all the household garbage produced in one day in Tokyo were piled into a square column with base 30 centimetres (12 inches) wide, it would be three times as high as Mount Everest.

♀ *EMERGENCY, HOT DOGS, JAPAN, MUMMIFICATION, TUNA*

TOLSTOY, Leo (1828–1910)

Tolstoy's *War and Peace* has about 460,000 words in Russian, but about 560,000 in English translation. In Russian *tolstoy* means 'fat'.

♀ *BICYCLE*

TOMATO

The first tomatoes imported into Europe were golden in colour, which led to them being nicknamed 'golden apples'. The Italian for tomato is *pomodoro* – 'apple of gold'. In Britain, however, tomatoes were considered poisonous and were not generally eaten until the middle of the 18th century. Until 1820, North Americans believed that tomatoes were poisonous.

Unripe tomatoes contain tomatine, which is toxic if eaten in large quantities. As they ripen, however, they lose all their tomatine.

There are nine main varieties of tomato: beefsteak, globe, plum, green, cherry, pear, currant, purple and striped.

♀ *FRUIT, GALILEI, HANGOVER, MARY I, PEACH, SOUP, SWEDEN*

TONGA

Tonga became known as the Friendly Islands after Captain Cook received an apparently friendly welcome there in 1773. However, according to one account by William Mariner, an English writer who lived in Tonga in the early

19th century, the diagnosis of friendship was not totally correct: it was just that the chieftains could not agree on how to kill him.

According to a paper in the *Lancet* medical journal in 2017, Tonga is the most obese nation in the world. It reported that over 90 per cent of adults in Tonga are either obese or overweight and almost a quarter have Type 2 diabetes.

COMMONWEALTH, FIJI, INDEPENDENCE DAY

TOOTH FAIRY

The earliest known reference to the tooth fairy was in a 'Household Hints' column in the *Chicago Daily Tribune* in September 1908. A reader, Lillian Brown, wrote about how the tooth fairy 'comes in the night to take away a tooth that has been taken out, and leave in its place a little gift'. The story was later popularised in 1927 by a children's play called *The Tooth Fairy* by Esther Watkins Arnold.

In 2008, the average rate paid for a tooth by the fairy in the UK was reported to be £1.22. By 2021, according to the journal *The Dentist*, it had risen to £3.42.

In 2012, a survey in the United States reported that the average price given by the tooth fairy was $3 per tooth. This figure was 15 per cent up on the previous year, making milk teeth one of the best investments in 2011.

A survey in 2019 reported that the tooth fairy leaves an average of $3.70 per tooth in the US, declining for the second year in a row after peaking above $4.50 in 2017. By 2020, however, according to a Delta Dental survey, it had risen again to a record $4.70 a tooth. According to Delta, the amount paid by the tooth fairy mirrors trends in the US economy.

SPAIN, TEETH

TOOTHACHE

The ancient Roman Scribonius Largus, in AD 47, was the first person to suggest that rotten teeth could be filled instead of extracted. He also claimed that decay could be removed painlessly with a knife.

'There was never yet philosopher that could endure the toothache patiently.' William Shakespeare, Much Ado About Nothing, *1598/9 (That play, incidentally, contains four occurrences of the word 'toothache', which does not appear in any other Shakespeare work.)*

ASPARAGUS, SHOES, ST APOLLONIA, TROUSERS

TOOTHPASTE

Paste to rub teeth clean dates back at least to ancient Egypt, where various concoctions were made for that purpose. Ash of burned ox hoofs, powdered egg shells, pumice and myrrh were among the ingredients used. More tastefully, the ancient Romans preferred powdered fruit, dried flowers and talcum powder, but were also known, more for abrasive qualities than taste, to use pumice, powdered flint or crushed oyster shell, often in a suspension of urine. The concoction was then applied first with fingers, but later twigs were used, then twigs with cloth wrapped round them, which were the earliest form of toothbrush.

The modern toothpaste tube was first marketed by Washington Wentworth Sheffield of Connecticut in 1892, but he cannot be regarded as their inventor as the collapsible metal tube was patented in 1841 by John Goffe Rand, an American artist living in England, as a handy way of storing his paints. Washington Sheffield's son Lucius had seen such paint tubes in use in France and through his observation the idea was adapted for toothpaste.

The history of modern toothpaste and toothbrushes is even vaguer. William Addis is often credited with the invention of the toothbrush around 1771. Some say he came up with the idea while in Newgate Prison, but at best this supposed innovation was a reinvention of an idea known to the Chinese since around 1500.

♀ LONGEVITY, TELEVISION

● TOOTHPICK

There is evidence that toothpicks go back to Neanderthal times, but their mass production began in 1869 with the invention by Charles Forster of Boston, Massachusetts, of a toothpick-making machine. He created demand for his product by having Harvard students loudly ask for toothpicks after eating their meals at local restaurants.

Great toothpick achievements include Joe King's feat of building a 7-metre (23 feet) high likeness of the Eiffel Tower out of 111,000 toothpicks, and a 5-metre (16-foot) long replica of the luxury liner *Lusitania* made by Wayne Kusy of Evanston, Illinois, with 193,000 toothpicks.

The world record for the smallest toothpick sculpture is held by Steven Backmann of San Francisco, who in 2014 made a model of the Empire State Building less than 2 centimetres high and 5mm wide out of shavings from a single toothpick.

♀ AGATHOCLES, BACON, MAINE, MOSAIC

● TOPLESSNESS

About two dozen women marched topless through the town of Portland, Maine, in 2010 to promote 'equal oppor-tunity toplessness'. Police said there were no incidents or arrests, as it is not illegal for a woman to be topless in Maine.

♀ BEAUTY

● TORTOISE

A tortoise named Jonathan that lives on the island of St Helena has been recognised not only as the world's oldest living land animal but also as the oldest tortoise ever. He is at least 190 years old and is blind and deaf but is reported to have good libido and to be still sexually active.

According to figures released in 2009, the Mojave Desert tortoise has been one of the top recipients of money spent by US state and federal agencies trying to save it from extinction. Between 1996 and 2006, more than $93 million was spent on managing the creature.

The saddleback tortoise has evolved a long neck and an arched shell which enables it to reach leaves 1.5 metres (5 feet) above the ground.

In 1997, Australian scientists announced an important discovery concerning the Fitzroy River tortoise, *Rheodytes leukops*: it breathes through its mouth on land and through its bottom when under water.

♀ AESCHYLUS, SPACE FLIGHT, TURTLE, YAWNING

● TOURISM

Modern tourism could be said to have begun on 5 July 1841, when Thomas Cook organised a special train to go from Market Harborough to Leicester and back, taking 570 members of his local temperance association to a gathering in Loughborough. It cost them a shilling each and was Cook's first publicly advertised trip.

What we might now call tourists,

however, had existed long before. There is some evidence of island-hopping in the Pacific some 20,000 years ago, though the sea levels may then have been low enough for them to have walked over.

In 1292, Marco Polo was definitely a tourist, even taking three and a half years over his sea voyage home rather than going back to work. Ibn Battuta was another inveterate traveller, who went on a pilgrimage to Mecca in 1326, then spent the next 30 years wandering around the entire Islamic world. It has been said that he travelled more than any other explorer of the time with a total of some 117,000 kilometres (73,000 miles).

The tourism industry, however, began with Thomas Cook. His inaugural one-shilling trip to Leicester soon developed into frequent such jaunts. A one-guinea excursion to Glasgow in 1845 even aroused such excitement that the first tourists there were welcomed with band music and salutes from a cannon. Cook's first package holiday abroad was a six-day trip to Paris, starting at London Bridge on 17 May 1861.

In some places, tourists were regarded with suspicion, particularly in Italy in 1865 where a journalist had claimed that a party of British holidaymakers were convicts the British government had dropped on the Italians after Australia had refused to accept them.

Tourism now earns about £106 billion a year for the UK economy, including about £8 billion a year in foreign currency. It is responsible for about 4 per cent of our GDP and provides nearly 3 million jobs.

Why do tourists do it? Psychology has little light to throw on the subject.

Sandor Ferenczi, a follower of Freud, wrote of the thrills and challenge of tourism, but it seems he was concerned primarily with mountain climbing.

According to a survey in 2014, the most common item left behind in a hotel by a tourist is sun cream, followed by clothing, souvenirs, towels, hair styling products, camera, footwear, inflatables, swimwear and jewellery. The item a tourist is most likely to break is a glass and they are most likely to steal a towel.

At a typical moment before Covid restrictions there were approximately 350,000 people, mostly tourists, flying in aeroplanes.

📍 *DRACULA, JAPAN, SMURFS, ST LUCIA*

⬤ TOWER BRIDGE

Tower Bridge, across the River Thames in London, was completed in 1894 at a cost of £1,184,000. Adjusted for inflation, that is almost £97 million at today's prices.

Tower Bridge is a 'bascule' bridge – a word that comes from the French for 'see-saw'.

Until 1977, the bridge was brown. In that year it was painted red, white and blue to celebrate the Silver Jubilee of Queen Elizabeth II.

The high-level walkways were closed in 1910, partly to deter suicides, but also because of their reputation as a haunt of prostitutes and pickpockets.

Prior to beginning a total repainting of Tower Bridge in London starting in 2009, it was calculated that 22,000 litres (4,800 gallons) of new paint would be needed.

Any ship wishing to have the bridge opened to let it pass underneath must give 24 hours' notice.

An average of two couples a month get married on Tower Bridge and one couple took a break from competing in the 2009 London Marathon to be wed on the bridge.

In 1952, the bridge began to open with a No. 78 double-decker bus still on it, forcing the vehicle to leap over the 0.9-metre (3-foot) gap. Nobody was hurt and the driver, Albert Gunton, was awarded £10 for his bravery.

⬤ TOWER OF LONDON

The last person to be executed at the Tower of London was Josef Jakobs, a German spy who was parachuted into England during the Second World War. He was shot at the Tower at 7.15am on 15 August 1941. He was seated in a chair for his execution, as he had broken his ankle on landing in Britain. Before Jakobs, the last execution at the Tower had been in 1916.

⚲ BOLEYN, HENRY VIII, POLAR BEAR, RAVEN, TOURISM, YEOMAN

⬤ TOWN CRIER

The Ancient and Honourable Guild of Town Criers is not as ancient as its title may suggest. In fact, it was founded in Hastings in 1978, though the post of town crier dates back many centuries.

The first World Championship of Town Crying was held in Halifax, Canada, in 1980.

The first European Women's Town Crying Championship was held in 2007.

The 11th World Town Criers Championship was held in Maryborough, Queensland, in 2005 and was won by Hans van Laethem of Ninove in Belgium. In 2019, the International Town Criers Championship was held in Holland, Michigan, and was won by John Markham of Ontario.

The British Town Criers' Championship in 2021 was held in silence because of the Covid epidemic. Entries were written and submitted by post, then judged by style and content instead of the usual 'three distinct parts of a cry' – sustained volume and clarity, diction and inflection, and content.

The record for the loudest town crier is held by Donald 'Bob' Burns, who was town crier of St George, Bermuda, at 113 decibels. He was the grand-nephew of the poet Robert Burns.

⬤ TRAFFIC

Delivering a judgement in 2006 on a case relating to a law designed to ease traffic congestion, a judge in Phoenix, Arizona, ruled that unborn children do not count when it comes to car occupancy. The case arose when a pregnant woman was fined $367 for 'improper use of a High Occupancy Lane'. Candace Dickinson appealed against the fine on the grounds that Arizona traffic laws don't define what a person is, so the child inside her womb justified her use of the lane. Judge Dennis Freeman said that his ruling was based on a common sense definition in which an individual occupies a separate and distinct space in a vehicle. 'The law is meant to fill empty space in a vehicle,' he said.

⚲ BALLET, BRAZIL, CARACAS, DEATHS, DUBLIN, HANDEL, TITS

⬤ TRAFFIC LIGHTS

The world's first traffic lights were a gas-powered contraption just off Parliament Square in London in December 1868, which had been erected to make it easier for MPs to cross a road to reach the House of Commons. The lights took the form of a revolving lantern with red and green signals, controlled by a lever that had to be operated by a police constable. The two arms meant Stop when extended horizontally and Caution when at a 45-degree angle. A police proclamation warned: 'All persons in charge of vehicles and horses are warned to pass over the crossing with due regard to the safety of foot passengers.'

The foot passengers, however, were not the ones with problems. The contraption exploded on 2 January 1869, causing severe injuries to the policeman, and the experiment was not repeated in other places. The Westminster signals were finally removed in 1872, and it was over half a century before Britain was ready to put its trust in traffic lights again.

The world's first automatic lights were invented by Earnest Sirrine of Chicago in 1910. They had no lights, but two signs saying 'Proceed' and 'Stop'. The first automatic red and green light system was invented in 1912 by Lester Wire of Salt Lake City.

On 5 August 1914, the United States had its first set of automatic traffic lights working in Cleveland, Ohio, at the crossroads formed by Euclid Avenue and 105th Street. They were red and green and included a warning buzzer. By 1918, New York had a set with red, green and amber, a colour scheme Britain also adopted for its first electric traffic lights in 1926 at the junction of St James's Street and Piccadilly.

The bulbs in Britain's traffic lights are responsible for 57,000 tons of carbon dioxide emissions a year.

℘ ALBANIA, LIFETIME

TRAINS

The earliest use of the word 'train' in the *Oxford English Dictionary* dates back to 1330. Its meaning then is given – prophetically, one might think – as 'tarrying, delay'. It was first used to describe a series of railway carriages coupled together in 1820.

According to the Oxford English Corpus, the adjectives most frequently used to describe 'train' are 'express' and 'highspeed', but the adjectives most likely to occur after the words 'train is' are 'due', 'late', 'delayed' and 'full'.

The longest straight stretch of railway in the world is a 485-kilometre (301-mile) piece of track in Australia.

℘ FLIGHT, MOOSE, MOSCOW, RAILWAY, STEPHENSON, UNDERGROUND

TRANSPLANTATION

The first successful corneal transplant was performed in Moravia by Dr Eduard Zirm in 1905; the first kidney transplant was by Dr Joseph Murray in Boston, Massachusetts, in 1954; the first heart transplant was in 1967.

The World Transplant Games have been organised under the aegis of the World Transplant Games Federation (WTGF) since 1978. The 22nd such Games were held in Newcastle-upon-Tyne and Gateshead in 2019 and attracted 2,400 competitors from 60 countries. The British team won by far the most gold medals with a total of 205, well ahead of the USA on 67 and Iran on 26.

Sadly, the 14th such games in Nancy, France, in 2003 saw the first death at such an event, which occurred in a badminton match when a contestant who had recovered from a successful kidney transplant collapsed and died of a heart attack.

After Russian surgeon Valery Agafonov had part of his pelvic bone transplanted in 1997 to replace a thumb mangled in an accident, bank officials said his signature was exactly the same as before.

The first hand transplants took place in France and the United States in 1999.

In 1979, the *National Enquirer* offered heart transplant pioneer Dr Christian Barnard $250,000 to transplant a human head. The offer was not accepted.

⚲ *BARNACLE, DONKEY, GRAPEFRUIT, KIDNEY, KNEES, UNICORN*

⬤ TRANSPORT

In 2001, Australian patent lawyer John Keogh was issued an innovation patent for a 'circular transportation facilitation device'. He applied for the patent to mock the new system Australia had just brought in to make it quicker and easier for people to register inventions. Keogh's description and diagrams, however, clearly claimed that he had invented the wheel.

The earliest known wheel is, in fact, to be seen on a pictogram in Uruk, Mesopotamia, dating back to around 3500 BC. It showed a sled followed by an almost identical sled on wheels.

The next important invention was the Sedan chair, a closed single-seater supported on poles and carried by two bearers. The poet Jane (or Jean) Elliott (1727–1805), was said to have been the last woman in Edinburgh to make regular use of her own Sedan chair.

In 1818, Denis Johnson of London patented the Velocipede – at first, a sort of hobby horse, though by 1850 the word was being used to describe a bicycle or tricycle. By 1869, cyclists were referred to as 'velocipedestrians'.

The credit for the first pedal-driven bicycle should probably be given to Kirkpatrick MacMillan, whose pedal, rod and crankshaft mechanism hit the roads of Dumfries in Scotland in 1839. Three years later, he rode the 113 kilometres (70 miles) into Glasgow and became one of the first traffic felons when he was fined 5 shillings for injuring a girl who ran across his path.

Gavin Dalzell of Lesmahagow, Lanarkshire, invented a pedal cycle around the same time. Some say he was seen riding it in 1836; others insist the first verified account was in 1845.

In 1888, Parliament gave bicycles full rights to use British roads, but until 1930 it was mandatory to ring a bell non-stop while cycling (though in the later years this was rarely enforced).

The petrol-driven car arrived in 1896 but all this time trains had been speeding ahead, with the world's first passenger service in 1830 and underground trains following in 1890.

Transport innovations registered at the European Patent Office which made less of an impact include the foldable and portable bicycle convertible into a shopping cart (1981), the sail propulsion bicycle (1983), a means of exercising dogs from a bicycle (1986), and a hang-glider with flapping wings in 2020.

⚲ *BUS DRIVERS, DOG, GLADSTONE, JAPAN, MOTORING, SWAZILAND*

⬤ TRANSVESTITES

In 1995, the Cultural Bureau in the city of Shen-yang, China, banned transves-tite shows on the grounds that they had no artistic merit.

In 1997, news from Sri Lanka reported that Sattambije Sriyaratne, 36, had been arrested for being a man. He had passed as a woman for three years and had even won an award as his country's best female entrepreneur.

TRAPPIST

The order known as Trappist was founded at La Trappe Abbey in Normandy in 1664. There are around 170 Trappist monasteries in the world, of which seven produce beer.

FRUITCAKE

TREADMILL

In 2006, Anchorage Zoo in Alaska became the world's first zoo to have a purpose-built treadmill designed for an elephant. The elephant's name was Maggie, and she had arrived at the zoo in 1983 as an infant when her herd in Kruger National Park in South Africa was culled. She joined Annabelle, an Asian elephant almost 20 years older than herself. In December 1997, Annabelle died at the age 33 of a chronic foot infection, leaving Maggie alone. Maggie then started putting on weight and the treadmill was designed as part of a diet and exercise programme.

DOG, PARAPSYCHOLOGY, ZOO

TREASON

Under the UK 1848 Treason Felony Act, it is a serious offence to publish an article advocating the abolition of the monarchy. In 2003, a challenge to the legality of this Act was raised by the *Guardian* newspaper, which intended to publish a series of articles in favour of establishing Britain as a republic. They argued that the 1848 Act was overruled by the 1998 European Human Rights Act, but the challenge was rejected by the House of Lords.

It is often claimed that it is officially an act of treason in the UK to stick a stamp with the Queen's head on it upside

down on an envelope. That is not true. It is an offence to perform any act with the intention of deposing a monarch, but sticking a stamp on upside down is unlikely to be seen as fulfilling that criterion.

Under the Treason Act of 1351, any of the following constituted an act of treason:

- Compassing or imagining the Death of our Lord the King, or of our Lady his Queen or of their eldest Son and Heir
- Violating the King's Wife or the King's eldest Daughter unmarried, or the Wife of the King's eldest Son and Heir
- Levying War against our Lord the King in his Realm
- Being adherent to the King's Enemies in his Realm, giving to them Aid and Comfort in the Realm, or elsewhere.

CAPITAL PUNISHMENT, PARLIAMENT

TREES

Trees are the longest-living organisms on Earth.

In one year, an acre of trees can absorb as much carbon as is produced by a car driven 14,000 kilometres (8,700 miles).

In Norse mythology, Yggdrasil is the name of the giant ash tree that links and shelters all the worlds and cosmologies.

In January 2022, a recently discovered species of evergreen tree in the tropical Ebo forest of Cameroon was named after the actor Leonardo DiCaprio. The *Uvariopsis dicaprio* tree is around 4 metres (13 feet) tall and has vibrant yellow-green flowers growing on its trunk. Fewer than 50 *U. dicaprio* trees have been identified and it is considered critically endangered. The name was chosen to honour DiCaprio's campaigning efforts to protect the forest from logging.

*'If I had eight hours to chop down a tree,
I'd spend six hours sharpening my axe.'*
Abraham Lincoln

⚲ CHRISTMAS, COCONUT, FORESTS, OLIVE,
OYSTER, RUSSIA

● TRICOLOUR

A new law was rapidly introduced in France in July 2010 after the publication of a photograph of a man wiping his bottom with the French tricolour flag they call La Tricolore. The law imposed a 1,500 euro fine on anyone caught trying to 'destroy, damage or use the flag in a degrading manner'. Publishing photographs of such acts would also be punished.

Previously, such behaviour was only an offence if committed during an event regulated by the public authorities. Now you cannot even wipe your bum on the French flag in private. The new law came after the bottom-wiping picture won a prize in a photo competition organised by a book and record shop in the city of Nice.

● TRILLION

When the words 'billion' and 'trillion' were first used in the 17th century, they meant a million million, and a million million million respectively. In the 18th century, the French and Americans started using 'billion' for a thousand million and 'trillion' for a thousand billion. The British have been doing the same since about 1960, so a trillion is now generally agreed to be 1,000,000,000,000.

At a rate of £100 a second, it would take over 700 years to pay off the UK National Debt of £2.38 trillion pounds (December 2021 figure).

A trillion pounds is 21 times the value of all the British banknotes and coins now in circulation.

The earliest known cave paintings date back to about 1 trillion seconds ago.

In January 2012, Malaysian oil magnate Kamal Ashnawi claimed to be the world's first dollar trillionaire.

If a trillion dollar bills were placed in a single pile, it would reach about a quarter of the way to the Moon, but the entire US National Debt would go to the Moon and back twice. On the other hand, if the trillion dollars were changed into one cent coins and they were put into a pile, it would stretch all the way to the Sun.

⚲ BEE, DEBT, GOOGLE, HOUSEWIVES, PI

● TRISTAN DA CUNHA

The island group of Tristan da Cunha in the Atlantic is the most remote community in the world. It is 2,437 kilometres (1,514 miles) from St Helena and 2,787 kilometres (1,732 miles) off the coast of Cape Town. There is no airstrip and the only way of getting there is a six-day boat trip from South Africa.

The islands were first sighted in 1506 by the Portuguese explorer Tristão da Cunha, who named the first island after himself. Nineteen miles to its south-west lies the unpopulated, extinct volcanic island called Inaccessible Island, which is now a wildlife reserve.

Potatoes were used as currency on the island of Tristan da Cunha until 1942. Four years later, a design for a one penny postage stamp was proposed which also had its local value on it as '4 potatoes'. Some of these were printed, but they seem never to have been officially accepted on letters.

TRIVIA

The word 'trivia' comes from the Latin for 'three roads' and is supposed to be characteristic of the mindless chatter that ensues when people stop to talk at crossroads.

⚲ SNOW

TROJAN HORSE

According to the ancient Greeks, there were 30 soldiers in the belly of the Trojan horse and two spies in its mouth.

⚲ PSYCHOLOGY

TROUSERS

Although the word 'trousers' dates back to 1599, the singular 'trouser', meaning one leg of a pair of trousers, dates back only to 1893.

In 2007, a former US judge lost a lawsuit against a dry cleaners which had lost his trousers. He had claimed $54 million (£34.4 million) damages for the false claims made in a sign displayed by the cleaners saying 'Satisfaction Guaranteed'. During the court case, he was reported to have broken down in tears when telling of the distress his lost trousers had caused. He later appealed against the decision but to no avail.

In October 1812, St John's and Trinity Colleges in Cambridge ordered that students appearing in hall or chapel in trousers or pantaloons should be marked absent. Loose-fitting breeches were the correct thing to wear. Similar views were held by Tsar Alexander I of Russia, who considered the wearing of trousers, instead of knee-breeches, to be subversive.

On 24 June 1985, Colonel Patrick Baudry of Air France, travelling on the Space Shuttle Discovery, announced his discovery that: 'In zero G you can put your trousers on two legs at a time.'

According to Sussex folklore, putting socks and trousers on right-leg first can prevent toothache. In Shropshire folklore, however, putting your trousers on right-leg first invites bad luck. Research has shown that right-handed men generally put trousers on with the right leg leading; left-handed men go left leg first.

'You should never have your best trousers on when you go out to fight for freedom and truth.' Henrik Ibsen

⚲ DECENCY, ELASTIC, POSTMEN, PUCCINI, TENNESSEE

TRUMAN, Harry S. (1884–1972)

The middle initial of Harry S. Truman did not stand for anything. As both his grandfathers had names beginning with 'S', he was given the bare initial to avoid having to choose between them. Strictly speaking, one should therefore not put a dot after the S in 'Harry S. Truman' as it is not short for anything, but Truman himself more often than not signed his own name with the dot as 'Harry S. Truman', so the official US government recommendation is to use a dot.

⚲ BOXING DAY, ELIZABETH II, HESITATION, WHITE HOUSE

TSETSE

Within one year, a tsetse fly may produce four generations of offspring, turning it from childless to a great-great grandparent. In a lifetime, a tsetse fly may produce 31 generations.

⚲ ZEBRA

TUATARA

The tuatara is a reptile found in New Zealand which has been classed as an endangered species since 1895. It has no ears, but has been shown to be able to hear.

In 2009, Henry, a New Zealand tuatara, become a father for the first time at the age of 111. For some time, Henry had had a reputation for aggression and was apparently not interested in sex, but all that changed after a cancerous growth was removed from his bottom. He mated in March 2008 with Mildred, 31 years his junior, who laid 12 eggs in June which gave birth to 11 surviving baby tuataras.

TUESDAY

Tuesday is named after the Norse God Tiw or Tyr. He was the god concerned with the formalities of war, especially treaties, and also the god of justice.

The Romans called Tuesday 'dies Martis', after Mars the god of war (the French, Spanish and Italians still call it 'Mardi', 'Martes' and 'Martedi' respectively), while the Angles and Saxons brought 'Tiwasdaeg' (Tuesday) to England in the 6th century. Why the Germans call Tuesday 'Dienstag' is unclear, but that may also have its origins with the god of war. Mars was sometimes called 'Mars Thingsus' (Mars the Assembly), and it has been suggested that 'Dien-' is a corruption of 'Thing-'.

The Welsh consider Tuesday to be a lucky day, but traditionally it is seen as unlucky by Greeks and Spaniards. According to northern English superstition, it is unlucky for a traveller to meet a left-handed person on a Tuesday. On other days, it is good luck to do so.

Analysis of parish records in Somerset shows that between 1640 and 1659 fewer seductions took place on a Tuesday than any other day of the week.

Sunday was the most common day for seduction, especially on the way back from church.

Californians have barbecues less often on Tuesday than any other day of the week and are also least likely to use a petrol-driven lawnmower on a Tuesday.

The actress Tuesday Weld was born on a Saturday.

'He respects Owl, because you can't help respecting anybody who can spell TUESDAY, even if he doesn't spell it right.' A.A. Milne, The House At Pooh Corner, 1928

BELGIUM, PANCAKE DAY, SHROVE TUESDAY

TUG-OF-WAR

Tug-of-war was an Olympic sport between 1900 and 1920, and the event led to a notable dispute at the 1908 Games in London in the first round when Liverpool Police scored a quick win over the US team. The Americans lodged a protest against their opponents' footwear. According to them, the British were wearing boots with steel spikes, cleats and heels which gave an illegally improved grip on the ground. The British insisted that they were standard-issue police boots and the protest was disallowed. The Americans then stormed out of the competition which resulted in gold, silver and bronze all going to teams from British police forces, presumably all wearing similar boots: London City Police won, Liverpool Police came second, and K Division Metropolitan Police were third. The winning City Police team later challenged the Americans to a contest in stockinged feet, but the challenge was not taken up.

Three members of the winning team, James Shepherd, Edwin Mills and Frederick Humphries, went on to represent Britain in the Olympics at both Stockholm in 1912 and Antwerp in 1920. In 1912, Sweden took gold with Britain winning silver as the only other team that entered; in 1920, five teams entered, with Britain winning ahead of the Netherlands and Belgium.

According to international rules, the rope in a tug-of-war contest must be between 100mm (4 inches) and 125mm (5 inches) in circumference.

TUNA

In 2019, the head of a Japanese sushi company paid $3.1 million (£2.5 million) for a giant tuna at the first new year's auction in Tokyo's new fish market. Kiyoshi Kimura bought the 278 kilogram (612 pound) bluefin tuna, which is an endangered species, paying more than twice his own previous record of $1.4 million, which he paid in 2013. 'I bought a good tuna,' Mr Kimura said after the auction. The amount he paid works out at £255 an ounce, which was roughly 20 times the price of silver on the same day.

♀ FISH, SANDWICHES

TUNISIA

The Roman name for the area now known as Tunisia was 'Africa terra', meaning 'land of the Afri', which was the dominant tribe resident there. The word 'Africa' eventually came to be applied to the whole continent.

When the film *Raiders of the Lost Ark* was shot in Tunisia, 300 television antennas had to be removed from homes in Kairouan to make a rooftop shot look as it did in 1936.

♀ SPAIN, TEMPERATURE

TURING, Alan Mathison (1912–54)

Mathematician, computer pioneer, code-breaker and grandson of the chief engineer of Madras Railways, Alan Turing was also an excellent marathon runner and finished fifth in the Amateur Athletic Association Marathon Championship on 25 August 1947 in a time of 2 hours, 46 minutes, 3 seconds. While working at Bletchley Park during the war, he would sometimes run the 64 kilometres (40 miles) to London to attend meetings at the War Office. He must also have been a good cyclist, for he cycled 96.5 kilometres (60 miles) to school when his first day at Sherborne in 1926 coincided with the General Strike. He did, however, break the journey with an overnight stay at an inn.

After the war, he was noted for cycling to work wearing a wartime gas mask when there was a high pollen count to avoid an attack of hayfever. At work, he chained his drinking mug to a radiator to prevent it being lost or stolen.

Alan Turing committed suicide in 1954 after being convicted of 'gross indecency with a male'. His death was caused by cyanide poisoning and a half-eaten apple found by his bedside is thought to have been the way he took the poison, though the apple was never tested. His favourite fairy story was *Snow White*, which also featured a poisoned apple.

The means of Turing's death, however, has nothing to do with the Apple computer logo of an apple with a bite taken out of it, despite frequent assertions that the logo was designed as a tribute to him. Rob Janoff, designer of the logo, says that Newton, Adam and Eve or Turing had nothing to do with it, and the only reason his apple has a bite taken out of it is to give a sense of scale so that the apple will not be mistaken for a cherry.

TURKEY (bird)

In Turkey, the turkey is called the 'American bird'. The correct collective noun for turkeys is a 'rafter'.

Turkeys arrived on British dinner plates around 1530. They were brought by Turkish merchants, which is why they were called 'turkeys'. But the birds did not come from Turkey. They were first domesticated in Mexico and were brought back after the discovery of America. The Turks were also confused, thinking the birds came from India, which is why the French call the bird *dinde*, as in d'Inde, meaning 'from India'. Another theory about the name 'turkey' is that Christopher Columbus, thinking he had found India, named the bird 'tuka', which is Tamil for 'peacock'.

More turkey is eaten per head of population in Israel than in any other country.

The red fleshy bit on a turkey's beak is called the snood; the pink growth on its neck is the caruncle.

⚷ *CHICKEN, DINOSAUR, DOUGHNUTS, ETIQUETTE, HUDSON, SHAKESPEARE*

TURKEY (country)

Turks eat more bread per head of population than any other nation. In 2000, it was estimated that the average person in that country ate 200 kilograms (440 pounds) of bread a year, which was about three times their own body weight. Research conducted in 2017, however, suggested that figure had reduced to just over 100 kilograms (220 pounds), but that still put Turkey well ahead of other countries. Bulgaria comes second, but the British eat most biscuits.

In June 1984, 17 people died in a road accident in Turkey caused by a coach driver trying to censor a love scene while behind the wheel. The screening of videotapes in such vehicles was then banned.

⚷ *COFFEE, COINS, ETIQUETTE, HITLER, QUINCE, TURKEY (bird)*

TURKMENISTAN

From 2001 to 2008, opera, ballet and the circus were banned in Turkmenistan as alien to Turkmen culture. Video games, smoking in public, listening to car radios, long hair on men and growing facial hair were also banned. In 2008, the ban on circuses and operas was reversed.

In 2001, 39 women and one man from the state carpet company in Turkmenistan completed the world's largest carpet, which weighed more than a ton and covered about 297 square metres (3,200 square feet). This record was thoroughly overtaken by a carpet made in Iran in 2007 for the Abu Dhabi mosque. It measures 5,360 square metres (57,694 square feet) but was originally about 6,000 square metres (64,583 feet), which was too big to fit into the mosque.

The Darvaza gas crater in Turkmenistan, which is also known as the 'gate of hell', was caused by Soviet geologists drilling for natural gas in 1971. When their equipment fell into the hole and gas began to escape, they set it on fire, expecting it to burn off in a day or two. It is still burning 50 years later.

⚷ *PRISONERS, UZBEKISTAN*

TURKS AND CAICOS ISLANDS

The Turks and Caicos were once part of the Bahamas and Jamaica, but on those countries gaining independence they became a territory in their own right, administered by Britain.

The Turks islands' name is derived from the Turk's Head cactus (*Melocactus intortus*). The Caicos islands' name comes from a Lucayan term *cayo hico*, meaning string of islands. Lucayans were the original inhabitants of the islands.

During the American Revolutionary War, George Washington is said to have personally requested salt from the Turks and Caicos because of its high quality.

Grand Turk was the first land reached by US astronaut John Glenn after the Mercury space mission in 1962.

The Turks and Caicos flag once had an igloo on it, because the flag designer copied a map-maker's error in confusing the salt mounds on the islands with igloos.

TURNSTILE

Under the Public Lavatories (Turnstiles) Act 1963, it is the duty of local authorities in the UK to abolish turnstiles in public lavatories and sanitary conveniences.

TURTLE

Strictly speaking, all tortoises are turtles, but not all turtles are tortoises. Tortoises are land-dwelling types of turtle.

There are 244 species of turtle in the world: seven sea turtle species, 180 freshwater species, and the rest land dwellers. In Britain, 'turtle' is generally used for saltwater species, 'terrapin' for freshwater varieties.

Turtles have no teeth.

A tortoise brought by Charles Darwin from the Galapagos died in Australia in 2008 aged 176. The Galapagos islands were named after their tortoises: *galapago* is an old Spanish word for 'tortoise'.

Turtles have existed for 200 million years.

Turtles mate at four in the afternoon and lay eggs at six.

♀ *ILLINOIS, MICHELANGELO, TERRAPIN, WATER SKIING*

TUSSAUD, Madame (Anne Marie Grosholtz) (1761–1850)

The first waxwork made by Madame Tussaud was of Voltaire in 1777.

Following the split of Brad Pitt and Angelina Jolie in 2016, the waxworks of the couple at Madame Tussauds in London were also separated. Around a decade previously, they were reported to be the only people with wax models in all eight Madame Tussauds museums. In 2006 in New York, Shiloh Jolie-Pitt became the first Madame Tussauds wax baby.

♀ *EARTHQUAKE, JACKSON Michael, TOURISM, WAX*

TWELFTH NIGHT

The Twelfth Day of Christmas and Twelfth Night is either 5 or 6 January, depending on whether you count Christmas Day as the first day of Christmas or do not start to count until Boxing Day.

In 567 the Council of Tours decreed that the entire period between Christmas and Epiphany should be celebrated, but including both Christmas Day and Epiphany adds up to 13 days.

In Sweden, Twelfth Night is celebrated on 6 January and is known as Thirteenth Day.

The song 'The Twelve Days of Christmas' was first published in English in 1780 without music.

When he died in 1794, the actor Robert Baddeley left a £100 bequest for a cake to be made for Twelfth Night celebrations at Drury Lane Theatre. The Baddeley Cake is served every year and is now matched to the show running at the theatre. When the theatre was showing *Charlie and the Chocolate Factory*, the cake was a Willy Wonka special. In 2022, it had five tiers and a *Frozen* theme. In 1888, both Oscar Wilde and Alfred, Lord Tennyson were reported to have attended the Baddeley Cake ceremony.

Twelfth Night is the only Shakespeare play to both begin and end with music. It is also the only Shakespeare play not to include the words 'child' or 'children'. Nowhere in the play is Twelfth Night or Christmas mentioned, though Sir Toby Belch does at one stage start to sing 'O the twelfth day of December …'.

The British used to celebrate Twelfth Night (6 January) with a drink called Lamb's Wool made from roasted apples, sugar and nutmeg in beer. The Dutch celebrate it with a midwinter horn-blowing competition dating back to 2500 BC.

Henry VIII, George Washington and George Bush (the elder) all celebrated Twelfth Night by getting married on that day, in 1540, 1759 and 1945 respectively. When Henry VIII saw his wife for the first time on their wedding day, he is said to have commented, 'You have sent me a Flanders mare.' Apparently he had been taken in by an over-flattering portrait of his bride by Hans Holbein the Younger.

CARPET, JOHNSON

TWENTY-NINE

The number TWENTY-NINE has precisely 29 straight lines in the letters used to spell it out. (To make this work, you have to write the Y with two straight lines and include the hyphen, or spell the Y with three lines and ignore the hyphen.) 29 is also the number of letters in the word 'floccinaucinihilipilification'.

DENTISTRY, LEAP YEAR

TWENTY-THREE

If there are 23 people in a room, there is a greater than even chance that two of them will share a birthday. The same is not true of 22 or fewer people.

The maximum number of people on a Grand Jury in the United States is 23.

There are 23 towns or cities in the United States called Moscow.

In Shakespeare's play *Hamlet*, Yorick's skull was buried for 23 years before Hamlet found it.

The expression '23 Skidoo' meaning 'scram' probably got its number from 23rd Street in New York, which contained ferries and stations for most services out of town.

According to a recent survey, 23 per cent of people store useless numbers of work contacts on their mobiles.

When a human baby is conceived, the egg and the sperm each contribute 23 chromosomes to the genetic make-up.

CAPITAL PUNISHMENT, IDES, STORIES

TWENTY-TWO

There are 22 letters in the Hebrew alphabet. According to St Isidore of Seville (who incidentally was recently proposed as Patron Saint of the Internet), God made 22 different things in the six days of Creation. On day one, he made unformed matter, angels, light, upper heavens, earth, water, air; day two, the firmament; day three, seas, seeds, grass, trees; day four, the sun, moon, stars; day five, fish, aquatic reptiles, birds; day six, wild beasts, domestic animals, land reptiles, man.

The Book of Revelation has 22 chapters. St Augustine's City of God was written in 22 books. The mystic significance of 22 is also reflected in a pack of tarot cards, which has 22 Major Trumps known as the Greater Arcana. There are also 22 balls in a game of snooker and 22 different meanings of 'fine' in the *Oxford Dictionary*.

Joseph Heller's great novel *Catch-22* had its title changed from 'Catch-18' shortly before publication.

The average American opens the fridge 22 times a day.

TWINS

Almost one in 30 babies born in the US in 2019 was a twin. Thirty years earlier, only one in 53 was a twin. The increase is put down to fertility treatment. Worldwide, the number of pairs of twins has risen since 1980 from 9 per thousand deliveries to 12 per thousand. Since any delivery of twins brings two babies, this means that worldwide, about one in 42 babies is a twin.

BUNKER, BURNS, BUSH George Walker, LEAP YEAR, PREGNANCY, SEX, SIAM

TWOPENCE

The first two-penny coin in England, known as twopence, tuppence or half-groat, was a silver coin minted from around 1450 to 1662. The current two-pence coin is legal tender up to 20p, so if you offer to pay 22p with eleven 2p coins, it may be refused.

The world's second postage stamp, after the Penny Black, was the Two Penny Blue in 1840. The postage fee then was one old penny (1d) for prepaid letters and twopence (2d) if the fee was collected from the recipient.

After decimalisation in 1971, the 2p coin carried the words 'new pence' until 1982.

The total value of all the 2p coins in circulation is over £131 million.

The herb *Lysimachia nummularia* is known as 'herb tuppence' or 'two-penny grass' from its rounded leaves.

The actress Tuppence Middleton is not related to the Duchess of Cambridge, but her name really is Tuppence after a nickname given by her grandmother to her mother.

TYPEWRITER

The longest common words that can be typed on the top row of letters of a typewriter or computer keyboard are 'proprietor', 'repertoire', 'perpetuity' and 'typewriter' itself. Less usual words include the plants 'pewterwort', 'pepperwort' and 'tetterwort' and the verb 'prerequire', which is to require as a pre-condition.

The left hand of a skilled typist does 56 per cent of the work.

BLYTON, LAVATORIES, PERU

TYRANNOSAURUS REX

The first Tyrannosaurus Rex was found by the fossil hunter Barnum Brown in Montana in 1902.

Three years later it was given the name 'Tyrannosaurus Rex', meaning 'Tyrant lizard king' by New York zoologist Henry Fairfield Osborn.

An average Tyrannosaurus Rex is thought to have been about 12 metres (39 feet) long, more than 6 metres (about 20 feet) tall, and probably weighed around 7 tons. The largest Tyrannosaurus Rex yet found is nicknamed 'Sue' and is in the Field Museum of Natural History in Chicago.

CHICKEN, DEAFNESS, DINOSAUR

UFO

Sixty-eight per cent of all UFO sightings are by men. The term 'Unidentified Flying Object' was coined by US air force officer Edward J. Ruppelt and first recorded in 1953. It quickly replaced 'flying saucer', which was first used in 1947, as the official term for such unidentified objects. Ruppelt was chosen in 1951 to head Project Grudge, the official US investigation into UFOs, which was replaced by Project Blue Book in 1953. Ruppelt died of a heart attack in 1960 at the age of 37.

NOVA SCOTIA, SPACECRAFT

UGANDA

The King of Toro in Uganda, Rudiki IV, was the world's youngest monarch in 1995 – aged three. His full name is Rukirabasaija Oyo Nyimba Kabamba Iguru Rukidi. The first of these names is a title meaning 'Greatest of men'. Despite this, his duties are limited to cultural events.

According to a news report from Kampala on 13 November 1988, Ugandan villagers lynched a local rain-maker after crops and homes in the Kabale district were destroyed by hail-stones and torrential rain. Villagers beat Festo Kazarwa to death because he had threatened to summon up hailstones if people did not show him more respect.

According to the figures in the *CIA World Factbook*, Uganda, Angola and Niger are the only countries on Earth in which more than half the male population are under 16. Niger is the youngest with a median age of 14.5 for men and 15.1 for women (14.8 combined). Uganda has a median age of 14.9 for men and 16.5 for women (15.7 combined).

BUGANDA, EXAMINATIONS, THUNDER

UK 2021

According to surveys published in the UK in 2021:

- 10 per cent of people want to wear flip-flops in the office;
- 20 per cent of people choose blue paint for some home decoration;
- 30 per cent of sexually active students have had an STD test while at university;
- 40 per cent of people think an animal's life is worth the same as a human life;
- 50 per cent of people perceive litter to be a big problem;

- 60 per cent of people aged 16–25 are very worried or extremely worried about climate change;
- 70 per cent of people say they would judge a town by its high street;
- 80 per cent of people recognise the positive impact that owning a dog can have on their mental health;
- 90 per cent of women have fantasised at some point during sex.

And one may well add:

- 100 per cent of all such survey results ought to be viewed with at least a modicum of scepticism.

UKRAINE

The national anthem of Ukraine begins with a line that means 'The glory and freedom of Ukraine Has Not Yet Perished'.

The area of Ukraine is about 608,647 square kilometres (235,000 square miles), making it the largest country totally within Europe. In 1887, a stone was erected in the town of Rakhiv in Ukraine, supposedly marking the geographical centre of Europe, a claim now thought dubious. Shortly after Ukraine gained independence from the old Soviet Union, it changed its currency from the karbovanets to the hryvna.

On 3 October 1995, the city council in the Ukrainian capital Kiev established a commission to ease confusion among postmen and delivery workers by renaming the 38 streets in the city that were all called 'Vostochnaya' (East).

In the Ukraine, ducks go 'krya-krya'.

 AQUARIUM, ISRAEL, POTATO

ULCER

Shakespeare only used the word 'ulcer' twice in his plays, once in *Hamlet* and once in *Troilus and Cressida*. However,

Hamlet also includes the word 'ulcerous', which also appears in *Macbeth* and *Timon of Athens*.

 ENGLISH, MOUSTACHE, VALENTINO

UMBRELLA

In ancient China, umbrellas protected against the sun, not the rain, while in ancient Egypt, an umbrella was a sign of rank.

The philanthropist and traveller Jonas Hanway is said to have introduced umbrellas into England in the 1750s, but they were used almost exclusively by women until the mid-19th century. Besides his umbrella achievements, Hanway was a fierce opponent of tea-drinking, which he accused of being 'pernicious to health, obstructing industry and impoverishing the nation'.

In the Peninsular War (1808–14), the Duke of Wellington issued an order forbidding officers to take umbrellas with them into battle.

1903 saw the invention of 'Pardoe's Improved Umbrella', an umbrella with mosquito net attached to protect from both rain and insects.

An often repeated story is told about an Italian who in 1969 was charged with selling grated umbrella handles as Parmesan cheese. This tale has been difficult to verify, but a report from Milan in 1962 concerned grated 'garbage and a plastic binder' being sold as Parmesan. It was reported that such trade had gone on at least since 1957 and none of the customers had complained.

In September 1978, Bulgarian writer and broadcaster Georgi Markov was fatally stabbed in London by an assassin using a poisoned umbrella.

The world's only Umbrella Cover Museum opened on Peaks Island off the coast of Maine in 1996. The curator is Nancy Hoffman, whose collection of umbrella covers now contains exhibits from 30 countries. Ms Hoffman's middle initial is '3', which she adopted after a mistyping.

In 2002, the number of umbrellas left behind on London's tube trains and buses was 11,277. In 2014, the number of lost umbrellas was given as 10,907. In 2019, the figure for lost umbrellas on London transport was given as 'over 7,000'.

⚲ *ELASTIC, RAIN*

UNDEAD

A conference was held at the University of Hertfordshire in April 2010 with the title 'Open Graves, Open Minds: Vampires and the Undead in Modern Culture'. Announced lectures included: 'Sullied Blood, Semen, and Skin: Vampires and the Spectre of Miscegenation' and 'Who Ordered the Hamburger with Aids?: Blood Anxiety in True Blood'. Delegates at the conference ate brownies and cakes out of a coffin during a tea break, while the dinner menu included 'deliciously blood-red soup, sucked from the veins of tortured tomatoes' and 'vegetables, freshly dug from the grave of a murderer, brought to life with a sensual crimson dressing of tomato and basil'.

A panel of literary vampire experts discussed such topics as 'Undead, unwed, but not unread: vampire fiction and chick-lit', 'Undead Victorians', 'Politics of the Undead' and 'The Gay Undead'. According to an article on the conference in the *Wall Street Journal*: 'In England in 1974, a man who thought he was being tormented by vampires choked to death on garlic.'

UNDERGARMENTS

In 2012, Zimbabwe became the third country in Africa to ban the sale of secondhand undergarments. The legislation made it illegal to import or sell 'articles of secondhand undergarments of any type, form or description, whether purchased, donated or procured in any other matter'. Commenting on the new law, one Zimbabwe newspaper described it as 'one of the best laws that our country has put in place in recent years'.

The Zimbabwean legislation closely followed that of Rwanda, which banned the sale of secondhand underwear at the end of 2011, and Ghana which banned it in 1994, but only began enforcing the law in 2011.

⚲ *UNDERWEAR*

UNDERGROUND

Forty-five per cent of the London Underground network is under the ground. The entire system serves 272 stations, carries around 1.35 billion passengers a year and includes 451 escalators (including 25 at Waterloo) and 202 lifts. At peak times, there are 543 trains in operation on the network. London has by far the longest underground railway in Europe with a total length of 402 kilometres (250 miles). The metro in Shanghai, however, is far longer at 803 kilometres (499 miles).

London's busiest Underground station in 2019 was King's Cross, with more than 88 million passengers starting or finishing journeys there. In 2020, with travel severely restricted by Covid, the busiest station was Stratford with only 25.1 million passengers.

The first baby born on an Underground train was in 1924 at Elephant & Castle on the Bakerloo line.

⚲ DUCK, LONDON, MACKEREL, MOLE, MONOPOLY, PIGEON

⬤ UNDERWEAR

Commenting on the case of a man who put out a fire at a home in Hartlepool in 2008 by smothering it with his aunt's size 12 knickers, a fire brigade spokesman said that the general principle of using a large, wet cloth to cover a grease fire was a sound one. As for using underwear, he said: 'Clearly it depends on what size you are, but I don't want to go there.'

Also in 2008, women in Canada were urged to send their underwear to the Burmese Embassy in Ottawa in protest at human rights violations. The organisers of the protest said that the ruling military junta in Burma believe a native superstition that contact with women's undergarments can sap a man's power.

In 2009, the Japanese cosmonaut Koichi Wakata became the first man to wear the same underpants in space for a month. He was testing a newly designed odour-free garment made specially for space travel. He only told his colleagues aboard the International Space Station about the experiment when he returned to Earth.

⚲ DECENCY, ELASTIC, MUSEUM, UZBEKISTAN, WAGNER, YETI

⬤ UNEMPLOYMENT

The first Unemployment Olympics were held in New York in 2009 and were open only to people who could supply evidence that they had lost their jobs. Events included Pin the Blame on the Boss (a variation on Pin the Tail on the Donkey) and Office-Phone Skee-Ball (hurling a black phone towards chalk goal marks on the pavement).

⚲ ANDORRA, COMMON COLD

⬤ UNICORN

The discovery in 2016 in Kazakhstan of the skull of an *Elasmotherium sibiricum*, also known as a Siberian unicorn, suggests that humans and some sort of unicorn may have been around at the same time. The one-horned Siberian unicorn was thought to have become extinct around 350,000 BC, but the recent finding has been dated to only 26,000 years ago.

The ancient Greeks wrote about unicorns, not as part of their mythology but in accounts of natural history. In ancient Rome, Pliny the Elder wrote of the 'very fierce, one-horned monoceros'. The Indus Valley civilisation, at around 3000 BC, sealed clay tablets with a unicorn emblem.

In the King James Bible, Old Testament, there are nine references to unicorns.

In the Middle Ages a unicorn was seen as a symbol of purity and grace, which could only be captured or tamed by a virgin. In those times, the tusk of a narwhal (a sort of toothed whale) was often sold as unicorn horn.

In the 1980s, a US patent was granted for a surgical procedure to create unicorns. It involved transplanting the horn buds of a goat to create one horn in the middle of the head. According to the application, it would 'render a unicorn of higher intelligence'.

The Greek physician Ctesias wrote a classic description of the unicorn around 400 BC. He described it as a fleet and fierce Indian wild ass with a white body, purple head, and a straight horn, a cubit long, with a white base, black middle and red tip. The unicorn is also mentioned in the writings of Aristotle and Aelian.

⚲ MARY, QUEEN OF SCOTS

UNION JACK

By a proclamation of James I of England (James VI of Scotland), the Union Flag was created on 12 April 1606, combining the crosses of St George of England and St Andrew of Scotland.

The cross of St Patrick was added in 1801 to form the Union Jack (or flag) we know today. Oliver Cromwell temporarily modified the flag by adding a Welsh harp in the middle.

Originally the flag was used only on ships at sea. As the flag on a ship is known as a 'jack', it became known as the Union Jack.

The insertion of thin white stripes separating the red cross from the blue background is called a 'fimbriation'.

In 2009, the UK government inadvertently flew the Union Jack upside down, which is a distress signal, at the signing of a trade agreement with China.

It was reported that China made the greatest number of Union Jacks waved at the 2011 royal wedding in England.

The width to length ratio of the Union Jack is officially 1:2, but 3:5 is also acceptable.

A 'Union Jack' is a nine-selection bet on a 3×3 grid, with a payout given for any line of three winners.

In 2010, it was reported that former UK Prime Minister Tony Blair owned a pair of silk Union Jack boxer shorts.

UNITED ARAB EMIRATES

The national sport of the United Arab Emirates is camel racing, and the national juice is camel milk.

 ⚲ *INCOME TAX, NUMBER PLATE, SHARJAH, SOUTH KOREA, STAMPS*

UNITED KINGDOM

The term 'United Kingdom' became official in 1801 when the parliaments of Great Britain and Ireland each passed an Act of Union, uniting the two kingdoms and creating the United Kingdom of Great Britain and Ireland. In 1931, it became the United Kingdom of Great Britain and Northern Ireland.

 ⚲ *MOZAMBIQUE, QUEENSLAND*

UNITED NATIONS

There are 193 members of the United Nations, following the admission of South Sudan in 2011. Seychelles is the only one of them whose name has no letters in common with 'Britain'.

The UN's Universal Declaration of Human Rights comprises 2,019 words. The EU's rules on giving ECO labels to toilet paper contain 4,442 words.

 ⚲ *CHAD, NORFOLK ISLAND, TOILET, VATICAN, ZIMBABWE*

UNITED STATES

The first US president to be born an American citizen was the 8th, Martin Van Buren (held office 1837–41). The seven before him were born British subjects.

The first US president to have been born in a hospital was Jimmy Carter (b. 1924, elected 1977).

The last US president to have had a beard was Benjamin Harrison, who left office in 1893, but William Howard Taft, who was president from 1909 to 1913, had a splendid moustache.

The tallest US president was Abraham Lincoln (elected 1861) at 1.9 metres (6 feet 4 inches). Lyndon Johnson was half an inch shorter. The shortest president was James Madison at 1.6 metres (5 feet 4 inches).

The only US president to have appeared in a shirt advertisement is Ronald Reagan, who promised that van Heusen shirts won't wrinkle ever!

The only US president to have been arrested and fined $20 for speeding on a horse-drawn carriage was Ulysses S. Grant in 1872.

The only US president to hold a patent was Abraham Lincoln. It was Patent No. 6469 awarded in 1849 for 'A Device for Buoying Vessels Over Shoals'. Lincoln had twice been stranded on riverboats that had run aground and his invention consisted of 'adjustable buoyant air chambers', which could be attached to the sides of a boat, then lowered into the water and inflated to lift the boat over obstructions. It was never produced and probably would not have worked anyway.

The heaviest president was William Taft (elected 1909), whose weight was estimated at various times to be between 300 and 350 pounds. He once got stuck in the bath at the White House and it took six men to lift him out. He promptly ordered a bigger bath.

From 1840 until 1960, all six US presidents who were first elected in a year ending in zero died in office. That pattern was broken by Ronald Reagan, elected in 1980, who survived an assassination attempt, and George W. Bush who was elected in 2000.

According to a retired FBI agent, during the Bush presidency there were 300 to 500 threats on the President's life each month.

⚲ *ALASKA, BROCCOLI, CHICKEN, HORSE-RADISH, OBESITY, RUGBY*

● UNIVERSITIES

Though Plato had opened his Academy in Athens around 387 BC, modern universities began in medieval Europe. They were called *studia generalia* and were designed to spread their reputation and influence as scholars travelled more widely, attracting students from all over Europe and providing qualifications recognised anywhere.

The guild of students and teachers within a *studium* was known as *universitas,* meaning 'the whole', or 'the universe', which, in due course, became the word for the entire institution.

The first university was established either at Salerno in the 9th century or, more reputably, at Bologna in the 11th. In its early days, Bologna saw itself as a guild of students in pursuit of learning, but Paris University, founded between 1150 and 1170, took a different view: it was a guild of teachers in pursuit of students, and this became the model for later universities, beginning with Oxford and Cambridge.

Scholars gathered at Oxford in the 12th century simply because it was a good place to cross the Thames by ford and roads from all over the country met there. In 1167, Henry II, during a squabble with Archbishop Becket, forbade English scholars to go to Paris, so they went to Oxford instead. The first formal college to be opened there was University College in 1249, which is often given as the date of the founding of Oxford University, though teaching had been going on there already for more than a century.

Meanwhile, the University of Cambridge was growing, boosted by an influx of disaffected Oxford students in 1209. Its first college was Peterhouse, founded in 1284.

In recent years, Oxford has produced most British prime ministers, while Cambridge gave the UK more Nobel Prize winners and spies. Of the 55 British prime ministers, 42 went to Oxford or Cambridge, three (Earl Russell, Neville Chamberlain and Gordon Brown) went to other universities (Edinburgh, Birmingham and Edinburgh again) and 11 (including Winston Churchill and John Major) did not go to university at all.

While Scotland (St Andrews in 1411) and Ireland (Dublin in 1591) were quick to open new universities, no more appeared in England until the 19th century. With many changes in terminology over the past 30 years it is difficult to give the precise number of universities in the UK now, but it is around 130, of which about 106 are in England.

⚲ *ALGERIA, BRADFORD, DEGREE, DUCK, HALITOSIS, JELLY, SEX WORK*

⬤ URANUS

William Herschel discovered the planet Uranus in 1781. When he died at the age of 83, he was just 87 days short of having lived for a period equal to one orbit of Uranus around the Sun. Herschel was also the first person to show that coral is not a plant, and in between his scientific investigations he composed 24 symphonies.

Uranus has 27 known moons, almost all of which are named after characters in Shakespeare's plays, unlike the moons of every other planet in the Solar System, which are named after characters in Greek and Roman mythology.

The two moons of Uranus that are not named after Shakespearean characters, Ariel and Umbriel, are named after sylphs in *The Rape of the Lock* by Alexander Pope. Ariel is the name of a sprite in Shakespeare's *The Tempest*, but Uranus's moon is named after Pope's Ariel.

Herschel discovered two of the moons of Uranus. Ten more of them were discovered in 1986 by the Voyager 2 mission.

⚲ *ASTRONOMY*

⬤ URINATION

In 2006, Danish artist Uwe Max Jensen was fined 1,000-kroner for pretending to urinate in public. Jensen claimed it was an artistic stunt, which was not meant to be indecent. He told the court that he had pretended to urinate by concealing a plastic bag containing water in his trousers and squeezing water on a wall. The court ruled that it wasn't necessary to establish whether he urinated or sprinkled water. It deemed his conduct obscene and unlawful, and fined him. He had initially been fined 2,000 kroner, but he refused to pay and the court reduced the fine by half.

Urination was an early word for the sport of diving.

Urine words in the *Oxford English Dictionary* include: all-flower-water (n.) cow urine used as an unspecified remedy; lant (v.) to add urine to ale in order to make it stronger; lotium (n.) stale urine used by barbers; puppy-water (n.) urine of a young dog used as a cosmetic.

According to Francis Bacon: 'We find also that places where men urine commonly have smell of violets. And urine, if one hath eaten nutmeg, hath so too.'

⚲ *DANDELION, PORONKUSEMA, VAGINA*

⬤ URSULA

The name Ursula is a diminutive of the Latin *Ursa*, so means 'little bear'.

Saint Ursula is the possibly legendary 4th century saint after whom the Virgin Islands were named. She was supposedly the daughter of a king named Dionotus in the kingdom of Dumnonia in south-west England. Betrothed to a governor in Gaul, she is said to have crossed the Channel with 11,000 virgin handmaidens, was blown across the sea quickly by a supposedly miraculous storm, and in thanks set off on a pilgrimage to Rome. On the way back, the group was attacked by the Huns, who killed Ursula and beheaded all the virgins.

Although the legend dates from the 4th or 5th century, there is no mention of the figure of 11,000 until the 9th century, and there is some suggestion that the number may be the result of a mistranslation and it may have been 11 virgins or possibly only one.

When Columbus discovered the Virgin Islands in 1493, he gave them the name 'Santa Ursula y las Once Mil Virgenes' (Saint Ursula and the 11,000 virgins).

Ursula was the 4,138th most popular name for a baby girl born in the United States in 2021.

♀ *VIRGIN ISLANDS*

URUGUAY

Uruguay is the only country that has the same letter three times in the first five letters of its name in English. It is also the only country in Latin America which is entirely outside the tropics.

UZBEKISTAN

Uzbekistan is the only county surrounded entirely by other countries whose names end in '-stan' (Afghanistan, Kazakhstan, Kyrgyzstan, Tajikistan and Turkmenistan).

Liechtenstein and Uzbekistan are the only countries that are doubly landlocked: not only are they totally inland, but none of the countries they border has a coastline either.

In Uzbekistan, handshakes take place only between two men. When a man greets an Uzbek woman, he should bow down to her with his right hand placed over his heart.

In January 2006, the authorities in Uzbekistan banned the sale of fur-lined underwear because of the 'unbridled fantasies' such items could provoke.

♀ *COINS, KYRGYZSTAN, SILKWORM*

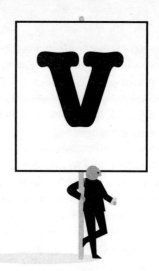

VAGINA

Kangaroos, like almost all marsupials, including koalas, wombats and Tasmanian devils, have three vaginas. The two outside ones carry sperm to the two uteruses, while the middle vagina is used for giving birth to the baby kangaroo.

To match this arrangement, most male marsupials have a bifurcated penis, allowing both outside vaginas to be impregnated simultaneously. Among marsupials, only the two largest species of kangaroo do not have a bifurcated penis.

Monotremes, including the platypus and echidna, also have a bifurcated penis. An echidna's penis in fact has four heads, none of which is used for urination.

⚲ *GRÄFENBERG, PREMATURE EJACULATION*

VAGRANCY

The Vagrancy Act 1824 was described as 'An Act for the Punishment of idle and disorderly persons, rogues and vagabonds'. Under its provisions, 'fortune-tellers setting out to deceive any of His Majesty's subjects' were officially deemed to be 'rogues and vagabonds'.

⚲ *FORTUNE-TELLING*

VALENTINO, Rudolph (1895–1926)

The first job of cinema heart-throb Valentino when he came to the United States in 1913 was as a gardener. He went on to take the romantic lead in many films, including *The Sheik* (1921), which was written by Mrs Edith Maud Hull, who was married to a pig-breeder named Percy.

The term 'Latin lover' was originally coined by Hollywood moguls for Valentino. His full name was Rodolfo Alfonso Rafaello Pierre Filibert Guglielmi di Valentina D'Antonguolla. He died of a ruptured ulcer at the age of 31. An estimated 100,000 mourners lined the streets at his funeral.

⚲ *BURIAL*

VAMPIRES

The earliest reference to vampires in England is often said to occur in Walter Map's *De Nugis Curialium* (*Of the Trifles of Courtiers*), written in 1190. This was some 700 years before Bram Stoker created Dracula, so it should be no surprise to learn that Walter Map did not actually mention vampires. The supposed reference to them is in two Welsh folk tales he recounts involving the dead rising from their graves. So they were more zombies than vampires.

Recent research links early references to vampirism to outbreaks of rabies, of which the symptoms may include sensitivity to light and garlic and a tendency to bite people.

In 1999 in the United States, 907 people took out insurance against turning into vampires or werewolves. In 2017, it was reported that 60,000 people took out insurance against being bitten by vampires and werewolves.

♀ GARLIC, UNDEAD

VAN GOGH, Vincent Willem (1853–90)

Van Gogh's 1889 *Self-Portrait with Bandaged Ear and Pipe* shows the artist apparently with his right ear bandaged, whereas it was the left ear that he partially cut off. The explanation seems to be that the artist used a mirror when painting the self-portrait.

Van Gogh assaulted his own ear after an argument with Paul Gauguin, but how much of the ear he sliced off is still a matter of dispute. Even those who met van Gogh very soon after the incident gave accounts ranging from the whole ear to a small piece of the lobe.

For more than a century, it was generally believed that van Gogh took the piece of ear to the local brothel where he thought he might find Gauguin, but in his absence he gave it to a prostitute called Rachel. Research in 2016 for Bernadette Murphy's book *Van Gogh's Ear* made some surprising revelations. First, the new findings strongly suggested that the name of the startled ear recipient was Gabrielle, not Rachel, and she was a maid, not a prostitute. Furthermore, a letter from the doctor who treated van Gogh was discovered,

containing a sketch of the damage done, strongly suggesting that he sliced off almost the entire ear.

Although van Gogh painted some 750 canvases and 1,600 drawings, he is said to have sold only one during his lifetime. *Red Vineyard at Arles* was bought by a friend for 400 francs.

When van Gogh's *Portrait of Dr Gachet* was sold at auction in New York in 1990 for $82.5 million, it was the highest price ever paid for a painting. Adjusting for inflation, it is now in 16th place.

♀ CÉZANNE

VANUATU

The first European to discover the islands of Vanuatu in the South Pacific was the Spanish explorer Captain Pedro Ferdinand De Quiros in 1605. He named them Tierra Australis del Espiritu Santo, believing he had discovered the great southern continent. The island he landed on is still called Espiritu Santo.

The next European to land there was the French explorer Louis Antoine de Bougainville in 1768. He called the islands the Cyclades, after the Greek islands so named, and he named a strait running between the islands after himself.

In 1774, Captain James Cook arrived and renamed the archipelago, consisting of some 83 islands, the New Hebrides after the islands off Scotland. It was known by that name until independence in 1980.

In 1839, the London Missionary Society sent two British missionaries to Vanuatu. When they arrived, they were quickly killed and eaten. Apparently, the standard baking time for cannibalism there was three to five hours, and the head of the victim was saved for the village chief. The last cannibal killing in Vanuatu is thought to have taken place in 1969.

There is a tradition in Vanuatu to celebrate the annual harvesting of the yam crop by jumping from high towers with vines attached to the ankles. This is thought to have been the origin of bungee jumping.

Diseases brought by missionaries and traders are thought to have caused the population to drop from about a million in 1800 to 45,000 in 1935. In 2020, it was back up to over 300,000.

Following a visit to Vanuatu by Queen Elizabeth II and Prince Philip in 1974, one tribe identified Prince Philip as the messiah referred to in an old legend. They formed the religious sect known as the Prince Philip Movement and have worshipped him ever since. A formal period of mourning followed his death in 2021.

In 2021, the World Risk Report placed Vanuatu at a higher risk of natural disaster than any other country. Despite this, the Happy Planet Index in 2019 placed Vanuatu second, behind Costa Rica, in its list of happiest countries on Earth.

⚲ *INCOME TAX*

⬤ VASECTOMY

A clinic in Oregon in 2008 had the idea of using the popular televised college basketball season to broadcast a radio advert for its service in providing vasectomies. 'You need an excuse ... to stay at home in front of the big screen,' the advert announcement began. 'It's snip city.' The sports radio station broadcasting the adverts promised to send each patient a recovery kit of sports magazines, free pizza delivery

and a bag of frozen peas to help reduce any swelling.

⚲ *THAILAND*

⬤ VATICAN

With an area of 0.44 square kilometres (0.17 square miles) and a population of 911, Vatican City is the world's smallest state. It has no coastline, no waterways, no natural resources and no airport, but has one heliport which is used only by the Pope and visiting heads of state.

The uniform of the Swiss Guard of Papal Defenders was originally designed by Michelangelo but, according to the Vatican tailor Ety Cicioni, there were no patterns and no instructions on how to make it when he arrived in 2000. By examining an existing uniform, he found that it can be made from 154 pieces. Each uniform weighs about 8 pounds, which is more than twice the weight of US army battle dress.

The Vatican chose the traditional date of the spring equinox, 25 March, as an appropriate day to launch its Internet site in 1997. It is also the day celebrated as the Annunciation of the Blessed Virgin Mary, when the arch-angel Gabriel told her she would bear a child. And according to some medieval theologians, 25 March was also the date of the Creation. In 1957, the European Common Market was created on 25 March.

Around 90 per cent of the crimes committed in Vatican City go unpunished. Because Vatican City has such a small resident population – about 500 people – and such a huge number of visitors –18 million a year – it has perhaps the world's highest per capita crime rate, the annual number of crimes varying between 1 and 1.5 per person.

Vatican City and Taiwan are the only countries that are recognised as independent states by the United Nations but are not UN members.

When Indian Hindu leader Pramukh Swami travelled for a meeting with Pope John Paul II at the Vatican in 1984, he was 63 years old, and for 46 years had devoutly kept to his vow not to interact directly with women. He was accompanied on his visit by nine other monks and a group of laymen, whose tasks included keeping women away from his route and guiding him with his eyes shut if any approached.

♀ *EXORCISM, FROG, GALILEI, HERON-ALLEN, LAUNDRY, STOCKINGS*

VEGETABLE

The estimated number of injuries caused by vegetables in the UK in 2005 and that required a trip to hospital was 14,149.

The word 'vegetable' dates back to the 15th century but does not occur in the King James Bible or in any of Shakespeare's plays.

♀ *BRUMMELL, CUCUMBER, FINLAND, PEAS, RHUBARB, WATERMELON*

VENEZUELA

Venezuela has won six Miss World contests, more than any country other than India, which also has six.

In 2019, Venezuela was third in the list of countries with most gun-related deaths, behind Brazil and the United States, but it rises to second (behind El Salvador) in the table of gun deaths per head of population.

Venezuela was given its name, which means 'little Venice', by Alonso de Ojeda in 1499.

♀ *BICYCLE, CARACAS, IMPLANT, JAMAICA*

VENICE

On 6 May 1996, gondoliers in Venice stopped serenading passengers following a ruling that singing would turn them into freelance musicians and therefore liable to contribute to a state pension fund. Breathalyser tests were introduced for Venetian gondoliers in January 2005. Police in the city said they wanted to tackle incidents of drunken rowing.

A survey in 2008 revealed that Venice is one of the worst cities in the world for romantic bust-ups, several of which were caused by the high cost of trips to the city.

In 2009, Venice, became the world's first city in which people could pay in advance online to go to public lavatories. Instead of the standard one euro fee per lavatory visit, tourists were told they could pay 7 euros online for 10 toilet visits over five days in high season, and 5 euros in the low tourist season. Bought offline at a toilet or other site, such tickets cost 9 euros and 7 euros.

♀ *BIRMINGHAM, CARNIVAL, PIGEON, SHROVE TUESDAY, VENEZUELA*

VENUS

Venus is the only planet that rotates in the opposite direction to its orbit around the Sun. Since Venus is visible in the morning and evening, it was once thought to be two separate stars called Eosphorus and Hesperus. The ancient Greeks were the first to realise they were identical.

It takes 225 Earth days for Venus to go round the Sun, and 243 Earth days to rotate once on its axis, so a Venusian day is longer than a Venusian year.

The ancient Mayans called Venus Kukulcan, the planet of warfare.

The atmosphere on Venus is 96 per cent carbon dioxide and the clouds are sulphuric acid. The atmospheric pressure is about 90 times as high as on Earth and would crush a human flat.

⚲ *APHRODISIAC, APRIL FOOLS, CLITORIS, EUROPE, MARS*

● VERMONT

If a hunter kills a moose in Vermont during the permitted hunting season, the moose must be tagged and reported. If a male moose is reported after it has been cut into parts, the antlers must also be presented and the scrotum containing the testicles must be left attached to the carcass or one of the hindquarters. If a female moose is reported in parts, the udder must be left attached to the carcass or one of the hindquarters.

⚲ *LICENCE PLATES, SALAMANDER*

● VIBRATOR

According to Rachel Maines in her 1998 book *The Technology of Orgasm: Hysteria, the Vibrator and Women's Sexual Satisfaction*, the vibrator was the fifth most common domestic item – after the sewing machine, fan, kettle and toaster – to be sold in a form that was powered by electricity.

Electric vibrators first appeared around 1880, but until the 1920s, according to Maines's account, they were considered respectable items of medical equipment and were used by physicians to treat cases of alleged hysteria in women. Only when vibrators began to appear in adult movies did attitudes towards them change.

● VICTORIA, Queen and Empress (1819–1901)

Queen Victoria had an African grey parrot called Coco which was taught to sing 'God Save The Queen'.

According to the editor of *Burke's Peerage*, Queen Victoria had terrible handwriting.

The flowers at Queen Victoria's funeral cost £80,000. Her direct descendants include Kaiser Wilhelm II, Alexandra (wife of Tsar Nicholas II), Queen Elizabeth II, the Duke of Edinburgh and the present monarchs of Spain, Norway, Denmark and Sweden.

At Osborne House, Queen Victoria's residence on the Isle of Wight, food was kept cold in an early refrigerator chilled by blocks of ice which were shipped over from North America. The ice was stored in a deep ice house on the grounds some distance from the main building.

⚲ *BEER, BREASTFEEDING, CHEESE, CHOCOLATE, COW, DENTISTRY*

● VICTORIA CROSS

The VC, the highest military order in the UK, was introduced on 29 January 1856 by Queen Victoria to honour acts of valour in the Crimean War. It has been awarded 1,358 times to 1,355 individual recipients, three winning it twice. The cross is inscribed 'For Valour'. Queen Victoria had this changed from the suggested 'For The Brave' as she considered all soldiers brave.

The jeweller Hancocks of London has made all the VCs awarded. More than an eighth of all VCs, a total of 176, are now owned by Lord Ashcroft and can be seen at the Imperial War Museum together with its own collection of 46 VCs.

Between 1861 and 1908, eight men had their VCs taken away after being convicted of crimes. These included theft of a colleague's medals, stealing a cow, desertion and bigamy. George V was strongly against forfeiture of a

Victoria Cross and said that, even if a man was hanged, he should wear his VC on the scaffold.

At any investiture, the VCs are presented first, taking precedence even over knighthoods.

A Royal Warrant in 1920 made it possible to award VCs to women, but this has never happened. Holders of the VC receive an annuity of £1,495 a year, which is free of tax.

FIRST WORLD WAR

VIENNA

In the mid-19th century, statistics at the Vienna General Hospital showed that pregnant women who were attended by a doctor ran an 18 per cent chance of dying in childbirth, while only 2 per cent of those attended by a midwife died. When this was pointed out by Ignaz Semmelweis, and doctors in one trial started scrubbing up with bleach, mortality rates dropped to between 1 and 3 per cent. Disapproving of Semmelweis's attempts to disrupt their normal procedure, however, some colleagues tricked him into visiting a lunatic asylum, where guards knocked him to the ground and forced him into a straitjacket. Two weeks later, Semmelweis died of gangrene and internal injuries caused by the beating.

Later, the term 'Semmelweis reflex' was given to the reflex-like rejection of new ideas because they contradict entrenched norms or practices.

With over 2.5 million plots in its central cemetery and a population of just under 2 million, Vienna is a city where the dead outnumber the living.

ACCORDION, COFFEE, SAUSAGES, ZOG I

VIETNAM

Of Vietnam's population of just over 86 million, an estimated 20 million are cyclists.

In 2011, police in Vietnam were banned from wearing black sunglasses, chatting, smoking or putting their hands in their pockets while on duty in public places.

BULL, DUCK, NOBEL PRIZE, SNIFFING, SUNGLASSES

VIKINGS

Although the Vikings did their marauding from the 8th to the 11th century, the word 'Viking' does not appear in English before 1807. Eric Bloodaxe (d. 954) was the last Viking ruler of Northumbria. Sweyn Forkbeard was King of Denmark, ruler of most of Norway, and King of England for five weeks before his death early in 1014. He was the father of the better-known King Canute. Sweyn Forkbeard did not have a forked beard – the name referred to the shape of his moustache.

Vikings are said to have used fleas as navigational tools, on the principle that fleas tend to jump northwards.

Trials in Viking society were decided by a jury of 12, 24 or 36 people, depending on the seriousness of the crime. Viking society had three classes: nobles, freemen and slaves.

In 1976, archaeologists found Viking remains in York (or Jorvik, as the Vikings called it), including a 10th-century woollen sock knitted on one needle.

Useful Viking word: 'scramasax' – a small knife for hand-to-hand combat.

CANTERBURY, HAMLET, SLAVERY

VIOLENCE

On 14 April 1989, police in Huddersfield reported that their research had confirmed that violent criminals could be calmed down by putting them in pink cells. In 2013, this was confirmed in Switzerland where 30 jail cells in the prison system were painted pink in an effort to calm aggressive inmates. The project was called 'Cool Down Pink'.

FOOTBALL, LAUGHTER

VIOLIN

The modern violin has been around for roughly 500 years, having evolved over thousands of years from stringed instruments known as the ravanstron, the rebec and the rabab. In the 16th century, the Medici family of Italy commissioned the great lute-maker Andrea Amati to build a small wooden stringed instrument that was as melodious as a lyre but was easy to carry around.

The word 'violin' comes from the medieval Latin word *vitula*, meaning 'stringed instrument'. Violins are typically made of spruce or maple wood. Over 70 different pieces of wood are put together to form the modern violin. Violin bows typically contain 150 to 200 hairs made of a variety of materials including nylon and horse hair. Violin strings were first made of sheep gut (commonly known as catgut), which was stretched, dried and twisted; other materials used have included solid steel, stranded steel or various synthetic materials, wound with various metals, and sometimes plated with silver.

Mr Christian Adam holds the world record for cycling backwards while playing the violin. In achieving this milestone, Christian played for 5.08 hours and covered a total distance of 60.45 kilometres (37.5 miles). This took place in 1963 on St Gallen highway in Switzerland, before the highway was fully open.

Playing the violin in normal fashion burns approximately 170 calories per hour.

Useful violin word: 'luthier' – a maker of stringed instruments.

HERON-ALLEN, LONDON, SKATES, VIOLIN SPIDER, VIVALDI

VIOLIN SPIDER

The brown recluse spider has nicknames such as brown fiddler, fiddleback spider and violin spider. The last of these comes from a distinct marking on the front of its body, which looks a lot like a violin. These spiders usually inhabit South California to West Arizona and in the majority of cases will not bite or attack humans. The brown recluse is a small, mellow creature that generally avoids conflict, but it does carry a hemotoxic venom that can be deadly and is normally released when the spider is pressed up against skin.

VIRGIN ISLANDS

The Virgin Islands is the correct name for what are commonly known as the British Virgin Islands. The 'British' is added to avoid confusing them with the Virgin Islands of the United States, which until 1917 were known as the Danish West Indies.

There are 100 women to every 82 men in the Virgin Islands, the highest female to male ratio in the world.

There are more than 20 times as many companies registered in the Virgin Islands as there are people living there.

JACKSON Michael, URSULA

VIRGINITY

According to a survey of 44 countries by Durex in 2012, the average age at which a person loses his or her virginity is highest in Malaysia (23.7) and lowest in Iceland (15.6). The US (18.0) and UK (18.3) were both close to the worldwide average.

According to medieval superstition, a woman could recover her virginity by giving birth to seven illegitimate children.

A male Emperor moth can smell a virgin female up to 11 kilometres (7 miles) away upwind.

⚲ HYPATIA, LOVE

VIVALDI, Antonio (1678–1741)

The Italian composer Antonio Vivaldi wrote over 500 concerti (including about 230 for violin and 38 for bassoon) as well as 46 operas and numerous sonatas and pieces of sacred music.

⚲ BACH

VOICE

In a research experiment at Nottingham University published in 2001, a sample of women were played tapes of the voices of 34 men and asked to judge their attractiveness, age, weight, muscular development and whether they had a hairy chest. The results showed that men with deep, sonorous voices are thought by women to be more attractive, older, heavier, more muscular and more likely to have a hairy chest than men with higher voices.

While the women subjects tended to agree with one another quite strongly in their assessments, measurements showed they were wrong on all counts except one: men with deep voices tend to be heavier than higher-pitched men.

'The frightened person has many voices.'
Finnish proverb

⚲ AIR HOSTESSES, BUGS BUNNY, CLEOPATRA, GEORGE V, MANGO, SEDUCTION

VOLLEYBALL

Volleyball was invented by William G. Morgan in Holyoke, Massachusetts, on 9 February 1895. He originally called the game 'mintonette'. He invented it because he thought basketball was too strenuous and violent. The game spread outside the US and Canada only in 1919 when the American Expeditionary Forces sent 16,000 volleyballs to their troops and allies.

Beach volleyball is the only Olympic sport with a rule prohibiting players from wearing too much. The uniforms must be a tight fit, and women's briefs must be cut on an upward angle towards the top of the leg. The side width must be at most 7 centimetres (2.75 inches).

According to the Fédération International de Volleyball, one in six of the world's population plays or watches indoor, beach or 'backyard' volleyball.

When a volleyball player is hit in the face by the ball hard enough to leave an imprint, it is called a 'tattoo'. Digging the ball out by extending a hand flat on the floor and bouncing the ball off the back of the hand is known as a 'pancake'.

The European Patent Office lists 2,568 volleyball-related patents, including 73 for beach volleyball.

Every year, around 100,000 Americans are treated in A&E for volleyball injuries.

⚲ LITHUANIA, SRI LANKA

VOLTAIRE (1694–1778)

The French writer/philosopher Voltaire (born François Marie Arouet) was 1.6 metres (5 feet 3 inches) tall and had a long nose. In 1717, at the age of 22, he was sentenced to 11 months in the

Bastille for writing a satirical verse in which he accused Phillipe II, Duke of Orléans, of incest with his daughter.

Voltaire is said to have drunk 50 cups of coffee a day.

♀ BOSWELL, MEDICINE, TUSSAUD

● VOODOO

In 2009, US electronics firm Radio Shack ordered its Mexican division not to distribute voodoo dolls wearing US soccer shirts. The dolls had been part of a promotion in a Mexican sports newspaper advising its readers to put pins in the dolls where they wanted to. The company said it could not support a situation that went against the national team.

● VOWELS

A vowel is 'a voiced breath modified by a definite configuration of the super-glottal passages, without audible friction' (Sweet, *A Primer of Phonetics*, 1890). 'Abstemious' and 'facetious' are frequently alleged to be the only two words in the English language that include all five vowels once each, in their correct alphabetical order. This is far from true: the full *Oxford English Dictionary* includes 16 such independent words. Here are the other 14:

Acheilous: without a lip; Adventious: an old form of adventitious; Aerious: of the nature of air; Affectious: affectionate; Anemious: of plants, growing in a windy situation; Annelidous: of the nature of a worm; Arsenious: of the nature of arsenic; Arterious: of an artery; Caesious: bluish or greyish green; Camelious: of a camel's hump; Fracedinous: pertaining to putrid fermentation; Materious: material; Placentious: disposed to please; Tragedious: full of tragedy.

Most of these words are described as archaic, obsolete or rare, but acheilous, arsenious and caesious are perfectly good modern words fit to hold their vowels high alongside abstemious and facetious.

The longest word that is spelt with a strict alternation of vowels and consonants is honorificabilitudinitatibus, which is defined as 'the quality of deserving honour and respect'. Shakespeare used the word in Act 5, Scene I of *Love's Labours Lost*.

The Canadian poet Christian Bok has written a novel, *Eunoia*, in which each of its five chapters uses only one of the five vowels, A, E, I, O, U. He is cautious about Y, which may be either vowel or consonant. Chapter O of his book is dedicated to Yoko Ono, whose Y is definitely consonantal. 'Eunoia', according to Bok, means 'beautiful thinking' and is the shortest word in English including all five vowels – but it is not in the *Oxford English Dictionary*. In Greek rhetoric, *eunoia* referred to the goodwill a speaker cultivates between performer and audience. Euoi is also not in the *OED*, but is allowed in Scrabble. It means 'a Bacchanalian cry of joy'.

♀ AA, BROWN, ENGLISH, IOWA, MACKEREL, MOZAMBIQUE, TENNIS

● VULTURE

In March 2009, the head of the regional government in Madrid petitioned the EU to relax the laws concerning the disposal of dead livestock because Spanish vultures were starving. Since 2002, when laws to stop the spread of mad cow disease were introduced, the countryside had been kept clear of carrion, which was one of the main sources of food for the vultures.

♀ AESCHYLUS, FLUTE, LUCK

VOODOO | VULTURE

WAGNER, Richard (1813–83)

According to the results of a survey into driving habits by the RAC published in 2007, Wagner's 'Ride of the Valkyries' is the piece of music that is most likely to make motorists – especially men – drive faster or take risks when behind the wheel.

Richard Wagner wore pink underwear. According to Mark Twain, his music was better than it sounds.

WALES

A Welsh language version of Scrabble was launched in 2005. It includes each of the two-letter combinations NG, DD, LL and RH on single tiles.

In 2008, a Welsh businessman living in Oxford was reported to have paid £27,500 at auction for the car number plate WEL 5H.

In the 19th century, nearly 14 per cent of the Welsh population had the surname 'Jones' and more than half the population were covered by only 10 surnames. The percentage of Welsh people named Jones in 2019 was 5.4.

There are four times as many sheep as people in Wales. In fact, Wales has 15 per cent of the total number of sheep in the European Union.

Coca-Cola launched its first Welsh language marketing campaign in 2000.

♀ *CHICKEN, LIECHTENSTEIN, OCTOPUS, TUESDAY, UK 2021, WELSH*

WALNUT

A walnut is the edible seed of a drupe, and thus not a true botanical nut. There are 21 species of walnut. The Romans called it 'Jupiter's acorn'.

The world production of walnuts in 2019 was 4.5 million tonnes, of which 56 per cent came from China, but the country with the highest per capita consumption of walnuts was the United States.

The Merry Wives of Windsor is the only Shakespeare play that mentions a walnut, though *Taming of the Shrew* has a reference to a walnut shell.

♀ *AUGUSTUS, SARDINE*

WALPOLE, Sir Robert (1676–1745)

Robert Walpole holds the record as the longest-serving British prime minister, with an uninterrupted run of nearly 21 years from April 1721 to February 1742.

♀ *DOWNING STREET, GEORGE I, GEORGE II, NETTLES*

WALRUS

The scientific name for the walrus is *Odobenus rosmarus*, which roughly means tooth-walking sea-horse.

Walruses can sleep in the water thanks to air sacs known as pharyngeal pouches on their throats that can be filled with up to 50 litres of air when they inflate. The walrus can then sleep in a vertical position, kept safe from drowning by these pillows.

According to research published in 2003, walruses use their right flippers eight times as much as their left when eating. Analysis of videotapes of walruses scooping up molluscs from the sea bed showed that the acts of scooping and flicking the molluscs to clean them were performed 89 per cent of the time with the right flipper and only 11 per cent with the left.

The collective noun for a group of walruses is a 'herd', a 'pod' or a 'huddle'.

⚲ *BACULUM, DINOSAUR, HOMOSEXUALITY, TEETH*

WAR

Over the past 5,000 years, an estimated 14,555 wars have taken place, killing approximately 25 billion people. Over the past 5,600 years, the world has been at peace for less than 300 years.

⚲ *BERWICK, DENTURES, HANDEL, KNIGHT-HOOD, UMBRELLA, WATERMELON*

WASHINGTON, George (1732–99)

Washington is said to have been the first American to breed jackasses and mules. He had a horse called Nelson or Old Nelson, which was a chestnut with a white blaze and white feet. The name of the horse had nothing to do with the English admiral but was named after the American soldier and statesman Thomas Nelson who gave the horse to Washington.

Having suffered from smallpox in his youth, Washington had his entire army inoculated against it in 1777. Among his other innovations was the feat of sending the first airmail letter – carried from Philadelphia to New Jersey by the balloonist Jean Pierre Blanchard.

The first First Lady, Martha Washington, would never have occupied that post if Betsy Fauntleroy had accepted on either of the occasions on which George Washington proposed to her first.

⚲ *AUSTRALIA, ICE CREAM, LIBRARY, TEETH, TWELFTH NIGHT*

WASP

The antennae of wasps are more sensitive than sniffer dogs' noses, and wasps can be trained to detect drugs or explosives, as Dutch scientists in November 2001 announced they had done. Furthermore, they said that training a wasp took only an hour, whereas dogs take six months. The disadvantage, as one of the researchers pointed out, is that wasps only live for a couple of months.

The world's smallest winged insect, the Tanzanian parasitic wasp, is smaller than the eye of a housefly.

⚲ *ACCIDENTS, CHRISTMAS, ICICLES, SKUNK, SNIFFING, STING*

WATER

An average human requires 1.5 gallons of water a day to survive indefinitely in a hot, exposed desert. A person can live about a month without food, but only about a week without water. The world record time to drink half a litre (17 fluid ounces) of water is 2.6 seconds.

⚲ *BEER, CAMEL, COLUMBUS, GABON, GOLD-FISH, LAVATORIES, OCEAN*

WATER-SKIING

Water-skiing was invented by
18-year-old Ralph Wilford Samuelson
in 1922. He first performed it in that
year in Lake City, Minnesota. Later, he
moved to Pine Island, Minnesota, where
he became a turkey farmer.

In 1972, the owner of an elephant
named Bimbo, aged seven, was awarded
$4,500 damages by the Californian
Supreme Court after it was claimed that
a road accident caused the elephant
to lose interest in dancing and water-
skiing. Bimbo was travelling in a trailer
that was involved in the accident. The
case was heard by a judge named Turtle.

WATERFALL

Waterfalls are grouped into 10 classes
based on the average volume of water
present on the fall.

Class 10 waterfalls include Niagara
Falls, Paulo Afonso Falls in Brazil and
Khone Falls in Cambodia.

BULLOCK, NIAGARA FALLS

WATERMELON

A watermelon is about 92 per cent
water. The first recorded watermelon
harvest took place around 5,000 years
ago in Egypt. Pictures of the fruit have
been found in paintings on the walls of
ancient buildings.

In the 4th century BC, during a
political debate, the Greek orator
and statesman Demosthenes had a
watermelon thrown at him by someone
in the audience. Placing a chunk of the
watermelon on his head, Demosthenes
thanked the thrower for providing him
with a helmet to wear in the war against
Philip of Macedonia.

The seedless watermelon was developed in 1939.

Although watermelons originated in
Africa, the country that produces most
of them is China and the biggest watermelon ever was grown by Christopher
Kent of Tennessee at the Operation
Pumpkin Festival in Ohio in 2013. It
weighed 159 kilograms (350.5 pounds).

Watermelon is the official state vegetable of Oklahoma, despite being a fruit,
not a vegetable.

Cordele, Georgia, claims to be Watermelon Capital of the World.

The average American eats over 7.7
kilograms (17 pounds) of watermelon
a year.

GEORGIA, LIBYA

WAX

On 1 December 1761, Marie Tussaud,
founder of Madame Tussauds
Waxworks, was born in Strasbourg. She
learnt wax modelling from her mother's
employer, Swiss physician Dr Philippe
Curtius, who made wax models for his
anatomy classes. During the French
Revolution, Marie Tussaud worked to
make death masks of guillotine victims.

Wax figures at Tussauds are made
2 per cent larger than their subjects
because wax shrinks.

The 1953 horror film *House of Wax*
was made in 3D, though its director
Andre de Toth was blind in one eye and
could not fully appreciate the effects.

In medieval times, pigment from
human earwax was used to illustrate
illuminated manuscripts. Human earwax
comes in two types. Ninety-seven per
cent of Europeans and Africans have
'wet' earwax, but East Asians have 'dry'
earwax. The gene controlling earwax
type was found in 2006 by Japanese
researchers, who discovered that earwax
type also correlates with armpit odour.

*BENTHAM, DICKENS, EARS, JACKSON Michael,
ST BERNARD, TUSSAUD*

WEATHER

According to Petronius, writing in AD 65: 'No living man has the right to cut his nails or hair on a ship; that is, unless the wind is blowing a hurricane.' If there is a hurricane at sea, however, another superstition recorded by Charles Darwin may explain its cause. In 1831, he recorded that the sailors on HMS *Beagle* believed that strong winds were caused by someone on shore keeping a cat shut up. At any moment, about 2,000 thunderstorms are going on somewhere on Earth; no research has been done to correlate these with confined cats.

Britain's worst ever storm was on 26 November 1703, when high winds and torrential rain killed an estimated 8,000 people in southern England.

Research published in 1990 showed that most violent crime rates increase in hot weather, while property crimes are not affected by the weather.

Useful weather verb: 'to driffle', which means 'to rain fitfully or in sparse drops'.

In January 2022, the National Weather Service in Miami issued a warning for people to beware falling iguanas. The unusually cold weather was causing many iguanas to freeze and stick to the branches of trees. Their metabolism slows and they lose consciousness and then drop from the tree.

'When two Englishmen meet, their first talk is of the weather.' Samuel Johnson, 1758

⚲ *GROUNDHOG DAY, METEOROLOGY, RAIN, ST SWITHUN, TIGER*

WEDDING

Italian couple Daniela Consolaro, 31, and Maurizio Andreosi, 40, were married in a shark tank in August 2004. The 14 sharks in the tank at the aquarium in Cattolica on the Adriatic coast were reported to be looking bored as the ceremony went on around them. The wedding was conducted by the mayor via a phone link. The couple said they chose to be lowered in a cage into the tank to draw attention to finning, the practice of cutting off fins for use in shark fin soup in Japan and elsewhere in Asia.

⚲ *BRIDEGROOM, CAT, CYBERSPACE, FASHION, IRAN, KUWAIT*

WEDDING RING

In October 2011, a Swedish woman found the wedding ring she had lost 16 years earlier around a carrot growing in her garden. Lena Paahlson said she had taken the ring off when cooking in her kitchen at Christmas 1995, but it went missing from the kitchen counter. She did not see it again until she was picking carrots in her garden in 2011 and found one with her ring around it. She thinks it must have fallen into the sink and been mixed with potato peelings that were composted or fed to sheep. This is believed to be a record for the length of time after which a missing ring has been found on a carrot.

⚲ *MARRIAGE*

WELLINGTON, Duke of (1769–1852)

Arthur Wellesley, later the first Duke of Wellington, was the son of Garret Wesley and Anne Wellesley. In his early years, he signed his name as Arthur Wesley, but his father died in 1781 and the family name was changed to Wellesley in 1798.

Although married and believed to have had several lovers, he maintained that 'no woman ever loved me; never in my whole life'. One of his alleged lovers was the French actress Marguerite George, who also had an affair with Napoleon. When asked to compare the two, she reputedly replied, 'The Duke was by far the more vigorous.' The Italian contralto Giuseppina Grassini is also thought to have had affairs with both Napoleon and Wellington but was discrete enough not to comment on their prowess.

As Prime Minister, Wellington rejected the idea of an underground railway in London on the grounds that the French army might use it to launch a surprise attack.

He is almost certainly the only man to have had a school (Wellington College), a tree (Wellingtonia) and a pair of boots (Wellingtons) all named after him.

ℙ *ADDRESS, DUELLING, HAIR, UMBRELLA*

● WELLINGTON BOOTS

The first wellington boots were made by Hoby of St James's Street for the Duke of Wellington, who asked for a boot hard-wearing for battle but comfortable at dinner.

The first rubber wellington was made in 1956 by American Henry Lee Norris in Scotland because he believed that the wet weather would boost sales.

The British sport of welly wanging – throwing wellingtons – started life as the 'gumboot and craters game' and was played by front-line soldiers in 1917. In 2006, Aberystwyth University experts created a machine that can hurl six wellies at a time up to 80 metres (262 feet).

In 2003, a wellington race took place in New Zealand, with 981 people running in their wellies. This record was thoroughly beaten in 2014 in Killarney, Ireland, when 3,194 people took part in a wellington boot race.

In 1900, New York millionaire Nathan Schwab ordered a pair of wellington boots for his dachshund.

In 2007, the biggest welly was built 8 metres (26 feet) high in North Queensland.

Writing on women's fashion in 1888, Oscar Wilde praised wellingtons for giving women more freedom.

Wellington boots with individual toes were first seen at the Chelsea Flower Show in 1995, where they were modelled by the Japanese garden designer Koji Ninomiya.

ℙ *SOCIALISM*

● WELLS, Herbert George (1866–1946)

The early life of H.G. Wells hardly suggested that he would become one of the greatest and most imaginative writers of his time. He was born the son of domestic servants, who later became small shopkeepers. He left school at 14 and was apprenticed to a draper, then a chemist, then another draper, but escaped a life of drudgery by winning a scholarship to study biology. After graduating from London University, he became a science teacher, then married his cousin, left her after three years and in 1894 ran away with a former student, Amy Catherine Robbins, who became his second wife in 1895.

In the same year, he published his first novel, *The Time Machine*, and a wealth of short stories and novels such as *War of the Worlds* and *The Invisible Man* followed.

According to the *Oxford English Dictionary*, his contributions to the English language include his being the first to use the phrases 'time-traveller' and 'atomic bomb'.

His last words are said to have been: 'Go away. I'm all right.'

In 1934, Wells, who suffered from diabetes, was co-founder of the Diabetic Association (now Diabetes UK).

The 2002 version of the film *The Time Machine* was directed by Simon Wells, the great-grandson of the author.

Four years before H.G. Wells was born, his father, Joseph Wells, became the first bowler to take four wickets in four balls in a county cricket match. He was playing for Kent against Sussex.

WELSH

In 2009, a road sign appeared on a street in Wales that must have confused Welsh speakers. It was bilingual, and the English read 'No entry for heavy goods vehicles. Residential site only'. Beneath this was an arrow, followed by the Welsh 'Nid Wyf yn y swyddfa ar hyn o bryd. Anfonwch unrhyw waith i'w gyfieithu', which was what came back when the sign-writers sent an email to a translator at Swansea Council. Unfortunately, what the Welsh means is: 'I am not in the office at the moment. Please send any work to be translated.'

꽃 *OCTOBER, NOVEMBER, UNION JACK, VAMPIRES, WALES*

WEREWOLVES

The idea of humans shapeshifting into bloodthirsty wolves on the night of a full Moon dates back at least to the 1st century when a case was mentioned by the Roman author Petronius. The high point of their history, however, had to wait another 1,500 years.

Between 1520 and 1630, some 30,000 people were reported to the French authorities as suspected of being werewolves. Two of the earliest were Pierre Burgot and Michel Verdun, who allegedly swore allegiance to the devil and claimed to have an ointment that turned them into wolves. These admissions may have been extracted under torture, which was the usual procedure for anyone accused of lycanthropy. After they confessed to transforming into wolves and brutally murdering several children, they were both burned at the stake, which was thought to be one of the few ways to kill a werewolf.

꽃 *LYCANTHROPY, VAMPIRES*

WESSEX

The origins of Wessex date back to the year 495 when the region was settled by Saxons under King Cerdic. His son (or possibly grandson) Cynric became King of the West Saxons in 519. King Cerdic is believed to be a direct ancestor of Alfred the Great, with 13 generations between them.

When Cnut the Great ruled England, he created the Earldom of Wessex, with Godwin as its first earl. Godwin was the father of Harold II, who inherited the title of Earl of Wessex when Godwin died in 1053. When Harold was killed at the Battle of Hastings in 1066, the Earldom of Wessex lapsed for more than 900 years. It was recreated in 1999 by Queen Elizabeth II for her youngest son, Prince Edward.

The full name of Prince Edward, Earl of Wessex, is Edward Antony Richard Louis: his initials spell his title: E.A.R.L.

꽃 *HAROLD II*

WHALE

The low-frequency call of the humpback whale is the loudest noise made by a living creature. The call of the humpback whale was louder than Concorde and can be heard from 500 miles away.

The grey whale migrates 12,500 miles

from the Arctic to Mexico and back every year. The large blue whale eats three tons of food a day. Its penis is 2–2.4 metres (7–8 feet) long.

Man, hoofed mammals, most marsupials and whales don't have a penis bone.

♀ DOYLE, MELVILLE, NARWHAL, PENIS, STURGEON

WHATEVER

For the third year in a row, a survey at the end of 2011 by the Marist College Institute for Public Opinion in New York revealed that the word 'whatever' was considered the most irritating verbal filler in conversation. The next two least favourite expressions were 'like' and 'you know', while fourth and fifth places were taken by 'just sayin'' and 'seriously'.

In 2019, a survey revealed that 'whatever' was still the most irritating word, hated by 34 per cent of Americans. The next most irritating were revealed as 'no offence' (20 per cent), 'dude' (16 per cent) and 'literally' (14 per cent).

According to a survey in 2018, the most annoying words in the UK were 'innit', 'like' and 'basically'.

WHEAT

In 1801, the astronomer William Herschel pointed out that there is a correlation between sunspot activity and the price of wheat.

♀ CARPET, PREGNANCY TEST, SANDWICH, YOGURT

WHEELCHAIR

A woman begging from a wheelchair in Monterrey, Mexico, in 2009, leapt to her feet and ran off when her husband smashed a shop window in an apparent attempt at burglary. The couple were arrested when they returned for the wheelchair.

♀ DRUNKEN DRIVING

WHISKERS

In May 2010, the Japanese town of Isesaki imposed a ban on whiskers, beards and facial stubble for anyone applying for a municipal service job. An official said that complaints had been received saying that facial hair is unpleasant. 'Although people tend to accept beards these days, officials should look like the public servants they are. That's our idea,' the official said. The announcement was made as part of the new 'Cool Biz' casual office dress rules, which allowed male staff to work without jackets and ties in summer in order to cut down on air-conditioning and reduce global warming.

♀ EPONYM, LION, SEA LION

WHISKY

Americans and the Irish call it 'whiskey'; Scots call it 'whisky'. When the British ask for 'whisky' they mean either malt whisky or a blend of several, which is what the Americans call Scotch. When Americans ask for 'whiskey' they have to specify Scotch, Irish, bourbon, Canadian, rye, a blend, or some other. In Scotch whisky the malted barley is dried over peat fires. In Irish whiskey, hot air is used.

Irish whiskey undergoes a triple process of distillation; Scotch is only distilled twice. The triple distillation raises the alcohol content from 8 per cent to 85 per cent. The spirit is then put in oak casks to mature for between three and 25 years. The whiskey starts as a colourless liquid but gains its colour and flavour from the wood.

At its peak, there were 400 distilleries in Ireland, but exports to the US were all but killed off by prohibition. Today only three distilleries are left. Finland and Iceland are the only countries where Irish whiskey outsells Scotch.

In Scottish Gaelic, the word *sgriob* means the itchiness felt on the upper lip just before taking a sip of whisky.

More Scotch whisky is sold in one month in France than Cognac in a year. Worldwide, Scotch whisky exports in 2019 earned Britain £155 every second.

♀ *ALCOHOL, ANAESTHETICS, PRESLEY*

● WHISTLING

Marie-Augustin, Marquis de Pelier of Brittany, was arrested in the spring of 1786 and charged with having whistled at Marie Antoinette as she was about to take her seat at the Comedie Francaise. The 22-year-old youth was kept incommunicado in Temple Prison for four years, then in 1790 he was secretly transferred to the dungeon of Lourdes. In 1814, his immediate release was ordered, but this coincided with the escape of Napoleon from Elba and the prisoner was forgotten again. Finally, in 1836, when Marie Antoinette had been dead for 43 years, the whistler, now 72, was freed and his landed property in Britanny was restored to him.

♀ *BURIAL, GROUNDHOG, OYSTER, QUEEN MARY*

● WHITE HOUSE

The White House is located at 1600 Pennsylvania Avenue in Washington, DC and was first built between 1792 and 1800 before being burnt down by the British in 1814 and rebuilt. The earliest known reference to the street as Pennsylvania Avenue is in a letter written in 1791 by Thomas Jefferson.

The name may have been given in compensation for the US capital city being moved from Philadelphia to Washington.

Originally called the 'President's Palace', this official residence of American presidents was named the 'Executive Mansion' in 1810, and renamed the 'White House' in 1902. It is 51 metres (168 feet) long, 46 metres (152 feet) wide (including porticoes) and 21 metres (70 feet) high with six floors, 132 rooms, 32 bathrooms, 147 windows, 412 doors, 28 fireplaces, 12 chimneys, eight staircases and three lifts, and it requires 570 gallons of paint to cover its outside surface. It has about 6,000 visitors a day and employs five full-time chefs. It also has a tennis court, jogging track, swimming pool, cinema, billiard room and bowling lane.

While the interior of the building was being renovated in the 1940s, President Harry S. Truman lived across the road in the President's Guest House, called Blair House, which itself has 119 rooms and an even larger floor area than the White House. When UK Prime Minister Tony Blair visited US President Bill Clinton in 1998, he stayed at Blair House, where he thanked the staff whom he described as 'quite tremendous – kind, thoughtful and helpful'.

The White House claims to be the world's only private residence of a head of state that is open to the public, free of charge.

♀ *BEER, EISENHOWER, FEBRUARY, POSTCODE, REAGAN, UNITED STATES*

● WHITTINGTON, Richard (c.1354–1423)

Sir Richard Whittington, MP and Lord Mayor of London, was the man on whom the story of Dick Whittington and his cat are based. The main differences between the true story and the tale, which became a popular pantomime in the 19th century, are that the real Whittington was four times Lord Mayor, not three, he wasn't ever poor, and there is no evidence that he ever had a cat.

One theory is that the 'cat' is all a misunderstanding, as the word 'cat' was also used for a merchant sea vessel at the time, and coming from a trading family, he may have arrived with a boat.

WIARTON WILLY

The town of Wiarton, home of the groundhog Wiarton Willy, Canada's answer to Punxsutawney Phil, faced severe embarrassment following the events of Groundhog Day in 1999. Visitors to the town were greeted with the sad news that Canada's official furry meteorological forecaster was dead, and a photograph was published of a dead albino groundhog, purported to be Willy, holding a carrot and lying face-up in a small coffin. Later, it was revealed that Willy's body had in fact been discovered in a severe state of decomposition some days before and he had been substituted in the photograph by the body of a previous Wiarton Willy who had been stuffed some years before.

WIFE-CARRYING

The Wife-Carrying Championships in Sonkajärvi, Finland, have been held annually since 1992 and have been the World Championships in Wife-Carrying since 1996.

The length of the official track is 253.5 metres (832 feet), and the surface is partially sand, partially grass and partially asphalt. The track has two dry obstacles and a water obstacle,

about 1 metre (3 feet) deep. The wife to be carried may be your own, the neighbour's, or you may have found her further afield; she must, however, be over 17 years of age. The minimum weight of the wife to be carried is 49 kilograms (108 pounds). If she is less than this, the wife will be burdened with a heavy rucksack such that the total weight to be carried is 49 kilograms (108 pounds).

The winner is the couple that completes the course in the shortest time, but if any contestant drops his wife, that couple will incur a penalty of 15 seconds per drop. The only equipment allowed is a belt worn by the carrier. Each contestant takes care of his/her safety and, if thought necessary, insurance. The rules also specify that all the participants must have fun.

From 1998 to 2008, the Championship resulted in 11 consecutive victories for Estonians, who in 2001 introduced a new and efficient style of carrying their partners. In place of the traditional piggyback or fireman's hold, they carried their wives upside down over their backs.

From 2009 to 2015, pairs from Finland took the title, with Russia winning in 2016 before Finland regained the title in 2017. In 2018 and 2019, however, the winners were Vytautas Kirkliauskas and Neringa Kirkliauskiene of Lithuania.

Traditionally, the first prize is the wife's weight in beer. More recently, this has been accompanied by a cash prize.

Since 2008, the UK, US, Australia and India have also held wife-carrying championships.

FINLAND

WIG

The ancient Egyptians around 350 BC wore wigs to cover their heads, which had been shaved to be free of vermin.

Mozart had a deformity of his left ear that he kept covered by a wig.

Queen Elizabeth I owned 150 wigs.

The word 'wig', however, only appeared in the English language around 1675. Before that it was always called by its full name, 'periwig'.

In 1765, wig-makers petitioned George III for financial relief, following a steep drop in demand for men's wigs. In February of that year, wig-makers marched through London to present the King with a petition demanding that certain professions should be forced to wear wigs. Noticing that few of the wig-makers were wearing wigs themselves, bystanders became furious at their demands that others should wear them and the march turned into a riot during which the wig-makers were forcibly shorn.

Demand for wigs was high, however, at the beginning of the 21st century when more wigs were made for *The Two Towers*, the second part of Peter Jackson's 'Lord of the Rings' trilogy, than for any other film in history.

The word 'bigwig' comes from the old tendency for the most important officials to wear the biggest and grandest wigs.

⚲ *HAT, LOUIS XIV, MERKIN, MOZART, SWIMMING*

WIGHT, Isle of

Until the late 1920s, it would have been theoretically possible for everyone on Earth to stand on the Isle of Wight at the same time without too much of a squash.

If all the world's 6.1 billion people had decided to see in the new millennium on the Isle of Wight on 1 January 2000, they would each have had the size of an A4 sheet of paper to stand on.

⚲ *ARTIFICIAL LEG, GHOSTS, TIGER, VICTORIA*

WILLIAM IV, King of Great Britain (1765–1837)

William IV became King in 1830 at the age of 64, on the death of his brother, George IV. He is the oldest person to have acceded to the British (or English) throne, but is expected to be overtaken by Prince Charles when he succeeds Queen Elizabeth II.

William IV had a reputation for eccentric behaviour, which included his habit of spitting in public. He joined the Royal Navy at the age of 13, but was thrown out for debauchery after being arrested in Gibraltar for brawling while drunk.

He cohabited for 20 years with the Irish actress Dorothea Jordan, who bore him 10 illegitimate children. Later in life, he married and apparently remained faithful to Princess Adelaide of Saxe-Meiningen, after whom the Australian city of Adelaide was named.

⚲ *EDWARD VIII, GEORGE IV*

WILSON

Until 2019 when Boris Johnson became UK Prime Minister, the only surname to have been held by both a US president and a British prime minister was Wilson: Woodrow Wilson, who was US President from 1913 to 1921, and Harold Wilson, who was UK Prime Minister from 1964 to 1970 and from 1974 to 1976.

If you arrange all the US presidents in alphabetical order, Woodrow Wilson comes last.

⚲ *BRADFORD, GNOME, PRIME MINISTER, REAGAN*

WIMBLEDON

An average match in the men's singles at Wimbledon lasts two and a half hours, of which the ball is in play for just 20 minutes.

The average match consists of 3.68 sets (2.26 for women); the average set is 9.86 games (8.92 for women); the average game is 6.35 points (6.56 for women). In men's matches, 81.8 per cent are won by the server. For women, the figure is 64.3 per cent.

The grass on the courts is cut to a height of exactly 8mm.

In the fortnight of the Wimbledon tennis championships each year, spectators consume: 300,000 cups of tea and coffee, 190,000 sandwiches, 150,000 glasses of Pimm's, 28,000 kilograms (27.5 tons) of strawberries, 7,000 litres (1,540 gallons) of cream and 30,000 portions of fish and chips.

In 2007, they also bought: 9,739 men's championship towels, 9,912 ladies' towels, 16,712 mini tennis-ball keyrings.

The players, in the meantime, work their way through some 40,000 balls. Until needed, the balls are stored at a temperature of 20°C (68°F).

In 2019, the total number of towels sold had risen to 27,419. In 2021, the previous difference in colour between men's and women's towels – green and purple for men, pink and turquoise for women – was dropped when it was announced that two green and purple towels would be provided for all players to continue the process towards sexual equality, which had begun with equal pay in 2007 and continued a few years later with an equal number of tweets about male and female players.

The Austrian Hans Redl played at Wimbledon from 1947 to 1956, despite losing an arm during the Second World War while he served with the German army at the battle of Stalingrad. He served by tossing the ball up with his racket which necessitated a change in the rules to let him touch the ball twice with his racket. Despite this, he reached the fourth round of the men's singles at Wimbledon in 1947.

John Isner's 253 km/h (157.2 mph) world record fastest serve would reach the Moon in 59 days 19 hours when the Moon is at its closest, and 66 days 19.6 hours when it is furthest away.

The longest ever tennis match was played in the first round at Wimbledon in 2010 when John Isner beat Nicolas Mahut 6–4, 3–6, 6–7, 7–6, 70–68. They were on court for 11 hours and five minutes and played 183 games.

Elizabeth Ryan, winner of 19 Wimbledon titles, died on 6 July 1979. The following day, Billie-Jean King overtook her record by taking her 20th title.

As well as the tennis, Wimbledon in south London has a Windmill Museum, which describes itself as a 'whimsical museum on windmill history'.

⚲ *BANANA, ELIZABETH II, GEORGE VI, KUWAIT, TENNIS, TIE-BREAK*

WINDOW

The window tax ran in Britain from 1696 until 1851. It was calculated from the number of windows in a house. All houses were charged at 2 shillings, properties with 10 to 20 windows paid 4 shillings, and those with more than 20 windows paid 8 shillings. Frugal house owners would block up their windows so they would qualify for a smaller fee. The abolition of window tax came after warnings from doctors that it resulted in ill-health through lack of light.

The world record for window-cleaning

is held by Terry Burrows of South Ockendon, Essex, with a time of 9.14 seconds for cleaning more than 3.9 square metres (6,000 square inches) of glass in three standard square office windows using a standard 29.8-centimetre (11.75-inch) long squeegee. Explaining his technique, Burrows said: 'It's not just about cleaning the windows. It's the actual coordination of moving from one window to the next.'

His equipment, however, fell well short of the record for the longest window-cleaning pole. A Bournemouth window-cleaning company set that world record in 2021 by washing windows with a pole 35 metres (115 feet) long.

BURGLARY, CARROT, GARBAGE, HAT, SNORING, WHEELCHAIR

WINDOW-SILL

It is illegal in the UK for anyone 'to order or permit any person in his service to stand on the sill of any window, in order to clean, paint, or perform any other operation upon the outside of such window', except in the case of windows in the basement.

WINE

St Vincent of Saragosa, the patron saint of wine who lived in the 3rd century and was martyred in AD 304, was teetotal. The reason for his wine patronage is unclear. According to one account, it is solely due to the French pronunciation of his name, which sounds like 'Vin-sang', which translates as 'wine blood'. Another explanation involves a legend of St Vincent and his donkey, which tells of their wandering through a vineyard where the donkey nibbled on nearby vines as St Vincent chatted with the workers. During that year's

harvest, the workers noticed that the vines 'pruned' by the donkey produced a better crop than the 'unpruned' vines. Thus, St Vincent and his donkey discovered the art of pruning grape vines.

Around 600 grapes are needed to make one bottle of wine.

ALCOHOL, BEETHOVEN, CHAUCER, ELEPHANT, GRAPE

WINNIE-THE-POOH

Winnie-the-Pooh first appeared in print on Christmas Eve 1925 in the *London Evening News*. The story was based on a bedtime tale Milne had told to his son, Christopher Robin. The bear was based on one of Christopher Robin Milne's toys and its name came from a Canadian grizzly bear named Winnie (short for Winnipeg) in London Zoo and a swan named Pooh which the Milnes used to feed.

The original toy was an Alpha Bear designed by Agnes Farnell and given to Christopher Robin on his first birthday in 1921. It was called Edward.

Winnie ille Pu, the 1958 Latin translation of *Winnie the Pooh*, is the only book in Latin ever to appear on the *New York Times* bestseller list. Since 1947, the original Pooh, Tigger, Kanga, Eeyore and Piglet have lived in America. They are now in the New York Public Library, despite Prime Minister Tony Blair lending his weight to an attempt to get them back to the UK in 1998.

A.A. Milne, creator of Winnie-the-Pooh, Tigger and all their friends, was born on 18 January 1882. 18 January 2022 was the 88th birthday of Raymond Briggs, the creator of *Fungus the Bogeyman* and *The Snowman*, and 18 January 1936 was the day on which *Jungle Book* author Rudyard Kipling died.

The annual World Pooh-sticks Championships have been held since 1984. The winner in 2018 was seven-year-old Innes Turnbull from Oxfordshire.

In 2017, China began blocking images of Pooh on social media, and in 2018 authorities also banned release of a Disney film of Winnie-the-Pooh. These decisions are thought to be connected with pictures of Pooh being used as a symbol of political dissent dating back to 2013, when an image of Chinese leader Xi Jinping walking with Barack Obama was compared with a picture of Pooh and Tigger.

MILNE, TUESDAY

WISCONSIN

Quite apart from the fame brought to this state by its hosting the biennial World Championship Cheese Contest since 1957, Wisconsin deserves praise for the achievement of Green Bay, which calls itself the Toilet Paper Capital of the World. In 1920, its soft, flushable toilet roll made its Northern Paper Mills the world's largest producer of toilet paper and, in 1935, they produced the first 'splinter free toilet paper' which they also called 'butt-painless toilet paper'.

In Connorsville, Wisconsin, it is illegal for a man to fire a gun while his partner is in the throes of sexual ecstasy.

In 1999, the Medical College of Wisconsin proudly published the results of 'the most comprehensive toilet-training study ever completed'.

Hawaii and Wisconsin are the only states with laws governing ice-cream container size.

In 1989, the world's biggest hamburger was made in Wisconsin, a 5,520-pounder, and in 1998 Wisconsin had the world's tallest stilts.

In 1999, a computer glitch was blamed for leaving the town of Oconomowok Lake in Wisconsin (population 505) off 2 million road maps. Inmates at five state prisons were employed to use stickers to put it back.

CHEESE, HAMBURGER, SPITTING

WISDOM, Norman (1915–2010)

The comedian and actor Norman Wisdom was the only person to have been awarded the freedom of the city of Tirana in Albania without also having won a Nobel Prize. The other two people to have been awarded the freedom of Tirana are Jimmy Carter and Mother Teresa.

In 1991, a French speaker in an agriculture committee of the European Parliament made a speech saying that Europe needed *la sagesse des Normands* (the wisdom of the Norman people) to deal with one particular problem. The simultaneous translation into English, however, stated that MEPs needed 'Norman Wisdom' to help them out. Unfortunately, the speaker did not understand the reason for the laughter so repeated the sentence, when the same translation was again greeted by laughter.

OSTRICH, OWL, UNIVERSITIES

WITCHCRAFT

The word 'witch' comes from the Saxon 'wicca', meaning 'wise one'.

Matthew Hopkins, the Witchfinder General from 1644 to 1647, had a remarkable record for detecting witches in England. His techniques usually began with searching for the Devil's mark on a woman; this would be a boil known as the third nipple. Cutting her with a blunt knife could also work, on the principle that if she didn't bleed she was a witch. Throwing her into a pond or river of which the water had been blessed was also sometimes used: if she floated, she was a witch, as witches had renounced their baptism, so holy water would reject them. Hopkins and his assistants were paid at a rate of £5 per witch detected.

In 2008, the last witch to have been beheaded in Europe was absolved as a victim of 'judicial murder' more than 200 years after her death. The parliament of the Swiss canton of Glarus voted unanimously to clear the name of Anna Goeldi, who was executed in 1782. She was a servant in the house of prominent burgher Johann Jakob Tschudi, and was convicted of 'spoiling' the family's daughter, causing her to spit pins and have convulsions.

The last people hanged for witchcraft in the UK were Mary Hicks and her nine-year-old daughter Elizabeth in 1716; the last in Scotland was Janet Horne in 1727.

The self-proclaimed Grand Warlock of Mexico predicted at the start of 2009 that the United States would pull troops out of Iraq in the course of that year and send them to the border with Mexico in an attempt to expand its territory. The previous year, Grand Warlock Vazquez had erroneously predicted that oil prices would be stable and that Cuba's Fidel Castro and singer Britney Spears would die.

♀ *JAMES I, JOAN OF ARC*

⬤ WIZARDRY

In October 2021, the city council of Christchurch, New Zealand, was reported to have ended its contract with Ian Brackenbury Channell, who is also known as the Wizard of New Zealand, after 23 years of service. A spokesman said that the city's 'promotional

landscape is changing'. The Wizard replied by calling the council 'a bunch of bureaucrats who have no imagination'.

⬤ WOLF

The last person to be killed by a wolf in Britain died in 1743. Grey wolves became extinct in England in 1486.

The ancient Roman festival of Lupercalia on 15 February, a fertility rite from which our own St Valentine's celebrations evolved, takes its name from *lupus* the Latin for wolf. Lupercal was the cave in which Rome's founders, Romulus and Remus, were said to have been brought up by wolves.

The tail of an average adult wolf is 47 centimetres (18.5 inches) long. In the winter it uses its tail to keep its face warm.

Canada has more wolves than any other country.

John Barry's score to the film *Dances With Wolves* was a favourite piece of music of Pope John Paul II.

Lord Baden-Powell, founder of the Boy Scouts and Wolf Cubs, was given the name 'Impeesa' by the Matabele, meaning 'The wolf that never sleeps'.

♀ *COMPUTATION, COSMETICS, JANUARY, ST VALENTINE*

⬤ WOLVERHAMPTON

The director of a dwarf management company said that he felt his dwarfs were a casualty of the current economic climate when he learned that a theatre in Wolverhampton was to use children in place of dwarfs in the Christmas pantomime of Snow White in 2011.

'It's not that expensive to hire dwarves,' Peter Burroughs of Willow Management said. 'They get between £700 and £750 a week, but their digs can cost around £300 a week, then they're taxed and they're no better off than anyone else.' He also said that using children instead of dwarfs spoils the magic for children in the audience.

Wolverhampton Wanderers has more letters in its name (22) than any other club in the English Football League, though it takes more key presses (24) to type the name of Brighton and Hove Albion.

WOMBAT

There are three species of wombat: the common wombat, the northern hairy-nosed wombat and the southern hairy-nosed wombat. The common wombat does not have a hairy nose. Wombats were first mentioned in English in 1798 by navigator Matthew Flinders. The word comes from the extinct Aboriginal Dharuk language. The oldest known drawing of a wombat is 4,000 years old in Australia's Wollemi National Park.

Like the kangaroo, the wombat is a marsupial, but unlike the kangaroo, the pouch in which a wombat keeps its baby faces backwards. This stops earth getting into the pouch when the mother wombat is burrowing into the ground.

During the Pleistocene age, giant wombats the size of a rhinoceros roamed southern Australia.

Although the wombat generally has only one baby, its pouch has two nipples.

A wombat's poo is cube-shaped; the wombat uses it for marking things on its territory.

♀ KOALA, VAGINA

WOMEN

According to the UN, there were 3,904,727,342 females in the world in 2021 compared with 3,970,238,390 males, which works out at 101.68 males to every 100 females. Until 1957, there were more females than males, largely owing to women having a longer life expectancy.

The sex ratio at birth is about 107 boys per 100 girls and males stay in the lead for every age group up to around the age of 60. For those over the age of 65, however, there are only 81.8 men per 100 women. In the 90–94 age group, women outnumber men by two to one, and for those aged 100 or more the ratio is four to one.

In the two most populous countries, China and India, males are in the majority, but in most other countries, females are in the lead. The Northern Mariana Islands have the highest female ratio with only 0.77 males per female. Worldwide, the average life expectancy stands at 68.5 years for men and 73.5 years for women.

Until 1922, under the common law 'doctrine of coercion', a woman in the UK who committed a crime in her husband's presence was presumed to have been coerced by him so was not guilty.

Every 90 seconds somewhere in the world, a woman dies in pregnancy or childbirth.

The average adult woman in the UK owns 19 pairs of shoes.

Car heaters, fire escapes, dishwashers, circular saws, chocolate chip cookies and rectangular bottomed paper bags were all invented by women. Only 58 women have been awarded Nobel Prizes compared with 885 men.

♀ ARISTOTLE, BOURDALOUE, CLEAVAGE, HAWKING, HIPS, MOTHERHOOD

WOODPECKER

According to research carried out in 1936, if you attach a false moustache to the face of a wild female woodpecker, a male woodpecker will attack her just as if she were a rival male. Northern flicker woodpeckers were used in this research and not green woodpeckers, the females of which have a black moustache naturally while males have red ones.

⚲ MANDELA

WOODS, Tiger (b.1975)

The golfer Tiger Woods was born on the penultimate day of 1975 and holed his first birdie on a 91-yard par three hole when he was six. His first names are Eldrick Tont.

WORDSWORTH, William (1770–1850)

William Wordsworth never wrote at a table or desk, but preferred sitting on a chair with a writing board on his arm. His usual meals were porridge or boiled mutton, though he was also partial to Cheshire cheese.

He slept in a half-sitting position, propped up on a bolster, and suffered from piles.

According to Thomas de Quincey, 'Wordsworth's legs were certainly not ornamental', while Robert Southey reported that Wordsworth had no sense of smell.

⚲ BLAKE, ST GEORGE

WORLD CUP

According to a survey taken just before the 2010 World Cup, only 5 per cent of Germans would prefer a night of passion with their loved one to watching Germany in the World Cup Final. Despite that, 38 per cent of respondents said they were not interested in football. The Argentine squad, however, were told by their team doctor that they may have sex on non-match days during the World Cup in South Africa, 'but with regular partners and without champagne or other drinks'. Argentina lost to Germany in the quarter-finals.

⚲ BANGLADESH, BHUTAN, FOOTBALL, MARADONA, SHIRT, TELEVISION

WORLD TELEVISION DAY

The date of 21 November was chosen by the UN in 1996 to be celebrated as World Television Day, as that was the day the first World Television Forum began in that year.

The resolution to create World Television Day was carried by 141 votes to nil with 11 abstentions. The abstentions included the USA, UK, Japan and Germany, all of whom thought that adding yet another day to the UN calendar was silly.

WORM

Experiments on the learning abilities of earthworms date back to work carried out in 1920 by the Dutch psychologist Van Oye, who taught worms to find food lowered into their bowls on pieces of wire. No further progress was made until around 30 years later when James V. McConnell and Robert Thompson at the University of Texas began some significant experiments in 1953.

They first confirmed Van Oye's finding that worms can indeed learn, doing this by turning a light on, then giving the worm an electric shock. After several repetitions, the worm began to contract – its normal reaction to pain – when the light came on. This simple conditioning experiment was evidence that the worm had a memory.

'It was while we were running our first experiment,' McConnell later wrote, 'that Thompson and I wondered aloud, feeling rather foolish as we did so, what would happen if we conditioned a flatworm, then cut it in two and let both halves regenerate. Which half would retain the memory?'

To find the answer, worms were taught something, then bisected. When they had grown back, both halves were found to have retained some of the memory. They forgot a little while regrowing, but then required less training than had originally been needed to reach the same level.

The next step was to teach a worm something, cut it in two, wait for the front end to regenerate, then slice that in two and this time wait for the back end to grow into a full worm. Result: a worm that wasn't present for the initial experiment. But still it seemed to remember some of what the original worm had been taught.

All this conformed with the Molecular Theory of Memory, which had been proposed around that time. The essential idea was that every new memory corresponds to a new molecule of RNA, which can be reproduced and spread through the organism, which is what led to the most dramatic experiments of all: worms were taught something, then minced and fed to uneducated worms.

A string of papers appeared in the early 1960s with titles such as: 'Is knowledge edible?', and McConnell launched a journal called *The Worm-Runner's Digest* containing a mixture of genuine research and satirical spoofs. The serious answer to the question about the edibility of knowledge appeared to be 'yes', which was unfortunate because, for a variety of reasons, the entire Molecular Theory of Memory was about to be ditched as totally misconceived. Another string of papers followed with titles such as 'Planaria: Memory

Transfer through Cannibalism Re-examined', which did their best to provide alternative explanations for the earlier results. The topic was then quietly abandoned and minced worm dropped from the menu of laboratories.

Linnaeus longissimus, the bootlace worm, is the longest animal on earth. In 1984, one found on the beach at St Andrews, Scotland, measured 55 metres (180 feet).

♀ MOLE, SNAIL, YODA

WRESTLING

In 1520 at the Field of the Cloth of Gold pageant near Calais, Francis I of France defeated Henry VIII of England in a wrestling match.

♀ CROCODILE, GUT BARGING, JELLY, LAOS, POTATO, PYTHON

WRIGHT, Orville (1871–1948) and Wilbur (1867–1912)

The first time Orville and Wilbur called themselves 'the Wright Brothers' was in 1889 when they started a printing firm. They moved into bicycle repair in 1893, and it was their work with bicycles that gave them the belief that a basically unstable vehicle could be controlled. It also provided the finances for their aeronautic experiments.

The Wright Brothers made the first powered flight of a heavier-than-air machine on 17 December 1903. Orville's inaugural flight of 36.5 metres (120 feet) was less than the distance between the wingtips of a Boeing 747. Their next two flights were 53 and 61 metres (175 and 200 feet), by Wilbur and Orville respectively, at a height of about 3 metres (10 feet) above the ground.

Neither Orville nor Wilbur ever married. As Wilbur once said, he 'did not have time for both a wife and an airplane'. Orville lost his front teeth in his youth after an incident involving a hockey stick and an ice-rink.

🔑 *BEE KEEPING*

⬤ WRIST

The scaphoid is one of eight bones in the wrist. The others are called trapezium, trapezoid, hamate, capitate, pisiform, triquetrum and lunate.

Between 60 and 70 per cent of all wrist-bone fractures are of the scaphoid. Its name comes from the Greek *skaphos*, meaning 'hollowed out' or 'a boat'. Its older name was 'navicular', from the Latin word for boat, *navis*. Actually its shape is more cashew nut than boat.

One recent invention designed to aid healing of scaphoid fractures is called the 'Herbert screw', which, according to one description, holds the pieces of the bone together 'like a shish kebab'. In 1991, Timothy Herbert, after whom the Herbert screw is named, wrote a 202-page book on *The Fractured Scaphoid*.

🔑 *CHIPS, LAVENDER, SIGN LANGUAGE, STONE, WRISTWATCH*

⬤ WRISTWATCH

Before the First World War, only women wore wristwatches. However, soldiers began wearing them in the war as a means of keeping their hands free for more important matters.

The earliest recorded use of the term 'wrist-watch' in English was by Baden-Powell in 1896 writing about the Matabele Campaign, when he advised that: 'Field-glasses, wrist-watch, buckles, and buttons should be dulled.'

🔑 *DOG*

⬤ WYCLIFFE, John (c.1320–84)

The religious reformer John Wycliffe died in 1384 of natural causes. Despite this, he was condemned as a heretic more than 30 years later in 1415, and in 1428 was burned at the stake posthumously along with his books. For the sentence to be carried out, Wycliffe's corpse was exhumed and burned and the ashes were thrown into the River Swift, which flows through Lutterworth in Leicestershire where he had died.

XANTHIPPE (5th century BC)

When the Greek philosopher Socrates married Xanthippe, he is said to have known of her reputation as a bad-tempered nagging woman, but married her to give himself practice at being patient.

There is a single reference to her in the works of Shakespeare, which is, as one might expect, in *The Taming of the Shrew*, where Petruchio refers to Kate as: 'as curst and shrewd as Socrates' Xanthippe'.

The *Oxford English Dictionary* lists the word 'Xantippe' (without an h in the middle) as meaning 'An ill-tempered woman or wife, a shrew, a scold.'

This is the only time Shakespeare uses a word or name beginning with X in any of his plays unless you count mentions of King Lewis XI in *Henry VI, Part III*.

XENOPHOBIA

Xenophobia – the fear of strangers or foreigners – is over 100 years old. The earliest use of the word recorded in the *Oxford English Dictionary* was in 1909.

PORK

XENOPUS

The name Xenopus comes from two Greek words meaning 'strange foot', which is very apt because it is a frog that has black claws on the three of the five toes of its hind legs, but it is not only its legs that are strange. Its eyes are on top of its head with circular pupils, looking upwards. They have no moveable eyelids, tongues or eardrums. Strangest of all, in 1931, the zoologist Lancelot Hogben discovered that female frogs of this species produced eggs when injected with the urine of a pregnant woman. A pregnancy test using these frogs was developed soon after.

XOLOITZCUINTLI

The Xoloitzcuintli, often known as Xolo for short, is the national dog of Mexico. In Aztec myth, the hairless variety of this dog is associated with the dog-headed god Xolotl, who was the god of fire, lightning and monstrosities and also gave his name to the axolotl.

YAK

Apart from being used as a beast of burden, the yak produces milk that may be processed to a cheese called chhurpi. It comes in a soft and a hard version, of which the latter is popular as a treat for dogs.

Butter made of yaks' milk is also an ingredient of the butter tea that is very popular in Tibet. It is also used in lamps and made into butter sculptures for religious festivities. Yak dung is also used as a fuel.

Yaks play a vital role in the recently introduced sport of yak skiing, which takes place at the Indian hill resort of Manali. The participant in yak skiing stands on skis at the foot of a hill holding a bucket of nuts. A rope is tied securely around his waist and its other end is taken up the hill by the organiser, where it is threaded over a pulley before being attached to a yak on the hilltop. When the rope is fixed, the skier rattles the nuts in the bucket, causing the yak to bound down the hill. Taking care to leave the bucket on the ground, the skier is then propelled uphill by the movement of the yak. The organiser says that the two most important things to

remember are not to rattle the bucket until the rope is securely attached, and not to forget to let go of the bucket after rattling it.

Yak skiing has no connection with yak polo, which is basically polo on yaks instead of horses and is played in Mongolia.

⚲ *HOBBITS, TIBET*

YAWNING

Research has shown that around one in three chimpanzees will yawn back when a human being yawns at them, and over 70 per cent of dogs will do so. Tortoises, however, do not yawn back when another tortoise yawns at them.

⚲ *GIRAFFE*

YEARS

2012 was the centenary of the first parachute jump from a moving aeroplane, the sinking of the *Titanic*, the invention of the electric blanket, and the 300th anniversary of the first recorded appearance of the word 'zig-zag' in English.

2013 was the first year since 1987 consisting of four different digits. In Jack London's novel *The Scarlet Plague*, first published in 1912, a disease known as the Red Death wipes out almost all the people on Earth in 2013.

2014 was the 1000th anniversary of the death of Sweyn Forkbeard, who was succeeded by his son Cnut (Canute) as King of England.

2015 was the 800th anniversary of King John signing the Magna Carta at Runnymede.

2016 was a great year for fans of binary numbers, in which 2016 is written as 11111100000.

2017 was the 300th anniversary of the first ballet in Britain.

2018 was the 200th anniversary of Mary Shelley's creation of Frankenstein.

2019 was the 200th anniversary of the birth of both Queen Victoria and her consort Prince Albert.

2020 was the centenary of the first recorded mention in English of the drink Cointreau.

2021 was the 400th anniversary of the Mayflower setting sail across the Atlantic from Plymouth.

2022, despite general turmoil across the globe, saw new world records set for most bananas in a shop display (over 70,000), most swimmers dressed in mermaid tails (388), most bungee jumps by one person in 24 hours (765) and most people dressed as vampires in the same place (1,369).

2023 has been declared the International Year of Millets by the UN.

YEMEN

According to local legend, Sana'a, the capital of Yemen, was founded by Shem, one of the sons of Noah. The only other countries with apostrophes in their capitals (in the usual English spellings) are Chad (N'Djamena) and Grenada (St George's).

According to legend, the Queen of Sheba, King Solomon's consort, was from Yemen. Her name was Queen Bilquis.

Ancient Yemen was known to the Romans as 'Arabia felix' which translates as 'happy Arabia'. In Roman times, Yemen was a major source of frankincense, myrrh and spices.

There is no minimum age for marriage in Yemen but sexual intercourse is forbidden to girls until an undefined time when it is 'suitable'.

In 2007, a 10-year-old Yemeni girl was reported to have walked into a courtroom to demand a divorce.

Yemen has competed in every summer Olympics since 1992 but has yet to win a medal. In 1992, Yemen was represented by eight men at the Olympics but since then has never sent more than four men and one woman.

CENTRAL AFRICAN REPUBLIC

YEOMAN

When the Tower of London appointed its first female beefeater in 2007, the official announcement made it clear that a female yeoman is still a yeoman. Her full title, it said, would be 'Yeoman Warder of Her Majesty's Royal Palace and Fortress the Tower of London, and Members of the Sovereign's Body Guard of the Yeoman Guard Extraordinary'. Moira Cameron was the first female yeoman in the 522-year history of the Tower.

YETI

The first report of a Yeti appeared in 1832 in the *Journal of the Asiatic Society of Bengal*, where the naturalist Brian Houghton Hodgson wrote of a hairy man-like biped that walked erect. As he pointed out, the Sherpa guides seemed familiar with the creature. Some claimed there were two yetis: 'dzu-teh', which is 2–2.4 metres (7–8 feet) tall, and 'meh-teh', which is only 1.5–1.8 metres (5–6 feet) tall. Both were said to have long arms that almost reached to the knees.

In 1889, the Scottish army surgeon, chemistry professor and professor of Tibetan Major Laurence Waddell found footprints in the snow one morning. His Sherpa guides told him they were the prints of a hairy wild man that was often seen in the area. Occasional reports of sightings continued and in September 1921, on a mountaintop near Tibet at 6,096 metres (20,000 feet), Lt Col C.K. Howard-Bury found footprints in the snow three times the size of a man's. The Sherpas told him that they were from 'a man-like thing that is not a man'. This description was mistakenly translated by a journalist as 'abominable snowman' and the name stuck.

The alternative name of 'yeti' came as a result of a sighting in 1925 by N.A. Tombazi, a British member of the Royal Geographical Society. He saw a creature stooping to pick at some bushes, then found 16 footprints, shaped like a man's, six or seven inches long and four inches wide. After this report, the creature became known as 'Yeti', from the Sherpa 'yeh-teh', meaning 'the thing'.

In 1959, mountaineer Peter Byrne visited a lamasery in Pangboche, Nepal, where the monks allowed him to examine something alleged to be the hand of a yeti. Byrne stole a finger and thumb from the hand, replacing them with a human finger and thumb that he had brought with him. The supposed yeti parts were smuggled into India where the actor James Stewart and his wife Gloria wrapped them in underwear to smuggle them to England.

Tests were inconclusive and the samples subsequently vanished.

On 30 June 1969, the headline appeared in the *US National Bulletin*: 'I was raped by the Abominable Snowman'.

YO-YO

The yo-yo was originally a Philippine jungle weapon, to be thrown at its target, then returned for re-use, rather like a faulty boomerang that had to be attached to a piece of string to ensure that it came back to its owner.

DICKENS

YODA

A worm discovered on the ocean floor has been named after the *Star Wars* character Yoda. *Yoda purpurata* was discovered 2.4 kilometres (1.5 miles) beneath the surface of the Atlantic and given its name after scientists noticed large lips on the sides of its head which reminded them of the Jedi master's floppy ears. The other part of the name is Latin for purple and describes its colour.

The name was announced in an issue of the journal *Invertebrate Biology* in 2012.

YODELLING

On 4 October 1988, the Bavarian Minister for the Environment, Alfred Dick, asked people not to yodel in the Alps because it might frighten the mountain eagle and the chamois and was therefore damaging to the environment.

Walter Scott would no doubt have agreed with him. In his journal for 4 June 1830, he wrote about an invitation to hear some yodelling: 'Anne wants me to go to hear the Tyrolese Minstrels, but though no one more esteems that bold and high-spirited people, I cannot but think their yodelling, if this be the word, is a variation, or set of variations, upon the tones of a jackass, so I remain to dribble and scribble at home.'

YOGURT

The *Oxford English Dictionary* lists 12 possible spellings for the word 'yogurt'.

The British spend about £1.3 billion a year on yogurt.

In 2006, the Supreme Court in South Korea upheld a lower court ruling convicting a dairy executive for an obscene event after three models had staged a nude performance with yogurt at a crowded Seoul art gallery in 2003. The models, caked in wheat flour, had used spray devices to squirt each other with yogurt, which washed off the flour to expose their bodies. The court ruled that the performance 'was obscene as the event's main purpose was commercial and it went beyond the point necessary to promote the product'.

℘ *BULGARIA, CHESS*

YOKO ONO (b. 1933)

Yoko Ono, the widow of John Lennon, was born on the day James 'Gentleman Jim' Corbett died: 18 February 1933. It was also the day the England football manager Bobby Robson was born.

Yoko Ono did not meet her father, who was a banker, until she was two years old, as he was transferred by his bank from Tokyo to San Francisco just before she was born.

In 2012, she became the 15th winner of the Oskar Kokoshka prize, Austria's most prestigious prize for contemporary art, and the first winner of that prize to have only one of the five vowels in her name.

Her first name, Yoko, means 'ocean child'.

℘ *LENNON, VOWELS*

YOM KIPPUR

A dispute broke out in Israel in 2010 over a custom called 'kaparot' dating back to at least the 7th century, which is performed by Ultra Orthodox Jews at Yom Kippur. The custom, which is part of a ritual to cleanse practitioners from sin before the Day of Atonement, involves ritually sacrificing a chicken after whirling it around above one's head. Some 2,000 Israelis in Tel Aviv signed petitions demanding an end to the public sacrifice of chickens.

YORK

It is not true that it is legal to shoot a Scotsman after dark in York with a bow and arrow, despite at least 2,000 sites on the Internet including this as a bizarre law that is still in existence. Nor, as many others maintain, is this only true on a Sunday, or only on all days of the week except a Sunday, nor does it only apply if the Scotsman is the one carrying the bow and arrow. And while we are on the subject, it is also not legal to shoot a Welshman with a crossbow from the grounds of Hereford Cathedral.

First, nobody has ever produced any evidence that such laws ever existed; second, even if they had existed, they would have been local ordinances rather than laws, overruled by British laws against murder; and third, there is a legal argument called the 'doctrine of implied repeal', which says that old laws should be disregarded when they are in conflict with later ones.

℘ *EARTHQUAKE, SMARTIES, VIKINGS*

ZAMBIA

Oral sex is illegal in Zambia. In 2001, a 65-year-old German tourist was sentenced to six years in jail for breaking this law. In his defence, Wolfgang Seifarth pleaded that he was not aware that he had been breaking Zambian law, but the magistrate ruled that ignorance of the law was no defence.

It is also illegal for tourists to photograph pygmies in Zambia.

In October 2001, a Zambian man applied for a divorce after he found a frog in a cup of tea his wife had made him. Andrew Nyoka, 28, explained to a community court: 'One time I found a frog in a cup of tea she had served me. That is the reason I went for another woman.' The judges granted him a divorce, saying it was clear the marriage could not be saved.

This seems in line with the advice given by Governor Welshman Mabhena of Zambia in March 1996 when he warned men against cooking or washing nappies. 'Our culture and tradition have a clear division of labour,' he said. 'There are certain household chores that just cannot be done by men.'

President Kaunda of Zambia once threatened to resign if Zambians did not cut down their consumption of beer.

HIPPOPOTAMUS, ZEBRA

ZEBRA

In 1898, the zoologist Lord Rothschild rode a carriage drawn by six zebras to Buckingham Palace in order to prove that zebras could be trained.

The coat of arms of Botswana is based on a shield supported by two zebras. One zebra is also holding an elephant's tusk, the other a stalk of millet. The zebra is the national animal of Botswana. There is also a very small zebra on the coat of arms of Zambia.

A cross between a zebra and a donkey may be known as a zebrinny, zebrula or zedonk, though zonkey, zebrass, zebronkey, zeass, zeedonk, zebadonk, zenkey, donbra and deebra have also been recorded. The generic name for crosses between zebras and horses or asses is zebroid or zebra mule.

In his *Origin of Species*, Charles Darwin reported a zonkey that apparently bred with a bay mare to produce what he called a 'triple hybrid.'

Zebras are considered to be black with white stripes rather than the other way round. There is no general agreement on the role played by the stripes, but as each zebra's stripe pattern is different, they play a role in mating behaviour by helping zebras recognise each other. It has also been suggested that they serve as camouflage in long grass, with lions unable to detect the black-and-white zebra stripes from grass stalks as they are colour blind. Research has also shown that zebras' stripes confuse blood-sucking tsetse flies.

BADGER

ZIMBABWE

Once part of the empire of Great Zimbabwe, then part of Matabeleland, then Southern Rhodesia, then the Republic of Rhodesia, Zimbabwe took the present form of its name in 1980. The name Zimbabwe derives from an expression meaning 'big house of stone' in the Shona language.

If you arrange the members of the United Nations in alphabetical order, Zimbabwe comes last.

At the 2004 and 2008 Olympics, Zimbabwe won two gold, four silver and one bronze medal – all by the swimmer Kirsty Coventry. Apart from that, Zimbabwe's sole Olympic medal was a gold won by the women's hockey team in 1980.

In 2003, the Zimbabwe dollar could be exchanged one-for-one with the US dollar. By 2007, the exchange rate had fallen to 30,000 per US dollar.

In 1994, Zimbabwe's President, Robert Mugabe, was made an honorary Knight Commander of the Order of the Bath by Queen Elizabeth II. This knighthood was revoked in 2008 over his 'abuse of human rights' and 'abject disregard' for democracy.

In 2009, the city council in Zimbabwe's capital, Harare, offered free graves for cholera victims.

BANANA, BOTSWANA, CARPENTRY, KYRGYZSTAN, UNDERGARMENTS

ZIPF, George Kingsley (1902–50)

The Harvard linguistics professor George Zipf made some profound discoveries on the statistical distribution of words. Here are two of the laws Zipf discovered:

Zipf's First Law: If the words in any large body of text are ordered according to the number of times they appear, and the position of each word in the list is then multiplied by its frequency, the result settles to a more or less constant figure. Example: in one large database of spoken English, the 35th most common word is 'very' which occurs 836 times; the 45th most common is 'see' with 674 hits; the 55th, 65th and 75th are 'which' (563), 'get' (469) and 'out' (422) respectively. If we multiply 35×836, and 45×674, and 55×563 and so on, the answers are 29,260, 30,330, 30,965, 30,485 and 31,650 respectively, which are remarkably close to one another. Only with the top and bottom few items on the list would one expect there to be any great divergence from this pattern.

Zipf's Second Law: In general, the shorter a word, the more often it will be used. Zipf puts this down to the 'Principle of Least Effort'. Example: roughly 50 per cent of English words used in any extended sample have only one syllable. Of the 20 words appearing most often in the Oxford English Corpus, two (a, I) have one letter, 10 (be, to, of, in, it, on, he, as, do, at) have two letters, five (the, and, for, not, you) have three letters, three (that, have, with) have four letters. None have five or more letters.

ZOG I, King of Albania (1895–1961)

King Zog of Albania (r. 1928–39) was the only national leader in modern times to return fire during an assassination attempt, when he fought off three assailants, wounding one of them, during a visit to the Vienna Opera House.

When in exile, he rented a floor at the Ritz Hotel in London and paid his bill in gold bullion bars.

His son, Crown Prince Leka, once bought Ronald Reagan an elephant from Harrods.

Before becoming King of Albania, Zog had served as Prime Minister (1922–24) and President (1925–28).

⚲ *ALBANIA*

ZOO

The first place in the world to be described as a 'zoo' was the London Zoological Gardens in Regent's Park. The title was first colloquially abbreviated to 'the Zoological' then 'the zoo', a term first used in 1847.

⚲ *BERLIN, COVID-19, EDINBURGH, HIPPOPOTAMUS, LLAMA, POLAR BEAR*

ZYZZYVA

Defined as 'a genus of tropical weevils (family Curculionidae) native to South America', zyzzyva became the last word in the *Oxford English Dictionary* in 2017. Until then, that honour had been held by zythum, a kind of malt beer in ancient Egypt.

A NOTE ABOUT THE AUTHOR

William Hartston graduated in mathematics at Cambridge but never completed his PhD in number theory because he spent too much time playing chess. This did, however, lead to his winning the British Chess Championship in 1973 and 1975 and writing a number of chess books and newspaper chess columns.

When William and mathematics amicably separated, he worked for several years as an industrial psychologist specialising in the construction and interpretation of personality tests. After 10 years writing a wide variety of columns for the *Independent,* he moved to the *Daily Express,* where he has been writing the Beachcomber column of surreal humour since 1998. In addition to writing about chess, he has written books on useless information, numbers, dates, sloths and bizarre academic research, including sexology.

Recently, his skills at sitting on a sofa watching television have been appreciated by viewers of the TV programme *Gogglebox,* but he has still not decided what he wants to be when he grows up.